CHILD ABUSE

A Multidisciplinary Survey

Series Editor

BYRGEN FINKELMAN, J.D.

A GARLAND SERIES

SERIES CONTENTS

VOLUME
7

PROTECTING ABUSED CHILDREN

PROTECTIVE SERVICES AND PROCEEDINGS, FOSTER CARE, TERMINATION OF PARENTAL RIGHTS

Edited with introductions by

BYRGEN FINKELMAN, J.D.

GARLAND PUBLISHING, INC.
New York & London
1995

Library of Congress Cataloging-in-Publication Data

Child abuse : a multidisciplinary survey / series editor, Byrgen
Finkelman.
    p.   cm.
    Includes bibliographical references and indexes.
    Contents: v. 1. Physical and emotional abuse and neglect
— v. 2. Sexual abuse — v. 3. Causes, prevention, and remedies
— v. 4. Short- and long-term effects — v. 5. Treatment of child
and adult survivors — v. 6. Treatment of offenders and
families — v. 7. Protecting abused children.
    ISBN 0-8153-1813-8 (v. 1 : acid-free paper). — ISBN
0-8153-1814-6 (v. 2 : acid-free paper). — ISBN 0-8153-1815-4
(v. 3 : acid-free paper). — ISBN 0-8153-1816-2 (v. 4 : acid-
free paper). — ISBN 0-8153-1817-0 (v. 5 : acid-free paper).
— ISBN 0-8153-1818-9 (v. 6 : acid-free paper). — ISBN 0-8153-
1819-7 (v. 7 : acid-free paper)
    1. Child abuse—United States.   I. Finkelman, Byrgen.
HV6626.52.C54   1995
362.7'62'0973—dc20   95-753
                                                   CIP

Printed on acid-free, 250-year-life paper
Manufactured in the United States of America

CONTENTS

PROTECTIVE PROCEEDINGS AND TERMINATION OF PARENTAL RIGHTS

SERIES INTRODUCTION

In 1960 Elizabeth Elmer said of child abuse "little is known about any facet of the problem and that methods for dealing with it are random and inadequate." She spoke of a "professional blind-spot" for abuse and of "the repugnance felt by most of our society for the entire subject of abused children."[1] Two years later, Dr. C. Henry Kempe and his colleagues brought national attention to the problem of child abuse with their article, "The Battered-Child Syndrome."[2] Prior to the publication of that landmark article, the literature on child abuse was almost non-existent. In the three decades since its publication, the research and literature on child abuse have become vast and daunting.

Social workers, psychologists, psychiatrists, counselors, and doctors have studied child abuse in great detail. As a result, we know that child abuse includes physical, emotional, and sexual abuse as well as neglect. Researchers have studied the causes of abuse from both the individual and societal perspectives. There are effective interventions for tertiary remediation of the problem, and there are many prevention models that hold out hope that child abuse can be stopped before it starts. Studies of the short- and long-term effects of child abuse show a range of maladies that include infant failure-to-thrive, learning disabilities, eating disorders, borderline personality disorders, violent behavior, delinquency, and even parricide. We now recognize the need for treatment of child victims, adult survivors, and adult perpetrators of all forms of abuse. Lawyers, legislators, and judges have grappled with the profusion of legal problems raised by protective services and proceedings, foster care, and the termination of parental rights to free abused children for placement in permanent homes. Legislatures have passed and amended statutes requiring various health, education and child care professionals to report suspected abuse, and they have dealt with the difficult problem of defining abuse and determining when the state should intervene to protect children from abusive parents. They have also struggled with the legal and psychological issues that arise when the child victim becomes a witness against his or her abuser. Even the Supreme Court has been called upon to sort out the constitutional rights of victims and criminal defendants and to determine the extent of government liability for failure to adequately protect children from abuse.

The articles in this series document our passage through five of the six stages that C. Henry Kempe identified in his 1978 commentary "Recent Developments in the Field of Child Abuse" as developmental stages in addressing the problem of child abuse:

> Stage One is denial that either physical or sexual abuse exists to a significant extent . . . Stage Two is paying attention to the more lurid abuse . . . Stage Three comes when physical abuse is better handled and attention is now beginning to be paid to the infant who fails to thrive . . . Stage Four comes in recognition of emotional abuse and neglect . . . and Stage Five is the paying attention to the serious plight of the sexually abused child, including the youngster involved in incest . . .

In spite of the voluminous research and writing on child abuse, the sixth and final of Kempe's stages, "that of guaranteeing each child that he or she is truly wanted, is provided with loving care, decent shelter and food, and first class preventive and curative health care," remains elusive.[3] There are many explanations for our inability to conquer the problem of child abuse. In reality, the explanation for our continued inability to defeat this contemptible social problem is as complex as the problem itself.

We continue to sanction the use of violence in the name of discipline. We put our societal stamp of approval on "punishment inflicted by way of correction and training" and call it discipline. But discipline also means "instruction and exercise designed to train to proper conduct or action."[4] It is not difficult to see the inherent conflict in these two definitions when applied to child-rearing. How can we "train to proper conduct or action" when we use physical punishment as a means of training, punishment that we would not inflict upon an adult under the same circumstances?

The courts and legislatures have been unable to find the correct balance between a family's right to privacy and self governance and the need of children for protection. We are unable or unwilling to commit sufficient revenue to programs that combat abuse.

There is also the tendency among many professionals working with abused children and abusive parents to view the problem and solution through specialized cognitive lenses. Doctors, social workers, lawyers, psychologists, psychiatrists, counselors, and educators are all striving to defeat child abuse. However, for the most part, these professionals focus on the problem of child abuse from the perspective of their own field of expertise. The literature on child abuse is spread throughout journals from these fields and in more specialized journals within these fields. It would be impossible for any single person to remain abreast of the developments in all other disciplines working toward a solution to child abuse. But it is also patently clear that the solution to the problem of child abuse is not going to come from any one individual or discipline. It is going to take professionals and lay people from all disciplines, working with knowledge from all disciplines.

An interdisciplinary examination is important in the fight against child abuse. The more professionals know about all aspects of the problem of child sexual abuse, the better equipped they will be to do work within their area of expertise. It is important, for example, for lawyers, working in the midst of the current backlash against child sexual abuse claims, to understand that there is a long history of discovery and repression of childhood sexual abuse. With a full understanding of why this backlash is occurring, lawyers and social service professionals can continue to effectively work against child sexual abuse.

Child abuse is a complex social problem. The issues confronted in these volumes are interconnected and overlapping. It is my hope that bringing together the articles in this series will aid in the fight against child abuse by facilitating a multidisciplinary search for a solution.[5]

NOTES

1. Elizabeth Elmer, M.S.S., "Abused Young Children Seen in Hospitals," *Social Work* 5(4), pp. 98–102 (October 1960).

2. C. Henry Kempe, M.D., F.N. Silverman, M.D., Brandt F. Steele, M.D. and others, "The Battered-Child Syndrome," *JAMA* 181, pp. 17–24 (1962).

3. C. Henry Kempe, M.D., "Recent Developments in the Field of Child Abuse," *Child Abuse & Neglect* 3(1), pp. ix–xv (1979).

4. *The Random House Dictionary of the English Language*, unabridged edition.

5. The articles in this collection may give the impression that child abuse and neglect and child sexual abuse are uniquely American

phenomena. They are not. There is a wealth of similar articles from almost every country imaginable. American sources have been used mainly because of the space limitations and because understanding the American child welfare system is vital to developing a cure for the problem.

VOLUME INTRODUCTION

The articles in this volume address the legal and psychological issues that arise in protective service proceedings, placement of abused children in foster care, and proceedings to terminate parental rights in a child.

As states became aware of greater numbers of children at risk for continued abuse by their parents it became the standard practice to place children in foster care. It was simply assumed that children were better off in foster care, and little thought was given to the quality or duration of their stay.

Delores Taylor and Philip Starr (1967), in their integrative review of clinical and empirical findings of foster parents, found a serious lack of knowledge about foster care. They could not determine whether foster care "is an outmoded social response to situations that have more adequate alternatives" or "an appropriate social response to many current situations." They found the evidence to be "complex and contradictory." We now know that foster care is not a good solution for many children and that it is actively harmful for others.[1]

There are many problems with the foster care system. On the most basic level, foster care fails to do what it was designed to do: provide a *temporary and safe* refuge for children who must be removed from their homes.

We know that most children who enter foster care never go home. Many of the more than one-half million children in foster care annually suffer abuse and/or neglect in their foster homes. Children are often placed in foster homes, even when the state agency has documented previous abuse in those homes.[2]

Children trapped within the foster care system have little or no power to change their situations. "Despite a wealth of scholarship and development of judicial doctrine, the legal rights of children placed under state care remain largely undefined."[3]

Arlene E. Fried (1993) discussed "the reform of child welfare systems achieved by class action litigation for injunctive relief and individual suits for damages to compensate children injured as a result of a child welfare agency's practices." She also reviewed the "treatment of supervised and foster children's rights in federal district and circuit courts and analyze[d] the Supreme Court's decision in *Suter v. Artist M.*" Fried "concludes that in order to alleviate the current crisis in the quality of care, the Supreme Court must clarify the dimensions of foster children's constitutional rights and render state child welfare agencies amenable to litigation that can lead to much-needed structural reform of state custody programs."[4]

Children who live in foster care exist in what is known in professional circles as "foster care limbo." They are not free to be adopted into permanent homes because their natural parents won't relinquish their parental rights and the state will not terminate them. Neither are they able to feel secure in their foster homes. We know that children need a secure and continuous relationship with a "psychological parent" for healthy emotional growth. Still, foster children are not permitted to form permanent attachments with foster parents. Some states flatly forbid foster parents to adopt children. In other states, children have been moved frequently from one foster home to another for no other reason than to prevent them from forming emotional attachments to their foster families. In one case, a 5½ year-old girl was removed from her foster care of the previous 4½ years so that she would not develop emotional ties that would inhibit her eventual return to her mother.[5]

Mendel Shapiro (1979) discussed some of the "statutory and judicial efforts to grant some degree of procedural protection against state interference with long-term foster families."[6] He pointed out that "efforts to come to terms with the reality of long-term foster care have been impeded to some extent by a perception that procedural protections for long-term foster families would merely institutionalize relationships resulting from the malfunctioning of the foster care system."[7]

Despite the fact that many states have enacted procedural statutes granting foster parents the right to a hearing either before or after removal of the foster child, this is not sufficient protection for long-term foster families. Shapiro argues that in cases "where the rights of the natural parents are not implicated, those long-term foster families that are the functional equivalent of the natural family should be accorded the same substantive protection constitutionally accorded the natural family." In other words "a foster child should be removed from his or her foster family only under conditions that would justify the removal of a child from his or her natural parents."[8]

Another attempt to solve the problem of foster-care limbo

involves avoiding the removal of children to foster care in the first place. Debra Ratterman (1986) asserted that:

> among the most important trends in current child welfare practice is the emphasis on improving services to enable children to remain in their homes rather than being placed in foster care.
>
> This emphasis is reinforced by the "reasonable efforts" requirements of the federal Adoption Assistance and Child Welfare Act of 1980 (P.L. 96-272). The Act requires that child welfare agencies provide services to prevent unnecessary placement and that, in each case, a court must determine that the state agency has made reasonable efforts to prevent or eliminate the need for placement.[9]

Edith Fein and Anthony N. Maluccio discussed permanency planning that "has been the guiding principle in child welfare" since the mid-1970s. They explain that "the concept took root in the landmark Oregon study, flourished in the Adoption Assistance and Child Welfare Act of 1980 (P.L. 96–272), and has now taken on the aura of dogma among child welfare workers."

They found that permanency planning seemed to be working well up until about 1984. Thereafter, the number of children in foster care began to creep up again as "some of the earlier successes were being reversed. The number of children in care was again rising, more very young children were entering care, and reentry rates were increasing suggesting repeated episodes of short-term care."[10]

Children whose homes can never be made safe face the prospect of perpetual foster care because they are not legally free for adoption into a new, permanent home.

The practice of adoption is an ancient one, but it was not part of the common law. The first adoption statutes in the United States were passed in the middle of the nineteenth century. These statutes, which generally required parental consent to an adoption, also permitted the court to dispense with parental consent under certain circumstances. These circumstances were not unlike those in current termination statutes and generally included abandonment and the judicial deprivation of parental custody due to neglect or cruelty, among other reasons. This, however, created a situation where parental rights were only terminated at the adoption proceeding, and if the judge was unwilling to terminate the parents' rights, the petitioning adoptive family, as well as the child, were caught in a situation where much emotional, and possibly financial, investment has been made, but to no avail.

In the mid-1950s, state legislatures began adopting statutory procedures to terminate parental rights to a child. These procedures permitted the termination of parental rights in order to free children for adoption before an actual adoption procedure was commenced. In this way, adoptive parents and children could avoid the problem under the old adoption statutes when parental rights were not terminated.

Still, the termination of a parent's rights in his/her natural child is considered a drastic measure. Many courts are loath to enter a termination order except in the most extreme cases. There is a difficult balancing of interests: society's interest in promoting and protecting biological families; the parents' interest in family autonomy and privacy; and children's interest in a safe, loving environment in which to grow.

Robert Borgman (1981) studied the relationships between termination of parental rights and permanency for children freed for adoption. His conclusions were not very promising. He determined that "an estimated 15%, the majority placed after age six . . ., will experience termination or disruption of the adoption and return to the placement agency . . ."[11] He also found that "much of the difficulty in permanency planning for children in this study appeared traceable to the instability and inappropriateness of the initial placement in foster family care. An alternative might have been an initial, time-limited placement in a small, professionally staffed group care facility accessible to visits by the child's parents." He also discovered that "the majority of children in this study strongly resisted adoption, either explicitly, or implicitly through the emergence or exacerbation of behavioral problems when adoption was proposed or took place." He identified behavioral problems in this context "as defenses against pain and grief about 'losing' the biological parents" and found that "for some children, permanent guardianship might have been more appropriate than adoption."

This is not surprising since children develop strong attachments to their parents however unfit their parents may be. This is due, in part, to the nature of children. It is also due, in part, to the strong societal messages that children receive telling them they should love their parents. The need on the part of children to maintain contact with their biological families is satisfied under permanent guardianship. With permanent guardianship, as with adoption, the biological parents lose custody of the child permanently. The permanent guardian is not supervised or controlled by the court or agency. However, Borgman points out, with permanent guardianship, "unlike adoption, parents and children retain residual rights specified in the court order granting the guardianship. These may include parents' and relatives' rights to visit the child, the child's right to retain the family name, and the right to inherit property from the family." Borgman praises permanent guardianship because it "allows children to expand relationships and broaden psychological identity without having to lose a heritage of relationships and rights."[12]

Dogart R. Leashore (1984/85) discussed the use of legal guardianship to help some of the 81% of the white children and 74% of the minority children in foster care who were not free for adoption in 1982. He applauded legal guardianship as a way of allowing children to become secure in a placement with a legal guardian family and obtain "the care and love all dependent children deserve" while still maintaining contact with his or her natural parents (if the parents so desire).[13]

Still, permanent guardianship is not in widespread use and termination of parental rights still rules the day. A disturbing issue that comes up in legal proceedings to terminate parental rights is the trend toward termination of parental rights of poor parents. This led to another trend discussed by Robert S. Catz and John T. Kuelbs (1973/4): the legal trend toward requiring the appointment of counsel for indigent parents in neglect and termination proceedings. The authors referred to this as "a rapidly developing area of case law that has received attention in both state and federal courts . . ." They found that an analysis of the constitutional arguments raised by this question "will demonstrate that the rights and interests of the parents which are jeopardized in a neglect or termination proceeding are such that due process and equal protection of the law demand that an indigent parent be given court appointed counsel." They argue that the "necessity for granting such a right becomes particularly apparent when one considers the seriousness and permanency of the consequences of such proceedings, the resources of the state in comparison with those of the parents, and the complexity of issues and questions involved in such proceedings."[14]

Unfortunately, the U.S. Supreme Court disagreed. In 1981, the U.S. Supreme Court, faced with the question of whether indigent parents have a constitutional right to state-paid counsel in these proceedings, said "no" in a 5-4 decision.[15] This decision was a low point for poor families since it sends a clear message that poverty may prove sufficient reason for termination of parental rights since the indigent are unlikely to possess the legal acumen to adequately represent themselves in termination proceedings.

Fortunately, many enlightened state legislatures have adopted statutes to protect indigent parents' rights. As of 1983, thirty-four states and the District of Columbia provide, by statute, for counsel for indigent parents in proceedings to terminate their parental rights.

There is no simple solution applicable to all cases where state intervention into a family occurs. The articles in this volume explore some of the problems that arise when the state intervenes on behalf of a child. One thing is clear: we must continue to strive for a solution to the problems faced by children until every child is guaranteed a safe, secure, and permanent home in which to thrive.

NOTES

1. Delores Taylor, Ph.D., ACSW, Philip Starr, MSW, "Foster Parenting: An Integrative Review of the Literature," *Child Welfare* 46(7), pp. 371–85 (July 1967).

2. Michael B. Mushlin, "Unsafe Havens: The Case for Constitutional Protection of Foster Children From Abuse," *Harvard Civil Rights-Civil Liberties Law Review* 23, pp. 199–280 (1988).

3. Arlene E. Fried, "The Foster Child's Avenues of Redress: Questions Left Unanswered," *Columbia Journal of Law & Social Problems* 26(3), pp. 465–90, 466 (Spr 1993).

4. Id. at 467.

5. *In Re Jewish Child Care Association*, 5 NY2d 222 (1959).

6. Mendel Shapiro, "Constitutional Protection of Long-Term Foster Families," *Columbia Law Review* 79(6), pp. 1191–1208, 1191. (1979).

7. Id. at 1191.

8. Id. at 1208.

9. Debra Ratterman, "Reasonable Efforts to Prevent Placement and Preserve Families: Judicial Determination of Reasonable Efforts," *Children Today* 15(6), pp. 26 and 30–32 (Nov–Dec 1986).

10. Edith Fein, and Anthony N. Maluccio, "Permanency Planning: Another Remedy in Jeopardy?" *Social Service Review* 66(3), pp. 335–48, 338 (Sept 1992).

11. Robert Borgman, "Antecedents and Consequences of Parental Rights Termination for Abused and Neglected Children," *Child Welfare* 60(6), pp. 391–404, 392 (Jun 1981).

12. Id. at 402.

13. Bogart R. Leashore, "Demystifying Legal Guardianship: An Unex-

plored Option for Dependent Children," *Journal of Family Law* 23, pp. 391–400, 400 (1984/5).

14. Robert S. Catz, and John T. Kuelbs, "The Requirement of Appointment of Counsel for Indigent Parents in Neglect or Termination Proceedings: A Developing Area," *Journal of Family Law* 13, pp. 223–44, 223–24 (1973/74).

15 *Lassiter v. Department of Social Services*, 452 U.S. 18 (1981).

FURTHER READING

Chemerinsky, Erwin. "Defining the 'Best Interests': Constitutional Protections in Involuntary Adoptions." *Journal of Family Law* 18, pp. 79–113 (1979–80).

Dobbs, Marian F. "Foster Care and Family Law: A Look at *Smith v. OFFER* and the Constitutional Rights of Foster Children and Their Families." *Journal of Family Law* 17, pp. 1–28 (1978–79).

Erickson, Nancy S. "Preventing Foster Care Placement: Supportive Services in the Home." *Journal of Family Law* 19, pp. 569–613 (1980–81).

Green, Arthur H. "Societal Neglect of Child Abusing Parents." *Victimology* 2(2), pp. 285–93 (1977).

Jones, Martha L. "Stopping Foster Care Drift: A Review of Legislation and Special Programs." *Child Welfare* 57(9), pp. 571–80 (1978).

Katz, Sanford N. "Foster Parents Versus Agencies: A Case Study in the Judicial Application of 'The Best Interests of the Child' Doctrine." *Michigan Law Review* 65, pp. 145–70 (1966).

Wald, Michael S. "State Intervention on Behalf of 'Neglected' Children: Standards for Removal of Children from Their Homes, Monitoring the Status of Children in Foster Care, and Termination of Parental Rights." *Stanford Law Review* 28(4), pp. 623–706 (1976).

Weinstein, Janet, et al. "Caring for our Children: An Examination of Health Care Services for Foster Children." *California Western Law Review* 26, pp. 319–49 (1990).

Weisman, Mary-Lou. "When Parents Are Not in the Best Interests of the Child." *The Atlantic Monthly* 274(1), pp. 42–63 (July 1994).

Foster Parenting: An Integrative Review of the Literature

A review of the literature on foster parenting reveals the serious lack of knowledge about this important social role, and the need for research to establish much that must be known in order to provide adequate foster homes.

**DELORES A. TAYLOR
AND PHILIP STARR**

An integrative review of clinical and empirical findings on foster parents was undertaken as part of a study of the foster family care program for emotionally disturbed children of Children's Services of Connecticut. Over the past 25 years, many reports of clinical studies of foster parents have appeared in the literature. There has, however, been little effort to build a knowledge base from previously published studies. Some authors have cited several other reports, but in general the literature is replete with duplications and contradictions, and many authors seem relatively unaware of previous work regarding the issues of foster parenting. We felt that it was important to integrate the findings and conclusions of previous reports in order to stimulate discussion and further study of the issues presented.

DELORES A. TAYLOR, Ph.D., ACSW, *is Research Director, Children's Services of Connecticut, Hartford, Connecticut.* PHILIP STARR, M.S.W., *is Research Associate, Children's Services of Connecticut. The authors wish to express their appreciation to Anthony Maluccio and David Christensen for their criticisms and contributions to this paper.*

The areas included in the review are as follows:

. . Recruitment problems.
. . Foster parent selection.
. . Motivation for foster parenthood.
. . Characteristics of foster parents who were recruited.
. . Definitions of the caseworker-foster parent relationships.
. . Training methods.
. . Adequacy of foster parent role performance.

Within each of these areas we were concerned with the following questions:

. . What were the basic similarities, differences, and contradictions in the various ways of viewing foster parents?
. . What value assumptions were made by the various authors?
. . Which findings have both clinical and empirical support?
. . What additional clarification and knowledge are needed?

We did not attempt to criticize the logic or methodology of the writings reviewed. The writers have contributed various levels of statements. A common theme was that of advocating action based on an author's generalizations from his thoughts and feelings. At another level some authors contributed their informal observations and experiences with foster parents. At a more formal level a number of authors reported the results of descriptive and exploratory studies. The only report of an experimental study was Soffen's.[1] Fanshel,[2] McCoy,[3] Wolins,[4] and

[1] Joseph Soffen, "The Impact of a Group Educational Program for Foster Parents," CHILD WELFARE, XLI (1962), 195–201.
[2] David Fanshel, *Foster Parenthood: A Role Analysis* (Minneapolis: University of Minnesota Press, 1966).
[3] Jacqueline McCoy, "The Application of the Role Concept to Foster Parenthood," *Social Casework*, XLIII (1962), 252–256.
[4] Martin Wolins, *Selecting Foster Parents* (New York: Columbia University Press, 1963).

1

others have used various concepts from social role theory, but there is no published attempt to explore conceptual strategies or develop models of the role and tasks of foster parenting.

Recruitment Problems

Clinical findings were in agreement that there is a dwindling supply of foster homes in relation to increasing demand for them.[5] Various authors emphasize different factors associated with this situation and present different solutions to the problem.

None of the findings should be viewed apart from a consideration of the present general population structure and the current job market situation. For example, there is a smaller proportion of persons within the age group from which foster parents are recruited than has been the case at any point in recent history. Numerous well-paying jobs are available to many of those persons within the group from which foster parents are usually recruited. Ougheltree indicates that factors that limit the number of potential foster homes for the Negro community are lack of adequate housing, relatively low economic status, frequent employment of women outside their homes, and distrust of social agencies.[6]

Within the present financial structure of foster care, it may be possible to reach out to different populations. Simsarian suggests that one good untapped resource is suburban families;[7] however, in a followup study of foster children, Murphy found that successful outcome was *not* associated with foster

5 L. John Bohman, "Methods of Recruiting Foster Homes and Ways to Enable Foster Parents to Help the Children," CHILD WELFARE, XXXVI (1957), 4–7; Gustave A. DeCocq, The Withdrawal of Foster Parent Applicants, mimeographed (San Francisco: United Community Council); Kenneth Dick, "What People Think About Foster Care," Children, VIII (1961), 48–52; Else Lowenstein, "Finding Foster Homes for Children," (unpublished master's thesis, New York School for Social Work, 1955); Callman Rawley, "The Relation of Administrative Policy and the Supply of Foster Homes," CHILD WELFARE, XXIX, No. 4 (1950), 7–9 ff.; Frances P. Simsarian, "Foster Care Possibilities in a Suburban Community," Children, XI, (1964), 97–102; Howard R. Stanton, "Mother Love in Foster Homes," Marriage and Family Living, XVIII (1956), 301–307; Nina Beck Tegethoff and Harriet Goldstein, "A Realistic Appraisal of Home Finding," CHILD WELFARE, XLI (1962), 255 ff.

6 Cornelia M. Ougheltree, Finding Foster Homes (New York: Child Welfare League of America, 1957).

7 Simsarian, op. cit.

homes located in suburban areas,[8] and Babcock indicates that suburban families presented difficulties in terms of agency travel time for purposes of agency supervision.[9]

Both Stanton [10] and Glassberg [11] indicate that new homes may be recruited by agencies if they do not stress motivation for foster parenthood. Stanton tested the assumption that high motivation for child care on the part of foster parents is essential to the child's healthy development within the family. A highly-motivated family is defined as one in which foster parents initiated and sustained considerable effort in becoming foster parents. A low-motivated home is defined as one in which the foster parents agreed to care for a foster child, although the agency had to initiate and sustain considerable effort in order to recruit the family. He found no statistically significant differences between the care given by the two groups, and concluded that agencies may have overstressed motivation as a criterion of foster parent selection.

Other authors stressed a lack of community knowledge regarding the functions of foster parents as a factor in their limited availability.[12] Empirical support is provided by Dick, who found that 43 percent of the families he studied had not heard, read, or seen any publicity about the agency's need for foster homes.[13] Simsarian found that all 60 of the suburban housewives she interviewed were uninformed about agency foster care programs.[14]

Bohman,[15] Rawley,[16] and Simsarian [17] seem to assume that community awareness of the need for foster homes, combined with public knowledge about the contribution of foster families, would lead to an increase in the availability of foster homes. Only Ougheltree presents evidence that indicates contin-

8 H. B. M. Murphy, "Foster Home Variables and Adult Outcomes," Mental Hygiene, XLVIII (1964), 587–599.

9 Charlotte G. Babcock, "Some Psychodynamic Factors in Foster Parenthood—Part I," CHILD WELFARE, XLIV (1965), 485–493, 522.

10 Stanton, op. cit.

11 Eudice Glassberg, "Are Foster Homes Hard To Find?" CHILD WELFARE, XLVI (1965), 453–460 ff.

12 Bohman, op. cit.; Glassberg, op. cit.; Rawley, op. cit.

13 Dick, op. cit.

14 Simsarian, op. cit.

15 Bohman, op. cit.

16 Rawley, op. cit.

17 Simsarian, op. cit.

uous concentrated publicity campaign was successful in recruiting foster homes.[18]

In contrast, Dick found that two thirds of the families he interviewed were not interested in becoming foster parents because they had children of their own to care for; 26 percent felt that agencies expected too much of people as foster parents.[19] DeCocq found that 16 foster parent applicants who withdrew their applications during the home study process were concerned about the agency's housing standards, the use of health clinics for foster children, attachment to the foster child, disciplining the child, visits from the natural parents, and the inadequacy of financial reimbursement for the cost of foster care.[20]

Glover has called for fair board rates, salaries, and fringe benefits for foster parents.[21] Miller,[22] Pratt,[23] and Wildy[24] describe projects in which foster parents are salaried or receive financial subsidy in addition to the usual agency board rate, medical and dental costs, clothing allowance, and other incidental expenses. They were in agreement that adequate financial compensation is necessary in order to recruit foster parents able to provide the demanding services required of them.

Glover argues that foster care can no longer depend upon the uncertain support of charity and local government; she recommends that, just as the Federal government has subsidized other local and national needs, it must appropriate funds for foster family care.[25]

Questions for further study include the following:

.. Would the provision of salaries increase the availability of foster homes?

.. Would publicity clarifying the nature of foster family care, and emphasizing the positive contribution of foster parent services increase the availability of foster homes?
.. What agency requirements are necessary? Are present requirements adapted to current market conditions?
.. Do agency expectations result in the rejection of potentially capable foster parents?

Foster Parent Selection

Three major issues are involved in the selection of foster parents: the requirements of foster home studies, foster parent-child matching, and the specific qualities sought in foster parents.

The areas most commonly considered as part of a foster home study were as follows:[26]

.. The social situation of the foster family.
.. The emotional content of that social situation for each of the family members.
.. The interrelationships of foster family members.
.. The ability of the foster family to make constructive use of casework services.

Charnley[27] and Lawder[28] say that, in offering their home to a child, most foster parents are seeking secondary psychological gains. In coming to the agency the foster parents are not seeking help with their problems, but want to provide a service in which secondary psychological gains are derived in the process of caring for children. Various clinicians contend, however, that some foster parents apply for a child as a means (perhaps unconscious) of seeking help with the resolution of their conflicts.[29] All the authors

---

[18] Ougheltree, op. cit.
[19] Dick, op. cit.
[20] DeCocq, op. cit.
[21] E. Elizabeth Glover, "Improving and Expanding Foster Care Resources," CHILD WELFARE, XLIV (1965), 244 ff.
[22] Clara Miller, "The Agency-Owned Foster Home," CHILD WELFARE, XXXIII (1954), 9–11 ff.
[23] Catherine Pratt, "Foster Parents as Agency Employees," Children, XIII (1966), 14–15.
[24] Lois Wildy, "The Professional Foster Home," in Foster Home Care for Emotionally Disturbed Children (New York: Child Welfare League of America, 1962), pp. 1–8.
[25] E. Elizabeth Glover, "Federal Grants-in-Aid and All Child Welfare Services," CHILD WELFARE, XLIV (1965), 64 ff.

[26] Esther Glickman, Child Placement through Clinically Oriented Casework (New York: Columbia University Press, 1957); Draza Kline, "Understanding and Evaluating a Foster Family's Capacity to Meet the Needs of an Individual Child," in Ner Littner et al., Changing Needs and Practices in Child Welfare (New York: Child Welfare League of America, 1960), pp. 23–35.
[27] Jean Charnley, The Art of Child Placement (Minneapolis: University of Minnesota Press, 1955).
[28] Elizabeth A. Lawder, "Toward a More Scientific Understanding of Foster Family Care," CHILD WELFARE, XLIII (1964), 57–63.
[29] Irene Josselyn, "Evaluating Motives of Foster Parents," CHILD WELFARE, XXXI (1952), 3–8; Lawder, op. cit.; Anthony N. Maluccio, "Selecting Foster Par-

stress the importance of understanding the nature and meaning of the foster family relationships in order to evaluate properly the foster parent applicants.

While specific emphases are attached by different authors to various aspects of the home study, the model for the study is the diagnostic assessment process as utilized in a child guidance or family agency setting. This model is based on an untested assumption that such an assessment is necessary for appropriate placement of foster children.

The problem of determining "appropriate placement" is connected with the issue of foster parent-child matching. A number of authors discuss different kinds of matching and derive different conclusions from their analyses. The findings, based on clinical and descriptive studies, are not entirely clear.

Kaplan and Turitz [30] and Cochintu and Mason [31] conclude that average foster homes can be used to serve both emotionally traumatized children and children with medical problems; the major factor in serving any child with special problems is not special abilities or needs on the part of the foster parents, but the availability of appropriate agency and community services. Rich's study of 32 foster homes may also be interpreted as suggesting that matching is unnecessary; she reports that foster families were equally successful in caring for every kind of child— "ordinary, disturbed or retarded." [32]

On the other hand, Fanshel [33] and Colvin [34] report findings that indicate that the

success of foster mothers with children of different temperaments and with handicaps is related to the personality characteristics of the mothers. For example, foster mothers with a high need for order seemed to be most effective with withdrawn children. [35]

The findings of Murphy and Babcock suggest that foster parents vary in their ability to care for young and older children. Murphy reports that the least successful foster mothers were those who preferred to care for preschool-age children. [36] Babcock reports that foster parents who were able to care most successfully for infants were frequently unable to withstand the anxieties and struggles characteristic of foster care of older children. [37]

Advocates of foster parent-child matching present three major arguments for their point of view. First, matching is seen as necessary to insure appropriate and relevant emotional interaction between foster parents and child. [38] Second, matching is seen as necessary to avoid sharp changes in standards of living for the child. [39] Third, matching is believed necessary in order to avoid the possibility of conflict for the child in relation to the integration of the natural and foster parents' expectations regarding discipline. [40]

Successful foster parent-child matching is thought of as involving the following:

.. An understanding of the child's patterns of interpersonal relationships. [41]

ents for Disturbed Children," *Children*, XIII (1966), 69–74; McCoy, "The Application of the Role Concept to Foster Parenthood," *op. cit.*; Ira L. Mintz, "Multi-Determined Motivations in Foster Parents," CHILD WELFARE, XLI (1962), 172–174.

[30] Lillian K. Kaplan and Lilly L. Turitz, "Followup Report on Treatment of Emotionally Traumatized Young Children in a Foster Home Setting," *American Journal of Orthopsychiatry*, XXXIV (1964), 581–583.

[31] Ann W. Cochintu and Winifred Mason, "Foster Homes for Children with Medical Problems," CHILD WELFARE, XL, No. 10 (1961), 26–28.

[32] Mabel Rich, "Foster Homes for Retarded Children," CHILD WELFARE, XLIV (1965), 392–394.

[33] David Fanshel, "Specializations Within the Foster Parent Role: A Research Report—Part II. Foster Parents Caring for the 'Acting Out' and the Handicapped Child," CHILD WELFARE, XL, No. 4 (1961), 19–23.

[34] Ralph W. Colvin, "Toward the Development of a Foster Parent Attitude Test," in *Quantitative Approaches to Parent Selection* (New York: Child Welfare League of America, 1962), pp. 41–53.

[35] *Ibid.*
[36] Murphy, *op. cit.*
[37] Babcock, "Some Psychodynamic Factors in Foster Parenthood—Part I"; Charlotte G. Babcock, "Some Psychodynamic Factors in Foster Parenthood—Part II," CHILD WELFARE, XLIV (1965), 570–577 ff.
[38] Babcock, "Some Psychodynamic Factors in Foster Parenthood—Part I"; Babcock, "Some Psychodynamic Factors in Foster Parenthood—Part II"; Colvin, *op. cit.*; Fanshel, *Foster Parenthood: A Role Analysis;* David Fanshel, "Specializations Within the Foster Parent Role: A Research Report—Part I. Differences between Foster Parents of Infants and Foster Parents of Older Children," CHILD WELFARE, XLI, No. 3 (1961), 17–21; Fanshel, "Specializations Within the Foster Parent Role: A Research Report—Part II," Kline, "Understanding and Evaluating a Foster Family's Capacity to Meet the Needs of an Individual Child"; George Mora, "Foster Families for Emotionally Disturbed Children," CHILD WELFARE, XLI (1962), 104–106.
[39] Charnley, *op. cit.*
[40] George C. Williston, "The Foster Parent Role," *Journal of Psychology*, LX (1963), 263–272.
[41] Colvin, *op. cit.*; Kline, "Understanding and Evaluating a Foster Family's Capacity to Meet the Needs of an Individual Child"; Mora, *op. cit.*

.. An understanding of the emotional makeup of the foster parents, with specific attention to possible vulnerable areas that may be reactivated by the particular relationship problems of a given child.[42]

.. An understanding of the vulnerable areas in the emotional makeup of the child that may be reactivated by the problems of the foster parents.[43]

The findings of Babcock,[44] Colvin,[45] Fanshel,[46] and Murphy[47] provide evidence that successful placements do occur with matching. There was also evidence that unmatched foster parents and children achieved success.[48] The clearest evidence suggests that differential results follow from the interaction effects of the child's age, the foster parent's capacity for tolerating certain kinds of behavior, and the support they receive from their own community involvement, agency and community services. Further study is isolating specific variables is indicated.

Whether or not they advocate foster parent-child matching, most writers stipulate basically similar qualities as essential to consider in foster parents recruited to care for neglected and dependent children, handicapped, and emotionally disturbed children. Implicit in statements of specific qualities sought in foster parents is a model generally associated with "ideal" behavior of middle-class families.

The following qualities are emphasized in foster parents:

.. Stability of character and stability in family units.[49]

.. The ability to give affection and care to a child in order to meet his needs.[50]

.. The ability to recognize the temporary nature of placement with the goal of helping the child return to his own home, if advisable.[51]

.. The ability to work cooperatively with the agency in fulfilling a shared responsibility.[52]

.. The capacity to be giving persons without expecting immediate love or gratitude from the child.[53]

.. An acceptance of the possibilities of change in the child's behavior.[54]

.. The ability to respond to a learning experience that includes the use of casework services.[55]

.. Considerable maturity in order to cope with the child's behavior and their own feelings in a constructive manner.[56]

---

42 Babcock, "Some Psychodynamic Factors in Foster Parenthood—Part I"; Babcock, "Some Psychodynamic Factors in Foster Parenthood—Part II"; Colvin, op. cit., Fanshel, "Specializations Within the Foster Parent Role: A Research Report—Part I. Differences between Foster Parents of Infants and Foster Parents of Older Children"; Fanshel, "Specializations Within the Foster Parent Role: A Research Report—Part II. Foster Parents Caring for the 'Acting Out' and the Handicapped Child"; Kline, "Understanding and Evaluating a Foster Parent's Capacity to Meet the Needs of an Individual Child"; Mora, op. cit.
43 Colvin, op. cit.; Kline, "Understanding and Evaluating a Foster Family's Capacity to Meet the Needs of an Individual Child"; Mora, op. cit.
44 Babcock, "Some Psychodynamic Factors in Foster Parenthood—Part I"; Babcock, "Some Psychodynamic Factors in Foster Parenthood—Part II."
45 Colvin, op. cit.
46 Fanshel, "Specializations Within the Foster Parent Role: A Research Report—Part II."
47 Murphy, op. cit.
48 Cochintu and Mason, op. cit.; Kaplan and Turitz, op. cit.; Rich, op. cit.

49 Child Welfare League of America Standards for Foster Family Care Service (New York: Child Welfare League of America, 1959); Wildy, op. cit.
50 Child Welfare League of America Standards for Foster Family Care Service; Miller, op. cit.; Wildy, op. cit.
51 Mary E. Flanagan, "Symposium, Part II: Social Factors Contributing to Character Disorders—Comments: How Foster Parents Can Help the Character Disordered Child," CHILD WELFARE, XXXVII, No. 5 (1958), 10-14; Peter Reinhold, "Letter to the Editor," Children, XIII (1966), 168.
52 Marian L. Chambers, "A Study of Twelve Foster Parents Who Applied to Board Children in 1946 and Discontinued in 1947 to See Why They Did Not Continue as Boarding Parents," (unpublished master's thesis, New School of Social Work, 1948); Dorothy Hutchinson, In Quest of Foster Parents (New York: Columbia University Press, 1943); Maluccio, op. cit.; Peter Reinhold, "Fostering the Troubled Child," Notes of an Institute Given at the New England Conference of the Child Welfare League of America, Providence, R.I., April 15, 1966; Wildy, op. cit.
53 Michael J. Begab, "Mental Retardation; The Role of the Voluntary Social Agency," Social Casework, XLV (1964), 457-464; Child Welfare League of America Standards for Foster Family Care Service; Hutchinson, op. cit.; Miller, op. cit.; Reinhold, "Fostering the Troubled Child."
54 Begab, op. cit.; Miller, op. cit.; Reinhold, "Fostering the Troubled Child."
55 Child Welfare League of America Standards for Foster Family Care Service; Maluccio, op. cit.; Reinhold, "Fostering the Troubled Child"; Reinhold, "Letter to the Editor"; Wildy, op. cit.
56 Child Welfare League of America Standards for Foster Family Care Service; Flanagan, op. cit.; Maluccio, op. cit.; Miller, op. cit.; Wildy, op. cit.

In addition, Wildy stresses the importance of previous training and practice in child care in order to provide the foster parents with a common core of knowledge and self-discipline.[57]

A critical issue is that of selecting "ideal" foster parents. The implication is aptly stated by MacDonald and Ferguson:

"The nation's 'potentially usable family' is not stable in time or space. It changes with the supply and demand for foster homes, the alternatives to foster-home care available in any given place, the kinds of children needing placement, and the resources of the agency for helping foster parents learn on the job." [58]

The problem in selecting foster families is still being defined in much the same way in 1966 [59] as it was in 1943,[60] but the social context has changed. The last 15 years has been a period in which foster family care has replaced the custodial institution as the placement of choice for large numbers of children, and there are increasing demands for foster parents to serve in specialized programs for emotionally disturbed and retarded children. New programs in foster family day care and homemaker services have placed further demands on the age group from which foster parents are usually drawn. Moreover, this age group is a declining proportion of the population.

The supply of prospective foster parents apparently has been reduced as a result of such factors as the increasing number of families living and working in cities where smaller homes are the rule, greater family geographic and social mobility, and the de-emphasis of the social utility of the maternal and homemaking roles of women.[61]

There is no quantity of readily available applicants as there may have been when the demand for foster parents was less. The problem is to find persons willing to be foster parents, to define the responsibilities of their task, to relate these responsibilities to program goals and to personal and training qualifications, and to provide the foster parents with financial and status rewards for their services.

Motivation for Foster Parenthood

Why should anyone wish to be a foster parent? Various writers have attributed the following motivations to foster parents:

.. Companionship of a child for themselves.[62]
.. Companionship for their own child.[63]
.. Compensation for the inability to adopt.[64]
.. Filling the void created by the death of a natural child.[65]
.. Identification with the unfortunate.[66]
.. Community service.[67]
.. Supplementing family income.[68]
.. Compensation for loss of own children who have left home.[69]
.. Undoing parental deprivation.[70]
.. General warmth for children.[71]

There has been much speculation about the motivation of foster parents. The interest in this area rests on the assumption that there is a relationship between motivation and adequacy of performance. The evidence, however, is not clear.

The level of motivation expressed in initiating application to become foster parents may be insignificant. Stanton finds no statistically significant difference in the child care provided by families who initiated application and families who responded to the agency's initiation.[72]

The content of expressed motivations may be important only in relation to caring for certain kinds of children. Murphy reports that mothers giving altruistic reasons for caring for children did a significantly better job

57 Wildy, *op. cit.*
58 Mary E. MacDonald and Marjorie F. Ferguson, "Selecting Foster Parents: An Essay Review," *The Social Service Review,* XXXVIII (1964), 316–327.
59 Maluccio, *op. cit.*; Reinhold, "Fostering the Troubled Child"; Reinhold, "Letter to the Editor."
60 Hutchinson, *op. cit.*
61 Beatrice Garrett, "Current Trends in Adoption and Foster Care," Paper presented at the New England Homefinder's Conference, Boston, February 17, 1965.
62 Josselyn, *op. cit.*
63 Babcock, "Some Psychodynamic Factors in Foster Parenthood—Part I"; Josselyn, *op. cit.*
64 Josselyn, *op. cit.*
65 *Ibid.*
66 Babcock, "Some Psychodynamic Factors in Foster Parenthood—Part I."
67 Josselyn, *op. cit.*
68 *Ibid.*
69 Babcock, "Some Psychodynamic Factors in Foster Parenthood—Part I."
70 Colvin, *op. cit.*; Fanshel, *Foster Parenthood: A Role Analysis.*
71 Colvin, *op. cit.*; Richard Kinter and Herbert Otto, "The Family Strength Concept and Foster Family Selection," CHILD WELFARE, XLIII (1964), 359–364 ff.
72 Stanton, *op. cit.*

with boys from "poor risk" backgrounds than mothers who did not give altruistic reasons. All mothers did equally well with "good risk" boys and with girls.[73] Babcock reports that those couples whose motivation for becoming foster parents was companionship for their own child were unable to take care of foster children once these children were no longer babies.[74]

The content of expressed motivations may not differentiate between accepted and rejected foster parents, but may differentiate between families the agency defines as being most and least adequate. Lowenstein reports that similar reasons for wanting a foster child were given by foster parents who were accepted and by those who were rejected.[75] On the other hand, Colvin[76] and Fanshel[77] indicate that a significant motivation among least adequate parents was that of undoing parental deprivation. Colvin[78] and Kinter and Otto[79] report that the most adequate foster parents used "love" and "give" in describing their reasons for wanting a foster child.

The effects of interaction among foster parent motivation, agency intervention, and the joys and trials of caring for certain kinds of foster children seem to be more complex than the empirical findings presented might suggest.

A number of clinical writers agree that motivations as expressed by prospective foster parents should be considered only as a starting point for the exploration of deeper motives.[80] They agree that a common fallacy to avoid is the idea that to know a motive is to know the outcome of a course of action. Instead, the assessment of foster parent motivation should result in an understanding of how the motives will be expressed in the foster parent-child relationship.

An emphasis on the satisfactions or dissatisfactions of individual motives in being foster parents may not prove to be very enlightening in our search for the conditions necessary to provide adequate foster care. It may be more fruitful to view foster care in relation to its accomplishments and failures in achieving the cooperative tasks of placement. This kind of social-organization view implies the development of an interactional frame of reference—a model of foster parenting in which one would examine the common purposes of foster families and social workers, the patterns and effects of their communication systems, and their ability and willingness to work together on behalf of the child.

At the present time, the closest approximation to this frame of reference can be developed from examining the characteristics of foster parents who were recruited, the caseworker—foster parent relationship, training methods, and the adequacy of foster parent role performance.

Characteristics of Foster Parents Who Were Recruited

The findings of descriptive studies of foster parents are not in agreement regarding the demographic characteristics of foster parents. Babcock,[81] De Fries,[82] and Rich[83] found that foster parents came from a segment of the population characterized by minimal educational and income levels. Ambinder found that foster parents had low verbal abilities (median Otis IQ ranging from 70 to 89) and reading levels below the ninth or tenth grade level.[84] On the other hand, Glassberg found that the median income of foster parents was the same as that of the Philadelphia metropolitan area, and that a total range of social and economic characteristics was represented by foster parents.[85]

---

[73] Murphy, op. cit.
[74] Babcock, "Some Psychodynamic Factors in Foster Parenthood—Part I."
[75] Lowenstein, op. cit.
[76] Colvin, op. cit.
[77] Fanshel, Foster Parenthood: A Role Analysis.
[78] Colvin, op. cit.
[79] Kinter and Otto, op. cit.
[80] Babcock, "Some Psychodynamic Factors in Foster Parenthood—Part I"; Charnley, op. cit.; Hutchinson, op. cit.; Josselyn, op. cit.; Lawder, op. cit.; Charlotte Towle, "Discussion of Evaluating Motives for Foster Parents," CHILD WELFARE, XXXI, No. 2 (1952), 8 ff.

[81] Babcock, "Some Psychodynamic Factors in Foster Parenthood—Part I."
[82] Zira DeFries, et al., "Foster Care for Disturbed Children—A Nonsentimental View," CHILD WELFARE, XLIV (1965), 73–84.
[83] Rich, op. cit.
[84] Walter J. Ambinder, Laura Fireman, and Douglas Sargent, "Verbal Abilities and Literacy Levels Required of Foster Parents," CHILD WELFARE, XLII (1963), 501–503.
[85] Glassberg, op. cit.

7

Babcock and Rich report that foster parents were family- and church-focused, rather than community-focused. They were apt to come from suburban or rural areas which are usually quite distant from the social and health resources of metropolitan communities.[86]

Jungries found that only 7 of the 45 foster parents he studied were able to use recommended child guidance services in a meaningful way by maintaining contact and supporting the child's therapy in a positive manner.[87] Ambinder and Sargent found that 73 percent of the disciplinary techniques used by foster parents were ineffective or harmful.[88]

From the available evidence it seems fairly clear that many foster parents may be expected to use child-rearing techniques different from those considered desirable by social agencies. Also, in many cases social agencies may seem to foster parents to be geographically isolated, too complex in terms of their expectations, and intrusive in their methods of providing services. In addition to whatever communications difficulties may be created as a result of the different psychological orientations to the child of social workers and foster parents, it seems fairly clear that a basic lack of understanding or even a misunderstanding about goals and means might follow from the foster parents' apparently low verbal and reading abilities.

These findings support the idea that recruited foster parents are unable to meet the expectations of the qualities sought for in foster parents, as identified above. The discrepancy between the ideal and the actual further suggests that conflicts are created for homefinders, foster care workers, and the recruited foster parents.

The nature and meaning of the husband-wife relationship of foster parents constitutes an area of disagreement in the literature. On the basis of reviews of 26 mental hygiene clinic records and 25 foster family records respectively, Markey and Noble,[89] and Babcock[90] found that the wife was the dominant figure in the marital relationship. Wineman also reports that the foster mother was the leader and the father was the follower.[91]

Charnley reports from her clinical experience that foster fathers tend to be passive and mothers tend to be domineering in their relationships with social workers.[92] Kohn[93] and Irons,[94] however, found that fathers were active in foster parent group meetings; Irons suggests that the "passive foster father" is a myth created by the predominant number of female workers in the field who work primarily with the foster mother.

Moreover, Markey and Noble, Charnley, and Babcock disagree as to the meaning of the foster mother's dominance in the husband-wife relationship. Markey and Noble interpret the wife's domination as pathogenic and interfering with the proper psychosexual adjustment of foster children. Charnley and Babcock argue that the foster father's passivity is an expression of mutual agreement regarding family roles, which results in foster mothers working directly with the caseworker on the problems related to foster children, with the father taking a secondary role in that task.

The lack of agreement in this area suggests the need for additional research, which should focus on the following questions:

.. What is the nature of the husband-wife relationship of foster parents?
.. Is this relationship a uniform one that characterizes all forms of interaction, or does it vary, depending upon the particular situation?
.. What are the effects of the relationship

---

[86] Babcock, "Some Psychodynamic Factors in Foster Parenthood—Part I"; Rich, *op. cit.*
[87] Jerome Jungries, Liller B. Green, and Matilda Kroll, "Foster Mothers in Child Guidance," CHILD WELFARE, XLI (1962), 147–152.
[88] Walter J. Ambinder and Douglas A. Sargent, "Foster Parents' Techniques of Management of Preadolescent Boys' Deviant Behavior," CHILD WELFARE, XLIV (1965), 90–94.

[89] O. B. Markey and Helen Nobel, "An Evaluation of the Masculinity Factor in Boarding Home Situations," *American Journal of Orthopsychiatry,* VI (1936), 258–267.
[90] Babcock, "Some Psychodynamic Factors in Foster Parenthood—Part II," *op. cit.*
[91] David Wineman, "Selecting and Matching of Foster Parents and Foster Children," mimeographed (Detroit: Merrill-Palmer Institute, 1964).
[92] Charnley, *op. cit.*
[93] Elaine A. Kohn, "A Joint Project for Providing Group Meetings for Foster Parents," CHILD WELFARE, XL, No. 5 (1961), 31–33.
[94] Lucia Irons, "Training of Foster Parents in Groups," mimeographed (Detroit: Merrill-Palmer Institute, 1966), pp. 26–28.

8

in relation to the child and the work with the agency?

Caseworker-Foster Parent Relationship

Most clinical writings are in agreement that the caseworker-foster parent relationship is not like a caseworker-client relationship. It is defined as being similar to a supervisor-staff relationship that focuses on education, support, and supervision of the foster parents.[95] Glickman suggests that, in a few cases, direct treatment of foster parents may be indicated in addition to the provision of advice and guidance.[96] Charnley indicates that interpretation may be an appropriate technique to use in discussion of foster parents' problems.[97]

Implicit in this definition of the relationship as being like that of a supervisor to staff members is the idea of a hierarchical organization of roles, with the social worker in a superior position and the foster parent in a subordinate one. Kline and Overstreet state that the final authority vested in the social worker causes the foster parent to view him as a judgmental person; the social worker is in a position to place a child with the foster parents, and he can punish the foster parents by criticism or by removal of the child.[98]

Rawley[99] and Radinsky[100] agree with Kline and Overstreet that the authority vested in the social worker is a problem inherent in the relationship between worker and foster parents. Rawley argues that this problem will be remedied when social workers view foster parents as equals and not as subordinates. Radinsky argues that the problem is inevitable and can only be remedied by group discussion meetings with foster parents. On the other hand, Kline and Overstreet believe that the caseworker's awareness of the final authority vested in his role will lead him to manage the foster parents' unrealistic expectations in a constructive way so that they interfere minimally with performance.

Aware of the dangers of replacement and the limited supply of available foster homes, Meyerowitz argues that the social workers identify with foster parents and use their authority to maintain the status quo.[101] She feels that if placement is viewed as a plan for helping the child and his parents achieve a better adjustment, social workers will be able to use their authority as a constructive positive force.

The only available data from foster parents reveals the following:

.. Fifty percent perceived the caseworker as a helpful person with ongoing supervisory responsibilities.
.. Twenty-five percent perceived the caseworker as a pastor or good uncle.
.. Thirteen percent perceived the caseworker as a homefinder.
.. Ten percent perceived the caseworker as an emergency repairman.
.. Twelve percent were confused (totals do not add up to 100 percent because more than one response per parent was possible).[102]

Ambinder interprets the hazy perceptions by foster parents of the caseworker's role as a problem in their relationship. None of the clinical writings address themselves adequately to this problem.

The review of these writings raises the following questions:

.. What responsibilities and decisions should social workers and foster parents have? Which responsibilities and decisions are unique? Which are shared?

---

[95] Babcock, "Some Psychodynamic Factors in Foster Parenthood—Part II"; Clare Britton, "Casework Techniques in Child Care Services," *Social Casework*, XXXVI (1955), 3–13; Charnley, *op. cit.*; Marcia T. Gedanken, "Foster Parent and Social Worker Roles Based on Dynamics of Foster Parenting," CHILD WELFARE, XLV (1966), 512–517; Glickman, *op. cit.*; Marie H. O'Connell, *Foster Home Services to Children* (New York: Child Welfare League of America, 1953; Rawley, *op. cit.*; Towle, *op. cit.*, Emily Mitchell Wires, "Some Factors in the Worker–Foster Parent Relationships," CHILD WELFARE, XXXIII, No. 8 (1954), 8 ff.

[96] Glickman, *op. cit.*
[97] Charnley, *op. cit.*
[98] Draza Kline and H. M. Overstreet, *Casework with Foster Parents* (New York: Child Welfare League of America, 1956).
[99] Rawley, *op. cit.*
[100] Elizabeth K. Radinsky, Bessie Schick Freed, and Helen Rubenstein, "Recruiting and Serving Foster Parents," in *Today's Child and Foster Care* (New York: Child Welfare League of America, 1963), 37–49.

[101] Hilda Meyerowitz, "Use of Authority in Child Placement," *The Jewish Social Service Quarterly*, XXXI (1955) 327–334.
[102] Walter Ambinder, *et al.* "Role Phenomena and Foster Care for Emotionally Disturbed Children," *American Journal of Orthopsychiatry*, XXXII (1962) 32–39.

.. What can social agencies and social workers do to help foster parents have a more adequate conception of the caseworker-foster parent relationship?

Training Methods

Foster parents face some common problems in fulfilling their roles. Frequently mentioned are:

.. Disciplining the foster child.[103]
.. Guiding the sexual development of the foster child.[104]
.. Sharing the foster child with his parents.[105]
.. Sharing the foster child with the agency.[106]

The most frequently mentioned way of helping foster parents deal with these problems is through on-the-job training by means of individual supervision and group discussion methods. The latter has been given increasing attention.[107]

Frequently mentioned benefits from the group approach are:

.. An awareness that other parents have similar questions and problems.[108]
.. An ability to discuss feelings and problems that were not discussed in individual contacts with the caseworker.[109]
.. Clarification of the respective roles of foster parents and social workers in the child's life.[110]

---

[103] Ambinder and Sargent, *op. cit.;* Nora S. House and Anna M. Koop, "Group Work in an Adolescent Boys' Foster Home Program," *The Catholic Charities Review,* L, No. 4, (1966), 6–13 Jacqueline McCoy and Jack Donahue, "Educating Foster Parents through the Group Process," CHILD WELFARE, XL, No. 3 (1961), 29–31.
[104] House and Koop, *op. cit.;* Markey and Noble *op. cit.;* McCoy and Donahue, *op. cit.*
[105] Chambers, *op. cit.;* Charnley, *op. cit.;* Jane Gaffney, "Are Foster Homes a Rare Resource?" CHILD WELFARE, XLIV (1965), 394–396; House and Koop, *op. cit.*
[106] Charnley, *op. cit.*
[107] Gaffney, *op. cit.;* House and Koop, *op. cit.;* Irons, *op. cit.;* Kohn, *op. cit.;* McCoy and Donahue, *op. cit.;* Radinsky, *et al., op. cit.;* Douglas A. Sargent, *A Progress Report of the Detroit Foster Home Project,* mimeographed (Detroit: Merrill-Palmer Institute, 1966). Soffen, *op. cit.;* Carolyn Thomas, "The Use of Group Methods with Foster Parents," *Children,* VIII (1961), 218–222.
[108] Gaffney, *op. cit.;* House and Koop, *op. cit.;* Kohn, *op. cit.;* McCoy and Donahue, *op. cit.;* Radinsky, *op. cit.*
[109] Irons, *op. cit.;* Kohn, *op. cit.;* Radinsky, *op. cit.*
[110] Gaffney, *op. cit.;* McCoy and Donahue, *op. cit.*

.. Raising the status of foster parents by giving them experiences in which they are viewed as colleagues and not as clients.[111]
.. Increasing the identification of foster parents with agency goals.[112]
.. Additional diagnostic clues for the social workers.[113]
.. Providing a check against professional omissions and policy problems.[114]

Kohn,[115] Thomas,[116] and Gaffney[117] agree that group meetings increase the foster parents' identification with the agency and, hence, increase the likelihood of retaining foster homes. Presumably, identification follows from:

.. Clarifying the roles of foster parents and social workers.
.. Providing educational material that helps foster parents to fulfill their roles.
.. Perceiving and treating foster parents as colleagues (as opposed to subordinates).

In addition, Gaffney specifies the helpfulness of writing and distributing a *Foster Parents Manual,* holding an annual reception honoring foster parents, and publishing a monthly *Newsletter to Foster Parents.*[118] The common theme implied in these approaches is the agency's tangible recognition of the valuable services that foster parents provide. This public recognition is rooted in the premise that everyone (foster parents included) enjoys knowing that his work is appreciated.

A significant area of disagreement is whether group training resulted in changes in child care. Sargent suggests that improvements in functioning appeared to be minimal and, when they did occur, they were apt to be slightly more prevalent among the foster fathers.[119] Soffen reports no significant changes in the relationship with the caseworker, motivation, family climate, adequacy of the home, or potential response of

---

[111] House and Koop, *op. cit.*
[112] Kohn, *op. cit.;* Soffen, *op. cit.;* Thomas, *op. cit.*
[113] Kohn, *op. cit.;* McCoy and Donahue, *op. cit.;* Radinsky, *op. cit.*
[114] Radinsky, Freed, and Rubenstein, *op. cit.*
[115] Kohn, *op. cit.*
[116] Thomas, *op. cit.*
[117] Gaffney, *op. cit.*
[118] *Ibid.*
[119] Sargent, *op. cit.*

the home to receiving foster children.[120] McCoy and Donahue state that foster mothers were able to utilize specific suggestions, but were unable to generalize to other situations or problems.[121]

In the only study that made use of an experimental and control group, Soffen [122] reports the following significant changes in the experimental training group:

.. Understanding the growth needs of children.
.. Ability to respond to growth needs.
.. Understanding the meaning of difficult behavior.
.. Ability to respond appropriately to difficult behavior.
.. Ability to respond appropriately to children's needs.

Although this review has highlighted the contributions of group discussions with foster parents as a supplement to individual services, two significant questions remain unanswered. First, if we expect foster parents to function as semiprofessionals, what kind of educational background, if any, should the agencies require of foster parents? Second, what should the content and timing sequence of an on-the-job training program be?

Though Wildly stresses the importance of foster parents having previous professional training in child care, she does not indicate what the components of that training should be.[123] Chambers and Foster describe the two-year certificate program for child care workers offered by the University of Pittsburgh.[124] How realistic is it to expect foster parents to involve themselves in a two-year training program?

Hromadka presents a schematic outline of the predominant and reinforcing child care techniques to be used in relation to different types of children's needs.[125] How applicable is his approach for foster parents? If applicable, could it serve as the core material for on-the-job training programs for foster parents?

Adequacy of Foster Parent Role Performance

Two major issues are presented in the literature in relation to the role performance of the foster parents: the definition of the foster parent role, and the adequacy of performance in that role.

In order to perform adequately, foster parents must know what agencies expect of them. A review of the literature reveals both a lack of clarity regarding role definition and disagreement between foster parents and social workers.

McCoy [126] and Williston [127] indicate that social workers perceive the roles of the foster parents as including the following components: foster parents act in an "as if" manner to the foster child; they are "partial" parents with limited responsibility; they share responsibility for the child with the social worker and the child's own parents; they care for the foster child and protect him, and the child is often unable to respond to that care and protection in a positive manner; the foster parents are temporary parents.

Williston argues, however, that foster parents define their own roles differently. He states that foster parents try to make the child over in their own image; they want the child to drop the affectional ties and identifications he has with his own family; they desire exclusive jurisdiction over the child and perceive other adults (natural parents and social workers) as unnecessary or as competitors.

Conflict in the role expectations and perceptions of foster parents is documented in the studies of Ambinder [128] and Wolins.[129] Ambinder's analysis of 50 interviews with foster parents reveals that 25 percent perceived their role as that of natural parents and 30 percent perceived their role as that of task-oriented specialists. Wolins reports

120 Soffen, op. cit.
121 McCoy and Donahue, op. cit.
122 Soffen, op. cit.
123 Wildy, op. cit.
124 Guinevere S. Chambers and Genevieve W. Foster, "Toward Improved Competence in Child-Care Workers—II: A Two-Level Training Program," Children, XIII (1966), 185–189.
125 Van G. Hromadka, "Toward Improved Competence in Child Care Workers: A Look at What They Do," Children, XIII (1966), 181–184.

126 McCoy, op. cit.
127 Williston, op. cit.
128 Ambinder, et al., "Role Phenomena and Foster Care for Emotionally Disturbed Children."
129 Wolins, op. cit.

that 77 percent of 93 foster parents defined their role as that of natural or adoptive parents, and 19 percent considered their role as being like that of relatives. Wolins also provides data from 78 close neighbors of the foster parents; their responses closely parallel those of the foster parents. Nineteen social workers responded quite differently, however. One third perceived the foster parent as a natural parent; one third perceived the role as unique; and the remainder perceived the role as either that of a relative or a paid agency employee.

A review of the literature regarding adequacy of role performance reveals that many of the foster parents recruited by social agencies have difficulty in fulfilling their responsibilities. Certain characteristics seem to be associated with different degrees of adequacy.

The most adequate foster parents:

.. Are younger.[130]
.. Use "love" and "give" in describing reasons for wanting a child.[131]
.. Have children themselves who seemed secure and well-adjusted.[132]
.. Have an understanding of children's behavior, and show warmth and appropriateness in relating to them.[133]
.. Are able to accept the child's own parents as significant persons in his life.[134]

Conversely, least adequate foster parents are older,[135] use "take" in describing reasons for wanting a child,[136] received low scores on parental competence,[137] have children of their own who were not secure and well-adjusted,[138] and had difficulty in accepting the natural parents as significant persons in the child's life.[139] In addition to these factors the least adequate foster parents:

.. Exercise strict and omnipotent control over the child's life.[140]
.. Reside in a suburban location.[141]
.. Express a strong preference for preschool children.[142]
.. Overemphasize academic performance.[143]
.. Reveal the undoing of parental deprivation as a significant motivation for becoming foster parents.[144]
.. Have own children younger than the foster child.[145]

Contradictory findings are reported in relation to an expressed preference for boys or girls. In Colvin's review of Etri's thesis, the most adequate foster parents expressed no preference.[146] On the other hand, Murphy reports that a preference for boys was associated with success with children from poor-risk backgrounds.[147]

A word of caution seems advisable. With very few exceptions, the data reported here are from social worker's judgments. There is considerable evidence that the social and psychological distance between social workers and foster parents tends to bias those judgments. For example, the findings of Ambinder,[148] De Fries,[149] and Babcock [150] suggest that inadequate performance may be associated with minimal education and occupational levels, but the definitions of adequate performance tended to reflect the bias of middle-class professionals. In addition, Dingman reports that social workers were able to predict the responses of caretakers only when the caretaker's attitudes were similar to those of social workers. Conversely, social workers were unable to predict

130 Colvin, op. cit.
131 Ibid.; Kinter and Otto, op. cit.
132 Joseph Kresh, "Factors Contributing to Successful Foster Motherhood: A Study of Foster Mothers Serving the Children's Bureau and Applicants Who Have Been Accepted by the Agency," (unpublished master's thesis, Adelphi School of Social Work, 1955).
133 DeFries, Shirley Jenkins, and Ethelyn C. Williams, op. cit.; Fanshel, Foster Parenthood: A Role Analysis; Soffen, op. cit.
134 Leslie W. Hunter, "Foster Homes for Teenagers," Children, XI, (1964), 243 ff.; Kresh, op. cit.
135 Colvin, op. cit.
136 Ibid.; Kinter and Otto, op. cit.
137 Fanshel, Foster Parenthood: A Role Analysis.
138 Kresh, op. cit.
139 Ibid.

140 Fanshel, Foster Parenthood: A Role Anaysis; Hunter, op. cit.; Josselyn, op. cit.
141 Murphy, op. cit.
142 Babcock, "Some Psychodynamic Factors in Foster Parenthood—Part I"; Babcock, "Some Psychodynamic Factors in Foster Parenthood: Part II"; Murphy, op. cit.
143 Hunter, op. cit.
144 Colvin, op. cit.; Fanshel, Foster Parenthood: A Role Analysis.
145 Chambers, op. cit.; Murphy, op. cit.
146 Colvin, op. cit.
147 Murphy, op cit.
148 Ambinder and Sargent, op. cit.
149 DeFries, Jenkins, and Williams, op. cit.
150 Babcock, "Some Psychodynamic Factors in Foster Parenthood: Part I"; Babcock, "Some Psychodynamic Factors in Foster Parenthood: Part II."

12

accurately the attitudes of caretakers who were not middle class.[151]

The review of the literature regarding adequacy of role performance of foster parents indicates that many foster parents recruited by agencies were unable to meet adequately the expectations of the qualities sought for in foster parents. This discrepancy raises the questions with which we began:

.. How realistic are the expectations for foster parents? What importance do they have for the role definition, status, and selection of foster parents? What importance do they have for training programs with the foster parents already recruited?
.. If expectations for foster parents are not realistic, what alternatives exist for specifying what the profession expects from foster parents?

Conclusions

Perhaps foster care is an outmoded social response to situations that have more adequate alternatives; in many ways our field is a captive of structures and systems that were designed for other purposes and in other times. Perhaps foster care is an appropriate social response to many current situations. As suggested here, the evidence is complex and contradictory. In trying to bring it together, our hope is to stimulate the search for answers from many different perspectives. Obviously our bias is for further research, and we have tried to formulate some of the components of the question, "What do we need to know in order to provide adequate foster homes?"

Equally obvious is a need for the clarification of objectives and of the means required to achieve those objectives. We have tended to assume that money, staff, and community acceptance are essential. If we had the maximum of all three "magic" ingredients, it is not at all clear what we would do with them. With insufficient resources, it is not entirely clear what we consider most essential. We consider it imperative for the field of child welfare to try to answer the questions raised in this paper.

---

151 H. F. Dingman, C. D. Windle, and S. J. Brown, "Prediction of Child-Rearing Attitudes," CHILD WELFARE, XLI (1962), 305–307 ff.

BIBLIOGRAPHY

AMBINDER, WALTER, et al., "Role Phenomena and Foster Care for Emotionally Disturbed Children." American Journal of Orthopsychiatry, XXXII (1962), 32–39.

——— and SARGENT, DOUGLAS A., "Foster Parents' Techniques of Management of Preadolescent Boys' Deviant Behavior." CHILD WELFARE, XLIV (1965), 90–94.

——— FIREMAN, LAURA, and SARGENT, DOUGLAS, "Verbal Abilities and Literacy Levels Required of Foster Parents." CHILD WELFARE, XLII (1963), 501–503.

BABCOCK, CHARLOTTE G., "Some Psychodynamic Factors in Foster Parenthood—Part I." CHILD WELFARE, XLIV (1965), 485–493 ff.

——— "Some Psychodynamic Factors in Foster Parenthood—Part II." CHILD WELFARE, XLIV (1965), 570–577 ff.

BEGAB, MICHAEL J., "Mental Retardation: The Role of the Voluntary Social Agency." Social Casework, XLV (1964), 457–464.

BOHMAN, L. JOHN, "Methods of Recruiting Foster Homes and Ways to Enable Foster Parents to Help the Children." CHILD WELFARE, XXXVI, No. 10 (1957), 4–7.

BRITTON, CLARE, "Casework Techniques in Child Care Services." Social Casework, XXXVI (1955), 3–13.

CHAMBERS, GUINEVERE S. and FOSTER, GENEVIEVE W., "Toward Improved Competence in Child-Care Workers—II: A Two-Level Training Program." Children, XIII (1966), 185–189.

CHAMBERS, MARIAN L., "A Study of Twelve Foster Parents Who Applied To Board Children in 1946 and Discontinued in 1947 To See Why They Did not Continue as Boarding Parents" (unpublished master's thesis, New York School of Social Work, 1948).

CHARNEY, JEAN, The Art of Child Placement. Minneapolis, University of Minnesota Press, 1955.

Child Welfare League of America Standards for Foster Family Care Service. New York, Child Welfare League of America, 1959.

COCHINTU, ANNE W. and MASON, WINIFRED, "Foster Homes for Children with Medical Problems." CHILD WELFARE, XL (1961), 26–28.

COLVIN, RALPH W., "Toward the Development of a Foster Parent Attitude Test," in Quantitative Approaches to Parent Selection (New York: Child Welfare League of America, 1962), pp. 41–53.

DECOCQ, GUSTAVE A., The Withdrawal of Foster Parent Applicants, mimeographed. San Francisco, United Community Council of San Francisco.

DEFRIES, ZIRA, JENKINS, SHIRLEY, and WILLIAMS, ETHELYN C., "Foster Care for Disturbed Children—A Nonsentimental View." CHILD WELFARE, XLIV (1965), 73–84.

DICK, KENNETH, "What People Think About Foster Care." Children, VIII (1961), 48–52.

DINGMAN, H. F., WINDLE, C. D., and BROWN, S. J.,

"Prediction of Child-Rearing Attitudes," CHILD WELFARE, XLI (1962), 305–307 ff.

FANSHEL, DAVID, *Foster Parenthood: A Role Analysis.* Minneapolis, University of Minnesota Press, 1966.

—— "Specializations Within the Foster Parent Role: A Research Report—Part I. Differences Between Foster Parents of Infants and Foster Parents of Older Children." CHILD WELFARE, XL, (1961), 17–21.

—— "Specializations Within the Foster Parent Role: A Research Report—Part II. Foster Parents Caring for the 'Acting Out' and the Handicapped Child." CHILD WELFARE, XL (1961), 19–23.

FLANAGAN, MARY E., "Symposium, Part II: Social Factors Contributing to Character Disorders—Comments: How Foster Parents Can Help the Disordered Child." CHILD WELFARE, XXXVII, No. 5 (1958), 10–14.

GAFFNEY, JANE, "Are Foster Homes A Rare Resource?" CHILD WELFARE, XLIV (1965), 394–396.

GARRETT, BEATRICE, "Current Trends in Adoption and Foster Care." Paper presented at the New England Homefinder's Conference, Boston, February 17, 1965.

GEDANKEN, MARCIA T., "Foster Parent and Social Worker Roles Based on Dynamics of Foster Parenting." CHILD WELFARE, XLV (1966), 512–517.

GLASSBERG, EUDICE, "Are Foster Homes Hard to Find?" CHILD WELFARE, XLIV (1965), 453–460 ff.

GLICKMAN, ESTHER, *Child Placement Through Clinically Oriented Casework.* New York, Columbia University Press, 1957.

GLOVER, E. ELIZABETH, "Federal Grants-in-Aid and *All* Child Welfare Services." CHILD WELFARE, XLIV (1965), 64 ff.

—— "Improving and Expanding Foster Care Resources." CHILD WELFARE, XLIV (1965), 244 ff.

HOUSE, NORA S. and KOOP, ANNA M., "Group Work in an Adolescent Boys Foster Home Program." *Catholic Charities Review,* L (1966), 6–13.

HROMADKA, VAN G. "Toward Improved Competence in Child Care Workers: A Look at What They Do." *Children,* XIII (1966), 181–184.

HUNTER, LESLIE W., "Foster Homes for Teenagers." *Children,* XI (1964), 234–243.

HUTCHINSON, DOROTHY, *In Quest of Foster Parents.* New York, Columbia University Press, 1943.

IRONS, LUCIA, *Training of Foster Parents in Groups,* mimeographed. Detroit, Merrill Palmer Institute, 1966.

JOSSELYN, IRENE, "Evaluating Motives of Foster Parents." CHILD WELFARE, XXXI, No. 2 (1952), 3–8.

JUNGRIES, JEROME, GREEN, LILLER B., and KROLL, MATILDA, "Foster Mothers in Child Guidance." CHILD WELFARE, XLI (1962), 147–152.

KAPLAN, LILLIAN K. and TURITZ, LILLY D., "Fol-

low-Up Report on Treatment of Emotionally Traumatized Young Children in a Foster Home Setting." *American Journal of Orthopsychiatry,* XXXIV (1964), 581–583.

KINTER, RICHARD, and OTTO, HERBERT, "The Family Strength Concept and Foster Parent Selection." CHILD WELFARE, XLIII (1964), 359–364 ff.

KLINE, DRAZA, "Understanding and Evaluating a Foster Family's Capacity to Meet the Needs of an Individual Child," in Ner Littner, *Changing Needs and Practices in Child Welfare* (New York: Child Welfare League of America, 1960), pp. 23–35.

—— and OVERSTREET, HELEN MARY, *Casework with Foster Parents.* New York, Child Welfare League of America, 1956.

KOHN, ELAINE, A., "A Joint Project for Providing Group Meetings for Foster Parents." CHILD WELFARE, XL, No. 5 (1961), 31–33.

KRESH, JOSEPH, "Factors Contributing to Successful Motherhood: A Study of Foster Mothers Serving the Children's Bureau and Applicants Who Have Been Accepted by the Agency" (unpublished master's thesis, Adelphi School of Social Work, 1955).

LAWDER, ELIZABETH A., "Toward A More Scientific Understanding of Foster Family Care." CHILD WELFARE, XLIII (1964) 57–63.

LOWENSTEIN, ELSE, "Finding Foster Homes for Children" (unpublished master's thesis, New York School for Social Work, 1955).

MACDONALD, MARY E., and FERGUSON, MARJORIE F., "Selecting Foster Parents: An Essay Review." *The Social Service Review,* XXXVIII (1964), 316–327.

MALUCCIO, ANTHONY N., "Selecting Foster Parents for Disturbed Children." *Children,* XIII (1966), 69–74.

MARKEY, O. B., and NOBEL, HELEN, "An Evaluation of the Masculinity Factor in Boarding Home Situations." *American Journal of Orthopsychiatry,* VI (1936), 258–267.

MCCOY, JACQUELINE, "The Application of the Role Concept to Foster Parenthood." *Social Casework,* XLIII (1962), 252–256.

—— and DONAHUE, JACK M., "Educating Foster Parents Through the Group Process." CHILD WELFARE, XL (1961), 29–31.

MEYEROWITZ, HILDA, "Use of Authority in Child Placement." *Jewish Social Service Quarterly,* XXXI (1955), 327–334.

MILLER, CLARA, "The Agency-Owned Foster Home." CHILD WELFARE, XXXIII, No. 9 (1954), 9–11 ff.

MINTZ, IRA L., "Multi-Determined Motivations in Foster Parents." CHILD WELFARE, XLI (1962), 172–174.

MORA, GEORGE, "Foster Families for Emotionally Disturbed Children." CHILD WELFARE, XLI (1962), 104–106.

MURPHY, H. B. M., "Foster Home Variables and Adult Outcomes." *Mental Hygiene,* XLVIII (1964), 587–599.

O'CONNELL, MARIE H., *Foster Home Services to Children: Helping the Child to Use Foster Care.*

New York, Child Welfare League of America, 1953.

OUGHELTREE, CORNELIA M., *Finding Foster Homes*. New York, Child Welfare League of America, 1957.

PRATT, CATHERINE, "Foster Parents as Agency Employees." *Children*, XIII (1966), 14–15.

RADINSKY, ELIZABETH K., FREED, BESSIE SCHICK, and RUBENSTEIN, HELEN, "Recruiting and Serving Foster Parents," in *Today's Child and Foster Care* (New York: Child Welfare League of America, 1963).

RAWLEY, CALLMAN, "The Relation of Administrative Policy and the Supply of Foster Homes." CHILD WELFARE, XXIX, No. 3 (1950), 7–9 ff.

REINHOLD, PETER, "Fostering the Troubled Child." Notes of an Institute Given at the New England Regional Conference of the Child Welfare League of America, Providence, R.I., April 15, 1966.

———— "Letter to the Editor." *Children*, XIII (1966), 168.

RICH, MABLE, "Foster Homes for Retarded Children." CHILD WELFARE, XLIV (1965), 392–394.

SARGENT, DOUGLAS A., *A Progress Report of the Detroit Foster Home Project*, mimeographed. Detroit, Merrill Palmer Institute, 1966.

SIMSARIAN, FRANCES P., "Foster Care Possibilities in a Suburban Community." *Children*, XI (1964), 97–102.

SOFFEN, JOSEPH, "The Impact of a Group Educational Program for Foster Parents." CHILD WELFARE, XLI (1962), 195–201.

STANTON, Howard R., "Mother Love in Foster Homes." *Marriage and Family Living*, XVIII (1956), 301–307.

TEGETHOFF, NINA BECK and GOLDSTEIN, HARRIET, "A Realistic Appraisal of Foster Home Finding." CHILD WELFARE, XLI (1962), 253–255 ff.

THOMAS, CAROLYN, "The Use of Group Methods with Foster Parents." *Children*, VIII (1961), 218–222.

TOWLE, CHARLOTTE, "Evaluating Motives of Foster Parents: Discussion." CHILD WELFARE, XXXI, No. 2, (1952), 8–9 ff.

WILDY, LOIS, "The Professional Foster Home," in *Foster Home Care for Emotionally Disturbed Children* (New York: Child Welfare League of America, 1962), pp. 1–8.

WILLISTON, GEORGE C., "The Foster Parent Role." *Journal of Psychology*, LX (1963), 203–212.

WINEMAN, DAVID, *Selecting and Matching of Foster Parents and Foster Children*, mimeographed. Detroit, Merrill Palmer Institute, 1964.

WIRES, EMILY MITCHELL, "Some Factors in the Worker-Foster-Parent Relationships." CHILD WELFARE, XXXIII, No. 8 (1954), 8–9 ff.

WOLINS, MARTIN, *Selecting Foster Parents*. New York, Columbia University Press, 1963.

RECEIVED MARCH 2, 1967

15

Legal Aspects of Foster Care*

SANFORD N. KATZ**

When a court separates a child from its biological parents and awards custody to a child welfare agency, the agency usually places the child with foster parents. Eventually, it is thought, the child will be reunited with its biological parents and the natural family relationship reestablished. Since there has been no judicial termination of all the biological parents' rights, both the court and the agency view the disposition as temporary and the legal rights of the natural parents are held in abeyance.[1]

Approximately 200,000 neglected children live with foster families in the United States in any given year.[2] While behav-

---

*This article will be published in slightly different form as Chapter 4 of the book *When Parents Fail: The Law's Response to Family Breakdown*, copyright © 1971 by Sanford N. Katz, to be published by Beacon Press.

**Professor of Law, Boston College Law School. Editor-in-Chief, Family Law Quarterly.

1. Court intervention usually involves withdrawing a natural parent's custodial rights. While this does not disturb the reciprocal inheritance rights of the child and its natural parents, it does affect the child's rights under certain legislation. See E. duFresne, *The Rights of Foster Children to Financial Benefits of Foster Parents Under Federal Statutes*, 7 J. FAM L. 613 (1968).

An interesting question is whether a natural parent could recover for the wrongful death of his natural child when that child is in the foster care of another as a result of court intervention. Or conversely, whether such a foster child could recover for the wrongful death of its natural parent.

2. S. Low, FOSTER CARE OF CHILDREN — MAJOR NATIONAL TRENDS AND PROSPECTS, U.S. DEPARTMENT OF HEALTH, EDUCATION AND WELFARE. Children's Bureau 1–2 (1966). "An estimated 287,200 children were living in foster care throughout the United States on March 31, 1965, either in foster family homes served by social agencies or in child welfare institutions for neglected, dependent, and emotionally disturbed children. The rate of children in foster care was 4.0 per 1,000 children under 18 years of age in the U.S. population. This estimate does not include a large, but unknown, number of children living in 'independent' foster family homes who were placed by parents, relatives or others without the assistance of a social agency. Nor does it include a much smaller, but also unknown number of children placed directly in foster family homes by juvenile courts (a practice that occurs to a significant extent only in a few States) or placed by other agencies that do not report to the Children's Bureau.

Assuming that the rate will continue to change in the direction and at the pace at

ioral scientists have developed a sociological profile of foster
care as an institution and a psychological and socioeconomic
portrait of foster parents,[3] the legal implications of the foster
family setting have received scant consideration. This article
will deal with these implications.

Institutional Origins and
Common Law Background

Little is known about the origins of foster care. Although fosterage was practiced among the Anglo-Saxons, the Welsh, and
the Scandinavians, the institution reached its peak of development in ancient Ireland.[4] An examination of the Irish institution reveals a sharp contrast between it and its modern
counterpart. Fosterage in ancient Ireland was based on a voluntary contract between natural parents and foster parents, both
usually members of the upper class.[5] The goals of the institution
were to provide a means of training children and, by forming
close bonds between families, to promote social cohesion.[6] Social status was the controlling factor in fosterage. In addition to
determining the fee that natural parents were to pay the foster
parents,[7] social status determined the legal obligations that attached to the network of relationships established, as well as
the nature of the food, clothing, training, and discipline the child
was to receive.[8]

Foster care, as the term is generally used today, is quite

---

which it was changing during the 1961–65 period, the number of children in foster care
in 1975 is projected to be 364,000, a 27 per cent increase over 1965 or an annual
increase of about 2 percent. The 1975 rate is estimated at 4.7 per 1,000 children.

The number of children in foster family homes on March 31, 1965, is estimated at
207,800, a rate of 2.9 per 1,000 children.

3. *See* D. FANSHEL, FOSTER PARENTHOOD (1966); E. WEINSTEIN, THE
SELF-IMAGE OF THE FOSTER CHILD (1960); M. WOLINS & I. PILIAVIN, INSTITUTION
OR FOSTER FAMILY (1967); C. Babcock, *Some Psychodynamic Factors in Foster
Parenthood* (pts. 1–2), 44 CHILD WELFARE 485, 570 (Nov. 1965, Dec. 1965); D.
Taylor & P. Starr, *Foster Parenting: An Integrative Review of the Literature,* 46
CHILD WELFARE 371 (July 1967).

4. W. HANCOCK & T. O'MAHONY, Preface to 2 ANCIENT LAWS AND INSTITUTES OF
IRELAND, SENCHUS MOR, Part II, XLVI (1896).

5. P. JOYCE, 2 A SOCIAL HISTORY OF ANCIENT IRELAND 14 (1913).

6. *Id.* at 17.

7. Commission for Publishing the Ancient Laws and Institutes of Ireland, 2 AN-
CIENT LAWS AND INSTITUTES OF IRELAND, SENCHUS MOR 151–5, Part II (1869).

8. *Id.* at 149–51.

different from the ancient Irish institution. It is an agency-supervised placement for children, generally from the lower and lower middle classes, whose natural parents are unable to provide them with proper care and who are therefore provided with substitute parents, most often recruited from the lower middle class.[9] Since foster care is theoretically a temporary arrangement, it is generally an alternative to institutional care, with the child receiving the advantages of a family setting[10] and the state benefitting economically.[11]

A foster parent is one who, although not legally related to the child by direct parental blood ties, nor decreed a parent in formal adoption proceedings, assumes the role of a parent. This status most commonly arises when a court awards guardianship and custody of a child to a child welfare agency which in turn delegates the parental role to persons chosen by the agency. Less commonly, foster status may arise in other ways. For example, a court may award guardianship and custody to persons other than the natural or adoptive parents, such as when a divorce court awards custody of a child to an aunt rather than to either of the spouses. Or it may arise as a result of persons who, because of legal defects in an adoption decree, are legally only adoptive parents. Finally, a person may be considered a foster parent if he or she cares for another's child through a formal or informal arrangement or by voluntarily caring for a foundling.

In these situations, the legal rights and duties of foster parents are determined by the common law doctrine of *in loco parentis*. Under this doctrine, persons holding themselves out as parents are held to similar, and often the same, standards as natural parents.[12] Courts use the *in loco parentis* doctrine to impose on foster parents the same responsibilities as natural parents with respect to providing their children with proper

9. *See* FANSHEL, *supra* note 3, at 23–7, 54–7; Taylor & Starr, *supra* note 3, at 377–9.

10. *See* S. PROVENCE & R. LIPTON, INFANTS IN INSTITUTIONS 143–66 (1962).

11. It is well known that the cost of maintaining a child in an institution far exceeds the cost of maintaining it in a foster family. For example, in Massachusetts it costs approximately seven times more per week to maintain a child in an institution than in a foster family.

12. Schneider v. Schneider, 25 N.J. Misc. 180, 52 A.2d 564 (Ch. 1947).

health, education, and environment conducive to the development of sound moral character.

Unless specifically decreed by a court, the parental right to legal custody does not attach to foster parents. In other words, foster parents seem to have more duties than rights. This statement, however, may be misleading, for foster parents do in fact enjoy the right to custody without benefit of the label. A *de facto* custodial interest develops in a foster parent when the foster relationship continues over a period of time. Courts are reluctant to interfere with this interest, and when they attempt to interfere, the foster parent is generally notified and given an opportunity to appear and defend his or her interest.[13] A continuing foster relationship, if secure and orderly, is typically protected against even a natural parent's unreasonable intrusion.[14] A natural parent who wishes to interfere with the foster parent relationship (established in ways other than through court or agency intervention) must, as any other individual, carry the burden of proving the foster parent's unfitness, as well as the burden of showing that the child's needs will be best served by a change in the custodial arrangement.[15]

Under certain conditions, a foster parent may terminate the relationship with a foster child. The most important of these conditions is that the foster parent must intentionally perform a positive act—which ordinarily implies obtaining the consent of all parties in interest—severing all aspects of the relationship.[16]

---

13. *See, In re* Adoption of Cheney, 244 Iowa 1180, 59 N.W.2d 685 (1953). *Contra,* James V. McLinden, Civil No. 13127 (D. Conn., filed May 23, 1969).

14. *See* Cummins v. Bird, 230 Ky. 296, 19 S.W.2d 959 (1929).

15. *See* State v. Knight, 135 So.2d 126 (La. App. 1961).

16. *See, e.g.,* Lewis v. United States, 105 F. Supp. 73 (N.D. W.Va., 1952); Leyerly v. United States, 162 F.2d 79 (10th Cir. 1947); Young v. Hipple, 273 Pa. 439, 117 A. 185 (1922).

The fact that a foster parent may terminate his relationship with his foster child more freely than either a natural or adoptive parent was used as the basis for applying less rigid standards for removing the foster child from the custody of its foster parents in State *ex rel.* Gilman, 249 Iowa 1233, 123S-39, 91 N.W.2d 395, 399 (1958): "The importance of the difference of the status of a natural or adoptive parent, on the one hand, and one merely standing in loco parentis, as in the case before us, is found in the fact that the defendant has made no attempt to adopt [his six-year-old foster child] during the several years he had custody of the child. He is still free to disavow his responsibility as a parent at any time. We do not say he has such an intent; but the right to do so and the possibility are there.

Viewing the entire picture, we think the trial court was amply justified in holding that

Announcing a decision to terminate the relationship while continuing to live with the child is insufficient.[17] A foster parent may not choose to honor the right to enjoy companionship, for example, and fail in the duty to provide support.[18]

The fact that a person has only a foster relationship with a child will ordinarily not relieve him of the obligation to provide financial support. In enforcing a foster parent's support duty, courts have held that persons acting in the role of natural parents assume the duties of natural parents.[19] Foster parents, therefore, may be required to reimburse those who undertake to support their foster children.[20]

Contractual Aspects of the Foster Parent-Child Relationship

A distinction must be drawn between the legal implications of the foster parent-child relationship that emerge from the common law doctrine of *in loco parentis* and the foster parent-child relationship created by agencies under court authority. The status of the individual chosen by an agency to become a foster parent hinges on whether the agency deems him to be an

---

the best interest of the child requires that the defendant be permanently deprived of custody, and the boy sent to a child-placing institution. From there he may eventually be placed in the home of suitable adopting parents, where he will have not only food, clothing and shelter, and love and affection, but security, with freedom from constant shifting about and from the uncertainties and unfavorable influences to which he has heretofore been subjected.

    17. *See* Capek v. Kropik, 129 Ill. 509, 21 N.E. 826 (1889); Schneider v. Schneider, 25 N.J. Misc. 180, 52 A.2d 564 (Ch. 1947).

    18. That there is a duty to support under these circumstances is evident from public welfare law. The "man-in-the-house" rule, or, as it is sometimes called, the "substitute parent" policy, was stated in People v. Shirley, 55 Cal. 2d 521, 524, 360 P.2d 33, 34 (1961): "[U]nder regulations of the State Board of Social Welfare a stepfather living in the home is responsible for the support of the mother of a needy child unless incapacitated and unable to support. . . . A man living in the home assuming the role of spouse has the same responsibility as that of a stepfather for the mother and the needy children. *See also* N. Pacht, *Support of Defendants in the District of Columbia: Part I,* 9 How. L. J. 20, 36–38 (1963); J. tenBroek, *California's Dual System of Family Law: Its Origin, Development, and Present Status, Part III,*17 STAN. L. REV. 614 (1965).

    19. *In re* Harris, 16 Ariz. 1, 140 P. 825 (1914); Howard v. Randolph, 134 Ga. 691, 68 S.E. 586 (1910); Faber v. Industrial Comm., 352 Ill. 115, 185 N.E. 255 (1933); Foreman v. Henry, 87 Okla. 272, 210 P. 1026 (1922); Rosky v. Schmitz, 110 Wash. 547, 188 P. 493 (1920); Ellis v. Cary, 74 Wis. 176, 42 N.W. 252 (1889). *See also In re* Adoption of Cheney, 244 Iowa 1180, 59 N.W.2d 685 (1953); Britt v. Allred, 199 Miss. 786, 25 So.2d 560 (1946); Hollis v. Thomas, 42 Tenn. App. 407, 303 S.W.2d 751 (1957); State *ex rel.* Gilroy v. Superior Court, 37 Wash. 2d 926, 226 P.2d 882 (1951).

    20. *See* Rudd v. Fineberg's Trustee, 277 Ky. 505, 126 S.W.2d 1102 (1939).

21

employee or whether he is a person simply selected by the agency to perform the function of a foster parent. Foster parents most commonly are not considered employees, but rather are persons unconnected with the agency's organization. Their rights and duties are determined by a placement contract, a standard-form agreement whose provisions are drafted by the agency and acquiesced in by the foster parents. The provisions of the contract normally supersede the common law doctrine of *in loco parentis*.

A further distinction should be drawn between the ostensible expectations of the foster parent-child relationship and the contractual basis which establishes it. As the Child Welfare League of America *Standards for Foster Family Care Service* states:[21]

> The ultimate objectives of foster family care should be the promotion of healthy personality development of the child, and amelioration of problems which are personally or socially destructive.
> Foster family care is one of society's ways of assuring the well-being of children who would otherwise lack adequate parental care. . . .
> Foster family care should provide, for the child whose own parents cannot do so, experiences and conditions which promote normal maturation *(care)*, which prevent further injury to the child *(protection)*, and which correct specific problems that interfere with healthy personality development *(treatment)*. Foster family care should be designed in such a way as:
> to maintain and enhance parental functioning to the fullest extent;
> to provide the type of care and services best suited to each child's needs;
> to minimize and counteract hazards to the the child's emotional health inherent in separation from his own family and the conditions leading to it;
> to make possible continuity of relationship by preventing replacements;
> to facilitate the child's becoming part of the foster family, school, peer group and larger community;
> to protect the child from harmful experiences;
> to bring about his ultimate return to his natural family whenever desirable and feasible.

These expectations should be compared with the harsh legalistic language in a representative foster care contract:[22]

> In consideration of being accepted as foster parents by the Agency we agree as follows:
> 1. The child placed with us will be accepted by us as a member of our family, and will receive our affection and care as foster parents. The Agency will furnish a monthly board payment, payable at the end of

21. Child Welfare League of America, Standards for Foster Family Care Service 6–7 (1959).
22. Cited in J. GOLDSTEIN & J. KATZ, THE FAMILY AND THE LAW 1021–22 (1965).

each month. At the time of placement, we will be notified of the specific rate for the child placed with us.

The Agency will provide for the child's clothing, medical and dental expenses.

We will be reimbursed for certain other expenditures made, as described in the Foster Parents' Manual, provided they have been previously authorized by the Agency.

2. We will notify the Agency of any change or plans for change in our own life, which may affect the child placed with us. This will include, but is not limited to vacation plans, illnesses, job changes, moving, and any change in the composition of our family.

3. We will notify the Agency immediately if the child placed with us becomes ill, and we will comply with the Agency's arrangements for medical and dental care.

4. We are aware that the Agency has the responsibility for making plans with regard to the child's relationship with his or her own relatives. We will cooperate with the arrangements made by the Agency worker for visits between the child and his or her own relatives.

5. We acknowledge that we are accepting the child placed with us for an indeterminate period, depending on the needs of the child and his family situation. We are aware that the legal responsibility for the foster child remains with the Agency, and we will accept and comply with any plans the Agency makes for the child. This includes the right to determine when and how the child leaves us, and we agree to cooperate with the arrangements made toward that end.

6. Should we find ourselves unable to continue giving foster care to the child placed with us, we will notify the Agency promptly, and will cooperate with the Agency in making the change of placement as easy as possible. For this reason, we will give the Agency as much time to make such change as is needed, unless our situation is emergent.

As can be seen from the provisions as set forth above, the stated goals of foster care, centering on the welfare of the child, the quality of the foster parent-child relationship, and the preservation of the natural parents' interests, are neither stated nor implied in the contract.

Because of the ambiguities inherent in the attempt to reconcile the goals of foster care programs with the provisions in placement contracts, conflicts inevitably arise between the agency and the foster parents. In resolving these disputes, the agency often asserts the provisions of the contract in support of its position and in opposition to the foster parents' assertion that they are furthering the very goals which foster care programs ostensibly seek to promote. Thus, disputes between agencies and foster parents raise grave doubts as to whether the best interests of the child are the paramount consideration in foster care programs, as well as whether foster parents are, in fact, viewed as "one of the crucial human resources for the care of children who must leave their own homes."[23]

The process by which these disputes are resolved and the considerations that bear upon their resolution are illustrated by the following two cases, *In re Jewish Child Care Association*[24] and *In re Alexander.*[25]

The Case of Laura

The history of Laura, the five-and-a-half-year-old whose custody was at issue in the New York case of *In re Jewish Child Care Association,* resembles that of many other children similarly involved in the struggle of foster parents to make permanent their relationship with their foster children over the objections of placement agencies. When Laura was thirteen months old, she was placed by the Jewish Child Care Association, a foster care agency, with Mr. and Mrs. Sanders, a childless couple in their thirties. Laura's mother, who was eighteen years old and unwed, had been unable to care for the baby at birth and had voluntarily placed her with the New York City Department of Welfare, which transferred the child's custody to the Jewish Child Care Association (hereafter referred to as the Agency).

At placement, the Sanderses were required to sign a document in which they accepted the standard conditions of foster care.[26] Among other things, the couple promised to give Laura affection and care, to follow the Agency's regulations regarding the boarding arrangement and any illnesses or changes in the family situation, and they agreed to cooperate with the Agency's plans for continuing a relationship with the child's natural mother. If the couple became unable to continue as foster parents, they promised to work with the Agency in making an orderly transition to another placement. The Sanderses acknowledged that they were accepting Laura for an in-

---

23. P. Hall, *Foreword to* D. FANSHEL, FOSTER PARENTHOOD v (1966).
24. 5 N.Y.2d 222, 183 N.Y.S.2d 65, 156 N.E.2d 700 (1959).
25. 206 So.2d 452 (Fla. 1968).
26. *See supra* note 22 and accompanying text.

determinate period and were aware that the legal responsibility for the child remained with the Agency.

During the first year after placement, the Sanderses spoke with the Agency about adopting Laura. They were told that adoption was not possible and were asked to help the child understand her relationship to her natural mother. The child had seen her natural mother once during the first year of placement. During the second year of foster care, the Sanderses again mentioned their desire to adopt Laura. The Agency refused to consider the proposal and required the couple, as a condition for keeping the child, to sign a statement acknowledging that they had the child only on a foster home basis. The Sanderses persisted in their efforts to adopt Laura, unsuccesfully seeking approval from the child's natural mother, grandmother, and other relatives. When the Sanderses requested permission to take Laura with them on an out-of-state vacation, the Agency refused, asserting that the child should be returned to her natural mother during that time. Laura, then four years old, had lived with the Sanderses for three years and had seen her natural mother only twice. She was not to see her mother again until the litigation over her custody began.

The Sanderses' constant efforts to adopt Laura, along with the Agency's belief that the couple had become too emotionally attached to the child, prompted the Agency to demand Laura's return. The couple refused and the Agency brought a writ of habeas corpus to obtain the child's release from the Sanderses' home. From the perspective of the foster parents, the Agency's decision to seek the writ was potentially beneficial for various reasons. It allowed the Sanderses to bypass administrative remedies and to obtain an immediate judicial review of the Agency's decision denying request for adoption. Considering their strained relations with the Agency, the Sanderses' chances for administrative relief would probably have been slim. Furthermore, since a habeas corpus proceeding is a method by which a court may explore the question of the child's welfare[27]

---

27. *See, e.g.,* New York *ex rel.* Halvey v. Halvey, 330 U.S. 610 (1947); Berry v Berry, 219 Ala 403, 122 So. 615 (1929); Porter v. Chester, 208 Ga. 309, 66 S.E.2d 729

beyond the narrow issue of the legal right to custody,[28] the fact that the Agency was Laura's legal guardian did not place it in a significantly advantageous position.

In the trial court proceedings to determine whether Laura's "best interests" would be served by a custodial change, the testimony was focused on the effect the proposed change would have on the child's natural mother as well as on the child's own physical and emotional well-being. The line of questioning at the trial seemed to be based on the assumption that the goal of the proceedings was to determine how Laura's needs could best be secured in light of the natural mother's inability to raise the child.

The trial judge heard testimony from the foster parents, representatives of the Agency, the Department of Welfare, and a psychiatrist. The Agency acknowledged that the Sanderses had taken good care of the child and were providing her with a comfortable home environment. However, it claimed that, because of the great love of the foster parents for the child, Laura should be removed from their custody and placed in a "neutral environment" where foster parents would be called "aunt" and "uncle" instead of "mother" and "father" and where "there would not be this terrible pull on the child between her loyalty to her foster parents and her mother."[29] In other words, the Agency did not claim that the foster parents were depriving the child of love, but rather that they were indulging her with too much love. The effect of their indulgence on the child, the Agency urged, was a strain on her relationship with her natural mother.

A large part of the trial consisted of the interrogation of a psychiatrist called by the foster parents. In his testimony, he analyzed the effect of a custodial change on Laura's emotional

---

(1951); Heuvel v. Heuvel, 254 Iowa 1391, 121 N.W.2d 216 (1963). Even the matter of child support may be explored. *Cf.* Howarth v. Northcutt, 152 Conn. 460, 208 A.2d 540 (1965) with Buchanan v. Buchanan, 170 Va. 458, 197 S.E. 426 (1938); Pugh v. Pugh, 133 W.Va. 501, 56 S.E.2d 901 (1949). But some jurisdictions limit the court's inquiry on habeas corpus to the narrow issue of the legal right to custody. *See, e.g.,* May v. Anderson, 345 U.S. 528 (1953) (Ohio).

28. *See* New York Foundling Hosp. v. Gatti, 203 U.S. 429 (1906); Pukas v. Pukas, 129 W.Va. 765, 42 S.E.2d 11 (1947).

29. 5 N.Y.2d 222, 227, 156 N.E.2d 700, 702, 183 N.Y.S.2d 65, 68 (1959).

development. In his opinion, the Sanderses' love for the child had positive rather than damaging emotional effects; indeed, Laura's removal from her foster parents would be detrimental to her emotional growth. He stated that latency was a critical period in a child's development and that, at Laura's age, she needed the security of the sustained relationship with her foster parents.

The trial judge apparently either was not sufficiently convinced by the psychiatric testimony or was persuaded by the Agency's argument that the child was becoming too attached to her foster parents, thus threatening her "relationship" with her natural mother. He decided to remove Laura from her foster parents and to allow the Agency to regain custody and place her in a "neutral environment."[30] After the intermediate appellate court affirmed the decision of the trial court,[31] the Sanderses appealed to the New York Court of Appeals, which held in favor of the Agency in a split (4–3) opinion.[32]

In the New York Court of Appeals' opinion, there is a discernible and major shift in emphasis from that found in the lower court's opinion. The trial court viewed the "best interests of the child" doctrine in terms of securing Laura's health needs in light of her natural mother's situation. The New York Court of Appeals interpreted "the best interests of the child" in terms of preserving the continuity of biological family loyalty.

To the majority of the Court of Appeals, the fact that the Sanderses were Laura's foster (rather than natural or future adoptive) parents was crucial. The court perceived foster parenthood as something less than full parenthood. By showing

---

30. Jewish Child Care Ass'n v. Sanders, 9 Misc. 2d 402, 172 N.Y.S.2d 630 (Sup. Ct. 1957), *aff'd*, 174 N.Y.S.2d 335 (App. Div. 1958), *aff'd*, 156 N.E.2d 700, 183 N.Y.S.2d 65 (Ct. App. 1959).

31. *Id.* The basis of the New York Supreme Court's opinion was as follows: "Respondents have, the court feels, become fond of the child to an extent which has resulted in an attempt by them to induce the mother to permit adoption by them; she has resisted these efforts and the conflict has resulted in this proceeding. The petitioner believes (quite correctly in the court's opinion) that it cannot suffer its established practice to be set at naught solely because respondents believe they can contribute more to the child's welfare than petitioner and the mother can.

The court does not believe that the best interest of this child will be served by the condonation of a disregard of their own obligations and agreements by the respondents, however well-intentioned they may be. *Id.* at 403, 172 N.Y.S.2d at 631.

32. 5 N.Y.2d 222, 156 N.E.2d 700, 183 N.Y.S.2d 65 (1959).

"extreme love," "affection," and "possessiveness" and by acting more like natural than foster parents, the Sanderses, in the court's estimation, had gone beyond the limits of their role as set out in the placement agreement. In essence, what the majority took as conclusive — namely, the "vital fact . . . that Mr. and Mrs. Sanders are not, and presumably will never be, Laura's parents by adoption,"[33] — was the very issue the court was to decide.

The court stressed its concern for preserving the natural ties between Laura and her mother. "[I]n considering what is in Laura's best interests," the court wrote, "it was not only proper, but necessary . . . to consider the facts in terms of their significance to Laura's eventual return to her own mother."[34] And later the court stated:

> What is essentially at stake here is the parental custodial right. Although Child Care has the present legal right to custody . . . it stands, as against the Sanders, [*sic*] in a representative capacity as the protector of Laura's mother's inchoate custodial right and the parent-child relationship which is to become complete in the future.[35]

Finally, in its concluding remarks, the court crystallized its views on the best interests of the child as follows:

> [T]he more important considerations of the child's best interests, the recognition and preservation of her mother's primary love and custodial interest, and the future life of the mother and child together are paramount.[36]

In addition, the court in *Child Care* was concerned with three considerations, all interrelated (but not necessarily related to the best interests of Laura): the preservation of the natural mother's rights; the sanctity of the placement contract; and the maintenance of the Agency's prestige and authority in the community. In the final remark of his opinion for the Court of Appeals, Chief Judge Conway came to grips with these issues. While the interests of Laura and her natural mother (but apparently not those of the foster parents) were of significant importance, what was paramount was the integrity of the law, as manifested in the child placement contract and in a private agency's administrative decisions. In order to maintain author-

---

33. *Id.* at 229, 156 N.E.2d at 703, 183 N.Y.S.2d at 70.
34. *Id.* at 228, 156 N.E.2d at 703, 183 N.Y.S.2d at 69.
35. *Id.* at 229, 156 N.E.2d at 703, 183 N.Y.S.2d at 70.
36. *Id.* at 230, 156 N.E.2d at 704, 183 N.Y.S.2d at 71.

ity, these administrative policies had to be affirmed and the child placement agreement enforced: "[T]he program of agencies such as Child Care . . . may not be subverted by foster parents who breach their trust."[37]

The majority in *Child Care* was concerned with symbols: Judge Conway seemed compelled to preserve the sanctity of legal doctrines and, indirectly, the reputation of a community institution, since the Sanderses had been a threat both to the integrity and the stability of the placement contract[38] and to the prestige of the Agency. To allow Laura to remain with her foster parents would have been to reward persons who failed to fulfill their promises and who had undermined the Agency's decision.[39] It seems that by protecting community institutions, the court shifted its focus from Laura's welfare to other matters: on a jurisprudential level, it was the continuity of legal doctrine; on a practical level, it was the prestige of a social service agency.

Child Care represents a legal struggle between a long-standing and dominant community institution of high prestige and a couple performing a function with low social status.[40]

---

37. 5 N.Y.2d 222, 230, 156 N.E.2d 700, 704, 183 N.Y.S.2d 65 (1959).

38. *But see* note 45 *infra* and accompanying text.

39. Subsequent to this case, another dispute between foster parents and an agency arose. After much publicity, the agency relented and the child was allowed to remain with her foster parents. *See In re* St. John, 51 Misc.2d 96, 272 N.Y.S.2d 817 (Family Ct. 1966), *rev'd sub nom.* Fitzsimmons v. Liuni, 26 App. Div.2d 980, 274 N.Y.S.2d 798 (3d Dep't 1966), *commented on* in II. Foster & D. Freed, *Family Law,* 19 Syracuse L. R. 478, 479–91 (1967); II. Foster & D. Freed, *Children and the Law,* 1966 Annual Survey of American Law 649, 660–61.

Apparently in response to the *Liuni* case, the New York State Legislature passed the following act: "Any adult husband and his adult wife and any adult unmarried person, who, as foster parent or parents, have cared for a child continuously for a period of two years or more, may apply to such authorized agency for the placement of said child with them for the purpose of adoption, and if said child is eligible for adoption, the agency shall give preference and first consideration to their application over all other applications for adoption placements. However, final determination of the propriety of said adoption of such foster child shall be within the sole discretion of the court, as otherwise provided herein." N.Y. Soc. Welfare Law § 383.3 (McKinney Supp. 1969).

40. D. Crystal, *What Keeps Us from Giving Children What We Know They Need?* 37 The Social Service Review 136, 137 (1953): "The plain fact is that foster-parenthood in our society—that is, being associated with a social agency for the purpose of rearing other people's children—evokes a series of negative associations in the mind of the public. . . . To be a foster-parent is to invite immediate practical questions from friends and neighbors as to economic motive, primarily, and in a sense to take on the stigma attached to being the recipient of 'welfare.' "

As a consequence, the child's best interests — theoretically the guiding principle in child custody cases — were subverted. Laura experienced two placements in addition to the Sanderses in a two-year period subsequent to the decision.[41] The outcome in *Child Care* is thus in direct contradiction to the theories of those child development specialists who would avoid multiple placements[42] because "the greatest damage to healthy psychological development is instability — and the kinds of impediments that interfere with the process of identity formation."[43]

The Case of Michael

Another illustration of the manner in which courts handle attempts by foster parents to adopt the children in their care is *In re Alexander,* a 1968 Florida case involving a two-year-old infant named Michael. Several days after he was born, a Florida Juvenile and Domestic Relations Court committed Michael to the Department of Welfare for subsequent adoption. Immediately after the Department was awarded custody, it placed the infant in the foster care of Mr. and Mrs. Alexander. As a condition of placement, the Alexanders were required to sign a Placement Agreement, stating among other things, that they would not attempt to adopt the child.[44]

Mr. and Mrs. Alexander were a couple in their late forties who had served as foster parents for the Department on previous occasions. Their annual income was about $5,000. Mr. Alexander held both a full- and part-time job. They lived in a modest home, neat and well kept. Although Mr. and Mrs. Alexander had no natural children of their own, Mrs. Alexander had four sons, ages twenty-three, twenty-eight, thirty, and thirty-four, by her first marriage. None of Mrs. Alexander's sons had completed high school. All except the youngest

---

41. *See* GOLDSTEIN & KATZ, *supra* note 22, at 1033–34.

42. A. Freud, *Psychoanalytic Knowledge and Its Application to Children's Services,* 5 THE WRITINGS OF ANNA FREUD: 1956–1965, 468 (1969).

43. L. Rapoport, *Safeguarding the Child's Best Interests: A Discussion* (unpublished paper presented at the American Orthopsychiatric Association Meeting, San Francisco, April 13, 1966). *See also* A. Freud, *supra* Ch. 3, note 3.

44. The Placement Agreement stated simply, "No action for adoption or guardianship may be taken." Brief for Appellant. Appendix at 1.

seemed to be having difficulties of one kind or another. At the time of this proceeding, Mrs. Alexander was a grandmother.

Mr. Alexander refused to allow his wife to work outside the home. Mrs. Alexander stated that as a consequence, she was limited to child rearing as a means of occupying her time; otherwise she would feel "restless" as well as unproductive. The role of a foster mother provided her with an opportunity to satisfy her own needs, including her maternal needs, and at the same time meet her husband's demands.[45]

During the two years that Michael lived with the Alexanders, Mr. and Mrs. Alexander sought to obtain the approval of the Department to adopt him. They were told that adoption was not possible because of the Placement Agreement which stated that they would not try to adopt the child,[46] and they were requested to return Michael to the Department. On advice of their counsel, the Alexanders surrendered the infant and the Department

---

45. *Id.* at 2–4.

46. The legal enforceability of a statement of this kind was at issue in Adoption of McDonald, 43 Cal.2d 447, 274 P.2d 860 (1954). In that case, foster parents signed an agreement with an adoption agency which included, among other provisions, a requirement that any request for adoption of the child placed with them had to be approved by the agency, and a stipulation that if after one year the agency was satisfied with the training of the child and the character of the foster parents' home, it would allow the adoption. The agreement further provided that the agency had the right to remove the child previous to legal adoption if at any time the circumstances warranted it. About eight months after the placement of the child, the foster father committed suicide. Later the agency demanded the return of the child. The foster mother refused to give up the child and peititoned a court for adoption without securing the agency's consent. The trial court granted the adoption, having concluded that the agency's consent was unnecessary.

One of the arguments which the agency made in its appeal to the California Supreme Court was that the foster mother was estopped from pursuing the adoption by virtue of the agreement she and her husband signed at the time of placement. Addressing himself to this argument, Justice Traynor wrote: "The [State] department [of Social Welfare] . . . has no power by regulation or otherwise to add to or detract from the rules for adoption prescribed in the Civil Code. . . . Thus, neither appellant, the department, the county agency, nor any private agency had the right by regulation or by agreement to deprive petitioner of the rights granted her by section 226 of the Civil Code to petition the court and have the court determine whether the petition should not be granted. If the department could give a licensed agency the right to control the adoption of a relinquished child, it could give such an agency the right to control the adoption of any child not subject to parental control. The statutory provisions governing adoption cannot be so circumvented.

In a proceeding such as this the child is the real party in interest and is not a party to any agreement. It is the welfare of this child that controls, and any agreement others may have made for its custody is made subject to the court's independent judgment as to what is for the best interests of the child." *Id.* at 461, 274 P.2d at 868; *see also* CAL. CIV. CODE § 224(n) (Supp. 1964).

immediately placed him in another foster home. The Alexanders immediately sought the advice of another lawyer, and when he urged them to resume their adoption efforts, the case was heard in a court located in the same county as the Department.

At the trial court level, the case raised the issue of the power of the Department to exclude the Alexanders from adopting Michael. This question was framed in terms of the necessity of the Department's consent to the adoption and the extent to which the Placement Agreement was to be enforced. Ancillary to these considerations was the question of whether the child's best interests would be served by the adoption. The Department argued the case principally on the technical legal issues of contract and procedural law. It urged the enforcement of the placement agreement, seeking thereby to oust the court from jurisdiction over the case. Alternatively, it raised the unsuitability of the Alexanders as adoptive parents, pointing to the fact that they were older than most adoptive couples and that their financial situation was not as secure as the Department would demand. The Alexanders argued that the Department, through its contract with them, could neither deprive the court of its right and duty to determine the child's best interests nor withhold its consent to the adoption. They also argued that they were fit parents for Michael.

The trial court decided in favor of the Alexanders. In a brief opinion, it upheld their contention that a welfare department could not divest the court of its inherent power to determine the ultimate best interests of a child, even though, as a legal matter, the authority to deal with the child on a day-to-day basis had been delegated to the Department.[47]

Subsequent to the decision of the trial court, the case received wide publicity in the local papers.[48] Thus, when the Department ultimately appealed the case, it was faced not only with the necessity of overcoming legal obstacles, but also with

---

47. *In re* Adoption, No. 155465-C (Fla. Cir. Ct., March 24, 1967). *See* Appendix.
48. Tampa Times, May 3, 1967, at 2, cols. 1–8; April 28, 1967, at 4, cols. 3–7; April 27, 1967, at 2A, cols. 1–8; Mar. 29, 1967, at 3, cols. 1–8.

the problem of strong local prejudice in favor of the Alexanders. The focus of the newspaper articles was naturally on the emotional aspects of the case. They stressed the personal qualifications of the Alexanders and their professed love for the child in contrast to the rigid bureaucratic position of the Department. The newspapers printed the opinions of local officials who portrayed the Welfare Department as cold blooded and "all knowing" and quoted a school principal as saying that "welfare workers had no concern for the welfare of children and their custody, and the only interest they have is in their rules."[49]

It is difficult to believe that these reports did not influence the appeals court when it decided to affirm the trial court by adopting its findings in toto.[50] Unlike some situations, for example *Child Care*, where the appeals court was removed physically and perhaps emotionally from local pressures, the appeals court in *Alexander* was located in the same community as the disputing parties — the Department, the foster parents, and the foster child.

The facts in *Alexander* represent the usual situation in cases where foster parents seek to adopt children placed in their care. However, because of the wide publicity given the case, it would not be fair to say that the court's disposition was truly representative. Nevertheless, it is possible to appraise the factors which probably influenced the decisionmaking process in both the court and the Department.

There are several aspects of the Department's handling of the case that violate basic precepts of child placement. Most importantly, the Department failed to implement the principle of continuity of care by immediately placing Michael in a permanent situation.[51] The Department knew when Michael was

---

49. Tampa Times, May 1, 1967.

50. For a discussion of the effects of mass media on child custody decisions, *see* S. Katz, *Community Decision-makers and the Promotion of Values in the Adoption of Children*, 38 THE SOCIAL SERVICE REVIEW 26, 37–39 (1964).

51. "Adoptive home placement is an important approach in providing maternal care as early as possible. The need for a permanent home early in the child's life cannot be overemphasized. The trend toward adoptive placements in the early weeks of life is increasing and has many advantages both for the infant and for the adoptive parents." S. PROVENCE & R. LIPTON, INFANTS IN INSTITUTIONS 164 (1962).

committed to it that the natural mother had given up all claims to the infant. Indeed, the court committed the infant to the Department for adoption. Nevertheless, instead of immediately seeking an adoptive couple for Michael, the Department placed him with the Alexanders, a couple chosen by foster care rather than adoption standards, and who were clearly informed that the arrangement was only temporary. It is difficult to understand why the Department chose this course of action, since none of the factors which would normally justify an interim placement prior to adoption — a child hard to place by virtue of its age or race, illness, legal complications, and so on[52] — was present in this case. Unfortunately, it is not uncommon for child welfare agencies to take this course of action and compound the error by allowing the temporary arrangement to continue indefinitely.

As was also the case in *Child Care,* the Department in *Alexander* used foster parents as boarding parents and was oblivious to the fact that emotional ties must inevitably develop between a child and its foster parents after years of living together. In each case the attachment should have been predictable. The Sanderses were a young childless couple eager to adopt a child; Mrs. Alexander was a woman known to have strong maternal needs. By resurrecting the Placement Agreement, the agencies in both cases sought to regain control over the situation and to give "law" precedence over normal human responses.

The result in *Alexander* is, or should be, more typical than that in *Child Care.* Theoretically, the court's role in child custody cases is that of *parens patriae.* As such, the court has a responsibility to make an independent examination of the facts to determine the best interests of the child. The courts in *Child Care* abdicated this responsibility and rested their decision on the Agency's findings. The courts in *Alexander,* on the other hand (if one disregards the possibility of publicity affecting their decisions), attempted at least to make an independent inquiry, and did not use the existence of the Placement Agreement as an

---

52. *See* A. Freud, *Cindy,* in GOLDSTEIN & KATZ, *supra* note 22, at 1051–53.

excuse for failing to do so, as the courts in *Child Care* seem to have done. If the courts in *Child Care* and *Alexander* had affirmatively sought to promote the best interests of Laura and Michael, they would have balanced a fundamental principle of child development — continuity of care — against the alleged limitations as adoptive parents of the Sanderses — emotional over-involvement — and the Alexanders — age and financial insecurity. Whether consideration of this principle would have altered the results in these cases is difficult to say, but a proper inquiry would at least have been made, and the responsibility of the courts to the children fulfilled.[53]

Conclusion

The cases of *In re Jewish Child Care Association* and *In re Alexander* illustrate the seemingly inevitable trend toward long-term placements. In both cases the placements were intended to be temporary, although in *Alexander* the child was available for adoption when the Department gained guardianship and custody. In both cases, by allowing the foster parents to establish strong emotional ties with the foster children, the agencies required the foster parents to assume roles that were almost inherently contradictory. The Sanderses and the Alexanders were expected to be substitute parents, providing everything that natural parents should provide, but to do so without themselves forming emotional attachments.

Both cases also illustrate another inconsistent attitude taken by agencies toward foster parents. On the one hand, agencies ask that foster couples care for a neglected child as they would their own. On the other hand, agencies attempt to maintain ultimate control over the foster parent-child relationship, basing

---

53. "Too often the courts have permitted themselves to become actors in a ceremony of official approval for whatever is being done or left undone for neglected children. Without sufficient or qualified staff to discover the needs of and the possibilities for children placed with foster agencies, the voluminous files loom larger than the child. The court is not made aware of the separation of siblings, the failure to work with the parents, and the failure to institute legal action on behalf of the child to free him for adoption and is given only a brief statement on why the child should be continued in placement. The lack of appropriate service by the social agencies, thus sanctioned and subsidized by court action, condemns countless children to emotionally arid lives." J. POLIER, THE ROLE OF LAW and THE ROLE OF PSYCHIATRY 119 (1968).

their authority on the fact that a court has committed a child to them. They emphasize that once a court has entrusted a child to their care, they are legally responsible for the child and answerable to the court. In practice, however, when a court grants the guardianship and custody of a child to an agency, the court neither oversees the process and standards by which the agency chooses foster parents, nor does it thoroughly or frequently review foster care placements.

Foster parents, however, are not as totally devoid of power as agencies sometimes assume. Not only does physical custody of a child give the foster parents certain legal advantages, but the doctrine of *in loco parentis* gives them something of a legal identity. A foster parent may be limited by a placement contra~ but these contracts do not necessarily set the actual legal dimen.,ions of his authority.

If foster care is used exclusively as a short-term living arrangement for a neglected child whose ultimate reunion with its natural parents is intended, it provides an agency, conscientiously seeking to promote the child's best interests, with an additional placement alternative to be used where natural care is temporarily undesirable and adoption inappropriate. When, however, foster care is used to provide a temporary home for a child eligible for adoption, it loses its unique properties and in fact often operates to defeat the child's best interests by breaking the continuity of care.

The Shuffled Child

And Foster Care

by Robert L. Geiser

By 1975, there will be 364,000 American children in foster care, five out of every 1000 children. The public stereotype of the foster child is of an orphan, committed by a court to a private charitable agency who cares for the child in an institution until he becomes an adult or else is adopted. This view could not be further from the truth.

Today's foster child is not an orphan. The child who has lost both parents through death is extremely rare in America, less than 1/10 of 1% of all children (about 70,000). Instead, the foster child is often referred to as an "Orphan of the Living." He has one or both parents alive, but is separated from them because of parental inability to care for him.

A child comes into foster care because of the psycho-social breakdown of his family. For 1/3 of the children, this is brought about by the mental or physical illness of a parent. Mental illness is the major factor and its effect on the family is profound because at least 40% of all foster children come from one-parent families. The parental illness deprives the child of his sole caretaker
Another third of foster children are in care because of

Robert L. Geiser is currently chief psychologist at the Nazareth Child Care Center in Jamaica Plain, Massachusetts. Previously chief psychologist in the Psychiatric Services for Children at the Tufts-New England Medical Center, he is the author of many magazine and journal articles on child psychology and education. His recent book on children in foster care, The Illusion of Caring, was published by Beacon Press in 1973.

problems in the family which render the parents incapable of raising children. Such factors are alcoholism, drug addiction, desertion, mental incompetence, incarceration of a parent in prison and sometimes just the unwillingness of a parent to continue caring for the child.

The remaining children in foster care are about equally divided between abused children and those where the child's own problems led to behavior which the parents cannot cope with or control. Clearly, foster care is necessitated by the failure of parents to meet the needs of children and rarely because of the child's own problems.

Many years ago most foster children were cared for in child welfare institutions run by private agencies. Today, over 80% of all children in foster care are placed with foster families and nearly 3/4 are public charges. Public welfare agencies make extensive use of foster family care — the cheapest type of foster care. The role of private agencies is confined almost solely to institutional care.

The domination of foster care by public agencies means foster care is now welfare and not charity. Foster care is primarily used for children of poor families. About 1/2 of the natural families of foster children are both unemployed and receiving public assistance. In spite of popular myths, the majority of the children are white and 3/4 of the children are legitimate.

Court commitments of children to foster care are not nearly as frequent as imagined. In Massachusetts, only about 1/4 of the children in foster care are permanently committed there by the courts. A handful more are temporarily placed by court order. Over 1/2 of the children are placed under voluntary arrangement between the parents and the public welfare agency. These children are in foster care without having gone through any court procedure to remove them from their parents.

The trend has been for state welfare agencies to use voluntary care and avoid court commitments. Legislation allows the public welfare department to place any child deemed in need of foster care. Application can be made by the parents, guardian, or any other person on behalf of the child, and in some cases, even by the child himself. The purpose of this approach is to make it easy for any child in need to receive foster care. The legal termination or limitation of parental rights weakens family ties and diminishes the parental sense of responsibility for the child. When the state takes the parents to court, it usually arouses strong feelings of bitterness,

(Continued on page 29)

resentment, and anger toward the state.

Once the child has been placed in care, the state's role is theoretically to rehabilitate the parents so that the child can be speedily returned home. The judicial route into care often destroys the state social worker's rapport with the parents, resulting in their rejection of state efforts to rehabilitate them. While these may seem like valid reasons for preferring the voluntary care arrangement, in fact this leads to a legal nightmare and is responsible for many of the destructive effects of foster care on children. This will be commented on later.

Two-thirds of the children in foster care are supposed to be in temporary care. For 3/4 of the children, the social work plan is eventually to reunite them with their parents. In these cases, parental rights are not legally terminated and consent for adoption is not obtained. Thus, the majority of children in foster care are technically not adoption candidates. Only about 3-5% of foster children are eventually adopted.

For most children, then, foster care is supposed to be short-term care by a foster family, necessitated by the breakdown of the child's natural family. It is supervised by a public welfare agency, frequently under an informal arrangement with the child's natural parents, with the intention in most cases of eventually returning the child to his family. Unfortunately, this is not what happens.

When a parent is unable, unwilling or unfit to care for his child and the state welfare department places him in foster care, it does not seem unreasonable to expect the state has the responsibility to nurture that child. But large, impersonal, bureaucratic welfare departments make poor parents. They are often inefficient, poorly administered, understaffed, overworked and inadequately financed. Lacking public support, they provide a cruel illusion of caring. Frequently foster care manages only to substitute public neglect for private neglect.

The state makes little effort to keep families from breaking up, to prevent the removal of children into foster care, or to rehabilitate the parents once the child is in care. Parental ties with their children are allowed to erode. Many parents have minimal contact with state welfare workers and some never see a worker once the child is placed. Within a year or so, the state may have lost contact and knowledge of almost half of the parents. Of those who do see a worker, only a handful feel the worker is committed to returning their child as quickly as possible. Placement for many children could have been prevented in the first place, had there been adequate day care facilities, homemaker services, and psychiatric counseling for parents.

The failure to rehabilitate parents means that foster care is not temporary. It becomes unplanned, long-term care. In 1971, in Massachusetts, the average length of stay in foster care was five years. Studies in other states report 1/3 of their foster children in care for over ten years and a half in care more than six years. For a ten-year-old child, that is over half of his life spent away from his parents.

Nor is this consistent foster care in one home. The average number of moves for a child in foster care placement is 2.7. Each move is another disturbing rupture of relationships. Some children are not moved but at least 1/3 have had from three to seven moves. The changes result from the collapse of the foster home placement because of the child's disturbed behavior and the lack of state support of foster parents in dealing with the child. Many children in foster care never see their social worker after placement, or see her only once or twice a year at best.

During these years in placement, more than 80% of the

children will never be returned to their natural parents, not even for a trial visit. Nor will the natural parents visit them or keep up contact. Less than 30% of the children are estimated to have parents who still show an interest in them. In short, placement in foster care, especially on a voluntary basis, may in effect, be parental abandonment of the child.

Technically, many of the children could be placed for adoption. Could be, that is, if the state obtained adoption releases from the parents. In some states laws exist allowing any child who has not had contact with his parents for a year to be freed for adoption without parental consent, but that depends upon the state petitioning for adoption release. Usually, however, the welfare department lacks an adequate tracking system to identify these children. How can you know about cases when 1/3 of the children are not even assigned to a social worker, when the worker hasn't seen the child for six months or where there is no record as to when a worker last visited the child? Many of the children have been on a worker's case list for less than a year, so s/he doesn't know the child, his/her parents or the foster family. In some welfare departments, 30% of the social work staff turns over each year, contributing further to the chaos.

Children who might be adopted also remain in foster care because there is not enough legal staff to initiate the petitions. Even when a petition is initiated, the probate

(Continued on page 35)

court delay in hearing it may run from one to three years. By the time things finally get done, the child is too old to adopt! Who wants to adopt a teen-ager?

Perhaps the greatest evidence of the kind of care a foster child receives is that 40% of these children suffer from handicaps.

A third of this group is emotionally disturbed, not surprising in view of the psycho-social pathology of the families from which they come and all that subsequently happens to them.

A quarter don't get evaluated and a large number of those who do, don't receive treatment. The state may care for the child's body, but it doesn't care for his mind.

Nor is the state's treatment of foster parents much better. There is little or no preparation or support for foster parents. A few meet the child before his placement; the rest do not. Three-quarters of the foster parents don't realize or are completely unaware of the extent of the handicaps of the child who will be placed with them. Only a handful receive any training prior to the child's placement. Foster parents also rarely see a social worker after placement.

There is considerable evidence that the present system of foster care increases rather than alleviates problems. A child who stays more than 18 months in foster care runs a considerable risk of becoming a professional foster child. The incidence of psychologic disturbances in foster children may run four to six times that of the general population. Seventy per cent of one sample of foster children showed marked aggressive behavior. Half, at least, of these children had serious school problems. Stealing, deviant sexual behavior, run-aways and overt suicide attempts figured in 1/3 to 1/10 of the group.

The major damage done by prolonged, unplanned foster care to children is their over-sensitivity to future rejections, confusion about their identity, and inability to form satisfactory emotional relationships with people. Sadly enough, when these children become adults and parents themselves, because they were not adequately parented, they cannot parent adequately. The cycle of physical and emotional damage to children goes through yet another generation. We had our chance to intervene and help the child and we failed to do so.

Foster care raises a number of legal issues of a practical nature. Voluntary placement is not doing what it was meant to do. Too many children are being abandoned in foster care. The children sit in a legal limbo partly because the state allows parents who do not show a continued interest in their child to retain parental rights, such as consent to adoption or the right to determine the child's religion. In the absence of clearcut guidelines for limiting parental rights and directing state intervention, the state is unable to make permanent care arrangements for the child. The state faces a legal stalemate with the parents. Obviously it is not in the child's best interests to return him to unrehabilitated parents, but then it is not in the child's best interests to remain indefinitely in "temporary" foster care, either.

If the concept of voluntary placements is to be retained, it would be advisable to do so only under a strict time limitation. For example, the state and parents would agree to a voluntary placement under a formal legal contract which would allow placement for a period not to exceed one year. The contract would specify exactly which rights the parents turned over to the state and which they reserved. If at the end of that year, the state had tried but failed to rehabilitate the family, parental rights could be terminated and the child freed for permanent placement.

The permanent placement would not necessarily have to be adoption. There is a need for a type of placement that would be planned, long-term foster care. This might be a form of quasi-adoption, perhaps subsidized, but the major change would be that the foster parents would have not only parental responsibilities as they now do, but also legally assigned parental rights. These rights would now have a standing in law superior to those of the biological parents. It does not make sense to have natural parents who are not interested in the child continue to have parental rights, while foster parents, willing to assume to duties of caring for the child, do not have the legal rights to enable them to carry out those duties within a stable parent-child relationship.

The state has shown itself repeatedly to be a poor guardian of the foster child, indeed, at times has even been guilty of violating its own neglect statutes. There is some merit in the idea of having an impartial advocate for each foster child, someone not connected with the state agency, but free to represent to best interests of the child as he sees them. This might be a social service project for some community service agency to consider.

It might be worthwhile to consider what might be done if, during the year a child was in foster care, the state did not make reasonable efforts to rehabilitate the parents. Parents have sued a school for failing to teach their child how to read, and a prisoner, found not guilty of a crime by reason of insanity and committed to a mental hospital for treatment, has sued for his release because he was not receiving the psychotherapy for which he had been committed. Surely there must be some way for a judge to return a damage action for the parents against the state for failure to provide rehabilitation services to the parents or treatment to a foster child, and compel the state to provide these services.

It is difficult to write about children these days without some involvement in the issue of children's rights. Many lawyers and mental health professionals talk about children's rights, but they seldom mean anywhere near the same thing by the phrase. Under the law children have few if any legal rights. The best interests of the child are usually equated with those of his parents.

The mental health professional means the rights of children to be wanted, to grow up in a healthy environment, etc. These are really special needs and interests of a psycho social nature. These might be justified on humanistic, religious or moral grounds, but not on legal grounds. They are relevant under the law to the best interests of a child, perhaps, but other than that the lawyer and the mental health professional approach the problem from very different points of view.

The basic difference between them is that the focus of the law is upon parents, while the mental health focus is upon the child. The law's focus is consistent with that of American culture which has always shown a reluctance to make a firm commitment to the welfare of all children.

The law's point of view derives from the middle ages and a time when children were viewed as nothing more than the prized possessions of their fathers. Gradually it has swung more and more to the child's side, either through extending to children some of the same legal rights that adults have or else by spelling out special needs and rights that are peculiar to children.

But the law and the mental health point of view will never coincide until America can decide just where its values lie, which is more important, to raise healthy, mentally sound children who can become productive citizens, or to continue to support a concept of parental rights even when they are clearly at odds with the child's well-being. Under the latter concept, the only right of a foster child is the right to live in limbo without a stable relationship with any caring adults.

(References available upon request)

The Interstate Compact on the Placement of Children

By Brendan Callanan and Mitchell Wendell

By the end of the 1974 legislative sessions, 24 states had enacted the Interstate Compact on the Placement of Children — nine of them in the past two years alone. Although the Compact has been working successfully among some of the states for well over a decade, there continues a marked upsurge of interest in it as its beneficial effects become more widely known. The courts normally labor under limitations which it is the purpose of the Interstate Compact to remove or ameliorate. An understanding of the assistance provided through the Compact begins with the situations they face in attempting to secure proper environments for children who for one reason or another do not have the love and security of a good family environment with their natural parents.

Courts have vital roles in the proper placement of children. The Interstate Compact on the Placement of Children is directly

Author's Addresses:
Mr. Brendan Callanan
Project Director
American Public Welfare Association
Suite 201
1155 16th Street, NW
Washington, DC 20036

Dr. Mitchell Wendell
Legal Consultant
American Public Welfare Association
Suite 201
1155 16th Street, NW
Washington, DC 20036

relevant to those roles involving the effective provision of services between the time of the initial placement and the consummation of the adoptive status, the finding of appropriate family or institutional homes for children determined to be dependent or neglected, institutional care and treatment of juveniles under adjudication of delinquency, and the enforcement of responsibility for child care and support during the continuance of placements.

The ability of the courts to provide protection for children and to facilitate services to them extends only as far as their jurisdictional reach. Within a single state, this is seldom a problem. But when a child who is a ward of the court, or who is otherwise being supervised, protected, cared for, or under a rehabilitative program pursuant to its process goes to another state, uncertainty and outright loss of control can occur. Because the all too frequent temptation in such situations is to dump the child and let the jurisdiction in which it is found work matters out as best it can, this result is not usually apparent in decided cases. Occasionally, however, courts have had reason to comment on related jurisdictional problems. (See *In re Adoption of Lunger*, 28 N.J. Super. 614 [1953]; *In re Blalock*, 283 N.C. 493 [1951]).

Courts have sought to ameliorate the territorial limitations on their jurisdiction in a variety of ways. In the case of adjudicated delinquents, they have simply refrained from making placements outside the state. In other instances, they have acted as though they really could control the situation even though the juvenile was sent to another state and have issued orders or prescribed programs as though their directives were binding. The motivations for this latter kind of action have been subject to varying interpretations. Some have thought this judicial conduct to represent irresponsibility in the manner of "sundown parole." Whatever the juvenile might do once out of the jurisdiction, he would be the problem of someone else. So long as the malefactor did not return, something had been accomplished. A more charitable view is that a court might take a chance, knowing that the best hope of help for the child was in a special institution or in a particular family environment found in another state. If compulsory process were thereafter found not to be necessary in the case, the absence of extraterritorial jurisdiction would not be put to the test. Further, if the order was phrased in authoritative language and seemed to express an ability to compel observance, the individuals concerned might believe that jurisdiction actually was maintained, even though a state line had been crossed.

The alternatives available in these situations have been unfortunate. Denial of a placement opportunity because the court has no power to protect it or to secure a return of the child if the undertaking proves unsuccessful reduces risks, but at the price of needed opportunities for the child rejected. On the other hand, the making of an unprotected placement runs the risk of creating a bad situation for which there is no satisfactory remedy.

In many contexts, the Full Faith and Credit Clause of the constitution is a sufficient reliance to overcome obstacles to the jurisdiction of state courts inherent in territorial limitations. However, the requirement that the courts of one state give full faith and credit to the public acts, records and judicial proceedings of the courts in other states is applicable only when the court has jurisdiction over both the parties and the subject matter at the time it must act. If a placement deteriorates after the child is already in another state, or if the adults in that other jurisdiction fail to discharge their responsibilities in connection with it, the fact that a court order may have originally made or allowed the interstate placement is unlikely to be of much help.

"The Interstate Compact on the Placement of Children provided many of the necessary answers that can make interstate placements as safe and orderly as those that occur within a single jurisdiction."

Nor is it a satisfactory answer to say that the courts and public welfare agencies in the state where the child is now present have the jurisdiction to assume full responsibility for the protection of and services to the child. In many instances, this is precisely the answer that good practice seeks to avoid. Aside from the initial promise of a satisfactory placement in the other state, the child often has no ties with the community in which the placement is made. Thus, to put responsibility on the state where the child is found when catastrophe has already struck may be the only available course, but it is unfair for both the child and the taxpayers of the community.

The Interstate Compact on the Placement of Children makes it unnecessary to run the risks or to choose between the undesirable alternatives just discussed. It does so because a compact is a device which can extend the jurisdictional reach of state courts and other public agencies to encompass the territory of all party states.

A compact has the force of statutory law in each party state because it is enacted by the legislature in each such jurisdiction. It is also a contract among the party states. (*Green v. Biddle*, 8 Wheat. 1 [1823]; *State ex rel. Dyer v. Sims*, 341 U.S. 522 [1950]). Consequently, it binds the state governments and all their instrumentalities to its observance and is also obligatory on private persons as are other statutes of the state. The specific meaning of these observations depends on the contents of the compact in question. In the case of the Interstate Compact on the Placement of Children, there are a number of benefits which flow from the application of its provisions. Before pointing them out, a word should be said to distinguish the instrument now under discussion from the Interstate Compact on Juveniles which has already been enacted by all 50 states and so is probably more familiar to juvenile court judges.

The Interstate Compact on Juveniles provides for two important kinds of service. It is the counterpart for children of the adult parole and probation compact and so makes it possible for juveniles adjudicated delinquent to receive parole or probation supervision in jurisdictions other than the one in which the adjudication took place. It also provides procedures for the return of children who have run away to other states but who have not otherwise committed any other acts which could be considered violations of law. Further, an amendment to the Interstate Compact on Juveniles provides a means of securing the equivalent of extradition for those children who are wanted for acts of delinquency rather than for the commission of crimes.

Also, the Interstate Compact on Juveniles made a start toward solving the problem of what to do with adjudicated delinquents for whom institutionalization in another state is desired, but it did not do so in a truly satisfactory manner. Article X of that instrument authorizes such interstate placements, but it does so in a way which, although not intentionally limiting, effectively confines the facilities that can be used to public institutions.

The reason is to be found in the phrasing of the Article. It authorizes party states to make agreements with one another for the confinement of juveniles by providing that a party state shall receive a delinquent juvenile "in one of its institutions." (Art. X,[3]). Further, the provision specifies the contents of the agreements, which must include among other things the rates to be charged.

The use of the word *of*, if narrowly construed, confines the meaning to facilities belonging to the party states. A private treatment or rehabilitation center may be *in* a state, but it cannot be an institution *of* the state.

Further, the requirement that agreements specify rates is feasible for party states setting charges for the use of their own facilities and programs but cannot be made effectively to govern private institutions which are not negotiators of or party to them.

As a practical matter, the real advantages of out of state confinement for an adjudicated delinquent are more likely to lie in the obtaining of services from private agencies than from public training schools or like institutions. The latter may be advantageously used when the purpose is to bring an adjudicated delinquent closer to his family or when a state without facilities of its own wishes to purchase space in the juvenile treatment facilities of other states. On the whole, however, the juvenile institutions of the several states, though subject to variations in quality, generally offer similar programs intended to meet the needs of the normal run of delinquents.

A substantial need is to serve the special problem delinquent who requires a sophisticated, highly individualized, experimental, or unusual program of care and treatment. There are all too few programs of such kinds. Most of those that do exist are conducted by private agencies — sometimes under religious auspices but also some secular organizations which happen to have become interested in providing services for problem children.

The Interstate Compact on the Placement of Children remedies the deficiency in coverage resulting from the restrictive wording of Article X of the Interstate Compact on Juveniles. It provides for the use of institutions *in* party states rather than for those *of* such states. It also allows placements by court order from the court which adjudges the delinquency to the receiving institution. No previous agreement between the states in which the courts and institutions are situated is necessary. Consequently, the only requisites for the effective use of the Interstate Compact on the Placement of Children to achieve the out-of-state confinement of an adjudicated delinquent with special needs is the willingness of the receiving institution to take the juvenile.

Procedurally, out-of-state institutionalization under the Interstate Compact on the Placement of Children is safeguarded by the requirement of a court hearing before the placement is made. As the result of the hearing and such other evidence as the court may have, the court must find that the out-of-state institutionalization is in the interest of the juvenile and that adquate facilities for meeting the juvenile's needs are not available within the state. Parenthetically, it should be noted that the key word is *available*. Unavailability may result as much from the fact that appropriate facilities or programs are full as from their nonexistence.

The parents or other guardian of a child must also have an opportunity to be heard on the question of out-of-state institutionalization. This proviso was thought wise for both policy and legal reasons. It is likely that if the result is to bring the adjudicated delinquent closer to home, the parents may desire it. If the conduct of the parents has not been such as to prompt termination of their custody rights for neglect or abuse of the child, it is probably desirable that they share as much as possible in the decision as to where the delinquent will be sent. This is especially the case because of the effort, embodied in the policies of all jurisdictions, to treat the delinquent as a young individual in need of help rather than as a criminal requiring punishment or the sterner aspects of an adult correctional program.

The requirement of a hearing is especially fortunate. Although the Compact was drafted before the line of decisions of which *In re Gault*, 387 U.S. 1 (1967), is the most celebrated, the need to provide basic elements of due process was recognized.

Two other and probably more numerous groups of children are served by the Interstate Compact on the Placement of Children. The first has inevitable involvement with the courts in every instance; the second contains cases in which such involvement occurs. Reference is made to children placed with would-be parents as a preliminary to a possible adoption, and children placed in foster care where no adoption is contemplated.

The steps in an adoption may be described thus:

1. Bringing the prospective parents and the child together. This involves identification of the persons involved and investigation to determine whether the would-be adoptive parents, the child, and the attendant conditions are propitious.
2. The placement and trial period. This should involve continuing investigation or testing of the interpersonal relationships and the suitability of the adoptive environment.
3. The finalization of the adoption, or the determination that it is inappropriate for it to be consummated.

For the first step of an adoption process, investigation is an essential ingredient. When the placement is interstate in character, a home study cannot be secured as a matter of right, except in those jurisdictions which are party to the Interstate Compact on the Placement of Children. The service is sometimes obtained on a courtesy basis, but this is a far different degree of assurance. If the necessary investigation is not forthcoming in a particular case, the court or other placing agency is faced with a choice — either to deny the prospective opportunity for adoption or to make the placement without safeguards. This is true because of the territorial limitations on jurisdiction previously discussed. On the other hand, in those states which have enacted the Compact, the requirement that the public authorities of the state into which the child is to be sent provide the preplacement investigation is both a statutory and a contractual obligation.

Whether the absence of supervision as a matter of right is considered a disadvantage during the continuance of the placement depends on how much monitoring of the placement is provided in practice by the agencies of the jurisdiction from which the placement originates. Although this is a matter of concern in all placements, it is particularly sensitive for an interstate situation because good practice would seem to encourage monitoring if in accord with the policies of either sending or receiving states.

At the time the court is considering the final decree of adoption, the need for reliable information on the course of the placement is especially acute. Only if it is available is the court in a satisfactory position to determine whether its decree should issue.

Except in those cases where a court has custody of a child in need of foster care, placements for this purpose are not likely to be its concern in the first instance. However, such placements can precipitate a number of questions of interest to the courts, especially if the placement breaks down or if the parties involved dispute the incidence of responsibility. If the entire transaction is within a single state, the laws of that jurisdiction will determine liabilities and will provide means of enforcing them. When an interstate placement for foster care has put the child in a different state from the one where the persons or agencies responsible for providing support or care are located, two kinds of problems can arise: (1) The laws of which jurisdiction apply, and (2) Can the courts or agencies with an interest in enforcement reach the parties in the other state who may have the responsibility. The Interstate Compact on the Placement of Children either obviates or reduces the severity of such problems from both the legal and practical points of view. It does so by specifically fixing responsibility. Article V (a) of the Compact reads in relevant part:

> The sending agency shall retain jurisdiction over the child sufficient to determine all matters in relation to the custody, supervision, care, treatment and disposition of the child which it would have had if the child had remained in the sending agency's state, until the child is adopted, reaches majority, becomes self-supporting or is discharged with the concurrence of the appropriate authority in the receiving state. Such jurisdiction shall also include the power to effect and cause the return of the child or its transfer to another location and custody pursuant to law. The sending agency shall continue to have financial responsibility for support and maintenance of the child during the period of the placement. Nothing contained herein shall defeat a claim of jurisdiction by a receiving state sufficient to deal with an act of delinquency or crime committed therein.

This is the governing law for interstate placements as among all jurisdictions which have enacted the Compact. Moreover, enforcement is possible on an interstate basis because the interstate compact is the constitutionally recognized device in our federal system for extending jurisdiction on an interstate basis.

Only one of the elements of the interstate problem to which the Compact is addressed has been handled successfully by a device other than the Interstate Compact on the Placement of Children. This is the matter of child support. Starting in the late 1940s, the several versions of the Uniform Reciprocal Enforcement of Support Act were enacted by all jurisdictions under the American flag. (See Clark, *Domestic Relations*, p. 206). However, the approach provided by these statutes is neither regulatory nor supervisory. It makes possible only the collection of support payments owed by an obligor on behalf of relatives for whom he or she has a legal obligation of support. However, the remedies provided by the Uniform Act are available only as among relatives by blood or marriage. Thus, the provision of foster care and the responsibilities of would-be adoptive parents not yet bound by a final decree are outside the perview of this type of statute.

Usually, we like to think of two clearly separable categories of placements — interstate and intrastate. Cases in each category may be treated according to their attributes, including their jurisdictional characteristics. However, foster parents and would-be adoptive parents increasingly cross from one category to the other. Adults who receive a child may initially be within the same state as the placing court or agency. But before the adoption is finalized, or while the child is still in need of foster care, employment necessities or other personal.factors may cause the adults to move. What was previously thought to be a legally and administratively simple intrastate placement must then either be disrupted or become an interstate placement with all of the jurisdictional infirmities already mentioned. However, in jurisdictions having the Interstate Compact on the Placement of Children, attendant problems are reduced to a minimum. Under the Compact, such circumstances can be construed to have produced an interstate placement, and the services and protections of the Compact apply.

There have been a variety of reasons why interstate placement problems have received little attention in the past. Perhaps first among them has been ignorance of the number of instances involved. With little law on the subject and few services or regulations, no one has known how many interstate placements there actually are. Children who are denied placement opportunities do not come to light as statistics, and those who fare badly come to the attention of public authorities only if their plight becomes aggravated and notorious enough to come before a court or is reported to a welfare department or the police.

Then too, there can be comfort in not looking beyond the borders of one's own jurisdiction. It is tempting to ignore or avoid problems that have no satisfactory answers because the solutions lie beyond the effective jurisdictional reach of the local courts or public agencies. The difficulty in all this is that it leaves too many children uncared for and in worse circumstances than they could experience if their properly supervised and investigated placement opportunities were made more numerous by the standardization of interstate placement procedures.

The Interstate Compact on the Placement of Children provides many of the necessary answers that can make interstate placements as safe and orderly as those that occur within a single jurisdiction. But at any given moment, the Compact is only as useful as the number of the jurisdictions which have it on their statute books and the size of the total territory and population in the party states. For Compact procedures to apply, both of the states involved in a placement transaction must be party to it. This effectiveness has grown substantially in recent years. The beginning of 1973 saw 15 states in the Compact. Less than two years later there were 24. The next legislative sessions in many of the remaining states will be actively pursuing enactment.

Alternatives to Absolute Termination of Parental Rights After Long-Term Foster Care†

Andre P. Derdeyn, * Andrew R. Rogoff,* * *and Scott W. Williams* ***

TABLE OF CONTENTS

* Associate Professor of Psychiatry and Pediatrics and Director of the Division of Child and Adolescent Psychiatry, University of Virginia Medical Center. B.A., Cornell University, 1959; M.D., University of Texas Southwestern, 1963.

** Member, Pennsylvania Bar. B.A., Yale University, 1974; J.D., University of Virginia, 1977.

*** Senior Staff Attorney, Charlottesville-Albemarle Legal Aid Society. B.A., Stanford University, 1970; J.D., Boston College, 1974.

† A portion of this Article is based upon the experience of the authors with an actual parental rights termination case. The names of all parties involved in that case have been changed to protect the anonymity of those parties.

I.   INTRODUCTION

The growing concern over the fate of children in foster care is one recent manifestation of this country's continuing interest in the welfare of its children. The rise in the number of children in "temporary" foster placements from 287,000 in 1965[1] to an estimated 364,000 in 1975[2] reflects increased protective service activity resulting in the removal of children from the parental home. Yet the continuing concept of foster care as a temporary placement prior to the child's returning home or being adopted is an idealized and outdated view of the system, for foster care is often many years in duration.

The present alternatives for placements after years of foster care are limited—foster children may be returned to parental custody, they may be adopted, or they may continue under foster care. Except in the unusual situation in which parents maintain contact with a child over many years and then resume custody, a child gains permanent and secure placement only through adoption. There is reason to question, however, whether absolute termination of the natural parents' rights and subsequent adoption constitute the optimal alternative for all children after long-term foster care.

This Article will explore in detail the variety of child placement arrangements, both within and outside the system, which can be tailored to meet the needs of children and their biological or foster parents. This examination will reveal numerous statutory reforms and recent judicial decisions that promise increasingly flexible approaches to the traditional custodial alternatives following long-term foster care. Particular emphasis will be devoted to the termination of parental rights case that first united the authors and confronted them with the fact that none of the traditional legal alternatives available to those children could adequately meet their emotional needs.

---

1.   Katz, *Legal Aspects of Foster Care*, 5 FAM. L.Q. 283 (1971).
2.   Geiser, *The Shuffled Child and Foster Care*, 10 TRIAL 27 (May/June 1974).

II. Foster Care and Continuity of Relationships

A. The Traditional Status of Foster Parents

Foster parents traditionally are considered employees of the agency with which they contract, with numerous duties and few rights.[3] When a foster parent attempts to contest removal of a child by the responsible welfare agency, or attempts to adopt a child against agency wishes, courts typically uphold the broad rights of biological parents and emphasize the limited nature of the placement contract between the foster parents and the agency.[4] Formulation of placement plans for the child, including plans for adoption, is left to the agency.[5]

The rationale for the traditional concept of the rights of foster parents vis-à-vis natural parents was articulated in In re *Jewish Child Care Association*.[6] Foster parents in that case appealed the lower court decision permitting a child care agency to remove from their custody a five and one-half year-old child who had spent four and one-half years in their care. The foster parents had accepted the girl under a standard agency agreement that the placement would be temporary and that the foster parents would prepare her for return to her biological mother. Before the first year ended, however, the foster parents decided to adopt the girl and actively pursued that course in direct conflict with agency rules and policies. The foster parents lost their battle to keep the child. In what Katz[7] sees as a subversion of the child's best interests, the court of appeals decided in favor of the agency, faulting the "extreme of love, affection, and possessiveness manifested by the [foster parents], togther [*sic*] with the conduct which their emotional involvement impelled."[8]

---

3. Katz, *supra* note 1, at 283-302.

4. Note, *The Rights of Foster Parents to the Children in Their Care*, 50 Chi.-Kent L. Rev. 86-102 (1973). In one representative situation the biological mother sought custody of her child, who had been with his foster parents from the age of three months to five years. The foster parents in turn attempted to terminate the mother's rights and to adopt the child. The court found that the foster parents "were bound by their agreement with the Department of Public Welfare" and that the "Department . . . was entitled to the possession of the child." Huey v. Lente, 85 N.M. 585, 591-92, 514 P.2d 1081, 1087-88 (1973). Thus the foster parents were accorded no legal standing, and custody was granted to the biological mother.

5. For instance, in *In re* Adoption of Runyon, 268 Cal. App. 2d 918, 74 Cal. Rptr. 514 (1969), a boy who had been with foster parents since the age of three days was removed from their home at the age of eight and placed with prospective adoptive parents. Although the foster parents also filed a petition for adoption, they were unable even to obtain a hearing on their petition. The court upheld the absolute statutory right of the agency to choose adoptive parents, and removal of the child was final.

6. 5 N.Y.2d 222, 156 N.E.2d 700, 183 N.Y.S.2d 65 (1959).

7. Katz, *supra* note 1, at 296.

8. *Id.* at 294.

This decision reflects a common judicial impression of foster care, in which the contractual view of foster care persists. A New York court recently disparaged the idea of a foster parent's right to custody as a notion by which "third-party custodians . . . acquire some sort of squatter's rights in another's child."[9] In an earlier decision, the same court admonished that "the temporary parent substitute must keep his proper distance at all costs to himself."[10] By tradition, then, foster care is defined as providing merely "substitute family care for a planned period for a child when his own family cannot care for him for a temporary or extended period, and when adoption is neither desirable nor possible."[11] Nevertheless, the assumption that foster care involves only temporary placement is not always correct.

B.   Duration of Foster Care Placements

The results of studies conducted in the last twenty years rebut the presumption that foster placements are uniformly short in duration.[12] In Maas and Engler's classic 1959 study[13] involving over 4000 children the authors demonstrated that more than half would remain in foster care for most of their childhoods. A 1973 Massachu-

---

9.   Bennett v. Jeffreys, 40 N.Y.2d 543, 552 n.2, 356 N.E.2d 277, 285 n.2, 387 N.Y.S.2d 821, 829 n.2 (1976). *See also* Organization of Foster Families v. Dumpson, 418 F. Supp. 277, 281 (S.D.N.Y. 1976) (three-judge court), *rev'd on other grounds sub nom.* Smith v. Organization of Foster Families, 431 U.S. 816 (1977) (Foster parents do not have a constitutional expectation that their roles "will not be abruptly and summarily terminated."); Spence-Chapin Adoption Serv. v. Polk, 29 N.Y.2d 196, 205, 274 N.E.2d 431, 436, 324 N.Y.S.2d 937, 945 (1971) ("To the ordinary fears in placing a child in foster care should not be added the concern that the better the foster care custodians the greater the risk that they will assert, out of love and affection grown too deep, an inchoate right to adopt."). *But see* Drummond v. Fulton County Dep't of Family & Children's Servs., 547 F.2d 835, 853, 855 (5th Cir.), *rev'd on rehearing en banc*, 563 F.2d 1200 (5th Cir. 1977); *In re* B.G., 11 Cal. 3d 679, 692-93, 523 P.2d 244, 253-54, 114 Cal. Rptr. 444, 453-54 (1974) (Foster parents, as de facto parents, are proper parties in a juvenile court review of foster placement and may "assert and protect their own interest in the companionship, care, custody and management of the child.").

10.   Spence-Chapin Adoption Serv. v. Polk, 29 N.Y.2d 196, 205, 274 N.E.2d 431, 436, 324 N.Y.S.2d 937, 945 (1971).

11.   CHILD WELFARE LEAGUE OF AMERICA, STANDARDS FOR FOSTER FAMILY CARE SERVICE 5 (1959). One must suspend disbelief while reading these standards because of the superhuman qualities they require of the model foster parent. Not only should such a person (1) love his or her foster child, (2) enjoy being a foster parent and (3) be able to maintain friction-free relationships with all people, but he or she should also "have the ability to accept the child's relationship with his parents and with the agency, without marked tendency to be overpossessive." *Id.*, standard 4.4 at 35.

12.   This fact is well-recognized in the literature. *See, e.g.*, Wald, *State Intervention on Behalf of "Neglected" Children: Standards for Removal of Children from Their Homes, Monitoring the Status of Children in Foster Care, and Termination of Parental Rights*, 28 STAN. L. REV. 625, 626 & n.7, 627 n.8 (1976).

13.   H. MAAS & R. ENGLER, CHILDREN IN NEED OF PARENTS (1959).

setts study revealed that the sixty percent of the children in care at the time of the study had been in care between four and eight years; the average stay was over five years.[14] In the Columbia University longitudinal study of children in foster care in New York City,[15] thirty-six percent remained in foster care at the end of five years.[16] About two-thirds of the children who had remained in care for five years had lost contact with their parents, and forty-six percent of the children remaining in care five years had experienced three or more placements.[17] Thus a great gulf exists between the myth that foster care readily terminates in return home or in adoption, and the reality that for many children foster care is interminable and may involve a significant number of placements.

C. *Judicial Recognition of the Foster Child-Foster Parent Relationship*

The emotional bonds that develop between foster parents and foster children often are indistinguishable from those existing between natural parents and their children. Because neither children nor foster parents have been parties to termination disputes, however, traditionally the courts have rarely recognized the emotional needs of foster children. Several recent cases, on the other hand, evidence a new trend in the legal status of foster parents. In *James v. McLinden*,[18] for example, a three month-old daughter of a heroin addict was placed with a forty-seven year-old woman who desired to raise the child. When the child was two years old, the welfare department filed a petition of neglect stating that the child had been abandoned by her parents and "is presently being cared for through an informal arrangement which is neither legal nor healthy."[19] The juvenile judge did not deem the mothering person a legal party to the proceeding and denied her entrance to the hearing. On application for injunction and declarative relief, however, the district court held that the woman's due process and equal protection rights had been violated, reasoning that:

---

14. A. GRUBER, FOSTER HOME CARE IN MASSACHUSETTS 72 (1973) (copy on file with the *Vanderbilt Law Review*).

15. S. JENKINS & M. NORMAN, BEYOND PLACEMENT: MOTHERS VIEW FOSTER CARE (1975). This study provided information concerning 624 children from 467 families with children in foster care. The children were under twelve years of age at first entry into foster care.

16. Fanshel, *Status Changes of Children in Foster Care: Final Results of the Columbia University Longitudinal Study*, 55 CHILD WELFARE 143, 145 (1976).

17. Fanshel, *Parental Visiting of Children in Foster Care: Key to Discharge?*, 49 SOC. SERVICE REV. 493, 496 (1975).

18. 341 F. Supp. 1233 (D. Conn. 1969).

19. *Id.* at 1234.

There is no sound reason to deny a person who has voluntarily assumed the obligations of parenthood over a child the same basic rights to due process a natural or legal parent possesses when the state intervenes to disrupt or destroy the family unit. "The policy of our law has always been to encourage family relationships, even those foster in character."[20]

Thus the court clearly recognized the bond that had developed between a non-biological parent and a child in her care.

In a second case[21] a relatively inexperienced agency worker determined that the atmosphere in a certain foster home was detrimental to a child who had lived there from the age of three weeks to nine years. At the request of the worker, the agency removed the child from the home. The lower court denied the foster parents' request for continued custody, but the appellate court upheld the rights of the foster parents and reversed the decision. The court noted that custody determinations should focus on the child's best interests rather than the rights of the placement organization. In this case the court deemed the effect of separating the child and his foster parents to be devastating.

A similar case[22] involved a five year-old boy who spent four years with a foster family. The child care agency ordered return of the child to the biological parents, and the lower court upheld this decision. On appeal, the reviewing court determined that despite the limited rights granted by the contract under which they cared for the child, the foster parents, as the de facto parents for four years, had the legal standing to file a petition raising the custody issue. The contract they had signed with the child care service was, therefore, held unenforceable. Despite the evidence that a greater concern regarding the needs and rights of children and their foster parents exists in today's courts, the current legal status of foster parents remains ambiguous.

D. The Current Ambiguous Status of Foster Parents

For some time foster parents and foster parent organizations have been seeking a greater part in decisionmaking regarding children in their care.[23] Even when foster placement is of long duration and the level of the child's contact with biological parents is low,

---

20. *Id.* at 1235.
21. Commonwealth v. Children's Servs., 224 Pa. Super. Ct. 556, 307 A.2d 411 (1973).
22. Stapleton v. Dauphin County Child Care Serv., 228 Pa. Super. Ct. 371, 324 A.2d 562 (1974). For a discussion of this case, see Note, *Increasing the Rights of Foster Parents,* 36 U. Pitt. L. Rev. 715, 718-24 (1975).
23. *See also* Reistroffer, *Participation of Foster Parents in Decision Making: The Concept of Collegiality,* 51 Child Welfare 25 (1972); Kurtis v. Ballou, 33 A.D.2d 1034, 308 N.Y.S.2d 770 (1970).

the status of the foster parent remains unclear. In 1977 the United States Supreme Court struck a blow to the rights of foster parents by upholding a New York statute authorizing removal of the child from the foster home without a prior full adversary administrative hearing.[24] The district court[25] had invalidated that provision of the statute on due process grounds, but the Supreme Court found only a limited liberty interest at stake and held that the established procedures were sufficient to protect those limited interests. Emphasizing that the relief sought in this case was purely procedural, the Court distinguished this case from those recognizing a right to family privacy in that "the State here seeks to interfere, not with a relationship having its origins entirely apart from the power of the State, but rather with a foster family which has its source in State law and contractual arrangements."[26] A concurring opinion dismissed the foster family's interest with even greater ease, stating that "[t]he family life upon which the State 'intrudes' is simply a temporary status which the State itself has created."[27] Clearly, then, conflict still exists between the emotional ties developed in a foster care situation and the long-established theories of the rights of natural parents.

E.   The Child's Needs and the Law of Child Custody After Long-Term Foster Care

The superior custody claim of a natural parent over a third party is ingrained in our cultural and legal tradition. The claim of the natural parent is supported by two doctrines which frequently are mutually reinforcing. The "parental right" doctrine holds that the natural parent has the right to custody in the absence of demonstrable detriment to the child.[28] The "best interests of the child" doctrine purports to give courts great latitude in determining placements. In reality, however, it often complements the "parental right" doctrine because judges assume that the best interests of the child are met when he or she is in the custody of the natural parent.[29]

---

24.   Smith v. Organization of Foster Families, 431 U.S. 816 (1977). The Court considered emotional issues in its determination that there was no liberty interest at stake.

25.   Organization of Foster Families v. Dumpson, 418 F. Supp. 277 (S.D.N.Y. 1976) (three-judge court).

26.   431 U.S. at 845.

27.   *Id.* at 863 (Stewart, J., concurring).

28.   For a general discussion of the evolution of the parental right doctrine, see Leavell, *Custody Disputes and the Proposed Model Act,* 2 GA. L. REV. 162, 165-78 (1968). American courts never accepted the harsh common law concept that gave a father almost unlimited right to custody. Nevertheless, until recently, courts have used property concepts in determining custody disputes. *Id.* at 166.

29.   *Id.* at 166, 178-81. *See* note 28 *supra.* For a summary of the disposition standards

For many children the limited and rigid custodial alternatives available after long-term foster care constitute an important part of the problem afflicting the foster care system. When the child cannot return to the biological parents' home, the standard options are either continued foster care or adoption, the latter alternative requiring termination of biological parents' rights regarding their children. No custodial question is more difficult than termination of parental rights, since the law also must serve parental interests. Termination is fraught with judicial resistance because of its absoluteness: parental rights are either sustained or severed.[30] This decision vexes judges. Also, it is unclear whether the child's interests might not sometimes better be served by a custody arrangement short of absolute severance. Providing children a permanent placement with adults who have a long-term commitment to them, as well as making possible some continuity with biological parents, optimally might meet the needs of some children.

In termination actions courts too often find that the parents' behavior or disabilities do not warrant absolute termination, but that the child's welfare requires continued foster care.[31] Although in many such cases it is unlikely that the parents will resume adequate parenting roles, the tradition of parental custody rights is so strong that these rights tend to prevail in any doubtful situation. Thus, courts face a recurring impasse that results in the often unsatisfactory compromise solution of continued foster care.

Decisions to intervene in children's lives are difficult to make because they involve value judgments as well as complicated legal, emotional, and practical issues. The morass of conflicting and often indeterminate interests is reflected in the definition of the best interest standard as "an empty vessel into which adult perceptions and prejudices are poured."[32] A 1971 Oregon case seeking termina-

---

prescribed by various state laws, see Mnookin, *Child-Custody Adjudication: Judicial Functions in the Face of Indeterminacy*, 39 L. & CONTEMP. PROB. 226 (1976). This Article does not attempt to address the differences in standards for termination of parental rights or the issues addressed at a termination hearing. For such a discussion, see Wald, *supra* note 12.

30. *See generally* Derdeyn & Wadlington, *Adoption: The Rights of Parents Versus the Best Interests of Their Children*, 16 J. AM. ACAD. CHILD PSYCH. 238 (1977). For a concise bibliography on the termination question, see Levine, *Foundations for Drafting a Model Statute to Terminate Parental Rights: A Selected Bibliography*, 26 JUV. JUST. 42, 46-56 (Aug. 1975). For a summary of state termination laws, see Katz, Howe, & McGrath, *Child Neglect Laws in America*, 9 FAM. L.Q. 1, 73-362 (1975). *See also* Areen, *Intervention Between Parent and Child: A Reappraisal of the State's Role in Child Neglect and Abuse Cases*, 63 GEO. L. J. 887, 928-30 (1975).

31. *See generally* Derdeyn, *A Case for Permanent Foster Placement of Dependent, Neglected, and Abused Children*, 47 AM. J. ORTHOPSYCH. 604 (1977).

32. Rodham, *Children Under the Law*, 43 HARV. EDUC. REV. 487, 513 (1973).

tion of rights of neglectful parents provides a good example of the ethical and legal quagmire such cases may entail. In *State v. McMaster*[33] the child had been placed with foster parents at age two months. The foster parents later wished to adopt, and when the child turned four the lower court effected termination of parental rights preparatory to adoption. The biological parents appealed. The Oregon Supreme Court noted that "the parents frequently quarrelled, [the biological father] never held a job more than a month and seldom that long, they were usually on welfare, and [the father] frequently left home with the welfare check, leaving [the biological mother] destitute."[34] Testimony suggested that the biological parents "would not allow [the] child to maximize her potential."[35] Yet the court was unwilling to terminate parental rights because this family's situation was not unusual enough to warrant such a drastic step:

> [T]he state of the [biological] family is duplicated in hundreds of thousands of American families,—transiency and incapacity, poverty and instability . . . . However, we do not believe the legislature contemplated that parental rights could be terminated because the natural parents are unable to furnish surroundings which would enable the child to grow up as we would desire all children to do . . . . The best interests of the child are paramount; however, the courts cannot sever . . . parental rights when many thousands of children are being raised under basically the same circumstances as this child.[36]

The court invalidated the termination but did not require transfer of custody to the biological parent. Thus the parental disabilities appeared to have justified the child's placement in foster care, but were not sufficient to warrant termination of parental rights. This impasse—judicial affirmation of parental rights coupled with judicial admission that the welfare of children may warrant custody in a foster parent—is one which significantly impairs the lives of thousands of children in foster care.

The termination issue creates substantial obstacles to proper attention to the needs of some children.[37] The either-or approach to termination results in inconsistent judicial decisions on similar sets of facts. In one illustrative case three siblings ranging in age from five to nine had spent three and one-half years in numerous, sepa-

33. 259 Or. 291, 486 P.2d 567 (1971).
34. *Id.* at 302, 486 P.2d at 572.
35. *Id.* at 303, 486 P.2d at 572.
36. *Id.* at 303-04, 486 P.2d at 572-73.
37. For the foremost legal and psychoanalytical theories in the field of child placement, see J. GOLDSTEIN, A. FREUD, & A. SOLNIT, BEYOND THE BEST INTERESTS OF THE CHILD (1973). These authors advocate legal recognition of the premise that the healthy development of each child requires continuity of the relationship with the adult who cares for him and meets his emotional and psychological needs. *Id.* at 31-32.

rate foster care placements. Their mother's whereabouts were unknown, and the welfare department petitioned to terminate the rights of the children's father. The court conceded the father's inability to establish an economically and emotionally stable home for the children. The decision was complicated, however, by the fact that the father periodically had demonstrated interest in the children; the oldest child, in fact, wished to remain with the father. Ultimately the court denied termination and adoption—attention to the children's emotional attachments and the father's legal rights precluded the children's securing of permanent homes.[38]

Reaching the opposite conclusion, however, does not always solve the problems of the child. In another case a child's need for stability and permanence was recognized and met at the cost to the child of a continuing relationship with a biological parent.[39] The parental rights of the mother of a six year-old girl were terminated when the court found the child to be permanently neglected. As the dissent pointed out, however, the mother displayed no intention of abandoning her child; she had, in fact, visited her regularly twice a month. The dissent observed that the mother had a "generally inadequate and defeatist attitude towards life," suffered a deeply ingrained "generalized lassitude," and noted that "any change of life style [was] fraught with fears and tension."[40] Notwithstanding these factors, he was reluctant to terminate the mother's rights because she might be helped to function at such a level that she could regain custody of her child. Facts in the record made it appear unlikely that the mother would become able to care for the child. Given this child's age and her mother's demonstrated interest, however, one can assume that the relationship with her mother was of considerable importance to the child. Severance of such a relationship is not likely to be the best alternative for the child's development. In this case, attention to the child's need for a permanent home with a capable parent outweighed the normally superior custodial right of the biological mother to retain custody.

The circumstances of children of divorced parents and foster children often are analogous. Children from disrupted families tend to develop their own immature and primitive fantasies about the cause of the disruption.[41] Following parental separation, death of a parent, or removal from the parental home, the child almost invari-

---

38.   State *ex rel.* Juvenile Dep't v. Crabtree, 23 Or. App. 183, 541 P.2d 1311 (1975).

39.   *In re* "Female" B., 49 A.D.2d 615, 370 N.Y.S.2d 672 (1975).

40.   *Id.* at 615, 370 N.Y.S.2d at 674.

41.   Derdeyn, *Children in Divorce: Intervention in the Phase of Separation,* 60 PEDIATRICS 20, 21-22 (1977).

ably entertains distorted fantasies of the absent parent. In these situations, as well, visits with non-custodial parents may be of great benefit. Authors addressing the value of contact with the non-custodial divorced parent have written that

> visitation precludes the need for nurturing any unwholesome and energy-consuming obsession with establishing a rendezvous with the non-custodial parent and provides an avenue by which the child can test the reality of images which are a product of his own fantasies and the impressions of others that have been communicated to him.[42]

Following long-term foster care, then, adoption is not always the most constructive legal or emotional alternative. The absoluteness of adoption makes it difficult for judges to justify terminating parental rights, and decisions which could lead to permanent placements are thus precluded. The either-or characteristic of adoption also may not be in the best interest of children who will benefit from maintaining contact with their past. Permanent and secure arrangements other than traditional adoption can and should be made for these children. Some courts and legislatures have begun addressing this need for alternative placement arrangements.

III. CASE REPORT

A case involving the termination of rights of the parents of two siblings in foster care brought the authors together and confronted them with the fact that none of the usual legal alternatives available to these children adequately met their emotional needs. The two children involved were Julie and Tom Jennings, twelve and ten years of age, respectively. The local welfare department removed them from their home because their parents neglected them severely. The father's alcoholism and the mother's limited ability to cope with family crises had led to a long history of Jennings family chaos, often the subject of welfare department intervention in the years prior to the removal of the children. They spent twenty-two months in the home of Mr. and Mrs. Wallace, who had two children of the Jennings children's approximate ages.

In this twenty-two month period, during which Mr. and Mrs. Jennings visited their children three times, the family court held numerous hearings in connection with the welfare department's petitions for permanent custody of the children. The court initially accepted the arguments for delay which were based on psychiatric testimony concerning the perceived needs of the parents for emo-

---

42.   Benedek & Benedek, *Postdivorce Visitation: A Child's Right*, 16 J. AM. ACAD. CHILD PSYCH. 256, 261-62 (1977).

tional and vocational counseling, and for time to arrange employment and adequate housing. As it became apparent that the parents were unable so to utilize the time granted and that the children were suffering from their status of uncertainty, the court denied motions for further extensions. Recognizing the presence of conflicting interests between the children's need for stable relationships with their adult caretakers and their parents' need for an opportunity to reorder their lives before being faced with the irreversible loss of their children, the court asked one of the authors to consult regarding final disposition of the children.

Julie and Tom Jennings, Mr. and Mrs. Wallace, and the Wallace children were interviewed by the psychiatric consultant. Julie and Tom were told that the purpose of the meeting was for the consultant to help the judge determine what decision would be best for them. Excerpts of the report to the court follow.

A.   Report of Psychiatric Consultation

(1)   Findings

Julie and Tom Jennings felt accepted and comfortable in the Wallace home and enjoyed comfortable relationships with the Wallace children. Both children volunteered examples of their biological parents' inadequate provision of basic needs (food and necessary medical care). They explained how different and how nice it was for the Wallaces to do such things as go to school to find out about their progress. Julie also mentioned that they could talk about any problem, regardless of its nature, with the Wallaces, unlike the situation with their biological parents.

In spite of their positive feelings about Mr. and Mrs. Wallace, however, both children also wished to return home. Tom simply wanted to return to his parents' home and could give no specific reason for his desire. Julie, more realistic than Tom about the problem, felt that her father had to stop drinking before this would be possible. They expressed concern about their parents and felt that returning to them would somehow make things better. Both children were aware of the Wallaces' concern for them, a concern they did not sense was manifested by their biological parents. Paradoxically, the children showed a protective concern for their biological parents and felt they should be home taking care of their biological parents.

Both children, when seen separately and asked to draw a picture of their family, drew idealized scenes. Julie seated the entire family at a meal and Tom drew the family playing baseball together. Tom drew his mother with a very sad face, saying it was because she did not see her children. He also expressed feelings of inadequacy by picturing himself with a baseball bat containing a hole so that the ball might pass through the bat even if he swung correctly. Tom felt that he *should* be back with his mother in order to make her feel better. Julie, a bit older, had the same feelings but believed that she had a better chance in life with the Wallaces. Both of these children felt guilty and responsible for their absence and, most directly, for making their mother sad. The obvious equation in their minds was that if they were to return to their parents, they would no longer have to feel guilty.

Notwithstanding the passage of twenty-two months, the arrangement presumably was temporary, and the children had always expected that they would return home. They clung to this hope because, from their point of view, there was no alternative to the current, "temporary" situation.

In terms of emotional realities, the children viewed their relationship with Mr. and Mrs. Wallace in a way approaching that of a parent-child relationship, muted somewhat by everyone's realization that this was supposed to be a temporary arrangement. The Wallaces were not financially able to adopt these children, although their attachment was strong, and they wished to continue to care for the children.

Julie and Tom felt cared for by Mr. and Mrs. Wallace, and they felt themselves to be, in essence, part of the Wallace family. At a fantasy level they expected that a return to their parents would provide some emotional relief, and therefore they wished to return home. The layman would find it unusual to see children of this age (ten and twelve years) invest so heavily in fantasy (reunion with biological parents) to the relative exclusion of reality (current loving relationship with the Wallaces).

(2)   Recommendation

The optimal situation for these children was continued care by Mr. and Mrs. Wallace under a permanent arrangement. These children would benefit from the knowledge that their home with the Wallaces was secure, so that both they and the Wallaces no longer would be limited in their relationships by their temporary state. The children, because of their feelings about their biological parents, should have the possibility of continuing contact with them. This was acceptable to Mr. and Mrs. Wallace.

The usual alternatives—(1) termination of parental rights with consequent availability for adoption, (2) continued foster care under the current arrangement, and (3) return to the custody of Mr. and Mrs. Jennings—had important shortcomings, since none of them matched the emotional realities of Julie and Tom Jennings' lives. Termination might offer Julie and Tom stability and continuity, assuming the Wallaces' ability to adopt. Because adoption did not appear possible, however, termination of parental rights introduced the possibility of an unacceptable eventuality—adoption by strangers. This would disrupt the relationship with the Wallaces and possibly separate the children from each other. Continued foster care also was unacceptable. The temporary nature of their current status impeded both the children and the Wallaces, in spite of a very successful relationship, in their commitments to each other. These children required a definitive resolution of their custody to help them invest more in current living and less in fantasy. The third alternative, return to the custody of the biological parents, was unacceptable also, because of the inability of the parents adequately to assume their parenting responsibilities. The wishes for family reunion were basically neurotic in character, and the children would not find the sought-for emotional relief by returning to their biological parents. They would, in fact, feel extremely anxious and unsupported if placed with their biological parents, and would suffer the loss of the only realistic parent-child relationship current in their lives.

The optimal resolution of this issue involved a truly permanent arrangement allowing these children to stay with the Wallaces. Regardless of whether Mr. and Mrs. Jennings' parental rights were formally terminated, a permanent settlement was needed which would cut off their access to the courts to intervene in the lives of these children, while still allowing the children to have contact with Mr. and Mrs. Jennings at the discretion of Mr. and Mrs. Wallace. The "temporary" nature of foster care was itself detrimental to these children at this time. They remained unsettled because of the temporary situation and very anxious regarding the upcoming trial. They required a final resolution of the current situation to free them from excessive involvement with the past and unrealistic hopes for the future.

B.   The Decision

The court did not adhere to the usual legal alternatives, but accepted instead the consultant's advice. Parental rights were terminated, the children remained in foster care with the Wallaces, and provision was made for the welfare department to arrange visits by the children with their biological parents at Mr. and Mrs. Wallace's request.

C. Follow-Up One Year Later

A year after the decision, the Wallaces had almost completed the process of subsidized adoption. Julie, then thirteen, wished to take the Wallace name but was concerned about her biological parents' possible anger. Tom, then eleven, had less enthusiasm for the adoption and wished to retain the Jennings name, which was agreeable to the Wallaces. The children had visited once with their mother, and Julie had a fairly active correspondence with her. Tom was writing his mother occasionally at the urging of his sister. The Wallaces continued to allow the children to visit their biological parents whenever they wished to do so. Julie spoke much more openly of her biological parents than did Tom, and was getting along very well academically and with peers. Although Julie felt duty and affection toward her biological parents, she had made firm attachments to the Wallace family and to her life with them. Tom remained overinvolved with the past, failing to make an optimum investment in his current life. Psychiatric intervention still was a possibility to help him modify his apparent feelings of guilt regarding his biological parents.

IV. RECENT DEVELOPMENTS IN THE LAW OF CHILD PLACEMENT

Critics of indeterminate decisionmaking standards often desire to shift back to the legislature the responsibility for formulating more definite criteria upon which judges may base their decisions.[43] On the other hand, the tradition of wide judicial discretion in complex custody determinations is still viable to some, including one judge who expressed her reservations about judicial determination this way: "[T]here can be no single or final definition that will encompass the myriad variations in the social histories, parental attitudes or actions, the conditions of the parents and the life prospects for the child."[44] Governmental branches are responding to the increasing recognition of the limitations imposed by the conventional options for placement of children after long-term foster care. State legislatures are considering new statutory schemes designed to give greater flexibility of choice. Courts, faced with the frustra-

---

43. *See generally* Mnookin, *Foster Care—In Whose Best Interest?*, 43 HARV. EDUC. REV. 599 (1973); Wald, *State Intervention on Behalf of "Neglected" Children: A Search for Realistic Standards*, 27 STAN. L. REV. 985 (1975).

44. *In re* P., 71 Misc. 2d 965, 969, 337 N.Y.S.2d 203, 208 (Fam. Ct. 1972).

tion of day-to-day family crises, have fashioned their own placements, as did the court in our case study. Additionally, commentators concerned with the limited nature of traditional child placements have suggested other alternatives, some of which may be implemented within existing statutory schemes.

A. *Legislative Developments*

(1) Legislative Encouragement of Adoption

The number of children available for adoption has decreased substantially in recent years.[45] Increasing acceptance of single parenthood, growing awareness of birth control methods, and the availability of medically safe and legally sanctioned abortions[46] contribute to this reduction. Increasingly, those available for adoption are older and minority children, both of whom are less readily adopted. In addition, some children tend to remain in foster care as a result of physical, medical, or emotional handicaps.[47]

Many states[48] have enacted subsidized adoption laws which provide financial assistance for expenses borne by people willing to adopt hard-to-place children.[49] These statutes

> provide a subsidy for a child when prospective adoptive parents are unable to assume full financial responsibility for the child during his minority. The subsidy would help with the costs of special medical care and with additional expenses incurred because of a child's continuing disabilities; facilitate adoption by many minority group families; minimize the special economic drain of rearing several children from the same biological family who should remain together.[50]

Subsidized adoption offers considerable potential for many children presently suffering from the indefiniteness of foster care. So far, however, it has not been widely exploited.[51] In an attempt to breathe

---

45. Derdeyn, *Adoption in Evolution: Recent Influences on Adoption in Virginia*, 70 S. Med. J. 168 (1977).

46. *Contra,* Maher v. Roe, 432 U.S. 464 (1977) (Court held that there is no constitutional requirement that public funds be used to finance abortions for indigent women).

47. Derdeyn, *supra* note 45, at 169.

48. Over forty jurisdictions now have subsidized adoption statutes, Katz & Gallagher, *Subsidized Adoption in America,* 10 Fam. L.Q. 3, 7 (1976).

49. Watson, *Subsidized Adoptions: A Crucial Investment,* 51 Child Welfare 220, 224 (1972).

50. Katz & Gallagher, *supra* note 48, at 4. One study found the costs of continued foster care and attendant administrative expenses to be less than the costs of subsidies to an adopting family. Child Care Association of Illinois, Subsidized Adoption: A Study of Use and Need in Four Agencies (1969) *as reported in* Katz & Gallagher, *supra* note 48, at 6. The savings in emotional costs through the provision of a permanent home to an otherwise homeless child cannot be estimated.

51. For instance, because of the peculiarities of Medicaid regulations (with regard to children requiring special medical or psychological attention) and the reluctance of both

life into the program and to encourage interstate adoptions, Senator Cranston recently introduced in the United States Senate a bill that will provide states with federal subsidies for such adoption subsidy payments.[52]

(2)   Recent Enactments

At least four states opt for some balance between rigid legislative edicts and open judicial discretion. In so doing they make substantial strides forward in providing workable guidelines for their courts and child care agencies.

(a)   California

The question whether to terminate parental rights is integral to the legal analysis of the permanent placement of children outside the home of their biological parents.[53] A termination hearing often provides the pivotal point in determining the nature and length of the placement which is legally available to the child. It is thus central to the problem of continuity of physical and emotional care for a child in foster care.

California addresses these problems by focusing on the duration of foster care, the effect on the child of a return to the parents, and the likelihood of the parents' prospective ability to adequately perform parental duties.[54] The legislature mandates an order of preference for placement determinations: (1) biological parents; (2) current caretakers irrespective of family relationships; and finally, (3) other "suitable" persons.[55] The prevalent requirement of a finding of *parental* unfitness has been eliminated in favor of a concentration on the interests of the child[56] in placement determinations. Even

---

foster parents and local welfare departments to move for adoptive placement when the adopting parents cannot afford traditional adoption, only thirty-five subsidized adoptions have taken place in Virginia as of May 1, 1977, although the law providing for them has been in force since 1974. Twenty-five of the children adopted under this plan were placed with their foster parents. (Based on a personal conversation with Mrs. Neville Weeks, adoption specialist, Virginia Department of Welfare, Richmond, Virginia.)

52.   S. 961, 95th Cong., 1st Sess., 123 CONG. REC. 3801-07 (March 9, 1977), *passed as amended, id.* 17,880 (October 27, 1977).

53.   This paper does not focus on removal, voluntary or otherwise, of children from biological parents. But trying to avoid that issue does not allow us to sidestep completely all the problems inherent in public intervention in the family. Only the question of initial state intervention may be escaped entirely. *See* Wald, *supra* note 12.

54.   CAL. CIV. CODE § 232(7) (West Supp. 1978).

55.   CAL. CIV. CODE § 4600 (West Supp. 1978).

56.   *Compare id. with* Rocka v. Roanoke County Dep't of Pub. Welfare, 215 Va. 515, 518, 211 S.E.2d 76, 78 (1975) (decision mandates that before terminating parental rights the court must find both that the parent is unfit and that the "best interest of the child" requires such termination).

with statutory guidelines that favor natural parents, the lower courts apparently endeavor to narrow the vestiges of parental preference with far greater frequency—at least in reported decisions[57]—than a reading of the statute would lead one to predict. Some courts ignore the statute altogether,[58] while others recognize its presence but base their decisions on "best interests" principles.[59] Significantly, knee-jerk affirmation of inchoate parental rights can no longer be expected.

Recently enacted California legislation focuses even more sharply on the length of time a child is out of the natural parents' home,[60] because permanent and continuous "parental" relationships are deemed essential to the child. Placements preferred include (1) adoption, (2) permanent foster care, and (3) guardianship. Though the state requires rehabilitation services for parents during the initial separation from their children, a premium is placed on prompt and final adjudication of the children's placement.

(b) Virginia

The Virginia legislature recently revamped its juvenile code, shifting significantly from its previous notion of supremacy of parental rights. Incorporating the idea that all persons develop close relationships when they associate with each other for a period of time, the statute expands the conventional "parent" concept to include all who stand in that role relative to a child, implying that the notion of "property" rights of biological parents in their children is distinctly on the wane.

The new enactment abandons the "best interests" and "welfare of the child" standards as the criteria for permanent termination of "residual" parental rights. In their place, the Code sets forth specific standards to guide judicial discretion. The neglect or abuse must be a "serious and substantial threat to [the child's] life, health or development," with no reasonable likelihood of a reformation of those conditions.[61] The presence of certain specified problems is deemed prima facie evidence of inability to correct the causes of

---

57. Professor Mnookin estimated that, during the late 1960's and early 1970's, "about one in every thousand cases where a California court has ordered foster care placement has resulted in a reported appellate opinion." Mnookin, *supra* note 43, at 609.

58. *E.g., In re* Adoption of Michelle Lee T., 44 Cal. App. 3d 699, 117 Cal. Rptr. 856 (1975).

59. *In re* Reyna, 55 Cal. App. 3d 288, 126 Cal. Rptr. 138 (1976).

60. S.B. 30 (codified in Cal. Welf. & Inst. Code § 366.5 (West Supp. 1978)) (described in Mnookin, *Foster Care Program*, 1 Children's Rights Report 6, 8-9 (March 1977)).

61. Va. Code § 16.1-283(B) (Supp. 1978).

the neglect or abuse. For example, a mental handicap or addiction to drugs (including alcohol) that interferes with child care duties and parental failure to use or to "respond" to rehabilitative services designed to prevent further abuse or neglect creates such a presumption.[62]

Here, too, prompt and final determinations are sought. Termination of parental rights follows parental failure, within twelve months, to maintain contact with children or to "remedy" the conditions that lead to the placement.[63] The required filing of a foster care plan[64] and the periodic review of foster care placements[65] are designed to eliminate indefinite foster care placements.

Interestingly, the Code avoids complete severance of parent-child relationships when a child over fourteen years of age objects.[66] In adding this provision, the legislature evidenced at least some understanding of the principles that led the *Jennings* court to terminate parental rights but still allow visitation for the children. Though strictly limited, this provision exemplifies the legislative opportunity to allow courts the flexibility to consider the psychological needs of children. The obvious remaining question is whether the courts will accept the opportunities offered them, or whether they will remain wedded to the restricted alternatives available in the past.

(c) Minnesota

In 1978 Minnesota joined the growing number of states whose legislatures are responding to the problem of conflict of rights in a termination procedure. Minnesota law[67] now requires a case plan for every child in foster care, either court ordered or voluntary. This plan must contain (1) reasons for placement, (2) responsibilities of the social service agency, (3) financial and visitation responsibilities of the parents, and (4) expected date of return home. The plan must be signed by the parents, the child placement agency, and if possible the child, and the plan must be reviewed every six months.

Under the statute parents have the right to counsel in the preparation of the case plan, and they must understand their obligations under it. As in the other states the notion of providing permanency for the child is central to the thrust of the statute. If a child is not

62. *Id.* § 16.1-283(B)(2).
63. *Id.* § 16.1-283(C).
64. *Id.* § 16.1-281.
65. *Id.* § 16.1-282.
66. *Id.* § 16.1-283(E).
67. 1978 MINN. LAWS ch. 602.

returned home within eighteen months, the agency is required to file a neglect, dependency, or termination petition.

(d) New York

Because the New York legislature recognizes as paramount the child's need for continuous emotional support from the adult care-taker, New York laws are perhaps the most heavily weighted in favor of the rights of foster parents.[68] Foster parents enjoy preferred status in adoption proceedings,[69] and are deemed interested parties in proceedings concerning the custody of their foster children.[70] So strong is this emphasis on permanent placement that revocation of foster placement is allowed if the foster parents fail, within six months of initial placement, to institute proceedings for adoption.[71] Children in foster care are subject to periodic reviews of their circumstances, with particular attention paid to the development or disintegration of their relationship with the biological parents.[72]

New York succinctly stated its position: long-term, indefinite foster care placement should be avoided. In its stead New York places prime importance on recognizing permanent emotional relationships that develop between children and adults in the foster home. Disappointingly, the available options are limited to continued foster care or adoption. For those children for whom either of these options is not perfectly suited, the legislature has offered no alternative.

(3) Model Acts

Drafters of two model acts hope to bring uniformity to the variety of state parental-rights-termination statutes. Each one addresses to some extent the dilemma of child placement alternatives.

Drafted by a group of juvenile court judges,[73] the Model Statute

---

68. N.Y. Soc. Serv. Law § 384-b(1)(b) (McKinney Supp. 1977).

69. *Id.* § 383(3) (McKinney 1976).

70. *Id.* Whether this section makes foster parents "parties" to an action in the normal sense, that is, entitled to notice and an opportunity to be heard, over whom jurisdiction is indispensable to any proceeding, is not clear from the statute. Clearly such status is preferred, since it is quite possible that foster parents are the only "parents" known to a child.

71. *Id.* § 384-b(3)(a) (McKinney Supp. 1977).

72. *Id.* § 392(2), (3), (5-a), (7) (McKinney Supp. 1977). New York's foster care program underwent a thoughtful analysis by Justice Brennan in Smith v. Organization of Foster Families, 431 U.S. 816 (1977). Though the failings of long-term, temporary foster care were deplored, the New York statutes withstood constitutional attack because the procedure available for questioning foster care placements and removals met the due process standards outlined in Mathews v. Eldridge, 424 U.S. 319, 335 (1976). 431 U.S. at 850-51.

73. Neglected Children Committee, National Council of Juvenile Court Judges, *Model Statute for Termination of Parental Rights,* 27 Juv. Just. 3 (Nov. 1976).

for Termination of Parental Rights[74] provides that the court, in determining whether parental rights in children should be ended, may consider whether the parent failed to stay in contact with his or her child. The court may consider the length and depth of the relationship existing within the foster family "to the extent that [the foster child's] identity is with that family."[75] The primary weakness of this proposal is that it provides no middle ground between termination of parental rights and continued foster care.

An Oregon reform proposal offers a wider range of choices.[76] After finding neglect or abandonment—carefully defined in the act—the court may choose from a variety of dispositional options. In addition to conditional and unconditional dissolution of the parent-child relationship, a court may sever parental control without terminating all rights. Such an order awards custody to another person or agency and "regulate[s] in the manner least detrimental to the child, the relationship between the child and the parent."[77] This kind of order, properly attuned to the child's relationships, supports the integrity of the foster family without severing the biological parent-child tie.

B. Permanent Placement Without Severance of Contact with Biological Parents: Case Law Developments

While new developments in the law of child placement probably occur every day, their impact is limited in that they occur most often in family courts such as the one that heard the *Jennings* case: a court not-of-record, which issues no written opinions, and from which only a de novo appeal is allowed. Such a decisionmaking process presents almost insurmountable difficulties in establishing reliable precedents. First, unless required to present written opinions, courts need not justify or explain admittedly difficult decisions, and they unintentionally may escape a degree of consistency in decisionmaking.

Second, the nature of the issues also militates against the establishment of sound legal principles through progressive decisions

---

74. The model statute bears the unmistakable imprint of the juvenile court judges. The preamble to the proposed act states that "all orders and judgments of the Juvenile Court shall be affirmed on appeal unless the trial court committed a gross abuse of discretion, legal error to the substantial prejudice of the appellant, or the judgment is clearly and manifestly against the weight of the evidence." *Id.* at 5.

75. *Id.*

76. Slader, Robart, & Pike, *Suggested Draft, Model Dissolution of Parent-Child Relationship Act*, § XXI (Metropolitan Pub. Defender's Office & Oregon Children's Servs. Div., April 1976) (copy on file with the *Vanderbilt Law Review*).

77. *Id.*

in child care cases. As Professor Mnookin has pointed out, issues of child custody and child placement involve decisions concerning interpersonal relationships and predictions about the future course of those relationships:

> A determination that is person-oriented and requires predictions necessarily involves an evaluation of the parties who have appeared in court . . . . The result of an earlier case involving different people has limited relevance to a subsequent case requiring individualized evaluations of a particular child and the litigants. Prior reported cases now provide little basis for controlling or predicting the outcome of a particular case.[78]

Perhaps the most instructive trend in the few reported cases is the movement toward increasingly flexible placements. Even the historically limited statutory schemes leave room for imaginative placements consistent with the developmental needs of a child. For example, an intermediate appellate court in Oregon reached, without the aid of specific statutory directives, a result that provided some of the benefits of adoption without a complete severance of contact with the biological parents.[79] Two children, subjected to a five-year period of custody skirmishes, rebounding placements, and uncertainty, finally were allowed to remain in the home of nonparent relatives who had provided the only comparatively constant relationship throughout the drama. That continuity enabled the court to override the historically impregnable parental claim to custody. The parents were allowed to visit.

Two recent English decisions also break traditional barriers to stepparent adoptions.[80] In both cases the courts found exceptional circumstances which allowed them to approve adoption and, at the same time, permit the non-adopting parent to maintain existing relationships with his child through continued visits. The differing religious, cultural, and racial heritages of the biological fathers were sufficient justifications for the courts to break new ground with their opinions.

In a third situation, involving disputes between parents and nonrelatives, courts are searching for the proper placement of children. In *Ross v. Hoffman*,[81] the court looked for and found "exceptional circumstances" to justify a finding that a "babysitter" of eight years, who had provided full time care five days each week, was the proper custodial "parent." While awarding custody to the

---

78. Mnookin, *supra* note 29, at 253.
79. Reflow v. Reflow, 24 Or. App. 365, 545 P.2d 894 (1976).
80. *In re* S, [1975] 1 All E.R. 109 (C.A. 1974); *In re* J, [1973] 2 All E.R. 410 (Fam. 1973).
81. 33 Md. App. 333, 340, 364 A.2d 596, 601 (Ct. Spec. App. 1976), *modified*, 280 Md. 172, 372 A.2d 582 (1977).

"babysitter," the judge found that the child's interests called for "liberal" visitation by the biological mother.

In *Bennett v. Jeffreys,*[82] in which a mother sought custody of an eight-year-old daughter whom she had placed in the care of another woman just after birth, the Court of Appeals of New York defined the conditions under which it can consider the best interests of the child with regard to a contest between a parent and a third party:

> The State may not deprive a parent of the custody of a child absent surrender, abandonment, persisting neglect, unfitness or other like extraordinary circumstances. If any of such extraordinary circumstances are present, the disposition of custody is influenced or controlled by what is in the best interest of the child. In the instant case extraordinary circumstances, namely, the prolonged separation of mother and child for most of the child's life, require inquiry into the best interest of the child.[83]

On remittitur, the family court awarded custody to the foster mother and visitation to the biological mother. The Supreme Court affirmed.[84]

The concept of continued contact with their children by non-custodial parents also finds official sanction in states that allow placement of a child with a guardian, one who has the "rights and responsibilities of a parent except for the duty to support" the child.[85] Guardianship allows the court to retain for the child a "familiar environment where the child has his emotional ties"[86] and does not force the judge to sever ties with the child's original family when that would be undesirable. Guardianship steers

> a course between the finality of a decree of adoption and dismissal of an adoption petition [when that would benefit the child]. Blood relationships may coincide with the psychological ties of the child. In such a situation, these ties are worthy of preservation, just as strong emotional attachments should not be severed, when they relate to de facto rather than natural parents.[87]

A California appellate court struck this balance in In re *Guardianship of Marino.*[88] In that case a child whose mother died soon after childbirth was raised in the family of his mother's sister "as if he were their own son."[89] After a six year silence, the father rediscovered an interest in his child and sought custody. Psychiatric

82. 40 N.Y.2d 543, 356 N.E.2d 277, 387 N.Y.S.2d 821 (1976).

83. *Id.* at 543, 356 N.E.2d at 280, 387 N.Y.S.2d at 823.

84. Bennett v. Marrow, 59 A.D.2d 492, 399 N.Y.S.2d 697 (1977).

85. Taylor, *Guardianship or "Permanent Placement" of Children,* 54 CALIF. L. REV. 741, 742-43 (1977).

86. Bodenheimer, *New Trends and Requirements in Adoption Law and Proposals for Legislative Change,* 49 S. CAL. L. REV. 10, 42 (1975). *See also* Taylor, *supra* note 85, at 745.

87. Bodenheimer, *supra* note 86, at 49 (footnote omitted).

88. 30 Cal. App. 3d 952, 106 Cal. Rptr. 655 (1973).

89. *Id.* at 954, 106 Cal. Rptr. at 656.

testimony suggested that **Mr.** Marino viewed his son Donald largely as a chattel,[90] and characterized Donald as a boy extraordinarily dependent upon his caretaker "parents."[91] Seeking Donald's continued healthy emotional development in his only "home," the court named Donald's caretakers his guardians. Despite the long period of neglect by the father, however, the court allowed him regular visitation.[92]

In each of these cases, then, a court structured a placement according to its perception of the emotional needs of the child,[93] basing its decision in part on the "exceptional" circumstances present in each case. Nevertheless, it was only in "unusual" cases that these courts felt free to construct placements tailored to the children's needs. In the majority of cases courts still feel constrained to adopt traditional dispositional alternatives. But close analysis of these decisions shows that in each one a court found it possible under *existing* law to fashion a remedy to meet a child's need for a permanent placement with caring adults and for continued communication with a non-custodial biological parent. Thus it seems clear that immediate solutions are possible even in states that have no prospect of legislative reform.

V. The Need for Flexible Dispositional Alternatives

Child custody law still lacks the kind of flexibility that might better suit the broad variety of issues confronting it. Courts should more freely utilize individual alternatives molded to fit the myriad situations in which children find themselves. They need not remain wedded to wooden legal categories into which children must be squeezed no matter how uncomfortable the fit. The absoluteness of termination of parental rights can in some instances be modified to afford stability to the foster or adoptive family, without necessarily costing the child continuity with his or her biological family.

Present adoption statutes are being applied in a social climate

---

90. The father asked the psychiatrist: "If you had an iron that belonged to you wouldn't you want it back?" *Id.* at 955, 106 Cal. Rptr. at 657.

91. *Id.* at 955, 956 & n.1, 106 Cal. Rptr. at 657, 658 & n.1.

92. The only foundation for such an outcome is found in the psychiatric testimony. *Id.* *See also* San Diego County Dep't of Pub. Welfare v. Superior Court, 7 Cal. 3d 1, 496 P.2d 453, 101 Cal. Rptr. 541 (1972).

93. Other examples of this individualized dispositional pattern arise in related areas: Mimkon v. Ford, 66 N.J. 426, 437, 332 A.2d 199, 204 (1975) (maternal grandparents allowed to visit a child even after adoption by the father's new spouse, such continued visits being beneficial to the child). *Contra,* Browning v. Tarwater, 215 Kan. 501, 524 P.2d 1135 (1974). *See generally* Note, *Visitation Rights of a Grandparent Over the Objection of a Parent: The Best Interests of the Child,* 15 J. Fam. L. 51 (1976).

very different from the one existing when they were enacted. The first general laws for adoption came into being in this country in the 1850's,[94] a time when there were great numbers of parentless children. Until very recently, adoption primarily involved infants surrendered voluntarily by their mothers. Presently, the same legal construct is expected to meet the needs of older, abused, and neglected children with memories of, and perhaps emotional ties to, biological parents. When the abused and neglected older child becomes a member of a new family by adoption, that family is by no means indistinguishable from the "natural" family, despite the implicit legal pronouncement to the contrary.

The absoluteness of the break with biological parents necessitated by termination of parental rights makes it extremely difficult for courts to make decisions in this area. All too often a judge will not terminate parental rights, and the child simply remains in foster care.[95] In the past, the central issue was the biological parent's right to "ownership" of the child. Society has progressed to the point that a non-biologically related adult can under certain circumstances attain "ownership." That absolute break, however, also has important emotional consequences, some of which are deleterious to both children and parents. Loyalty conflicts generated by hostile and competing adults can be quite crippling for younger children.[96] For older children, on the other hand, some contact with biological parents may be of value, whether they remain in stable foster care or are adopted. There is no sound reason to continue in the belief that adoption requires that biological parents be banished, or that a child's emotional connections with biological parents preclude the creation of healthy and stable placements.

Courts now recognize that emotional damage is an inevitable by-product of the uprooting of a child from his "psychological parents"—regardless of their biological tie to the child—and his placement with a parent figure who has had little or no contact with the child.[97] Still, judges find it difficult to ignore the pleas of persons claiming an "interest" in children despite their lack of an emotional relationship. A sympathetic description of this situation is provided by Judge Polier in her characterization of the clash which occurs when an attempt is made to terminate the rights of an adult who, but for biology, is a stranger to the child:

---

94. *See generally* H. WITMER, E. HERZOG, E. WEINSTEIN, & M. SULLIVAN, INDEPENDENT ADOPTIONS: A FOLLOW-UP STUDY (1963).

95. Derdeyn, *supra* note 31.

96. J. GOLDSTEIN, A. FREUD, & A. SOLNIT, *supra* note 37.

97. *See In re* Reyna, 55 Cal. App. 3d 288, 301, 126 Cal. Rptr. 138, 147 (1976).

> The parent may never have provided a home, may have maintained no real contact with the child, and may have no plans for making a home for the child. Still, the possible termination of parental rights comes as a jolt and is seen as punishment, forfeiture of what is theirs, and as a threat to self-esteem which must be fought.[98]

While such parental "interest" should be accorded less importance than the child's need for adequate parenting, the adult's assertion of rights in these types of cases is not, by definition, inimical to the child's welfare.[99] Even when a permanent placement with caring adults is secured, termination of parental rights followed by adoption is not always preferable to an arrangement allowing knowledge of or contact with biological parents.[100]

Some change is already taking place in the law. Foster children[101] and their foster parents[102] are being accorded standing to sue or at least to be heard in order to protect their interests. Creative custodial arrangements are being devised, as in the English cases coupling adoption with visitation.[103] Legislatures, too, are being asked to expand their placement guidelines. The Oregon Model Dissolution of Parent-Child Relationship Act allows for the suspension of those parental rights which are inconsistent with the least detrimental alternative available to the child.[104] The Oregon Model Act arguably requires that courts enumerate the rights, interests, and responsibilities that a parent possesses in and for his or her child. Such an enumeration will not be an easy process. Some elements that might be considered either in adoption or permanent foster care are (1) the right to be kept informed about one's child's progress; (2) an expectation of visitation, but only at the child's (or the court's or the guardian's) option; (3) a limited or conditional right of visitation vested in the parent; (4) a duty to contribute support; and (5) a right to limited or conditional custody. In considering individual cases courts can determine which components of the parent-child relationship should be preserved.

---

98. *In re* P., 71 Misc. 2d 965, 966, 337 N.Y.S.2d 203, 205 (Fam. Ct. 1972). *See also* H. CLARK, THE LAW OF DOMESTIC RELATIONS § 17.5 (1968); Derdeyn, *Child Custody Consultation,* 45 AM. J. ORTHOPSYCH. 791, 793 (1975).

99. Derdeyn, *Child Abuse and Neglect: The Rights of Parents and the Needs of Their Children,* 47 AM. J. ORTHOPSYCH. 377, 384-85 (1977).

100. Derdeyn, *supra* note 31.

101. Organization of Foster Families v. Dumpson, 418 F. Supp. 277 (S.D.N.Y. 1976), *rev'd on other grounds sub nom.* Smith v. Organization of Foster Families, 431 U.S. 816 (1977).

102. Drummond v. Fulton County Dep't of Family & Children's Servs., 547 F.2d 835, 854 (5th Cir.), *rev'd on rehearing en banc,* 563 F.2d 1200 (5th Cir. 1977); Reflow v. Reflow, 24 Or. App. 365, 545 P.2d 894 (1976).

103. *See* text accompanying note 80 *supra.*

104. *See* text accompanying note 76 *supra.*

Provisions must be made to insure that judges render written opinions and that all interested parties are given the opportunity to participate in the proceedings. In addition to biological parents, foster parents and children also are proper parties to termination and custodial adjustment proceedings.[105] After this proceeding, the court should be required to make written findings of fact and conclusions of law. An explanation of the course chosen helps insure a reasoned decision by a judge who must, for the record, consider the various alternatives that he or she ultimately rejects. It also makes an appellate court's task of review easier.[106]

Courts not infrequently face a situation wherein children placed long ago in foster care still feel or need an attachment to their parents. The current adoption practice of severing any and all connections with the biological parents may be extremely unsettling to these children, as it would have been to the *Jennings* children. Even when children are assured of a permanent home with their foster parents, either through permanent foster care or adoption, contact with their biological parents encourages a sense of continuity of self and the development of realistic attitudes[107] toward their biological parents and themselves. In such cases, the children should have a right to visit, a right vested in the child and under the control of the adoptive or permanent foster parents. Virginia did not have a provision for permanent foster care at the time of the *Jennings* trial,[108] but the *Jennings* court constructed an approximation of permanent foster care by terminating rights of the *Jennings* parents, continuing the placement of Julie and Tom Jennings in the Wallace home, and defining the children's right to visit their biological parents.

Most decisions cite "exceptional circumstances" to justify their creativity, flexibility, or deviance from traditional parental rights and standard custodial alternatives. The situation of the *Jennings* children, however, is by no means a unique one for children in foster care: for many there continues to be a memory of and an attachment

105. *See* Drummond v. Fulton County Dep't of Family & Children's Servs., 547 F.2d 835 (5th Cir.), *rev'd on rehearing en banc*, 563 F.2d 1200 (5th Cir. 1977); Organization of Foster Families v. Dumpson, 418 F. Supp. 277 (S.D.N.Y. 1976), *rev'd on other grounds sub nom.* Smith v. Organization of Foster Families, 431 U.S. 816 (1977); Katzoff v. Superior Court, 54 Cal. App. 3d 1079, 127 Cal. Rptr. 178 (1976).

106. Mnookin, *supra* note 29, at 279; Watson, *The Children of Armageddon: Problems of Custody Following Divorce*, 21 SYRACUSE L. REV. 55, 74 (1969). An example of sloppy oral decisionmaking is apparent in *In re* Guardianship of Marino, 30 Cal. App. 3d 952, 960, 106 Cal. Rptr. 655, 660-61 (Ct. App. 1973).

107. Wald, *supra* note 12, at 672.

108. Subsequent to the *Jennings* trial, Virginia's revision of the juvenile code included a provision for permanent foster care. VA. CODE § 63.1-206.1 (Supp. 1978).

to biological parents who are extremely unlikely ever to be able to care for them. These alternatives—the permanent care of a child by non-biological parents and a child's continuing relationship with biological parents—need not be mutually exclusive, and need not continue to present such a block to making dispositions in accordance with children's historical and emotional realities. It is possible to construct dispositions that afford the child the needed stability of a continuous placement and still avoid severing the child's connections with his or her past.

Constitutional Protection of Long-Term Foster Families

Foster home care is designed to provide a temporary refuge for children removed from the homes of natural parents who are unable or unwilling to care for their offspring.[1] A foster placement is intended to last only until the child's natural parents are again able to provide permanent care for the child or until the natural parents' rights are terminated and the foster agency secures a permanent adoptive home.[2] In most cases, however, the agency either experiences long delays or fails altogether to achieve a permanent solution for the future of foster children, most of whom neither return to their natural parents nor find an adoptive home.[3] As a result, long-term family relationships frequently evolve out of "temporary" foster placements, and foster parents often resist agency attempts to remove a foster child from their home.[4]

This Note assesses the legal rights of long-term foster families. After describing the problems of long-term foster care, the Note examines recent statutory and judicial efforts to grant some degree of procedural protection against state interference with long-term foster families. It then evaluates the adequacy of these efforts in light of constitutional requirements, concluding that the Constitution mandates a threshold level of due process protection based on a familial "liberty" interest similar to that of a natural family. Finally, the Note argues that in certain limited circumstances procedural protections will be inadequate, and that in these circumstances foster families should be protected by a substantive constitutional right to family integrity.

---

1. See CHILD WELFARE LEAGUE OF AMERICA, STANDARDS FOR FOSTER FAMILY CARE SERVICE 5 (1959); COMMITTEE ON THE OFFICE OF ATTORNEY GENERAL, NATIONAL ASSOCIATION OF ATTORNEYS GENERAL, LEGAL ISSUES IN FOSTER CARE 1 (1976) [hereinafter cited as LEGAL ISSUES IN FOSTER CARE]. Children can be placed in foster care voluntarily or involuntarily after a determination of neglect or abuse. See Katz, Legal Aspects of Foster Care, 5 FAM. L.Q. 283 (1971). The majority of foster children are placed voluntarily. See Levine, Caveat Parens: A Demystification of the Child Protection System, 35 U. PITT. L. REV. 1, 29 (1973); Mnookin, Foster Care: In Whose Best Interest?, 43 HARV. EDUC. REV. 599, 601 (1973) [hereinafter cited as Foster Care].
When a child is placed in foster care, the natural parents typically retain guardianship, while the foster care agency assumes legal custody of the child. The agency, in turn, delegates its responsibility for day-to-day care to the foster parents. See, e.g., N.Y. SOC. SERV. LAW § 383(2) (McKinney 1976), § 384-b(4) (McKinney Supp. 1978-1979).
2. Continued abuse or neglect of the child are generally sufficient grounds for the termination of parental rights. See generally Wald, State Intervention on Behalf of "Neglected" Children: Standards for Removal of Children from Their Homes, Monitoring the Status of Children in Foster Care, and Termination of Parental Rights, 28 STAN. L. REV. 623 (1976). A foster child may not be placed for adoption until the rights of the natural parents have been terminated.
3. See note 10 and accompanying text infra.
4. See, e.g., Smith v. Organization of Foster Families for Equality & Reform, 431 U.S. 816 (1977); Drummond v. Fulton County Dep't of Family & Children's Servs., 547 F.2d 835, rev'd on rehearing en banc, 563 F.2d 1200 (5th Cir. 1977), cert. denied, 437 U.S. 910 (1978).

I. Long-Term Foster Care

Foster care agencies are public or state-chartered private institutions operated under state guidelines.[5] In most cases, the structure of a state's foster care system reflects the basic notion that foster home placements are not intended to be permanent, and the system is designed to allow the agency to act promptly both to meet the foster child's immediate needs and—once the natural parents' rights have been terminated—to take advantage of promising adoption opportunities.[6]

Thus, prospective foster parents are not subject to selection criteria as strict as those applied to prospective adoptive parents, the supposedly temporary nature of foster placement requiring only assurance that the child's physical needs will be provided for in a relatively stable environment.[7] Moreover, the foster care agency is generally invested with broad discretion to remove a child from its foster home;[8] many agencies even require foster parents to agree in writing to surrender the child to the agency on demand.[9]

In reality, most foster children live with their foster families for at least several years.[10] Most foster care systems, however, fail to provide for the special problems that arise once a "temporary" placement turns into a long-term relationship.[11] Strong emotional ties can be expected to develop among members of a long-term foster family,[12] and an involuntary severance

---

5. *See, e.g.*, N.Y. Soc. Serv. Law § 371(10) (McKinney Supp. 1978-1979), which defines the term "authorized agency" and requires that all private agencies submit to state inspection. In addition to private agencies, N.Y. Soc. Serv. Law § 371(18) (McKinney 1976) provides for public institutions to care for children who cannot be provided for at their own homes.

6. *See, e.g.*, N.Y. Soc. Serv. Law § 383(2) (McKinney 1976).

7. *See* Legal Issues in Foster Care, *supra* note 1, at 11.

8. *See, e.g.*, N.Y. Soc. Serv. Law § 383(2) (McKinney 1976), which provides that "any . . . authorized agency may in its discretion remove such child from the home where placed or boarded." New York does provide for administrative and judicial review of agency decisions. *See* notes 27-29 and accompanying text *infra*.

9. *See, e.g.*, Iowa Code Ann. § 238.42 (West 1969), which requires such agreements. In other states, such agreements, while not statutorily required, are common practice. *See, e.g.*, Drummond v. Fulton County Dep't of Family & Children's Servs., 563 F.2d 1200, 1203 (5th Cir. 1977) (en banc), *cert. denied*, 437 U.S. 910 (1978); *In re* Jewish Child Care Ass'n, 5 N.Y.2d 222, 225, 156 N.E.2d 700, 701, 183 N.Y.S.2d 65, 67 (1959).

10. The majority of foster children are neither reunited with their natural parents nor placed in an adoptive home. Fanshel, *The Exit of Children From Foster Care: An Interim Research Report*, 50 Child Welfare 65 (1971); Foster & Freed, *Family Law*, 19 Syracuse L. Rev. 478, 490 (1967). A study of 624 foster children conducted at Columbia University found that at the end of five years 36.4% were still in foster care; 56.1% were discharged; 4.6% were placed in adoptive homes; and 2.9% were placed in mental institutions or training schools. Fanshel, *Status Changes of Children in Foster Care: Final Results of the Columbia University Longitudinal Study*, 55 Child Welfare 143 (1976). Evidence presented to the court in Organization of Foster Families for Equality & Reform v. Dumpson, 418 F. Supp. 277, 281 (S.D.N.Y. 1976), *rev'd sub. nom.* Smith v. Organization of Foster Families for Equality & Reform, 431 U.S. 816 (1977), indicated that the median stay for a foster child in a foster home in New York was more than four years.

The Florida legislature found that seven out of ten foster children do not return to their natural families after one year of foster placement. Fla. Stat. Ann. § 409.168(1) (Harrison 1979).

11. Some state legislatures have begun to deal with this problem by providing procedural protections for long-term foster families. *See* notes 27-32 and accompanying text *infra*.

12. The existence of such ties has been explicitly recognized by the Supreme Court. *See*

of those ties can result in severe and lasting psychological damage to family members. This is particularly true in the case of the foster child,[13] who, under current theories of child development, needs a secure and continuous relationship with a "psychological parent" to ensure healthy emotional growth.[14] Yet the agency's broad discretion provides little formal assurance that such factors will be considered when a removal decision is made. Indeed, the more relaxed standard applied for the selection of foster parents increases the likelihood that, once a long-term foster family relationship develops, the agency will resist an attempt by the foster parents to retain or adopt their foster child.[15] An agency may even be inclined to remove a foster child from an emotionally supportive foster placement simply to forestall the development of an intimate family relationship before the child's future status is finally resolved.[16]

In reaching decisions with respect to placement or removal, an agency is generally required to adhere to a "best interests of the child" standard.[17]

Smith v. Organization of Foster Families for Equality & Reform, 431 U.S. 816, 844-45 n.52 (1977) (pointing to the "undisputed fact that the emotional ties between foster parent and foster child are in many cases quite close, and undoubtedly in some as close as those existing in biological families").

13. *See, e.g.,* L. STONE & J. CHURCH, CHILDHOOD AND ADOLESCENCE, A PSYCHOLOGY OF THE GROWING PERSON 531 (3d ed. 1975) (concluding that foster children who are moved from home to home "develop a sense of repeated loss and rejection, and often become victims of psychopathology"). The authors go so far as to suggest that for some children at least, including the emotionally disturbed, quality institutional care is preferable to a foster care system that, by constantly transferring children from home to home, prevents them from forming secure emotional attachments. *Id.* at 531.

14. The notion of psychological parenthood has gained wide acceptance since the appearance of J. GOLDSTEIN, A. FREUD & A. SOLNIT, BEYOND THE BEST INTERESTS OF THE CHILD (1973), which defines the psychological parent as:

one who, on a continuing, day-to-day basis, through interaction, companionship, interplay, and mutuality, fulfills the child's psychological needs for a parent, as well as the child's physical needs. The psychological parent may be a biological . . . , adoptive, foster, or common-law . . . parent, or any other person. There is no presumption in favor of any of these after the initial assignment at birth.

Id. at 98. Under this view, a separation of child and psychological parents can cause trauma. *Id.* at 40-42. *See also* A. Freud & D. Burlingham, *Infants Without Families: Reports on the Hampstead Nurseries,* in 3 THE WRITINGS OF ANNA FREUD 183 (1973), *quoted in* J. GOLDSTEIN, A. FREUD & A. SOLNIT, *supra,* at 138:

Observers seldom appreciate the depth and seriousness of this grief [of separation] of a small child. Their judgment of it is misled for one reason. This childish grief is short-lived. Mourning of equal intensity in an adult person would have to run its course throughout a year; the same process in the child between 1 and 2 years will normally be over in 36 to 48 hours. It is a psychological error to conclude from this short duration that the reaction is only a superficial one and can be treated lightly.

Short of trauma, the "limbo of permanent temporariness" places great emotional strains on the foster child and the foster family. *See, e.g.,* Fiaste, *Rocky Road From Foster Care to Adoption,* reproduced in *Foster Care: Problems and Issues: Joint Hearing Before the Subcomm. on Children and Youth of the Senate Comm. on Labor and Public Welfare and the Subcomm. on Select Education of the House Comm. on Education and Labor,* 94th Cong., 1st Sess. 883 (1975).

15. *See* LEGAL ISSUES IN FOSTER CARE, *supra* note 1, at 11.

16. *See, e.g., In re* Jewish Child Care Ass'n, 5 N.Y.2d 222, 183 N.Y.S.2d 65, 156 N.E.2d 700 (1959).

17. The statutes of at least 23 states require that child custody decisions be based on "the best interests of the child." *See* Mnookin, *Child-Custody Adjudication: Judicial Functions in the Face of Indeterminacy,* 39 LAW & CONTEMP. PROB., Summer 1975, at 226, 243 n.81 [hereinafter cited as *Child Custody Adjudication*]. Even states that do not explicitly

This standard, which is also commonly applied by courts when judicial decisions are sought,[18] thus serves as the principal safeguard against abuse by an agency of its power to intervene in foster family relationships. As an expression of the fundamental goal in foster care decisionmaking, the standard is naturally difficult to fault, but as a practical guide it has some serious shortcomings. In the first place, given the unpredictability of the factors affecting the human psyche, courts and social workers must of necessity resort to their own subjective values—and prejudices—in determining a child's best interest.[19] The risks created by this subjective element are compounded by the fact that the determination may be made without the full participation of the foster parents. Moreover, agencies and courts applying the "best interests" standard often focus on the child's future best interest, rather than on the protection of the child's current relationships.[20] While there are generally accepted standards for determining whether a child's present needs are met,[21] scholars agree that attempts to determine a child's future best interest must yield indeterminate results.[22] Some recent judicial applications of the standard have revealed a heightened concern for the child's present psychological interest,[23] but these decisions do not obviate the basic weak-

---

require application of the "best interests" standard appear to rely on it implicitly in granting agencies discretionary authority to remove children from foster homes. *See, e.g.,* Drummond v. Fulton County Dep't of Family & Children's Servs., 563 F.2d 1200, 1203, 1205-07 (5th Cir. 1977) (en banc), *cert. denied,* 437 U.S. 910 (1978).

18. *See* note 23 *infra.*

19. *See, e.g.,* Bennett v. Jeffreys, 40 N.Y.2d 543, 356 N.E.2d 277, 387 N.Y.S.2d 821 (1976); *In re* Jonathan D., 97 Misc. 2d 859, 412 N.Y.S.2d 733 (Fam. Ct. 1978); *In re* Suzanne Y., 92 Misc. 2d 652, 401 N.Y.S.2d 383 (Fam. Ct. 1977). *See generally Child Custody Adjudication, supra* note 17, at 226. The same author in *Foster Care, supra* note 1, describes a simulation study in which three experienced judges were given the files of 94 children from 50 families and asked to decide the children's disposition. The judges agreed in less than half the cases, and "[e]ven in cases in which they agreed on the decision, the judges did not identify the same factors as determinants, each seeming to operate to some extent within his own unique value system." *Id.* at 619.

20. *See. e.g.,* Drummond v. Fulton County Dep't of Family & Children's Servs., 563 F.2d 1200 (5th Cir. 1977) (en banc), *cert. denied,* 437 U.S. 910 (1978).

21. *See generally* Areen, *Intervention Between Parent and Child: A Reappraisal of the State's Role in Child Neglect and Abuse Cases,* 63 GEO. L.J. 887 (1975).

22. *See generally Child Custody Adjudication, supra* note 17. The indeterminacy of the "best interest" standard not only affects the role of the family court judge but also undermines the efficacy of the foster child/attorney relationship. Although legal representation for children is a central goal of the children's rights movement, *see* Dembitz, Book Review, 83 YALE L.J. 1304, 1312 (1974), the child's lawyer is in no better position to determine his client's future best interests than any other participant in the controversy. *See* Mlyniec, *The Child Advocate in Private Custody Disputes: A Role in Search of a Standard,* 16 J. FAM. L. 1, 13 (1977-1978); *cf.* Veazey v. Veazey, 560 P.2d 382, 387-90 (Alaska 1977) (child's attorney must make his own inquiry into his client's best interests, and is not required to advocate the position taken by his "client of tender years").

23. *See, e.g.,* Bennett v. Jeffreys, 40 N.Y.2d 543, 356 N.E.2d 277, 387 N.Y.S.2d 821 (1976); *In re* Jonathan D., 97 Misc. 2d 859, 412 N.Y.S.2d 733 (Fam. Ct. 1978); *In re* Suzanne Y., 92 Misc. 2d 652, 401 N.Y.S.2d 383 (Fam. Ct. 1977). These cases evince a greater willingness, in applying the "best interests of the child" standard, to permit termination of the rights of the natural parents even when they are considered fit. By identifying the "best interests" standard with current notions of psychological development, the approach taken in these decisions would permit "no fault" termination of parental rights if removal of the child would be emotionally detrimental. Other judicial developments in this area are described in Boskey & McCue, *Alternative Standards for the Termination of Parental Rights,* 9 SETON HALL L. REV. 1 (1978).

nesses of the standard itself.   Efforts to go beyond the limited protection afforded by "best interests" determinations are considered in the next section.

II.   EVOLVING PROTECTIONS FOR LONG-TERM FOSTER FAMILIES

A.   *State Statutory and Judicial Approaches*

Efforts to come to terms with the reality of long-term foster care have been impeded to some extent by a perception that procedural protections for long-term foster families would merely institutionalize relationships resulting from the malfunctioning of the foster care system.[24]

However, growing public awareness [25] of the fact that foster family relationships are now predominantly long-term and that disruption of such relationships may inflict permanent psychological harm on foster children has begun to be reflected, in at least some states, in the law governing foster care.   In addition to the judicial decisions referred to above,[26] several state legislatures have enacted procedures specifically designed to consider the interests of long-term foster families.   In New York, foster parents whose foster child has resided with them for at least twenty-four months are recognized as parties in interest at the mandatory annual family court review of the status of their foster child.[27]   The state also grants foster parents who have had actual custody of a child for eighteen months the right to a post-removal hearing [28] from which departmental review is available.[29]   Florida's recently revised child placement statutes adopt a similar approach.[30]   Wisconsin and Pennsylvania have established even broader protections for foster parents.   In Wisconsin, any decision affecting foster parents of children may be appealed under "fair hearing procedures." [31]   In Pennsylvania, administrative regulations require a hearing prior to all removals from foster placements of thirty days or more.[32]

---

24. *See, e.g.*, Smith v. Organization of Foster Families for Equality & Reform, 431 U.S. 816, 862 (1977) (Stewart, J., concurring) (arguing against the view that "breakdowns of the New York [foster care] system must be protected or forever frozen in their existence by the Due Process Clause of the Fourteenth Amendment").

25. *See, e.g., Foster-Care Fiasco*, NEWSWEEK, Mar. 5, 1979, at 94.

26. *See* note 23 *supra.*

27. N.Y. SOC. SERV. LAW § 383(3) (McKinney 1976).

28. N.Y. SOC. SERV. LAW § 392(2)(c) (McKinney Supp. 1978-1979).

29. N.Y. SOC. SERV. LAW § 400(2) (McKinney Supp. 1978-1979).

30. *See* FLA. STAT. ANN. §§ 409.165, .168, .168(4)(b) (Harrison 1979) (requiring a periodic review of the status of foster children and granting foster parents standing to appear and assert their interests).

31. WIS. STAT. ANN. § 48.64(4)(a) (West Supp. 1978).

32. Children and Youth Manual of the Department of Public Welfare § 4335 (1975). The Pennsylvania regulatory enactment was preceded by an opinion of the State Attorney General, Termination of Long-Term Foster Placements, [1974] PA. OP. ATT'Y GEN. No. 32, which addressed the constitutional dimension of the issues involved in long-term foster care. The opinion declared that procedural protections were constitutionally required, noted the "fundamental" nature of the right to companionship of one's child, and emphasized the Supreme Court's focus on "the reality of the emotional bonds, not the formalities," when evaluating relationships. *Id.* at 117.

These recent judicial and legislative attempts to provide some protection for long-term families are important, though preliminary, efforts by the states to deal with the implications of long-term foster care. The procedural safeguards enacted by states such as New York and Pennsylvania guarantee at least that foster parents' views on removal will be formally heard by the agency. There is no assurance, however, that such safeguards will ever be widely available. More importantly, even if they were, adequate protection for long-term foster families still would not be assured. The adoption of new procedures may be interpreted as a legislative directive to give more careful consideration to the impact of disrupting long-term foster relationships in custody and removal decisions, but even under the modified procedures, foster agencies retain broad discretion over the ultimate decision.[33] The agencies, moreover, will generally continue to rely on the "best interests of the child" standard, with its inherent weaknesses and limitations.[34] As long as that standard continues to govern foster agency decisionmaking, modifications in custody and removal procedures alone can provide no guarantee either that individual decisions will adequately focus on the foster child's present, discernible psychological needs, or that adequate attention will be given to the importance of the foster relationship if that relationship is not seen as in the child's future "best" interest. As far as the courts are concerned, the fact that some decisions applying the "best interests of the child" standard have recently revealed special sensitivity to the foster family relationship[35] is no guarantee that those courts will continue to apply the standard in such a fashion or that such an approach will be widely adopted.

These shortcomings of state law protections for foster families must be placed in proper perspective. In most cases, state procedures permitting foster parents a minimal opportunity to be heard may sufficiently protect the interests at stake, especially where the foster relationship has been relatively short, where the child is relatively mature, or where the interests of the natural parents command competing attention. But these procedures are neither universal nor uniform; nor is it clear, as will be considered below, that procedural safeguards alone can satisfactorily protect the special interests of long-term foster families in all circumstances.

B. *Procedural Due Process Protection*

The limited availability and scope of state protections for long-term foster families have led foster parents dissatisfied with agency procedures and decisionmaking to seek the uniform and potentially more expansive procedural protections of the due process clause[36] of the federal Constitution. To

---

33. The agency's discretion is not explicitly affected by the modified procedures. *See, e.g.,* N.Y. Soc. Serv. Law § 383(2) (McKinney 1976), *quoted* in note 8 *supra.*
34. *See text* accompanying notes 17-22 *supra.*
35. *See* note 23 and accompanying text *supra.*
36. An alternative approach has been based on the argument that state interference with long-term foster families violates the equal protection clause of the fourteenth amendment.

establish that their interests come within the scope of the clause, foster parents have advanced two principal arguments. One has sought to demonstrate a protected "property" interest,[37] based on the contention that "the realities of the foster care system . . . justify [foster parents'] expectation that their role as foster parents will not be abruptly and summarily terminated."[38] The property argument has not, however, proved persuasive,[39] largely because the contractual nature of the foster family relationship precludes any legitimate anticipation of permanence sufficient to qualify the parents' interest as a protected claim of "entitlement."[40] More generally, courts understandably hesitate to characterize relationships with children as "property" interests, with the implication that children are "mere chattels"[41] or that one set of parents "may acquire some sort of squatter's rights in another's child."[42]

The other argument, which has proved more effective, is based on the assertion that state custody and removal procedures are inadequate to protect an asserted "liberty" interest of the foster family.[43] This argument identifies

---

This argument is viable only if it is assumed that long-term foster families are constitutionally entitled to the same substantive rights and protections as natural families.

Where interracial foster placement is at issue equal protection concerns may be more prominent, although in *Drummond v. Fulton County Dep't of Family & Children's Servs.,* see notes 55-72 and accompanying text *infra,* the court rejected an equal protection challenge. 563 F.2d 1200, 1204-06 (5th Cir. 1977) (en banc), *cert. denied,* 437 U.S. 910 (1978). On whether race is a legitimate factor in adoption and custody proceedings see Grosman, *A Child of a Different Color: Race as a Factor in Adoption and Custody Proceedings,* 17 BUFFALO L. REV. 303 (1968).

37. The concept that individuals may acquire a protected "property" interest in a government benefit has been a key component of modern procedural due process doctrine, which has extended procedural guarantees to nontraditional forms of "property." Board of Regents v. Roth, 408 U.S. 564, 571-72 (1972). The Supreme Court has, for example, recognized due process interests in the receipt of expected welfare payments, Goldberg v. Kelly, 397 U.S. 254 (1970), and the continuation of government employment, Perry v. Sindermann, 408 U.S. 593 (1972). *See generally* Reich, *The New Property,* 73 YALE L.J. 733 (1964).

38. Organization of Foster Families for Equality & Reform v. Dumpson, 418 F. Supp. 277, 280-81 (S.D.N.Y. 1976), *rev'd sub nom.* Smith v. Organization of Foster Families for Equality & Reform, 431 U.S. 816 (1977).

39. The argument was explicitly rejected by the district court in Organization of Foster Families for Equality & Reform v. Dumpson, 418 F. Supp. 277, 280-81 (S.D.N.Y. 1976), *rev'd sub nom.* Smith v. Organization of Foster Families for Equality & Reform, 431 U.S. 816 (1977). The parents did not pursue it on appeal, *see* 431 U.S. at 839. However, much of the Supreme Court's analysis of the parents' asserted "liberty" interest, *see* notes 51 & 52 and accompanying text *infra,* relies on concepts more appropriate to a property argument. Justice Stewart's concurrence, in particular, confounded liberty and property reasoning, *see* note 52 *infra.*

40. Characterization of nontraditional interests as property subject to due process protection requires a showing of a "legitimate claim of entitlement" rather than simply "an abstract need or desire" or a "unilateral expectation." Board of Regents v. Roth, 408 U.S. 564, 577 (1972). Thus, mere "hopes to continue a relationship with" a foster child have been held not to amount to a property interest. Kyees v. County Dep't of Pub. Welfare, 600 F.2d 693, 697 (7th Cir. 1979). *See generally* L. TRIBE, AMERICAN CONSTITUTIONAL LAW §§ 10-8 to -19 (1978); Reich, *supra* note 37.

41. Organization of Foster Families for Equality & Reform v. Dumpson, 418 F. Supp. 277, 282 (S.D.N.Y. 1976), *rev'd sub nom.* Smith v. Organization of Foster Families for Equality & Reform, 431 U.S. 816 (1977).

42. Bennett v. Jeffreys, 40 N.Y.2d 543, 552 n.2, 356 N.E.2d 277, 285 n.2, 387 N.Y.S.2d 821, 829 n.2 (1976)

43. The assertion of a familial "liberty" interest involves two distinct levels of constitutional inquiry. Of concern in this section is the identification of an interest that must be accorded *procedural* protection under the Constitution. Beyond this is a possible determination that an interest is entitled to *substantive* protection. The Supreme Court has acknowledged

the interests of the long-term foster family in maintaining its privacy and integrity with the traditionally protected core liberty interest in "the right of the individual to . . . marry, establish a home and bring up children." [44] The essential claim made by foster parents is that the same procedural safeguards that have traditionally limited state interference with natural families should be extended to foster families that act as the functional and psychological equivalent of natural families.

Although majorities on two federal courts have rejected this argument in specific instances,[45] the Supreme Court has explicitly left the question open, suggesting that, at least in limited circumstances, long-term foster families might be entitled to some constitutional protection.[46]

1. Smith v. Organization of Foster Families for Equality & Reform (OFFER.)[47] In *OFFER,* the Supreme Court rejected a claim by an association of foster parents that the New York procedures governing removal of foster children from foster homes violated the procedural due process rights of foster parents.[48] Although the Court avoided deciding whether a foster relationship could ever constitute a liberty interest entitled to constitutional protection by holding that the New York procedures adequately protected whatever familial interest a foster parent might have in such a relationship,[49]

---

in this context that "recognition of a liberty interest in foster families for purposes of the procedural protection of the Due Process Clause would not necessarily require that foster families be treated as fully equivalent to biological families for purposes of substantive due process review." Smith v. Organization of Foster Families for Equality & Reform, 431 U.S. 816, 842 n.48 (1977).

Although many of the Court's decisions on familial interests have dealt with substantive rights, *see* note 80 and accompanying text *infra,* it has also made clear that procedural due process protections apply to family activities and relationships. *See, e.g.,* Moore v. City of E. Cleveland, 431 U.S. 494, 499-502 (1977); Cleveland Bd. of Educ. v. LaFleur, 414 U.S. 632, 639-40 (1974).

44. Meyer v. Nebraska, 262 U.S. 390, 399 (1923). *See* L. Tribe, *supra* note 40, § 10-8, at 506-08.

45. Kyees v. County Dep't of Pub. Welfare, 600 F.2d 693 (7th Cir. 1979); Drummond v. Fulton County Dep't of Family & Children's Servs., 563 F.2d 1200 (5th Cir. 1977) (en banc), *cert. denied,* 437 U.S. 910 (1978). *See* text accompanying notes 55-72 *infra.*

46. *See* notes 47-54 and accompanying text *infra.*

47. 431 U.S. 816 (1977).

48. The Organization of Foster Families specifically challenged the constitutionality of N.Y. Soc. Serv. Law §§ 383(2), 400 (McKinney 1976) and 18 N.Y. Codes, Rules & Regs. § 450.14 (1974). Section 383(2) authorizes the agency to remove "in its discretion" a foster child from a foster home. Section 450.14 of the Codes, Rules and Regulations provides that absent an emergency, the agency must notify the foster parents of the proposed removal ten days before action is taken, after which the foster parents may request a conference with the Social Services Department and retain custody of the child until the conference is held. If the conference results in a decision unfavorable to the foster parents, the child may be removed, and the foster parents may obtain an adversary administrative hearing.

49. 431 U.S. at 847-56. The Court reached this conclusion by applying the test set down in Mathews v. Eldridge, 424 U.S. 319, 335 (1976), which identifies the "specific dictates" of due process by considering three "distinct factors": first, the private interest that will be affected by official action; second, the risk of an erroneous deprivation of such interest through the procedures used, and the probable value, if any, of additional or substitute procedural safeguards; and, finally, the government's interest, including the function involved and the fiscal and administrative burdens that the additional or substitute procedural requirements would entail. 431 U.S. at 848-49.

the Court's opinion, by Justice Brennan, did discuss the legal and constitutional status of the foster family and its relationship to the natural family.[50]

The Court emphasized that unlike natural families, which derive their existence apart from the state, the foster family is the product of a temporary contractual arrangement between the state and the foster parents.[51] Under this contractual view, foster parents have no justifiable expectation that the foster placement will be allowed to mature into a legally protected permanent relationship. Although this reasoning seems more appropriate to the evaluation of a claimed "property" interest, the Court evidently found the expectable impermanence of the relationship fatal even to the assertion of a "liberty" interest. It took the view that the "limited recognition" given to foster families under New York law and the foster care contracts could not be seen to create "any but the most limited constitutional 'liberty' in the foster family."[52]

Nonetheless, the Court was evidently unwilling to exclude the foster family altogether from the ambit of constitutional protection. While focusing on what it perceived to be significant differences between foster and natural families, the Court acknowledged that biological relationships are not the exclusive determinant of the existence of a family.[53] Most significantly, the Court recognized that, at least when a child who has never known his natural parents is placed in a foster home as an infant and remains there for several years, the foster family will hold the same place in the emotional life of the child and perform the same socializing functions as a natural family.[54] Thus, despite its contractual view of the foster family relationship, the *OFFER* Court's recognition of these realities of foster care suggests that it might, in a limited context, be prepared to extend to long-term foster families some of the procedural and even substantive protection hitherto reserved for the natural family.

2. Drummond v. Fulton County Department of Family & Children's Services.[55] In *Drummond,* a custody dispute between foster parents and a foster care agency, a mixed-race foster child who had resided with his white foster parents continuously for nearly two years[56] was removed by the agency in accordance with a procedure that did not allow participation by either the foster parents—who sought to adopt the child—or any independent

---

50. *Id.* at 838-47.
51. *Id.* at 845.
52. *Id.* at 846. In a concurring opinion, *id.* at 856-63, Justice Stewart rejected the majority's suggestion that the Court might, in some circumstances, treat the foster family as equivalent to the natural family for procedural due process purposes. His opinion draws heavily on notions of statutory entitlement, which also influenced the majority's apparent reluctance to invest the foster family with procedural protection. *Id.* at 860 (Stewart, J., concurring).
53. *Id.* at 844 (majority opinion).
54. *Id.*
55. 408 F. Supp. 382 (N.D. Ga. 1976), *aff'd en banc,* 563 F.2d 1200 (5th Cir. 1977), *cert. denied,* 437 U.S. 910 (1978). The *Drummond* decision has been followed by the Seventh Circuit, *see* Kyees v. County Dep't of Pub. Welfare, 600 F.2d 693 (7th Cir. 1979).
56. 563 F.2d at 1203.

representative of the child.[57]   The rights of the child's natural mother had been terminated on the ground of parental unfitness and the agency had been unable to find a permanent adoptive home.   Despite the strong recommendation by the agency's own staff social worker that the foster parents be allowed to adopt the child,[58] the agency ordered removal based on its belief that the child should be raised in a black family.   The Drummonds challenged the removal decision in federal court,[59] arguing—in conjunction with a court-appointed representative for their foster child [60]—that the agency's procedures interfered with the liberty interest shared by foster parent and child in the foster relationship without providing due process of law.[61]   The Court of Appeals for the Fifth Circuit initially upheld the Drummonds' claim,[62] but after rehearing en banc reversed the panel decision.[63]

Like the Supreme Court's opinion in *OFFER*, on which it relied, the final *Drummond* opinion stressed the significance of the administrative and

---

57. *Id.* at 1204.   The agency employed an informal decisionmaking process.   It began with visits to the prospective adoptive home by a social worker, who kept recorded impressions of the visits.   Subsequent office interviews were conducted by the agency's staff.   The file thus developed was considered at an agency staff meeting, where the final decision was made. *See also* Note, *Long-Term Foster Parents and Children Have No Protectable Interest in Their Relationship,* 29 MERCER L. REV. 1137 n.2 (1978).   In the aftermath of the *Drummond* litigation, the Fulton County agency adopted revised procedures for dealing with the grievances of foster parents, providing for four levels of appeal.   *Id.* at 1137.

58. 547 F.2d at 837, 848.   The social worker focused on the fact that the child was obviously thriving in the loving family environment created by the Drummonds, and recommended adoption despite reservations about the Drummonds' race, age, lack of education, and overly protective attitude.

59. They also challenged the agency's action in state court.   *See* Drummond v. Fulton County Dep't of Family & Children's Servs., 237 Ga. 449, 228 S.E.2d 839 (1976).

60. The child's representative, who intervened during preparation for appeal, *see* 547 F.2d at 835, 855-56, supported the parents' assertion of a familial liberty interest, but he argued in addition that the child had a separate liberty interest, personal to himself, in the form of a "right to a stable environment." 563 F.2d at 1208. This right, the representative argued, required that the child be given a hearing prior to any removal decision, "particularly in light of the significant literature which indicates a traumatic effect of such moves on young children." *Id.* Concededly novel, this argument relied on an analogy to cases according procedural due process rights to minor defendants in juvenile court proceedings, specifically *In re* Gault, 387 U.S. 1 (1967) (minor defendants in juvenile court proceedings have due process rights), and McKeiver v. Pennsylvania, 403 U.S. 528 (1971) (same). Pointing to the foster agency's status as the child's legal guardian and its efforts to act in the child's best interest, the court rejected the analogy as an inappropriate model for a nonadversary proceeding in which the minor is not a defendant whose liberty is at stake. 563 F.2d at 1208-09.

61. The Drummonds raised this argument for the first time on appeal. 563 F.2d at 1206. In the district court the Drummonds claimed only that the agency's reliance on racial considerations deprived them of equal protection under the law. 408 F. Supp. at 383. This claim was rejected both by the district court, *see id.,* and by the court of appeals, *see* 563 F.2d at 1204-05.

The Drummonds' principal due process argument was based on the claim that they were their foster child's "psychological parents," and that they were therefore entitled to the constitutional protections accorded natural parents, including, presumably, the substantive right to family privacy. 563 F.2d at 1206. Their claim focused, however, on the alleged deprivation of due process caused by the agency's constitutionally defective procedures.

The Drummonds advanced a second argument based on the assertion that the decision to remove the child would "[cast] a stigma upon their reputation," *id.* at 1207, thereby invading a different liberty interest. The court, however, found insufficient grounds to characterize the agency's action as defamatory, *id.* at 1208.

62. 547 F.2d 835 (5th Cir. 1977).

63. 563 F.2d 1200 (5th Cir. 1977) (en banc), *cert. denied,* 437 U.S. 910 (1978).

contractual sources of the foster relationship, reasoning that "[t]rue liberty rights do not flow from state laws, which can be repealed by action of the legislature. Unlike property rights they have a more stable source in our notions of intrinsic human rights." [64] The rights asserted by the Drummonds, the court concluded, did not meet these standards, and accordingly did not amount to a liberty interest "of full-fledged constitutional magnitude" deserving of due process protection. Under these circumstances, the court held, the agency procedures were adequate to protect whatever less substantial interests the plaintiffs may have had in the foster relationship.[65]

In its characterization of the interests actually at stake in the case, the *Drummond* majority's opinion suffers from a basic inconsistency. The court noted Justice Brennan's [66] intimation in *OFFER* that a foster family might under certain circumstances be the functional equivalent of a natural family,[67] and it acknowledged that its conclusion might not be applicable to all foster family "situations."[68] In fact, however, the Drummonds' "situation" closely paralleled the particular circumstances identified by Justice Brennan in *OFFER*. The child involved, having never known his natural parents,[69] had been placed in foster care as an infant (aged less than one month) and had remained continuously with the same foster parents for nearly two years.[70] In this case, then, the Drummond foster family undoubtedly performed the same emotional and socializing functions as a natural family and should accordingly have been provided at least minimal procedural due process protection. A dissenting opinion by Judge Tuttle [71] took this view, concluding that the standards set in *OFFER* permitted recognition of the Drummonds' interests as protected by the requirements of procedural due process. To the majority's contention that the agency's procedures were sufficient to protect any due process interests that might exist, Judge Tuttle responded that the majority "trivialize[d] due process beyond recognition." [72]

3. *Identifying a Protectable Liberty Interest.* Even if doubts about the *Drummond* majority's reasoning are resolved in favor of its conclusion that no interests of "full-fledged constitutional magnitude" were involved in that

---

64. *Id.* at 1207.
65. *Id.* at 1210-11.
66. In this connection, it may be worth noting that although the Supreme Court denied certiorari to the Drummonds, 437 U.S. 910 (1978), Justice Brennan, author of the Court's opinion in *OFFER*, and Justice White voted to grant certiorari.
67. 563 F.2d at 1209.
68. *Id.* at 1207. The court purported to limit its conclusion to "only those [situations] in which a child placement agency charged with the custody of a child, places that child for temporary care." *Id.* The meaning of this limitation is by no means clear, especially since in *Drummond* itself the "temporary" care had lasted for two years.
69. The panel decision refers to the Drummonds as "the only parents [the child] had known during his infancy." 547 F.2d at 853. The record gives no indication that the child's natural parents maintained any contact with him after his foster placement.
70. Justice Brennan stipulated "several" years in *OFFER*. *See* text accompanying note 54 *supra*.
71. 563 F.2d at 1212-19. Judge Tuttle also wrote the panel decision that had initially upheld the Drummonds' claim.
72. *Id.* at 1217.

case, the decision is not incompatible with the recognition of a right of at least some long-term foster families to procedural protection under the due process clause.[73] As indicated earlier, the basis of such a right is the existence of a liberty interest in family integrity, an interest that precludes arbitrary state interference with relationships between parents and child.[74] This interest, which has been given unambiguous recognition in the case of natural families, should be no less demanding of respect where foster families fulfill, or may reasonably be presumed to fulfill, the same socializing and emotional functions normally performed by natural families. At a minimum, then, the due process clause should be deemed to require an opportunity for a long-term foster family to show that it is functioning as the equivalent of a natural family. This requirement should certainly apply to the families identified by Justice Brennan in *OFFER*—those in which a child was placed in a foster home as an infant, never knew his natural parents, and remained in the foster home for "several" years. A right to a hearing may also be found where other facts give rise to a reasonable presumption that family-like ties have arisen—as, for example, where an older child has been with foster parents for an exceptionally long time. Such families should have an opportunity to show that they are, in fact, equivalent to a natural family.

The specific procedural requirements in any given case must be determined on the basis of a weighing of individual, state, and efficiency interests.[75] Because a basic objective of procedural due process is to protect against erroneous or improper assessment of the facts on which decisions are based,[76] it seems minimally necessary that states accord to foster parents notice of a proposed removal, a statement of reasons, and an opportunity to participate in a hearing with agency officials before a final decision is reached. To assure the adequacy of the foster parents' participation, due process would also require provision for preremoval judicial review of agency decisions. Beyond these requirements, however, the interests of the state and considerations of efficiency suggest that legislatures should have scope to define the extent of procedural protection deemed appropriate. States might, for example, fully meet their constitutional responsibilities without instituting procedures as detailed and formal as those enacted in New York.

Recognition that long-term foster families—at least those encompassed within the *OFFER* dictum—are entitled to due process safeguards would assure a stable and uniform nationwide threshold of procedural protection. At the same time, it would not unduly interfere with substantive state policies, including the state interest in ensuring that foster care agencies can act quickly and efficiently to respond to what those agencies determine to be the best

---

73. As previously discussed, *see* note 43 *supra,* a distinction may be drawn between interests entitled to procedural protections and those substantively protected against governmental invasions in all but extraordinary situations. *See* notes 83-86 and accompanying text *infra.*

74. *See* notes 43 & 44 and accompanying text *supra.*

75. *See* Mathews v. Eldridge, 424 U.S. 319, 335 (1976), *discussed in* note 49 *supra.*

76. *See, e.g.,* Kyees v. County Dep't of Pub. Welfare, 600 F.2d 693, 697 (7th Cir. 1979).

interests of the children in their custody. The weighing of interests mandated by the Supreme Court may thus be the most appropriate means to protect the interests of most long-term foster families without undermining the overall efficiency of a state's foster care system. In some circumstances, however, a foster family may have become so nearly indistinguishable from a natural family that procedural guarantees alone may be inadequate. Such guarantees leave largely unaffected the broad discretion generally granted to foster care agencies in custody and removal decisions,[77] as well as the application of the problematic "best interests of the child" standard.[78] To this extent, procedural due process may not sufficiently protect the *substantive* rights of familial privacy and integrity that some long-term foster families may validly claim.[79] The circumstances under which such rights may arise are examined in the next section.

III. LONG-TERM FOSTER FAMILIES AND THE SUBSTANTIVE RIGHT TO PRIVACY

A. *The Constitutional Protection of Familial Relationships*

The Supreme Court has long recognized that there exists a "private realm of family life which the state cannot enter."[80] In *Griswold v. Connecticut*,[81] the Court articulated a constitutional "right to privacy" assimilating earlier decisions [82] that had granted substantive protection against government interference in certain intimate personal decisions and family relationships. Unlike the procedural protections afforded "liberty" interests, which merely limit the manner in which the government can interfere with family relations, inclusion of these relations within the constitutionally protected zone of privacy bars government interference in all but the "most compellingly justified instances." [83] In its characterization of this right of familial privacy the Court has made clear that the constitutional significance of the family relationship derives from the importance of the function it traditionally performs and from emotional intimacy, as well as from biological relationships.[84] Thus, relationships included within this protected zone have not been limited to nuclear or traditional family arrangements. Constitutional protection has

---

77. *See* note 8 *supra.*
78. *See* note 17 *supra.*
79. *See* notes 99-104 and accompanying text *infra.*
80. Prince v. Massachusetts, 321 U.S. 158, 166 (1944). *See also* Wisconsin v. Yoder, 406 U.S. 205, 231-33 (1972) (right to keep children out of school for religious reasons); Griswold v. Connecticut, 381 U.S. 479 (1965) (right to use contraceptives); Pierce v. Society of Sisters, 268 U.S. 510, 534-35 (1925) (right to educate children in religious schools); Meyer v. Nebraska, 262 U.S. 390, 399-401 (1923) (right to instruct children in foreign languages).
81. 381 U.S. 479, 485 (1965).
82. In particular, the Court cited Meyer v. Nebraska, 262 U.S. 390 (1923), and Pierce v. Society of Sisters, 268 U.S. 510 (1925), as forerunners of the view that a constitutionally protected zone of family privacy exists. 381 U.S. at 482.
83. *See* L. TRIBE, *supra* note 40, § 11-1, at 565.
84. Wisconsin v. Yoder, 406 U.S. 205, 231-33 (1972); Prince v. Massachusetts, 321 U.S. 158, 166 (1944).

been extended both to the relations between parents and their illegitimate children [85] and to members of a biologically connected extended family.[86] It is in the latter context that the Court, in a plurality opinion, most clearly set out its rationale for protecting familial relationships and its basis for determining the kinds of relationships likely to be included in the term "family" for privacy purposes.

In *Moore v. City of East Cleveland,*[87] the Supreme Court, finding that an extended family was within the zone of familial relations protected by the right of privacy, held that a local ordinance limiting occupancy of residential housing units to nuclear families violated the constitutional rights of an extended family residing in a unit covered by the ordinance involved. In reaching its decision, the Court focused on the family's "deeply rooted" place in the nation's history and tradition [88] and on the vital functions long performed by the family in American society—the passing on, from one generation to the next, of "our most cherished values," [89] and the provision, for family members, of "mutual sustenance" and a secure home life.[90] Since, in the Court's view, the extended family was similar in historical stature and functionally equivalent to the nuclear family, the Court refused to terminate the protection of family rights at the "arbitrary" boundary of the nuclear family.[91] Moreover, although not faced with the question, the Court indicated that it considered adoptive families as within the constitutionally protected zone, suggesting that for privacy purposes a "family" need not always be based on a biological relationship.[92]

B. *The Constitutional Protection of the Foster Family*

Although foster families are a relatively modern phenomenon, the long-term foster family relationship created by the malfunctioning of the foster care system can, as has been noted above, fulfill both the socializing and emotionally supportive roles performed by more traditional family structures. Where this is the case—that is, where foster parents have become the child's "psychological parents" and where the rights of the natural parents have been terminated—long-term foster families should be deemed "fam-

---

85. Stanley v. Illinois, 405 U.S. 645 (1972) (unmarried father). *See also* Levy v. Louisiana, 391 U.S. 68 (1968), where the Court struck down a Louisiana statute denying an illegitimate child the right to bring a wrongful death action for the death of his mother. The Court, in language evocative of current notions of psychological parenthood, declared that "[t]hese children, though illegitimate, were dependent on [their mother]; she cared for them and nurtured them; they were indeed hers in the biological and in the spiritual sense." *Id.* at 72.
86. Moore v. City of E. Cleveland, 431 U.S. 494 (1977).
87. *Id.*
88. *Id.* at 503 & n.12.
89. *Id.* at 504.
90. *Id.* at 505.
91. *Id.* at 502.
92. *See also* State v. Baker, 158 N.J. Super. 536, 386 A.2d 890 (App. Div. 1978), *aff'd,* 81 N.J. 99, 405 A.2d 368 (1979) (reaching a similar conclusion based on state constitutional law).

ilies" for substantive constitutional purposes. Under such circumstances, a foster child should be removed from a foster home only when removal from a natural home would be justified.

1. *The Long-Term Foster Family as the Historical and Functional Equivalent of the Traditional Family.* Foster families are not of the same historical stature as either biological or adoptive families; they are not relationships "deeply rooted" in our country's history and have not *traditionally* performed the socializing and emotionally supportive functions pointed to by the Court in *Moore.*[93] However, foster families are now frequently called on to perform such roles, and, as previously noted, a number of states have begun to recognize both the importance and the implications of the long-term relationships that result.[94] The statutory safeguards enacted in these states evidence a concern that such relationships—even though their existence testifies to the failure of the adoption system to solve the problems of parentless children—not be improperly disturbed once they have, in fact, arisen. Moreover, it is not only tradition but also "recognition of the basic values that underlie our society" that should define the "[a]ppropriate limits on substantive due process." [95] The decisive question, therefore, should be whether long-term foster families do effectively serve as the functional equivalent of traditional "deeply rooted" family relationships.[96]

The answer to this question is clear: long-term foster families not only may develop deep emotional attachments, but may also provide a foster child with the educational and supportive benefits considered central to the family relationship. In this regard, *Moore's* functional approach to the family relationship dovetails with Justice Brennan's suggestion in *OFFER* that long-term foster parents might "hold the same place in the emotional life of the foster child, and fulfill the same socializing functions, as a natural family."[97] Moreover, like many extended family arrangements of the kind found subject to protection in *Moore,* foster families tend to arise in times of adversity,[98]

---

93. *See* notes 87-92 and accompanying text *supra.*
94. *See* notes 25-32 and accompanying text *supra.*
95. Moore v. City of E. Cleveland, 431 U.S. 494, 503 (1977).
96. In this regard, see L. TRIBE, *supra* note 40, § 15-21, at 988 (arguing that constitutional law should "facilitat[e] the emergence of relationships that meet the human need for closeness, trust, and love in ways that may jar some conventional sensibilities but without which there can be no hope of solving the persistent problem of autonomy and community"). This thesis is more fully developed in Wilkinson & White, *Constitutional Protection for Personal Lifestyles,* 62 CORNELL L. REV. 563, 623-24 (1977), which the *Moore* Court cited with approval. 431 U.S. at 504 & n.13.
97. 431 U.S. at 844.
98. 431 U.S. at 505. The majority of foster children come from poor homes, and are surrendered by their parents because of some breakdown in the family structure. *See Foster Care, supra* note 1, at 607. One study of foster placement in New York lists the major reasons for voluntary foster placement: mental illness of the parent—22%; unwillingness or inability to continue or to assume care for the child—19%; child behavior—16%; neglect or abuse—14%; desertion or abandonment—8%; physical illness of the parent—11%; family dysfunction—9%. S. JENKINS & E. NORMAN, FILIAL DEPRIVATION AND FOSTER CARE 55 (1972).

when the breakdown of a nuclear family calls for assistance from a broader network of friends and relatives, or, failing such help, from the state.

2. *Defining the Substantive Rights of Long-Term Foster Families.* To be accorded a substantive constitutional right of familial privacy, a long-term foster family must at the outset satisfy the threshold requirements for recognition of procedural due process protection.[99] This will ordinarily entail a showing that the foster child was placed with the family as an infant, did not know his natural parents, and has remained with the foster family for a period in excess of a year.[100]

Beyond this threshold, the foster parents must be able to show that they have in fact become the child's psychological parents [101] and that the family group actually serves as the social and psychological equivalent of a natural family.[102] Such a showing rests upon an assessment of the child's present emotional needs and relationships rather than upon application of the more ambiguous "best interests of the child" standard with its essentially future orientation. A finding of psychological parenthood should obviate any need to undertake a "best interests" analysis in all but the most extraordinary circumstances.

A showing of psychological parenthood is thus necessary, but it is not sufficient by itself to establish a substantive right of privacy. The final consideration that must be taken into account is the status of the natural parents' rights with respect to the child. Where the natural parents are dead or unknown, or where their rights have been relinquished or legally terminated, the interests of the foster family may be deemed unchallenged and a right of privacy recognized. But where the natural parents have not given up or been deprived of their rights, the assertion of a substantive foster family right might be incompatible with the competing and also fundamental interests of the natural parents. Specifically, an irreconcilable conflict arises where

---

99. *See* notes 36-79 and accompanying text *supra.*

100. Statutory specification of a period of time as a minimum requirement may be a legitimate exercise of legislative classification, inoffensive to equal protection, provided it is reasonable. Such a classification would serve a valid state purpose in protecting foster care agencies from abuses by foster parents—who are not screened as carefully as adoptive parents, *see* note 15 and accompanying text *supra*—seeking to use foster care as a "short form" method of adoption.

It would, however, be difficult for a court to determine as a general proposition at precisely what point a foster placement turns into a protected long-term arrangement. In a given case, a court might look to the expectations of the natural parents at the time of the placement, to the age of the child, *see* J. GOLDSTEIN, A. FREUD & A. SOLNIT, *supra* note 14, at 40, or to statutes relating to procedural rights, *see, e.g.,* N.Y. SOC. SERV. LAW § 383(3) (McKinney 1976). *Cf.* Roe v. Wade, 410 U.S. 113 (1973) (judicially created standards for determining when fetus becomes viable).

101. *See* note 14 and accompanying text *supra.*

102. In *Smith v. Organization of Foster Families for Equality & Reform,* the Court avoided passing on the merits of the concept of psychological parenthood, finding that

> this case turns, not on the disputed validity of any particular psychological theory, but on the legal consequences of the undisputed fact that the emotional ties between foster parent and foster child are in many cases quite close, and undoubtedly in some as close as those existing in biological families.

431 U.S. at 844-45 n.52. The Court's approach in *OFFER,* does not, however, appear to differ in any significant respect from the psychological parenthood analysis.

the natural parents, while retaining their rights, have maintained contact with the child. Under these circumstances, it may be impossible to establish that the foster parents have become the child's exclusive psychological parents. In fact, under these conditions the concept of psychological parenthood provides little useful guidance.[103]

Admittedly, determining whether a natural parent/child relationship is sturdy enough to compete with the interests of the foster family requires a factual inquiry into an ill-defined area. Once this threshold determination is made, however, there will generally be no need for a full-scale evaluation of the child's "best interests." The presumption in such cases, as long as the natural parents have regained their capacity to care for the child, must be in favor of the child's return.[104] Acknowledging the superiority of the natural parents' interest reflects the most basic social values, and is in any event essential to the effective functioning of the foster care system. To disregard the natural parents' claim, or even to subject them to a burden of establishing that the child's best interest lies with them, would deter the voluntary removal of children from unhealthy family situations. Natural parents temporarily unable to care for their children would risk their permanent loss by agreeing to a foster placement that lasted a long time, regardless of their efforts to retain emotional ties with the child.

On the other hand, where the natural parents have made no effort to preserve a relationship with the child while in foster care, their subsequent assertion of a competing family interest is unlikely to have merit. The foster parents may well have become exclusive psychological parents, even if the natural parents' rights have not been terminated. In such a case, the foster family should be recognized as having a substantive right of privacy.

CONCLUSION

The failure of the foster care system to assure the timely permanent placement of foster children has led to the formation of long-term foster families that serve as the functional equivalent of natural families without commensurate constitutional protection. The fact that these families represent a failure of the system does not justify ignoring the legitimate personal and familial interests of foster parents and children who have established a long-term relationship, especially where the relationship has matured to the

---

103. *See Child Custody Adjudication, supra* note 17, at 280; Strauss & Strauss, Book Review, 74 COLUM. L. REV. 996, 1001-02, 1007-08 (1974).
104. This presumption is given statutory expression in New York in a provision asserting the legislative policy that
> it is generally desirable for the child to remain with or be returned to the natural parent because the child's need for a normal family life will usually best be met in the natural home and . . . parents are entitled to bring up their own children unless the best interests of the child would be thereby endangered.
N.Y. SOC. SERV. LAW § 384-b(1)(a)(ii) (McKinney Supp. 1978-1979). *See* Smith v. Organization of Foster Families for Equality & Reform, 431 U.S. 816, 823 (1977).

extent that the foster parents have become the foster child's psychological parents.

To assure a measure of protection to long-term foster parents, many states have enacted procedural statutes granting such parents the opportunity to be heard at a formal hearing before a foster child can be removed from their home. While these procedural innovations are welcome developments, they fall short of providing full protection to the interests involved. At least where the rights of the natural parents are not implicated, those long-term foster families that are the functional equivalent of the natural family should be accorded the same substantive protection constitutionally accorded the natural family. In such situations a foster child should be removed from his or her foster family only under conditions that would justify the removal of a child from his or her natural parents.

Mendel Shapiro

LEGAL ESSAY

DEMYSTIFYING LEGAL GUARDIANSHIP: AN UNEXPLORED OPTION FOR DEPENDENT CHILDREN

by Bogart R. Leashore*

I. INTRODUCTION

Over the last decade, considerable attention has been given to the perils and pitfalls of traditional foster family care for dependent children. Child welfare professionals increasingly advocate leaving children with their biological families, if feasible, and returning children to their families or pursuing adoption[1] if removal from the home was necessary. Nevertheless, too many children remain "adrift" in foster care. For example, recent national estimates of the number of children in foster care range from 243,000 to 502,000.[2] The percentage of foster care children who are minorities has ranged from 35% to 46% during the last few years, while 25% of the total number of children in foster care are reportedly handicapped.[3]

---

* B.A., 1968, Xavier University; M.S.W., 1970, Howard University; Ph.D., 1979, University of Michigan; Director, Urban Studies Program, Howard University.
[1] See generally, V. PIKE, S. DOWNS, A. EMLEN, G. DOWNS & D. CASE, PERMANENT PLANNING FOR CHILDREN IN FOSTER CARE: A HANDBOOK FOR SOCIAL WORKERS (1977); Stein & Gambrill, Facilitating Decision Making in Foster Care: The Alameda Project, 51 SOC. SERV. REV. 502 (1977); Jones, Stopping Foster Care Drift: A Review of Legislation and Special Programs, 57 CHILD WELFARE 571 (1978); Gill, The Foster Care Adoptive Family: Adoption for Children Not Legally Free, 54 CHILD WELFARE 712 (1975); Howe. The Ecological Approach to Permanency Planning: An Interactionist Perspective, 62 CHILD WELFARE 291 (1983); Miller, Fein, Bishop, Stillwell & Murray, Overcoming Barriers to Permanency Planning, 63 CHILD WELFARE 45 (1984).
[2] P. MAZA, ADMINISTRATION FOR CHILDREN, YOUTH & FAMILIES, U.S. DEPT. OF HEALTH & HUMAN SERV., No. 1 (Dec. 1983).
[3] Id.

95

A 1982 national survey found that only 21% of the total number of dependent children in substitute care were free for adoption;[4] 81% of the white children and 74% of the minority children were not free for adoption.[5] Similarly, among the handicapped children, 71% were not free for adoption.[6] Thus, while the national thrust for adoption may be increasing the number of children being adopted, it cannot be the plan of care for those children who are not legally free for adoption. They are likely to remain in foster care if they are not returned to their biological parents, but in some instances legal guardianship may be a more desirable option. Legal guardianship, however, has received little attention in the literature and is generally underutilized by the courts and child welfare practitioners. The purpose of this essay is to examine how legal guardianship might be transformed into a viable alternative to foster care and, perhaps, to adoption.

II.   What Is Legal Guardianship?

With regard to children, "guardianship" is generally defined in terms of a specific set of powers which are assigned by the court.[7] These powers over the child may include the authority to consent to marriage, to enlistment in the armed services, and to ordinary medical treatment. When the legal guardian is given custody of the child, the guardian may be granted other powers and duties by the court, including the right and duty to protect, train and discipline the child; the duty to provide food, clothing, shelter, education, and ordinary medical care; the right to determine where and with whom the child shall live; and the right, in an emergency, to authorize surgery or other extraordinary medical care.[8]

Under some guardianship arrangements, where the guardian has custody but parental rights have not been terminated, biological parents may retain the right to visit and consent to adoption, as well as the responsibility for support of the child.[9] This type of guardianship should be differentiated from the sort of guardianship contemplated when the

---

[4] P. Maza, Administration for Children, Youth & Families, U.S. Dept of Health & Human Serv., No. 2 (Dec. 1983).
[5] *Id.*
[6] *Id.*
[7] *See* Foster Children in the Courts 154-55 (M. Hardin ed. 1983).
[8] *Id.*
[9] *Id.* at 155.

court has determined that neglect or dependency exist.[10] In that case, guardianship may be awarded to an agency or individual if parental rights are terminated and adoption is anticipated. Under those circumstances, guardianship is not a permanent legal placement option, but instead a transitional status before adoption.

Other types of guardianship, with or without custody, are awarded by courts other than juvenile courts. For example, "probate guardianship" may be awarded by a court that has jurisdiction over estates and conservatorships. In probate guardianship, the guardian is awarded control over a child's estate, property, or person. Typically, probate guardianship over a child occurs if a child's parents die or become incapacitated and someone assumes legal control of the child. This type of guardianship is not limited to relatives.[11]

The situations and purposes for which guardianship may be imposed are numerous; however, in the context of child welfare and the care of dependent children, and for purposes of this essay, legal guardianship is court-assigned authority and responsibility for the child over a designated time period, imposed to provide for the child's physical, social, and emotional needs. Furthermore, the scope of this essay is limited to situations in which physical custody is awarded to the guardian, so that the guardian plays a role comparable to, but not identical to, foster or adoptive parents.

III. WHY LEGAL GUARDIANSHIP?

Legal guardianship for dependent children can be designed to benefit the child, the biological parents, and the guardian. Many of these benefits can best be understood in the context of the separation trauma, sense of loss, and subsequent identity conflicts which emerge when temporary or permanent placement becomes necessary.

The emotional bonds and attachments between children and their biological families are real, despite negative interactions such as child abuse or neglect, and these ties are not easily broken, nor should they be in many cases. Even when the parent is ambivalent toward or rejecting of the child, this may be the only relationship in which the child feels a sense of belonging and security. Despite efforts of child welfare

---

[10] *Id.*
[11] *Id.* at 155-57.

experts, in involuntary child placement, children regard the child placement agency and its personnel as responsible for depriving them of
their families.[12] Even in instances of voluntary placement, the child
may view the agency as the perpetrator of the separation.[13] Corres-
pondingly, the removal of a child from his home can have a devastating
impact on parents. For example, a study of the parents of children
in foster care found that these parents frequently experienced feelings
of sadness, worry, nervousness, emptiness, anger, bitterness,
thankfulness, relief, guilt, and shame.[14] These feelings were felt by both
mothers and fathers with no statistically significant differences between
parents, except that shame was experienced by more fathers than
mothers.[15] This impact might be lessened if parents understood that
their active and constructive involvement in the child placement process is not only desired, but necessary in most cases. Guardianship provides the opportunity for such involvement since parents could assist
and participate in the process of designating a legal guardian. A par-
ticipatory approach can do much to alleviate the parental fears, hostility,
helplessness, and sense of loss that often accompany separation.[16]

Though adoption has traditionally been used as a placement option for dependent children, and while it is generally viewed as ''in
the best interests of the child'' when successful adoptive placements
occur, research has shown that identity problems are not infrequent
in adopted persons.[17] This is reflected in the surge of adoptees who
search for their biological families. It may be preferable to place children
under a legal guardianship with relatives or significant others rather
than placing them for adoption with strangers. This approach would
avoid some of the identity loss that seems to accompany placing children
with unrelated foster or adoptive parents. Those who oppose or are
indifferent toward the increased use of legal guardianship for dependent children might argue that the state is already the guardian and

---

[12] *See* Pollock, *The Meaning of Parents to the Placed Child*, 36 CHILD WELFARE 8, 8-9 (Apr. 1957).
[13] *Id.* at 9.
[14] *See* Jenkins, *Separation Experiences of Parents Whose Children are in Foster Care*, 48 CHILD WELFARE 334-40 (1969).
[15] *Id.* at 335-36.
[16] Pollock, *supra* note 12, at 10-11.
[17] For an excellent and comprehensive review of the professional literature in this area, see Sorosky, Baran & Pannor, *Identity Conflicts in Adoptees*, 45 A. J. ORTHOPSYCHIATRY 18 (1975).

that therefore there is no need for a legally appointed guardian. However, in reality, while the state is often given custody of dependent children, others must provide for the child's day-to-day needs. Under present policies and practices, foster parents fill that need, but are not authorized to do much else in terms of specific powers. Furthermore, it is often unclear whether state agencies have authority to delegate these day-to-day decisions to foster parents.[18] Until recently, foster parents have been legally little more than "a hired hand of the child welfare agency which placed the child."[19] This absence of clear-cut authority in foster parents creates potential for uncertainty. As their powers are difficult to define, so are their rights, as the following discussion indicates.

The case of *Smith v. Organization of Foster Families*[20] illustrates some of the complex issues related to foster family care. Specifically, the Organization of Foster Families for Equality and Reform (OFFER) and several families filed a class action attacking New York statutes which allowed the state to remove children from foster homes without a preremoval hearing. Although the district court ruled that the New York statutes infringed on the constitutional rights of foster children,[21] the United States Supreme Court later reversed the decision.[22] Two major conclusions result from this case:

> (1) a preremoval conference with the agency empowered to remove the foster child will satisfy due process requirements even if such a conference is available only on the request of the foster parents and (2) if the foster family has a liberty interest within the scope of the fourteenth amendment, a system of periodic review which becomes effective only after eighteen months of foster care is constitutionally adequate to protect that interest.[23]

The *Smith* decision leaves open the potential for disruptive changes in the foster care relationship without input of all interested parties.

---

[18] *See generally* D. DODSON, THE LEGAL FRAMEWORK FOR ENDING FOSTER CARE DRIFT: A GUIDE TO EVALUATING AND IMPROVING STATE LAWS, REGULATIONS AND COURT RULES (1983).
[19] Katz, *The Changing Legal Status of Foster Parents*, 5 CHILDREN TODAY No. 6, p. 11 (1976).
[20] 431 U.S. 816 (1977).
[21] *Id.* at 822.
[22] *Id.* at 856.
[23] George, *The Power of Foster Parents to Prevent the Removal of Their Foster Children*, 21 J. FAM. L. 115, 124-25 (1982).

Furthermore, it creates uncertainty in a relationship that requires stability.

Another factor in favor of legal guardianship for dependent children is the recent attention given to civil liability for inadequate foster care. For example, some children have been abused or neglected by their foster parents, while other children have been placed in foster homes that cannot meet their needs.[24] Generally, child welfare agencies and workers are held liable when the state has custody of the child and negligence occurs in the selection of foster parents and/or supervision of the placement.[25] The appointment of legal guardians satisfactory to the parents, the courts, state agencies, and the child might ameliorate the risk that the state would incur liability for inadequate care.

Finally, legal guardianship may be a useful alternative to meet the special needs of minorities. Racial matching and interracial adoption continue to be important issues in child placement. With the decline in the number of white children available for adoption, there has been an increased interest in interracial adoption. This has led to considerable controversy.[26] Some black social workers have expressed opposition to placing black children in white homes because they feel that children so placed will have problems with identification and developing coping skills needed to combat racism.[27] It should be noted that laws which prohibited interracial adoption have been eliminated, although race remains a relevant factor in some jurisdictions.[28] Legal guardianship offers an option that will allow opponents and supporters of interracial adoption an opportunity to redirect their energies toward "the best interests of the child." Legal guardianship need not have the finality of adoption nor does it require severance of biological family ties. Furthermore, it "leaves the door open" for biological family members to resume the care of dependent children later.

As a second consideration, informal adoption or "absorption" of children by grandparents, aunts, uncles, and others is a significant

---

[24] Besharov, *Malpractice in Child Placement: Civil Liability for Inadequate Foster Care Services*, 63 CHILD WELFARE 195 (1984).

[25] For an example, see Vonner v. State, 273 So. 2d 252 (La. 1973).

[26] *See* Ballard, *Racial Matching and the Adoption Dilemma: Alternatives for the Hard to Place*, 17 J. FAM. L. 333 (1979).

[27] *Id*. at 338.

[28] *Id*. at 340-52.

and important pattern in many black families.[29] Informal adoption has been defined as the process by which dependent children are informally reared by adults who are not their natural or formal adoptive parents. The parent surrogates may or may not be related to the children.[30]

Research on black families and informal adoption has shown that children are most likely to be informally adopted at very early ages; two out of three black families with only informally adopted children have provided homes for at least two children; a majority of informally adopted children were born in-wedlock; only approximately twelve percent of informally adopted black children are related to the head of the household; and factors which account for informal adoption include separation and divorce of parents, parental death or illness, and economic hardship.[31] While many of these informal adoptions can be transformed into formal adoptions,[32] others could also be transformed into legal guardianship arrangements. Thus, the legal status of the parties could be made more certain without the absolute finality of adoption. Legal guardianship provides flexibility unavailable when adoption is the placement choice, but helps maintain stability frequently missing in foster care placement.

IV. Rights and Responsibilities of the Parties

Child development experts, social workers, and others generally agree that children need to establish and maintain relationships with psychological or biological parents in a stable and nurturing environment.[33] Nevertheless, legal rights for children when their biological parents cannot or will not provide needed care must also be firmly established. Several legal areas need attention, including the legal right, if any, that attaches the child to the biological parent(s), the liberty right of the child not to be moved from one placement to another without a prior hearing, the right to be placed in the least restrictive setting, and the right to a guardian-ad-litem or legal advocate.[34] Whether or not these are constitutionally protected rights, guidelines to delineate

[29] *See* R. Hill, Informal Adoption Among Black Families 1-3 (1977).
[30] *Id.* at 9.
[31] *Id.* at 41-50
[32] *Id.* at 86.
[33] *See generally* Children's Defense Fund, Children Without Homes (1978); J. Goldstein, A. Freud, & A. Solnit, Beyond the Best Interests of the Child (1973); Pollock, *supra* note 12; Rest & Watson, *Growing Up in Foster Care*, 63 Child Welfare 291 (1984).
[34] *See* R. Gottesman, The Child and the Law (1981).

the rights of children when the court appoints a legal guardian are mandated for the protection of all parties involved.

Although guardianship should clearly state the rights and responsibilities of the guardian, the extent of these rights and responsibilities may be unclear. While it is generally expected that the guardian will provide for the child's physical, social, and emotional needs, specific authority to consent to medical care, to participate in educational planning, to consent for a driver's license, and to make other important decisions should also be assigned by the court. Moreover, the guardian, like the child, should be protected against arbitrary removal of the child from placement. However, legal preference for returning the child to the biological parent, if and when they become able to resume care, requires that their rights be considered at every stage in the process of naming a guardian.

Legal guardianship does not terminate the relationship between the children and their blood relatives. Indeed, "the child does not lose one family when he gains legal recognition of another."[35] For example, in the case of *In re Guardianship of Marino*,[36] a mother died shortly after the birth of a child who was subsequently raised by the mother's sister. Six years later, the father of the child expressed an interest in and sought custody of the child. The father had very little contact with the child prior to seeking custody although seven other children were in his care. The court ruled that the child should remain in the sister's home in order to avoid harm to his emotional development. A guardianship petition was granted to the aunt and the father was allowed regular visitation.[37]

One observer notes that, except in cases of termination of parental rights, biological parents of dependent children may retain the right to visit, the obligation to support the child, and the right to initiate court proceedings regarding the child. Like their children, biological parents should also have the right to legal counsel.[38] Similar rights could be afforded parents whose children are wards of legal guardians.

Besides protecting the rights of the children, the guardians, and the parents, the legal guardianship process should include procedural

---

[35] *See* Bodenheimer, *New Trends and Requirements in Adoption Law and Proposals For Legislative Change*, 49 S. CAL. L. REV. 10, 42 (1975).
[36] 30 Cal. App. 3d 952, 106 Cal. Rptr. 655 (1973).
[37] *Id.* at 957, 106 Cal. Rptr. at 658.
[38] *See generally* DODSON, *supra* note 19.

safeguards to assure that state agencies supervise and review the status of the child and his family, and obtain or regain custody of the child if necessary. Similarly, procedural guidelines ought to limit or delineate the agency's ability to remove a child without a prior court order.[39]

For those who need and desire financial assistance to provide care for the child, guardianship subsidies, comparable to adoption subsidies, should be made available. In addition, when needed, medical care should be made available, especially if the child has a handicapping condition or other health-related problems.[40] Maintenance subsidies to help meet ordinary day-to-day expenses, and special service subsidies for such items as medical and psychological services are sometimes available to aid adoptive parents.[41] As in the case of adoption, guardianship subsidies should be considered for hard-to-place children. It seems likely that relatives or others might have an interest in and a capacity for providing needed care as custodial guardians but lack adequate financial resources. A subsidized guardianship program would enable those most interested to fill the gap in the child's family structure. For those who argue that subsidized guardianship is costly, it must be noted that it is also costly to maintain children in foster care. In any case, the value of a stable and loving family for children cannot be measured in dollars and cents.

Agency responsibilities in legal guardianship arrangements can also include periodic contact with the guardian and the child to ascertain the child's well-being, and periodic reports to the court about the child's development. Agencies could also be given responsibility for arranging and monitoring visitation between biological parents and the child, for providing ongoing services directed toward returning the child to the biological parent(s), and resolving issues related to the child, the family, or the guardian.

V.   Conclusions

To date, legal guardianship as a plan of care for dependent children has been greatly underutilized. If legislatures and agencies took action to clearly define specific rights and responsibilities of dependent children, their legal guardians, and biological parents, then legal guardianship

---

[39] *Id.*

[40] *Id.*

[41] *See* Byrne & Bellucci, *Subsidized Adoption: One County's Program*, 61 Child Welfare 173 (1982).

could provide a useful alternative in dependent child placement. Subsidies could facilitate the placement of children with appropriate guardians.

The significance of guardianship for dependent children was highlighted over a decade ago.[42] Though agencies are said to act in loco parentis, they do not and cannot provide the actual day-to-day care for the child. Furthermore, child care workers and others often view biological parents in negative terms, and may have little regard for the parent-child ties.[43] In spite of the conscious or subconscious association made between guardianship and death,[44] dependent children should be in the care of individuals, preferably relatives or adults known to the child, who do not deny the existence of biological parents nor the ties that children may have with them. Legal guardians may be well-suited to that role. The misapprehension that guardianship is associated with death should make way for recognition that all children need protection, care, guidance, and love, regardless of whether the biological parents are alive or dead.

Although legal guardianship cannot be the panacea for resolving all of the issues related to placing dependent children, it can serve to abate some of the problems associated with foster care and adoption. Ties with biological families can be sustained and even strengthened if the parents participate in the selection of the guardian. Many of the problems facing adopted persons who know little about their birth families can be avoided with legal guardianship. Problems associated with parental visitation can be eliminated under legal guardianship. Civil liability for inadequate foster care may also be diminished. Additionally, it may be easier for agencies to appoint legal guardians who are the same race as the child, thus avoiding problems that may arise in interracial adoption and foster care. Far too much time, energy, and resources have been devoted to foster care and adoption, neither of which are satisfactory remedies for all dependent children. Legal guardianship provides another option—an option that should be thoroughly investigated by members of the legal and social work professions. Interested parties should collaborate to develop effective and efficient use of legal guardianship as another means for providing the care and love all dependent children deserve.

[42] *See* Appelberg, *The Significance of Personal Guardianship For Children in Casework*, 49 CHILD WELFARE 6 (1970).
[43] *Id.*
[44] *Id.*

Reasonable Efforts to Prevent Placement and Preserve Families

Defining Active and Reasonable Efforts To Preserve Families

by Robert J. Hunner

Combined with other significant changes, two federal laws—the active efforts provisions of the Indian Child Welfare Act of 1978 (P.L. 95-608) and the reasonable efforts provisions of the Adoption Assistance and Child Welfare Act of 1980 (P.L. 96-272)—are changing the face of foster care and child welfare services in the United States. In order to expand understanding of these "efforts" provisions, Northwest Resource Associates in Seattle, Washington, was awarded a grant from the Children's Bureau and the Administration for Native Americans, OHDS, to develop a guide that would describe delivery of services related to these emerging elements of child welfare services.

The Indian Child Welfare Act of 1978 was designed "to protect the best interests of Indian children and to promote the stability and security of Indian Tribes and families." Child welfare workers are required to make active efforts to provide remedial services and rehabilitative programs designed to prevent the breakup of Indian families. The

Adoption Assistance and Child Welfare Act of 1980 requires that reasonable efforts be made to prevent or eliminate the need for placement.

Some distinctions between the two acts should be pointed out.

Under the provisions of the Indian Child Welfare Act, the court must be satisfied that active efforts have been made to provide remedial services and rehabilitative programs and that these efforts have proven unsuccessful. Without the finding of active efforts, a child may not be removed. Under P.L. 96-272, the court must be satisfied that reasonable efforts were made to prevent removal of a child or to reunify children already separated from their families. Unless the court has determined that these reasonable efforts were made, states and Indian tribes may not claim federal funding for the placement of those children who are otherwise eligible for federal financial participation. Compliance with this provision is monitored by federal auditing and a program review process.

This is not the case with the Indian Child Welfare Act. There is no federal auditing or program review to ensure that the active efforts provisions are being appropriately implemented, and there are no financial considerations that apply to compliance.

These "efforts" provisions—while instituted in the laws of many states and included in established policies and procedures under which child welfare workers operate—have been applied differently in different jurisdictions. Undoubtedly, this reflects the need to distinguish between the words "active" and "reasonable": That is, given that the different words were used, it would seem that different levels, kinds or intensities of effort were expected.

As Northwest Resource Associates grappled with these distinctions in developing the guide, we eventually agreed that for implementation purposes, in order for an effort to be a reasonable one, it must be active. It is possible that an effort could be active without being reasonable, such as in a situation of inappropriate or ineffective case planning and referrals. Active efforts, therefore, must also be reasonable.

While the two concepts may seem simple and direct, they involve complex combinations of investigative and assessment skills, professional judgment, effective case planning, the availability of appropriate service resources and sensitivity to the ethnic and cultural background of the child and family.

One way to understand the efforts concepts is to examine their intents: to protect children from abuse and neglect; to promote the provision of services that support families; to preserve families; and to reinforce cultural identities. Both Acts imply that foster care should be reserved for those children for whom no other alternative will provide the necessary protection. Thus, the efforts provisions obligate those who intervene in families to do so only when necessary; to reach their decisions about families and risks to children only after careful assessment and evaluation; to use the least intrusive, family-strengthening and supportive services that will reduce or eliminate risks to children; and, whenever possible, to provide this support and these services at the appropriate point in time and with the intensity necessary to eliminate the need for out-of-home placements of children.

Assessment and evaluation of the family situation is essential to satisfy the reasonable and active efforts requirements. Unless the family assessment has been thorough and accurate, no subsequent efforts can be considered either active or reasonable.

The development of a case plan, preferably done jointly by the child welfare worker and the parent(s), is also an important element in the efforts requirements. The case plan must be related to the risks to the child. After a family has been identified as needing protective services, there is sometimes a tendency in child welfare to begin to address all of the family's problems rather than those that are placing the child at risk of abuse or neglect.

Active and/or reasonable efforts go beyond simply offering services to a family. The obligation of the child welfare worker is that she or he encourage and assist the parents in using a service. This involves making the service accessible by providing a convenient location, a desirable time, and transportation and child care, if necessary. The intensity of the effort and the diligence of the child welfare worker must be appropriate to the needs of the parents as they relate to the risks to the child.

These efforts must also be appropriate to the family's ethnic, racial or cultural background and delivered in a context that is comfortable and sensitive to the family. Experience in child welfare services indicates that successful assistance to families stems from, and is affected by, the extent to which the worker is able to identify cultural strengths upon which to build an appropriate case plan. Respect for cultural and ethnic differences and recognition of the potential of this diversity to enhance the worker-client relationship are vital aspects of reasonable and active efforts.

The timing of the various elements of the effort must also be considered. Because a large proportion of child abuse and neglect cases involves alcohol or drug abuse by

the child's caretaker, it is usually ineffective to provide services until drug or alcohol dependency or addiction are successfully addressed first. In these cases, then, providing the necessary treatment before other interventions becomes part of the reasonable or active effort.

Another set of variables complicates the efforts discussion. Since each child welfare case is unique, efforts will, necessarily, vary depending on the specifics of the case. Different efforts would be considered active or reasonable depending on such factors as the child's age, the cultural background of the family, the capacities of the parents, the kind(s) of abuse or neglect, the strength of the extended family and the availability of other significant supporting individuals. For example, the efforts required to assist a family with a disabled or handicapped child would probably differ from those needed by a family where the child is developing normally.

Sometimes, too, efforts must be directed toward the child as well as the parent. Children who are at risk of out-of-home placement as a result of their behavior—such as violence toward themselves or others, or drug or substance dependency or addiction—should be the direct recipients of active or reasonable efforts, along with their parents.

Resource availability is also an issue. A child welfare worker may determine that a specific service option, such as a Homebuilders type of intensive in-home services, is indicated for a family to avoid an out-of-home placement. If this resource is not available in the community and its absence places the child at continued risk, the caseworker must decide whether or not to petition the court to place the child in foster care with the justification that active or reasonable efforts have been made.

It is our opinion that this action should be taken only when all other options have been exhausted. For

example, intensive in-home services may be indicated as necessary. But if this resource does not exist in the community, or if there is a long waiting list, it would be both active and reasonable to secure an approximation of this service, such as crisis intervention combined with a parent aide and a homemaker. In the absence of a parent aide or homemaker, a short-term alternative might be found by drawing on a member of the parent's extended family or church. Another option would be for the caseworker to recruit volunteers to provide this kind of service. While exploring these alternatives places an additional demand on the worker's time and resources, such efforts to avoid a placement are reasonable, and certainly active.

What is enough? What is reasonable? The questions will continue to arise and are among the issues addressed in the recently published guide, *Active and Reasonable Efforts to Preserve Families: A Guide for Delivering Services in Compliance with the Indian Child Welfare Act of 1978 (P.L. 95-608) and the Adoption Assistance and Child Welfare Act of 1980 (P.L. 96-272)* (see accompanying box). Based on an extensive review of the literature on effective interventions, it contains detailed descriptions of service options that have been shown to reduce risks to children and prevent out-of-home placements.

The guide is designed to be used by a variety of professionals and volunteers concerned with the reasonable and active efforts requirements. For example, it can serve as a case planning and management tool for child welfare workers, assisting them in documenting reasonable and active efforts that they have undertaken with a family as well as providing suggestions for alternate interventions. Juvenile and tribal court judges can document efforts made to prevent placements and determine the extent to which these efforts were reasonable and active.

We expect that administrators will find the guide helpful in defining policies and procedures related to implementing the efforts provisions, as well as in evaluating programs, allocating resources and promoting the enhanced availability of intensive in-home services. The guide can also serve as a planning document to identify innovative methods of providing services to families in communities that lack resources. Finally, we expect the guide to assist foster care case reviewers in monitoring reasonable and active reunification efforts. ■

Robert J. Hunner is Executive Director, Northwest Resource Associates, Seattle, Washington.

Reasonable Efforts to Prevent Placement and Preserve Families

Editor's note: In 1985, the Children's Bureau funded four projects to provide resources and technical assistance to judges and the courts around the determination that "reasonable efforts" have or have not been made to prevent the need for placement. Results of two of the projects are described in the following articles. The two other projects are being conducted by the University of Tennessee ("Defining Reasonable Efforts: A Project to Unify Judicial and Agency Approaches") and the National Council of Juvenile and Family Court Judges ("Placement Prevention Training").

Judicial Determination of Reasonable Efforts

by Debra Ratterman

Among the most important trends in current child welfare practice is the emphasis on improving services to enable children to remain in their own homes rather than being placed in foster care. This emphasis is reinforced by the "reasonable efforts" requirements of the federal Adoption Assistance and Child Welfare Act of 1980 (P.L. 96-272). The Act requires that child welfare agencies provide services to prevent unnecessary placement and that, in each case, a court must determine that the state agency has made reasonable efforts to prevent or eliminate the need for placement.

The Foster Care Project, a part of the American Bar Association's National Legal Resource Center for Child Advocacy and Protection, began a special study on state implementation of "reasonable efforts" one year ago under a grant from the Children's Bureau. The purpose of the project is to develop guidelines to help child welfare agencies and courts understand reasonable efforts requirements and to prevent the unnecessary placement of children.

The study was completed in July, and we are just beginning to analyze the information collected. This article will review some of the preliminary findings and recommendations for agencies and courts.

A Study of "Best Practices"

The study was conducted by an attorney/social worker team consisting of Project Director Mark Hardin and myself—an attorney—of the Foster Care Project, Professor Theodore J. Stein of the

(Continued on page 30)

26

Judicial Determination *(Continued from page 26)*

State University of New York—Albany and Research Assistant Gary Comstock. The team studied both courts and agencies, visiting sites identified as having effective approaches in implementing reasonable efforts. The "best practices" of these agencies will be used in developing manuals for agencies and courts.

Prior to these site visits, the Foster Care Project conducted a review of state laws and agency policies on preventive services and efforts to avoid unnecessary placement. Pilot studies were also conducted in Richmond, Virginia, and Wilmington and Dover, Delaware. The programs and courts chosen for the study were Santa Cruz, California; Jacksonville, Florida; Rochester, New York; Davenport and Tipton, Iowa; Portland, Oregon; and Cloquet and St. Cloud, Minnesota.

The study utilized five methods of obtaining data: compiling state and local policy, interviewing, reviewing casefiles, viewing hearings, and conducting a time study. The teams spent a week in most states, interviewing judges, agency or county attorneys, caseworkers, agency supervisors, parents' and children's attorneys, guardians ad litem, court-appointed special advocates and service providers about their experiences with reasonable efforts and the court process. In the case

reviews, we looked for good documentation of efforts to provide preventive services by the caseworker and of the judge's findings. The time study measured the time spent by caseworkers at various tasks related to reasonable efforts in order to determine the amount of time that could reasonably be spent in preventing placement.

Practical Approaches to Implementing Reasonable Efforts

The agencies and courts that we studied provided some unique examples of methods to best implement the reasonable efforts requirement. Each program had special strengths, and each participant in the process—judges, administrators, supervisors, caseworkers and attorneys—could play a critical role in preventing unnecessary placement.

We found that judges who were knowledgeable concerning preventive and reunification services were better able to evaluate agency efforts. Background in child welfare—as a juvenile probation officer, for example—is extremely helpful to a judge in formulating intelligent questions, determining whether the agency had made reasonable efforts and ordering alternative service programs. Judges can also urge the agency to initiate new

service programs for special groups. In Florida, the agency began a special program for adolescents in response to a judge's concern over the lack of alternatives for adolescent status offenders who have been abused.

Judicial oversight of reasonable efforts has had the strongest impact on agency practice where judges review agency efforts thoroughly and critically, not hesitating to make negative determinations of reasonable efforts in extreme cases. One judge found that making an occasional negative determination had a great impact on casework and services to keep families together, but had little impact on agency funding. The financial impact was slight because the judge made negative determinations in a very small proportion of cases and the agency was nearly always able to correct the problem and get a positive determination in a relatively short time, thus allowing the federal matching funds to resume. Interestingly, there was not a single site in our study where judges found a lack of reasonable efforts in a substantial proportion of cases. Where negative determinations were made, they were limited to situations that were viewed by judges as extreme lapses in casework and services.

In some states, judges play an

important role in the passage of state statutes mandating a judicial determination of reasonable efforts. In New York, a special amendment going beyond the federal requirement, requiring such a determination in voluntary placement cases, was prompted by judges who felt this type of judicial oversight was necessary to assure service delivery to these families. In addition, the state Permanency Planning Task Forces sponsored by the National Council of Juvenile and Family Court Judges have been instrumental in educating judges on legal issues related to reasonable efforts.

Concerted agency efforts to communicate with the juvenile court seem to be necessary in order to consistently meet the new reasonable efforts requirement. Joint meetings with agency officials and judges are helpful in establishing new procedures and guidelines for documenting efforts. Some agencies use their "court liaisons" or "court workers," who are knowledgeable about court procedure and who compile information on specific cases for court hearings, to aid in implementing the judicial determination. The court workers are charged with assuring that the judge is receiving enough information to make the determination intelligently and that the determination is actually made in every case. If these workers uncover noncompliance or systematic problems, this information is passed on to supervisors or administrators who may take it up with the court.

Many of the agencies recognize the importance of documenting preventive services in obtaining a favorable judicial determination. Some systematically include this information in the petition or court report. An extensive set of forms including information on reasonable efforts has been an integral part of the New York agency's success in implementing the requirement.

Judges who were knowledgeable concerning preventive and reunification services were better able to evaluate agency efforts.

Another fundamental element of reasonable efforts is the availability of a comprehensive array of service alternatives for families. Although this depends largely on state law and financial support, one agency was able to expand and improve services by organizing the community, bringing together public and private agencies, churches and community groups in preventing and treating child abuse. Another program was also able to provide a broad range of services by carefully defining its service needs, encouraging the creation of private service providers in the community and carefully targeting its available funds on service gaps. Relationships with outside service providers are geared to the goals of reasonable efforts, and these collaterals are expected to provide documentation of their efforts to the agency and the court.

We found that in many cases the availability of certain specialized services, such as treatment for addicted babies, is increasingly important to making reasonable efforts. Since adolescents often require a different approach than young children, some agencies have initiated special programs for this group. Many communities need service

providers that focus on black and other minority families.

Agencies view homemaker services as most important and useful in many types of cases. Homemakers are used by many of the programs we studied to provide hands-on training to parents and also to evaluate the situation in the home.

Programs in smaller population areas have special problems related to the stigma that clients feel when accepting services from public agencies. When one rural program found that the state cars that workers used for home visits were observed by neighbors and therefore created embarrassment and resentment on the part of many clients, the agency shifted to unmarked cars in an effort to maintain the families' confidentiality.

We observed a number of interesting examples of flexibility in dealing with different family situations to avoid unnecessary separations of children and parents. In one case, an agency placed a child and her young adult mother with a foster family in order to provide supervision and role modeling without separating parent and child.

Agency attorneys also have an important role in implementing reasonable efforts. They can provide a necessary link between the agency and the court, informing the court of the agency's resources and constraints and informing the agency of the court's expectations. At one site, the county attorney, a former social worker, uses her expertise to prepare cases showing reasonable efforts. She also uses the reasonable efforts determination to document the agency's provision of services at later hearings. When seeking to terminate parental rights, factual findings that recount services provided and parental failure to respond prior to removal provide important evidence that agency efforts were adequate. This kind of documentation is much more effective and easy to present when

112

Many of the agencies recognize the importance of documenting preventive services in obtaining a favorable judicial determination.

placed in the court record.

At some sites, parents' and children's attorneys attempt to use the reasonable efforts determination to help their clients get necessary services. By being prepared to urge the judge to make a negative determination, they can sometimes convince the agency to leave the family intact and provide additional services to their clients. Legal aid programs that represent parents are also able to assure that state legislation on reasonable efforts is being applied and initiate lawsuits to enforce it. Guardians ad litem and court-appointed special advocates are also important in filling in advocacy "gaps" in some of the programs we visited. They were able to argue for additional services, and their recommendations had more influence with the judges.

Preliminary Conclusions

From the information gathered from the study, we are beginning to articulate guidelines for the judicial determination of reasonable efforts. Even though situations that require intervention and service alternatives vary on a case-by-case basis, there are some general principles that should guide judges and caseworkers.

Review of preplacement services by courts is very new and has a long way to go. More progress has been made in the review of reunification services, since many judges have already been fulfilling this role in termination of parental rights cases and thus can extend their expertise to foster care review. However, extension of these skills to preventive services is more of an innovation, and there is a need for

further training of judges on the judicial determination of reasonable efforts to prevent placement. Courts which already devote a substantial amount of time and attention to child welfare cases are most able and willing to implement reasonable efforts in a meaningful way.

The judicial determination of reasonable efforts is still a relatively new area for agencies. We found that most of the agencies that had progressed the farthest in implementing the federal requirements had early policies related to the prevention of unnecessary foster care. These agencies have changed worker attitudes so that foster care is considered a last resort, and they had long recognized the need to expand service options for abused children and their families to avoid unnecessary separation of families.

Agencies appear to respect courts that closely scrutinize their efforts to avoid placement, where the judge is viewed as competent, realistic and not hostile. Agencies generally consider it a burden to be thoroughly reviewed by the judge on reasonable efforts, but where this review is done thoroughly and competently, it seems to reinforce the morale and competency of caseworkers. Accountability is a necessary element of professionalism. Skilled workers will feel vindicated by positive determinations and gain from judicial input about service expectations.

Documentation of efforts both within the agency and for the courts is also critical for successful implementation of reasonable efforts. Although uniform documentation of the reasonable efforts determination is necessary for full compliance, the use of "boilerplate" provisions in court orders raises the

issue of whether the spirit of the law is being met.

The enlistment of agency counsel in pursuing the objectives of reasonable efforts is an important but underutilized aspect of implementation. Agencies should call upon their attorneys to educate judges and advocate in court on the necessity of the reasonable efforts judicial determination. Advocates for parents and children and guardians ad litem should also address these issues to increase clients' access to services.

The reasonable efforts requirement is a significant reform in the effort to shorten the length of time children spend in foster care. Preventive services need to be encouraged, because treating a family while the child is in the home is generally more effective than working with parents while the child is in placement. Earlier and more frequent court oversight of agency services leads to quicker resolution of the family's problems, or clarifies earlier the intractability of these problems. More documentation of services to the family at earlier stages of the legal proceedings will aid in another aspect of permanency planning: the termination of parental rights when problems cannot be resolved. Because of the important benefits to children in crisis, the implementation of reasonable efforts determinations needs to be a strong priority of both agencies and courts. ■

Debra Ratterman is Assistant Staff Director of the American Bar Association Foster Care Project, Washington, D.C. The contents of this article should not be construed as official policy of the American Bar Association.

32

113

UNSAFE HAVENS: THE CASE FOR CONSTITUTIONAL PROTECTION OF FOSTER CHILDREN FROM ABUSE AND NEGLECT

*Michael B. Mushlin**

Introduction

In a midwestern community not long ago, a one-year-old girl who required constant medical attention for epileptic seizures was sent by a state child welfare department to a foster home known by the state to be inadequate.[1] In fact, the caseworker assigned by the state to supervise the home had recommended that the department not use this "marginal" setting except on a temporary, short-term basis. Children sent to this home in the past had been "ill clothed" and had not received attention for medical problems. The warning was ignored. When the child's caseworker reported that the foster parents were not bringing the child to her scheduled medical appointments, again the child welfare department did not respond. Finally, after two and one-half years and pressure from the child's physician, the child was removed from the foster home. By this time, the child, now three and one-half, had not received treatment for her epilepsy and was also experiencing other medical problems.[2] Even after an official finding of abuse by the state was registered against the home for its failure to care for this child, the state

---

* Professor of Law, Pace University. B.A. 1966, Vanderbilt University; J.D. 1970, Northwestern University.

I am grateful for the thoughtful editorial assistance and encouragement of Professor Donald L. Doernberg. I am also grateful for the assistance of Professors Norman B. Lichtenstein, M. Stuart Madden, David Rudenstine, Barbara Salken and Merril Sobie. I also wish to express my appreciation for the research assistance of Susan DeGeorge, Talay Hafiz, Shelley Halber and Laura Hurwitz. Finally, I am thankful for the support and encouragement of my wife, Thea Stone.

[1] G.L. v. Zumwalt, 564 F. Supp. 1030 (W.D. Mo. 1983) (cited in D. Caplovitz & L. Genevie, Foster Children in Jackson County, Missouri: A Statistical Analysis of Files Maintained by The Division of Family Services 86–87, case 5.2 (July 21, 1982) (unpublished report)).

[2] The child was experiencing constant diarrhea and had not been toilet trained. In addition, she was so emotionally deprived that, although she was three and one-half, she had not been taught how to kiss. *Id.* at 87.

continued to use the foster home without interruption as a place-ment for abused and neglected children.

In the same state, another foster child was assaulted while in foster care. The state knew of the attack, but did nothing. Within four months, the child was sexually abused by the foster father in the same home.[3] In a third foster home, a four-year-old girl was whipped by her foster mother and made to stand with her hands extended over her head for thirty minutes. The child was being punished for being dirty. Although the case-worker determined that the child had been beaten, and reported this to her superiors, no action was taken and the child was returned to the home.[4]

In another part of the country, a troubled young boy who wet his bed was placed in a foster home. The foster mother, frustrated at her inability to control his behavior, sought help from the state's child welfare agency. Her pleas were ignored. The situation deteriorated until one night the foster mother forced the child to "drink his urine."[5]

None of these cases received public attention, nor were any of them the subject of reported court decisions or large damage awards. Each, however, is an example of the stark reality of life in foster homes[6] for too many of the nation's half-million[7]

---

[3] *Id.* at 87, case 5.3.

[4] *Id.* at 89, case 5.6.

[5] Gil, *Institutional Abuse of Children in Out-of-Home Care*, 3 Child and Youth Services 7, 10 (1981).

[6] Foster family care is distinguished from institutional care and adoption in that "the foster family care is designed to be temporary and to offer the child care in a family setting." A. Kadushin, Child Welfare Services 425 (1967). In this Article, the term "foster care" is used to refer to foster family care arrangements.

Once it is determined that a child can no longer remain in her original home, state law usually places the child in the custody of the state or local department of child welfare. R. Horowitz & H. Davidson, Legal Rights of Children 358 (1984). The child welfare agency normally selects and licenses adults to serve as foster parents. *Id.* at 361–65. The foster family then often enters into a contractual arrangement with the agency that requires the foster parents to care for the child under the direction and supervision of the agency. *Id.* A typical foster family is a middle-aged, working or lower-middle class family that owns its own home and has agreed to undertake the responsibility of foster care parenting out of either a need for extra cash or an altruistic desire to help needy children. Mnookin, *Foster Care—In Whose Best Interest?*, 43 Harv Educ. Rev. 599, 610 (1973) [hereinafter Mnookin, *In Whose Best Interest?*]; A. Gruber Children in Foster Care: Destitute Neglected . . . Betrayed 151–74 (1978); T. Festinger, No One Ever Asked Us . . . A Postscript to Foster Care 270–71 (1983).

[7] For the years 1977 to 1983, estimates have varied from 273,913 to 502,000. T Tatara, *Characteristics of Children in Substitute and Adoptive Care: A Statistical Sum*

foster children. This Article assesses constitutional rights of foster children to protection. In the last twenty-five years, the number of children in foster care has increased fivefold.[8] The foster care program now ranks with prisons, mental institutions and juvenile detention and treatment centers as a major state-operated custodial program.[9]

The Article argues that foster children have an equal, if not greater, claim to federal judicial protection from harm while in state care than do institutionalized persons who are already accorded significant protections.[10] Yet, in stark contrast to

---

mary of the VCIS National Child Welfare Data Base 30, table 2 (1985). In 1983, the latest year for which data are available, the American Public Welfare Association estimated that 447,000 children were served by the nation's foster care system. *Id.* at 32, table 3. Of that number, sixty-nine and one-half percent were sent to foster family homes. *Id.* at 62. The remainder resided in group homes or institutions. *Id. See also* F. Kavaler & M. Swire, Foster-Child Health Care 1 (1983); Children's Defense Fund, Children Without Homes: An Examination of Public Responsibility to Children in Out-of-Home Care 2 (1978); Lowry, *Derring-Do in the 1980's: Child Welfare Impact Litigation After the Warren Years*, 20 Fam. L.Q. 255, 275 (1986).

[8] Besharov, *Foster Care Reform: Two Books for Practitioners* (Book Review), 18 Fam. L.Q. 247 (1984) [hereinafter Besharov, *Foster Care Reform*]. Three major reasons have been offered to explain the expansion in the use of foster care. R. Mnookin, In the Interest of Children 69 (1985) (decrease in use of institutions for abandoned and neglected children) [hereinafter Mnookin, In the Interest]; Besharov, *The Misuse of Foster Care: When the Desire to Help Outruns the Ability to Improve Parental Functioning*, 20 Fam. L.Q. 213, 215 (1986) (increase in births to young single mothers unable to raise their children) [hereinafter Besharov, *The Misuse of Foster Care*]; Besharov, *Child Protection: Past Progress, Present Problems, and Future Directions*, 17 Fam. L.Q. 151, 153–55 (1983) (increase in child abuse and neglect reporting systems) [hereinafter Besharov, *Child Protection*]. Almost eight times as many children are reported to state officials as suspected victims of abuse or neglect than were reported in 1960. *Id.* at 151. Still, it is likely many children who ought to be in substitute care are not, either because their cases are not reported or because of the failure of the child welfare system to respond to legitimate pleas for protection of endangered children. *Id.* at 161 (estimates 50,000 cases of observable injuries not reported in 1979).

It is also likely, however, that some children go into foster care unnecessarily. Children's Defense Fund, *supra* note 7 at 15–18 (lack of family services). Mnookin, *In Whose Best Interest?*, *supra* note 6, at 619–20 (vagueness of statutes permits class, race, and lifestyle biases to affect decisions).

[9] *See* Bureau of the Census, U.S. Dep't of Commerce, Statistical Abstract of the United States 174, chart 307 (107th ed. 1987) (503,601 state and federal prisoners). *Id.* at 171, chart 301 (223,551 held in jails). *Id.* at 100, chart 159 (220,700 mental health inpatients). *Id.* at 171, chart 299 (51,402 juveniles in public custody, 34,112 in private custody). *Id.* at 99, chart 158 (132,235 in-state facilities for the mentally retarded).

[10] Other commentators have surveyed problems in foster care. Two articles offer arguments for a foster child's right to safety. *See* Donella, *Safe Foster Care: A Constitutional Mandate*, 19 Fam. L.Q. 79 (1985); Comment, *Child Abuse in Foster Homes: A Rationale for Pursuing Causes of Actions [sic] Against the Placement Agency*, 28 St. Louis U.L.J. 975 (1984). Other articles have considered issues such as the standards for placement, the right of foster children and foster parents to remain together, and

scores of decrees entered to protect institutionalized persons from physical harm, there is but one reported federal case[11] that has enforced by injunctive decree a constitutional right of foster children to protection from harm while in foster care.

The six sections of this Article present the case for direct federal court involvement in aiding foster children who are at risk of abuse and neglect while in foster care. Section I discusses the extent of abuse and neglect in foster care as well as the structural causes of this maltreatment. It also explains the inevitable failure of the political branches of government to confront the problem. Section II describes the constitutional right to safety and surveys the judicial treatment of that right, including the lack of development of the right for children in foster care. Section III discusses differences between children in foster family care and institutionalized persons, and argues that none of the differences can account for the failure to accord foster children the benefits of the right to safety. Section IV explores the appropriate remedy for the right to safety for foster children, and it demonstrates that damage remedies are inadequate because their availability is severely circumscribed by a variety of immunity doctrines, and because even if they were available, monetary awards deflect attention from the root causes of abuse and neglect of foster children. This section presents the case for structural injunctions as the most practical remedy.

---

the entitlement of foster children to permanence through either a prompt return home or adoption. *See, e.g.,* Besharov, *The Misuse of Foster Care, supra* note 8; Dobbs, *Foster Care and Family Law: A Look at* Smith v. OFFER *and the Constitutional Rights of Foster Children and Their Families,* 17 J. Fam. L. 1 (1979); Mnookin, *In Whose Best Interest?, supra* note 6; Musewicz, *The Failure of Foster Care: Federal Statutory Reform and the Child's Right to Permanence,* 54 S. Cal. L. Rev. 633 (1981); Wald, *State Intervention on Behalf of "Neglected" Children: Standards for Removal of Children from their Homes, Monitoring the Status of Children in Foster Care, and Termination of Parental Rights,* 28 Stan. L. Rev. 623 (1976).

[11] G.L. v. Zumwalt, 564 F. Supp. 1030 (W.D. Mo. 1983) (consent decree). A case is now pending in federal court that squarely presents the issue of whether or not foster children are entitled to injunctive relief designed to vindicate their right to be protected from harm. L.J. v. Massinga, Civ. No. 84-4403 (D. Md. filed Dec. 1984). On July 27, 1987, a preliminary injunction was granted in that case. *See infra* note 169. The case now awaits final trial and disposition. In addition, a class action raising the issue of the constitutional right of foster children to safety is now pending before a state court. Janet T. v. Morse, S-359-86 WNM (Sup. Ct. Vt. filed Aug. 29, 1986). Thus, it seems likely that in the near future courts will be required to determine for the first time whether it is appropriate to assert jurisdiction to fashion structural injunctive decrees for the protection of foster children.

Section V discusses whether federal courts are the appropriate forum to address the right to safety for foster children. Until the 1960's, federal courts declined to become involved in cases involving custodial conditions because of a self-imposed abstention policy called the "hands-off" doctrine.[12] Under that doctrine, courts deferred entirely to the judgments of administrators.[13] The awakening of interest in the rights of the confined led to the erosion of that doctrine.[14] In 1974, the Supreme Court announced definitively that the hands-off doctrine was inconsistent with constitutional principles, saying that "there is no iron curtain drawn between the Constitution and the prisons of this country."[15] Since then, lower federal courts have almost routinely intervened on behalf of the institutionalized, at least when necessary to protect against the most severe conditions of confinement.[16] Section V concludes that federal courts should also be the appropriate forum for foster care right-to-safety cases, and argues that none of the judicially created abstention doctrines bar them.

The final section of the Article proposes five basic guidelines which, if followed, would maximize the potential effectiveness of district courts in making foster care safe. The Article concludes that federal judicial involvement offers the promise of benefitting children in foster care by materially improving a system that thus far has resisted reform. Without judicial scrutiny, the abuse and neglect that many children suffered in their

---

[12] See Comment, *Beyond the Ken of Courts. A Critique of Judicial Refusal to Review the Complaints of Convicts*, 72 Yale L.J. 506 (1963). *See also infra* notes 112–113 and accompanying text.

[13] Zeigler, *Federal Court Reform of State Criminal Justice Systems: A Reassessment of the* Younger *Doctrine from a Modern Perspective*, 19 U.C. Davis L. Rev. 31, 56 (1985) (citing cases).

[14] *See, e.g.*, A. Neier, Only Judgment: The Limits of Litigation in Social Change 170–71 (1982).

[15] Wolff v. McDonnell, 418 U.S. 539, 555–56 (1974). Professor Zeigler dates the demise of the hands-off doctrine a decade earlier, to Cooper v. Pate, 378 U.S. 546 (1964). *See* Zeigler, *supra* note 13.

[16] *See, e.g.*, Pugh v. Locke, 406 F. Supp. 318 (M.D. Ala. 1976), *modified sub nom.* Newman v. Alabama, 559 F.2d 283 (5th Cir. 1977), *rev'd in part sub nom.* Alabama v. Pugh, 438 U.S. 781 (1978) (prison); Morgan v. Sporat, 432 F. Supp. 1130 (S.D. Miss. 1977) (juvenile detention facility); Wyatt v. Stickney, 344 F. Supp. 387 (M.D. Ala. 1972), *modified sub nom.* Wyatt v. Aderholt, 503 F.2d 1305 (5th Cir. 1974) (mental hospital); New York State Ass'n for Retarded Children v. Rockefeller, 357 F. Supp. 752 (E.D.N.Y. 1973) (institution for the mentally retarded); Hamilton v. Schiro, 338 F. Supp. 1016 (E.D. La. 1970) (prison).

original homes will continue after the state places them in foster care. For these children, the temporary, substitute family system imposed on children in foster care by the state will not be a haven, but a hell.

I. The Problem of Abuse and Neglect in Foster Home Placements

Foster care is intended to provide a temporary, safe haven for children whose parents are unable to care for them.[17] Too often, however, this purpose is not realized. Frequently, foster children are exposed to abuse and neglect by foster parents, and to serious injury due to the failure of the system itself to provide for stable care, or to attend to the children's medical problems. The failure of foster care programs to follow appropriate minimum standards that would ensure the care and protection of children has led to increased rates of foster care abuse and neglect. Despite the considerable costs, to both the children affected and to society generally, the political process has been unresponsive to calls for reform of foster care systems.

A. Types of Abuse and Neglect

Whatever the reason for placement, foster children have not had a normal upbringing. By definition, the bonds to a foster child's permanent family have been disrupted. Foster children suffer disproportionately from serious emotional, medical and psychological disabilities.[18] To compound matters, it is well-established that they are at high risk of further maltreatment while in foster care.[19] Foster children, therefore, are especially vulnerable individuals, prone to become victims unless special

---

[17] Child Welfare League of America, Standards for Foster Family Services 8 (1975); Musewicz, *supra* note 10, at 637.

[18] A. Gruber, *supra* note 6, at 182; D. Caplovitz & L. Genevie, *supra* note 1, at 37, table 2.3; P. Ryan, Analyzing Abuse in Family Foster Care: Final Report 59 (1987).

[19] P. Ryan, *supra* note 18, at 59 and authorities cited therein; Vera Institute of Justice, Foster Home Child Protection 31–32 (Feb. 1981) (unpublished report) (Children who were abused in foster care were three times as likely to have entered foster care because of parental abuse than children who were not abused); D. Caplovitz & L. Genevie, *supra* note 1, at 100 (Children with several emotional, intellectual or physical difficulties tended to be at higher risk of abuse or neglect).

care is taken to protect them. Two broad categories of mistreatment of these children have been identified.

1. Foster Family Abuse and Neglect

No one knows how many children are abused or neglected while in foster care,[20] but the problem is more widespread than is currently acknowledged. Children in foster family care have been reported severely beaten[21] and killed.[22] In addition, cases in which children have been subjected to bizarre punishments[23] or parental neglect[24] are common.

Foster children seem peculiarly vulnerable to sexual abuse. This is a special problem because, by definition, there is no permanent kinship bond in foster care. As a result, the traditional incest taboo does not operate.[25] The lack of permanent ties[26] combined with the cultural and class gaps that often exist between foster families and foster children, also can create an explosive environment in which expressions of verbal hostility often erupt.[27]

While foster care has been frequently criticized for other reasons, some observers claim that, at the very least, children

---

[20] Vera Institute of Justice, *supra* note 19, at 43. *See also* P. Ryan & E. McFadden, National Foster Care Education Project: Preventing Abuse in Family Foster Care 11, 14 (1986).

[21] Vera Institute of Justice, *supra* note 19, at 8–9 (use of belts, switches, electric cords, dog leashes, bread boards and broomsticks).

[22] *See* Vonner v. State Dep't of Pub. Welfare, 273 So. 2d 252 (La. 1973) (foster child beaten to death); D. Caplovitz & L. Genevie, *supra* note 1, at 94–95, case 5.14 (child killed by foster mother's boyfriend); Vera Institute of Justice, *supra* note 19, at v (foster child beaten to death by his foster mother).

[23] B. Warren & G. Bardwell, *G.L. v. Zumwalt, Case Record Monitoring, April 11, 1983 through June 30, 1984: Final Report* 52–54 (Apr. 24, 1985) (unpublished report on file with author) (children forced to stand in the center of a room for up to thirteen and one-half hours at a time, made to use a tin can for a toilet, locked in a basement, toilet-trained by being forced to stand with their pants over their heads); D. Caplovitz & L. Genevie, *supra* note 1, at 88, case 5.4.

[24] D. Caplovitz & L. Genevie, *supra* note 1, at 64 (children received only two meals a day and bitten by bedbugs); Vera Institute of Justice, *supra* note 19, at 13–14 (children smelled of "urine and vomit" and were "continually hungry").

[25] P. Ryan, *supra* note 18, at 60. An additional factor accounting for the higher level of sexual abuse in foster care is that a large number of foster children were sexually abused in the past. *Id.* at 105. *See also* B. Warren & G. Bardwell, *supra* note 23, at 53–54, case 549.

[26] *See supra* note 6 and accompanying text.

[27] B. Warren & G. Bardwell, *supra* note 23, at 54, 64, cases 549, 536, 660 (citing cases in which foster parents have called their child a "dummy," said, "I feel sorry for you," and talked negatively about the child's mother).

in foster care are protected from a high risk of abuse and neglect of the type just described.[28] The evidence, however, does not bear out these hopes. One study reported that the rate of substantiated abuse and neglect in New York City foster family care was more than one and one-half times that of children in the general population.[29] A national survey of foster family abuse and neglect, completed in 1986 by the National Foster Care Education Project, revealed rates of abuse that, at their highest, were over ten times greater for foster children than for children in the general population.[30]

As high as the reported rate is, a much higher level of abuse and neglect actually occurs than that officially reported. In 1979, a San Francisco group undertook a project to educate child welfare officials in a six-county area to discover unreported abuse occurring in foster care homes.[31] Within a two-year period, seventy-five cases of either physical abuse and neglect or

----

[28] *See* Mnookin, *In Whose Best Interest?*, *supra* note 6, at 632.

[29] Vera Institute of Justice, *supra* note 19, at 63–64 (49 abused children per 1,000 in general population and 77 per 1,000 for children in foster family care).

[30] The number of complaints ranged from 3 per 1,000 homes to 67 per 1,000 homes. Substantiated abuse complaints ranged from 1.2 per 1,000 to 27 per 1,000. P. Ryan & E. McFadden, *supra* note 20, at 11. According to the United States Department of Health and Human Services, the rate of maltreatment of children in 1978 for those 34 states reporting on the subject was 2.55 per 1,000. Department of Health and Human Services, National Analysis of Official Child Neglect and Abuse Reporting 10–11, Table 2 (1978).

Unfortunately, the reported statistics on foster family abuse studies are not widely known. Comment, *supra* note 10, at 976 ("Statistics indicate that the percentage of abused children who suffer at the hands of foster parents is 'miniscule,' a mere 0.3%. . . .") (quoting Note, *The Challenge of Child Abuse Cases: A Practical Approach*, 9 J. Legis. 127, 139 (1982)). The statistic that only .3 percent of all reported abuse cases involve foster parents is not terribly illuminating for several reasons. First, it represents only the raw number of substantiated abuse cases involving foster children, without comparison to the number of foster parents generally. Therefore, it does not supply the relationship between the number of foster parents and those who are abusive, a figure that is relevant where, as here, one is interested in knowing the risk of abuse to any given foster child. Obviously, the overwhelming majority of American children are not cared for in foster homes.

Second, the percentage does not disclose how many foster children were abused by foster parents. Since multiple placements are not rare, see *infra* note 38 and accompanying text, and since many foster homes are not closed despite reports of abuse and neglect, *see supra* notes 1, 5 and 8 and accompanying text, it is reasonable to assume that there is a greater than one-to-one relationship between abusing foster parents and abused foster children.

Third, the report deals with only substantiated cases of foster parent abuse and neglect. This statistic does not include children who are harmed by "program" abuse. *See infra* note 35 and accompanying text.

[31] Gil, *supra* note 5, at 8.

sexual abuse were reported from the area. In the past, "virtually no reports had been documented" through the official child abuse reporting system.[32] Another study found that one state foster care agency neglected to report sixty-three percent of the cases of suspected child maltreatment to the central registry of child neglect, even though such reports were mandated by state law.[33]

The actual amount of abuse and neglect may be much greater than anyone imagines. One study attempted to account for unreported or uninvestigated abuse and neglect in assessing the risk of abuse and neglect in foster boarding home care. The study concluded that forty-three percent of the children studied had been placed in an unsuitable foster home, and that fifty-seven percent of the children in the foster care system who were examined were at serious risk of harm while in foster care.[34]

2. Program Abuse

Another equally dangerous form of mistreatment results when the foster care system itself fails to provide children with a stable and secure home setting, or when it does not provide for the child's medical, psychological and emotional needs. This type of mistreatment has been termed "program abuse."[35]

a. Stability of Care

Children entering foster care placement inevitably experience the pain of separation from their family setting no matter how inadequate that setting has been.[36] The substitute experi-

---

[32] *Id.* at 8–9.

[33] D. Caplovitz & L. Genevie, *supra* note 1, at 83–84, table 5.1. The study also reported that in over forty percent of the cases, the agency did not so much as undertake an internal investigation to determine whether or not the suspicion of abuse reported by its own caseworker was true. *Id.* at 84–85. A follow-up study three years later revealed that the same agency failed to report, for external investigation, seventy-four percent of the suspected incidents of child mistreatment in the sample group. B. Warren & G. Bardwell, *supra* note 23, at 50–51, chart 3.

[34] D. Caplovitz & L. Genevie, *supra* note 1, at 59–69, 82–98. The study based these calculations upon an examination of over 800 case records maintained for 194 randomly selected foster children placed in care within a five year period prior to March of 1981. *Id.* at 96.

[35] Gil, *supra* note 5, at 10.

[36] *Id.*

ence created in its place compounds that trauma if it does not provide a stable home environment.[37] Unfortunately, foster home placements are frequently extremely unstable. Often foster children are shuffled from home to home without any opportunity to form an attachment with an adult caretaker. Stays in four or more foster homes are common.[38] Aside from the trauma entailed by this movement, the likelihood that the child will be abused at some time during his stay increases with each move.[39]

b. Medical Care

As the substitute parent, the child welfare program assumes responsibility for the child's medical and psychological care.[40] All children need medical care, but the need is acute for foster children who are less healthy than any other identifiable group of youngsters in the United States.[41] The provision of treatment cannot await the end of a foster care placement.

Nevertheless, medical care systems for foster children are inadequate "to manage effectively even simple and common child health problems."[42] For example, a comprehensive study of the medical status of foster children found that many of the pre-school age foster children studied had not received vaccinations for the prevention of childhood diseases.[43] Fourteen percent had received no medical examination upon admission to foster care, and the average physical exam was incomplete.[44] Forty-seven percent of the children had visual problems that

---

[37] D. Fanshel & E. Shinn, Children in Foster Care: A Longitudinal Investigation 137 (1978).

[38] See D. Caplovitz & L. Genevie, supra note 1, at 20–24; Children's Defense Fund, supra note 7, at 41; A. Gruber, supra note 6, at 67–68.

[39] See, e.g., Vera Institute of Justice, supra note 19, at vi (reporting that twenty-eight percent of victims of foster family abuse had been in three or more foster homes as compared to only thirteen percent of foster children generally).

[40] Child Welfare League of America, supra note 17, at § 3.10.

[41] F. Kavaler & M. Swire, supra note 7. The authors undertook an extensive independent evaluation of the physical condition of 668 New York City foster children. See also A. Gruber, supra note 6, at 73 (Massachusetts); D. Caplovitz & L. Genevie, supra note 1, at 35–37 (Kansas City).

[42] F. Kavaler & M. Swire, supra note 7, at 149.

[43] Id. at 143. These findings have been confirmed. See, e.g., D. Caplovitz & L. Genevie, supra note 1, at 41–43.

[44] F. Kavaler & M. Swire, supra note 7, at 142.

had not been evaluated by an optometrist.[45] Over forty percent needed dental care but had not been to a dentist.[46] Only one-fourth of the children who had identifiable emotional or developmental problems had received treatment.[47] When children had received medical attention, it often was inadequate. For example, sixty-one percent of the children who received glasses were given inadequate prescriptions.[48] Based upon these data the authors concluded that "[t]he system for providing health care to foster children is woefully inadequate both in New York State and in the country."[49]

In light of the high level of both foster family abuse and neglect and program abuse, "[t]he assumption that a child is removed from an abusive or neglectful home and placed in a safe environment can no longer be taken at face value. . . ."[50] Indeed, the threat of abuse and neglect of children in foster family care must be considered to be "acute and widespread."[51] Given the state's responsibility to these children, this situation is inexcusable.[52]

B. The Causes and Costs of Maltreatment

Although all of the facets of abuse and neglect of foster children have not been examined, enough is known to dispel notions that foster care maltreatment is inevitable or that responsibility for maltreatment rests entirely with foster parents. Instead, there is a growing body of evidence that links foster family abuse and neglect to the state child welfare agencies that fail to meet minimum professional standards.[53] Such standards

---

[45] *Id.* at 146.

[46] *Id.*

[47] *See also* D. Caplovitz & L. Genevie, *supra* note 1, at 38; A. Gruber, *supra* note 6, at 89, 183.

[48] F. Kavaler & M. Swire, *supra* note 7, at 146.

[49] *Id.* at 185. *See also* Shor, *Health Care Supervision of Foster Children,* LX Child Welfare 313, 318 (1981) (Maryland foster care agencies).

[50] Gil, *supra* note 5, at 8.

[51] P. Ryan & E. McFadden, *supra* note 20, at 14.

[52] *See also* Vera Institute of Justice, *supra* note 19, at 64.

[53] *See* Child Welfare League of America, *supra* note 17; American Public Welfare Association, Standards for Foster Family Systems for Public Agencies (1975). *See also* Cavara & Ogran, *Protocol to Investigate Child Abuse in Foster Care,* 7 Child Abuse and Neglect 287, 293 (1983); P. Ryan, *supra* note 18, at 7; Vera Institute of Justice, *supra* note 19, at 33–34.

require the careful screening and licensing of potential foster care applicants,[54] training of those who are chosen for the job,[55] careful matching of foster children with foster parents,[56] and regular, continual supervision by competent caseworkers[57] of the foster care placement.[58] Supervision by trained caseworkers fulfills two crucial functions. First, it allows the agency to meet its "obligation to ascertain whether the child is receiving care in accordance with accepted standards, and in relation to his needs."[59] Second, supervision promotes the competence of foster parents by relieving anxieties aroused by the child's behavior, increasing understanding of the child by supplying information and promptly providing supportive help. Training, casework support and consultation with social workers are often esential for foster parents to understand and guide foster children. Absent these forms of state back-up, foster parents can find the behavior of foster children "baffling or inexplicable," or may feel they are in an endless "struggle for control."[60] Professional standards also provide for the elimination of foster home

---

[54] *See, e.g.,* American Public Welfare Association, *supra* note 53, at 55–56; Child Welfare League of America, *supra* note 17, at § 4.16; Vera Institute of Justice, *supra* note 19, at 33.

[55] Foster children are not easy to handle, because often they have been sexually or physically abused in the past. They present their caretakers with patterns of behavior that are extremely upsetting and provocative to persons not prepared to cope with them. Compliance with professionally recognized standards would require the availability of training programs for foster parents. Child Welfare League of America, *supra* note 17, at § 4.4. *See also* American Public Welfare Association, *supra* note 53, at 64; P. Ryan, *supra* note 18, at 99–100, 105, recommendations 2, 15; Vera Institute of Justice, *supra* note 19, at 33–36.

[56] The failure of a foster care agency seriously to consider prior to placement whether a particular child should live with a particular set of foster parents is often the direct cause of the maltreatment of foster children. Child Welfare League of America, *supra* note 17, at § 3.9. *See also* Vera Institute of Justice, *supra* note 19, at 36–37.

[57] *See, e.g.,* American Public Welfare Association, *supra* note 53, at 64; Child Welfare League of America, *supra* note 17, at § 4.4; P. Ryan, *supra* note 18, at 105–06, recommendations 17–19; Vera Institute of Justice, Protection of Children in Foster Family Care: A Guide for Social Workers (March 10, 1982) (unpublished article); P. Ryan, *supra* note 18, at 3.

[58] Child Welfare League of America, *supra* note 17, at § 4.27. The Child Welfare League standards require that the agency maintain personal contact with the child once a month for the first year, after which personal contact every other month may be sufficient. *Id.* at § 4.28. Regular supervision is also stressed in the literature of foster family abuse and neglect. *See, e.g.,* American Public Welfare Association, *supra* note 53, at 65; P. Ryan, *supra* note 18, at 103, recommendation 11; Vera Institute of Justice, *supra* note 19, at 39–42.

[59] Child Welfare League of America, *supra* note 17, at § 4.27.

[60] P. Ryan, *supra* note 18, at 59–60.

overcrowding,[61] strict bans on improper punishment,[62] and prompt referrals for outside investigation of all suspicions of maltreatment by foster parents.[63]

Failure to follow professional standards results in increased foster family abuse and neglect. One study connected the lack of training of foster parents, foster home overcrowding, the failure to match foster children with appropriate parents and the failure to visit foster homes regularly with the abuse of foster children.[64] Another study linked the failure to refer allegations of abuse and neglect to the proper authorities for investigation and the failure to follow up on suspicions of abuse with the continuation of foster child abuse.[65]

These failures of the foster care system, and the corresponding abuse and neglect of foster children, have a serious, detrimental effect on society. Injuries inflicted upon foster children will not heal easily since often the abused foster children have already been harmed in their permanent homes.[66] Society has a humanitarian interest in the prevention of such unnecessary suffering, and a strong utilitarian interest in reducing crime and dependency. A negative foster care experience does little to advance these interests; indeed, it contributes to later antisocial and dependent behavior.[67] Then-Justice Rehnquist described the significance to society of protecting children from

---

[61] Child Welfare League of America, *supra* note 17, at § 4.7.

[62] Vera Institute of Justice, *supra* note 57, at 17–20 (Condoning corporal punishment raises the risk of severe injury to foster children. In addition, foster children are more likely to interpret physical punishment as rejection which, in turn, reinforces their poor self image.).

[63] Gil, *supra* note 5, at 8. *See also* P. Ryan, *supra* note 18, at 107–08, recommendation 22.

[64] Vera Institute of Justice, *supra* note 19, at 2.

[65] Gil, *supra* note 5, at 9. *See also* Office of the City Council President, The Foster Care Pyramid: Factors Associated with the Abuse and Neglect of Children in Foster Boarding Homes 2, 53–55, 60–64, 69–73 (1982) (study found that inadequate home studies, reference checks and procedures to decertify deficient foster homes correlated with abuse and neglect).

[66] Vera Institute of Justice, *supra* note 57, at 5–7 (citing J. Segal, *Child Abuse: A Review of Research Families Today* 1 (1979)). *See also* Comment, *supra* note 10, at 979 (and authorities cited therein).

[67] R. Flowers, Children and Criminality 101 (1986) (and authorities cited therein); D. Gurak, Center for Policy Research, Foster Care Experience Among Incarcerated Adults 19 (June 1977) (unpublished report). By contrast, there is evidence that foster children who have had a satisfactory experience in foster care fare as well as children in the general population. T. Festinger, *supra* note 6, at 199–209.

abuse: "[C]hildren who are abused in their youth generally face extraordinary problems developing into responsible productive citizens. . . . Few could doubt that the most valuable resource of a self-governing society is its population of children who will one day become adults and themselves assume the responsibility of self-governance."[68] Nevertheless, the legislative and executive branches of government have not responded to calls for foster care reform.

C. The Failure of Reform: Legislative and Executive Default

Although severe deficiencies in the foster care system have been spotlighted almost from its start,[69] the American foster care system has developed a remarkable immunity to reform. It has been the subject of studies at the state and national level,[70] yet little appreciable improvement has resulted. In 1979, the president of the Children's Defense Fund, Marian Wright Edelman, concluded that the conditions in the foster care system of the United States remained a "national disgrace."[71] In the same year, the National Commission on Children in Need of Parents,[72] issued its unanimous verdict that "[w]ith some admirable exceptions, the foster care system in America is an unconscionable failure, harming large numbers of the children it purports to serve."[73] While these condemnations concern the full gamut of issues posed by the administration of foster care, the specific issue of abuse and neglect of foster children in foster family placements has not been overlooked.[74]

It is not difficult to understand why the American foster care system has been so roundly criticized. Foster care systems.

---

[68] Santosky v. Kramer, 455 U.S. 745, 789–90 (1982) (Rehnquist, J., dissenting).

[69] See, e.g., A. Gruber, supra note 6, at 9 (1930 White House conference marking establishment of national foster care program); A. Kadushin, supra note 6, at 411 (citing Lewis, Long-Time and Temporary Placement of Children in Selected Papers in Casework 40 (1951) (by the 1950's foster care was failing to fulfill its purpose)); H. Mass & R. Engler, Jr., Children in Need of Parents (1959).

[70] Children's Defense Fund, supra note 7; National Commission of Children in Need Of Parents, Who Knows? Who Cares? Forgotten Children in Foster Care (1979); A. Gruber, supra note 6 (Massachusetts foster care system).

[71] Children's Defense Fund, supra note 7, at xiii.

[72] National Commission on Children in Need of Parents, supra note 70, at 4.

[73] Id. at 5.

[74] See supra notes 21–27, 29, 31–34, 64–65 and accompanying text. But see supra notes 28, 30 and accompanying text.

are administered by staffs that are "overburdened, poorly paid and often unprepared professionally"[75] for the difficult work they are called upon to perform. Lack of financial support has led to a system that is poorly organized and usually lacks even the most basic information about its own operation.[76] Foster parents as well receive inadequate financial and professional support. Payments offered to foster parents are often less than the cost of caring for the basic needs of the child; inadequacy of these payments adds financial stress to the burdens of being a foster parent.[77] Funding is especially important if foster care placements are to be made safe. Money is needed for additional trained social workers to screen carefully and regularly supervise foster homes, to train foster parents and to ensure that an adequate number of foster parents are available to avoid overloading foster homes with more children than they can handle.[78] Funds must also be allocated to hire medical personnel to supervise and implement a decent medical care system.[79] Abuse of children who come under the state's care for protection is the "inevitable result of inadequate funding."[80] Without additional aid, it would be almost impossible for change to occur even if there were a commitment to it by people in the system.

One must ask why foster care is "least favored by the legislature."[81] Here, too, the answer is not difficult to discern. Foster care is a service almost always reserved for the children of the poor,[82] and, in most states, foster care is disproportionately used by minority children[83] who, not unexpectedly, have encountered discrimination in the foster care system.[84] The dis-

---

[75] National Commission on Children in Need of Parents, *supra* note 70, at 6.

[76] Lowry, *supra* note 7, at 257.

[77] National Commission on Children in Need of Parents, *supra* note 70, at 21. *See also* A. Gruber, *supra* note 6, at 172.

[78] *See supra* notes 54–61 and accompanying text.

[79] *See supra* notes 40–49 and accompanying text.

[80] Besharov, *Protecting Children from Abuse: Should It Be a Legal Duty?*, 11 U. Dayton L. Rev. 509, 546 (1986).

[81] Lowry, *supra* note 7, at 274.

[82] Mnookin, *In Whose Best Interest?*, *supra* note 6, at 607 and sources cited therein; F. Kavaler & M. Swire, *supra* note 7, at 47. *See* Lowry, *supra* note 7, at 257.

[83] National Commission on Children in Need of Parents, *supra* note 70, at 25. *Accord*, Children's Defense Fund, *supra* note 7, at 49–52; Lowry, *supra* note 7, at 257; Dobbs, *supra* note 10, at 4.

[84] *See, e.g.*, Player v. Alabama Dep't of Pensions and Security, 400 F. Supp. 249, 255 (M.D. Ala. 1975), aff'd, 536 F.2d 1385 (5th Cir. 1976) (finding black children in the

parate treatment of minorities also appears to mean that they run an even greater risk of abuse and neglect in foster care than other foster children.[85] While other parents experiencing difficulties with child rearing can rely on private school and paid professional support, the poor and the underclass must resort to their local child welfare agency.

It is difficult to imagine a more powerless group of people than foster children. They are largely unrepresented in the court proceedings that lead to their placement.[86] Living without the protection of their parents, they are completely at the mercy of the persons who may also be responsible for maltreating them.[87] They do not vote; they lack the developmental ability to organize. Their voices, assuming they are old enough to speak, cannot be heard. Whatever happens to them, therefore, happens outside of the zone of public scrutiny.

The pressure that exists for improvements in foster care systems focuses on issues other than maltreatment. Supporters of foster care reform, responding either to the concerns of natural parents, or to those of foster parents concerned about adoption, have concentrated on the states' over-reliance on foster care rather than on the issue of safety within the foster care system. Natural parents and their advocates have exerted pressure for preventive services that would limit the need for foster care by requiring the state to aid families in distress before taking a child away.[88] These services can include day care, homemaker services, parent training, transportation, clinical services and assistance in obtaining housing.[89] Advocates of

Alabama foster care system were not given equal treatment in referrals to specialized placements); Wilder v. Bernstein, 645 F. Supp. 1292 (S.D.N.Y. 1986) (consent decree designed to ensure that all children, regardless of race or religion, are served by the New York City foster care system on a "first come-first served" basis). *See also* Children's Defense Fund, *supra* note 7, at 49–54.

[85] D. Caplovitz & L. Genevie, *supra* note 1, at 99–100, table 5.5 (black children are more likely to be abused or neglected in foster care).

[86] *See* R. Horowitz & H. Davidson, *supra* note 6, at 296–99, § 7.17, 368, § 9.06 (Foster children usually have no voice in voluntary placements. There are minimal or no procedural rights at periodic review proceedings.).

[87] *See supra* note 6 and accompanying text, and *infra* notes 203–04 and accompanying text.

[88] Wiltse, *Current Issues and New Directions in Foster Care*, in Child Welfare Strategy in the Coming Years 67 (A. Kadushin ed. 1978); Stein, *An Overview of Services to Families and Children in Foster Care*, in Foster Children in the Courts 420 (M. Hardin ed. 1983).

[89] *See, e.g.*, N.Y. Comp. Codes R. & Regs. tit. 18, § 423.2 (1987).

adoption have called for "permanency planning" designed to speed children though foster care by promptly returning them to their original homes, or, if that is not practicable, by terminating parental rights and placing the child for adoption.[90]

Yet even if these reforms are successful,[91] "there will always be some children—the orphans, the abandoned, and the severely abused—for whom substitute care outside of their homes will be necessary."[92] Coalitions for preventive services and permanency planning have not addressed the issue of maltreatment of foster children, perhaps because they would not be the direct beneficiaries of such reform. Without an ally who will materially or politically gain from the change, the plea for protection of those children who will end up in foster care will remain no more than a soft whisper. Whether the courts should fill this void must now be considered.

D. The Call for Judicial Involvement

Courts would provide a great benefit to society were they to become involved in foster care reform both by preventing the indignity of abuse and by protecting foster children's fu-

---

[90] Maluccio & Fein, *Permanency Planning: A Redefinition*, 62 Child Welfare 195, 197 (1983). The call for permanency planning from the legal and social work communities has been loud and persistent. *See, e.g.,* Christoff, *Children in Limbo In Ohio: Permanency Planning and the State of the Law*, 16 Cap U.L. Rev. 1 (1986) and sources cited therein; New York Task Force on Permanency Planning for Children in Foster Care, Permanency Planning: A Shared Responsibility (March 1986); Mnookin, *In Whose Best Interest?*, *supra* note 6, at 633–35.

[91] Advocates who have called for child welfare reforms in the areas of preventive services and permanency planning have begun to obtain at least some legislative results. In 1980, Congress passed the Adoption Assistance and Child Welfare Reform Act of 1980, Pub. L. No. 96–272, 94 Stat. 500 (provides financial incentives to encourage states to strengthen preventive services and permanency planning). *See* 42 U.S.C. § 675. For a comprehensive analysis of the provisions of the Act, see Allen, Golubock & Olson, *A Guide to The Adoption Assistance and Child Welfare Reform Act of 1980* in Foster Children in the Courts 577 (M. Hardin ed. 1983).

Legislative reform focusing on the promotion of a permanent family bond has also taken place at the state level. In 1976, California passed the Family Protection Act, S.B. 30, 1977 Cal. Legis. Serv. 977 (West), and in 1979, New York passed the Child Welfare Reform Act of 1979, 1979 N.Y. Laws 610, 611. *See* A. English, Foster Care Reform, Strategies for Legal Services Advocates to Reduce the Need for Foster Care and Improve the Foster Care System 83–97 (1981).

[92] A. English, *supra* note 91, at 4.

tures.[93] Yet, federal courts are understandably reluctant to become involved[94] in protracted endeavors, such as would be required in large scale institutional reform of this kind, unless they perceive that the need to do so is great. Some have argued that federal courts should not intervene in such matters unless intervention is necessary to protect the rights of "discrete and insular" minorities[95] who lack access to the normal political process.[96] As one commentator put it: "The judicial obligation to enforce the rights of the politically powerless is at the heart of the American political system."[97] Expressed differently, federal judicial intervention is appropriate when important constitutional rights are implicated, when the institution itself has proven resistant to change through more traditional legislative or executive means, and where the change requested is "critical to the quality of American life."[98] The case for the exercise of judicial discretion to ensure protection of foster children is compelling under any of these formulations.

As discussed below, the right to protection occupies a critical niche in our system of government; it has historic roots in our philosophical conception of the fundamental role and justification for government's existence.[99] If any group in society is denied the right to protection, it is difficult to imagine how it can enjoy any other right. Yet, foster children are powerless to obtain the right for themselves.[100] Involvement by the federal

---

[93] T. Festinger, *supra* note 6, at 262–64. *See also* Besharov, *The Misuse of Foster Care*, *supra* note 8, at 218–19, (quoting M. Wald, Protecting Abused/Neglected Children: A Comparison of Home and Foster Care Placement 12–13 (1985)).

[94] The power of a federal court to grant affirmative relief is discretionary. Comment, *Confronting the Conditions of Confinement: An Expanded Role for Courts in Prison Reform*, 12 Harv. C.R.-C.L. L. Rev. 367, 385–86 (1977); Tennessee Valley Auth. v. Hill, 437 U.S. 153, 193 (1978). *See generally* D. Dobbs, Law of Remedies 108–11 (1973).

[95] The term "discrete and insular minorities" was first used by Chief Justice Stone in his now famous footnote in United States v. Carolene Products, 304 U.S. 144, 152 n.4 (1938), to describe those groups that most require judicial protection in order to enjoy their constitutional rights. *See also* J. Ely, Democracy and Distrust 73–179 (1980); Cover, *The Origins of Judicial Activism in the Protection of Minorities*, 91 Yale L.J. 1287 (1982).

[96] *See* J. Ely, *supra* note 95, at 135–36; R. Mnookin, In The Interest, *supra* note 8, at 37–41; Swygert, *In Defense of Judicial Activism*, 16 Val. U.L. Rev. 439, 443 (1982).

[97] Comment, *supra* note 94, at 386.

[98] Zeigler, *supra* note 13, at 39.

[99] *See infra* notes 106–110 and accompanying text for a discussion of the historic roots of the right to safety.

[100] Professor Mnookin has observed that children as a group may not qualify for

courts in advancing the right to protection is thus consistent with the notion of the limited intervention of the federal judiciary.

An additional motivation justifying judicial involvement in foster care reform is the long history of solicitude to the needs of children. Children, because of their obvious dependency, need special protection.[101] As long ago as 1944,[102] the Supreme Court recognized the state's strong interest in safeguarding children from abuse.[103] This interest is reflected in a virtually unbroken line of Supreme Court opinions upholding state actions that might otherwise have been unconstitutional, but that were saved by the need to protect children.[104]

Having examined the nature and scope of the problem, the foster care system's resistance to change through the legislature or the executive, and the consistency of judicial involvement in foster care reform with principles of judicial intervention, the next section examines which substantive rights justify judicial involvement.

II. The Constitutional Right to Safety

In 1982, a unanimous court in *Youngberg v. Romeo* held that the state owes an "unquestioned duty" to provide reasonable safety for all residents of a state institution for the mentally

---

special protection as a discrete and insular minority because of the "multitude of potential and part-time spokesmen [sic] for children." Mnookin, In The Interest, *supra* note 8, at 41. Whatever may be said of children generally, however, foster children are a discrete and insular minority, especially where a claim for which they have no obvious allies is concerned.

[101] Mnookin, In the Interest, *supra* note 8, at 31.

[102] Prince v. Massachusetts, 321 U.S. 158 (1944).

[103] *Id.* at 168–69 (upholding law that prohibited children from selling magazines in a public place).

[104] New York v. Ferber, 458 U.S. 747 (1982) (upholding New York law prohibiting knowing promotion of sexual performance by children even if it is not obscene); H.L. v. Matheson, 450 U.S. 398 (1981) (upholding notification and consultation barriers to the exercise of the right to an abortion for an immature minor which would be unconstitutional if applied to an adult); Ginsberg v. New York, 390 U.S. 629, *reh'g denied*, 391 U.S. 971 (1968) (upholding criminal statute prohibiting sale to minors of material that would not be obscene if sold to adults).

Taken together, these decisions establish a right unique to children to be protected from "endangering surroundings and influences." S. Davis & M. Schwartz, Children's Rights and the Law 73 (1987).

retarded.[105] Unquestioned though the right may be, recognition of its existence developed quite slowly and it continues to lack clear standards defining its scope. Nevertheless, the right to safety has deep roots in American legal and philosophical thought. This section briefly traces the origin of the right, its development in lower federal courts and in the Supreme Court, and provides a brief comment on the standards that courts have used to determine whether or not the right has been violated, and concludes with a discussion of the application of the right to foster children.

A. The Development of the Right to Safety

1. The Origin of the Right

The right to safety for the institutionalized invoked by Justice Powell in *Youngberg* can be traced as far back as Blackstone, Cooke and Hobbes—progenitors of modern American law—all of whom recognized that the first function of government is protection of the governed. In *Leviathan*, Hobbes' seminal seventeenth century work, Hobbes asserted that government's primary purpose and responsibility is protection. This is so, he wrote, because men live under governments for their own preservation.[106] In *Calvin's Case*,[107] Cooke, Chief Justice of the King's Bench, explained the basic terms of the modern social compact: in exchange for "true and faithful ligeance" the government undertakes the duty of protection.[108] And Blackstone ranked the "right to personal security" as the primary right each citizen possesses.[109] The right to personal security "consists in . . . uninterrupted enjoyment of . . . life . . . limbs . . . body . . . health, and . . . reputation."[110]

---

[105] 457 U.S. 307, 324 (1982). While there were two concurrences in addition to the majority opinion in *Youngberg*, the Court did not divide on this issue. *See infra* text accompanying note 145.

[106] T. Hobbes, Leviathan (1651).

[107] [1608] 4 Co. Rep. 1 (K.B.).

[108] *Id.* at 4b.

[109] 1 W. Blackstone, Commentaries 129.

[110] *Id.* at 300. This conception of the centrality of the right of protection has not changed in modern times. In 1918, Justice Oliver Wendell Holmes authored an article identifying four conditions that make up the "necessary elements in any society." O.W.

2. The Early Prison Cases

Despite its deep jurisprudential underpinnings, the right to safety has been recognized only recently as an enforceable constitutional right of the institutionalized. Although the Sixth Circuit suggested that the government had a duty to protect prisoners from assault or injury,[111] as late as 1944, the hands-off doctrine effectively precluded litigation to enforce this right.[112] The hands-off doctrine was a judicially created concept that commanded federal courts to abstain from examining prison matters,[113] as prisons were considered the exclusive domain of the Congress and of the state governments.[114]

By the late 1960's and early 1970's, however, federal courts, responding to the Supreme Court's receptive approach to civil rights cases, slowly began to lower the barrier to judicial review of institutional conditions. During that time period, several courts held that inmates have an eighth amendment right to be protected from harm.[115] The eighth amendment's "evolving stan-

---

Holmes, *Natural Law*, in Collected Legal Papers 310, 312 (1920). The most important of these, in Holmes' view, was "some protection for the person." *Id*. In Miranda v. Arizona, 384 U.S. 436 (1966), Justice White stated that "[t]he most basic function of any government is to provide for the security of the individual and of his property." *Id*. at 539 (White, J., dissenting). In a report to the American Bar Association in 1981, Chief Justice Warren Burger identified "protection and security" as a "theme [that] runs throughout all history." W. Burger, Annual Report to the American Bar Association 2 (Feb. 8, 1981) *reprinted in* 67 A.B.A. J. 290 (1981). For a thorough account of the historic underpinnings of the right to safety and its roots, see Willing, *Protection by Law Enforcement: The Emerging Constitutional Right*, 35 Rutgers L. Rev. 1, 22–54 (1982).

[111] Coffin v. Reichard, 143 F.2d 443 (6th Cir. 1944).

[112] The hands-off doctrine was invoked even where inmates' safety was at stake. *Ex parte* Pickens, 101 F. Supp. 285, 287, 290 (D. Alaska 1951) (The complaint alleged that the facility was overcrowded and unsanitary, and that given the locked exits, a coal stove presented an inescapable situation in the event of a fire. The court considered conditions a "fabulous obscenity" but dismissed the complaint.).

Two recent cases dealing with the right to safety in penal facilities may foreshadow a return to considering such complaints non-justiciable. *See* Davidson v. Cannon, 474 U.S. 344 (1986); Daniels v. Williams, 474 U.S. 327 (1986), discussed *infra* note 153.

[113] Comment, *supra* note 10, at 507. The pull of the doctrine was so strong that even claims of racial discrimination were not cognizable. *See* United States *ex rel.* Morris v. Radio Station WENR, 209 F.2d 105 (7th Cir. 1953). *See also* Note, *Constitutional Rights of Prisoners: The Developing Law*, 110 U. Pa. L. Rev. 985 (1962).

[114] *See, e.g.*, Banning v. Looney, 213 F.2d 771 (10th Cir. 1954), *cert. denied*, 348 U.S. 859 (1954).

[115] *See* Jackson v. Bishop, 404 F.2d 571, 579 (8th Cir. 1968) (use of a strap to beat prisoners as a disciplinary measure violated the eighth amendment's proscription against cruel and unusual punishment). *See also* Holt v. Sarver, 309 F. Supp. 362 (E.D. Ark.

dards of decency" were violated when prison officials failed to manage their system in a way which minimized the high risk of violence in the prison. The standards for application under the eighth amendment varied: some courts based relief from unsafe prison conditions on a visceral "shocking to the conscience" test;[116] others based their interpretations on the observation that the state must exercise ordinary care in the custody of prisoners.[117]

In 1974, Justice White sounded the Supreme Court's death knell to the "hands-off" doctrine in a single line: "[T]here is no Iron Curtain between the Constitution and the prisons of this country."[118] With the demise of the "hands-off" doctrine, lower courts were free to consider right-to-safety cases without jurisdictional hindrance. As time passed, lower courts established that the right to safety followed an inmate into prison. Those decisions explain that the right protects inmates not only from deliberate abuse by their keepers, but also from conditions which make inmates open to violence by their fellow inmates.[119]

1970), Woodhous v. Virginia, 487 F.2d 889, 890 (4th Cir. 1973) (standards for adjudicating the right to safety in a prison context: "(1) whether there is a pervasive risk of harm to inmates from other prisoners, and, if so, (2) whether the officials are exercising reasonable care to prevent prisoners from intentionally harming others or from creating an unreasonable risk of harm.").

[116] Meredith v. Arizona, 523 F.2d 481, 483 (9th Cir. 1975); Holt v. Sarver, 309 F. Supp. 362, 380 (E.D. Ark. 1970).

[117] Muniz v. United States, 280 F. Supp. 542, 546 (S.D.N.Y. 1968). This theory is derived from common law doctrine that places a duty upon prison officials to provide for the protection of prisoners who are placed in their charge. See Restatement (Second) of Torts § 20 (1965); W. Prosser & W. Keeton, Torts 1048 (5th ed. 1984). In Estelle v. Gamble, 429 U.S. 97 (1976), the Court similarly found that prison authorities have a constitutional duty to provide prisoners with medical care: "[D]eliberate indifference to serious medical needs of prisoners constitutes the 'unnecessary and wanton infliction of pain.'" Id. at 104, (quoting Gregg v. Georgia, 428 U.S. 153, 173 (1976)). Several lower federal courts have utilized this theory as a basis for affording prisoners relief from rampant prison violence. See, e.g., Ramos v. Lamm, 639 F.2d 559 (10th Cir. 1980), cert. denied, 450 U.S. 1041 (1981); Grubbs v. Bradley, 552 F. Supp. 1052, 1122 (M.D. Tenn. 1982).

[118] Wolff v. McDonnell, 418 U.S. 539, 555–56 (1973).

[119] See, e.g., Hoptowit v. Ray, 682 F.2d 1237, 1250 (9th Cir. 1982); Little v. Walker, 552 F.2d 193 (7th Cir. 1977), cert. denied, 435 U.S. 932 (1978).

Extensive relief has been granted, effectuating that right. Among the types of relief ordered are (a) increases in staff, see, e.g., Jones v. Diamond, 636 F.2d 1364 (5th Cir. 1981); Ruiz v. Estelle, 503 F. Supp. 1265 (S.D. Tex. 1980), aff'd in part and rev'd in part, 650 F.2d 555 (5th Cir. 1981), aff'd in part and rev'd in part, 666 F.2d 854 (5th Cir. 1981), aff'd in part and rev'd in part, 679 F.2d 1115 (5th Cir. 1982); (b) improvements to staff training programs, see, e.g., Grubbs v. Bradley, 552 F. Supp. 1052, 1128 (M.D. Tenn. 1982); and (c) classification of inmates by dangerousness, see, e.g., Jones v.

3. The Right in Other Institutional Settings

While the right to safety was first articulated in the context of prisons, and has been most fully developed there, it has been implemented in other institutional settings as well. In 1973, a federal district court held that a class of residents of the Willowbrook State School for the Mentally Retarded had the right "to reasonable protection from harm."[120] The court distinguished this right to safety from a right to treatment, which it declined to recognize. Courts since have followed the Willowbrook decision, applying it in other institutionalized settings as well. It is now firmly established that the mentally ill and retarded,[121] residents of state juvenile training schools,[122] suspects in police custody[123] and pretrial detainees[124] have a constitutional right to protection.

Diamond, 636 F.2d 1364, 1374 (5th Cir. 1981); Grubbs v. Bradley, 552 F. Supp. 1052, 1060 (M.D. Tenn. 1982).

In some cases, in order to ensure the right to protection, courts have ordered modifications to the structure of an institution or, if necessary, that the institution, or some part of it, be closed. *See, e.g.,* Dimarzo v. Cahill, 575 F.2d 15 (1st Cir. 1978); Martino v. Carey, 563 F. Supp. 984 (D. Or. 1983) (court ordered progress reports on renovations and their impact on violative conditions); Benjamin v. Malcolm, 564 F. Supp. 668 (S.D.N.Y. 1983).

See also Robertson, *Surviving Incarceration: Constitutional Protection from Inmate Violence,* 35 Drake L. Rev. 101 (1985–86); Plotkin, *Serving Justice: Prisoners' Rights to be Free From Physical Assault,* 23 Clev. St. L. Rev. 387 (1974); Note, *Inmate Assaults and Section 1983 Damage Claims,* 54 Chi.-Kent L. Rev. 596 (1977).

[120] New York State Association for Retarded Children, Inc. v. Rockefeller, 357 F. Supp. 752, 758 (E.D.N.Y. 1973). *See* New York Association for Retarded Children v. Carey, 393 F. Supp. 715 (E.D.N.Y. 1975) (consent decree encompassing protection from harm caused by physical injury as well as from conditions causing the deterioration, or preventing the development, of an individual's capacities), *modification denied,* 551 F. Supp. 1165 (E.D.N.Y. 1982), *aff'd in part and rev'd in part,* 706 F.2d 956 (2d Cir.), *cert. denied,* 464 U.S. 915 (1983).

See also D. Rothman & S. Rothman, The Willowbrook Wars (1984).

[121] *See, e.g.,* Society for Good Will to Retarded Children v. Cuomo, 737 F.2d 1239 (2d Cir. 1984); Association for Retarded Citizens v. Olson, 561 F. Supp. 473 (D.N.D. 1982), *aff'd,* 713 F.2d 1384 (8th Cir. 1983); Welsch v. Likins, 373 F. Supp. 487 (D. Minn. 4th Div. 1974), *aff'd in part, vacated and remanded in part,* 550 F.2d 1122 (8th Cir. 1977).

[122] Santana v. Collazo, 533 F. Supp. 966 (D.P.R. 1982), *modified,* 714 F.2d 1172 (1st Cir. 1983), *cert. denied,* 466 U.S. 974 (1984); Pena v. New York State Div. for Youth, 419 F. Supp. 203 (S.D.N.Y. 1976), *aff'd,* 708 F.2d 877 (2d Cir. 1983); Martarella v. Kelley, 349 F. Supp. 575 (S.D.N.Y. 1972).

[123] City of Revere v. Massachusetts Gen. Hosp., 463 U.S. 239, 245 (1983).

[124] Duran v. Elrod, 760 F.2d 756 (7th Cir. 1985); Jones v. Diamond, 636 F.2d 1364 (5th Cir. 1981).

As in prison cases, the right is most frequently implemented by courts in class action suits seeking injunctive relief, rather than in individual suits for damages where the plaintiff's claim often founders on one or more of the various immunity doctrines.[125] The injunctive relief that has been granted has provided significant reforms in several institutional contexts. Courts have ordered institutions for the mentally retarded or ill to make structural improvements,[126] decrease their population,[127] hire more staff,[128] institute staff training programs[129] and provide training of residents.[130] In pretrial detention decisions, courts have been willing to close jails where deemed necessary to ensure safety.[131]

Since the eighth amendment does not apply outside the context of prison,[132] courts have relied on different theories to support the right to safety for those in non-penal institutions. The due process clause of the fourteenth amendment is most frequently invoked. For confinement to meet constitutional stan-

---

[125] *See, e.g.,* Harlow v. Fitzgerald, 457 U.S. 800 (1982) (The Court rejected the previous standard which permitted a finding of liability based on proof that the official acted in bad faith. Instead, the Court held that the individual must prove that her clearly established constitutional right was violated by the defendant). Given the uncertainty as to the standard governing the right to safety, see *infra* notes 149–153 and accompanying text, this is a difficult burden indeed. Harper v. Cserr, 544 F.2d 1121, 1124 (1st Cir. 1976). *But see* Gann v. Schramm, 606 F. Supp. 1442 (D. Del. 1985) (official immunity denied where officials at state mental hospital violated the well-known constitutional right to a safe environment for those involuntarily committed to mental institutions).

[126] Rone v. Fireman, 473 F. Supp. 92, 132 (N.D. Ohio 1979) (physical improvements in the facility to provide an appropriate environment for the mentally retarded).

[127] Woe v. Cuomo, 638 F. Supp. 1506, 1517 (E.D.N.Y. 1986) (enjoining additional patients from being admitted to the Bronx Psychiatric Center); New York State Ass'n for Retarded Children v. Carey, 393 F. Supp. 715, 717 (E.D.N.Y. 1975) (requiring sharp reduction in the population of Willowbrook to a capacity of 250 beds or less).

[128] *See, e.g.,* New York State Association For Retarded Children v. Rockefeller 357 F. Supp. 752, 769 (E.D.N.Y. 1973).

[129] *Id.* at 768 (consent decree increased staffing and training provision). *See also* Rone v. Fireman, 473 F. Supp. 92, 133–34 (N.D. Ohio 1979).

[130] In the Willowbrook case, the consent decree mandated individually designed instruction for residents. New York State Ass'n for Retarded Children v. Carey, 596 F.2d 27, 31 (2d Cir. 1979) (programs to include education, physical therapy, speech pathology and audiology services). *See also* Association for Retarded Citizens v. Olson, 561 F. Supp. 473, 494 (D.N.D. 1982), *aff'd,* 713 F.2d 1384 (8th Cir. 1983).

[131] *See, e.g.,* Rhem v. Malcolm, 377 F. Supp. 995 (S.D.N.Y. 1974); Inmates of Suffolk County Jail v. Eisenstadt, 360 F. Supp. 676, 689–90 (D. Mass. 1973) (Charles Street Jail deemed unfit by failing to meet a standard of "basic humanity toward men" and ordered replaced).

[132] Ingraham v. Wright, 430 U.S. 651, 664 (1977) (the eighth amendment was "designed to protect those convicted of crimes").

dards, the conditions of confinement must bear some relationship to its purpose.[133] If, as in the case of the mentally ill, confinement is to treat and protect, the deprivation of liberty lacks constitutional support when it fails to advance those purposes.[134]

4. The Supreme Court's Treatment of the Right to Safety

Although the Supreme Court has not decided a prison case in which it awarded relief which focused directly on the right to safety,[135] it has endorsed lower court orders that provided affirmative relief on that ground. In *Bell v. Wolfish*[136] and *Rhodes v. Chapman*,[137] the Court approved a number of lower federal court opinions that granted relief from "deplorable" conditions in some of the country's oldest and worst prisons and jails.[138] Several of these lower court orders had implemented the right to safety.[139]

---

[133] Some states base the institutionalization on the *parens patriae* theory. *Parens patriae* refers to the inherent power of a state to "provid[e] care to its citizens who are unable . . . to care for themselves." Addington v. Texas, 441 U.S. 418, 426 (1979). *See, e.g.,* Welsch v. Likins, 373 F. Supp. 487, 496 (D. Minn. 1974), *aff'd in part and vacated and remanded in part*, 550 F.2d 1122 (8th Cir. 1977) (The court cited approvingly the language of the doctrine, but did not explicitly mention *parens patriae*). For a history of the *parens patriae* theory, see Custer, *The Origins of the Doctrine of* Parens Patriae, 27 Emory L.J. 195 (1978); Rendleman, Parens Patriae: *From Chancery to the Juvenile Court*, 23 S.C.L. Rev. 205 (1971). The Supreme Court has imposed constitutional limits on the doctrine by holding that when the state exercises this power it must take steps to ensure that the exercise of the state's power bears some relationship to its purpose. Jackson v. Indiana, 406 U.S. 715 (1972).

[134] Halderman v. Pennhurst State School & Hosp., 446 F. Supp. 1295 (E.D. Pa. 1977), *aff'd in part, rev'd in part*, 612 F.2d 84 (3d Cir. 1979) (en banc), *rev'd on other grounds*, 451 U.S. 1 (1980).

[135] The Supreme Court has denied relief in two individual damage claims involving the right to safety in prisons and jails. *See infra* note 153.

[136] 441 U.S. 520 (1978).

[137] 452 U.S. 337 (1981).

[138] *Bell,* 441 U.S. at 539 n.20; *Rhodes,* 452 U.S. at 345 n.11, 346–47, 352 n.17.

[139] The *Rhodes* majority cited with approval the following lower court decisions that had granted relief which included implementation of the right to safety in prison: Ramos v. Lamm, 639 F.2d 559 (10th Cir. 1980), *cert. denied*, 450 U.S. 1041 (1981); Williams v. Edwards, 547 F.2d 1206 (5th Cir. 1977); Gates v. Collier, 501 F.2d 1291 (5th Cir. 1974); Pugh v. Locke, 406 F. Supp. 318 (M.D. Ala. 1976), *aff'd as modified*, 559 F.2d 283 (5th Cir. 1977), *rev'd in part on other grounds*, 438 U.S. 781 (1978) (per curiam).
  In *Bell,* the majority, without specification, approved of lower court decisions which "have condemned . . . sordid aspects of our prison systems." 441 U.S. at 562. *See also* Hudson v. Palmer, 468 U.S. 517, 526–27 (1984); Hutto v. Finney, 437 U.S. 678, 681 (1978); Holt v. Sarver, 309 F. Supp. 362, 381 (E.D. Ark. 1970).

In 1982 the Supreme Court explicitly recognized the right
to safety in the context of institutionalized mentally retarded
persons. *Youngberg v. Romeo*[140] was a damage action brought
on behalf of a thirty-three-year-old retarded man with the mental
capacity of an eighteen-month-old child. Romeo, confined involuntarily to the Pennhurst State Hospital, was "injured on
numerous occasions, both by his own violence and by the reactions of other [inmates] to him."[141] Romeo's mother brought
suit on his behalf against Pennhurst's director and two supervisors, alleging at least sixty-three incidents of violence against
him. In an amended complaint, Romeo sought compensation for
the failure to be protected and provided "treatment or programs
for his mental retardation."[142]

Following a jury verdict for the defendants, Romeo appealed to the Third Circuit, complaining that the trial court's
charge defined his rights as stemming only from the eighth
amendment. The trial court, drawing on the Supreme Court's
eighth amendment cases, had charged that liability would not
attach for Romeo's injuries unless the defendants had been
"deliberately indifferent" to his needs.[143] The Third Circuit reversed, holding that Romeo's right to safety was found in the
fourteenth amendment, not the eighth, and that only "substantial
necessity" could justify abridging it. The court also held that
the right was broad enough to encompass Romeo's claim for
treatment.[144]

Although the Supreme Court vacated and remanded the
decision by the Third Circuit, the majority nevertheless held
that the right to safety for the institutionalized was an "unquestioned duty" of the state and was one of the "essentials of care
that the state must provide."[145] Justice Powell observed:
"[W]hen a person is institutionalized—and wholly dependent on
the state . . . [there is] a duty to provide certain services."[146]
The majority included the right to safety within the "historic

---

[140] 457 U.S. 307 (1982).
[141] *Id.* at 310.
[142] *Id.* at 311.
[143] *Id.* at 312 n.11 (citing Romeo v. Youngberg, 644 F.2d 147, 155, 160, 169 (3d Cir,
1980)).
[144] 644 F.2d 147, 156, 160, 164.
[145] 457 U.S. at 324.
[146] *Id.* at 317.

liberty interests" essential to ensure a person's bodily integrity from unnecessary invasion by the state, thus qualifying the right to safety for substantive protection under the due process clause.[147] The right survives involuntary commitment, and since the mentally retarded, unlike convicts, have not been guilty of any wrongdoing, the Court intimated that their rights may be even greater than those of prisoners.[148]

While the Court had little difficulty identifying the right to safety as a substantive due process entitlement of the involuntarily confined, it struggled to articulate a clear standard for determining when the right had been violated. The Court rejected the "deliberate indifference" standard used in prison right-to-safety cases and by the district court in *Youngberg*.[149] On the other hand, the Court rejected the Third Circuit's "substantial necessity" test as well.[150] It is not entirely clear what test the Court adopted in its place. Justice Powell stated that courts should balance "the liberty [interest] of the individual" in safety against "the demands of an organized society."[151] Restrictions on liberty that are "reasonably related to legitimate government objectives" are not unconstitutional even if they result in a "lack of absolute safety."[152] Just what "relevant state interests" Justice Powell had in mind for this balance are not readily apparent from his opinion.[153] Despite the uncertainty

---

[147] *Id.* at 315–16.

[148] *Id.* at 321–22.

[149] 457 U.S. at 321–22.

[150] *Id.* at 322.

[151] *Id.* at 310.

[152] *Id.* at 319–20.

[153] The Court postulated that the denial of training might violate Romeo's right to safety if training were necessary to relieve his aggressive behaviors. The standard the Court used to make the determination of the amount of training required is whatever "an appropriate professional would consider reasonable to ensure his safety." *Id.* at 324. The Court thus attached a "presumption of correctness" to the judgment of the "qualified" persons in charge of Romeo's care.

It is by no means clear how such a standard applies in a typical class action right-to-safety case that arises from a lack of proper supervision, staff, or training, or from the failure to classify individuals by dangerousness or to erect more structures for safe confinement. *See supra* notes 126–30 and accompanying text. These conditions occur because of a lack of funds to operate an adequate facility and a generalized lack of concern for the welfare of the inmates. Since such conditions normally are not the product of distinct professional judgments concerning the treatment to be given a specific individual, it is not easy to determine from the Court's opinion the standard a court should apply in a typical right-to-safety case.

In two recent decisions, Daniels v. Williams, 474 U.S. 327 (1986), and Davidson v. Cannon, 474 U.S. 344 (1986), the Court held that negligent failure to protect an inmate

about the appropriate standard, the Court's opinion leaves little doubt that a constitutional right to safety is included in the notion of substantive due process, which is applicable not only to prisoners but also to retarded persons who depend upon the state for the necessities of life, and who are, supposedly, confined for their own welfare. Is there any inherent reason for this right to be limited to those dependent on the state by reason of their institutionalization? The next subsection briefly explores that question.

5. The Development of the Right to Safety Beyond Institutional Walls

Inspired perhaps by *Youngberg*, the lower federal courts have recently expanded the boundaries of the right to safety beyond institutional walls. In *Jensen v. Conrad*,[154] for example, the Fourth Circuit, in dicta, noted that the state owes a constitutional duty to protect a child who had been reported to state child protection workers as abused. There arose a duty to take steps to prevent further harm from occurring, the court held, from the moment the state became aware of the child's plight.[155]

The Seventh Circuit has also recognized this right to safety.[156] That court had held that the Constitution protects persons who, while not in state custody, are nevertheless placed by the state in a position of danger and then left defenseless. When the state, by its actions, throws a person in such a "snake-pit," the fourteenth amendment's guarantee of due process is triggered.[157] *White v. Rochford*[158] is a classic example of this idea. On a cold day the Chicago police stopped a car driven by a man transporting his two young nephews and cousin. The uncle was arrested and taken by police escort to the station for processing, but the car and the children were left on the shoulder

---

from harm while incarcerated does not violate the due process clause. Curiously, neither the *Daniels* nor *Davidson* majority cited or addressed *Youngberg*.

[154] 747 F.2d 185 (4th Cir. 1984), *cert. denied*, 470 U.S. 1052 (1985).

[155] 747 F.2d at 194.

[156] Bowers v. DeVito, 686 F.2d 616 (7th Cir. 1982); White v. Rochford, 592 F.2d 381 (7th Cir. 1979).

[157] *Bowers*, 686 F.2d at 618.

[158] 592 F.2d 381 (7th Cir. 1979).

of a busy eight-lane expressway despite the uncle's pleas. After exposure to the cold, the children decided to flee. Luckily, they escaped with their lives. The two older children were traumatized, but not physically injured. The five-year-old, an asthmatic, was hospitalized for one week following the incident. The children sued, seeking damages for their emotional and physical injuries. The Seventh Circuit held that these facts, if true, violated the right to safety even though the children were not in state custody: "[Leaving] helpless minor children subject to inclement weather and great physical damage without apparent justification . . . [is] a patently clear intrusion upon personal integrity."[159] From the opinions it is not unreasonable to expect that the Supreme Court would recognize some constitutional right to safety for those not in state custody, but the question is not free from doubt and it is by no means clear what the parameters of that right would be.[160]

B. The Lack of Development of the Right to Safety in the Foster Care Field

Although the right to safety is well-established for other persons in state custody such as prisoners, mentally ill and retarded persons, foster children have not yet received much benefit from the right. *G.L. v. Zumwalt*[161] is the only case in which final relief was provided to a class of foster children predicated on a constitutional right-to-safety theory,[162] and that case has limited precedential value because it was a consent

---

[159] *Id.* at 384.

[160] Several recent Circuit Court decisions further complicate this question. *Compare* DeShaney v. Winnebago County Dep't of Social Services, 812 F.2d 298 (7th Cir. 1987) (reckless failure by welfare authorities to protect a child from a parent's physical abuse did not violate the Constitution) *and* Estate of Gilmore v. Buckley, 787 F.2d 714 (1st Cir. 1986) (no liability imposed on state for murder committed by inmate furloughed from the House of Corrections who independently conceived of and executed the murder) *and* Bradberry v. Pinellas County, 789 F.2d 1513 (11th Cir. 1986) (swimmer suffered no constitutional deprivation due to insufficient numbers of lifeguards or inadequately trained lifeguards) *with* Ellsworth v. City of Racine, 774 F.2d 182, 185 (7th Cir. 1985), *cert. denied*, 106 S. Ct. 1265 (1986) ("When a municipality puts an individual in a position of danger from private persons and then fails to protect that individual, it cannot be heard to say that its role was merely a passive one.").

[161] 564 F. Supp. 1030 (W.D. Mo. 1983).

[162] *See supra* note 11 and accompanying text.

decree issued prior to trial.[163] There is only one case in which damages were awarded to a foster child based on the right to safety.[164] In addition, there are no reported decisions granting final injunctive relief to protect foster children from abuse and neglect in foster home placements. The limited case law suggests a judicial reluctance to accept the notion that foster children should be beneficiaries of this right.

Taylor v. Ledbetter[165] illustrates this trend. On behalf of a two-year-old girl, plaintiff sued the Gwinnett County, Georgia Department of Family and Children's Services for severe injuries that occurred while the child was in foster care. Plaintiff alleged that the child had been beaten by her foster mother and then given an overdose of unnecessary medication which caused her to become permanently comatose. The suit claimed that defendants had violated the child's constitutional right to safety by failing to investigate adequately the foster home before placing the child, by failing to supervise the foster home, and by failing to provide complete medical information to the child's physicians.[166]

The original panel in *Taylor* affirmed the district court's dismissal of the complaint for failure to state a claim upon which relief could be granted. The court characterized plaintiff's arguments as "reflect[ing] a misunderstanding of the role of federal courts."[167] Although the injuries to the child were obviously "serious," the court expressed its belief that "[f]ederal courts should exercise great caution in becoming involved in the decisions of state and local officials charged with the custody and welfare of children."[168] Thus, the court articulated what

---

[163] Generally, a consent judgment is binding only on the parties to the action. Green v. International Business Mach. Corp., 37 Ill. App. 3d 124, 345 N.E.2d 807 (1976). The Supreme Court, therefore, recently indicated that the provisions of a decree, even in a civil rights case, need not be fashioned strictly in accordance with governing law. Local 93, International Ass'n of Firefighters v. City of Cleveland, 106 S. Ct. 3063, 3077 (1986). *See also* Comment, Local Number 93, International Association of Firefighters v. City of Cleveland: *A Consent Decree Is Not an Adjudicated Order for Purposes of Title VII*, 20 Akron L. Rev. 547 (1987).

[164] *See supra* note 11 and *infra* notes 175–180 and accompanying text.

[165] 791 F.2d 881 (11th Cir. 1986), *aff'd in part, rev'd on rehearing*, 818 F.2d 791 (11th Cir. 1987) (en banc).

[166] 791 F.2d at 882.

[167] *Id.* at 883.

[168] *Id.* at 884. The opinion made no mention of *Youngberg.* Indeed, it referred to

amounted to another federal abstention doctrine. Although the Eleventh Circuit, sitting en banc, recently reversed the panel decision and held that the complaint should not have been dismissed, it left for further proceedings whether or not the child's claim "constitutes a liberty interest protected by the due process clause."[169]

Only in the Second Circuit has the right to safety been squarely recognized and enforced in the foster care context. In *Brooks v. Richardson*, the first reported case to discuss this issue, a district judge in the Southern District of New York refused to dismiss the pro se complaint of a mother who maintained that her child had been abused and neglected for over five years while in foster care.[170] The claim survived a motion to dismiss because "[a] child who is in the custody of the state and placed in foster care has a constitutional right to at least humane custodial care."[171] The court noted that the purpose of foster care is to protect the child from harm in his permanent

---

the "deliberate indifference" standard which the Supreme Court in *Youngberg* specifically rejected as insufficient for persons not convicted of crime. 457 U.S. at 312 n.11. In Atchley v. County of DuPage, 638 F. Supp. 1237 (N.D. Ill. 1986), and Gibson v. Merced County Dep't of Human Resources, 799 F.2d 582 (9th Cir. 1986), two other right-to-safety claims were rejected. In *Atchley*, the claim was rejected because the defendant was responsible for committing the child to foster care but did not have responsibility to supervise the foster home in which the injury occurred. 638 F. Supp. at 1240. In *Gibson*, the court assumed, without deciding, that a foster child has a constitutionally protected right to be free from harm. 799 F.2d at 589. However, the court found no denial of the right since the defendant's act of removing the child from the home of the foster parents, without their consent, appeared reasonable.

[169] Taylor v. Ledbetter, 818 F.2d 791, 795 (11th Cir. 1987) (en banc). In addition to the *en banc* opinion in *Taylor*, two recently decided cases granting preliminary relief to foster children indicate that the pendulum may now be swinging in the direction of recognition of the constitutional rights of children in foster care to safety. In Doe v. New York City Dep't of Social Services, 86 Civ. 4011 (MJL) (S.D.N.Y. Sept. 24, 1987) (granting motion for preliminary injunction), the court determined that the failure to obtain foster home placements immediately for children taken into state custody and the housing of these children overnight in social services offices violated plaintiffs' constitutional rights. Slip op. at 101. In L.J. v. Massinga, No. JH-84-4409 (D. Md. July 27, 1987) (granting motion for preliminary injunction), the court held that the plaintiffs, children in the Baltimore foster care system, were likely to prevail on their claims that they had a right to safety under Title IV-B and IV-E of the Social Security Act and the fourteenth amendment. Slip op. at 27–30. Pending final determination, the court awarded relief requiring the defendants to monitor foster homes, to provide appropriate medical care to foster children, to refer complaints of mistreatment for investigation, and to submit a plan to the court for the review of the continued licensing of any foster home in which a child had been maltreated. *Id.* at 53–54.

[170] Brooks v. Richardson, 478 F. Supp. 793 (S.D.N.Y. 1979).
[171] *Id.* at 795.

home. Given this purpose, the court stressed that it would be "ludicrous if the state, through its agents, could perpetrate the same evil"[172] that the placement in foster care was designed to prevent.

It was not until the Second Circuit's decisions in *Doe v. New York City Department of Social Services*[173] however, that a court actually awarded damages in a disputed case involving the right to safety. A foster child who had been beaten and sexually abused by her foster father sued, claiming that her plight had been or should have been known to the foster care agency responsible for her care.[174] In *Doe I*, the circuit court reversed a jury verdict for the defendants on the grounds that the district court had incorrectly instructed the jury on the plaintiff's constitutional rights.[175] In *Doe II*,[176] the court again reversed the trial court, this time for improperly setting aside a $225,000 jury verdict.[177] Although it found for plaintiff, the *Doe* court did not identify the source of the constitutional right it invoked and it did not discuss the rationale for finding that the right applied in a foster care setting in either of its two opinions. The Court of Appeals referred to attributes of foster care that it intimated might render the application of right-to-protection concepts developed in the prison field unduly burdensome to foster care administrators. The court distinguished foster care from other institutions on several grounds.

First, other institutions have "closer and firmer lines of authority running from superiors [to] subordinates . . . than

---

[172] *Id.* at 796.

[173] 649 F.2d 134 (2d Cir. 1981), *cert. denied*, 464 U.S. 864 (1983) (*Doe I*) and 709 F.2d 782, *cert. denied*, 464 U.S. 844 (1983) (*Doe II*).

[174] For a graphic description of the facts, see Doe v. New York City Dep't of Social Services, 649 F.2d 134, 137–40 (2d Cir. 1981), *cert. denied*, 464 U.S. 864 (1983).

[175] The *Doe I* court held that the lower court "erroneously conveyed the impression that deliberate indifference and negligence were mutually exclusive[,]" *id.* at 143, when in reality, repeated acts of negligence could be perceived as "evidence of indifference." *Id.* at 142. The Second Circuit also attached great significance to the defendants' failure to comply with their statutory duty to report allegations of abuse for investigation. This failure, the court held, could constitute deliberate indifference to plaintiff's welfare. *Id.*

[176] 709 F.2d 782, *cert. denied*, 464 U.S. 844 (1983).

[177] On remand, the jury found for plaintiff, but the same district judge set aside the verdict leading to the second appeal. Again, the Court of Appeals reversed, this time holding that there was sufficient evidence "of deliberate indifference respecting one very significant aspect of her welfare, the protection from abuse" to sustain the verdict. *Id.* at 790–92.

[those that] exist in the foster care context, particularly in respect of [sic] the relationship between agency personnel and the foster parent."[178] In addition, the court asserted that information is not as easily gained about the treatment of foster care children as it can be in other settings since there are only "occasional visits" to foster homes by agency social workers.[179] Finally, the court attached significance to the relationship between foster parents and foster care agencies which the court felt was less "unequivocally hierarchical than is the case with prison guards and a warden."[180]

Despite these supposed differences, the *Doe I* court applied the deliberate indifference standard adopted by the Supreme Court for eighth amendment prison claims. The court apparently did not feel the need to articulate a standard that would accord foster children greater protection than prisoners. Indeed, the weight of the court's logic cuts in the opposite direction.

A curious kind of constitutional vacuum, therefore, seems to exist with respect to foster children. Aside from a single and largely unexplained damage award, and a solitary consent decree, foster children remain the sole identifiable group held in the grip of the state still not accorded the benefits of the fundamental constitutional protection of safety.[181] Several factors may account for this strange state of affairs.

First, as even the *Doe* court suggested, foster care is seen as a particularly benevolent service run by the state with the best of intentions.[182] Prisons, jails, mental institutions, and homes for the retarded have long been regarded as dumping grounds for persons who are despised by society.[183] It is relatively easy for the judicial mind, once freed from the shackles of the hands-off doctrine, to imagine abuses taking place in these

---

[178] *Doe I*, 649 F.2d at 142.

[179] *Id.*

[180] *Id.*

[181] *See supra* notes 119, 121–24, 164 and accompanying text.

[182] The *Doe* court observed that where the child is placed in a foster home, there is a tendency "to respect the foster family's autonomy and integrity [and to] . . . minimize intrusiveness, given its goals of approximating a normal family environment for foster children." 649 F.2d at 142.

[183] *See* Halderman v. Pennhurst State School & Hosp., 446 F. Supp. 1295, 1299 (E.D. Pa. 1977) (quoting W. Wolfensberger, The Origin and Nature of Our Institutional Models 3 (1975)) *aff'd in part, rev'd in part*, 612 F.2d 84 (3d Cir. 1979) (en banc), *rev'd on other grounds*, 451 U.S. 1 (1980).

dark places; the same is not true for foster care. When children are taken from their parents out of an expressed concern for their welfare, and, following removal, are placed in a seemingly normal home for care by civilians who have volunteered for the job, one is not automatically concerned. The supervision of the placement is done not by wardens or jailers, but by social workers, the very epitome of a helping profession.[184] It is hard to grasp the idea that here, too, abuses can occur, and that when they do they are largely unchecked by the state.

Second, flowing from the idea that only good intentions are at work in the foster care field, is the corollary notion that decisions with regard to foster care require a type of decision-making skill which is not appropriately the subject of judicial review. After all, the job of a foster care agency involves nothing less than child rearing, a discipline whose complexity has generated scores of theories and occupied the attention of numerous scholars. It may have been this thought that motivated the Supreme Court in a case involving the due process rights of a foster child and a foster parent to remain together, to declare that foster care administration involves "issues of unusual delicacy . . . where professional judgments regarding desirable procedures are constantly and rapidly changing."[185]

Even in *Doe*, these factors surfaced and influenced the court's decision. The court stated that given the goal of establishing a normal home for the child the court should "minimize intrusiveness" into the foster family.[186] The Ninth Circuit exercised a similar caution when it proclaimed a "need for flexibility [in foster care] in order to accomplish what is best for [the] child."[187]

Third, in addition to the courts' reluctance to entertain right to safety cases, litigators do not seem to press claims to safety in foster care with the same vigor that they exert in the prison

---

[184] *See* Wyman v. James, 400 U.S. 309, 322–23 (1971). H. Ginott, Between Parent and Child 215–16 (1965).

[185] Smith v. Organization of Foster Families for Equality and Reform, 431 U.S. 816, 855 (1977). There is a parallel between this reasoning and underlying concepts of judicial and prosecutorial immunity, such as that expressed by the Court in Imbler v. Pachtman, 424 U.S. 409 (1976), and Stump v. Sparkman, 435 U.S. 349 (1978).

[186] *Doe I*, 649 F.2d at 142.

[187] *Gibson*, 799 F.2d at 589.

and mental health fields. Their hesitancy may be accounted for by the fact that there are fewer public interest lawyers working in the foster care field than in the other fields where this issue has been litigated,[188] and the few that are in the field have primarily chosen to concentrate on other pressing issues which foster care administration raises, including questions of permanency planning and preventive services, often to the exclusion of right-to-safety concerns. Success in a right-to-safety case will not provide a permanent home for the children, only a safer placement while they remain in temporary care.[189] Thus, both the dearth of lawyers pursuing the issue and the reluctance of the courts to entertain the claims have combined to create a barrier between foster children and the constitutional promise of safe custodial conditions. It is now necessary to consider whether any principled reasons exist that might render the right to safety inapplicable to foster children.

III. The Search for a Principled Basis for Withholding the Right to Safety

There are three possible explanations for denying a constitutional right to safety to foster children while providing it to other groups or persons cared for by the state. First, children in foster family care are not institutionalized. Second, foster children come into state care voluntarily. Finally, foster children may be subject to the Supreme Court's ruling in *Ingraham v. Wright*,[190] which held that school children do not have an eighth amendment right to be protected from physical harm by their custodians. This section analyzes whether any of these proposed differences between foster children and other groups provide a

---

[188] In 1980, there were approximately 700 public interest lawyers working in 117 public interest law centers. Mnookin, In the Interest, *supra* note 8, at 45. Less than seven percent of these lawyers concern themselves with children's issues, a number smaller than a "medium-sized law firm in Denver, Colorado." *Id.* at 49.

[189] *See supra* notes 170–174 and accompanying text, and *infra* notes 200–201 and accompanying text. Public interest lawyers in other fields are not always put to such a hard choice. If public interest lawyers in the prisoners' rights field, for example, were forced to choose between litigation that would lead to the release of some of their clients because of invalid convictions or litigation to improve the living conditions of all of their clients while they are in prison, there might never have been the extensive case law on prison reform.

[190] 430 U.S. 651 (1977).

principled basis for a determination that foster children are not eligible for the constitutional protection of the right to safety, and demonstrates that they do not.

A. Custody Without Institutionalization

Children in foster family care do not reside in large communal custodial settings like prisons or mental institutions.[191] Moreover, because of their age, children in foster care would be under the control of an adult whether or not they were placed in foster care. In this sense, children in foster care differ from institutionalized adults who, but for their confinement, would be free to do what they wished and live where they pleased.

These factors were important to the Supreme Court in *Lehman v. Lycoming County Children's Services*,[192] which held that a foster child was not in "custody" for purposes of the habeas corpus jurisdiction of the federal court. The case arose when a mother brought suit, on behalf of her three sons, to challenge the constitutionality of a Pennsylvania statute under which the state obtained custody of her children and terminated her parental rights.[193] Without reaching the merits, the Court held that habeas corpus did not lie because the children "are not prisoners . . . [who] suffer any restrictions imposed by a state criminal justice system."[194] Justice Powell for the majority stated that foster children:

---

[191] *See supra* note 6 and accompanying text.

[192] 458 U.S. 502 (1981).

[193] Ms. Lehman placed her three sons in the custody of the Lycoming County Children's Services Agency, which placed them in foster homes. She visited her sons monthly, but did not request their return for three years, at which time the Lycoming County Children's Services Agency initiated parental termination proceedings. The district court terminated her parental rights based on Ms. Lehman's "limited social and intellectual development" and her "five-year separation from the children." *Id.* at 504. The Pennsylvania Supreme Court affirmed the ruling. *Id.* at 505.

Ms. Lehman sought review in the United States Supreme Court by a writ of certiorari rather than by appeal. Review was denied. Lehman v. Lycoming County Children's Services, 439 U.S. 880 (1978). She then sought a writ of habeas corpus pursuant to 28 U.S.C. §§ 2241, 2254 in the United States District Court of the Middle District of Pennsylvania, requesting a declaration of invalidity of the Pennsylvania statute under which her parental rights were terminated, a declaration that she was the children's legal parent, and an order releasing the children into her custody. *Id.* at 505–06. The district court dismissed the petition, without a hearing, on jurisdictional grounds. This dismissal was affirmed by the Third Circuit, sitting en banc. *Id.* at 506.

[194] *Id.* at 510.

are in the "custody" of their foster parents in essentially the same way, and to the same extent, other children are in the custody of their natural or adoptive parents. Their situation in this respect differs little from the situation of other children in the public generally; they suffer no unusual restraints not imposed on other children.[195]

In *Child v. Beame*,[196] the district court made a similar observation in the course of dismissing a foster child's claim to a constitutional right to adoption. The court stated that:

the attempt to equate the child plaintiff's status while in the foster care of the state with those who are taken into custody under a civil commitment because of mental illness, physical retardation, incorrigibility or similar causes is somewhat farfetched. The civilly committed have been deprived of their liberty by the state while the state's action in taking the child plaintiffs into foster care, whether with an institution or foster parent, is not a deprivation of liberty. The state has merely provided a home in substitution for the one the parents failed to provide.[197]

These cases, however, do not stand for the proposition that foster children are insufficiently deprived of liberty to invoke judicial review of the conditions of their care. First of all, neither *Lehman* nor *Child* were challenges to the living conditions of foster care. Instead, both courts were confronted with claims that questioned the very presence of the children in foster care.[198] In *Child*, the court made this distinction clear when it noted that "plaintiffs do not question the living conditions in

---

[195] *Id.* at 510.

[196] 412 F. Supp 593 (S.D.N.Y. 1976).

[197] *Id.* at 608.

[198] In both *Lehman* and *Child*, the complaints were not related to the conditions of the foster care placement, but to the fact or duration of placement, respectively. In *Lehman*, the fact of placement in foster care was at issue since plaintiff's parental rights were terminated upon her request to have her children released to her from foster care. In *Child*, plaintiff children alleged a deliberate policy of keeping children in foster care settings without seeking adoptive homes. 412 F. Supp. at 596.

their foster homes."[199] But in a right-to-safety case, the plaintiff does not rely upon a liberty claim of restricted movement, as was the case in both *Lehman* and *Child*. Rather, the claim concerns the substantive due process liberty interest in being held safely.[200] The key to the existence of a right to safety lies in the recipient's dependence upon the state for the maintenance of a safe living environment,[201] not in the recipient's assertion that the state cannot restrict his liberty at all.

For example, prisoners cannot choose who they want to provide needed medical care, what they will eat, or with whom they will share their living quarters. These decisions, made by their keepers, will, in large measure, determine the quality of their lives. It is this dependence on the state for the very essentials of life, not the fact of institutionalization, that has prompted the courts to recognize the entitlement to safety in the institutional context.[202]

Foster children, like prisoners, rely on the state for shelter, clothing, food, and freedom from physical abuse or neglect. Although they may not be held in large institutional settings, they are just as dependent on the state for their needs as are prisoners. This similarity is not diminished because the state chooses to act through private agents in the foster care context. Surely, if the state maintained a group home for children on state property, providing two adults per child, it would be most difficult to distinguish the children's situation from that of prisoners. In that circumstance, the state, having institutionalized the children, would presumably be compelled to comply with the constitutional requirements, including the right to safety, applicable to institutionalized persons generally.[203] Regardless of the locus of confinement, the sole purpose for the state's intervention into the children's lives is protection.[204] Both the

---

[199] *Id.* at 608.

[200] *See supra* notes 145–148 and accompanying text.

[201] Estelle v. Gamble, 429 U.S. 97, 103 (1976) ("An inmate must rely on prison officials to treat his medical needs; if the authorities fail to do so, those needs will not be met. In the worst cases, such a failure may actually produce physical . . . torture. . . . In less serious cases, denial of medical care may result in pain and suffering.")

[202] *See, e.g.,* Estelle v. Gamble, 429 U.S. 97, 103 (1976); Halderman v. Pennhurst State School & Hosp., 446 F. Supp. 1295, 1318 (E.D. Pa. 1977), *aff'd in part, rev'd in part*, 612 F.2d 84 (3d Cir. 1979) (en banc), *rev'd on other grounds*, 451 U.S. 1 (1980).

[203] *See supra* note 146 and accompanying text.

[204] *See, e.g.,* Conn. Gen. Stat. Ann. § 17-38a (West 1987) ("The public policy of

rationale for foster care placement and the dependence on the state emphasize the absurdity in excluding foster children from the constitutional protection from harm merely because they are not institutionalized in the traditional way.

Lehman's discussion of the liberty implications of foster family placement is inapposite to a right-to-safety analysis for another reason: *Lehman* dealt solely with a question of statutory, not constitutional, construction. There the issue for decision was whether a foster child's movement was sufficiently restricted such that a federal habeas corpus petition would lie. The Court held that, for purposes of habeas corpus, the children were not in "custody,"[205] and that the mother, therefore, could not seek a federal court order to obtain their release from care. A right-to-safety case involves a different issue. In contrast to a habeas corpus petition, which is calculated to review the legality of custody, a right-to-safety case questions not the fact of confinement, but the conditions of confinement.[206] Thus, *Lehman* is not authority for the proposition that foster children lack a constitutional right to be protected, but only that the federal habeas corpus statute is not the way to assert such a right.

B. Voluntary Placement and the Right to Safety

The overwhelming majority of foster care placements are voluntary, meaning that the child's parents have consented to a

---

[the] state is: To protect children whose health and welfare may be adversely affected through injury and neglect; to strengthen the family and to make the home safe for children by enhancing parental capacity for good child care; to provide a temporary or permanent nurturing and safe environment for children when necessary. . . ."); Mass. Gen. Laws Ann. ch. 119 § 1 (West 1987); N.Y. Soc. Serv. Law § 395 (McKinney 1983) (a public welfare district shall be responsible for the welfare of children residing or found in its territory who are in need of public assistance, support and protection); Fla. Stat. Ann. § 409.145 (West 1986). *See also supra* note 17 and accompanying text. Courts have expressed this purpose as well. *See, e.g.,* Brooks v. Richardson, 478 F. Supp. 793, 795–96 (S.D.N.Y. 1979).

[205] *Lehman,* 458 U.S. at 511.

[206] In Preiser v. Rodriguez, 411 U.S. 475 (1973), the Court confirmed that the Civil Rights Act, 42 U.S.C. § 1983, can be used to challenge the conditions of confinement. Habeas corpus, 28 U.S.C. § 2241 (1966) is the appropriate device with which to challenge the propriety of confinement.

placement.[207] Consent to foster care occurs when physical or mental illness, economic problems or other family crises make it impossible for parents—particularly single mothers—to provide a stable home life for their children.[208] Often the consensual placement follows a state-sponsored investigation into conditions of a deteriorating home caused by these pressures. Other times, a parent may seek government help.[209] In either event, the normal concomitant of foster care for most children is the consent of their parents. In this sense, children enter foster care in a manner that is quite different from the means by which other groups normally enter state control. Prisoners, to take the most obvious example, do not as a routine matter ask to be imprisoned.[210]

The decision by the Supreme Court in *Youngberg* can be understood as supporting the notion that the distinction between voluntary and involuntary institutionalization is significant. In no fewer than eleven places in the majority opinion, Justice Powell stated that the due process right to safety which the Court was recognizing for the first time applied to the involuntarily committed.[211] Given the emphasis by the Court on the involuntary nature of the confinement, one must ask whether the entitlement to safety in foster care should depend on, or be

---

[207] *See* Areen, *Intervention Between Parent and Child: A Reappraisal of the State's Role in Child Neglect and Abuse Cases*, 63 Geo. L.J. 887, 921–22 (1975) (as many as 50% voluntary placements); A. Gruber, *supra* note 6, at 138 (Studies from New York and elsewhere estimate the percentage of voluntary placements between 50 and 90%. In Massachusetts, 58.8% of the placements are voluntary); Mnookin, *In Whose Best Interest?*, *supra* note 6, at 601; Musewicz, *supra* note 10, at 639; Information Services, Characteristics of Children in Foster Care, New York City Reports, table 11 (1976).

[208] Smith v. OFFER, 431 U.S. 816, 824 (1977).

[209] A. Kadushin, *supra* note 6, at 316. Voluntary placement in foster care is usually a two-part process. Initially parents and a local social service official enter a voluntary placement agreement (VPA), which sets forth the terms and conditions of a child's care and transfers the custody of the child from the parent to the authorized agency.

If a child will be in custody for more than 30 days, the social services official must obtain judicial approval of the VPA. The judge must be shown that the parents voluntarily and knowingly entered the VPA, that they were unable to provide adequate care at home, and that the child's best interests would be promoted by placement in foster care. Joyner v. Dumpson, 712 F.2d 770, 773 (2d Cir. 1983); Smith v. OFFER, 431 U.S. 816, 824 n.9 (1977).

[210] Even prisoners who voluntarily enter guilty pleas are not choosing to come under state control. A guilty plea voluntarily and intelligently given is a defendant's choice among several limited alternatives; it is a bargain with the prosecutor for what is seen as the "least bad" option. North Carolina v. Alford, 400 U.S. 25, 31–39 (1970).

[211] 457 U.S. at 310, 312, 313, 314, 315, 316, 318, 321, 322.

influenced by, the voluntary nature of most foster care place-ments.[212] For three reasons, it should not.

First, characterizing foster care placements as voluntary is highly questionable; certainly they are not voluntary for the person under care. The children themselves have no more choice about placement than an involuntarily committed pris-oner or mental patient. They are rarely asked whether they desire to be in foster care,[213] and it is not clear that they should be asked. It is impossible to believe that all but a small per-centage of children would have the maturity and ability to make an informed judgment.[214] No rational system would seek the consent of a three-year-old, for example, as a condition of un-dertaking his care. As then-Chief Justice Burger put it: "[M]ost children, even in adolescence, simply are not able to make sound judgments concerning many decisions, including their need for medical care or treatment."[215]

Yet even the choice for the foster child's parent is largely illusory as well. Many parents reluctantly agree to relinquish custody temporarily in the face of a clear inability to care for their child by themselves.[216] This is particularly true of impe-cunious parents, since, unlike the middle class who can arrange for alternatives when family problems occur, "the poor have

---

[212] Consent can sometimes make a difference. In Joyner v. Dumpson, 712 F.2d 770 (2d Cir. 1983), for example, the Second Circuit rejected a facial challenge to the loss of parental control entailed in the New York State scheme for voluntary foster care placement. The court relied in part upon the absence of evidence that consent was coerced and in part on the idea that the state could constitutionally condition consent to foster care on the diminution of parental rights. Id. at 777–82. But the court's ruling was limited. It made plain that if, on remand, plaintiffs' allegations of a "Dickensian portrait of the New York foster care system" were true, and if it was a system that "greedily grasps control over every child placed within its domain," the result might be different despite the presence of consent. Id. at 783. Joyner, therefore, does not support the argument that consent to placement, in and of itself, eliminates the obligation of the state to comply with the Constitution.

[213] In his study, Gruber found that twenty-seven percent of the children voluntarily placed in foster care were opposed to the decision. A. Gruber, supra note 6, at 141. The lack of weight of the child's preference is reflected in most state statutes dealing with foster care, where either the child's consent is not sought or is sought for limited purposes only after he reaches a certain age (commonly 14). See, e.g., Minn. Stat. § 260.245; Ohio Rev. Code Ann. § 2151.353 (Baldwin 1987); N.J. Stat. Ann. § 30:4c-11 (West 1981); Mass. Gen. Laws Ann., ch. 119, § 23 (West 1958).

[214] One study found that almost half of all foster children were too young to under-stand the reasons that they were placed in foster care. A. Gruber, supra note 6, at 141.

[215] Parham v. J.R., 442 U.S. 584, 603 (1979).

[216] See supra notes 208–09 and accompanying text.

little choice but to submit to state-supervised child care when family crises strike."[217] Voluntariness of placement is illusory for another reason: the state social worker who investigated the home may have threatened the parent with the permanent loss of the child unless there was "consent" to temporary placement.[218] Whereas punitive and coercive techniques are usually expressly prohibited, pressure is often seen by the caseworker as legitimate. Thus the area between free choice and unacceptable coercion often is unclear.[219]

It is a small wonder that most parents in this predicament opt for voluntary placement. They must either consent to the placement, retaining some chance of having the child returned later, or refuse consent and face the prospect of defending a state-sponsored child protection proceeding in the local family court, which, if they lose, significantly diminishes the possibility of retaining parental rights.[220] Even in those cases where the consent is genuine, it cannot reasonably be understood to be a voluntary decision to expose a child to unsafe conditions.[221] Indeed, such a decision would constitute child abuse as that term is defined in most state laws.[222]

---

[217] Smith v. OFFER, 431 U.S. at 834. *See also* Association for Retarded Citizens v. Olson, 561 F. Supp. 473, 484 (D.N.D. 1982), *aff'd*, 713 F.2d 1384 (8th Cir. 1983).

[218] Mnookin, *In Whose Best Interest?*, *supra* note 6, at 601.

[219] Levine, *Caveat Parens: A Demystification of the Child Protection System*, 35 U. Pitt. L. Rev. 1, 12–13 (1973). *See also* Musewicz, *supra* note 10, at 639 (such parents are "frequently uneducated and without legal advice except for that offered by the social worker encouraging the placement").

[220] Mnookin, *In Whose Best Interest?*, *supra* note 6, at 601. *See also* Children's Defense Fund, *supra* note 7, at 18; Levine, *supra* note 219, at 23–24.

[221] The government may not condition the receipt of these, or any, benefits on the non-assertion of a constitutional right even if the benefits are considered a "mere privilege." L. Tribe, American Constitutional Law 510 (1978). *But see* Town of Newton v. Rumery, 107 S. Ct. 1187 (1987), where the Court held lawful a knowing and intelligent waiver of the right to file a civil rights complaint in exchange for dismissal of criminal charges.

[222] Such treatment would, for example, constitute neglect under New Jersey law: "Neglect of a child shall consist in any of the following acts, by anyone having the custody or control of the child: . . . failure to do or permit to be done any act necessary for the child's physical or moral well-being." N.J. Stat. Ann. § 9:6-1 (West 1976). *See also, e.g.*, Mass. Gen. Laws Ann. ch. 119 § 1 (West 1958); Conn. Gen. Stat. § 17-38a (West 1975). Federal standards also suggest that exposure to unsafe conditions constitutes abuse or neglect. Placing a child in such conditions, for example, falls within the definition of child abuse and neglect given in the Child Abuse Prevention and Treatment Act: "[C]hild abuse and neglect means the physical or mental injury, sexual abuse or exploitation, negligent treatment, or maltreatment of a child under the age of eighteen . . . by a person who is responsible for the child's welfare under circumstances which

The second reason that the constitutional right to safety should not depend upon the voluntariness of the placement is that the right, as even the *Youngberg* Court appears to have recognized, is too basic to depend upon that factor alone. The Supreme Court's reasoning in *Youngberg* itself, notwithstanding its repeated use of the term "involuntarily committed," suggests that the right to safety encompasses the voluntarily as well as the involuntarily confined. Relying on precedent, the Court stated: "If it is cruel and unusual punishment to hold convicted criminals in unsafe conditions, it must be unconstitutional to confine the involuntarily committed—who may not be punished at all—in unsafe conditions."[223] "An individual's liberty is no less worthy of protection merely because he has consented to be placed in a situation of confinement."[224] If a person lost all claim to constitutional protection because he consented to confinement, "the state arguably could chain confined residents to their beds and administer wanton physical beatings without violating the constitution. This . . . represents a complete abdication of the state's constitutional duty to respect the rights of all its citizens to fundamental liberty."[225]

Third, the right to safety must apply to voluntary admissions because of the established constitutional principle that a state must administer constitutionally even those services which it only provides voluntarily.[226] Similar treatment by the Supreme

---

indicate that the child's health or welfare is harmed or threatened thereby. . . ." 42 U.S.C. § 5102 (1982). This act and other federal child protection acts are discussed in D. Besharov, The Abused and Neglected Child: Multi-Disciplinary Court Practice 11–33 (1978).

[223] 457 U.S. at 315–16. Furthermore, "[among] the historic liberties so protected was a right to be free from, and to obtain judicial relief for, unjustified intrusions on personal security." *Ingraham v. Wright*, 430 U.S. at 673. *See also* Association for Retarded Citizens v. Olson, 561 F. Supp. 473, 485 (D.N.D. 1982), *aff'd* 713 F.2d 1384 (8th Cir. 1983).

If Justice Powell really meant to limit the right to safety to the involuntarily confined, he picked a strange case in which to do it. Romeo was committed by court order on petition of his mother, his sole caretaker, who stated that she could no longer care for him. Chief Justice Burger, in his concurrence, was not wrong when he said that "the state did not seek custody of respondent; the family understandably sought the state's aid to meet a serious need." 457 U.S. at 329.

[224] Association for Retarded Citizens, 561 F. Supp. at 485.

[225] *Id. See also* Society for Good Will to Retarded Children v. Cuomo, 737 F.2d 1239, 1245 (2d Cir. 1984).

[226] *See* Perry v. Sindermann, 408 U.S. 593, 597 (1972). This principle has been relied upon in several cases dealing with voluntary and involuntary confinement. *See*,

Court of the state provision of education illustrates this principle. The Supreme Court has repeatedly held that there is no right to compel a state to establish a system of free education for its citizens.[227] However, the Court has also held that once it elects to provide such a system, it must administer that system in conformity with constitutional commands.[228] Similarly, although there is no recognized affirmative constitutional right to the provision of foster care,[229] the state, having chosen to provide the service, is obligated to administer it constitutionally.[230]

In short, since most children cannot consent to foster care, since few parents truly consent to foster care, since none consent to unsafe care for their children, since safety is too important to be bartered or dependent on the voluntary nature of the service, and since the provision of a service by the state must be administered constitutionally, the constitutional right to safety must follow all children into care regardless of whether or not their placement is voluntary.

C. Ingraham v. Wright *and the Constitutional Right to Safety*

Ingraham v. Wright[231] held that the eighth amendment does not protect school children from excessive corporal punishment.[232] The Court also held that children may be physically punished by their teachers without a prior due process hearing.[233] Taken together, these holdings might suggest that foster children also lack constitutional protection from physical abuse,

---

e.g., Youngberg, 457 U.S. at 315–16; Society for Good Will to Retarded Children v. Cuomo, 737 F.2d at 1245–46.

[227] San Antonio Indep. School Dist. v. Rodriguez, 411 U.S. 1, 29–39 (1973), and cases cited therein.

[228] Goss v. Lopez, 419 U.S. 565 (1975).

[229] *See* Child v. Beame, 412 F. Supp. 593, 602 (S.D.N.Y. 1976).

[230] *See* Society for Good Will to Retarded Citizens v. Cuomo, 737 F.2d 1239, 1246 (2d Cir. 1984). Indeed, most state foster care laws do not even discuss distinctions between voluntary and involuntary placement when dealing with the level of care to which the foster child is entitled. *See, e.g.,* N.Y. Soc. Serv. Law §§ 358a, 372a, 372c (Consol. 1978); Minn. Stat. Ann. § 257.071 (West 1982); Ohio Rev. Code Ann. § 3107.02 (Baldwin 1987); N.J. Stat. Ann. § 30.4C (West 1981); Mass. Gen. Laws Ann., ch. 119, § 23 (West 1969).

[231] 430 U.S. 651 (1977) (In a 5-4 decision, Justice White—joined by Justices Brennan, Marshall and Stevens—filed a sharp dissent in which they decried the majority opinion).

[232] *Id.* at 662–71.

[233] *Id.* at 672–82.

but such a result is not compelled by either the reasoning or result of *Ingraham*.

Ingraham does not foreclose right-to-safety cases for foster children because the rationale the Court used for holding that school children do not require constitutional protection from physical abuse does not apply to foster care. *Ingraham* placed great emphasis on the openness of the public schools and the watchfulness of school children's parents. Schools, the Court also pointed out, are not closed, twenty-four-hour-a-day institutions.[234] These factors, which the court found make mistreatment of school children unlikely, were contrasted with the case of prisons, where the eighth amendment does apply. Judicial scrutiny of penal conditions engendered by eighth amendment commands is important precisely because prisons are institutions not usually open to public view, and because, as a group, prison inmates are powerless and friendless.[235]

For purposes of constitutional protection and judicial intervention, foster children have more of the attributes of prisoners than of school children. Like prison, and unlike school, foster care is a total institutional setting. No school bell rings for foster children each day releasing them from care. Foster children, unlike school children, cannot rely on the watchful eyes of their parents to protect them from abuse; they are in foster care precisely because their parents cannot care for them.[236]

The Court in *Ingraham* also held that procedural due process protection is not required before corporal punishment may

---

[234] *Id.* at 670. In an interview with Bill Moyers broadcast the evening before his resignation from the Supreme Court, Justice Powell, the author of the majority opinion, offered this additional insight into the Court's reasoning:

I knew from my own experience in public education that the public schools are quite public in the sense that PTA's—Parent Teacher Associations—school board meetings are open to the public and parents come and testify before the school board. I've sat through some long evenings with parents complaining about this or that, that if there were any abuse of this provision of the Florida Statute (providing for corporal punishment) that pressure would immediately or promptly be brought on the particular school to correct it. And I just thought it was not a situation for the judicial system of our country to become involved in.

The Search for the Constitution, Interview with Justice Lewis Powell (PBS broadcast, June 25, 1987) (transcribed by author).

[235] *Ingraham*, 430 U.S. at 669.

[236] *See supra* notes 6, 8, 17, 87 and accompanying text.

be inflicted because physical punishment of school children is
generally "unremarkable in physical severity."[237] Civil and criminal state remedies were more than adequate to control those
few instances in which excessive punishment of school children
did occur.[238] Unfortunately, the same cannot be said of foster
care. The same factors that render foster care more akin to a
prison or juvenile detention facility than a school also provide
an environment in which serious abuse goes unchecked and
may remain unknown to the outside world.[239]

The *Ingraham* Court limited itself to plaintiff's eighth
amendment and procedural due process claims;[240] it expressly
stated that it had no occasion to decide whether "corporal punishment of a public school child may give rise to an independent
cause of action to vindicate substantive rights under the Due
Process Clause."[241] Since the *Ingraham* record did not disclose
widespread abuse, the issue was not before the Court. The
problem of foster family abuse, however, does raise this unre-
solved issue.[242]

IV. The Search for a Remedy for Violence in Foster Care

It is well-established that for every right there should be a
corresponding remedy.[243] It is particularly important to find an

---

[237] *Ingraham*, 430 U.S. at 677.

[238] *Id.* at 672–82.

[239] As suggested *infra*, state tort remedies in this field are not adequate. *See infra*
notes 245–73 and accompanying text.

[240] For a comparison of procedural due process and substantive due process, *see
generally* J. Nowak, R. Rotunda & J. Young, Constitutional Law 324–25, 416–24 (2d
ed. 1983).

[241] 430 U.S. at 679 n.47. This distinction explains how the Court in *Youngberg*
could hold that the right to safety for the mentally retarded flows from the substantive
provision of the fourteenth, and not from the eighth, amendment. 457 U.S. at 314–15
& n.16. The Court has similarly held that rights of pretrial detainees derive from the
due process clause, not the eighth, amendment. *See, e.g.*, Block v. Rutherford, 468
U.S. 576 (1984); Bell v. Wolfish, 441 U.S. 520 (1979).

[242] In a post-*Ingraham* decision, the Fourth Circuit held that school children have
a substantive due process right to be protected from corporal punishment that amounts
to "brutal and inhumane abuse of official power literally shocking to the conscience."
Hall v. Tawney, 621 F.2d 607, 613 (4th Cir. 1980). *See also* Doe "A" v. Special School
Dist. of St. Louis County, 637 F. Supp. 1138 (E.D. Mo. 1986); Brooks v. School Bd.
of Richmond, 569 F. Supp. 1534, 1536 (E.D. Va. 1983).

[243] *See* Marbury v. Madison, 5 U.S. (1 Cranch) 137, 163 (1803) (The laws of the
United States furnish remedies for the violation of vested legal rights.).

effective remedy for violence in foster care. Without the basic right to safety, the dignity of the foster child and his ability to develop into a mature, functioning adult are diminished.[244] This section canvasses the available remedies for foster care violence, and demonstrates that the structural injunction, not the damage action, offers the only effective remedy for violence in foster care.

A. The Unavailability of Damage Actions

Abused foster children are increasingly turning to state damage actions for compensation for the injuries that they have suffered. Some of these suits, which have survived pretrial dismissal,[245] reveal a formidable array of state tort law barriers to ultimate success. Foremost among these is the common law doctrine of sovereign immunity. In its purest form, the doctrine bars a suit against a state agency providing a governmental service.[246] Suits are permitted in the doctrine's more modern version, but only if the plaintiff can show that the governmental activity sued upon is ministerial rather than discretionary.[247] The theory of this distinction is that the state ought to be free to carry on its wide-ranging activities unimpeded by the risk of liability for decisions that involve its discretionary, policymaking functions.[248]

In jurisdictions that recognize the modern sovereign immunity doctrine, a key issue in a suit brought by an abused foster child is whether or not an agency's actions involved

---

[244] *See supra* notes 66–68 and accompanying text.

[245] *See, e.g.,* Mayberry v. Pryor, 134 Mich. App. 826, 352 N.W.2d 322 (1984), *rev'd,* 422 Mich. 579, 374 N.W.2d 683 (1985) (summary judgment in favor of foster parents reversed); Zink v. Dep't of Health and Rehabilitative Services, 496 So. 2d 996 (Fla. App. 1986) (summary judgment in favor of the defendant reversed).

[246] Osborn v. Bank of the United States, 22 U.S. (9 Wheat.) 738 (1824). *See generally* W. Prosser & W. Keeton, *supra* note 117, § 131 at 1044.

[247] *See, e.g.,* Koepf v. County of York, 198 Neb. 67, 251 N.W.2d 866 (1977). Despite important variations, all states retain immunity from suits that result from discretionary governmental activities. The variations are as follows: a few states retain total immunity from suit; some still preclude suits by individuals in courts, but have created administrative agencies that have the authority to decide claims against the state; others have consented judicially to suits in only a very limited class of cases. Most states, however, allow suits for non-discretionary activities that cause injury. W. Prosser & W. Keeton, *supra* note 117, § 131, at 1044.

[248] *Id.* at 1039.

discretionary decisionmaking. If the court finds that they did, sovereign immunity bars the suit regardless of the agency's negligence. The courts that have examined the issue have split on whether the conditions of foster care placement involve this judicially protected discretion. Several jurisdictions have held that there is no sovereign immunity,[249] because there is no discretion involved in the foster care supervision process. Others, however, have applied sovereign immunity.[250] These courts, pointing to the "delicate and complex judgments" required of foster care agencies,[251] and alluding to foster care as an altruistic governmental service[252] entitled to a high degree of judicial deference, have shielded agencies from "hindsight scrutiny by the courts."[253]

Even in jurisdictions that do not accord sovereign immunity to foster care agencies, however, recovery is difficult. The agency may escape liability by shifting its portion of the blame for the injury to the foster parents.[254] Having done so, it is then able to avoid responsibility for the injury under the doctrine of respondeat superior, on the ground that foster parents are not employees of the state.[255] The policy reasons that one court assigned for this result are revealing. That court held that the legislature could not have intended that foster parents be regarded as state employees because: "A legal theory conferring employee status on foster parents . . . would place an intolerable burden on the state and might well diminish the beneficial effect of the foster care program."[256]

---

[249] See, e.g., Koepf v. County of York, 198 Neb. 67, 251 N.W.2d 866 (1977); National Bank of South Dakota v. Leir, 325 N.W.2d 845 (S.D. 1982).

[250] Brown v. Phillips, 178 Ga. App. 316, 342 S.E.2d 786 (1986); Walker v. State, 104 Misc. 2d 221, 428 N.Y.S.2d 188 (1980); Pickett v. Washington County, 31 Or. App. 1263, 572 P.2d 1070 (1977); Jiminez v. County of Santa Cruz, 42 Cal. App. 3d 407, 116 Cal. Rptr. 878 (1974).

[251] Pickett v. Washington County, 31 Or. App. 1263, 1268, 572 P.2d 1070, 1074 (1977).

[252] Id. at 1268, 572 P.2d at 1074.

[253] Id.

[254] See, e.g., Blanca v. Nassau County, 103 A.D.2d 524, 480 N.Y.S.2d 747 (1984), aff'd sub nom. Blanca C. By Carmen M. v. Nassau County, 65 N.Y.2d 712, 481 N.E.2d 545, 492 N.Y.S.2d 5 (1985); Parker v. St. Christopher's Home, 77 A.D.2d 921 (1980).

[255] See, e.g., New Jersey Property-Liability Ins. Guar. Ass'n v. State, 184 N.J. Super. 348, 446 A.2d 189 (1982), rev'd, 195 N.J. Super. 4, 477 A.2d 826, cert. denied, 99 N.J. 188, 491 A.2d 691 (1984); Kern v. Steele County, 322 N.W.2d 187 (Minn. 1982).

[256] New Jersey Property-Liability Ins. Guar. Ass'n v. State, 195 N.J. Super. 4, 16, 477 A.2d 826, 833 (1984).

Even when sovereign immunity is not invoked, or blame is shifted to foster parent negligence, the courts have resisted finding negligent supervision by the agency. In *Koepf v. County of York*,[257] for example, the Supreme Court of Nebraska affirmed a directed verdict in favor of a foster care agency. In that case, a fourteen-month-old child had died from severe physical injuries inflicted by his foster parent. Four months prior to the child's death, the agency had been told that the foster mother was not emotionally stable and that she did not take good care of the child.[258] Expert testimony also revealed that the foster mother was on medication for "physiological depression and mental confusion."[259] Finally, there was testimony that three weeks before the child was killed, he appeared at a state court hearing with bruise marks on his body.[260] Despite this substantial evidence of agency negligence, the Nebraska Supreme Court agreed that this was still not enough evidence to submit the case to a jury.

Sovereign immunity, the unavailability of respondeat superior, and the courts' reluctance to find an agency negligent in its supervisory capacity make the opportunity for recovery against an agency slight. They do not preclude damage actions against the foster parents themselves, or the individual caseworker assigned to the case. The chance of recovery, however, is slim there as well.

In several jurisdictions, foster parents are immune from suit for negligent supervision of their foster children,[261] on the theory that foster parents stand in the place of permanent parents and therefore are entitled to the same family immunity.[262] If this "loco parentis"[263] doctrine of parental immunity is applied, no

---

[257] 198 Neb. 67, 251 N.W.2d 866 (1977).

[258] Id. at 76, 251 N.W.2d at 872.

[259] *Id.*

[260] *Id.*

[261] Brown v. Phillips, 178 Ga. App. 316, 342 S.E.2d 786 (1986); Goller v. White, 20 Wis. 2d 402, 122 N.W.2d 193 (1963).

[262] *In re* Diane P., 120 N.H. 791, 424 A.2d 178 (1980); Rutkauski v. Wasko, 286 A.D. 327, 143 N.Y.S.2d 1 (1955); Hush v. Devilbiss Co., 77 Mich. App. 639, 259 N.W.2d 170 (1977); Thomas v. Inmon, 268 Ark. 221, 594 S.W.2d 853 (1980).

[263] "Loco parentis" refers to a person "who intentionally accepts the rights and duties of natural parenthood with respect to a child not his own." *In re* Diane P., 120 N.H. 791, 424 A.2d 178 (1980) (citing Niewiadomski v. United States, 159 F.2d 683, 686 (6th Cir. 1947), *cert. denied*, 331 U.S. 850 (1947)). *See generally* 59 Am. Jur. 2d *Parent and Child* § 77 (1987).

judgment can be awarded for negligence against foster parents for their failure to maintain a safe home. Even if the parental immunity doctrine is not invoked, however, the chance of a recovery remains slight. Foster parents, normally drawn from the ranks of moderate-income families, are often judgment proof,[264] and as they are not considered state employees, the states do not indemnify them for judgments entered against them.[265]

Suits under state law against individual, state-employed caseworkers, while theoretically possible in states without sovereign immunity doctrines, also are not likely to succeed because state-employed caseworkers are generally judgment-proof.[266] Federal civil rights damage actions are unavailing as well, because the Supreme Court has approved several imposing eleventh amendment,[267] qualified immunity,[268] and *Monell*

---

[264] *See* Cathey v. Bernard, 467 So.2d 9, 10 (La. App. 1985).

[265] New Jersey Property-Liability Ins. Guar. Ass'n v. State, 184 N.J. Super. 348, 446 A.2d 189, *rev'd*, 195 N.J. Super. 4, 477 A.2d 826, *cert. denied*, 99 N.J. 188, 491 A.2d 691 (1984).

[266] Note, *A Damages Remedy for Abuses by Child Protection Workers*, 90 Yale L.J. 681, 695 (1981).

[267] *See* Hans v. Louisiana, 134 U.S. 1 (1890) (state immunity); Pennhurst State School and Hosp. v. Halderman, 465 U.S. 89 (1984) (state immunity); Brandon v. Holt, 469 U.S. 464 (1985) (official immunity). For the latest version of the enormous controversy over the scope of the eleventh amendment, compare the majority decision written by Justice Powell with Justice Brennan's dissent in Welch v. State Dep't of Highways, 107 S. Ct. 2941 (1987). For a sampling of the scholarly debate, see Shapiro, *Wrong Turns: The Eleventh Amendment and the Pennhurst Case*, 98 Harv. L. Rev. 61 (1984); Fletcher, *A Historical Interpretation of the 11th Amendment: A Narrow Construction of an Affirmative Grant of Jurisdiction Rather than a Prohibition Against Jurisdiction*, 35 Stan. L. Rev. 1033 (1983); Field, *The Eleventh Amendment and Other Sovereign Immunity Doctrines* (pts. 1 & 2), 126 U. Pa. L. Rev. 515 (1978), 126 U. Pa. L. Rev. 1203 (1978).

[268] An individual action for damages against a state official may be defeated because of a qualified immunity that shields the defendant from liability for good faith violations of constitutional rights, except those that were clearly established at the time of the conduct which forms the basis of the cause of action. Harlow v. Fitzgerald, 457 U.S. 800 (1982). *See also supra* note 125 and accompanying text. Given the lack of development of the right to safety for foster children, it is possible that a damage claim would fail on that ground, at least initially. Jensen v. Conrad, 747 F.2d 185 (4th Cir. 1984), *cert. denied*, 470 U.S. 1052 (1985) (right-to-safety case against state officials for failure to protect a child from known risk of harm by parent dismissed because right to protection is not clearly established). *See also* Comment, *Defining the Scope of the Due Process Right to Protection: The Fourth Circuit Considers Child Abuse and Good Faith Immunity*, 70 Cornell L. Rev. 940 (1985).

doctrine[269] barriers to recovery in actions that charge violations of federal constitutional rights,[270] or "constitutional torts."[271]

Although there have been several recent ground-breaking opinions that appear to raise the possibility of liability,[272] the impediments to recovery remain formidable. The number of money recoveries for foster care abuse is minuscule compared to the extent of actual abuse, and in those few cases in which judgments have been obtained, the amount of the judgment is quite low. Research has uncovered only four cases in which damages have been awarded on state-created tort actions for foster care abuse. The judgments granted in these cases range from a low of $4,500 for the death of a foster child to a high of $46,000. The total amount obtained for all of these cases is a paltry $85,500.[273] Even if the outlook for damage actions were more promising, they have other serious drawbacks which make them unattractive vehicles for reform of the foster care system.[274] The next subsection explains why damage actions, even if theoretically obtainable, are not a promising avenue of reform.

---

[269] In a constitutional tort action a municipality is not liable for acts of its employees unless the actions were pursuant to a deliberate municipal policy. Monell v. Dep't of Social Services, 436 U.S. 658 (1978). This is not to say that recovery is impossible, as the *Doe* case discussed earlier shows. *See supra* notes 173, 175–77 and accompanying text.

[270] For a discussion of the various barriers to recovery for constitutional tort actions, see Spurrier, *Federal Constitutional Rights: Priceless or Worthless? Awards or Money Damages Under Section 1983*, 20 Tulsa L.J. 1, 26 (1984).

[271] "Constitutional torts" is the term used by Professor Christina Whitman to describe such damage actions. Whitman, *Constitutional Torts*, 79 Mich. L. Rev. 5, 7 (1980).

[272] Several courts have rejected the doctrine of sovereign immunity and have allowed suits against states, counties, placement agencies or social workers to proceed. *See supra* note 249. Other courts have held that suits were not barred by parental immunity, since the foster parents were not considered to have *loco parentis* status. Andrews v. Ostego County, 112 Misc. 2d 37, 446 N.Y.S.2d 169 (1982); Mayberry v. Pryor, 422 Mich. 579, 374 N.W.2d 683 (1985).

[273] Vonner v. State Dep't of Pub. Welfare, 273 So. 2d 252 (La. 1973) (wrongful death, $4,500); Little v. Utah State Div. of Family Serv., 667 P.2d 49 (Utah 1983) (wrongful death, damages of $20,000 plus funeral expenses and costs); Cathey v. Bernard, 467 So. 2d 9 (La. App. 1985) (wrongful death and survival action, total of $15,000 awarded); Jenks v. State, 507 So. 2d 877 (La. App. 1987) (case settled for $46,000). A review of reported tort damage awards contained in *National Jury Verdict Review and Analysis* failed to disclose any unofficially reported judgments. Even when the *Doe* case—the only other known award—is added, the total recovery from the American legal system for the extensive amount of abuse and neglect in foster care is only $310,500.

[274] For a less pessimistic view of the case law, see Comment, *supra* note 10, at 979–84.

B. The Inadequacy of Damage Actions

Individual damage actions, even if available, are not useful mechanisms for obtaining reform. They tend to focus attention, myopically, on individual culpability for past actions instead of on detection and correction of institutional deficiencies that contribute to the maltreatment of foster children. By its nature, a claim for damages examines past wrongs. It seeks to compensate for an injury which has already occurred.[275] By contrast, an equitable action for an injunction seeks to prevent harm from occurring in the first instance.[276]

Because an individual damage action is concerned with the culpability of the assigned caseworker or foster parent for the abuse suffered by the child, rather than with the system itself, it is unlikely that a damage claim will bring attention to the root causes of the problem. It thus diverts attention from the real culprit in the drama: the state's failure to fund and maintain an adequate foster care system.

With the real problem obscured, two contradictory and unhelpful tendencies compete for attention. The first is to shift blame for the danger to children onto overworked caseworkers or poorly selected and ill-trained foster parents.[277] Such charges are often unfair as these people often lack the support or environment to do an acceptable job. Furthermore, this shift of focus diverts desperately needed funds from structural reform to individual payments that change nothing in the system.

Moreover, the fear of liability may influence qualified people who might otherwise be attracted to this form of public service to seek other kinds of work. Those who do enter or remain in the field may engage in what has been called "defensive social work,"[278] a term referring to practices followed because of a desire to avoid liability rather than to advance the interests of the children.[279] Workers in the system may find

---

[275] See Restatement (Second) of Torts § 821 (B)(i) (1979); P. Schuck, Suing Governments 15 (1983).

[276] See Restatement (Second) of Torts § 821 (B)(i) (1979); Rothstein v. Wyman, 467 F.2d 226, 241 (2d Cir. 1972); P. Schuck, supra note 275, at 15–16.

[277] See D. Besharov, The Vulnerable Social Worker 15, 65, 133. Cf. Whitman, supra note 271, at 60.

[278] D. Besharov, supra note 277, at 138. Cf. Whitman, supra note 271, at 53.

[279] See D. Besharov, supra note 277, at 136–38.

themselves saddled with a conflict of interest: their understandable desire to avoid personal liability versus the best interests of the children dependent on their services. This second tendency is even more dangerous than the first as it may lead courts, reluctant to impose liability upon "vulnerable" caseworkers, foster parents, or agencies, to render decisions, such as *Koepf*,[280] that restrictively define the range of protections guaranteed to foster children.[281] Another form of defensive social work is immobilized decisionmaking. The whole system will collapse if liability precludes responsible decisionmaking in areas such as reporting and investigating suspected cases, the adequacy of foster parents, and termination of parental rights.[282]

The final casualty of a regime focused solely on the question of individual responsibility is the loss of public education that attends a more broad-based examination of societal fault in the foster care system.[283] For similar reasons, Professor Christine Whitman recommended that for civil rights actions generally, "the time has come to admit that equitable actions may be a [more] preferable form of judicial redress" than damage actions for the vindication of constitutional rights.[284] Thus, even if the chances of obtaining damage awards were better, individual damage actions, which operate only after the injury has occurred, are not useful mechanisms for obtaining the structural reform of foster care systems that is needed to ensure the right to safety in foster care. Examination of the structural injunction, undertaken in the next section, demonstrates its superiority as a form of relief in the foster care area.

C. The Structural Injunction

"Structural" or "institutional injunctions"[285] grant broad, detailed relief as a remedy to constitutional violations in the

---

[280] Koepf v. County of York, 198 Neb. 67, 251 N.W.2d 866 (1977).

[281] *Cf.* Whitman, *supra* note 271, at 41–47.

[282] *Id.* at 138.

[283] D. Besharov, *supra* note 277, at 159.

[284] Whitman, *supra* note 271, at 47–48. *But see* Levine, *Social Worker Malpractice: A New Approach Toward Accountability in the Juvenile Justice System*, 1 J. Juv. L. 101 (1977).

[285] See, e.g., Rudenstine, *Institutional Injunctions*, 4 Cardozo L. Rev. 611 (1983) (using the term "institutional injunctions" to describe equitable orders entered in cases involving state and mental institutions); Chayes, *The Role of the Judge in Public Law*

operation of government-run services. The structural injunction focuses prospectively on changing organizational behavior.[286] Beginning with *Brown v. Board of Education*,[287] and coming to maturity in later school desegregation cases,[288] the structural injunction has since been used by federal courts in a wide variety of civil rights contexts.[289]

Structural injunctions have been the subject of substantial judicial[290] and scholarly[291] comment, and remain highly contro-

---

Litigation, 89 Harv. L. Rev. 1281, 1281–84 (1976) (terming the cases "Public Law" litigation); Robertson, *supra* note 119, at 146 (terming the relief ordered "Structural Injunctions Directed at Inmate Violence"); Fiss, *Foreword: The Forms of Justice*, 93 Harv. L. Rev. 1 (1979) (terming the litigation "Structural Reform" litigation); Diver, *The Judge as Political Powerbroker: Superintending Structural Change in Public Institutions*, 65 Va. L. Rev. 43, 49 (1979) (terming the cases "Institutional Reform" litigation); Note, *Complex Enforcement: Unconstitutional Prison Conditions*, 94 Harv. L. Rev. 626 (1981) (distinguishing cases seeking "complex enforcement" through a detailed injunction to "transform a social institution" from "discrete adjudication," which involves only an application of legal forms to particular instances of wrongdoing).

[286] Robertson, *supra* note 119, at 146, and authorities cited therein.

[287] 347 U.S. 483 (1954), 349 U.S. 294 (1955). *Brown* has been frequently mentioned as the progenitor of all modern structural injunction cases. *See, e.g.,* Rudenstine, *Judicially Ordered Social Reform*, 59 S. Cal. L. Rev. 451 (1986); Rosenberg & Phillips, *Institutionalization of Conflict in the Reform of Schools: A Case Study of Court Implementation of the PARC Decree*, 57 Ind. L.J. 425 (1982).

[288] *See* P. Dimond, Beyond Busing: Inside the Challenge to Urban Segregation (1985); Taylor, *Brown, Equal Protection, and the Isolation of the Poor*, 95 Yale L.J. 1700, 1709–12 (1986); Moss, *Participation and Department of Justice School Desegregation Consent Decrees*, 95 Yale L.J. 1811 (1986). Important desegregation cases of the last decade include Milliken v. Bradley, 418 U.S. 717 (1974); Columbus Bd. of Educ. v. Penick, 443 U.S. 449 (1979); Dayton Bd. of Educ. v. Brinkman, 443 U.S. 526 (1979).

[289] *See, e.g.,* Levy v. Urbach, 651 F.2d 1278 (9th Cir. 1981) (institution for treatment of persons suffering from leprosy); French v. Owens, 538 F. Supp. 910 (S.D. Ind. 1982) (prisons); Rhem v. Malcolm, 432 F. Supp. 769 (S.D.N.Y. 1977), *aff'd in part*, 527 F.2d 1041 (2d Cir. 1975) (jails); Morgan v. Sproat, 432 F. Supp. 1130 (S.D. Miss. 1977) (juvenile detention facility); Welsch v. Likins, 373 F. Supp. 487 (D. Minn. 1974) *aff'd in part*, 550 F.2d 1122 (8th Cir. 1977) (mental institution); New York State Ass'n for Retarded Children v. Rockefeller, 357 F. Supp. 752 (E.D.N.Y. 1973) (institution for the mentally retarded); Pennsylvania Ass'n for Retarded Children v. Pennsylvania, 334 F. Supp. 1257 (E.D. Pa. 1971), *adopted*, 343 F. Supp. 279 (E.D. Pa. 1972) (special education).

[290] Compare, for example, the majority, concurring and dissenting opinions in Rhodes v. Chapman, 452 U.S. 337 (1981). At the close of the October 1986 term, four of the sitting justices generally opposed structural injunctions while four approved of them. Justice Scalia has yet to address this topic as a justice of the Supreme Court. Justice Powell's resignation will do nothing to lessen the controversy. For a discussion of the clash of views among the current justices, see Rudenstine, *supra* note 285. Lower federal judges have also addressed this topic. Lasker, *Judicial Supervision of Institutional Reform*, 5 Crim. Just. Ethics 2, 79 (1986); Weinstein, *The Effect of Austerity on Institutional Litigation*, 6 L. and Hum. Behav. 145 (1982); Johnson, *Observation — The Constitution and the Federal District Judge*, 54 Tex. L. Rev. 903 (1976).

[291] Among the major works favoring the use of structural injunctions are A. Neier, *supra* note 14; Rudenstine, *supra* note 285; Eisenberg & Yazell, *The Ordinary and the*

versial. Opponents contend that they violate the separation of powers, erode federalism barriers, and compromise democratic principles. Supporters counter, often with arguments drawn from history, that the use of broad equitable federal injunctive powers does not represent a radical departure from the traditional judicial role. But the criticism most often uttered in opposition to this form of relief is that "courts lack the expertise and administrative capacity necessary to improve"[292] large bureaucratic governmental systems such as the foster care system.

No doubt there are serious impediments to effective implementation of a decree calling for safe treatment of foster children. Implementation may require substantial restructuring of a large, bureaucratic institution. Reform will require piercing the institutional veil, for unless the will to change is transmitted to the caseworkers who select and supervise the foster homes, and to the foster parents themselves, the right to safety will be a chimera.[293] Moreover, organizational and psychological change alone will be insufficient. Safety will come only at a price. Increased appropriations will be needed to hire and train more and better-qualified caseworkers and foster parents and to provide support services for foster parents and children.[294]

The only remedy that holds significant promise of accomplishing this feat is a structural injunction. In contrast to the limited possibilities for success with damage actions, the evidence suggests that structural injunctions do engender improvements. Of course, the benefits are not felt overnight; change is often measured by "inches and centimeters" rather than "leaps

---

Extraordinary in Institutional Litigation, 93 Harv. L. Rev. 465 (1980); Fiss, *supra* note 285; Goldstein, *A Swann Song for Remedies: Equitable Relief in the Burger Court*, 13 Harv. C.R.-C.L. L. Rev. 1 (1978). Works criticizing this form of relief include Horowitz, *Decreeing Organizational Change: Judicial Supervision of Public Institutions*, 1983 Duke L.J. 1265; Diver, *supra* note 285; Mishkin, *Federal Courts as State Reformers*, 35 Wash. & Lee L. Rev. 949 (1978); Frug, *The Judicial Power of the Purse*, 126 U. Pa. L. Rev. 715 (1978); Nagel, *Separation of Powers and the Scope of Federal Equitable Remedies*, 30 Stan. L. Rev. 661 (1978).

[292] Comment, *supra* note 94, at 388.

[293] *See supra* notes 277–78 and accompanying text. *See also* Lowry, *supra* note 7, at 279.

[294] *See also* Zeigler, *supra* note 13, at 40–42 (review of the authority that holds that inadequate resources cannot be used as an excuse to avoid compliance with constitutionally guaranteed rights).

and bounds."[295] The cases involving prison violence exemplify the successful use of structural injunctions.[296]

In a law review article, Professor James E. Robertson recently surveyed the results of four prison cases in which structural injunctions designed to reduce prison violence were obtained.[297] He found that with the passage of time and vigorous efforts at implementation, the decrees "result[ed] in a significant lessening of prison violence."[298] Similar results have been obtained in the implementation of structural injunctions dealing with other concerns. Prison systems in general have been reshaped,[299] and institutions for the mentally ill and the mentally retarded have been drastically altered.[300] Moreover, the available evidence on cases that have addressed educational issues indicates that compliance with judicially ordered reform is ob-

---

[295] Rebell, *Implementation of Court Mandates Concerning Special Education: The Problems and the Potential*, 10 J.L. & Educ. 335, 355 (1981). *See also* Note, *The* Wyatt *Case: Implementations of a Judicial Decree Ordering Institutional Change*, 84 Yale L.J. 1338, 1356 (1975).

[296] A decree seeking to reduce prison violence is, if anything, more difficult to implement than one concerned with foster parent abuse and neglect. Prisons are typically populated with adults who have demonstrated a proclivity for extreme violence. Robertson, *supra* note 119, at 106. *See also* H. Toch, Police, Prisons and the Problems of Violence, 53 (1977), *cited in* Robertson, *supra* note 119. The existence of an active and violent prison subculture is well known and amply documented. *Id.* at 108–09 and authorities cited therein. If significant results can be obtained in that inherently volatile environment, then positive change should be possible in the more benign setting of foster family care. Although it is true that the state has less control over the happenings in a civilian foster home than in the highly regimented setting of a prison, there are ample means available for the control of violence in foster care. *See supra* notes 53–65 and accompanying text. If these safeguards are followed, there is every reason to believe that foster care mistreatment can be greatly minimized with less effort than would be required to achieve safety in prisons.

[297] Robertson, *supra* note 119, at 146–55.

[298] *Id.* at 154. *See, e.g.*, Feliciano v. Barcelo, 497 F. Supp. 14 (D.P.R. 1979). *Feliciano* involved the Puerto Rico prison system. In 1981–82, there were 49 deaths and 75 serious injuries in the Puerto Rico prison system. By 1983–84, the numbers had declined to one death and 17 serious injuries, one-seventh the rate prior to the judgment. Robertson, *supra* note 119, at 153, citing a letter from Cirilo Castro Penaloza, Acting Administrator, Administracion de Correccion, Puerto Rico (Undated, postmarked Feb. 1985); Holt v. Sarver, 300 F. Supp. 825 (E.D. Ark. 1969); Hamilton v. Schiro, 338 F. Supp. 1016 (E.D. La. 1970); Palmigiano v. Garrahy, 443 F. Supp. 956 (D.P.R. 1977), *remanded*, 599 F.2d 17 (1st Cir.), *aff'd*, 616 F.2d 598 (1st Cir. 1979), *cert. denied*, 449 U.S. 839 (1980).

[299] *See generally* M. Harris & D. Spiller, After Decision: Implementation of Judicial Decrees in Correctional Settings (1977).

[300] *See* D. Rothman & S. Rothman, *supra* note 120 (successful implementation of the Willowbrook remedial decree resulted in the community placement of half of the facility's residents; it also brought about positive changes in the state's policy regarding the care of retarded persons).

tainable.[301] In all these areas, the initial recalcitrance of defendants to obey the decree was overcome by patient, yet persistent, efforts by courts and by plaintiffs' attorneys.

Structural injunctions tend to bring benefits which are broader than those strictly related to literal compliance with court orders. The "focused compulsion"[302] engendered by a structural law suit causes policy makers to attend to problems that they would otherwise ignore.[303] Moreover, the cases themselves may "sensitize . . . the public . . . to the need for . . . reform."[304] By serving the traditional federal judicial role of the community's "sensitive conscience,"[305] the courts have stimulated other branches of government to act responsively to the needs highlighted by the decrees.[306] In the child welfare field, this "informing function"[307] of institutional litigation would be particularly valuable. Structural injunctions, despite the difficulty of enforcement, would "focus attention on the systemic nature of problems plaguing child welfare."[308]

Even if the potential benefits of the structural injunction were less clear, the case for granting structural injunctions would still be compelling. Given the lack of realistic alternatives,[309] it would be a default of constitutional responsibility for

---

[301] M. Rebell & A. Block, Educational Policy Making and the Courts 65 (1982) (compliance achieved in most of 41 randomly selected education decrees not involving desegregation). The results of school desegregation decrees are less clear. *Compare* United States Civil Rights Commission, Fulfilling the Letter and Spirit of the Law: Desegregation of the Nation's Schools, Letter of Transmittal (1976) (communities in which desegregation proceeds without major incident far outnumber those like Boston and Louisville) *with* H. Kalodner & J. Fishman, Limits of Justice: The Court's Role in School Desegregation (1978) (case studies of several school desegregation cases where the level of compliance was minimal). The spotty results in school desegregation cases may be explained by their high visibility and the tremendous amount of opposition they receive.

[302] Rebell, *supra* note 295, at 344 n.26.

[303] Johnson, *The Role of the Federal Courts in Institutional Litigation*, 32 Ala. L. Rev. 271, 273–79 (1981).

[304] Comment, *supra* note 94, at 392. *See also* Jacobs, *The Prisoners' Rights Movement and Its Impacts: 1960–80*, in N. Morris & M. Tonry, Crime and Justice: An Annual Review of Research 459 (1981).

[305] Weinstein, *supra* note 290, at 151.

[306] Note, *Implementation Problems in Institutional Reform Litigation*, 91 Harv. L. Rev. 428, 463 (1977). For an example of how this phenomenon has already occured in foster care litigation, see *infra* note 388 and accompanying text.

[307] A. Neier, *supra* note 14, at 237.

[308] D. Besharov, *supra* note 277, at 159. *See also* Lowry *supra* note 7, at 275.

[309] *See supra* notes 81–92.

the courts not to attempt to enforce foster children's crucial constitutional right to safety. One commentator, who surveyed the somewhat disappointing results of the federal courts' efforts to achieve desegregation in our nation's schools, observed not long ago that "[f]or all the faults that have characterized adjudication, it is not possible to conceive of a constitutional system in which no institution of government is prepared to declare and enforce constitutional rights."[310] Structural injunctions are clearly the remedy of choice for the problem of violence in foster care. The question arises as to the appropriate forum for assertion of such claims. The next section addresses that question.

V. The Search for a Forum

Both federal and state courts have jurisdiction to entertain right-to-safety cases.[311] But, if a structural injunction is the preferable remedy to enforce the right to safety against foster care violence, federal courts are the better forum in which to vindicate that right. Federal courts historically have been called upon to protect the constitutional rights of citizens from encroachments by state officials. While state courts have in recent years become more active participants in the dialogue of constitutional adjudication,[312] they lack the institutional attributes necessary to overcome the bureaucratic and political obstacles to the achievement of a safe foster care system. This section discusses the superiority of federal courts as a forum for right-to-safety cases and explains why two abstention doctrines that operate to close federal courts to some claims—the domestic relations exception and the *Younger v. Harris* doctrine—are not applicable to right-to-safety cases.

---

[310] H. Kalodner & J. Fishman, *supra* note 301, at 23.

[311] Maine v. Thiboutot, 448 U.S. 1, 11 (1980) (section 1983 actions may be brought in the state courts). *See also* Martinez v. California, 444 U.S. 277, 283 n.7 (1980); M. Schwartz & J. Kirklin, Section 1983 Litigation: Claims, Defenses and Fees 15 (1986).

[312] *See* Brennan, *State Constitutions and the Protection of Individual Rights*, 90 Harv. L. Rev. 489 (1977); Collins, *Looking to the States*, Nat'l L.J., S-2 (Sept. 29, 1986). *See also* Recent Developments in State Constitutional Law (P. Bamberger ed. 1985).

A. The Superiority of Federal Courts

Since the passage of the fourteenth amendment and the Civil Rights Act of 1871, federal courts have been seen as the "fundamental protectors of . . . federal rights."[313] The primary basis for confidence in the federal courts in this role is the protection provided by the Article III requirement of lifetime appointment for federal judges.[314] This requirement largely insulates the federal judiciary from the political process, giving federal judges the level of independence needed to counter the majoritarian tendencies—expressed through elected officials[315]—to tolerate a substandard system of foster care. Since state judges often lack this electoral independence,[316] they are subject to political pressures that dilute their ability to order and supervise reform of state institutions, such as the foster care system.[317] Unlike a case where a single individual is raising a single constitutional issue, the judge in a foster care reform case is asked to oversee the fundamental restructuring of a major social service system in order to guarantee an entire class essential constitutional rights.[318]

Staying power and independence are central to redressing the injustices of foster care systems. The deficiencies in foster care are not easily correctable; they arise in large part because of bureaucratic inertia and a lack of commitment by elected officials to the allocation of sufficient resources to provide the services truly needed to protect the children in care. It is all too easy for legislators to forget the needs of foster children when

---

[313] M. Redish, Federal Jurisdiction: Tensions in the Allocation of Judicial Power 1 (1980). See also Pulliam v. Allen, 466 U.S. 522, 541 (1983) (continued to recognize the importance of a federal forum for the protection of federal rights); Mitchum v. Foster, 407 U.S. 225 (1972) (reemphasized that federal courts play a crucial role in the protection of federal rights); Whitman, supra note 271, at 24 n.114 (citing Allen v. McCurry, 449 U.S. 90, 105 (1980). See also Puerto Rico v. Branstad, 107 S. Ct. 2802 (1987).

[314] U.S. Const. art. III, § 1 ("The judges . . . shall hold their offices during good behavior."). See also Neuborne, The Myth of Parity, 90 Harv. L. Rev. 1105, 1127–28 (1977) (removal only by impeachment means maximum insulation from majority pressures).

[315] Neuborne, supra note 314, at 1127–28.

[316] State judges are ordinarily elected for a fixed term. See generally Neuborne, supra note 314, at 1122.

[317] Neuborne, supra note 314, at 1127–28 and authorities cited therein.

[318] See supra notes 302–08 and accompanying text.

lobbyists press them for more popular services such as police, fire protection and education.

There are other reasons why federal courts provide a superior forum to state courts for foster care right-to-safety cases. First, state judges, as a group, are less likely to be as familiar with federal law as federal judges are.[319] Most of the state judge's time is spent adjudicating claims that arise solely under a particular state's laws. In contrast, federal judges spend the bulk of their time adjudicating federal claims. For this reason, federal judges have much greater familiarity with federal constitutional problems.[320] Second, federal judges tend to have what Professor Neuborne terms a "psychological set"[321] that disposes them to be more receptive to constitutional claims. They are "heirs of a tradition of constitutional enforcement."[322]

Without the familiarity with federal law, support and time, environment of receptivity, and the political independence that characterize the federal judiciary, it is difficult to envision consistent, appropriate decisions in foster care right-to-safety cases. This is not to say that state judges are uniformly unable to handle competently foster care reform cases. In fact, there are instances in which state judges have done so.[323] However, given the added obstacles that they must overcome to achieve the results required, foster care reform cases belong in federal court.[324] The following section examines whether either of two

---

[319] Neuborne, *supra* note 314, at 1121–24.

[320] M. Redish, *supra* note 313, at 2. Another reason that the federal courts seem better suited to address the right-to-safety cases is that the work load of state judges is much greater than that of their federal colleagues. Neuborne, *supra* note 314, at 1122.

[321] Neuborne, *supra* note 314, at 1124.

[322] *Id.*

[323] *E.g., In re* P., No. 78J04583 and No. 78J04584, slip. op. (Ky. 1983), *cited in* Moraine, *Making Foster Care Work*, 4 Cal. Law. 24, 53 (1984); Palmer v. Cuomo, 121 A.D.2d 194, 503 N.Y.S.2d 20 (1986).

[324] It has been argued that there is empirical support for the notion of parity between federal and state courts. Solimine & Walker, *Constitutional Litigation in Federal and State Courts: An Empirical Analysis of Judicial Parity*, 10 Hastings Const. L.Q. 213 (1983). The data from that study, however, do not support the conclusion that state courts are as competent to handle class action right-to-safety claims for structural injunctive relief as are federal courts. The data were drawn from reported decisions without apparent differentiation between individual and class claims, or between established and as-yet-unestablished rights. *Id.* at 238. Individual adjudications of established rights differ from the class claims of previously unrecognized rights pertinent to the problem of foster care abuse. In such uncharted waters, the sympathy, independence and expertise of federal judges is especially important. Whitman, *supra* note 271, at 24

major abstention doctrines would prevent the federal courts from examining foster care reform cases.

B. Abstention Is Inappropriate in Right-to-Safety Cases

In *Younger v. Harris*,[325] the Supreme Court gave new life to an abstention doctrine applicable to civil rights cases.[326] The *Younger* doctrine is an exception to the general duty of federal courts to enforce federal law and "fearlessly protect"[327] federal constitutional rights from encroachment by state officials.[328] *Younger* instructs district courts to refrain from adjudicating properly presented federal constitutional issues when the relief sought would result in halting a state criminal proceeding, unless plaintiffs can demonstrate "extraordinary circumstances."[329] As long as federal plaintiffs have an opportunity to present their claim in the state criminal trial, and are not suffering irreparable injury, then the federal court should abstain.[330] Justice Black explained that "Our Federalism"[331] is the driving force behind

---

n.114. In addition, the authors report that federal courts uphold federal claims in a greater percentage of cases than do state courts. Solimine & Walker, *supra*, at 240, table II (federal courts uphold federal claims in 41% of cases, compared with 32% in state courts). For the views of other commentators who favor the availability of federal forums for vindication of federal rights, see Doernberg, *There's No Reason for It; It's Just Our Policy: Why the Well-Pleaded Complaint Rule Sabotages the Purposes of Federal Question Jurisdiction*, 38 Hastings L.J. 597, 647–50 (1987); Mishkin, *The Federal "Question" in the District Courts*, 53 Colum. L. Rev. 157, 168 (1953). For a contrary view, see Bator, *The State Courts and Federal Constitutional Litigation*, 22 Wm. & Mary L. Rev. 605 (1981).

[325] 401 U.S. 37 (1971).

[326] The abstention doctrine now commonly associated with *Younger* traces its roots back to *In re* Sawyer, 124 U.S. 200 (1888). *See generally* Zeigler, *An Accommodation of the* Younger *Doctrine and the Duty of the Federal Courts to Enforce Constitutional Safeguards in the State Criminal Process*, 125 U. Pa. L. Rev. 266, 269–82 (1976) (tracing the history of the nonintervention doctrine of *Younger* and arguing that the Supreme Court's interpretation of the doctrine differs during periods of judicial activism and judicial restraint).

[327] Parker v. Turner, 626 F.2d 1, 6 (6th Cir. 1980).

[328] Mitchum v. Foster, 407 U.S. 225, 242 (1972) (The Court described federal courts "as guardians of the people's federal rights—to protect the people from unconstitutional action under color of state law."). *See also* Morial v. Judiciary Comm. of La., 565 F.2d 295, 298–99 (5th Cir. 1977), *cert. denied*, 435 U.S. 1013 (1978).

[329] *Younger*, 401 U.S. at 53.

[330] *Id.* at 43–45.

[331] *Id.* at 44.

the doctrine.[332] The Supreme Court has steadily enlarged the boundaries of this highly controversial doctrine by holding that the underlying policies dictate restraining federal involvement not only when state criminal proceedings are pending, but also during civil proceedings in which the state is a party in its "sovereign capacity."[333]

Indeed, the doctrine creates an enclave of virtual immunity from lower court enforcement of federal constitutional rights. Federal courts have justified the application of the *Younger* doctrine as necessary to prevent the unseemliness of allowing a state court defendant to come "running into federal court seeking an adjudication of his rights and/or an injunction halting the criminal prosecution."[334] To permit federal jurisdiction in such a case is considered undesireable because it would seem to imply that the state judiciary is unable or unwilling to enforce federal rights.[335] In addition, the bifurcation of the state case

---

[332] Two other forms of abstention in use in federal courts today do not apply to right-to-safety cases or would require expansion of existing doctrines to apply: *Pullman* abstention and *Burford* abstention. *See* Railroad Comm'r of Texas v. Pullman Co., 312 U.S. 496 (1941); Burford v. Sun Oil Co., 319 U.S. 315 (1943). *Pullman* only applies when one case raises both a federal constitutional question and an unclear question of state law, the resolution of which might modify the federal question or obviate the need to decide it. A right-to-safety case generally raises only a federal issue. Moreover, applying *Pullman* abstention would require waiting for the state court's decision on the state issues hypothetically involved, decisions that could theoretically remain pending during the child's entire time in foster care and permitting the harm to the foster child to persist.

Similarly, *Burford* abstention, in which the federal court defers to the state court to avoid interference with complex state administrative activities, usually by dismissing the action, would be inapplicable in right-to-safety cases. The *Burford* doctrine had been designed to apply to administrative actions, while right-to-safety cases deal with judicial issues. 319 U.S. at 332. *See generally* C. Wright, The Law of Federal Courts § 52 (4th ed. 1983) (describing four variations of the abstention doctrine); Redish, *Abstention, Separation of Powers, and the Limits of the Judicial Function*, 94 Yale L.J. 71 (1984).

[333] Trainor v. Hernandez, 431 U.S. 432, 444 (1977). Over the years, the Supreme Court has applied the doctrine to civil proceedings in which the state seeks civil enforcement, *id.*, proceedings regulating the conduct of attorneys, Middlesex County Ethics Comm. v. Garden State Bar Ass'n, 457 U.S. 423 (1982), proceedings dealing with civil contempt, Juidice v. Vail, 430 U.S. 327 (1977), proceedings concerning child custody, Moore v. Sims, 442 U.S. 415 (1979) and, most recently, proceedings dealing with posting bonds pending appeal in a purely private case, Pennzoil Co. v. Texaco, Inc., 107 S. Ct. 1519 (1987).

[334] Parker v. Turner, 626 F.2d 1, 3 (6th Cir. 1980).

[335] *See* Huffman v. Pursue, Ltd., 420 U.S. 592, 604 (1975) (stressed that federal court interference with a state's process is "an offense to the State's interest," and "can readily be interpreted 'as reflecting negatively upon the state court's ability to enforce constitutional principles.'"), *reh'g denied*, 421 U.S. 971 (1975) (quoting Steffel v.

that results when federal courts take jurisdiction of a case already in a state court threatens to throw the administration of state criminal justice into confusion.[336]

The doctrine's boundaries were enlarged in *Moore v. Sims*.[337] There a sharply divided Court applied the *Younger* abstention doctrine to state child-protection proceedings. The plaintiffs in *Moore* were suspected of abusing their children. State officials had removed the children from school and placed them involuntarily in foster care, without notice to the parents and without a hearing pursuant to the Texas Family Code Act. The plaintiffs challenged the constitutionality of several sections of the code.[338] After several unsuccessful attempts to obtain a hearing before the state courts, plaintiffs turned to federal court and secured injunctive relief.[339] The Supreme Court, however, found that the district court should have abstained, as the enjoined state court proceedings touched on matters which are "a traditional area of state concern."[340] Because the state has a vital interest in "quickly and effectively removing the victims of child abuse from their parents,"[341] and because the child protection proceedings, under state abuse and neglect laws, are "in aid of and closely related to state criminal statutes,"[342] the Court held that the *Younger* doctrine was applicable. Finding none of the exceptions to the doctrine satisfied, the Court ordered abstention.[343]

Thompson, 415 U.S. 452, 462 (1974). *See also* Juidice v. Vail, 430 U.S. 327 (1977) (applying the *Younger* doctrine to halt the federal court's interference in the state contempt process).

But see, e.g., Redish, *The Doctrine of* Younger v. Harris: *Deference in Search of a Rationale*, 63 Cornell L. Rev. 463, 482–84 (1978) (rejecting the need for deference to avoid insulting state courts).

[336] *Trainor*, 431 U.S. at 446. *See also* Moore v. Sims, 442 U.S. 415, 429–30 (1979) (noting that when federal courts intervene, they deprive the state judiciary of an opportunity to develop state policy); Wells, *The Role of Comity in the Law of Federal Courts*, 60 N.C.L. Rev. 59 (1981).

[337] 442 U.S. 415 (1979).

[338] Sections of chapters 11, 14, 15, 17, and 34 in Title 2 of the Texas Family Code were challenged. *See* Note, Moore v. Sims: *A Further Expansion of the* Younger *Abstention Doctrine*, 1 Pace L. Rev. 149 (1980).

[339] *Moore*, 442 U.S. at 418–22.

[340] *Id.* at 435.

[341] *Id.* (quoting Sims v. State Dep't of Pub. Welfare, 438 F. Supp. 1179, 1189 (S.D. Tex. 1977)).

[342] *Id.* at 423, (quoting Huffman v. Pursue, Ltd., 420 U.S. 592, 604 (1975)).

[343] *Id.* at 433–35.

Although *Moore v. Sims* concerned an attempt by parents to regain custody of their children, courts have since interpreted the decision as requiring the application of the *Younger* principle to all family court proceedings.[344] While one must therefore ask whether the *Younger* doctrine applies or should apply to foster child right-to-safety cases, an examination of the policies underlying the doctrine reveals that the answer is no. The *Younger* doctrine developed as a response to special cases where the state's interest in enforcement of its own laws outweighs the strong federal interest in the federal court enforcement of federal constitutional rights.[345] In right-to-safety cases, the important constitutional rights at stake outweigh any possible interference with the state's law enforcement interests. In such a context, the balance tips against *Younger* abstention because the predicate for the doctrine's applicability is missing.

Federal prison reform cases provide an appropriate analogy. Cases concerning prison conditions have never been considered subject to the *Younger* doctrine,[346] primarily because plaintiffs in these cases do not seek to overturn their convictions or to shorten their incarceration. Thus, federal involvement in these cases does not interfere with any pending state proceedings. The same is true of foster care right-to-safety cases, which concern the quality, not the existence of the placement.

The analogy to prison cases, however, is not perfect. Unlike prisoners, whose case is closed upon conviction, foster children remain subject to judicial proceedings,[347] even if their parents

---

[344] *Id.* at 425, 430. District courts have based their opinions on a broad understanding of *Moore. See, e.g.,* Brown v. Jones, 473 F. Supp. 439, 443–46 (N.D. Tex. 1979).

[345] Trainor v. Hernandez, 431 U.S. 434, 444 (1977); Juidice v. Vail, 430 U.S. 327, 334–35 (1977).

[346] In the few prison cases that have dealt with abstention issues, *Younger* abstention has been rejected. Campbell v. McGruder, 580 F.2d 521, 525 (D.C. Cir. 1978) (abstention did not prevent federal court from granting injunctive relief to pretrial detainees in case of unconstitutional facility conditions); Ramos v. Lamm, 639 F.2d 559, 564–65 (10th Cir. 1980) (prison conditions case where *Pullman, Burford,* and *Younger* abstention were held to be inappropriate).

[347] Adoption Assistance and Child Welfare Act of 1980, Pub. L. No. 96-272, 94 Stat. 500 (codified as amended in scattered sections of 42 U.S.C.) (states must institute a procedure whereby review of the child's placement occurs at least once every eighteen months); Social Security Act § 47(a)(1), 42 U.S.C. § 67(a)(1) (Supp. 1981) (the purpose of the Adoption Assistance and Child Welfare Act of 1980 is to expeditiously either return the child to his parents, or to arrange for the child's adoption). *See, e.g.,* N.Y.

have consented to placement. The child's case will generally remain available for family court review during the time the child is in foster care.[348] The difference between a foster care case and a prison conditions case, then, is that a foster care right-to-safety case touches on collateral areas that, at least theoretically, are usually within the purview of cases already in state courts.

The Supreme Court has sent contradictory messages whether *Younger* applies to such collateral matters. On one hand, in *O'Shea v. Littleton*,[349] the Court approved application of the abstention doctrine where the relief sought would broadly affect state criminal court judicial practices and procedures.[350] On the other hand, in *Gerstein v. Pugh*,[351] the Court refused to apply *Younger* to an action seeking preliminary hearings for a class of pre-trial detainees.[352] Lower courts attempting to distinguish *Gerstein* and *O'Shea* have reached seemingly irreconcilable results.[353] The agony of their efforts may explain what

---

Soc. Serv. Law § 392 (Consol. 1984 & Supp. 1986) and *infra* note 348 and accompanying text (a reviewing body may inquire into the child's foster care placement and order improvement if needed).

[348] M. Hardin, Foster Children in the Courts 623 (1983). *See* N.Y. Soc. Serv. Law § 392(10) (Consol. 1984 & Supp. 1986) (requires the court to possess continuing jurisdiction in the case of children who are continued in foster care; rehearings must occur at least every twenty-four months). *See also* Miss. Code Ann. § 43-15-13 (Supp. 1986); Tex. Fam. Code Ann. § 18 (Vernon 1986).

[349] 414 U.S. 488 (1974).

[350] *Id.* at 500–01 (even though the plaintiffs did not seek to enjoin any pending criminal proceeding, the Court held that the relief sought—a day-to-day audit of state court practices—was within the *Younger* prohibition since it would have thrust the federal court into the role of "receiver" of the state court system).

[351] 420 U.S. 103 (1975).

[352] *Id.* at 108 n.9.

[353] Lower federal courts have consistently found *Younger* applicable to collateral challenges to the absence of a hearing or standards in state bail-setting procedures, Muda v. Busse, 437 F. Supp. 505 (N.D. Ind. 1977); to the use of social histories prior to adjudication in family court juvenile delinquency proceedings, J.P. v. DeSanti, 653 F.2d 1080 (6th Cir. 1981); to the absence of appointed counsel in child support contempt matters, Parker v. Turner, 626 F.2d 1 (6th Cir. 1980); and to failure to adjourn a criminal trial on Friday, which the defendant observed as his sabbath, N.J. v. Chesmard, 555 F.2d 63 (3d Cir. 1977). However, other courts have determined that *Younger* is not implicated when the collateral attack is on preventive detention practices of family court judges, Coleman v. Stanziam, 570 F. Supp. 679 (E.D. Pa. 1983), *app. dismissed*, 735 F.2d 118 (3d Cir.), *cert. denied*, 469 U.S. 1037 (1984), or concerns the right to bail pending appeal of a criminal conviction, Abbott v. Laurie, 422 F. Supp. 976 (D.R.I. 1976), or relates to the practice of indefinitely confining a juvenile pursuant to an unclear family court order, A.T. v. County of Cook, 613 F. Supp. 775 (N.D. Ill. 1985).

prompted then-Justice Rehnquist to comment that the Court's *Younger*-based decisions map a "sinuous path."[354]

The path is easier to follow in right-to-safety cases. In every case in which a federal court has abstained from examining a federal claim on *Younger* grounds because, as a collateral matter, the claim involved a family court case, the federal claim involved an attack on the procedures followed by the state court.[355] At least for foster care cases, there is a relevant distinction between *Gerstein* and *O'Shea*. *Gerstein* was directed not at state criminal prosecutions, but at the narrow legality of pre-trial detention without a probable cause hearing.[356] *O'Shea*, on the other hand, was a broad-based attack on the Cairo, Illinois, criminal justice system.[357] Since right-to-safety cases do not challenge state court procedures, a foster care right-to-safety case bears a greater similarity to *Gerstein* than to *O'Shea*, because it challenges only the legality of the conditions of foster care, not the placement proceedings themselves.

When a federal court changes the procedures to be used in a state proceeding by, for example, ordering the appointment of counsel in a support order proceeding,[358] it comes dangerously close to intruding on the overriding state interest in conducting its own judicial proceedings. *Younger* is designed, in part, to avoid federal displacement of the state court "in supervising the conduct of trials in state court."[359] This displacement can occur when the federal challenge is to a collateral matter. The effect of a federal injunction which alters a state procedure is to transfer control of the case from a judge in one system to a judge in another system.[360] Such a transfer can create the same type of confusion and inefficiency as would an injunction against the state proceeding itself.

---

[354] Steffel v. Thompson, 415 U.S. 459, 479 (1973) (Rehnquist, J., concurring).

[355] *See infra* notes 363–64 and accompanying text.

[356] 420 U.S. at 108.

[357] 414 U.S. at 499.

[358] Parker v. Turner, 626 F.2d 1 (6th Cir. 1980).

[359] N.J. v. Chesmard, 555 F.2d at 68 (3d Cir. 1977).

[360] *See also* J.P. v. DeSanti, 653 F.2d 1080, 1084 (6th Cir. 1981) (allowing federal suits would "clearly interfere" with the procedures of the juvenile court system); Brown v. Jones, 473 F. Supp. 439, 448 (N.D. Tex. 1979) (observing that without the *Younger* application, a party would continually move to stop a procedure, never allowing any action to get to court).

Equitable relief in right-to-safety cases does not pose these dangers. A federal court order to improve a foster care system in no way interferes with the local family court process. It neither dictates the procedures that the state court should follow nor limits the range of disposition alternatives that the state judge may consider. The overriding purpose of a family court foster care proceeding is to determine whether or not foster care placement is necessary, and, if it is, to determine when and by what means it should be terminated.[361] That purpose is not disturbed by a right-to-safety injunction. The state's interest in the integrity of its own proceedings, therefore, is not compromised by federal injunctive relief protecting the safety of foster children. Indeed, relief not only leaves intact the state interest in protecting children, but also enhances it by improving the quality of the foster care program.[362]

Lower federal courts confronting *Younger* issues in family court and foster care matters have applied the doctrine in a manner consistent with this analysis. Thus, cases seeking to enjoin the use of certain family court procedures have been dismissed,[363] but the courts have refused to apply *Younger* where, as in a right-to-safety case, the plaintiff does not seek to enjoin the state proceeding or to interfere with family court proceedings.[364]

---

[361] M. Hardin, *supra* note 348, at 86; Guttenberger, *Foster Placement Review: Problems and Opportunities*, 83 Dick. L. Rev. 487, 491 (1979) (footnote omitted). *See also* Mass. Gen. Laws Ann., ch. 119, § 26 (Law Co-op Supp. 1987); N.Y. Soc. Serv. Law § 392 (Consol. 1984); Ohio Rev. Code Ann. § 5103.151 (Baldwin 1984 & Supp. 1986); Va. Code Ann. § 16.1-282 (1950 & Supp. 1987).

[362] L.H. v. Jamieson, 643 F.2d 1351 (9th Cir. 1981). The mere existence of an available, but unutilized, state forum has never been enough to authorize *Younger* abstention. Under 42 U.S.C. § 1983, the federal remedy for constitutional injury is supplemental to the state remedy. *See* Monroe v. Pape, 365 U.S. 167 (1961); Blackmun, *Section 1983 and Federal Protection of Individual Rights—Will the Statute Remain Alive or Fade Away?*, 60 N.Y.U. L. Rev. 1 (1985).

[363] *See, e.g.*, L.H. v. Jamieson, 643 F.2d 1351 (9th Cir. 1981); J.P. v. DeSanti, 653 F.2d 1080 (6th Cir. 1981); Haag v. Cuyahoga County, 619 F. Supp. 262 (N.D. Ohio 1985); Brown v. Jones, 473 F. Supp. 439 (N.D. Tex. 1979).

[364] *See, e.g.*, L.H. v. Jamieson, 643 F.2d 1351 (9th Cir. 1981); A.T. v. County of Cook, 613 F. Supp. 775 (N.D. Ill. 1985). *A.T.* and *L.H.* are illustrative. In *A.T.*, the plaintiff sought release from the indefinite confinement that resulted when he was confined pursuant to a family court order that allowed him to be "released upon request of the child's parent or other responsible adult." 613 F. Supp. at 776. The court held that *Younger* was not applicable because plaintiffs challenged what happened after the

There are two additional reasons why *Younger* should not relegate right-to-safety cases to the state courts. *Younger* does not apply either when there is no adequate remedy in the state court proceeding or when the plaintiff is suffering great and immediate irreparable harm.[365] In the right-to-safety context, both exceptions to *Younger* usually apply. First, a single family court judge, in a single case, is unlikely to have either the perspective or the authority to fashion relief that will improve the quality of the foster care system. The only question normally considered by the judge (and the only one that can be considered) is whether the child belongs in foster care, and if so, when and under what conditions release is appropriate.[366] This yes-no, in-out approach is very different from what a right-to-safety decision requires. In such cases, a judge must consider not simply the child's status, but also the quality of the child's placement in the foster care system. Most state statutes provide neither procedures nor remedial power for family court judges to address these questions.[367]

Second, foster children do suffer great and immediate irreparable harm when their right to safety is violated. Unlike a *Younger* situation, where the cost, anxiety and inconvenience of having to defend against a criminal charge does not qualify

---

family court judge had ruled. The injunction requested, therefore, did not duplicate, disrupt or insult the state judiciary. *Id.* at 778.

In *L.H.*, the plaintiff class sought additional funding for private agencies that care for children in the state's custody. The court refused to dismiss on *Younger* grounds even though there were foster care review proceedings, in which plaintiffs could have raised this claim, pending for all members of plaintiff class. The court noted that plaintiffs were not seeking to enjoin those proceedings. It also found that the relief requested "may enrich the variety of disposition alternatives available to a juvenile court judge." 643 F.2d at 1354.

[365] *Younger*, 401 U.S. at 45.

[366] *See supra* note 361 and accompanying text.

[367] Section 392 of New York's Social Service Law is an example of how little a family court judge can do to improve safety for foster children during placement. Family courts have four options: they can return the child to his parent, free the child for adoption, continue the existing foster care, or direct the adoption in the foster family home itself. Application of Social Services Official, 89 A.D.2d 534, 452 N.Y.S.2d 612 (1982); *In re* L., 77 Misc. 2d 363, 353 N.Y.S.2d 317, *modified on other grounds*, 45 A.D.2d 375, 357 N.Y.S.2d 987 (1974). Family courts are not given the task of overseeing an agency's efforts and should avoid substituting their judgment for the commissioner's. They should not choose between adequate plans or design their own plans, but should merely satisfy themselves that the placement plans of the Commissioner are adequate. *In re* Damon A., 61 N.Y.2d 77, 459 N.E.2d 1275, 471 N.Y.S.2d 838 (1983); *In re* Commissioner of Social Services *ex rel.* Riddle v. Rapp, 127 Misc. 2d 835, 487 N.Y.S.2d 477 (1985).

as a great and immediate irreparable harm, and unlike the possibility of having a child removed from parental custody during the pendency of the action,[368] violations of the right to safety cannot be rectified or minimized by subsequent review. When safety is at stake, every moment counts. Loss of life itself may be at stake—certainly, health and emotional well being are.[369] With the potential damage so great, the *Younger* rationale for delay is not persuasive.[370]

Younger, therefore, cannot bar a right-to-safety case in the foster care field any more than it bars a right-to-safety case involving prisoners. The policies that have led federal courts to close their doors to a limited number of federal constitutional cases are not contravened by right-to-safety cases. For the federal courts to abstain in such cases is for them to abdicate their responsibility to enforce federal rights.

C. The Domestic Relations Exception is not a Jurisdictional Barrier to Right-to-Safety Cases

"Poorly defined and unevenly applied,"[371] the domestic relations exception is a judge-made doctrine which permits federal courts to decline to exercise diversity jurisdiction when to do so might embroil them in family disputes. In its most extreme expression of the concept, the Supreme Court described the doctrine as impelled by the notion that "[t]he whole subject of the domestic relations of husband and wife, parent and child, belong to the laws of the States and not to the laws of the United States."[372]

Several rationales have been offered for the doctrine, which constitutes a major restriction of federal jurisdiction. It has been

---

[368] *Younger*, 401 U.S. at 46; *Moore*, 442 U.S. at 434–35.

[369] *See supra* notes 19–27 and accompanying text.

[370] *Younger* justified its abstention rule by, among other things, assuming that courts of equity should not act in a restraining manner if the "moving party has an adequate remedy at law and will not suffer irreparable injury if denied equitable relief." 401 U.S. at 43–44. *See also* Trainor v. Hernandez, 431 U.S. 434, 440–42 (1977) (resting on the assumption that subsequent review and remedy at law can, except in the face of great and immediate injury, satisfactorily ameliorate any harm done to the moving party).

[371] Atwood, *Domestic Relations Cases in Federal Court: Toward a Principled Exercise of Jurisdiction*, 35 Hastings L.J. 571, 573 (1984).

[372] *In re* Burrus, 136 U.S. 586, 593–94 (1890).

said that the domestic relations exception is justified by the strong state interest in family law matters, by the state courts' superior competence in divorce and custody cases,[373] and by a fear of the possibility of incompatible decrees in divorce and child custody cases involving continuing judicial supervision.[374] Some federal courts also have expressed discomfort at the prospect of becoming involved in these often acrimonious proceedings.[375]

The doctrine is generally confined to diversity jurisdiction cases where, absent the doctrine, a state law claim could be brought in federal court solely because the parties reside in different states. On occasion, however, federal courts have declined to adjudicate claims involving domestic disputes even when they are otherwise properly brought under the federal question jurisdiction of the federal courts.[376] A recent panel opinion of the Eleventh Circuit suggested that the domestic relations doctrine might apply in a right-to-safety case.[377] But the doctrine, which has dubious credentials in any setting,[378] has no place in right-to-safety cases.

---

[373] *See, e.g.,* Buechold v. Ortiz, 401 F.2d 371, 373 (9th Cir. 1968); Phillips, Nizer, Benjamin, Krim and Ballon v. Rosenstiel, 490 F.2d 509, 516 (2d Cir. 1973) (quoting C. Wright, Federal Courts 84 (2d ed. 1970)).

[374] *See, e.g.,* Lloyd v. Loeffler, 694 F.2d 489, 493 (7th Cir. 1982) (recognizing that "the exercise of federal jurisdiction will create a potential for inconsistent decrees"); Sutter v. Pitts, 639 F.2d 842, 844 (1st Cir. 1981) ("there is an obvious likelihood of incompatible state and federal decrees").

[375] *See, e.g.,* Thrower v. Cox, 425 F. Supp. 570, 573 (D.S.C. 1976) ("vexatious" field of family law warrants separate courts; "the federal court system should allow [state courts] that dubious honor exclusively"); *see also* Wand, *A Call for the Repudiation of the Domestic Relation Exception to Federal Jurisdiction,* 30 Vill. L. Rev. 307, 385–87 (1975).

[376] *See, e.g.,* Peterson v. Babbitt, 708 F.2d 465, 466 (9th Cir. 1983) ("[t]here is no subject matter jurisdiction over these types of domestic disputes"); Zak v. Pilla, 698 F.2d 800, 801 (6th Cir. 1982) (even a valid claim under 42 U.S.C. § 1983 should be "dismissed by a federal district court for lack of jurisdiction"). *But see* Franks v. Smith, 717 F.2d 183, 185 (5th Cir. 1983) ("[t]he mere fact that a claimed violation of constitutional rights arises in a domestic relations context does not bar review of those constitutional issues"). The Supreme Court has not expressly stated that the domestic relations exception does not apply to cases brought under federal question jurisdiction. However, the Court has not invoked this exception in cases challenging the constitutionality of a child's placement or treatment in foster care. *See, e.g.,* Moore v. Sims, 442 U.S. 415 (1979); Smith v. OFFER, 431 U.S. 816 (1977).

[377] Taylor v. Ledbetter, 791 F.2d 881, 884 (11th Cir. 1986), *aff'd in part, rev'd in part on rehearing,* 818 F.2d 791 (11th Cir. 1987) (en banc).

[378] *See* Atwood, *supra* note 371; Wand, *supra* note 375; Comment, *Federal Jurisdiction and the Domestic Relations Exception: A Search for Parameters,* 31 UCLA L.

After *Erie Railroad v. Tompkins*,[379] a federal court's only substantive concern in most diversity cases is to apply state law in an even-handed manner.[380] In that limited context, the domestic relations exception, despite its questionable pedigree, serves reasonably well. Without it, a potential out-of-state litigant in a state divorce or custody matter could escape adjudication of her dispute in the state tribunal to which it is assigned by state law. For example, if litigants, in such an instance, can avoid the state tribunal, the potential for disruption and inefficiency is greater than when a tort action is brought in federal court. Unlike tort or contract matters, family law enforcement is generally entrusted to a specialized tribunal,[381] and family law cases often involve emotional matters of unique state concern.[382] In domestic relations matters, the risk of inconsistent adjudications by judges untrained in the intricacies of local law—ever-present in all diversity jurisdiction cases—becomes too high a price to pay for the theoretically impartial forum that diversity jurisdiction is designed to obtain.

The balance, however, changes significantly when the litigation is brought to vindicate federal rights. No longer must the court weigh the relative importance of an impartial federal forum for the adjudication of a pure state law claim against the disruption to the state system caused by the provision of the alterna-

---

Rev. 843 (1984); Note, *The Domestic Relations Exception to Diversity Jurisdiction: A Re-Evaluation*, 24 B.C.L. Rev. 661 (1983). Much of the criticism of the exception (which originated from dicta in two Supreme Court opinions) questions whether the exception is justified. Atwood, *supra* note 371, at 592–93; Wand, *supra* note 375, at 359–85; Note, *supra*, at 684–91. Critics have also condemned the inconsistent application of the exception. Atwood, *supra* note 371, at 573; Wand, *supra* note 380, at 387; Comment, *supra*, at 855–72; Note, *supra*, at 676–84.

Although authorities debate whether the exception should be redefined or abolished, most agree that it should not extend to cases brought under federal question jurisdiction. Wand, *supra* note 375, at 392; Comment, *supra*, at 882; Atwood, *supra* note 371, at 626. An extension of this sort would preclude federal courts from deciding important constitutional issues that were intended to be within their jurisdiction. Wand, *supra* note 375, at 392–93; Comment, *supra*, at 882–83.

[379] 304 U.S. 64 (1938).

[380] *Id.* at 71 (previously "the laws of the several States" under section 34 of the Federal Judiciary Act of September 24, 1789 did not include common law).

[381] H. Clark, The Law of Domestic Relations in the United States 284 (1968); Armstrong v. Armstrong, 508 F.2d 348, 350 (1st Cir. 1974).

[382] An example is the *Baby "M"* case, involving surrogate parenting arrangements. *In re* Baby "M", 217 N.J. Super. 313, 525 A.2d 1128 (1987), *cert. granted*, 107 N.J. 140, 526 A.2d 203 (1987).

tive forum. In right-to-safety cases, the clash is between the overriding duty of federal courts to enforce and uphold constitutional rights, and the state's interest in having its courts hear these cases. The addition of the federal constitutional component changes the result of the abstention inquiry.

> Federal courts should be most sensitive to their institutional responsibility to accept jurisdiction assigned to them by Congress when considering domestic relations cases that raise substantial federal constitutional or statutory claims. The domestic relations limitation, of dubious validity even in diversity cases, is wholly inappropriate in actions founded on a federal question.[383]

Accordingly, most courts and commentators take the position that the domestic relations exception is appropriately restricted to diversity cases.[384]

There is another reason why the doctrine should not apply in right-to-safety cases on behalf of foster children: none of the principles that the domestic relations exception is designed to uphold are threatened by the invocation of federal jurisdiction. The right to safety concerns the quality, not the fact or the duration, of a child's placement in foster family care. The articulation and maintenance of this right by federal courts will not interfere with divorce cases, intrude on competency regarding family matters or have a major impact on child custody arrangements.[385]

Thus, since there are no genuine obstacles to the provision of a federal forum for the vindication of a foster child's federally secured constitutional right to safety, and since a structural injunction granted by a federal court is the preferred remedy, the concluding section of this article considers guidelines for fashioning and administering the appropriate injunctive relief if foster care systems are to be made safe.

---

[383] Atwood, *supra* note 371, at 625–26.
[384] *See supra* note 378 and accompanying text.
[385] *See supra* notes 361–62 and accompanying text.

VI. Guidelines for Effective Structural Injunctions

Unfortunately, a precise recipe for success in obtaining implementation of complex injunctive decrees does not exist.[386] This is certainly true for foster care. There is only a single federal structural injunction dealing with safety in foster care: the order in *G.L. v. Zumwalt*.[387] But *G.L.* is still in post-judgment litigation,[388] so courts and lawyers confronting foster care right-to-safety cases do not have a completed record of other cases in the foster care field to draw upon. However, there are many mature structural injunctions in other, closely related, fields that present similar implementation questions.[389] Important lessons emerge from the extensive experience in those cases about what the court and the parties involved in the case must do to increase the chances that a structural decree will be effective. This section discusses five guidelines derived from those cases that, if followed, materially increase the probability of successfully implementing a structural injunction that protects the right to foster care safety while preserving the independence and integrity of the court.

A. *Continued Involvement of Plaintiffs' Counsel*

Institutional judgments are not self-executing. Child welfare agencies have been resistant to reform and, if the past is any guide, there is no reason to think that merely hortatory court

---

[386] Lowry, *supra* note 7, at 280.

[387] 564 F. Supp. 1030 (W.D. Mo. 1983). *See supra* note 11 and accompanying text.

[388] Under the terms of a supplemental consent decree, the court approved the establishment of an outside body composed of three persons to assist the parties' compliance with the decree. G.L. v. Zumwalt, Supplemental Consent Decree, at 2–7 (July 29, 1985). The Committee, as that body is called, currently is engaged in monitoring the decree. In addition, soon after the decree was entered, the state legislature passed a law establishing a state children's commission which, among other things, was specifically charged with reporting to the legislature annually on compliance with the decree. H.B. 256, 82nd Gen. Assembly, 1st Reg. Sess., 1973 Mo. Laws 504.

[389] There is a growing literature, primarily in the form of case studies, on the effect of structural injunctions. *See, e.g.,* Alpert, *Prison Reform by Judicial Decree: The Unintended Consequences of* Ruiz v. Estelle, 9 Just. Sys. J. 291 (1984); Champagne & Hass, *The Impact of* Johnson v. Avery *on Prison Administration*, 43 Tenn. L. Rev. 275 (1976); M. Harris & D. Spiller, *supra* note 299; Mnookin, In the Interest, *supra* note 8; Note, *supra* note 295; M. Rebell & A. Block, *supra* note 301; D. Rothman & S. Rothman, *supra* note 120, at 66–89.

orders will be treated more seriously than other calls for change
that are almost always ignored. An institutional injunction case,
therefore, cannot end at final judgment. Indeed, the victory that
accompanies attainment of an institutional injunction must be
seen by plaintiffs' counsel as only a way station on the road
toward the achievement of the clients' goal.

Several case studies of institutional reform litigation in
other areas stress the importance of an active role for the plaintiffs' counsel. David and Sheila Rothman in their study of the
Willowbrook litigation, for example, identify the constant involvement of plaintiffs' counsel, whose "energies did not flag"
over the decade or more of active post-judgment monitoring, as
having contributed in a major way to the successful implementation that was achieved in that case.[390] An American Bar Association study of compliance with court orders in prison reform
cases made a similar observation when it commented that "[i]t
is logical to conclude that compliance would not have occurred
as quickly or in the ways that it did if plaintiffs' attorneys [in
these cases] had not been monitoring actively."[391] Thus, the first
essential element to increase the probability of compliance with
a structural injunction is the continuing involvement of plaintiffs' attorney in the post-judgment proceedings.[392]

B. A Specific Decree

The decree itself must be detailed and specific. It is not
enough to declare that the plaintiff foster children have the right
to be protected from harm; the court must specify what the
foster care system must do to effectuate the right. A concrete
decree focuses the parties and the court on the deficiencies in
the system that caused the problem. Decrees should be quantitative and precise and should provide specific tasks, possibly

---

[390] D. Rothman & S. Rothman, *supra* note 120, at 356–57.

[391] M. Harris & D. Spiller, *supra* note 299, at 396.

[392] Where the administration of the decree is left to the parties, the burden of
reporting non-compliance usually falls on the plaintiff's attorney. Special Project, *The
Remedial Process in Institutional Reform Litigation*, 78 Colum. L. Rev. 784, 824 (1978).
See also Note, *supra* note 295 at 1366, ("more active participation by the attorneys for
the plaintiffs and amici might have compensated for some of the deficiencies of the . . .
[monitor] that emerged during the implementation process").

along with timetables for achieving them. If nonobjective standards and goals are provided, intermediate, objective standards should also be outlined.[393] *G.L.* is a model of this type of decree.[394]

The *G.L.* decree dealt with fifteen different aspects of the problem, including caseworker case loads, foster parent compensation, medical and dental examinations, selection and supervision of foster homes, and investigations of suspected instances of foster parent abuse and neglect. For each topic, the decree provides standards for gauging the defendants' performance. For example, the defendants must maintain accurate medical records for each child including, at minimum, a complete medical history, all medical, dental and eye examinations, all inoculations and prescribed medication and indications as to when the next exam should occur.[395] The decree does more than simply declare that foster homes be supervised regularly by trained caseworkers; it specifies a minimum acceptable frequency for the visits.[396]

While a court must avoid excessive detail that will enmesh it in the minutiae of child care management,[397] it is important that its order not be so general that it fails to provide effective relief. A decree that prescribes specific standards for the defendants to meet saves the court and the parties from later time-consuming and frustrating disputes about what constitutes compliance with the decree.[398] A court formulating a decree has the opportunity to seek the input of the defendants. Since the decree is normally not issued until well after the initial determination

---

[393] Lottman, *Enforcement of Judicial Decrees: Now Comes the Hard Part*, 1 Mental Disability L. Rep. 69, 74 (1976); Note, *supra* note 306, at 457.

[394] The district court in that case published the consent decree that it approved because of the "assistance this case may render other courts considering similar questions." G.L. v. Zumwalt, 564 F. Supp. 1030, 1030 (W.D. Mo. 1983). Publishing *G.L.* was an unusual but not unprecedented event. *See, e.g.,* Goldsby v. Carnes, 365 F. Supp. 395, 396 (W.D. Mo. 1973); Wyatt v. Stickney, 344 F. Supp. 373 (M.D. Ala. 1972).

[395] *G.L.*, 564 F. Supp. at 1038.

[396] *G.L.*, 564 F. Supp. at 1034.

[397] *Cf.* Procunier v. Martinez, 416 U.S. 396, 404 (1973) ("problems of prisons . . . [are] not readily susceptible of resolution by decree"). *See also* Bell v. Wolfish, 441 U.S. 520, 531 (1978); Jones v. North Carolina Prisoners' Union, 433 U.S. 119, 126 (1976).

[398] Special Project, *supra* note 392, at 817–18 (addresses the advantages and disadvantages of a detailed decree).

of liability, and since the defendants have the right to comment on it without prejudicing their right to appeal, there is no impediment to seeking their assistance.[399] For the same reasons, the defendants have an incentive to come forward. Used wisely, the defendants' participation in the decree formulation process can be beneficial. By incorporating defendants' suggestions the court "encourages voluntarism" and "cooperative approaches."[400] It also becomes more fully informed about the practical consequences of its decree, and by encouraging the defendants' participation, it helps blunt the criticism that the judiciary lacks "relevant information"[401] needed to formulate feasible remedies for systemic constitutional injuries.

An additional and important benefit of a detailed decree is that it aids the court and parties in gauging the progress, or lack thereof toward compliance. The American Bar Association's study of prison cases revealed the practical significance of detailed structural decrees. The authors commented that the "clear and unambiguous" nature of a decree contribute[s] to compliance in that it gives "the plaintiffs' attorneys objective standards by which to measure failure to comply," and more importantly, it "contribute[s] to the belief (by defendants) that the judge [is] committed to achievement of compliance."[402]

C. The Need for Monitoring

In addition to its substantive provisions, the decree must provide for monitoring the defendants' performance. Monitoring

---

[399] See, e.g., Taylor v. Board of Educ., 288 F.2d 600, 604 n.2 (2d Cir.), cert. denied, 368 U.S. 940 (1961).

For example, in Tatum v. Rogers, 75 Civ. 2782 (CBM) (S.D.N.Y. February 20, 1979) (available August 20, 1987 on LEXIS, Genfed Library, Dist file), an action challenging the New York State Division of Criminal Justice Services maintenance and use of its computerized criminal history information system, the court, after finding that the plaintiff class's constitutional arguments were justified, directed the defendant agency to prepare a feasibility study to advise the court and plaintiffs' counsel how the vast defects in defendant's data base and procedures could be corrected.

[400] Lasker, supra note 290, at 79. Judge Lasker, who has presided over several significant structural decrees involving all the major pretrial detention facilities in New York City, concludes that this approach avoids "unnecessary intrusion" by the judiciary. Id. at 79.

[401] Robertson, supra note 119, at 148. See also Note, supra note 306, at 439 (participation by the defendants can "enhance the likelihood of compliance with whatever standards are chosen").

[402] M. Harris & D. Spiller, supra note 299, at 189.

allows the court and the parties to determine the extent to which defendants have implemented the decree.[403] Moreover, it forces the defendants to confront their obligation to change the system to comply with the decree. Unless defendants deliberately abdicate all responsibility, monitoring educates them about the system that they are responsible for running.

There are several methods utilized by the courts to monitor decrees. One is for the court merely to retain jurisdiction, leaving plaintiffs' counsel solely responsible for monitoring. This method is generally coupled with provision for the plaintiffs' counsel to have access to the institutional records, documents and other relevant materials in the defendants' possession.[404] In addition, most courts require the defendants to submit regular reports detailing the progress of implementation.[405] The general consensus is, however, that this alone is not an effective method of implementation.[406] An example of the ineffectiveness of the method is *Mills v. Board of Education of the District of Columbia*.[407] In *Mills*, the court ordered the Board of Education to provide suitable education for the handicapped. Over the next three years, the plaintiffs were unsuccessful in obtaining compliance.[408] As a result, the court, on motion of the plaintiffs, appointed a special master.[409] A special master may have a broad range of power, including fact-finding, reporting and making recommendations, negotiating disputes between the parties, acting as an arbitrator, and in some cases, issuing orders binding the parties.[410] Although controversial, the use of masters in

---

[403] Note, *supra* note 306, at 440; Special Project, *supra* note 392, at 824–37.

[404] This device has been used frequently as an adjunct to the retention of jurisdiction. *See, e.g.,* G.L. v. Zumwalt, 564 F. Supp. 1030, 1042 (W.D. Mo. 1983); Lottman, *supra* note 393, at 69–70.

[405] The drawback of this device is that it depends on the "accuracy or completeness of information provided by administrators." Note, *supra* note 306, at 441. Reliability is often suspect because defendants may exaggerate compliance or base the reports on "inadequate record keeping systems." *Id.* at 442.

[406] Note, *supra* note 306, at 441. This method typically leaves enforcement up to an overworked plaintiffs' counsel whose lack of time and financial backing can hamper the enforcement effort. Lottman, *supra* note 393, at 70.

[407] 348 F. Supp. 866 (D.D.C. 1972).

[408] Rebell, *supra* note 295, at 337–38.

[409] *Id.* at 338.

[410] Nathan, *The Use of Masters in Institutional Reform Litigation*, 10 Toledo L. Rev. 419, 421 (1979). Schwimmer v. United States, 232 F.2d 855, 865 (8th Cir.), *cert. denied*, 352 U.S. 833 (1956) (quoting *ex parte* Peterson, 253 U.S. 300, 312 (1920)). *See*

institutional reform cases has been considered "highly effective" by some commentators.[411]

A third method of monitoring used by the courts, and one somewhat less intrusive than a master, is the appointment of a monitor. In contrast to the role of a master, a monitor's powers are usually more limited. In a typical case the monitor serves as the court's "'eyes and ears' during the implementation process,"[412] but is not vested with direct responsibility for implementation.[413] In *Wyatt v. Stickney*,[414] a case involving the rights of the mentally ill and retarded in Alabama, Judge Frank Johnson used this device when he appointed a Human Rights Committee to oversee compliance. The committee was effective to the extent that two years after the order there had been a substantial improvement in safety, sanitation and habitability of the facility,[415] but many other provisions of the order had not been successfully addressed.[416] In the *G.L.* case, after attempts at monitoring by the plaintiffs' counsel proved unsuccessful, the court ordered the appointment of a blue ribbon commission with powers similar to the Human Rights Committee used by Judge Johnson.[417] Thus, while there continues to be much debate about which form of monitoring is most effective,[418] and concrete recommendations in this area cannot be made reliably, there can be no debate that some method of examining defendants' conduct after entry of the decree is crucial.

D. The Role of the District Judge

The district judge must be actively involved to ensure successful implementation of a structural injunction. By relying

---

generally Kaufman, *Masters in the Federal Courts: Rule 53*, 58 Colum. L. Rev. 452 (1958).

[411] Nathan, *supra* note 410, at 421; Special Project, *supra* note 392, at 835.

[412] Note, *supra* note 295, at 1360.

[413] *Id.* at 1361.

[414] 325 F. Supp. 781 (M.D. Ala. 1971), *aff'd sub nom.* Wyatt v. Aderholt, 503 F.2d 1305 (5th Cir. 1974).

[415] Note, *supra* note 295, at 1378.

[416] *Id.*

[417] The Committee, a three-person body appointed by the parties, has been given a budget with which to hire a professional staff person. G.L. v. Zumwalt, Supplemental Consent Decree, at 2-7 (Filed July 29, 1985).

[418] *See, e.g.,* Nathan, *supra* note 410, at 461-64; Special Project, *supra* note 392, at 809; Harris, *The Title VII Administrator, A Case Study in Judicial Flexibility,* 60 Cornell L. Rev. 53, 62-74 (1974).

upon counsel, and, if appropriate, court-appointed monitoring adjuncts, the court can avoid the appearance of administrative involvement, which has been criticized by opponents of structural injunctions. Activity should not be confused with partisanship. The court need not shed the mantle of independence and become identified as a partisan "powerbroker"[419] in order to be effectively involved. The judge sits to resolve disputes among the parties in the post-judgment phase of litigation just as dispassionately and objectively as prior to judgment. The key to success here is not that the judge identifies with one side or the other—of course, she should not—but that the court not end its involvement merely because a judgment has been entered.

A clearly communicated willingness of the court to use its powers to enforce its decree is paramount. Without this, the natural reluctance of defendants to comply is reinforced. Of all the variables associated with institutional compliance with structural injunctions, this is the one that appears to be predictive.

A study of one of the major early prison condition cases, involving the entire Arkansas prison system, *Holt v. Sarver*,[420] concluded that transcending all other factors that influenced compliance was the "district court's expectation that defendants would comply with all of the court's order."[421] By contrast, the study of *Hamilton v. Schiro*[422] by the same research team identified the district judge's apparent satisfaction with the slow and incomplete efforts of the defendants to achieve compliance as a cause of the less than positive results achieved in that case.[423] If, despite the result of the trial, the judge does not appear to take the decree seriously, then neither will those responsible for its implementation.[424]

---

[419] The pejorative term "powerbroker" was first used in this context in Diver, *supra* note 285.

[420] 309 F. Supp. 363 (E.D. Ark. 1970).

[421] M. Harris & D. Spiller, *supra* note 299, at 90. *See also* D. Rothman & S. Rothman, *supra* note 120, at 356 (attributing successful implementation of the Willowbrook litigation in large part to the efforts of the district judge).

[422] 338 F. Supp. 1016 (E.D. La. 1970).

[423] M. Harris & D. Spiller, *supra* note 299, at 283. Failure of judicial involvement has been affirmatively linked to poor compliance results by others. *See, e.g.,* Mnookin, In the Interest, *supra* note 8, at 351; Altman, *Implementing a Civil Rights Injunction: A Case Study of* NAACP v. Brennan, 78 Colum. L. Rev. 739, 750–51 (describing how the "lack of judicial responsiveness" hindered enforcement of the decree).

[424] M. Harris & D. Spiller, *supra* note 299, at 27 (study concluded that the single

E. The Need for Flexibility

Finally, the decree must be flexible enough so that unanticipated consequences can be dealt with through modification of its terms if necessary. Any attempt, whether judicial, legislative or executive, to reform an institution as complex as a modern social services bureaucracy is likely to produce unintended consequences.[425] The decree in *G.L. v. Zumwalt*, for example, limited the number of children permitted in any single foster home to six,[426] because of concern that overcrowded foster homes were more likely to become centers of maltreatment than foster homes that were not overcrowded. While in the abstract this provision seems sensible,[427] in practice it produced difficulty.

Several excellent foster homes were caring for more than six *G.L.* class members when the decree was entered. In order to comply with the literal language of the decree, defendants would have had to remove children doing well in their homes. The disruption and anxiety caused these children would have outweighed any benefit that they might have gained from being sent to smaller foster families. The Federal Rules of Civil Procedure provide a mechanism by which an injunction can be modified when it is not having its intended effect.[428] In *G.L.* this was not necessary, as plaintiffs' counsel agreed to permit the

---

most important factor to a successful implementation effort was the judicial determination to see that compliance was obtained).

[425] Note, *The Modification of Consent Decrees in Institutional Reform Litigation*, 99 Harv. L. Rev. 1020, 1033 (1986). A structural injunction, like any significant organizational change, often produces unintended results. *Id.* at 1034. *See also* Horowitz, *supra* note 291, at 1305.

See also Wyatt v. Stickney, 325 F. Supp. 781 (M.D. Ala. 1971), *aff'd sub nom.* Wyatt v. Aderholt, 503 F.2d 1305 (5th Cir. 1974) (unintended consequences—boredom and anxiety among the patients—resulted when, in order to comply with the decree, the hospital was unable to allow the residents to work because it could not afford the compensation).

[426] *G.L.*, 564 F. Supp. at 1036.

[427] *See supra* note 61 and accompanying text.

[428] Fed. R. Civ. P. 60(b)(5) & (6); C. Wright, *supra* note 332, at 661. As early as 1932, Justice Cardozo stated that a "continuing decree of injunction directed to events to come" should be understood to be "subject always to adaptation as events may shape the need." United States v. Swift & Co., 286 U.S. 106, 114 (1932). *See also* United States v. Karahalias, 205 F.2d 331 (2d Cir. 1953). Lower courts have continued to rely on Cardozo's principles. *See, e.g.,* Nelson v. Collins, 659 F.2d 420, 424 (4th Cir. 1981) (en banc). *See also* Jost, *From Swift to Stotts and Beyond: Modification of Injunctions in the Federal Courts*, 64 Tex. L. Rev. 1101 (1986).

children to remain in these homes providing that no others were sent to them until they had shrunk, by attrition, to the required size.[429] The court and parties need always be ready to modify the decree to avoid detrimental, unintended consequences.[430]

These guidelines are, of course, general. They do not begin to answer the many specific questions that any serious effort at implementation of a right-to-safety decree will present.[431] They do serve, however, to identify at least the major tasks that must be attended to if implementation is to be achieved. If these tasks are undertaken, given the record of effectiveness obtained for structural decrees in other settings, there is reason to be hopeful that a federal court can achieve its function of assuring that the constitutional right to safety is provided to foster children.

Conclusion

The time has come to recognize that foster children have a right to safety while in foster care. Foster care is intended to be a temporary refuge for children whose parents cannot care for them. But in practice, more often than has been acknowledged by many observers, foster care is not safe. Abuse and neglect of foster children occur at levels that far exceed in quantity and magnitude what a reasonably run system of care should produce. State-countenanced mistreatment of innocent children has serious ramifications for society. The infliction of harm on children who have suffered the trauma of parental default retards or even eliminates their potential for normal development. However, the political process has proven to be ineffective in alleviating this problem. Foster children, drawn largely from the disadvantaged and from minority groups, sim-

---

[429] See Letter from plaintiffs' counsel to defendants dated February 3, 1984, at 4 (on file with author).

[430] Examples of court-ordered modifications of structural injunctions include New York State Ass'n For Retarded Children v. Carey, 393 F. Supp. 715 (E.D.N.Y. 1975), modification denied, 551 F. Supp. 1165 (E.D.N.Y. 1982), aff'd in part and rev'd in part, 706 F.2d 956 (2d Cir. 1983), cert. denied, 464 U.S. 915 (1983); Goldsby v. Carnes, 365 F. Supp. 395 (W.D. Mo. 1973), modified, 429 F. Supp. 370 (W.D. Mo. 1977). For a criticism of the over-eagerness of some courts to modify decrees when implementation becomes difficult, see Shapiro, The Modification of Equitable Decrees: A Critical Commentary, 50 Brooklyn L. Rev. 459 (1984).

[431] See supra notes 293–95 and accompanying text.

ply do not have access or influence to move the executive or legislative branches of government to increase the funding needed to bring about change. As a practical matter, the courts must become involved if foster care is to function as it is intended.

The basis for judicial involvement is clear. The right to safety has deep roots in American jurisprudential thought. During the past two decades, federal courts have developed and implemented the right for every group of persons held under state custody other than foster children. Ironically, foster children are the one group with the most to gain from recognition of this fundamental right.

This article demonstrates that it is not possible to construct a logical distinction between foster children and other groups that have been afforded the benefits of the right to safety. To make the right to safety effective, a court must be able to fashion prospective relief with the flexibility to take into account the wide range of factors that can stimulate the organizational change needed. Experience with right-to-safety cases for other groups shows that only the structural injunction provides the court with these tools. Federal courts have historically served as the forum for the protection of citizens' constitutional rights from abridgement by the state. Therefore, they are the preferred forum for foster care right-to-safety cases. Reform of foster care will not come easily or quickly. But, if the guidelines offered in this article for courts and parties are followed, experience from other structural injunction cases demonstrates that federal courts have it in their power to make foster care, at last, the haven it was always intended to be.

CALIFORNIA WESTERN LAW REVIEW

VOLUME 26	1989-1990	NUMBER 2

Making Reasonable Efforts in Child Abuse and Neglect Cases: Ten Years Later

ALICE C. SHOTTON*

INTRODUCTION

In 1980, Congress enacted the Adoption Assistance and Child Welfare Act, commonly referred to as Public Law 96-272. The Act was heralded by child advocates across the country as a major step in reforming our languishing child welfare systems. The law required child welfare agencies to implement several reforms in their systems in exchange for federal funds.[1] A key provision of the law, but perhaps the least understood, requires child welfare agencies to make "reasonable efforts" to maintain children with their families or, if this is not possible, to make reasonable efforts to reunify the child with the family. The law also mandates that a juvenile court scrutinize the agency's "efforts" in every case to determine whether they were "reasonable." The statute, however, and accompanying regulations, did not define reasonable efforts.[2]

A major objective of Congress in requiring states to make reasonable efforts was "preventing the unnecessary separation of children from their families by identifying family problems, assisting families in resolving their problems, and preventing breakup of the family where the prevention of child removal is desirable and

---

* B.A., UCLA, 1970; Elementary Teaching Credential, California State University at Northridge, 1972; J.D., Southwestern University School of Law, 1979. Staff Attorney, Youth Law Center, San Francisco. Research assistance by: Kadijah R. Muhammad, Legal Intern, Youth Law Center, Fall 1989; student at U.C.L.A. Law School (J.D. expected 1990).

1. Pub. L. No. 96-272, June 17, 1980, 94 Stat. 500 (*see generally* 42 U.S.C. 620 *et seq.*). *See also* Allen, *A Guide to the Adoption Assistance and Child Welfare Act of 1980*, in FOSTER CHILDREN IN THE COURTS (M. Hardin, ed.) American Bar Association, 1983, for a detailed discussion of the requirements of P.L. 96-272.

2. *See* § IIA, *infra*, for a further discussion of a definition of "reasonable efforts."

possible. . . ."[3]

This article will summarize the statutory, regulatory, judicial and programmatic steps that have been taken in the last decade to implement reasonable efforts in our child welfare systems. The article will also present a definition of "reasonable efforts" for use in individual cases and will analyze model legislation from various states as guidance for other states considering incorporating reasonable efforts language into their juvenile codes. Finally, the article will suggest trends and goals for the the 1990s.

I. LEGISLATIVE HISTORY OF THE REASONABLE EFFORTS REQUIREMENT

Before passing P.L. 96-272, Congress heard testimony over a five-year period about our country's treatment of abused and neglected children and their families. The most striking fact presented was the astonishing number of children who were being removed from their families and placed in foster care, many for the entire duration of their childhoods. By 1977, the foster care population was estimated to be as high as 502,000.[4] While lost in a system that could neither return them to their families nor place them with adoptive parents, these children often moved from foster home to foster home, becoming more and more disturbed with each move.

At the same time as Congress was listening to testimony about our dysfunctional child welfare systems, a handful of programs around the country were experimenting with new ways to work with families in crisis. The most notable of these groups was Homebuilders, located in the state of Washington. Homebuilders' model is a short-term program which provides intensive services to families in their homes, and is considered by many as state-of-the-art child welfare practice.[5]

These intensive family service programs were experiencing substantial success in keeping crisis-ridden families intact. They responded to these families almost immediately upon referral and had staff available on a 24-hour basis who could go to the family's home, rather than requiring the family to come to a program office. These programs demonstrated that by utilizing the appropriate tools, many families previously thought "hopeless" could actually provide adequate homes for their children. This new faith in working with troubled families, coupled with the demonstrated

---

3. 42 U.S.C. § 625.
4. *Keeping Families Together: The Case for Family Preservation*, The Edna McConnell Clark Foundation 1 (1985).
5. *Id.* at 8-13.

harms of children growing up in foster care, helped inspire the reasonable efforts requirement.

II. PROBLEMS WITH IMPLEMENTATION OF THE REASONABLE EFFORTS REQUIREMENT

A. Lack of a Definition

Unfortunately, neither Congress nor the Department of Health and Human Services (HHS), the federal agency charged with overseeing the implementation of P.L. 96-272, defined the term "reasonable efforts". HHS has, however, issued a regulation listing suggested preventive and reunification services states should consider when developing their state plans.[6] Nevertheless, it is up to the states and their court systems to define the term. Many advocates of child welfare reform believe that the lack of a definition has been a significant obstacle to implementation even several years after the reasonable effort requirement became law. Only a few states have attempted to define "reasonable efforts" in their statutes. These states include Florida, Minnesota, and Missouri. Each of these statutes, however, uses the same general wording. They define "reasonable efforts" as "reasonable diligence and care" by the agency (Florida[7]), "due diligence" by the agency (Minnesota[8]), and "reasonable diligence and care" by the division (Missouri[9]). Missouri's statute has additional language requiring that the agency's diligence and care be made to "utilize all available services related to meeting the needs of the juvenile and the family." Minnesota's additional language is similar—the agency must exercise due diligence "to use appropriate and available services to meet the needs of the child and the child's family. . . ."[10] Florida's statute, in contrast, "assumes the availability of a reasonable program of services to children and their families."[11]

While these definitions are a helpful first step in defining reasonable efforts, it is proposed that the following three-step defining process will improve reasonable efforts determinations in individ-

---

6. 45 C.F.R. § 1357.15(e)(2) (1986) (These services include: (1) twenty-four hour emergency caretakers and homemaker services; (2) day care; (3) crisis counseling; (4) individual and family counseling; (5) emergency shelters; (6) emergency financial assistance; (7) temporary child care to provide respite to the family; (8) home-based family services; (9) self-help groups; (10) services to unmarried parents; (11) mental health, drug and alcohol abuse counseling, vocational counseling or vocational rehabilitation; and (12) post-adoption services).
7. FLA. STAT. ANN. § 39.41(4)(b) (West Supp. 1988).
8. MINN. STAT. ANN. § 260.012(b) (Supp. 1990).
9. MO. ANN. STAT. § 211.183(2) (Vernon Supp. 1990).
10. *See supra* note 8.
11. *See supra* note 7.

ual cases. The steps include: (1) identifying the exact danger that puts the child at risk of placement and that justifies state intervention; (2) determining how the family problems are causing or contributing to this danger to the child; and (3) designing and providing services for the family that alleviate or diminish the danger to the child. If any one of these steps is missing, it is unlikely that the efforts made on behalf of the family will be reasonable.

For example, suppose the child is severely malnourished and that this is the primary reason the child is at risk of placement and the agency is involved with the family. The agency, in order to make reasonable efforts to prevent that placement, must try to determine how the family situation is contributing to, or causing, the malnutrition. It may be because the parent is ignorant of nutrition, because the parent is depressed and unable to prepare meals, or because the parent is addicted to drugs and is too preoccupied with fulfilling the drug craving to prepare meals. In order to take the third step, however (that of designing and providing services to this child's family), it is clear that the relationship between the parent and the child's condition must be explored. If the parent is not preparing meals because he or she is depressed, sending in a homemaker to work with the mother on meal preparation may be futile. Instead, arranging counseling would be a much more reasonable effort.

B.   Lack of Guidelines for When Judicial Findings of Reasonable Efforts Must Be Made

The federal statute and regulations also fail to clarify when, during the court process, judges should make reasonable efforts determinations. States are again required to decide when and how often the judicial determination should be made. Only California has added reasonable efforts language to every section of its juvenile code which deals with juvenile court hearings, from detention hearings to termination hearings.[12] Ohio has recently added language requiring courts to make "reasonable efforts" determinations at every court hearing where the court is either removing a child from his home or continuing that child's placement in foster care.[13]

While the majority of state statutes that deal with the timing of judicial findings do specify more than one stage of the court process at which the determination should be made, none are as all-

---

12.   CAL. WELF. & INST. CODE §§ 306, 319, 361, 366.21(e), 366.21(f), 366.22(a) (West Supp. 1990), and CAL. CIV. CODE § 232(a)(7) (West Supp. 1990).
13.   OHIO REV. CODE ANN. § 2151.419(A) (Anderson 1989).

encompassing as California's or Ohio's.[14] Both California's and Ohio's statutes recognize the importance of the agency making reasonable efforts throughout the time a child is in placement, acknowledging that such vigilance is necessary to prevent the foster care limbo Congress was so concerned about when passing P.L. 96-272.

C. Consequences of Failing to Make Reasonable Efforts

Substantial misunderstanding exists regarding the consequences under P.L. 96-272 of an agency's failure to make reasonable efforts in a particular case. The only ramification that Congress intended was that the child welfare agency could not legally claim federal matching funds for the child's stay in foster care pursuant to Title IV-E for that period of time when a court found reasonable efforts to be lacking.[15] Many have incorrectly believed that a failure to make such efforts under the federal law prevents the agency from removing the child from a dangerous home situation, or else, requires the agency to return the child to an unsafe home if the child is already in placement. Unfortunately, the confusion also has led several states to pass statutes requiring reasonable efforts to be shown before removing a child.[16]

The result of this confusion is that many judges simply ignore the reasonable efforts requirement or else make positive findings based on inaccurate or incomplete information. For many judges, determining whether reasonable efforts have been made involves little more than checking a box on a court form, with no discussion of the issue. It is important to stress that P.L. 96-272 has never tied the state's ability to remove children from their parent's home to the reasonable efforts requirement. The child's safety is always paramount. Only federal funding for the child's placement is in jeopardy when reasonable efforts are lacking.

---

14. *See, e.g.*, FLA. STAT. ANN. §§ 39.402(2), (9), (10), 39.41(2)(a) (West 1988); IND. CODE ANN. §§ 31-6-4-6(e), 15.3 (West 1986)); IOWA CODE ANN. §§ 232.52(6), .95(2)(a)(West 1985), § 232.102(3)(b) (West Supp. 1989); MINN. STAT. § 260.012(b) (Supp. 1990); MISS. CODE ANN. §§ 43-21-301(4)(c), -309(4)(c), -405(6), -603(7) (Supp. 1989); OR. REV. STAT. §§ 419.577(3)(b)(B) (1989); VA. CODE §§ 16.1-252(A), (E)(2), -279(A)(3)(c), (C)(5)(c), (E)(9)(c) (Supp. 1988); WASH. REV. CODE ANN. §§ 13.32A.170(1)(d), .34.060(6)(a), .130(1)(b) (Supp. 1989); WIS. STAT. ANN. § 48.21(5)(b)(West 1987), §48.355(2)(a) (West Supp. 1989).

15. HHS, Human Development Serv., Policy Announcement, ACYF-PA-84-1 (Jan. 13, 1984), p. 4.

16. *See infra* note 37.

D. Emergency Situations

Another area of confusion concerns whether or not a child can be removed in an emergency situation if no reasonable efforts have been made. Here again, HHS has left it to the states to define an emergency situation and its relationship to the reasonable efforts determination. Several states have passed statutes and developed court rules that contain special language regarding the agency's role in making reasonable efforts in an emergency situation.[17] California's statute is again illustrative:

> Where the first contact with the family has occurred during an emergency situation in which the child could not safely remain at home, even with reasonable services being provided, the court shall make a finding that the lack of preplacement preventive efforts were reasonable.[18]

This statute makes two things clear in emergency situations: (1) no child should ever be left in a dangerous situation, and (2) reasonable efforts must always be considered, even in an emergency.

Faced with a removal where the agency is claiming an emergency existed and wants the judge to excuse the lack of preventive efforts, the judge should scrutinize the following:

(1) Is this truly an emergency? Even in a legitimate emergency, there is the question of degree. The fact that the agency labels the case an "emergency" does not eliminate the need for judicial scrutiny. At a minimum, the agency should do whatever time allows. Some examples of efforts that can be made even in an emergency include: removal of a perpetrator, rather than the child; locating relatives who can care for the child; and use of homemaker, respite care, emergency funds and intensive in-home services based on the Homebuilders model.

(2) Has the agency been involved with the family on prior occasions? Judges and attorneys may need to press for accurate information on any prior contacts the agency has had with the family. This should include asking the family whether they had requested help on prior occasions, and if so, what was the agency's response. If there were prior contacts, is the emergency the result of the

---

17. *See* ARK. CODE. ANN. § 9-27-335(c)(3) (Supp. 1986); CAL. WELF. & INST. CODE § 319 (West Supp. 1990); CAL. JUV. CT. R. 1446 (a) (1990); FLA. STAT. ANN. §§ 39.402 (B)(a), 39.41(4)(B) (West Supp. 1988); ILL. ANN. STAT. ch. 37, para. 803-12(3) (Smith-Hurd 1989); LA. CODE. JUV. PROC. ANN. art. 87(F) (West 1988); MISS. CODE ANN. §§ 43-21-301(4)(c)(ii), -309(4)(c)(ii), -603(7)(b)(1989); MO. ANN. STAT. § 211.183(1) (Vernon Supp. 1990); OKLA. STAT. ANN. tit. 10, § 1104.1(d)(2)(1987); VA. CODE §§ 16.1-252(E)(2)(1988).

18. CAL. WELF. & INST. CODE § 319 (West Supp. 1990); *see also*, MINN. STAT. § 260.172 (Supp. 1990). (If court finds agency's efforts have not been reasonable, but further efforts could not permit child to safely remain at home, court may still authorize or continue removal.)

agency's failure to make reasonable efforts on those prior occasions?[19]

E.   *Interplay With Other State Statutes*

Confusion as to how the requirement interplays with other state statutes also has hampered implementation. These other statutes include mandatory reporting statutes, removal statutes, and termination of parental rights statutes. They are discussed in detail below.

1.   Mandatory Reporting Statute

Since 1964, every state has enacted a statute requiring the reporting of suspected child abuse and neglect.[20] The range of persons who must report the abuse/neglect has expanded over the years and now includes a variety of individuals involved with children.[21] Likewise, the types of abuse and neglect which must be reported have increased in most states to include physical abuse, physical neglect, sexual abuse, and emotional maltreatment.[22] Obviously, these statutes have greatly increased the number of children who come to the attention of child welfare agencies and who, consequently, may be at risk of being removed from their homes. Nevertheless, just as the report itself does not justify removal, neither does it negate the need to make reasonable efforts.

This is true regardless of who the reporting person is. It is not uncommon for agency workers to feel pressured to accommodate the opinion of the reporter. For example, a physician may be concerned about a child's injuries and the parent's role in the child receiving those injuries. While the physician may feel strongly

---

19. For a further discussion of reasonable efforts and emergencies, *see* Ratterman, *Reasonable Efforts to Prevent Foster Placement: A Guide to Implementation* (2nd ed., 1987), American Bar Association, at 13-14.

20. *See, e.g.,* CAL. PENAL CODE §§ 11164 to 11174.3 (West Supp. 1990); MASS. GEN. LAWS ANN. ch. 119, §§ 51A *et seq.* (West Supp. 1989); FLA. STAT. ANN. §§ 415 *et seq.* (West Supp. 1988); OHIO REV. CODE ANN. tit 21, § 2151.421 (Anderson 1989).

21. *See, e.g.,* CAL. PENAL CODE § 11166 (West Supp. 1990) (following persons covered: any child care custodian, health practitioner, or employee of a child protective agency who knows or reasonably suspects child is abused shall report to child protective agency; any commercial film and photographic print processor who has knowledge of, or observes in professional capacity, child engaged in sexual act shall report; any other person who has reasonable suspicion child has been abused may report); FLA. STAT. ANN. § 415.504 (West Supp. 1988) (any person, including, but not limited to, health or mental health professionals; school, childcare, or social workers; or law enforcement officers, who knows or has reasonable cause to suspect that a child is abused or neglected, must report by calling a statewide toll-free number).

22. *See, e.g.,* CAL. PENAL CODE §§ 11165.1 to 11165.4 (West Supp. 1990) (statutes cover sexual abuse, assault and exploitation; neglect; willful cruelty or unjustifiable punishment of a child; and unlawful corporal punishment or injury).

that the child should not be removed from the parents' custody, the worker has a legal obligation to make an independent investigation of the case and also to make reasonable efforts to prevent the child's removal.

2. Child Removal Statutes

Every state has statutory guidelines outlining when a governmental agency can remove children from their parents custody. These statutes cover a range of removal situations, including emergency law enforcement removals, social worker removals, and removals initiated or authorized by court order. While the reasons justifying removal differ somewhat from state to state, they generally require that the child be in imminent danger of substantial harm and that the parents are unable to protect the child from that harm.[23]

As with the mandatory reporting statute, the crucial point to stress is that even though the statutory grounds for removal exist in a case, this does not generally excuse an agency from its obligation under federal law to make reasonable efforts to prevent that removal. At the same time, the failure to make reasonable efforts does not prevent a state from removing a child from a dangerous situation. Rather, if the failure to provide services is found to be unreasonable, it will only result in a lack of federal funding for the child's placement until reasonable efforts are made. Unfortunately, at least ten states' statutes make removal conditional upon a finding that reasonable efforts have been made.[24] It would appear that judges in these states may be hard-pressed to make a negative reasonable efforts determination in cases where the child is clearly at risk but no services exist or none have been sought out to keep the child safely in the home.

3. Statutory Grounds Justifying No Reunification Services

At least one state, California, has passed a statute outlining grounds that can justify not providing a family with reunification services.[25] If these grounds are proven at the dispositional hearing

23. *See, e.g.*, CAL. WELF. & INST. CODE § 319 (West Supp. 1990.)
24. *See* FLA. STAT. ANN. §§ 39.402 (2), (8)(a) (West 1988); GA. CODE ANN. § 24A-2701 (Supp. 1988); ILL. ANN. STAT. sch. 37, para. 803-12, (Smith-Hurd 1989); IOWA CODE ANN. §§ 232.52(6), .95 (2)(a) (West 1985); ME. REV. STAT. ANN. tit. 15, § 3314 (1)(C-1) (Supp. 1989); MISS. CODE ANN. §§ 43-21-301 (4)(c), - 309(4)(c), -603(7)(a) (Supp. 1989); N.Y. SOC. SERV. LAW §358-a(3) (McKinney Supp. 1990); Va. Code §§ 16.1-251(A)(2), -252(e)(2) (Supp. 1988); WASH. REV. CODE ANN. §§13.32A.170(1)(d), 13.34.060(6)(a)(Supp. 1989); WIS. STAT. ANN. §§ 48.355(2)(a)(West Supp. 1989).
25. CAL. WELF. & INST. CODE § 361.5 (West Supp. 1990).

by clear and convincing evidence, the court may choose not to order reunification services but rather to proceed to a permanency planning hearing within 120 days.[26] By California court rule, the dispositional hearing for children already detained generally must take place no later than 15 days from the date of the detention order.[27] This means that in specified cases within a very short time, generally a matter of a few months from the time a child is removed, the agency may be relieved from working to reunify the family.

The grounds in California's statute that can justify no reunification services include: (1) parent's whereabouts unknown; (2) mental disability of parent as defined in the termination statute; (3) child previously made a dependent for physical/sexual abuse and being removed again for additional physical/sexual abuse; (4) parent convicted of causing the death of another child through abuse or neglect; and (5) child under five and a victim of severe physical abuse.[28]

The intent behind the passage of this statute was to lend some guidance to child welfare agencies in deciding which families should be reunified.[29] It was also a recognition that, given the scarcity of resources, some families would probably never be able to be reunified within California's short statutory time periods. Nevertheless, even these families have the right to have the agency make reasonable efforts to prevent removal and to reunify up to the time of the dispositional hearing. From the time the agency first became involved with the family, the need to make reasonable efforts existed. At the very least, these families have the right to have the worker make every effort to place the child with a relative. More than anything, this type of statute allows the court to decide much sooner than in most cases when the worker no longer needs to make reasonable efforts.

In 1986, an appellate court decision, *In Re Clarence I.*,[30] appears to have encouraged the legislature to pass this statute. In that case, the mother appealed the termination of her parental rights as to her son. The trial court had ruled that attempting to reunify this family was inappropriate because of the severity of the child's injuries, the felony convictions of the parents, the par-

---

26. California uses the term "permanency planning hearing" instead of the term "18 month dispositional hearing" found in P.L. 96-272 § 475(5)(c).

27. Cal. Juv. Ct. Rules 1447, 1451 (1990).

28. Cal. Welf. & Inst. Code § 361.5 (b)(West Supp. 1990).

29. The author bases this assertion on her extensive contact with judges, child welfare workers, and others involved in California's dependency systems over the past several years.

30. 180 Cal. App. 3d 279, 225 Cal. Rptr. 466 (Ct. App. 1986).

ents' psychological evaluations, and another agency's written report.

The mother's sole challenge on appeal was that the trial court had failed to order family reunification services, as required under both case law and court rules, prior to terminating her parental rights. The appeals court held the court rule applied only to juvenile court proceedings and thus was inapplicable to this superior court challenge.[31] It stated that a decision to order reunification services was within the sound discretion of the trial court, and that the court was not required to order them prior to terminating the parental relationship.[32]

The court of appeal affirmed the trial court's determination that it would have been inappropriate to attempt to reunite this family and return the child to his parents, with whom he would have likely suffered additional serious bodily injury or perhaps death.

It is unclear whether other states will follow California's example in statutorily defining which families need not be provided reunification services. Many judges in California report hesitance in applying the statutory guidelines, unsure whether the statute provides the necessary due process to families.[33] As of this date, there is no reported case law challenging the application of the statute.

4. Termination of Parental Rights Statutes

Many state termination statutes contain a requirement that a family be provided or at least offered reasonable services before their parental rights can be terminated. Generally, this requirement is coupled with the condition that the child has been in out-of-home placement for a certain period of time and other conditions that may differ from state to state.[34]

The reasonable services required by these statutes are arguably the same as the reasonable efforts required by federal law. A termination case generally involves a history of family problems,

---

31. 180 Cal. App. 3d at 281, 225 Cal. Rptr. at 467.
32. *Id.* at 283, 225 Cal. Rptr. at 468.
33. *See supra* note 29.
34. *See, e.g.,* CAL. CIV. CODE § 232(2)(a)(7) (West Supp. 1990); LA. REV. STAT. ANN. § 13:1601(D(4), (F)(4) (West 1989); MINN. STAT. ANN. § 260.221(b)(5) (Supp. 1990); N.Y. SOC. SERV. LAW § 384-b (McKinney 1983 & Supp. 1986); N.C. GEN. STAT. § 7A-289.32(3) (1989); R.I. GEN. LAWS § 15-7-7 (1985); S.D. CODIFIED LAWS ANN. § 26-8-35.2 (1989); WIS. STAT. ANN. § 48.415 (West Supp. 1989). The following are state statutes where reasonable efforts *may* be considered at termination. ALA. CODE § 26-18-7(a)(6) (1986); KAN. STAT. ANN. § 38-1583(b)(7) (1986); MONT. CODE ANN. § 41-3-609(2)(g) (1989); NEB. REV. STAT. § 43-292(6) (1988); NEV. REV. STAT. § 128.106(7) (Supp. 1989); N.H. REV. STAT. ANN. § 170-C:5(V)(b) (Supp. 1989); OR. REV. STAT. § 419.523(2)(1989); TENN. CODE ANN. § 37-1-147(e)(2) (Supp. 1989).

agency work to assist the family, and the parent's response to this assistance. A number of thorough and objective reasonable efforts findings made by a judge throughout the life of a case establishes a meaningful judicial record which can streamline the court process at termination and move the child more quickly into a permanent living situation. On the other hand, the lack of meaningful reasonable efforts determinations during the case's progress or negative determinations can delay or defeat a termination proceeding and cause the child to remain in foster care limbo.

F. *The Role of Law Enforcement*

Another major obstacle to implementation in many jurisdictions is the interplay between law enforcement and child welfare agencies. Far too often, there is little or no coordination or established protocols between the two agencies when a report of child abuse or neglect is made. Often, law enforcement responds alone to the initial report. Many law enforcement officials are not trained in the reasonable efforts requirement and have little access to current information on available services to keep the family intact. As a result, police often remove a child rather than look for alternatives that might allow a child to remain safely at home.

It is important to stress that no matter who responds to a child abuse report, the federal reasonable efforts requirement still applies. Therefore, it is incumbent on state and local child welfare agencies to develop a means of working with law enforcement to insure that reasonable efforts are made before removal.

III. APPLICATION TO DELINQUENT CHILDREN

Depending on the type of placement, the reasonable efforts requirement may apply to cases involving delinquent children. When children are placed in eligible facilities such as family foster care homes or non-secure group homes, reasonable efforts to prevent placement must be made as a condition to receive federal funding for the placement. Children placed in secure, correctional-type facilities are not covered by the reasonable efforts requirement.[35] A handful of states—Iowa, New York, and Virginia—have passed statutes mandating that reasonable efforts be made before a delinquent child is placed in foster care.[36]

---

35. For a further discussion of delinquents, as well as status offenders and the reasonable efforts requirement, *see* Ratterman, *supra* note 19, at 5-6.

36. IOWA CODE ANN. § 232.52.6 (West 1985); N.Y. FAM. CT. ACT § 352.2(2)(b) (McKinney Supp. 1986); VA. CODE § 16.1-279(e)(9)(c) (Supp. 1988).

IV. State Reasonable Efforts Statutes

While P.L. 96-272 required states to implement a number of changes in their child welfare and juvenile court systems, the federal law does not require states to incorporate these changes into their juvenile codes. By 1986, however, at least twenty-one states had passed legislation addressing the court's determination of reasonable efforts.[37] Since 1986, only a few states have passed similar legislation.[38]

At least four states—California, Minnesota, Missouri and Ohio—have adopted comprehensive statutory reasonable efforts schemes that go beyond the technical requirements of the federal law.[39] All are examples of model legislation. Under California's statutory scheme, judicial findings of "reasonable efforts" are tantamount to due process. If seeking to terminate parental rights, the agency in many cases must prove to the court that it made "reasonable efforts" throughout the case. The court is required by statute to make a reasonable efforts determination at virtually every court hearing in the case, beginning at detention, and again at disposition, six and twelve month reviews, the eighteen month permanency planning hearing, and culminating at the termination hearing.[40]

Minnesota's recently-enacted statute offers perhaps the greatest guidance in statutorily defining "reasonable efforts." It defines the

---

37. Ark. Code Ann. § 9- (Supp. 1985); Cal. Welf. & Inst. Code §§ 319, 361(c), 11404 (West Supp. 1989); Fla. Stat. Ann. § 39.402, -.408, -.41 (West 1988); Ga. Code Ann. § 24A-2701(c) (Supp. 1988); Ill. Ann. Stat. ch. 37, para. 803-12(Smith-Hurd 1989); Ind. Code Ann. §§ 31-6-4-6, -10, -15.3, 31-6-11-10 (West 1989); Iowa Code Ann. § 232.52, -.95, -.102 (West 1986); Kan. Stat. Ann. §§ 38-1542(f), -1543(i), -1563(h) (1986); La. Stat. Ann. Code Juv. Pro. (Supp. 1988) art. 87 (West 1988); Me. Rev. Stat. Ann. tit. 15, §§ 3314-1, 3317 (Supp. 1989); Mass. Gen. Laws Ann. ch. 119, § 29C (West Supp. 1989); Miss. Code Ann. § 43-21-301, -309, -405, -603 (Supp. 1989); Mo. Ann. Stat. § 211.183 (Vernon Supp. 1990); Nev. Rev. Stat. § 432B-360 (1986) §, -550 (Supp. 1989); N.M. Stat. Ann. § 32-1-34 (1989); N.Y. Soc. Serv. Law § 358-a, N.Y. Fam. Ct. Act §§ 352.2, 754 (McKinney Supp. 1990); Okla. Stat. Ann. tit. 10 § 1104.1 (1987); Or. Rev. Stat. §§ 419-.576 -.577 (1989); Va. Code § 16.1-251, -252, -279(A)(3)(c), (C)(5)(c), (E)(a)(c) (Supp. 1988); Wash. Rev. Code Ann. § 13.32A.170, -.34.060, -.34.130 (Supp. 1989); Wis. Stat. Ann. § 48.21 (West 1987), §§ 48-355, -.38 (West Supp. 1989).

38. *See, e.g.*, Minn. Stat. § 260.012 (Supp. 1990); Neb. Rev. Stat. § 43-1315 (1987); and Ohio Rev. Code Ann. § 2151.419 (Anderson 1989).

39. Cal. Welf. & Inst. Code §§ 306, 319, 361(c), 366.21(e), 366.21(f), 366.22(a), (West Supp. 1990) and Cal. Civ. Code § 232(a)(7) (West Supp. 1990); Minn. Stat. §§ 260.012(b), -.155, -.172, -.191 (Supp. 1990); Mo. Ann. Stat. § 211.183 (Vernon Supp. 1990); and Ohio Rev. Code Ann. § 2151.49 (Page 1988) (provides for the suspension of sentence).

40. Cal. Welf. & Inst. Code §§ 319 (detention), 361(c) (disposition), 366.21(e) (six-month reviews), 366.21(f) (12-month reviews), 366.22(a) (West Supp. 1990) (18-month permanency planning), and Civ. Code § 232(a)(7) (West Supp. 1990) (termination of parental rights).

term as "the exercise of due diligence by the responsible social service agency to use appropriate and available services to meet the needs of the child and the child's family" to prevent removal, or reunify if removal is necessary.[41] The statute states that the "agency has the burden of demonstrating that it has made reasonable efforts."[42] The juvenile court, on the other hand, must make findings and conclusions as to the provision of "reasonable efforts." The statute gives courts the following guidelines in scrutinizing the services offered or provided to a particular child and family: Were the services relevant to the child's safety and protection, adequate to meet the child's and family's needs, culturally appropriate, available and accessible, consistent and timely, and realistic under the circumstances?[43]

Ohio amended its juvenile code in 1988 to require the court to make written findings of fact regarding reasonable efforts at court hearings where the court is either removing a child from his home or continuing that child's placement in foster care.[44] These hearings include detention, adjudication, and disposition. In its written findings of fact, the court must "briefly describe the relevant services provided by the agency to the family of the child and why those services did not prevent the removal of the child from his home or enable the child to return home."[45]

Some state reasonable efforts statutes use the term "available" when describing the services which the agency must use in making reasonable efforts. California's statute, for example, requires the judge at the detention hearing to determine on the record whether reasonable services were provided to prevent or eliminate removal and whether services are "available" which would prevent the need for further detention.[46] Arguably, the term "available" limits the agency's duty to make reasonable efforts. However, P.L. 96-272 requires close scrutiny of such terms. If an agency claims a particular service is unavailable, the judge should inquire as to whether the lack of the service is reasonable. The legislative purpose behind the reasonable efforts requirement is to encourage states to increase their preventive and reunification services to families in need. Attorneys and other child advocates should push courts and legislatures to see that these services are developed.

---

41. MINN. STAT. § 260.012(b) (Supp. 1990).
42. *Id.*
43. MINN. STAT. § 260.012(c) (Supp. 1990).
44. OHIO REV. CODE ANN. § 2151.419 (Anderson 1989).
45. *Id.*
46. CAL. WELF. & INST. CODE § 319 (West Supp. 1990).

V. REASONABLE EFFORTS' RELATION TO THE INDIAN CHILD WELFARE ACT

In 1978, shortly before the passage of P.L. 96-272, Congress passed the Indian Child Welfare Act, P.L. 95-608 (ICWA). Like P.L. 96-272, the ICWA was passed because of Congress' concern over the excessive number of Indian children removed from their homes. As part of its statutory scheme, the ICWA requires child welfare agencies to make "active efforts" to provide services "designed to prevent the breakup of the Indian family" before they could place a child in foster care or terminate parental rights.

Defining "active efforts" is perhaps as problematic as defining reasonable efforts. However, clearly both requirements apply to Indian children removed from their homes. One source has concluded that "for an effort to be a reasonable one, it must be active. It is possible that an effort could be active without being reasonable, such as in a situation of inappropriate or ineffective case planning and referrals. Active efforts, therefore, must also be reasonable."[47]

While both statutes require close scrutiny into service delivery, the ICWA has an added purpose—to preserve and maintain Indian tribes and cultures—as well as to protect individual families. In addition, unlike the reasonable efforts requirement, in ICWA cases the agency must prove to the court that active efforts have been made before it can remove an Indian child from its family. In contrast, an agency's failure to demonstrate reasonable efforts under P.L. 96-272 only results in the state and Indian tribes being unable to claim federal funding for the child's placement.[48] A final important distinction between the two statutes is that P.L. 96-272 is enforced through federal monitoring, not by the stipulation that a child may not be removed.

At least one state—Minnesota—has attempted to incorporate both reasonable efforts and active efforts into their juvenile codes.[49] Its language reads as follows:

> In a proceeding regarding a child in need of protection or services, the court, before determining whether a child should continue in custody shall also make a determination, consistent with section 260.012 as to whether reasonable efforts, or in the case of an Indian child, active efforts, according to the Indian Child

---

47. Active and Reasonable Efforts to Preserve Families: A Guide for Delivering Services in Compliance with The Indian Child Welfare Act of 1978 (P.L. 95-608) and The Adoption Assistance and Child Welfare Act of 1980 (P.L. 96-272), Northwest Resource Associates, Seattle, Washington (1986).

48. See supra § IIIC for a further discussion on the ramifications for failing to make reasonable efforts under P.L. 96-272.

49. MINN. STAT. § 260.172 (Supp. 1990) (subdivision 1(c)).

Welfare Act of 1978, United States Code, title 25, section 1912(d), were made to prevent placement or to reunite the child with the child's family, or that reasonable efforts were not possible. The court shall also determine whether there are available services that would prevent the need for further detention.

VI. CASE LAW

The appellate courts are more and more becoming a source of direction for defining reasonable efforts in individual cases. This is not surprising, given the lack of legislative guidance, both federal and state, in defining the term. Further, given the inherent discretion in the word "reasonable" — what is reasonable for one person may not be reasonable for another — court decisions in individual cases are vital.

In a recent survey of over 1,200 juvenile court judges from around the country, 44 judges responded that they had made at least one negative reasonable efforts finding during their tenure on the bench.[50] Several of these judges reported that they had made numerous negative findings, with one noting that he had probably made over 100 such findings. The judges reported a variety of reasons for their findings. The reasons most often cited included lack of counseling or parenting classes, no case plan or failure to provide clear directions to parents in the case plan, and lack of agency contact with the family. Other services judges found lacking included mediation, in-home family preservation services, medical evaluations, substance abuse treatment, transportation, homemakers, respite, and failure to comply with visitation arrangements.

In one case, the judge based his negative finding on the fact that the agency failed to develop the case based on the child's individual situation but, rather, relied on the fact that the child's siblings had been properly removed to justify this child's removal.

Those judges making negative findings reported making such findings at all stages of the proceedings, including detention, disposition, 6-12-18 month reviews, and termination of parental rights.

Only a handful of cases now exist that address the issue of reasonable efforts in juvenile dependency cases prior to the termination of parental rights stage. In *Interest of S.A.D.*,[51] the appellate

---

50. This survey was conducted by staff at the Youth Law Center in the summer of 1989. The judges were sent a two-page survey form which contained questions such as: Have you ever made a negative finding of reasonable efforts and, if so, how many times, in what type of case, and at what kind of hearing?

51. 382 Pa. Super 166, 555 A.2d 123 (Pa. Super. Ct. 1989).

court expressed great concern over the agency's failure to make reasonable efforts to keep an eighteen-year-old mother together with her fourteen-month-old daughter. The mother had herself sought help from the agency because she had no money and no housing. Rather than getting help with either, she was told that her only alternative was to "voluntarily" place her baby with the agency while she looked for housing. She did so and, a few weeks later, after finding a job at $3.60 per hour and a place to stay with the family of a friend, she asked the agency to give her child back. The agency refused, saying that she needed "her own place to live,"[52] even though no one from the agency had visited the home where mother was staying.

The agency's evidence of reasonable efforts consisted of the following worker testimony:

> Q. What assistance has been provided?
> A. Well, housing of her child, getting [Mother] hooked up with Community Services, providing her bus pass and things so she can come visit with her child, getting her hooked up with the Salvation Army, which in turn put her up in a motel for a short time.
>
> We have been working with her and encouraging her to get out to D.P.A., get on assistance, seek employment, and encouraging her to find her own place to live.[53]

After a lengthy discussion of the background and purpose behind the federal reasonable efforts requirement, the court concluded:

> Our review of the record reveals a very young, unwed mother, lacking financial resources and housing who was unemployed. The mother, in a responsible fashion, turned to CYS to obtain assistance to provide and care for her child. There is no evidence that this young mother in any way neglected or abused her child. CYS has failed to present clear and convincing evidence to establish dependency and has failed to make reasonable efforts to prevent the separation of the mother and child.
>
> A fundamental purpose of the Juvenile Act is to preserve family unity whenever possible. The Act limits the Commonwealth's course of interference with the family unit to those cases where the parents have not provided a minimum standard of care for the child's physical, intellectual and moral well-being. *In Interest of Pernishek*, 268 Pa. Super. 447, 408 A.2d 872 (1979). It is well-settled that the Juvenile Act was not intended to provide a procedure to take the children of the poor and give them to the rich, nor to take children of the illiterate and crude and give them to the educated and cultured, nor to take the children of the weak and sickly and give them to the strong and healthy.

---

52. *Id.* at 170, 555 A.2d at 125.
53. *Id.* at 173, 555 A.2d at 127.

Neither will this court tolerate the separation of a young child from a parent to protect agency funding.[54]

The court then reversed the order of dependency and remanded the case with instructions that the child be returned to her mother.

In another pre-termination decision, a Missouri appellate court reversed and remanded a case because the dispositional order removing four children from their mother's custody lacked the determination that the agency had made reasonable efforts to prevent the removal. In *Interest of A.L.W., L.R.W., A.M.W. and H.A.K.*,[55] the court carefully reviewed Missouri's reasonable efforts statutory scheme, including its emergency removal provision which deems reasonable efforts to have been made "if the first contact with the family occurred during an emergency in which the child could not safely remain at home even with reasonable in-home services."[56] The court strongly rejected the agency's contention that because a child abuse hot line call coded as "emergency" sent the worker to the family's home, the agency was deemed to have made reasonable efforts under the statute. The court held:

> It is compromise to the safety of the child even with reasonable in-home services that determines the emergency, and not any pseudo-emergency of the hot line. The statute does not mean for the hot line to preempt the role of evidence and adjudication. The contention of such emergency made by the juvenile officer . . . is made all the more tenuous by lack of any allegation of emergency to the court.[57]

Perhaps the most extensive discussion of reasonable efforts is by a juvenile court in an unreported decision. In *Matter of A Child*,[58] upon the mother's motion, the Juvenile Department of the Circuit Court of Multnomah County reviewed the foster care placement of a six and a half-year-old disabled child, and the services rendered to her family. At the time of the hearing, the child had been in out-of-home care for approximately nine months. The court's order addressed only whether the child welfare agency had made reasonable efforts to eliminate the need for removal of the child from her home and to make it possible for the child to return home.

The state's first contention was that neither Oregon nor federal law compelled a reasonable efforts finding at a review hearing re-

---

54. *Id.* at 176, 555 A.2d at 128-29. (citations omitted.).
55. 773 S.W. 2d 129 (Mo. Ct. App. 1989).
56. *Id.* at 133.
57. *Id.* at 134.
58. No. 88178 (Circuit Court for the State of Oregon for Multnomah County, Juvenile Dept.) (Nov. 26, 1986).

quested by a parent. Specifically, the state argued that the hearing was gratuitous, since it was not in response to the agency's report, or a statutorily required six, twelve, or eighteen month review. The court rejected this claim on both federal and state grounds. It held that P.L. 96-272 intended frequent and thorough review of children in foster care, and that state law, while not requiring more hearings, encouraged them.[59]

The state also argued that a reasonable efforts finding is not necessarily in the best interests of the child because it only directly impacts the federal matching funds to the child welfare agency. The court rejected the argument, holding that close scrutiny of the services offered to reunite a family could only be in the child's best interest.[60]

The state also asserted that the reasonable efforts required by the referee at the shelter hearing in this case (medical exam of the child and interview of child's grandmother as possible placement for child) were all that were required in the case. The court, however, found these services to be few and incomplete for a reasonable efforts finding for a child who already had been in agency care for nine months. The court held that the state's contention flew in the face of both the language and legislative history of P.L. 96-272.

Finally, the court, after closely scrutinizing all agency efforts, held that it had not made reasonable efforts to provide either preventive or reunification services to the family. The court based this holding on the following:

(1) The family was not formally referred to parenting classes, a critical service identified for this family, until nine months after the child was removed from the home;[61]

(2) The agency was too slow in providing family and marital counseling and offered no adequate explanation for why it had not offered its intensive family counseling from the outset;[62]

(3) The agency's efforts to arrange a medical appointment for the mother to determine if she needed medication superseded and interfered with the provision of necessary individual counseling for the mother;[63]

(4) The agency failed to provide frequent and appropriate visitation, because it did not attempt unsupervised, extended, overnight and weekend visits which the court deemed entirely appro-

---

59. *Id* at 2-4.
60. *Id.* at 4-5.
61. *Id.* at 8-10.
62. *Id.* at 10.
63. *Id.* at 10-11.

priate;[64] and

(5) The child's medical exam was not to be considered a reunification service, as it was not given for other than routine purposes.[65]

Virtually all other reported appellate cases to date that define "reasonable efforts" or "reasonable services" do so in the context of a termination of parental rights proceeding. In these cases, the courts explain the efforts/services that an agency must have made before the courts will grant the permanent severance of parents' right to the care and custody of their children. In spite of the fact that these cases involve reasonable efforts or services mandated by state termination statutes, they are still extremely relevant in defining reasonable efforts under P.L. 96-272. The remaining cases in this article are termination cases.

As set out in P.L. 96-272's legislative history, Congress passed the reasonable efforts requirement because such efforts were considered to be good social work practice and because of the importance of the constitutional right to family integrity. Certainly these are the same reasons states pass statutes requiring agencies to make reasonable efforts before courts can terminate parental rights. Particularly in light of the lack of an adequate definition of reasonable efforts in either the federal act or accompanying regulations, how courts define the concept at termination is helpful to anyone assessing the requirement in individual cases.

A. *Engaging Families In Accepting Services*

Courts have recently begun to scrutinize more closely the role of child welfare agencies in engaging families to accept and participate in services in individual cases. Many child welfare workers want to know what their duty under the reasonable efforts requirement is in engaging families to accept services. A question often asked by workers is whether just handing a client a telephone number of a service provider is sufficient. The answer, of course, depends on the facts of the individual case. In some cases, handing a client a phone number is sufficient if the client is actually able to follow up and make the call. In others, the worker may need to call for the client and arrange an appointment, and, in still others, the worker may need to actually take the client to the appointment.

As one court has noted:

The question of what constitutes "reasonable efforts" is one

---

64. *Id*. at 12.
65. *Id*. at 12.

which cannot be answered by a definitive statement. Instead, it must be answered on the basis of any given factual situation, for it is clear that services which might be reasonable in one set of circumstances would not be reasonable in a different set of circumstances.[66]

Even though courts need to assess reasonable efforts on a case by case basis, they differ greatly in how intensively they delve into the efforts actually made in a case. Some courts list the problems of the family, enumerate the family's failings in addressing their problems, and tally what the agency did to help the family, with little integration among the three.

A 1986 Missouri case, *In the Interest of AMK*,[67] demonstrates this approach. In that case, the mother appealed the termination of her parental rights to her four children. The basis of the termination was the mother's inability to properly support her children. She argued, among other things, that the child welfare agency had failed to use reasonable, diligent and continuing efforts to help her rectify those conditions which led to the removal of her children.

The court of appeal rejected the mother's argument based on the evidence before it. When the agency intervened, the family had inadequate food, clothing, and electricity, and eviction was imminent. The mother's employment was sporadic and at best her monthly earnings were $180, insufficient to cover food, housing, utilities, and clothing costs. The court found the evidence sufficiently clear, cogent and convincing of the mother's inability to rectify the conditions for termination.

In reaching this result, the court first enumerated the agency's reasonable efforts on behalf of the family: providing food and housing, obtaining a placement for the family at a residential home which taught parenting skills and self-sufficiency, referring the mother to community service programs and psychological counselors, and arranging visits with the mother and her children. The agency also offered to help the mother apply for public food and housing benefits such as AFDC and food stamps.

The court then cited the following actions of the mother as evidence of her further failure to rectify her problems: (1) leaving a 6-month residential treatment program after 1 week; (2) missing community service meetings; (3) having only minimal attendance at her therapy sessions; (4) not completing financial assistance applications; and (5) cancelling visits with her children and not see-

66. In the Matter of Myers, 417 N.E.2d 926, 931 (Ind. App. 1981).
67. 723 S.W.2d 50 (Mo. Ct. App. 1986).

ing them regularly.[68]

While the court in this case goes into some detail about the family's problems/failures and the agency's efforts to help, it fails to make the vital connection between the problems/failures and the agency's efforts. For example, the court notes that the mother had only minimal attendance at therapy sessions. The court did not, however, discuss *why* the mother failed to attend. Was it because the service was not accessible in terms of transportation, cultural appropriateness, and acceptance?[69] Was appropriate childcare provided? The mother clearly was poverty-stricken. Were the services free of charge or was she required to pay all or a portion of the cost?[70]

Likewise, in *In re Kathleen*,[71] the mother placed her child in voluntary foster care, and the local child welfare agency devised a reunification plan. The mother complied with that part of the plan requiring her to find gainful employment and an apartment, and to maintain weekly visits with her daughter, but failed to seek counseling.

Approximately two years later, the mother admitted to dependency, and a new reunification plan was developed. The plan involved increased visitation and required the mother to participate in counseling. She again failed to attend counseling sessions, despite problems that surfaced during visitation.[72]

The mother's parental rights were terminated under a state statute which permits termination when a child has been in state care for at least six months, and when the agency has made "reasonable efforts . . . to encourage and strengthen the parental relationship."[73] The court found that the agency had made reasonable efforts by urging the mother to participate in counseling, and that her failure to do so indicated the impossibility of reunification, thus justifying the termination of her parental rights.

This case again demonstrates a court's failure to take the agency to task about just what efforts it made to help the mother

---

68. *Id.* at 52.

69. *See, e.g.*, Matter of Jose F., 178 Cal. App. 3d 1141, 224 Cal. Rptr. 239, 245 (1986) (case ordered not published) (Court discusses in detail how the agency did not make services accessible for the mother, including excuses offered by the social worker at trial that counseling "could not 'realistically' be considered due to Mrs. V's work hours, the number of children she had and the limited availability of counseling programs for Spanish-speaking persons.")

70. Several other cases take this same approach, without integrating the needs/failures of the family with the efforts made by the agency. *See, e.g.*, Matter of V.M.S., 446 N.E.2d 632 (Ind. Ct. App. 1983) and In the Matter of the Welfare of CD, CT, MT, and ST, 393 N.W.2d 697 (Minn. Ct. App. 1986).

71. 460 A.2d 12 (R.I. 1983).

72. *Id.*

73. *Id.*

participate in counseling. The lower court should have inquired of the mother as to why she refused to engage in counseling—in what way did the agency "urge" her to participate? Was the counseling actually designed to overcome the mother's problems? Just what were the mother's problems? If "problems" did "surface during visitations", did the agency attempt to have a trained family counselor supervise and work with the mother during the actual visits?

In contrast to these cases, the court in *In Matter of Jones*,[74] took a much more critical look at the agency's role in assisting the family. In that case, the parents appealed the termination of their parental rights to their child. Subsequent to the child's removal from the home, the parents had minimal visitation and contact with the child. The father was frequently unemployed, and the parents maintained a substandard living arrangement. The lower court found that the parents had moved frequently and failed to maintain contact with the child welfare agency. The lower court further found that the agency had assisted the parents in paying their medical bills, and had referred them to a consulting center for parenting training and homemaking skills.

In reversing the termination order, the court of appeal found that the agency had merely informed the parents of what actions should be taken in order to facilitate the return of the child. Despite the fact that the parents had changed residences and employment, the court held that the agency was not excused from providing services and, in fact, should have assisted the family in obtaining a stable residence. In addition, the agency's failure to ensure that the homemaker actually made visits and that the parents received parenting training indicated that the agency did not make reasonable efforts to assist the family in reunification.[75]

Other appellate courts have overturned termination decisions because the agency only evaluated the parent's shortcomings, without considering what the agency did to remedy these shortcomings. One New York court held that a parent's failure to maintain contact with the child or plan for its future cannot be

---

74. 436 N.E.2d 849 (Ind. Ct. App. 1982).

75. *See also Matter of Loretta*, 114 A.D.2d 648, 494 N.Y.S.2d 232 (N.Y. App. Div. 1985). (Three siblings had been in foster care most of their lives; agency's original case plan provided for weekly visitations and individual and family counseling; at termination, court determined mother's participation in plan insufficient because she attended only twenty of the sixty-six counseling sessions over an eighteen-month period, and did not regularly visit the children. Court terminated parental rights, and mother appealed. On appeal, while remanding case for other reasons, court held agency's arrangements for counseling and visits, and providing transportation to and from these meetings, were "not only extensive but consistent with the statute" requiring "diligent efforts to encourage and strengthen the parental relationship.") 474 N.Y.S. 2d 421, 61 N.Y.2d 368.

judged without considering the agency's statutory duty to make diligent efforts to encourage or strengthen the parental relationship. The court further found that many New York agencies failed to provide adequate services and in fact interfered with reunification.[76] The court also held that the child welfare agency "must affirmatively plead in detail and prove by clear and convincing evidence that it has fulfilled its statutory duty to exercise diligent efforts to strengthen the parent-child relationship and to reunite the family."[77]

Relying on this language, another New York court, in scrutinizing a reunification plan, held that the agency "should be sensitive to the particular needs and capabilities of the parents . . . and should not be unrealistic in light of the financial circumstances of the parents." These "responsibilities are not one-sided, for the parents are obligated to cooperate with the [agency] . . ."[78]

B. Reasonable Efforts and the Mentally Disabled Parent

Several cases have addressed the issue of reasonable efforts and the mentally disabled parent. A California appellate court recently handed down perhaps the most detailed decision as to what services must be explored in the case of a developmentally disabled parent. In *In re Victoria M.*,[79] the appellate court scrutinized the reunification services offered to a mother who had tested as mildly mentally retarded in 1980 with an I.Q. of 58. Her I.Q. was again measured in 1987 at 72, in the borderline range of intelligence. The mother appealed the termination of her parental rights as to three of her children.

The children had originally been removed for lack of adequate housing. However, the dependency petition was sustained on the grounds of parental neglect because the children, when removed, were found to have lice and scabies, and one child had a burn wound which became infected due to lack of proper attention.

The appellate court reversed the termination order because of the agency's failure to make reasonable efforts. In elaborating, the court noted that the agency failed to tailor services to the mother's intellectual limitations. It also failed to help the mother with the very problems that were the basis of the dependency petition—the children's lice, scabies, and infected wound. Further, while the mother lacked housing, the agency made almost no effort to assist

---

76. In the Matter of Sheila G., 462 N.E.2d 1139 (N.Y. 1984).
77. *Id.* at 474 N.Y.S.2d at 430, 61 N.Y.2d at 385, 462 N.E.2d at 1148.
78. In the Matter of Lisa L., 117 A.D.2d 931, 499 N.Y.S.2d 237 (N.Y. App. Div. 1986).
79. 207 Cal. App. 3d 1317, 255 Cal. Rptr. 498 (1989).

her in finding a place to live. One worker explained his failure in this regard was based on his understanding that the children's grandmother was helping the mother find housing. Another worker reported he had discussed the housing authority with mother and told her to read the newspaper and "keep her eyes open" as she drove about town. The court also faulted the agency for never referring the mother to the appropriate regional center which provides specialized services to developmentally disabled persons.

In another California case, *In re Venita L.*,[80] the parents of a three-year-old child appealed from the court's decision terminating reunification services and ordering a petition freeing the child from her parents' custody to be filed. The court of appeal reversed.

The child had originally been placed in foster care when her mother had been hospitalized in a psychiatric unit. The father lived in a motel at the time and said he could not provide a home. As a result of these circumstances, the agency devised a reunification plan requiring therapy, suitable residence, and regular visitation. In a little more than a year, the parents' reunification plans had been amended five times. The father's plan required participation in Alcoholics Anonymous, due to repeated episodes of violent drunken behavior.

In reversing and remanding the case, the court, while not making light of the father's alcohol abuse, determined that this was not the basis for the initial dependency. It further found that mother had substantially complied with reunification efforts, but that the lower court ignored those efforts and instead focused on the father's alcohol problems.

In *Matter of Catholic Guardian Society*,[81] a mother classified as mildly retarded appealed the termination of her parental rights to her four children. In denying the termination petition, the appellate court held that (1) the agency had not made the diligent efforts required by statute;[82] and (2) the evidence did not establish that the mother's mental retardation precluded her from caring for the children for the foreseeable future.

The court noted that diligent efforts did not exist where the agency had not provided general psychiatric or psychological services or specialized services for mental retardation. The court also found that the mother's passive behavior during visits did not establish a substantial and continuous failure to maintain contact

80. 191 Cal. App. 3d 1229, 236 Cal. Rptr. 859 (1987).
81. 131 Misc. 2d 81, 499 N.Y.S.2d 587 (N.Y. Fam. Ct. 1986).
82. 499 N.Y.S.2d at 592.

with the children, and that present incap..city to care for children because of mental retardation does not, ipso facto, demonstrate a future incapacity.

In *State ex rel. Juv. Dept. v. Habas*,[83] the child had been placed in state custody at birth because of the mother's periodic bouts of manic depression requiring medication and hospitalization. After the mother completed parenting classes, the child was returned to her, contingent upon the agency immediately supplying her with homemaker services and a day nurse. When the child had been home sixteen days, but before any services had been provided, the mother suffered a depressive episode and left the child alone for several hours. When found, the child was in good health except for a severe diaper rash. The agency determined the mother to be a good parent when not in the midst of a depressive bout, but unfit during such episodes.

The trial court had granted termination based on (1) the mother's mental illness which rendered her incapable of caring for her child; and (2) the mother's failure to effect a lasting adjustment after reasonable efforts by the agency. This decision was affirmed by the court of appeals, and mother appealed to the supreme court.

The supreme court reversed the termination order, holding that the agency had failed to show that the mental illness made it impossible for the parent to care for the child in the future and that the agency had failed to make reasonable efforts to provide services. The court noted that the failure to provide services appeared to have been due to "some administrative confusion as to which of two counties was to provide the services."[84]

In *Matter of Star A.*,[85] the child welfare agency appealed the trial court's dismissal of proceedings it instituted to terminate a mother's parental rights as to her two children, who were removed while the mother was hospitalized for mental illness. She was subsequently rehospitalized on several occasions. The agency attempted to arrange psychiatric counseling for the mother on at least two occasions, but made no further efforts to do so, feeling such efforts would be futile since the mother had been receiving services from other agencies and had not been cooperative with them.

The court on appeal found that the agency had not made "diligent efforts to encourage and strengthen the parental relationship" as required by state law, and held that the agency could not

---

83. 299 Or. 177, 700 P.2d 225 (Or. 1985).
84. *Id.* at 186, 700 P.2d at 230.
85. 55 N.Y.2d 560, 450 N.Y.S.2d 465, 435 N.E.2d 1080 (N.Y. 1982).

simply predetermine that efforts would be futile.

The dissent, however, found that the intent of the statute was to ensure permanency for children, that there was no possibility of the children being reunited, that efforts would in fact have been futile, and that therefore the court should have ruled for the agency and terminated parental rights.[86]

C. Reasonable Efforts and Housing

For many families, the lack of adequate housing is the primary reason for state intervention and removal of their children. Many court decisions have addressed this situation and have been fairly sympathetic to the families' situation. For example, in *In the Matter of Derek W. Burns*,[87] a nineteen-year-old mother, who had been in foster care since one month of age, appealed a family court's decision terminating her parental rights to her two-year-old son on the grounds of inadequate planning for the child's physical needs. When her child was born, the mother had turned to the child welfare agency for help in finding housing. As a condition of agency assistance, she was required to place her child in "voluntary" foster care for ninety days.

The mother, upon turning eighteen and relying on the terms of the voluntary placement agreement, notified the agency that she was terminating the arrangement and taking her child with her to live elsewhere. The agency refused and the child was eventually forcibly taken from the mother and placed in foster care.

An agency case worker then established a case plan calling for the mother to attend counseling and parenting classes, to attend weekly visits with her son, and to secure adequate housing and day care. Because the mother was not able to maintain a stable living arrangement for at least six months, the agency initiated, and the court granted, a termination of parental rights petition. The supreme court reversed, holding that the agency had neither provided the mother with meaningful case plans outlining reunification guidelines, nor made reasonable efforts to provide preven-

---

86. *See also* In the Matter of Appeal in Pinal County, 729 P.2d 918 (Ariz. Ct. App. 1986), where the appellate court held that any reunification efforts for the mother, diagnosed as a chronic paranoid schizophrenic, would be futile based on expert testimony that the child would be at risk with the mother in unsupervised settings. *See also* In the Matter of Christine Tate, 67 N.C. Ct. App. 89, 312 S.E.2d 535 (N.C. App. 1984) (Court upheld termination of mother's parental rights where mother suffered from drug and alcohol abuse and mental problems. Court held that agency had made significant efforts to assist mother by referring her to mental health centers, helping her with housing and employment, and monitoring her case. The court further found that mother had not made "substantial progress." Although she had made some efforts to work with her child, "substantial progress" requires a positive result from these efforts.)
87. 519 A.2d 638 (Del. 1986).

tive and/or reunification services. Even though the sole reason for the child's transfer to agency custody was lack of housing, the case plan did not indicate any housing assistance services.

In *In the Matter of Enrique R.*,[88] the child was not released from foster care to live with his grandmother solely because she could not obtain adequate housing. (She had applied for public housing in 1980 and, because her application was lost, was forced to file again in 1984.) All parties agreed that the maternal grandmother was a fit person to provide the child a permanent home and could provide access to both the child's parents while they underwent drug therapy.

The court recognized the negative effects of prolonged foster care upon children, and the duty of the agency to take all steps necessary to implement the state's goal of permanency for foster children. The court found that return of the child to his maternal grandmother satisfied that goal, with the exception of inadequate housing. Relying on state law and agency regulations, the court ordered the agency to assist the grandmother in obtaining adequate housing. Such assistance was to include writing letters, making phone calls, and taking legal action on the grandmother's behalf to secure a preference in tenant selection for public housing.

In another New York case, *In the Matter of Jason S.*,[89] the agency appealed the court's dismissal of a petition to terminate the mother's parental rights. The appellate court affirmed, holding that the agency failed to establish that it had actively aided the mother in her search for suitable housing—the primary obstacle preventing the return of the child. Additionally, the court found that the agency failed to work with the mother to strengthen and encourage her relationship with her child, even though she often showed little interest in having regular contact with her child.

D.   Parent-Child Visitation and Reasonable Efforts

Visitation between parent and child has been shown in numerous studies to be one of the most important, if not *the* most important, reunification service.[90] No foster care case is complete without a complete discussion of the visitation arrangements existing for the family. One commentator, after in-depth interviews with

---

88.   129 Misc. 2d 956, 494 N.Y.S.2d 800 (N.Y. Fam. Ct. 1985).

89.   117 A.D.2d 605, 498 N.Y.S.2d 71 (N.Y. App. Div. 1986).

90.   *See, e.g.*, Fansel, D., *On the Road to Permanency*, CWLA, New York, 1982 (Children visited frequently are more likely to be released from foster care); WEINSTEIN, E., THE SELF-IMAGE OF THE FOSTER CHILD, Russell Sage Foundation, New York (1960) (Frequent visiting is associated with emotional well-being of children and parents).

selected caseworkers in several states, found that to a great extent planned visit frequency is beyond the parents' control. Rather, frequency is much more the result of such things as agency policy and resources, where the child is placed, the cooperation of the foster parents, and caseworker attitudes and assessment of the case.[91]

In spite of these findings, only a few courts clearly enunciate and evaluate an agency's reasonable efforts in the area of visitation.[92] Far more common is the situation where visitation is only briefly alluded to, often by holding the parent responsible for problematic visits.[93]

One case, however, that has closely scrutinized an agency's efforts in the visitation area is *In re Kristina L.*[94] This case was an appeal by parents of the termination of their parental rights to their middle child. The child had spent all but her first six months in foster care, where she had been placed for failure to thrive. The mother had no visits with her child for three months after the child entered foster care and visits began only because the mother requested them. For several months, the mother had only hour-long visits with her infant daughter every other week. The trial court terminated parental rights based on the fact that the child had bonded to her foster parents, and that future bonding with her biological parents was impossible.

The Rhode Island Supreme Court reversed for the following reasons: (1) the state's failure to prove that the parents were unfit; (2) the trial court's failure to find that the child was likely to suffer physical or emotional harm if she were returned to her family; (3) the parents cooperated with the child welfare agency; and (4) the agency failed to make reasonable efforts to reunify the family.

The supreme court, in its decision, noted that it was not surprising that the child had bonded with her foster family in light of the "totally inadequate" visitation schedule arranged by the agency.

The court went into a detailed discussion of the visitation sched-

---

91. Hess, P., Case and Context: Determinants of Planned Visit Frequency in Foster Family Care. CWLA, New York, Vol. LXVII, No. 4, July/August, 1988.

92. *See, e.g.*, In Re Kristina L., 520 A.2d 574 (R.I. 1987); In the Matter of a Child, No. 88178, (Circuit Court for the State of Oregon For Multnomah County, Juvenile Dept.) (Nov. 26, 1986).

93. *See, e.g.*, Matter of V.M.S., 446 N.E.2d 632 (Ind. Ct. App. 1983) (Termination upheld in case where agency asserted in termination petition, among other things, that parents' behavior while visiting their children did not demonstrate adequate parental relationship); Matter of Christine Tate, 312 S.E.2d 535 (N.C. Ct. App. 1984)(Court upheld termination based on following: (1) child did not cry when visits ended; (2) parent did not complete entire visits; (3) parent had completed only seven visits in the past year; and (4) mother showed an inability to provide a stable environment.)

94. 520 A.2d 574 (R.I. 1987).

ule the agency arranged for the family over a four year period. It described this schedule as "insufficient at best and sometimes nonexistent."[95] The agency had to cancel many visits because there was no worker to transport the child or because of car troubles. The child's first overnight visit was canceled because the mother was unable to get a crib for her daughter. Finally, after the child had been in foster care for four years, the family entered a reunification program with another agency that took over the visitation schedule. The program worked intensively with the family and greatly increased the length and number of visits. With the new schedule, the child adjusted well to the increased visits and no longer became upset and vomited before the visits took place, as was the case when the social service agency arranged them.

The court also was concerned that, in spite of the parents cooperating with the agency and showing their care and concern for the child, their rights were terminated. The court noted that the mother had taken the child to three different hospitals when she was an infant in an attempt to determine why the baby was not gaining weight, and had also participated in counseling sessions, visited the child, attended a parenting program, and at times "went beyond what was required" for reunification.

The supreme court determined that the agency's keeping the child from her family for six years for reasons as insignificant as dirty dishes and laundry and an awkwardness between mother and child was unacceptable, and ordered the family court to oversee the reunification of the family. In its decision, however, the court encouraged the foster family to continue to play a part in the child's life.

In scrutinizing a visitation schedule in a particular case, there are a number of questions that judges, lawyers, social workers, and others can ask. First and most important, how soon did visits begin after a child's removal? The time between removal and the first visit is a crucial one. Both children and parents can experience a great deal of fear not knowing what has happened to each other. If several weeks elapse before the first visit, a judge should question whether the agency's efforts in this regard were reasonable.

One should also ask how often do visits take place and how long do they last. Often parents must travel a great distance to visit. Short visits may not seem worth the effort. Also, are the visits supervised? Is this justified by the facts of the situation? Where do the visits take place? Is the setting in as home-like a setting as

---

95. 520 A.2d at 581.

possible or in the agency offices?

E. Impact Litigation and Reasonable Efforts

A few class actions have been brought challenging a child welfare system's failure as a whole to make reasonable efforts to preserve or reunify families. In *Grant v. Cuomo*,[96] four named plaintiffs and three non-profit corporations sued New York state and municipal officials, seeking class certification, declaratory relief and a mandatory injunction requiring defendants to perform duties imposed upon them by New York's child welfare laws. Specifically, plaintiffs alleged that defendants failed to make preventive services available for families with children being considered for foster care, and failed to provide protective services to children in danger of child abuse.

The New York Supreme Court held that since defendants availed themselves of federal funding for child welfare programs, they were bound by federal mandates. Specifically, defendants were required to (1) make *reasonable efforts* to keep children with their families prior to placing them in foster care; and (2) implement a service plan for children being considered for foster care, including short and long term goals, services required by the child, the manner in which they will be provided, alternative plans, and preventive services.

The following year another New York court took on New York City's child welfare agency. In *Martin A. v. Gross*,[97] several families sued the agency, arguing that it had failed to provide them with preventive services sufficient to avoid foster care placement for their children. To support their argument, plaintiffs cited state law which required the agency to provide day care, homemaker services, parent training, and aid in transportation, clinic services, and 24-hour access to emergency shelter, cash and goods. They also challenged the 90-day limit on emergency shelter services.

The New York Supreme Court granted the families' motions for preliminary injunction, holding that defendants had a mandatory duty to conduct thorough evaluations, develop meaningful service plans and identify the services to be provided. The court also ordered the agency to implement a plan that was consistent with its legal obligations, and enjoined the state from imposing the 90-day limitation on emergency shelter since it conflicted with the purpose of preventive services law. The court

---

96.   130 A.D.2d 154, 518 N.Y.S.2d 105 (N.Y. App. Div. 1987) *aff'd* 73 N.Y.2d 820 (1988).

97.   138 Misc. 2d 212 (N.Y. Sup. Ct. 1987), *aff'd* N.Y.L.J. Sept. 29, 1989, at 21, col. 1 (App. Div. 1st Dept.), motion for leave to appeal dismissed, 72 N.Y.2d 1041.

noted that providing emergency shelter for longer than 90 days may, for example, wipe out the need for foster care placement altogether or reduce it substantially.

VII. The Role of Attorneys in Implementing Reasonable Efforts

All attorneys in a dependency action, regardless of whether they represent the child welfare agency, the parents, or the child, play a key role in the implementation of reasonable efforts. While the agency has the duty to make the reasonable efforts and the court has the duty to determine whether the agency does this, it is the attorneys who must investigate the agency's assertions of reasonable efforts and challenge these assertions where appropriate. Judges rely on attorneys to flesh out the services offered and/or provided to the families and to present the evidence that will provide a basis for the reasonable efforts determination.

All attorneys, regardless of who their client is, should investigate the removal of a child from the family or, if already removed, investigate the reunification efforts of the agency.[98] In investigating a child's removal, attorneys must find out the circumstances under which the child was taken from the family. They should inquire about the family's prior contacts with the agency, who made the removal decision, the basis for the removal, and particularly the specific harm the removal was designed to prevent; and what alternatives, including in-home services and placement with relatives, were considered prior to removal.[99] They must then present appropriate evidence to the juvenile court.

VIII. Social Policy Considerations

A. Funding Issues

As mentioned previously, the intent of P.L. 96-272 and the reasonable efforts requirement in particular was to combat the foster care limbo to which far too many of our abused and neglected children were being subjected. It was hoped that by putting some of the monies being spent for foster care placement into preventive services for the families of these children, the problem of foster

---

98. *See, e.g.,* Cal. Welf. & Inst. Code § 317(e) (West Supp. 1990). Many jurisdictions are also drafting standards and practice guidelines for attorneys in dependency actions. *See, e.g.,* Faye Kimiera, ed., *Attorney's Manual For Handling Child Abuse and Neglect Cases in Hawaii*, Hawaii State Bar Association, 1989.

99. For a more detailed discussion of the attorney role, *see Making Reasonable Efforts: Steps for Keeping Families Together*, The Edna McConnell Clark Foundation, at 11-40 (1987).

care drift could be addressed. The rationale from a funding stand-point was that it would be more cost-effective to pay for preventive services than for years of a child's substitute care in a state-paid placement.[100]

While the intent of P.L. 96-272 has not been realized for all children in the child welfare system, it is still considered both good social work practice and cost-effective. Studies of intensive in-home service programs throughout the country bear this out. For example, a study done for the Maryland Department of Human Resources sifts through financial data on out-of-home placements, staff salaries, and in-home services to demonstrate the cost-effectiveness of intensive in-home services for Maryland families.[101] The Adoption Assistance and Child Welfare Act of 1980 permits states to transfer unused federal foster care funds into preventive services programs.[102] This is a direct financial incentive to states to shift their resources away from placement and toward services enabling families to stay together.[103]

California is currently experimenting with providing financial incentives to counties to increase their efforts in providing services to prevent removal or enhance reunification. In 1988, Under A.B. 558, three pilot counties were permitted to shift 10% of their projected AFDC-FC foster care funds into family maintenance and reunification services. As of this writing, those agencies implementing A.B. 558 report being very optimistic about the legislation's success in keeping troubled families intact.[104]

B.   Conflict Between Child Rescue Philosophy and Family Preservation Philosophy

Child welfare practice in the United States prior to the passage of P.L. 96-272 was largely based on a child rescue philosophy, with little focused effort made by agencies to prevent the breakup

---

100. *See*, Allen, *A Guide to the Adoption Assistance and Child Welfare Act of 1980*, in FOSTER CHILDREN IN THE COURTS (M. Hardin, ed.) American Bar Association, 1983, p.2.

101. "Measuring the Cost-Effectiveness of Family-Based Services and Out-of-Home Care", Institute of Urban and Regional Research and National Resource Center on Family-Based Services, School of Social Work, University of Iowa (June 1983); *see also*, "Evaluation of Nebraska's Intensive Services Project", the National Resource Center on Family-Based Services, School of Social Work, University of Iowa (March 1984).

102. Social Security Act §§ 474(c)(2), (4), 42 U.S.C. §§ 674(c)(2), (4).

103. Ratterman, et al., *Reasonable Efforts To Prevent Foster Placement: A Guide To Implementation*, (2d ed., 1987) American Bar Association, 1; and Allen, et al., *A Guide to the Adoption Assistance and Child Welfare Act of 1980*, in FOSTER CHILDREN IN THE COURTS (Mark Hardin, ed.) American Bar Association, 585, 605 n.68 (1983).

104. Telephone interview with Jeanne Newton, Family Preservation Specialist, Department of Public Welfare, Solano County, California (January 28, 1990).

of families and a child's subsequent placement into foster care. The intent of the child rescue philosophy was to insure that no child was left in an unsafe situation. While well-intentioned, this philosophy often doomed children to years of drift in foster care, with little or no hope of being placed in a permanent home. It also neglected or failed to recognize the harm that separation can cause to both children and their parents.[105]

Public Law 96-272, in contrast, is primarily based on a family preservation philosophy. This philosophy has as its starting point the belief that a child's biological family is the placement of first preference and that "reasonable efforts" must be made to preserve this family as long as the child is safe. Where these efforts fail and the child must be removed, the family preservation philosophy holds that reasonable efforts must still be made to reunify the child with the family.

Clearly, these two philosophies place very different emphases on the value the biological family has to a particular child. For many who have worked in the child welfare field prior to the passage of P.L. 96-272, switching to a radically different view of the value of working with the biological family has not been easy. For still others who generally believe in family preservation, implementing it in their day-to-day practice has been a challenge. The lack of adequate federal and state funding hinders implementation. Further, many times inflexible agency policies and funding streams help keep family preservation practice from becoming a reality in many jurisdictions.

CONCLUSION

Ten years ago, Congress passed the reasonable efforts requirement as a key part of a comprehensive statutory scheme to reform our child welfare systems. To date, no system has completely implemented the reforms necessary to make reasonable efforts a reality and only a handful have made substantial progress in adequately serving our families in crisis. Nevertheless, P.L. 96-272, including its reasonable efforts requirement, will surely remain the law for at least the next decade. By the year 2000, the federal statute will be amended and its provisions made stronger. State legislatures will continue to pass and strengthen their statutory schemes requiring compliance with reasonable efforts and other reforms of P.L. 96-272. However, it is predicted that the greatest change and progress will be focused on the courtrooms across the country. Both trial and appellate judges will be faced with an

---

105. *See supra* note 4.

ever-greater number of challenges to child welfare practices on behalf of our nation's at-risk children. One hopes the courts will respond to and meet that challenge.

Permanency Planning: Another Remedy in Jeopardy?

Edith Fein
Hartford, Connecticut

Anthony N. Maluccio
Boston College

The course of the child welfare reform permanency planning is discussed. Background, achievements, and unanticipated effects of permanency planning are reviewed, and some directions for thinking about the current crisis in child welfare are suggested.

Since the mid-1970s, permanency planning has been the guiding principle in child welfare. The concept took root in the landmark Oregon study,[1] flourished in the Adoption Assistance and Child Welfare Act of 1980 (P.L. 96-272), and has now taken on the aura of dogma among child welfare workers. When a new concept becomes so accepted, examination of how it is operating and whether it is fulfilling its original promise is vital. The typical course of institutional reform repeats itself time and again. At one point, a reform movement is created to correct deplorable practices in one area of society's functioning. The reform flourishes for a while, and its acceptance soon leads to complacency. Benign neglect permits the proliferation of unintended negative consequences of the reform, institutional indifference and negligence follow, and then pressure for a new reform builds.

As a consequence of such a process, permanency planning may have become another remedy in jeopardy. In considering the question, we will review some achievements and unanticipated effects of per-

Social Service Review (September 1992).

manency planning and suggest not solutions but directions for thinking about the role of permanency planning in child welfare in the future.

Background of Permanency Planning

Child welfare and its practice of foster care have always had a place in the story of the human family. Modern child welfare practices can be traced to the middle of the nineteenth century, when the movement originated "to seek out and to rescue" children who were neglected or cruelly treated.[2] Agencies devoted to the rescue of children were modeled after the animal rescue societies, and a common outcome of the investigation of complaints was placement in an institution.[3] From these institutions, and from almshouses and orphanages, children were often placed with surrogate families who could use their labor or to whom they were indentured. The first choice for placement was a rural, preferably farm, family, which provided free care for the children.[1]

By the 1920s, however, with changing social and economic conditions (the relative decrease in farm families, an increasing divorce rate, and larger numbers of women working outside the home), the use of "boarding homes" was replacing the free foster care that had previously existed.[5] By the time of the Depression, free foster family care was a thing of the past, and orphanages and similar institutions now had to pay board for the youngsters in their care if they were to be placed with a family. Moreover, the Social Security Act of 1935, with its support to families with dependent children, weakened the economic grounds for taking children from their parents. Concern for children began to be focused on efforts to protect them from abuse and neglect rather than rescue them from poverty. By this time, the growth of social casework and the influence of psychoanalytic theory led to the expectation that parents could be rehabilitated to care for their children appropriately, and the perception of foster care as child rearing by a substitute family on a temporary basis gradually evolved.

By the 1970s, following research findings documenting the "drift" of children in foster care,[6] a movement emerged to provide permanence for children coming to the attention of the child welfare systems. The previously mentioned Oregon project demonstrated various strategies for attaining permanence. With the institutionalization of the permanency planning movement in the 1980 Adoption Assistance and Child Welfare Act, and the consequent emphasis on maintaining children in their own families or in another permanent family through adoption, foster family care came into dispute.[7] Although in the early 1980s up to 40 percent of the children in care had been there 2 years or more, foster care was no longer officially viewed as a viable long-term alternative for children who were removed from their biological families.[8] Moreover, what data exist support the belief of child welfare workers that the permanency planning movement's impetus to prevent placement and reunify removed children with their biological families has been "successful" enough to result in a foster care system in which the most difficult youngsters remain:[9] typically those who are older, who come from disorganized or poorly functioning families, and who display multiple behavioral, developmental, and other problems and needs.[10] As a consequence, administrators, practitioners, and others are increasingly underscoring the need for further reforms: specialized or therapeutic foster family–based treatment homes, improved services to all children in care, and the professionalization of foster parenting.[11] In addition, recognition is growing that service systems are not as responsive as they should be to the special needs and qualities of minority children and families, who are disproportionately represented in the child welfare system.[12]

The Current Situation in Permanency Planning

The 1980 Adoption Assistance and Child Welfare Act was designed to end the drift of children in foster care, encourage planning for permanency for each child through options ranging from return to biological parents to adoption and long-term foster care, provide oversight to move cases through the child welfare system, and develop preventive services to avert family breakdown.[13] The current situation is bitterly disappointing in view of the hopes raised by the legislation. In the following sections, we will discuss some results of permanency planning and some unanticipated effects that may contain the seeds for new reform efforts.

Numbers in Care

Until 1984, the legislation seemed to be working, and, up to that point, the permanency planning movement was considered a success. Although accurate data do not exist, federal government estimates based on voluntary reporting by the states suggest that, by 1983, the number of children in out-of-home care decreased dramatically from the 1977 high of over half a million to less than a quarter of a million.[14] The length of time in care also decreased substantially. The number of children in care for more than 2 years dropped from 58 percent in 1977 to 47 percent in 1982, the median time in care dropped from 31 to 21 months, and the average time in care dropped from 47 to 35 months.[15] The prevalence rate, that is, the number of children in care as a proportion of the number in the general population, declined from 7.7 per 1,000 to four.[16] If the 1977 rate had continued, there would have been 485,000 children in care in 1982 instead of 243,000.[17]

As children moved out of care more readily, those remaining were the ones with whom the system had the most difficulty. They were older, more had special needs, and minority representation was greater than that in the general population.[18] The disproportionate number of minority youngsters in foster care was especially disturbing, particularly because minority adolescents were underrepresented.[19] This suggested that younger minority children were entering care in disproportionately large numbers and that minority adolescents were not receiving child welfare services. Minority overrepresentation among adolescents incarcerated or in psychiatric facilities underscores the seriousness of the problem.[20]

By the latter half of the 1980s, some of the earlier successes were being reversed. The number of children in care was again rising, more very young children were entering care, and reentry rates were increasing, suggesting repeated episodes of short-term care.[21] As shown in an extensive analysis of caseloads in New York State, foster care reentry contributed substantially to the rise in foster care caseloads.[22] The stability and continuity sought for children by the permanency planning movement were fast disappearing. As was observed with deinstitutionalization in mental health services, unintended consequences were becoming evident in foster care.

Since 1984, the reversal in trends has been accelerating. The astronomic rise in reports of child abuse and neglect is stretching the state systems to the breaking point. Already burdened by such debilitating socioeconomic forces as substance abuse, family violence, babies born with Acquired Immune Deficiency Syndrome (AIDS), teenage pregnancy, homelessness, and the gap between rich and poor, state children's agencies are increasingly coming under attack by parents' groups, child welfare professionals, and legal groups willing to undertake litigation on behalf of children.

Prevention of Placement

Earlier certainties about the ability of permanency planning to guide the rescue of children from the worst excesses of the child welfare system are being challenged by new insights. For example, child welfare workers have long been aware that permanency planning should begin before a child is removed from the home. Nevertheless, federal legislation mandating reasonable efforts on the part of state agencies to prevent placement has foundered due to difficulty in specifying what constitutes reasonable effort and the slow growth of prevention services.[23] Although prevention services, which have become nearly synonymous with the family preservation services movement, are rapidly growing in most states, [24] the approximately 2 million cases of child abuse reported in recent years and the almost quarter of a million new entries into foster care in 1988 suggest that efforts to prevent placement are falling far short of their mark.[25]

Though the concept of preventive services was written into P.L. 96-272, the funding to implement that concept has been insufficient. Family preservation and family resource services for families whose children are at imminent threat of removal have been popular prescriptions for the crisis in numbers faced by the state agencies. Their justification has been their cost-effectiveness in reducing days in foster care. But without adequate funding, these solutions remain short-term, crisis-oriented, and stopgap and lack ongoing support for families. We shall have to learn again, as if another lesson were needed, that underfunded services provide only short-term gain.

Moreover, questions should be raised about the underlying philosophy of family preservation as a proposed solution. The family preservation movement stresses the provision of intensive, time-limited services to families whose children face imminent risk of removal from their homes.[26] "Imminent removal" is a useful and essential concept, but one difficult to define; thus the imprecise nature of the entry criterion of imminent removal calls into question the measures of program success. Recent studies in California, New Jersey, and elsewhere show mixed results regarding the effectiveness of family preservation services in preventing out-of-home placement.[27] In addition, various authors are calling for more sophisticated research into a range of outcomes other than placement prevention, particularly qualitative measurement of child and family functioning.[28] An additional question is whether emphasizing the concept of imminent removal leads to the neglect of the more fundamental need to provide preventive or early intervention services.[29] An analogous situation in medical services would be to propose that the way to treat cancer is to wait until it becomes life threatening.

Family Reunification

Similar questions may be raised about the current emphasis in child welfare on family reunification, which involves a complex process affected by numerous characteristics of the child, family, and service.[30] As with prevention of out-of-home placement, services that enable youngsters to remain in their homes once they are reunified are sorely lacking.[31] From 55 percent to 73 percent of children in substitute care are returned to their families annually.[32] Services to help a family maintain its functioning after reunification, however, typically last less than 6 months and exist as special intensive programs in only 37 states.[33] The lack of family maintenance programs is an unfortunate correlate of the increasing number of children reentering foster care each year.[34]

In addition, the case of family reunification illustrates a pattern of responding rigidly and simplistically to complex issues in the field of child welfare. Family reunification reflects an either/or approach: either the child is returned to the birth family or is consigned to out-of-home placement. Fluid connections between those options are not supported.[35] As a result of this system, many children go back and forth between their families and foster or institutional placements with no sense of continuity; termination of parental rights is often accomplished without the reality or even the prospect of adoption; and, in effect, the children are often left in limbo.

As with deinstitutionalization, family reunification and preservation have unintended consequences, the most recognizable being the illusion that the programs are dealing with the problems of out-of-home placement although they fail to attack the basic difficulties that have decimated family life. Family income is the best predictor of a child's removal from the home,[36] and permanency planning is a limited response to a complex set of systemic problems in such areas as employment, housing, health, and education.

Kinship Care

Kinship care, that is, the placement of children with their relatives, is rapidly increasing throughout the country as a form of permanency planning. This trend largely accounts for the recent explosion in foster care entries in Illinois and New York, and the suggestion has been made that kinship care is the most stable type of placement.[37]

As pointed out by the National Commission on Family Foster Care, the phenomenon of kinship care raises a number of issues, such as licensing and other regulatory procedures, administration of services, payments and other supports to the relatives as foster parents, roles of relatives, and relationship between care givers and the child's parents.[38] In particular, negative aspects of kinship care include inadequate efforts to rehabilitate the biological family, overburdening relatives with the demands of children with special needs, and abusing kinship care in order to save funds, without sufficient regard for the individual needs of children and their families.

Adoption

Adoption statistics are difficult to obtain. The dramatic increase in federal adoption subsidies, from under half a million dollars in 1981 to $7 million in 1983, greatly increased the support of adoptions, particularly of special-needs children.[39] In 1981, approximately 19,000 children received adoption subsidies; by 1983, the number had grown to 31,400.[40] Yet adoption was the permanency planning goal for only 14 percent of the children in care in 1984, and only 11 percent actually were adopted.[41] Adoption is particularly unlikely for adolescents and for minority children of any age.[42] Thus, despite the stated preference for adoption as a permanency planning alternative, it is an unrealistic hope for the vast majority of youngsters in care.

Partly in response to the lack of families for children awaiting adoption, growing emphasis has been placed on adoption by foster parents.[43] Foster parents are increasingly encouraged to adopt children in their care, in contrast to the practice wisdom of not long ago, which raised questions about the motivation of foster parents interested in adopting their foster children. Yet after-care supports and services for foster parents who adopt special-needs children are sorely lacking despite adoption subsidies.[44] Without services, disruption of adoptions becomes a concern. Although the overall rate of adoption disruption is low, older children and those with more placements and more time in foster care are more vulnerable.[45] They are increasingly the children in the adoption pool, leading to the expectation that disruptions may increase in coming years.

Adolescents in Foster Care

The proportion of adolescents in foster care increased rapidly in the 1980s, "as the permanency planning movement has been successful in keeping younger children out of care, reuniting them with their biological families following placement, or placing them in adoption or other permanent plans."[46] According to one report, approximately 40 percent of the 275,000 youngsters in residential and foster family settings in 1984 were between 13 and 20 years of age.[47]

Although the increase in the proportion of adolescents in care has slowed due to the rise in younger-child placements in the late 1980s, adolescents are still represented in large numbers in the foster-care population. They constitute three different groups: those who were placed at an early age and have remained in the same foster home, those who were placed at an early age and have been moving from one placement to another, and those who were placed for the first time as teenagers, usually because of behavioral or relationship problems.[48] On reaching majority age, most of these adolescents typically are discharged to some form of independent living for which they are poorly prepared. Sensitivity to their needs led to expanded programs, stimulated in part by federal enactment of the Independent Living Initiative of 1986 (P.L. 99-272) and the subsequent infusion of federal funds to develop services focused on preparing young people in care for "emancipation" or "independent living."[49]

The concept of independent living, however, has been criticized for its various negative connotations or consequences. Critics claim it creates unrealistic and unfair expectations in adolescents, foster parents, and practitioners; it regards the need of adolescents to connect with other human beings as a sign of weakness; and it places the burden of preparing for adulthood largely on adolescents themselves.[50] Agencies have come to appreciate the seriousness of a number of challenges in serving adolescents, including the need to begin preparing youth earlier in their placements; flexible funding for work-study programs; better vocational assessment, training, and support; adequate health care; and the provision of emotional and financial resources for the move into adulthood.[51]

The permanency planning movement did not anticipate the needs of youth moving out of care. In addition to often being emotionally, intellectually, and physically delayed, these young adults generally have limited family and social supports and, to a much greater extent than children with biological family connections, must depend on the kindness of strangers to make their way in the world.

Race and Ethnicity

Minority youth in general are at high risk in this country. In 1989, over 40 percent of black and 36 percent of Hispanic children were living in poverty, and minority youth constituted 60 percent of the juveniles in public custody facilities.[52] In particular, as already noted, the foster-care population includes a disproportional and expanding number of children, youth, and families of color. Moreover, substantial evidence exists that minority children who enter the child welfare system are at greater risk of adverse consequences, such as longer duration in care, than their white counterparts.[53]

A recent study of children in long-term foster family care supported findings about the vulnerabilities of minority children and families.[54] Black children and youth had fewer contacts with their biological families than white youngsters; Hispanic and black children were more likely to be placed in transracial foster homes than white children; and minority children were more likely to enter care at a younger age and stay longer. Minority status bestows greater risk for biological and foster families as well. Compared to white families, minority biological families had greater need for services and visited their children less often. Minority foster families were poorer, more needed public housing and public assistance, and fewer were likely to receive services.

Only limited federal efforts have been made to promote child welfare services that are particularly responsive to the needs of ethnic minority children. Not enough attention has been paid to using flexible program funds to address housing, utility, and other environmental needs that prevent family reunification or contribute to a child's removal from the home. Agencies have been slow to examine their cultural and ethnic competencies, both as organizational cultures and in respect to staff recruitment and training.[55] Because minority status confers greater vulnerability in many areas on those about to enter, or who are already in, the child welfare system, extraordinary efforts need to be made to redress the vulnerabilities and inequities.

Other Effects

The permanency planning movement has espoused such practices as goal-directed, timely decison making to move youngsters back to their biological families or into adoption as quickly as possible. The efficacy of these practices is being strained by the troubled youngsters and families coming into the child welfare system. Child welfare workers are becoming aware that children's reactions to separation and loss are not readily resolved,[56] that sexual abuse can be treated therapeutically but with no confidence in the effectiveness of the treatment,[57] and that attachment is a much more complicated phenomenon than previously perceived. There is some question about whether the damage to personality development can ever be undone if adequate attachments do not occur during infancy.[58]

Currently, as noted earlier, there are no accurate data, much to our national shame, on how many children are in foster care or are affected by the child welfare system, but various estimates place the number between 300,000 and 500,000 children.[59] Although the numbers themselves are shocking, even more disturbing is the realization that the child welfare "system" is no system at all. The lack of federal leadership in promoting professional standards of practice and effective policy initiatives has permitted 50 separate state "systems" to operate. Services to children and families are fragmentary, the promise of funding for adequate preventive services has never been fulfilled, and the press of substance abuse and housing problems is forcing child welfare into overwhelming crisis.[60] The children's agencies in each state are overwhelmed by the number of cases, caseworkers are inadequately trained and responsible for too many children, and the resources for assisting families (such as public housing, prenatal care, and drug-treatment programs) are insufficient for the demand.[61] Each state struggles to meet the minimum level of compliance with federal regulations necessary to continue the flow of dollars, while the quality of care children receive is hotly debated.

Conclusion

The failures of family preservation and reunification as major components of permanency planning can be likened to the outcomes of deinstitutionalization for the mentally ill. When the original conditions and client populations change, the remedies are no longer applicable.

Permanency for children is difficult when the families with whom the children are to be reunited are struggling daily with poverty, homelessness, domestic violence, and substance abuse. It is doubtful whether the term "family," defined as a unit of adults devoted to rearing the young, can be applied when the adults do not care adequately for their children.

Concern is growing that permanency planning is not fulfilling its promise because of mechanistic imposition of the desirable options mandated by the federal legislation. The "spirit" of permanency planning, it is feared, has been ignored as states have institutionalized the concept, a phenomenon analogous to what occurred in the past when the reform movement of moral treatment for the mentally ill was transformed into the state hospital system.[62]

The seriousness of the problems being confronted by the children and families who need help and the inadequate institutional response to their needs have created the crisis now faced in child welfare. Society, therefore, is at an important point where it must make decisions about public policy concerning children. Problems exist on many levels. Some must be addressed to make the present system operate better, some require a reordering of priorities to create a more consolidated and integrated system with more responsive service delivery, and others demand a rethinking of basic assumptions in order to design a more reasonable system.

A more effective continuum of foster caring is imperative. The children who come to the attention of the child welfare system need an individualized response to their particular family situations. Some may need brief respite care, some a diagnostic placement for a short time, others specialized therapeutic care, and still others long-term foster-care placement. Children and families all need a continuum of resources, more flexible and more sensitive to their needs than the categorically designed and funded "continuum of services" with which we are currently familiar.

Long-term foster care is an especially important part of this continuum of resources. Though long discredited as a permanency planning option, long-term care, if properly supported, can be a reasonable alternative in situations in which reunification or adoption is inappropriate.

To plan an effective role in child welfare, however, foster care needs to be viewed as a service to families rather than as a substitute for families. No solutions to child welfare issues will be viable without supports to families. These include adequately compensated employment, availability of housing, accessible medical care, and perhaps decriminalization of substance abuse to remove the economic incentive for drug dealing. Other supports are also important, such as good day care, parenting education, and readily available mental health services. As was noted over a decade ago, "permanency planning cannot substitute for preventive services and for increased investment in our children."[63]

On another level, we must recognize the complexity of human beings and that the instruments that measure functioning and the policies that guide interventions only approximate the complexity. Instruments and policies apply to populations in the aggregate with some adequacy of fit, but they are of limited use when applied to individuals.[64] When we apply our carefully designed policies, we must appreciate that informed judgment is the best tool we have for dealing with individuals. We must move away from the search for simple answers to complex questions.

Finally, as an adjunct to these suggestions, it is vital to begin thinking the unthinkable and to desentimentalize the concept of the biological family. Children need adults to attach to in order to experience relationships, become socialized, and grow to be functioning members of society. If, despite society's best supports, the adults biologically related to the child cannot provide this nurturing, the best interests of the child and society require that essential connections be made in other ways.

In sum, encounters with the nostrums of the past and recent experience with P.L. 96-272 indicate that panaceas are nowhere to be found. The complexity of human interactions precludes simple solutions, and the certainty of having solved a problem is destined to elude our grasp. These considerations, however, are not negative. They help define the dimensions of the problem and provide a challenge to those who choose to work seriously with children, society's most precious resource.

Notes

1. Jane Lahti, Karen Green, Arthur Emlen, Jerry Zendry, Quentin D. Clarkson, Marie Kuehnel, and Jim Casciato, *A Follow-up Study of the Oregon Project* (Portland, Oreg.: Portland State University, Regional Research for Human Services, 1978).

2. Paul Gerard Anderson, "The Origin, Emergence, and Professional Recognition of Child Protection," *Social Service Review* 63, no. 2 (June 1989): 222–44.

3. Leroy Pelton, *For Reasons of Poverty: An Evaluation of Child Welfare Policy* (New York: Praeger, 1989).

4. Marshall B. Jones, "Crisis of the American Orphanage, 1931–1940," *Social Service Review* 63, no. 4 (December 1989): 613–29.

5. Anderson (n. 2 above), p. 223.

6. Henry S. Maas and Richard E. Engler, *Children in Need of Parents* (New York: Columbia University Press, 1959).

7. Lahti et al. (n. 1 above).

8. Federal Register, "Fiscal Year 1984 Coordinated Discretionary Funds Program" (Washington, D.C.: Department of Health and Human Services, Office of Human Development Services, October 18, 1983).

9. Charles P. Gershenson, "Child Welfare Research Notes #7, 8, 11, 13" (Washington, D.C.: Department of Health and Human Services, Administration for Children, Youth and Families, 1984–86).

346   Social Service Review

10. Peter J. Pecora, James K. Whittaker, and Anthony N. Maluccio, *The Child Welfare Challenge: Policy, Practice and Research* (New York: Aldine de Gruyter, in press).

11. Robert P. Hawkins and James Breiling, eds., *Therapeutic Foster Care: Critical Issues* (Washington, D.C.: Child Welfare League of America, 1989); Joe Hudson and Burt Galaway, eds., *Special Foster Family Care: A Normalizing Experience* (New York: Haworth, 1989); Patricia Ryan, "Increased Federal Funding for Foster Parent Education," *Fostering Ideas* 4, no. 1 (1990): 1; Edith Fein, Anthony N. Maluccio, and Miriam Kluger, *No More Partings: An Examination of Long-Term Foster Family Care* (Washington, D.C.: Child Welfare League of America, 1989).

12. Analogies can be drawn between the development of child welfare practice and changes in care for the mentally ill. For the mentally ill, early reforms included protective confinement in almshouses, physical cures, moral treatment, the growth of the mental hygiene movement and the state hospitals, and, currently, deinstitutionalization. In child welfare, changes encompassed the establishment of foundling homes, rescue of children and their placement into free foster care, the growth of orphanages and paid boarding homes, and currently permanency planning and its belief in the ability of parents to rehabilitate. In each of these social initiatives, the reforms contained unintended consequences whose proliferation led to the need for further reforms.

13. Anthony N. Maluccio, Edith Fein, and Kathleen Olmstead, *Permanency Planning for Children* (London and New York: Tavistock, 1986).

14. Gershenson, "Child Welfare Research Notes" (n. 9. above).

15. Ibid.

16. Ibid.

17. Ibid.

18. Ibid.; Tina L. Rzepnicki, "Recidivism of Foster Children Returned to Their Own Homes: A Review and New Directions for Research," *Social Service Review* 61, no. 1 (March 1987): 56–70.

19. Fein, Maluccio, and Kluger (n. 11 above); Shirley Jenkins and Beverly Diamond, "Ethnicity and Foster Care: Census Data as Predictors of Placement Variables," *American Journal of Orthopsychiatry* 55, no. 2 (April 1985): 267–76; Toshio Tatara, "Characteristics of Children in Foster Care," *Division of Child, Youth, and Family Services Newsletter, American Psychological Association* 12, no. 3 (1989): 16–17.

20. Donna M. Hamparian, Joseph M. Davis, Judith M. Jacobson, and Robert E. McGraw, *The Young Criminal Years of the Violent Few* (Washington, D.C.: Office of Juvenile Justice and Delinquency Prevention, U.S. Department of Justice, 1985); Edmund V. Mech, "Out-of-Home Placement Rates," *Social Service Review* 57, no. 4 (December 1983): 659–67.

21. Theodora Ooms, *The Crisis in Foster Care: New Directions for the 1990s* (Washington, D.C.: American Association for Marriage and Family, Research and Education Foundation, 1990).

22. Fred Wulczyn, "Caseload Dynamics and Foster Care Reentry," *Social Service Review* 65, no. 1 (March 1991): 133–56.

23. M. S. Jellinek, J. M. Murphy, J. Bishop, F. Poitrast, and D. Quinn, "Protecting Severly Abused and Neglected Children," *New England Journal of Medicine* 323, no. 23 (1990): 1628–30; James R. Seaberg, "Reasonable Efforts: Toward Implementation in Permanency Planning," *Child Welfare* 65 (1986): 469–79.

24. "States Make Great Advances in Implementing Family Preservation Services," *Frontline Views: Newsletter of the Family Preservation Clearinghouse* 1 (November 1, 1990): 1–3; James K. Whittaker, Jill Kinney, Elizabeth Tracy, and Charlotte Booth, eds., *Reaching High-Risk Families: Intensive Family Preservation in Human Services* (New York: Aldine de Gruyter, 1990).

25. For child abuse data, see Ooms (n. 21 above); for 1988 foster care entries, see Richard P. Barth and Marianne Berry, "A Decade Later: Outcomes of Permanency Planning," in *The Adoption Assistance and Child Welfare Act of 1980: The First Ten Years*, ed. North American Council on Adoptable Children (St. Paul: North American Council on Adoptable Children, 1990).

26. Elizabeth Cole and Joy Duva, *Family Preservation: An Orientation for Administrators and Practitioners* (Washington, D.C.: Child Welfare League of America, 1990).

27. Charles P. Gershenson, "Observations of Family Preservation Services Evaluations."

Frontline Views: Newsletter of the Family Preservation Clearinghouse 1 (November 1, 1990): 6–7; Leonard Feldman, *Evaluating the Impact of Family Preservation Services in New Jersey* (Trenton, N.J.: New Jersey Division of Youth and Family Services, Bureau of Research, Evaluation, and Quality Assurance, 1990); Ying-Ying Yuan, Walter R. McDonald, C. E. Wheeler, David L. Struckman-Johnson, and Michele Rivest, *Evaluation of AB 1562 In-Home Care Demonstration Projects* (Sacramento, Calif.: Walter McDonald & Associates, 1990); Kristine Nelson, "Random Thoughts," *Research Exchange* 1, no. 1 (Fall 1991): 2–3.

28. Tina L. Rzepnicki, John R. Schuerman, and Julia II. Littell, "Issues in Evaluating Intensive Family Preservation Services," in *Intensive Family Preservation Services: An Instructional Sourcebook*, ed. Elizabeth M. Tracy, David A. Haapala, Jill Kinney, and Peter J. Pecora (Cleveland: Case Western Reserve University, Mandel School of Applied Social Sciences, 1991), pp. 117–42; Mark W. Fraser, Peter J. Pecora, and David A. Haapala, *Families in Crisis: The Impact of Intensive Family Preservation Services* (New York: Aldine de Gruyter, 1991); Peter H. Rossi, *Evaluating Family Preservation Programs: A Report to the Edna McConnell Clark Foundation* (New York: Edna McConnell Clark Foundation, 1991); Kathleen Wells and David E. Biegel, eds., *Family Preservation Services: Research and Evaluation* (Newbury Park, Calif.: Sage Publications, 1991).

29. Anthony N. Maluccio, "The Optimism of Policy Choices in Child Welfare," *American Journal of Orthopsychiatry* 61, no. 4 (1991): 606–9.

30. Robert M. Goerge, "The Reunification Process in Substitute Care," *Social Service Review* 64, no. 3 (September 1990): 422–57.

31. Jellinek et al. (n. 23 above); Jane Aldgate, Anthony N. Maluccio, and Christine Reeves, *Adolescents in Foster Families* (London: B. T. Batsford, 1989).

32. Tatara (n. 19 above); Edith Fein, Anthony N. Maluccio, Virginia J. Hamilton, and Darryl E. Ward, "After Foster Care: Outcomes of Permanency Planning for Children," *Child Welfare* 62, no. 6 (1983): 485–562.

33. Barth and Berry, "A Decade Later" (n. 25 above).

34. Wulczyn (n. 22 above).

35. Barbara A. Pine, Robin Krieger, and Anthony N. Maluccio, "Family Preservation: An Overview, " in *Together Again: Family Reunification in Foster Care*, ed. Anthony N. Maluccio, Robin Krieger, and Barbara A. Pine (Washington, D.C.: Child Welfare League of America, in press).

36. Duncan Lindsey, "Factors Affecting the Foster Care Placement Decision: An Analysis of National Survey Data," *American Journal of Orthopsychiatry* 6, no. 2 (1991): 272–81.

37. Wulczyn (n. 22 above); Fred Wulczyn and Robert Goerge, *Public Policy and the Dynamics of Foster Care: A Multi-state Study of Placement Histories* (Chicago: University of Chicago, Chapin Hall Center for Children, 1990); Goerge (n. 30 above).

38. National Commission on Family Foster Care, *A Blueprint for Fostering Infants, Children and Youth in the 1990s* (Washington, D.C.: Child Welfare League of America, in collaboration with the National Foster Parent Association, 1991).

39. Barth and Berry, "A Decade Later" (n. 25 above).

40. Penelope L. Maza, "Trends in Adoption Assistance: Child Welfare Research Note #12" (Washington, D.C.: Department of Health and Human Services, Administration for Children, Youth, and Families, 1984).

41. Maximus, Inc., *Child Welfare Statistical Fact Book, 1984: Substitute Care and Adoption* (Washington, D.C.: Foster Care Information System, 1984).

42. Ibid.

43. William Meezan and Joan F. Shireman, *Care and Commitment: Foster Parent Adoption Decisions* (Albany: State University of New York Press, 1985).

44. Edith Fein, Michael J. Dunne, and Lynne Kimmel, *The Fullness of a Dream: Report to the Connecticut Department of Children and Youth Services* (Hartford, Conn.: Department of Children and Youth Services, 1988).

45. Urban Systems Research and Engineering, Inc., *Evaluation of State Activities with Regard to Adoption Disruption* (Washington, D.C.: Urban Systems Research and Engineering, 1985), found disruption rates of 6–20 percent; Richard P. Barth and Marianne Berry, *Adoption and Disruption: Rates, Risks, and Responses* (New York: Aldine, 1988), found that 11 percent of adoptions disrupted; and Trudy Festinger, "Adoption Disruption: Rates

348   Social Service Review

and Correlates," in *The Psychology of Adoption*, ed. David M. Brodzinsky and Marshall D. Schechter (New York: Oxford University Press, 1990), found disruption rates of 12–14 percent.

46. Anthony N. Maluccio, Robin Krieger, and Barbara A. Pine, eds., *Preparing Adolescents for Life after Foster Care: The Central Role of Foster Parents* (Washington, D.C.: Child Welfare League of America, 1990), p. 6.

47. American Public Welfare Association, "Voluntary Cooperative Information Systems" (Washington, D.C.: American Public Welfare Association, 1985).

48. Fein, Maluccio, and Kluger (n. 11 above).

49. Edmund V. Mech, ed., "Special Issue: Independent-living Services for At-Risk Adolescents," *Child Welfare* 67 (1988): 483–634.

50. Maluccio, Krieger, and Pine, eds., *Preparing Adolescents* (n. 46 above).

51. Ibid.; Mech, ed. (n. 49 above).

52. For poverty figures, see Children's Defense Fund, *The State of America's Children, 1991* (Washington, D.C.: Children's Defense Fund, 1991); for juvenile figures, see Barbara Allen-Hagen, "Public Juvenile Facilities: Children in Custody, 1989," *Juvenile Justice Bulletin* (January 1991), pp. 1–10.

53. Mary I. Benedict, Roger B. White, Rebecca Stallings, and David A. Cornely, "Racial Differences in Health Care Utilization among Children in Foster Care," *Children and Youth Services Review* 11 (1989): 285–97; Fein, Maluccio, and Kluger (n. 11 above); Leon W. Chestang, "The Delivery of Child Welfare Services to Minority Group Children and Their Families," in *Child Welfare Strategy in the Coming Years*, DHEW Publication no. (OHDS) 78-30158 (Washington, D.C.: U.S. Department of Health, Education, and Welfare, 1978), pp. 169–94; Patricia T. Hogan and Sau-Fong Siu, "Minority Children and the Child Welfare System: An Historical Perspective," *Social Work* 33 (1988): 493–98; Lenore Olsen, "Services for Minority Children in Out-of-Home Care," *Social Service Review* 56, no. 4 (December 1982): 572–85.

54. Fein, Maluccio, and Kluger (n. 11 above).

55. James W. Green, *Cultural Awareness in Human Services* (Englewood Cliffs, N.J.: Prentice-Hall, 1982); Elaine Pinderhughes, *Understanding Race, Ethnicity and Power: The Key to Efficacy in Clinical Practice* (New York: Free Press, 1989).

56. Sally E. Palmer, "The Separation Experiences of Foster Children" (paper presented at the annual meeting of the American Orthopsychiatric Association, New York, 1989); Ron Molin, "Future Anxiety: Clinical Issues of Children in the Latter Phases of Foster Care," *Child and Adolescent Social Work* 7, no. 6 (1990): 501–12.

57. Karen Bander, Edith Fein, and Gerrie Bishop, "Evaluation of Child Sexual Abuse Programs," in *Handbook of Clinical Intervention in Child Sexual Abuse*, ed. Suzanne M. Sgroi (Lexington, Mass.: Heath, 1982), pp. 345–76.

58. Daniel Johnson and Edith Fein, "The Concept of Attachment," *Children and Youth Services Review* 13, nos. 5 and 6 (1991): 397–412; Quincy Howe, Jr., *Under Running Laughter* (New York: Free Press, 1991).

59. Select Committee on Children, Youth and Families, U.S. House of Representatives, *No Place to Call Home: Discarded Children in America* (Washington, D.C.: U.S. Government Printing Office, 1989).

60. Ooms (n. 21 above).

61. Sheila B. Kamerman and Alfred J Kahn, *Social Services for Children, Youth, and Families in the U.S.* (Greenwich, Conn.: Annie E. Casey Foundation, 1989).

62. Kathleen Wells, "Eagerly Awaiting a Home: Severely Emotionally Disturbed Youth Lost in Our Systems of Care," *Child and Youth Care Forum* 20, no. 1 (1991): 7–18.

63. Anthony N. Maluccio, Edith Fein, Jane Hamilton, Jo Lynn Klier, and Darryl Ward, "Beyond Permanency Planning," *Child Welfare* 59, no. 9 (1980): 528.

64. Tina Adler, "Seeing Double? Controversial Twins Study Is Widely Reported, Debated," *APA Monitor* 22, no. 1 (1991): 1, 8.

The Foster Child's Avenues of Redress: Questions Left Unanswered

ARLENE E. FRIED[*]

I. INTRODUCTION

Though the actual number of children in foster care fluctuates constantly,[1] the estimated number of children over whom the state temporarily assumes legal custody is expected to climb from 343,000 in 1988 to over 550,000 by 1995.[2] Child abuse and neglect, poverty, homelessness, and substance abuse are among the causes of the rising number of children placed in state custody[3] when not properly cared for by their parents.[4] But systemic failures of child welfare agencies, evidenced by their inability to offer safe and well-supervised placements, often result in abuse and neglect in the foster home.[5] The pervasiveness of "program abuse," which results in harm to children in foster care systems that are poorly administered, also prevents the system from providing for a child's medical, psychological, emotional, and

---

* Writing & Research Editor, Colum. J.L. & Soc. Probs., 1992-93.

1. H.R. Rep. No. 395, 101st Cong., 2d Sess. 84-85 (1990) [hereinafter House Report] (stating that accurate data regarding the number of children in foster care is unavailable).

2. Id. at 18-19.

3. Id. at 26-32. See also Celia W. Dugger, Troubled Children Flood Ill-Prepared Care System, N.Y. Times, Sept. 8, 1992, at A1 ("The upsurge in homelessness in the last decade, fueled by crack and AIDS, has not only led to the destruction of thousands of families and produced a huge influx of children into the foster care system, it has also contributed to an extraordinary new set of deprivations and emotional traumas.").

4. See Marcia Lowry, Derring-Do in the 1980s: Child Welfare Impact Litigation After the Warren Years, 20 Fam. L.Q. 255, 256 (1986).

5. See Michael B. Mushlin, Unsafe Havens: The Case for Constitutional Protection of Foster Children from Abuse and Neglect, 23 Harv. C.R.-C.L. L. Rev. 199, 205-07 (1988) (indicating that there is some evidence that children in foster care are more likely to be abused and neglected than those in the general population).

245

educational needs.[6] These failures are "destroying salvageable human beings"[7] and perpetuating and building an "underclass" of nonproductive future citizens.[8]

Despite a wealth of scholarship and development of judicial doctrine, the legal rights of children placed under state care remain largely undefined. A surge in litigation over the last decade has culminated in the Supreme Court's decision in *Suter v. Artist M.*,[9] which denied children supervised by a state child welfare agency a private cause of action under the Adoption Assistance and Child Welfare Act of 1980 ("AACWA" or "the Act")[10] to compel state administration of federally mandated services. The Court determined that children who are in danger of abuse or neglect and who are under the supervision of a child welfare agency, as well as children in foster care, lack adequate standing to bring suit to enforce the provisions of the AACWA.[11] The Court's earlier decision in *DeShaney v. Winnebago County Department of Social Services*[12] held that a state did not have an affirmative duty under the Fourteenth Amendment[13] to provide for and protect children supervised by a state welfare agency in

---

6. Id. at 207 (describing "program abuse" as the injury resulting from foster care systems that offer unhealthy and unsafe placements in which children's important needs are not met (citing Eliana Gil, Institutional Abuse of Children in Out-of-Home Care, 4 Child & Youth Services 7, 10 (1982))).

7. Lowry, supra note 4, at 257. The author noted:
Child welfare systems take these children of the poor and, in many instances, complete what poverty and discrimination have begun, destroying salvageable human beings and producing yet another generation of the economically dependent and socially and psychologically unfit. Grown up, these former foster children fill our mental hospitals, our jails and our welfare rolls.
Id.

8. See Jonathan Freedman, Foster Child: A Generation of Neglect, a Legacy of Loss, L.A. Times, Apr. 9, 1990, at B5:
Building an underclass is hard work. It costs a lot of money to make sure that children don't get the care they need. It costs money in administration of neglect, in ordering care that won't be given (because the state doesn't pay for services it requires), and in punishing child-abusers for continuing the cycle of abuse that they inherited.

9. 112 S. Ct. 1360 (1992).

10. Pub. L. No. 96-272, 94 Stat. 500 (1980) (codified as amended at 42 U.S.C. §§ 620-628, 670-679a (1988)) (providing federal matching funds to states for foster care and adoption services).

11. *Artist M.*, 112 S. Ct. at 1370.

12. 489 U.S. 189 (1989).

13. U.S. Const. amend. XIV (providing that "[n]o State shall . . . deprive any person of life, liberty, or property, without due process of law").

their homes.[14]	*DeShaney*, however, left open the question whether a state is constitutionally obligated to provide adequate care and safety to foster children in its custody.

The need to define the legal rights of children placed in state custody is critical. The cases and commentary cited in this Article paint "a bleak and Dickensian picture of life under the auspices of [a child welfare agency]."[15] This Article discusses the reform of child welfare systems achieved by class action litigation for injunctive relief and individual suits for damages to compensate children injured as a result of a child welfare agency's practices. The implications of *Suter v. Artist M.*, recent litigation trends, and the current status of children's rights and avenues of redress are addressed. Part II traces the treatment of supervised and foster children's rights in the federal district and circuit courts and analyzes the Supreme Court's decision in *Suter v. Artist M.* Part III outlines the constitutional doctrine surrounding the rights of both supervised and foster children. Part IV examines the legal distinction between children voluntarily placed in foster care and children so placed by the court. Finally, the Article concludes that in order to alleviate the current crisis in the quality of care, the Supreme Court must clarify the dimensions of foster children's constitutional rights and render state child welfare agencies amenable to litigation that can lead to much-needed structural reform of state custody programs.

II. Federal Statutory Rights

A. THE ADOPTION ASSISTANCE AND CHILD WELFARE ACT OF 1980

The notion of legal rights for foster children is not new. "The rights of helpless children who are wards of the state has a history going back to the Magna Carta and beyond."[16] Because children are dependent, whether on their parents or on others entrusted

---

14. *DeShaney*, 489 U.S. at 202.

15. B.H. v. Johnson, 715 F. Supp. 1387, 1389 (N.D. Ill. 1989) (quotation in text referring to the Illinois Department of Children and Family Services). See Freedman, supra note 8, at B5 (referring to foster care in Los Angeles County: "Foster care in the richest metropolis of the richest state of the richest nation in the world resembles a Third World nightmare.").

16. Eugene D. v. Karman, 889 F.2d 701, 712 (6th Cir. 1989) (Merritt, C.J., dissenting), cert. denied, 496 U.S. 931 (1990).

with their care, they are vulnerable and helpless as individuals. It is a blight on our society when children receive less care and face greater danger after becoming wards of the state than before being taken into custody.[17]

Many efforts to define the legal rights of foster children have centered on statutory sources of law. In an attempt to reduce the amount of time children spend in foster care, Congress passed the AACWA[18] with a mandate "to lessen the emphasis on foster care placement and to encourage greater efforts to find permanent homes for children either by making it possible for them to return to their own families or by placing them in adoptive homes."[19] Section 671(a)(15) requires the agency charged with executing the Act to use "reasonable efforts" to avoid placement when possible and to reunify children in foster care with their families.[20] Other provisions require case plans and reviews for each child to ensure appropriate supervision and placement.[21] The statute requires states to provide preventive and reunification services, thereby reducing costly foster care expenditures, in order to receive federal subsidies.[22]

The purpose of the "reasonable efforts" requirement of the AACWA is to prevent unnecessary placement in foster care when children could remain at home if appropriate services were available to families.[23] A House committee report identified the "reasonable efforts" provision as the "core of the law and the premise behind preventive programs."[24] Federal oversight is vested in the Department of Health and Human Services by

---

17. See House Report, supra note 1, at 2 (describing "alarming" findings, "agencies in crisis, and services that are failing families and children").

18. Pub. L. No. 96-272, 94 Stat. 500 (1980) (codified as amended at 42 U.S.C. §§ 620-628, 670-679a (1988)).

19. S. Rep. No. 336, 96th Cong., 1st Sess. 1 (1979), reprinted in 3 U.S.C.C.A.N. 1448, 1450 (1980).

20. 42 U.S.C. § 671(a)(15) (1988) (requiring that states have a plan that "provides that, in each case, reasonable efforts will be made (A) prior to the placement of a child in foster care to prevent or eliminate the need for removal of the child from his home, and (B) to make it possible for the child to return to his home").

21. 42 U.S.C. § 675(1) (1988) describes a case plan, and § 675(5)(B) defines and states the goals of a case review system.

22. See 45 C.F.R. §§ 1356.21, 1357.15 (1992) (regulations promulgated by the Department of Health and Human Services describing case plan guidelines and services to be made available in order to comply with the AACWA reasonable efforts requirements).

23. Debra Ratterman et al., Reasonable Efforts to Prevent Foster Placement 1 (2d ed. 1987).

24. House Report, supra note 1, at 81.

allocation of the power to withhold federal funds for noncompliance.[25] The statute is silent as to whether it creates a private right of action for the child-beneficiaries. This silence has led to litigation.

B. PRIVATE RIGHTS OF ACTION UNDER THE AACWA

In 1983, the First Circuit addressed the propriety of a private cause of action for violations of statutory rights created by the AACWA. In *Lynch v. Dukakis*,[26] the plaintiff class of foster children charged the Massachusetts child welfare agency with "systemic malfeasance."[27] The First Circuit refused to lift a lower court's injunction requiring the state agency to assign a caseworker within 24 hours of the child coming into its care, to limit the caseworkers' caseloads, and to comply with the case plan and review requirements of the AACWA.[28] The court held that a private right of action existed for state violations of the AACWA under 42 U.S.C. § 1983,[29] which creates a cause of action against any person who, acting under color of state law, abridges rights created by the Constitution and laws of the United States. The court declined to find that the AACWA, by giving the Secretary of Health and Human Services enforcement discretion with the power to withhold federal funds,[30] precluded private enforcement of the

---

25. 42 U.S.C. § 671(b) (1988) states in part:
[I]n any case in which the Secretary finds, after reasonable notice and opportunity for a hearing, that a State plan which has been approved by the Secretary no longer complies with the provisions of subsection (a) of this section, or that in the administration of the plan there is a substantial failure to comply with the provisions of the plan, the Secretary shall notify the State that further payments will not be made to the State under this part, or that such payments will be made to the State but reduced . . . .

26. 719 F.2d 504 (1st Cir. 1983).

27. Id. at 512.

28. Id. at 508. These requirements were included in the district court's injunction because they were considered necessary in order to comply with the case plan and case review system provisions in the Act. See also supra note 21.

29. 42 U.S.C. § 1983 (1988) states:
Every person who, under color of any statute, ordinance, regulation, custom or usage, of any State or Territory or the District of Columbia, subjects, or causes to be subjected, any citizen of the United States or other person within the jurisdiction thereof to the deprivation of any rights, privileges, or immunities secured by the Constitution and laws, shall be liable to the party injured in an action at law, suit in equity, or other proper proceeding for redress.

30. 42 U.S.C. § 671(b). For the text of § 671(b), see supra note 25.

statute.[31]   That same year, a New Mexico federal district court[32] reached the same conclusion as to the viability of § 1983 claims for state violations of the AACWA.[33]

Five years later, the Fourth Circuit took the identical position in *L.J. v. Massinga*,[34] sustaining an injunction[35] in a § 1983 case involving a plaintiff class deprived of their statutory rights to case plans and review systems.[36]   The court concluded that the maintenance of private suits furthered Congress' intent that the plaintiff children receive the services mandated by the AACWA.[37]

In 1991, however, a district court for the Eastern District of Louisiana held that a plaintiff class of present and potential foster children could not maintain a § 1983 cause of action for statutory violations of the AACWA, nor would the court imply a right of action under the Act itself.[38]   The court employed the standard set forth in *Wilder v. Virginia Hospital Ass'n*[39] to determine the viability of a § 1983 claim, stating that "Congress must have intended for the statute to benefit the putative plaintiffs and the statute must create a binding obligation on the recipient [of federal funds] . . . . In addition, the statute must not be so vague or amorphous to evade enforcement by the courts."[40]   The court concluded that the plaintiff class of present and potential foster

---

31. *Lynch*, 719 F.2d at 511.

32. Joseph A. v. New Mexico Dep't of Social Servs., 575 F. Supp. 346 (D.N.M. 1983).

33. A consent decree settled the injunctive and declaratory claims by defining specific procedures to restructure the practices of the child welfare agency involving social worker training, supervision and caseload sizes, planning and review, adoption matching, adoption screening and placement, legal services, information and record-keeping systems, staff qualifications, and citizen review boards. Id. at 354-65.

34. 838 F.2d 118 (4th Cir. 1988), cert. denied, 488 U.S. 1018 (1989).

35. See L.J. v. Massinga, 699 F. Supp. 508, 540 (D. Md. 1988). United Press International reported that in addition to the consent decree implementing improvements in Baltimore's foster care system as a result of L.J. v. Massinga, several children in that suit recovered $575,000 in damages for injuries suffered as a result of the agency's practices. Lawyers Say Foster Care Lagging, UPI, Mar. 20, 1990, *available in* LEXIS, Nexis Library, UPI File.

36. *L.J.*, 838 F.2d at 123.

37. See *L.J.*, 699 F. Supp. at 536 ("Congress . . . created requirements it thought essential to protect the welfare of foster children. The Commonwealth voluntarily undertook to fulfill those requirements as a condition of receiving federal money . . . . [In granting the injunction, this court] gives realization to the will of Congress and protection requested by those Congress intended to protect.").

38. Del A. v. Roemer, 777 F. Supp. 1297 (E.D. La. 1991).

39. 496 U.S. 498 (1990).

40. *Del A.*, 777 F. Supp. at 1305 (citing Wilder v. Virginia Hosp. Ass'n, 496 U.S. 488, 509 (1990)).

children had no standing to bring a § 1983 suit for state violations of the AACWA because the plaintiff children were not the intended beneficiaries of the funding statute,[41] and the vague "reasonable efforts" requirement on the part of the state to comply with the statutory provisions provided no objective benchmark for a court to use in enforcing the statute.[42]

The district court for the Northern District of Illinois struggled with the question of enforceable rights created by the AACWA in a number of cases within a short span of time. In 1989, the district court held in *B.H. v. Johnson*[43] that the plaintiff class of children who are or who will be in foster care have enforceable rights under the AACWA to case plans and reviews, which they can pursue via § 1983 or through a right of action implied from the Act.[44] The court deemed the statutory provision requiring "reasonable efforts" to prevent unnecessary placement and to reunify the family[45] too vague to be enforceable.[46] The court distinguished its finding that the children had an enforceable entitlement to case plans and reviews on the basis that the statute specifically mandated these obligations.[47] But the court's distinction is illusory, because the two provisions of the Act are interdependent. The AACWA directs that the "reasonable efforts" provision is to be implemented through the use of case plans and case reviews which specify the services to be provided to an individual child and family. The case plans and reviews are therefore the means to be used to realize the "reasonable efforts" goals. A few months later, the same court[48] again held that because the "reasonable efforts" requirement of the AACWA is too amorphous, the Act does not create for the plaintiff class of foster

---

41. Id. The court identified the state as the intended beneficiary of the AACWA since the state receives funding for compliance with the Act. Id.

42. Id. at 1308.

43. 715 F. Supp. 1387 (N.D. Ill. 1989).

44. Id. at 1402.

45. 42 U.S.C. § 671(a)(15) (1988).

46. *B.H.*, 715 F. Supp. at 1401.

47. 42 U.S.C. § 671(a)(16) (1988) requires "a case plan . . . for each child receiving foster care maintenance payments . . . [and] a case review system . . . with respect to each child." See *B.H.*, 715 F. Supp. at 1402.

48. Aristotle P. v. Johnson, 721 F. Supp. 1002 (N.D. Ill. 1989).

children a right enforceable under § 1983 to compel efforts to reunify families.[49]

The same district court modified its position on this issue later in the year. Citing its decision in *B.H. v. Johnson*,[50] which determined that children have a private right to enforce the statutory provisions requiring case plans and reviews, the court in *Artist M. v. Johnson*[51] held that "there is nothing to distinguish among the several statutory requirements to suggest that one is less mandatory than the others."[52] Expressly disagreeing with the conclusion reached in *B.H. v. Johnson*,[53] the court held that the "reasonable efforts" provision[54] is one readily enforced by courts and is enforceable by the plaintiff children under § 1983 or directly under the Act.[55]

The following year, the district court reiterated that position, holding that impoverished parents in need of adequate housing whose children are in foster care have a right under § 1983 to enforce the AACWA's "reasonable efforts" requirements to prevent unnecessary placement and to reunify families.[56] Citing a number of state court cases,[57] the court indicated that the "reasonable efforts" requirement of the AACWA is enforceable and not too ambiguous when utilized in proceedings to terminate parental rights.[58] The court pointed out that preventing unnecessary foster care placement not only would benefit the

---

49. Id. at 1010-12 (finding that the statute provides the state with the flexibility necessary to develop administrative procedures it deems appropriate).

50. 715 F. Supp. 1387 (N.D. Ill. 1989).

51. 726 F. Supp. 690 (N.D. Ill. 1989), aff'd, 917 F.2d 980 (7th Cir. 1990), rev'd sub nom. Suter v. Artist M., 112 S. Ct. 1360 (1992). See also infra part II.C.

52. *Artist M.*, 726 F. Supp. at 695.

53. Id. at 695 n.6.

54. 42 U.S.C. § 671(a)(15) (1988).

55. *Artist M.*, 726 F. Supp. at 697.

56. Norman v. Johnson, 739 F. Supp. 1182, 1186-87 (N.D. Ill. 1990) (issuing a mandatory preliminary injunction in an attempt to remedy systemic violations). The court stated that "[c]ourts are accustomed to enforcing reasonableness standards and state actors and others are accustomed to being required to comply with such standards." Id. at 1187.

57. Id. at 1186.

58. Id. ("The state cases have held that the [AACWA] requires the provision of affirmative services to help reunify the family, including, in appropriate circumstances, providing housing, monetary assistance for obtaining housing, and assistance in finding housing.").

plaintiffs and their families but would be in the "public interest" as well.[59]

The district court for the District of Columbia also has considered the scope of private enforcement rights under the AACWA. In April 1991, a class action suit brought on behalf of present and potential foster children sought injunctive relief under § 1983 for violations of the AACWA.[60] The plaintiff class reported systemic violations and consistent noncompliance by the District of Columbia's Department of Human Services. The court held that not only the children in foster care, but those at risk of needing placement, were entitled to relief for the statutory violations committed by the child welfare agency.[61]

Thus, in the decisions addressing the issue of private enforcement rights under the AACWA, the trend had been toward finding such entitlements. This past year, however, the Supreme Court reversed the direction of the case law and put an end to private actions brought to enforce the provisions of the AACWA when it decided *Suter v. Artist M.*[62]

---

59. Id. at 1190-91. The court stated:

[T]he defendant will save money if, by giving these plaintiffs modest assistance, it can get their children out of the foster care system. The public interest in this case is clearly expressed in the [AACWA]: unnecessary foster care placement is detrimental to the individuals involved and to the public.

Id. See also House Report, supra note 1, at 89 (explaining that the emphasis on prevention services in the AACWA, if implemented, would be less expensive than the out-of-home care that results otherwise or the injuries that occur from crisis situations).

60. LaShawn A. v. Dixon, 762 F. Supp. 959 (D.D.C. 1991). The court found:

In almost every area of the federal law, the District's child welfare system is deficient. It fails to investigate reports of abuse and neglect in a timely manner; it fails to provide services to children and families; it fails to make appropriate foster care placements; it fails to develop case plans; and it fails to assure a permanent home for the children in its care, among other things.

Id. at 989.

61. Id. at 990. The enforcement of the resulting consent decree is currently being overseen by the district court. See Ruben Castaneda, Foster Care Takeover Threatened, Wash. Post, July 31, 1992, at C5 (discussing the problems that U.S. District Judge Thomas Hogan is having in the implementation of the consent decree and the resulting threat to appoint a person to run the agency if changes are not forthcoming quickly). The Supreme Court's decision in Suter v. Artist M. will no longer permit the type of private right of action enforced in LaShawn v. Dixon. See infra part II.C.

62. 112 S. Ct. 1360 (1992). See also discussion in part II.C.

C. *SUTER V. ARTIST M.*

The facts of *Suter v. Artist M.*[63] paralleled those of similar cases nationwide testing the enforceability by private plaintiffs of the provisions of the AACWA.[64] Seeking an injunction mandating state compliance with the Act, the plaintiff class of children[65] charged the Illinois Department of Children and Family Services ("DCFS") with failing to employ "reasonable efforts" in assigning caseworkers to children delegated to its care.[66] The Seventh Circuit affirmed the decision of the district court in favor of the children, maintaining that the plaintiff class could sustain a private cause of action either under § 1983 or the Act itself.[67]

On appeal, the Supreme Court focused on the statute's "reasonable efforts" language as the crucial element determinative of the Act's enforceability in a private cause of action.[68] At oral argument,[69] Justices Scalia and Stevens pressed the attorney for the state of Illinois regarding the assertion that the language imposed too "vague and amorphous" a standard to be enforced by a court.[70] The Justices referred to an analogous standard in the Sherman Act prohibiting "unreasonable restraint of trade,"[71] which the courts often interpret without difficulty.[72] The state's attorney stressed the agency's need for "flexibility," and the Deputy Solicitor General, appearing for the United States as amicus curiae in support of the state of Illinois, maintained that what constitutes "reasonable efforts" is a social policy determination more

---

63. 112 S. Ct. 1360 (1992).

64. See supra part II.B.

65. The plaintiff class consisted of present and potential foster children who were the subjects of juvenile court petitions, in the custody of or in a home supervised by the DCFS, and who were without caseworkers for an extended period of time. Artist M. v. Johnson, 917 F.2d 980, 983 (7th Cir. 1990).

66. Artist M. v. Johnson, 917 F.2d 980, 983 (7th Cir. 1990), rev'd sub nom. Suter v. Artist M., 112 S. Ct. 1360 (1992). The "reasonable efforts" requirement is found in 42 U.S.C. § 671(a)(15) (1988). See supra note 20.

67. *Artist M.*, 917 F.2d at 991-92.

68. *Artist M.*, 112 S. Ct. at 1370.

69. Suter v. Artist M., 60 U.S.L.W. 3427 (U.S. Dec. 17, 1991) (reporting on the highlights of the case presented at oral argument).

70. Id.

71. See Sherman Act, 15 U.S.C. §§ 1-7 (1988).

72. *Artist M.*, 60 U.S.L.W. at 3427.

appropriately left to the state agency.[73] In its opposing brief, the class of children subject to DCFS supervision argued that the state agency, by systematically failing to assign caseworkers to children in its care, had not exercised any independent judgment as to what constituted "reasonable efforts." The class contended that since caseworkers are responsible for implementing the "reasonable efforts" requirements, and the requisite caseworkers had not been assigned, the DCFS had failed to make any effort at all to prevent unnecessary removal or to reunite families.[74]

The issue of whether the "reasonable efforts" language provides sufficient guidance to a court in enforcing the statute goes directly to the critical question of congressional intent. Did Congress intend to create an enforceable right when it mandated that child welfare agencies employ "reasonable efforts" in implementing the statute? Or did it expect the Department of Health and Human Services, with its power to discontinue funds if states failed to enforce the AACWA,[75] to be the only monitoring mechanism?[76] It is interesting to note, as did Justice Scalia during oral argument, that the Secretary has never cut off funds for noncompliance with the Act.[77] Thus, the effectiveness of the power to withhold funds to compel state compliance with the AACWA has never been proven.[78]

Chief Justice Rehnquist's majority opinion[79] overturned the Seventh Circuit decision, finding no private right of action under

---

73. Id. See also Brief for the United States as Amicus Curiae at 9, Suter v. Artist M., 112 S. Ct. 1360 (1992) (No. 90-1488) (indicating that there is no "objective benchmark" to measure reasonable efforts).

74. Brief for Respondents at 22-36, Suter v. Artist M., 112 S. Ct. 1360 (1992) (No. 90-1488).

75. 42 U.S.C. § 671(b) (1988). See supra note 25.

76. See Brief for the United States as Amicus Curiae, supra note 73, at 5 (stating that "[t]he Act does not provide for any private causes of action. Instead, it directs the Secretary to discontinue or reduce a State's funding upon a determination that an approved plan no longer complies . . . .").

77. Suter v. Artist M., 60 U.S.L.W. 3427 (U.S. Dec. 17, 1991).

78. Additionally, federal oversight is only superficial. See House Report, supra note 1, at 82:

HHS conducts only 'paper' audits of these protections . . . . [R]eviewers look to see if there is a judicial determination that 'reasonable efforts' have been made or if the child has a case plan in his file; they do not look beyond the finding or plan to determine if reasonable efforts were actually made, appropriate services provided, or whether states actually follow case plans.

79. Suter v. Artist M., 112 S. Ct. 1360 (1992). This was a seven-to-two decision, with Justices Blackmun and Stevens dissenting. Id. at 1362.

either the AACWA or § 1983.[80] Because the AACWA did not provide "guidance . . . as to how 'reasonable efforts' are to be measured . . . it is a directive whose meaning will obviously vary with the circumstances of each individual case."[81] The Court also drew a negative implication from § 672(e), which specifically provides that " 'no Federal payment may be made under this part' for a child voluntarily placed in foster care for more than 180 days unless within that period there is a judicial determination that placement is in the best interest of the child."[82] The Court reasoned that, had Congress intended to compel states to comply with specific requirements, it would have employed specific language such as that employed in § 672(e), rather than the vague "reasonable efforts" directive.[83]

Artist M. appears to conflict with the Court's 1990 decision in *Wilder v. Virginia Hospital Ass'n*,[84] which held that health care providers could enforce, under § 1983, the Boren Amendment to the federal Medicaid Act requiring states to establish "reasonable and adequate" rates for reimbursement to health care providers.[85] Rehnquist distinguished *Wilder* by explaining that the Boren Amendment and the regulations outlining procedures to determine rates were more specific than the "vague" language of the AACWA.[86] Unlike the Boren Amendment, the AACWA provided "[n]o further statutory guidance . . . as to how 'reasonable efforts' are to be *measured*."[87] The *Artist M.* Court held that the

80. Id. at 1363.
81. Id. at 1368. See also Sue Suter, Ruling in the Best Interest of Children, Chi. Trib., May 14, 1992, at C26 (discussing the necessity of a flexible, "case-by-case" determination of what constitutes "reasonable efforts").
82. *Artist M.*, 112 S. Ct. at 1369 n.12 (relating, as an example of specific language imposing explicit requirements on a state, the provisions of 42 U.S.C. § 672(e) (1988)).
83. Id.
84. 496 U.S. 498 (1990).
85. 42 U.S.C. § 1396a(a)(13)(A) (1988).
86. *Artist M.*, 112 S. Ct. at 1368 (citing Wilder v. Virginia Hosp. Ass'n, 496 U.S. 498, 519 n.17 (1990)).
87. Id. (emphasis added). Note that, although a method of *measuring* "reasonable efforts" is not provided in the statute or regulations, the Department of Health and Human Services did promulgate regulations specifying guidelines and suggested services that child welfare agencies should utilize in order to comply with the AACWA. 45 C.F.R. §§ 1356.21, 1357.15 (1992). The Court acknowledged that these regulations list services and describe what must be included in a case plan, but concluded that the regulations are not specific enough to "provide notice to the States that failure to do anything other than submit a plan with the requisite features, to be approved by the Secretary, is a further condition on the receipt of funds from the Federal Government." *Artist M.*, 112 S. Ct. at 1369.

regulations promulgated by the Department of Health and Human Services only require the states to submit to the Department an appropriate case plan to qualify for receipt of federal funds under the AACWA.[88] The Court further held that, consistent with the legislative history that indicated Congress intended the states to self-regulate,[89] the only enforcement mechanism available to ensure state compliance is the power of the Secretary to withdraw or reduce federal funds for failure to submit and adhere to a case plan.[90]

In his dissenting opinion, Justice Blackmun stressed the similarity of the "reasonable efforts" standard of the AACWA to the "functionally identical" statutory provision at issue in the *Wilder* case.[91] Blackmun also criticized the majority for foreclosing the possibility of a § 1983 suit without applying standards set out in established precedents "to determine whether a statute has created a right enforceable under § 1983."[92] As the *Wilder* Court asserted, in order to foreclose a § 1983 action to enforce a statute, a party must "demonstrate 'by express provision or other specific evidence from the statute itself that Congress intended to foreclose [§ 1983] enforcement.' "[93] As for the majority's conclusion that the "reasonable efforts" clause proved too "vague and amorphous" for a court to enforce, Justice Blackmun wrote that "[f]ederal courts, in innumerable cases, have routinely enforced reasonableness clauses in federal statutes,"[94] and the majority's view that the Secretary's power to discontinue funds is a preclusive "enforcement mechanism" is contradicted by established law.[95]

---

88. 112 S. Ct. at 1369.

89. Id. at 1369 n.15.

90. Id. at 1368.

91. Id. at 1370-71 (citing Wilder v. Virginia Hosp. Ass'n, 496 U.S. 498 (1990)).

92. Id. at 1371 ("I cannot acquiesce in this unexplained disregard for established law."). For a discussion of Supreme Court cases prior to Suter v. Artist M. that provided an analytical framework for determining when a federal statute creates an enforceable right, see Martin A. Schwartz, Reviewing Federal Statutes under § 1983, Revisited, N.Y. L.J., June 16, 1992, at 3.

93. *Artist M.*, 112 S. Ct. at 1376 (quoting *Wilder*, 496 U.S. at 520-21).

94. Id. at 1374.

95. Id. at 1376 (citing Rosado v. Wyman, 397 U.S. 397 (1970)). In Rosado v. Wyman, the Supreme Court held that "[i]t is . . . peculiarly part of the duty of this tribunal . . . to resolve disputes as to whether federal funds allocated to the States are being expended in consonance with the conditions that Congress has attached to their use." *Rosado*, 397 U.S. at 422-23.

By refusing to recognize a right to private enforcement of the AACWA, the Court has restricted enforcement of the Act to the one entity that consistently has refused to exercise its authority in the face of substantial statutory violations and systemic state failures to provide for children in its care — the Department of Health and Human Services.[96]   Thus, by virtue of the Court's decision in *Artist M.*, judicial review of state failures to implement the provisions of the AACWA is foreclosed.

III. CONSTITUTIONAL RIGHTS

Because the plaintiff class in *Artist M.*[97] consisted of both foster children in the custody of the state and children under the supervision of the child welfare agency due to reports of abuse and neglect,[98] a due process argument[99] could not be made[100] as a result of the Supreme Court's holding in *DeShaney v. Winnebago County Department of Social Services.*[101]   *DeShaney,* decided in 1989, held that due process only protects children from deprivations of liberty by state actors,[102] and a child injured at home while under the supervision of the child welfare agency has not suffered injury as a result of state action.[103]   The petitioner in *DeShaney* attempted to convince the Court that, by assuming the responsibility of supervising children in the home, the state had entered into a "special relationship" with the children and therefore owed them a duty of care commensurate with cases in which state action is found.[104]   While successful in other arenas,

---

96. See Ruth Marcus, Court Shuts Out Foster Care Children; Private Suits to Force States to Maintain Families Are Barred, Wash. Post, Mar. 26, 1992, at A3 (reporting on a comment by Marcia Lowry, the Director of the Children's Rights Project of the ACLU, in which she contended that "leaving it up to [the Department of Health and Human Services] to police state foster care systems presented state officials with a 'blank check' to violate the law").

97. Suter v. Artist M., 112 S. Ct. 1360 (1992).

98. See supra note 65.

99. See supra note 13.

100. See Artist M. v. Johnson, 917 F.2d 980, 983 n.5 (7th Cir. 1990) (stating that the class of plaintiffs at home under DCFS supervision would be barred from asserting a substantive due process claim by the holding in DeShaney v. Winnebago County Dep't of Social Servs., 489 U.S. 189 (1989)).

101. 489 U.S. 189 (1989).

102. Id. at 197.

103. Id. at 196-97 (holding that the State's failure to protect a child from injury by private individuals while under State supervision does not violate the Due Process Clause).

104. Id. at 197.

the *DeShaney* Court found the "special relationship" doctrine inapplicable to the constitutional claims of children in their homes against a state welfare agency.

The result in *DeShaney* is important for two reasons. First, it forecloses the opportunity for children under state supervision, but not in foster care, to pursue constitutional claims against an agency or its officials for failure to protect them. Combined with the result in *Suter v. Artist M.*, these same children also are foreclosed from judicially enforcing their statutorily created rights. The *Artist M.* Court denied both supervised and foster children a right of action under the AACWA. But, for supervised children, enforcement of the provisions of the AACWA was their only available means of legal redress for the appalling conditions of their care, other than the route foreclosed in *DeShaney*. Second, *DeShaney* impacts on the constitutional claims of foster children only by implication. In a footnote, the *DeShaney* Court explained:

> Had the State by the affirmative exercise of its power removed Joshua from free society and placed him in a foster home operated by its agents, we might have a situation sufficiently analogous to incarceration or institutionalization to give rise to an affirmative duty to protect.[105]

Thus, *DeShaney* left the door open to foster children to bring suit against the state for violations of their due process rights under the Fourteenth Amendment.

Since 1989, the Supreme Court consistently has denied certiorari in cases brought by foster children seeking to enforce their constitutional rights.[106] But the proliferation of circuit court decisions in the area of substantive due process rights of foster children is likely to compel a decision by the Supreme Court.

---

105. Id. at 201 n.9.
106. Meador v. Cabinet for Human Resources, 902 F.2d 474, (6th Cir.), cert. denied, 498 U.S. 867 (1990); Eugene D. v. Karman, 889 F.2d 701 (6th Cir. 1989), cert. denied, 496 U.S. 931 (1990); Milburn v. Anne Arundel County Dep't of Social Servs., 871 F.2d 474 (4th Cir.), cert. denied, 493 U.S. 850 (1989); Taylor v. Ledbetter, 818 F.2d 791 (11th Cir. 1987), cert. denied, 489 U.S. 1065 (1989); L.J. v. Massinga, 838 F.2d 118 (4th Cir. 1988), on remand, 699 F. Supp. 508 (D. Md. 1988), cert. denied, 488 U.S. 1018 (1989). With many cases to choose from in which the Supreme Court could have determined the rights of foster children, it is interesting to note that the Court selected a case where the plaintiff class included supervised children. Thus, the class was therefore precluded by *DeShaney* from asserting a due process claim.

Though most circuits have supported the existence of such claims by foster children, differences in defining the proper scope of such claims abound.

A. LEGAL REDRESS UNDER SUBSTANTIVE DUE PROCESS

In *Estelle v. Gamble*,[107] a prisoner brought a § 1983 action for violation of his Eighth Amendment rights[108] when he was denied adequate medical care while in state custody. The Supreme Court held that a state's "deliberate indifference" to an affirmative obligation of care gives rise to a constitutional claim.[109] The Supreme Court further held in *Youngberg v. Romeo*[110] that an involuntarily committed mental patient had a substantive due process liberty interest in a safe environment, freedom from bodily restraints, and reasonable training to ensure this safety and freedom.[111] The Court acknowledged the patient's "right to adequate food, shelter, clothing, and medical care."[112] These cases are clearly relevant to the claims of foster children in the custody of the state who allege unsafe conditions and inadequate food, clothing, shelter, and medical care. As in the case of prisoners and institutionalized patients, foster children are completely dependent on their caretakers and incapable of providing for their own health and safety.

In most cases, the circuits have supported the protection of foster children on substantive due process grounds.[113] The Second Circuit, in *Doe v. New York City Department of Social Services*,[114] held that a foster child had a right to damages under § 1983 for the child welfare agency's violation of her constitutional right to safety if the agency was deliberately indifferent to the

---

107. 429 U.S. 97 (1976).
108. U.S. Const. amend. VIII (prohibiting the use of "cruel and unusual punishment").
109. 429 U.S. at 104-05. In concluding that deliberate indifference to a prisoner's medical needs is a violation of the inmate's constitutional rights, the Court stated that "[a]n inmate must rely on prison authorities to treat his medical needs; if the authorities fail to do so, those needs will not be met." Id. at 103.
110. 457 U.S. 307 (1982).
111. Id. at 319.
112. Id. at 315 (footnote omitted).
113. But see Milburn v. Anne Arundel Dep't of Social Servs., 871 F.2d 474 (4th Cir.), cert. denied, 493 U.S. 850 (1989). See also infra notes 129-139 and accompanying text.
114. 649 F.2d 134 (2d Cir. 1981), cert. denied, 464 U.S. 864 (1983).

known risk of injury at the hands of her foster parent.[115] Similarly, the Eleventh Circuit decided in *Taylor v. Ledbetter*[116] that a foster child has a liberty interest in a safe environment, and failure to protect the child from an abusive foster parent violated the child's right to substantive due process.[117] Following *Doe v. New York City Department of Social Services*, the Seventh Circuit decided *K.H. v Morgan*,[118] which held that a foster child has a substantive due process right to be protected from a foster parent that the agency knows or should know is dangerous to the child's physical or mental health.[119]

The Sixth Circuit in *Eugene D. v. Karman*,[120] however, refused to recognize the constitutional claim of a foster child, noting that the Supreme Court had yet to decide whether the status of a child in a state-licensed foster home "is sufficiently analogous to institutionalization to give rise to a constitutionally imposed affirmative duty to protect."[121] The dissent in *Eugene D.* challenged the majority's logic, scornfully questioning why a child has no constitutional rights to care and safety simply because the state chose a foster home rather than an institutional setting for placement.[122] Six months later, in *Meador v. Cabinet for Human Resources*,[123] the Sixth Circuit reversed its position, pointing to a footnote in *DeShaney*[124] to indicate that a foster

---

115. Id. at 145.

116. 818 F.2d 791 (11th Cir. 1987), cert. denied, 489 U.S. 1065 (1989).

117. Id. at 797. The court noted:

We believe the risk of harm is great enough to bring foster children under the umbrella of protection afforded by the fourteenth amendment. Children in foster homes, unlike children in public schools, are isolated; no persons outside the home setting are present to witness and report mistreatment. The children are helpless. Without the investigation, supervision, and constant contact required by statute, a child placed in a foster home is at the mercy of the foster parents.

Id.

118. 914 F.2d 846 (7th Cir. 1990), on remand, K.H. v. Suter, 765 F. Supp. 432 (N.D. Ill. 1991). The court regarded this case as "materially identical" to Doe v. New York City Dep't of Social Servs., 649 F.2d 134 (2d Cir. 1981). K.H. v. Morgan, 914 F.2d at 852.

119. 914 F.2d at 850.

120. 889 F.2d 701 (6th Cir. 1989), cert. denied, 496 U.S. 931 (1990).

121. Id. at 711.

122. Id. at 714.

123. 902 F.2d 474 (6th Cir.), cert. denied, 498 U.S. 867 (1990).

124. 489 U.S. at 201 n.9. For the language of the footnote, see text accompanying supra note 105.

home placement would give rise to an affirmative duty for the state to protect the foster child.[125]

The position taken by the Fourth Circuit is the most surprising. In 1988, the court awarded a plaintiff class of foster children an injunction compelling the Baltimore Department of Social Services to remedy systematic deficiencies in placement supervisions and medical care on the basis of the defendant's violation of the children's Fourteenth Amendment rights.[126] But, the following year, the same court held in *Milburn v. Anne Arundel County Department of Social Services*[127] that a child repeatedly abused by his foster parent had no private cause of action under § 1983 for violations of his Fourteenth Amendment rights. The state agency was aware of the danger because it received hospital reports reporting the child's injuries on four separate occasions, yet each time the agency returned the child to the same foster home.[128] The *Milburn* court cited *DeShaney* in holding that the child could not claim the protection of the Fourteenth Amendment against private violence.[129] The court considered the foster child to be in the custody of the foster parents and not in the custody of the state, and it was the foster parent, not the state, who inflicted the violence.[130]   The court further drew a distinction between the rights of a child placed by a court in foster care and those of a child "voluntarily" placed in foster care by his parents.[131]   As contrasted with the situation postulated in a footnote in *DeShaney*,[132] the state defendant in *Milburn* did not remove the child from free society to place him in a foster home operated by its agents.[133]

The Fourth Circuit's opinion that foster parents are not state actors greatly limits the constitutional protection to which foster

---

125. *Meador*, 902 F.2d at 476 (holding that the plaintiff foster children had a substantive due process right to be free from unnecessary harm in a foster home, where the agency was "deliberately indifferent" to their safety).

126. L.J. v. Massinga, 838 F.2d 118 (4th Cir.), on remand, 699 F. Supp. 508, 539 (D. Md. 1988), cert. denied, 488 U.S. 1018 (1989).

127. 871 F.2d 474 (4th Cir.), cert. denied, 493 U.S. 850 (1989).

128. Id. at 475.

129. Id. at 476.

130. Id. at 476-77.

131. Id. at 476. See infra text accompanying note 169.

132. 489 U.S. at 201 n.9. For the language of the footnote, see text accompanying supra note 105.

133. *Milburn*, 871 F.2d at 476.

children should be entitled.[134] Pointing to the agreement between the foster parents and the state, the *Milburn* court concluded that the contract provided only "general guidelines" concerning the home, leaving the foster parents with a great deal of discretion in parenting. With only a perfunctory licensing procedure approving the home, the court considered the connection between the state and the foster parents to be too tenuous and thus deemed the abuse of the child an act of private violence.[135]

By focusing on the relationship between the foster parents and the state, rather than on the special relationship between the state and the foster child, the Fourth Circuit ignored the obligations of the agency toward the child, the relationship of dependency the custody situation creates, and the supervisory responsibilities an agency cannot disregard. Ironically, the *Milburn* court noted that the state's contract with the foster parents called for the agency to provide for "board, medical care, clothing and supervision of the child during his placement."[136] Though the court treated this clause and the cursory approval of the foster home as evidence that the foster parents were not agents of the state, the clause clearly emphasizes the affirmative duties the state had assumed toward the child and highlights the special relationship implied by the arrangement.

The treatment of a foster child's substantive due process rights at the district court level is also inconsistent. At a minimum, courts have determined that substantive due process requires that a foster child be provided with adequate shelter and treatment. Thus, a New York federal district court held in *Doe by Johanns v. New York City Department of Social Services*[137] that the city's night-to-night program, whereby children are "repeatedly kept in city offices during the day, don't know where they will sleep at night and carry their possessions from place to place in plastic

---

134. See also Del A. v. Roemer, 777 F. Supp. 1297, 1317-18 (E.D. La. 1991) (stating that a foster parent is a state actor only when the state places the child in a home it knows or should have known is unsafe. "Outside of this narrow case, foster parents are not agents of the State." (citing K.H. v. Morgan, 914 F.2d 846 (7th Cir. 1990))). Note that the court strains the description of the foster parent in order to limit the inference of state action, rather than choosing to maintain that the standard of deliberate indifference on the part of the agency has not been met. This may reflect the court's reluctance to admit to the existence of constitutional rights for foster children.

135. *Milburn*, 871 F.2d at 477.

136. Id.

137. 670 F. Supp. 1145 (S.D.N.Y. 1987).

garbage bags,"[138] deprives foster children of their substantive due process rights by neglecting to provide clean clothing, adequate food, bathing and toilet facilities, and education.[139]

The district court for the Northern District of Illinois decided two cases with opposite results in 1989. *B.H. v. Johnson*[140] held that the plaintiff class had no substantive due process right to parent or sibling visits, nor to adequate caseworkers or placement in the "least restrictive setting," because the Fourteenth Amendment does not impose obligations upon the state to provide substantive services.[141]   The court did conclude, however, that the plaintiff class had a substantive due process right "to be free from unreasonable and unnecessary intrusions upon their physical and emotional well-being, while directly or indirectly in state custody, and to be provided by the state with adequate food, shelter, clothing and medical care . . . ."[142] But, in *Aristotle P. v. Johnson*,[143] the court found that foster children had a liberty interest in sibling relationships.   By pursuing policies which impaired that interest, the state agency injured the children's emotional well-being and violated substantive due process rights to sibling visitation.[144]

Two significant class actions in 1991 alleging systemic malfeasance in the administration of child welfare agencies also produced different outcomes. A Louisiana federal district court in *Del A. v. Roemer*[145] stated that though foster children are constitutionally entitled to the substantive due process right of "reasonable physical safety,"[146] as decided by the Supreme Court

---

138. Id. at 1146.
139. Id.
140. 715 F. Supp. 1387 (N.D. Ill. 1989).
141. Id. at 1397.
142. Id. at 1396.
143. 721 F. Supp. 1002 (N.D. Ill. 1989).
144. Id. at 1009-10 (stating that "[t]he fact that the plaintiffs' injuries are psychological rather than physical is of no moment"). The court did not directly attempt to reconcile this holding with the different one reached in the same district regarding sibling visitation just a few months earlier in B.H. v. Johnson, 715 F. Supp. 1387 (N.D. Ill. 1989). It conceived of the deprivation of sibling visitation as an injury to a child in state custody, 721 F. Supp. at 1009-10, rather than viewing sibling visits as an allocation of state resources for the purpose of family reunification.
145. 777 F. Supp. 1297 (E.D. La. 1991).
146. Id. at 1318. The court stated that children in state custody have a right to "adequate food, shelter, clothing, and medical care[,] . . . freedom from bodily restraint and any training necessary to ensure their safety . . . ." Id.

in *Youngberg v. Romeo*,[147] they do not have a substantive liberty interest in emotional and psychological safety[148] or placement in the least restrictive setting.[149] In contrast, a federal district court for the District of Columbia in *LaShawn v. Dixon*[150] viewed the viability of a constitutional claim as essential to ensure that the District could not avoid enforcement of an injunction by declining federal funding under the AACWA.[151] In ordering injunctive relief that restructured the operation of the child welfare agency, the court held that the foster children possessed substantive due process rights to physical safety, to freedom from psychological and emotional harm, and "[t]o the extent that certain services, such as appropriate placement and case planning, are essential to preventing harm to the children in the District's custody, . . . the children have a constitutional liberty interest in those services."[152]

Thus, though most of the circuits conclude that foster children possess substantive due process rights to care and protection, the district court cases differ in defining the precise scope of these rights. Although the Fourth Circuit's determination in *Milburn*[153] may influence other circuits, the clear weight of authority against the court's finding, as well as the difficult logic of its decision, render such an occurrence unlikely. Despite the fact that district courts have acknowledged foster children's substantive due process rights, some courts may continue to limit these rights to the bare minimum of physical safety.[154] Until the Supreme Court grants certiorari in a case concerning the constitutional rights of foster children, the status of these children's access to legal redress and the precise scope of their constitutional claims will remain uncertain.

---

147. 457 U.S. 307 (1982).
148. *Del A.*, 777 F. Supp. at 1319.
149. Id. at 1319-20.
150. 762 F. Supp. 959 (D.D.C. 1991).
151. Id. at 990-91.
152. Id. at 993.
153. 871 F.2d 474 (4th Cir.), cert. denied, 493 U.S. 850 (1989).
154. See *Del A.*, 777 F. Supp. at 1318-20, discussed in supra notes 145-149 and accompanying text.

IV. The Rights of Children Voluntarily Placed in Care

Children "voluntarily" placed in the custody[155] of a child welfare agency by their natural parents comprise a large segment of the foster care population.[156] Many parents so place their children because they are unable to care for them due to financial problems, substance abuse, or physical or psychological disabilities.[157] Some legal discussion has considered whether the distinction between voluntary and involuntary placement is relevant to a finding of a constitutional imperative on the part of the state to provide adequate care.[158] But differentiating on the basis of the voluntary nature of placement is problematic. In instances where a report of abuse or neglect has been filed, the voluntary nature of a parent's consent may be suspect.[159] In establishing substantive due process rights for a patient of a state

---

155. The use of the term "custody" as a description with legal implications raises certain questions. First, is a child in a foster home in the "custody" of the state or in the "custody" of the foster parents? In Milburn v. Anne Arundel County Dep't of Social Servs., 871 F.2d 474 (4th Cir. 1989), the voluntarily placed child is said to be in the "custody" of his foster parents. See supra note 133 and accompanying text. In New York State, a parent who voluntarily places a child retains "legal custody" while the agency has "physical custody." Joseph R. Carrieri, The Ways the Foster Child Comes into Foster Care, in The Foster Child 1989: From Abandonment to Adoption at 19, 22-23 (PLI Litig. & Admin. Practice Course Handbook Series No. 151, 1989) [hereinafter The Foster Child 1989]. In contrast, a voluntary placement agreement in Pennsylvania gives the county agency "legal custody." Melissa A. Lengyel, Comment, Foster Child Abuse in Pennsylvania: Pursuing Actions Against the County Placement Agency, 94 Dick. L. Rev. 501, 514 (1990).

156. *Mushlin*, supra note 5, at 237 (citing studies and authorities indicating that "[t]he overwhelming majority of foster care placements are voluntary").

157. The Foster Child 1989, supra note 155, at 23.

158. See, e.g., DeShaney v. Winnebago County Dep't of Social Servs., 489 U.S. 189, 201 n.9 (1989); Milburn v. Anne Arundel Dep't of Social Servs., 871 F.2d 474, 476 (4th Cir.), cert. denied, 493 U.S. 850 (1989); Taylor v. Ledbetter, 818 F.2d 791, 797 (11th Cir. 1987), cert. denied, 489 U.S. 1065 (1989). See also Martin Guggenheim, The Effect of Tort Law on Child Welfare Liability, in Liability in Child Welfare and Protection Work: Risk Management Strategies 83, 86 (Marcia Sprague & Robert M. Horowitz eds., 1991); Mushlin, supra note 5, at 237-42; Daniel L. Skoler, A Constitutional Right to Safe Foster Care? Time for the Supreme Court to Pay Its I.O.U., 18 Pepp. L. Rev. 353, 379-80 (1991).

159. See Amy Sinden, Comment, In Search of Affirmative Duties Toward Children Under a Post-*DeShaney* Constitution, 139 U. Pa. L. Rev. 227, 256 (1990) ("The extent to which such a parent at a time of crisis may be subtly coerced or intimidated by a social worker who, with the authority of the state behind her, confidently pronounces placement to be 'in the best interest of the child' is impossible to measure."). See also Smith v. Organization of Foster Families for Equality and Reform, 431 U.S. 816, 833-34 (1977) (describing the lack of informed consent and the threat of neglect proceedings accompanying voluntary placement decisions).

mental hospital, *Youngberg v. Romeo*[160] emphasized the fact that the patient had been involuntarily committed, despite the fact that the patient's mother had petitioned the court to commit her child to an institution.[161] Thus, the line between "voluntary" and "involuntary" blurs in attempting to identify if the state is the cause of an individual's placement. Additionally, though a parent may voluntarily place a child in state custody, the child has not necessarily consented to the arrangement.[162]

Taylor v. Ledbetter[163] also emphasized the involuntary manner in which a child enters foster care, holding the situation to be analogous to prison and mental hospital commitment.[164] *DeShaney v. Winnebago County Department of Social Services*[165] raised the "voluntary" issue in a footnote[166] and stressed that a state's action that causes a "restraint of personal liberty . . . trigger[s] the protections of the Due Process Clause."[167] The Court considered significant the fact that when the state, "by the affirmative exercise of its power," removes children from their homes, "an affirmative duty to protect" may arise.[168] In its interpretation of *DeShaney*, the Fourth Circuit held a voluntarily placed foster child not to be entitled to redress for the child welfare agency's failure to protect him from abuse of which it was aware, in part because "[t]he State of Maryland by the affirmative exercise of its power had not restrained the plaintiff's liberty."[169]

Thus, voluntarily placed foster children who may be totally dependent on the child welfare agency are considerably disadvantaged in the protection they are afforded by the courts.

---

160. 457 U.S. 307 (1982).

161. Id. at 309.

162. See Guggenheim, supra note 158, at 86. The author noted:

It is true that the way in which a child enters the foster care system is significant from the parent's perspective, but that difference is immaterial from the perspective of the child. Once a child is in foster care, regardless of the method by which s/he entered the system, it is difficult to conclude that some children have federal rights which protect them against harm while others have no such federal rights.

Id.

163. 818 F.2d 791 (11th Cir. 1987), cert. denied, 489 U.S. 1065 (1989).

164. Id. at 797.

165. 489 U.S. 189 (1989).

166. Id. at 201 n.9.

167. Id. at 200.

168. Id. at 201 n.9.

169. Milburn v. Anne Arundel County Dep't of Social Servs., 871 F.2d 474, 476 (4th Cir.), cert. denied, 493 U.S. 850 (1989).

The Fourth Circuit's decision provides a perverse incentive for a child to remain in a parent's inadequate charge until the situation has deteriorated to the point where the state will forcibly remove the child into its own custody. Only then would the state be constitutionally required to provide the foster child with adequate shelter and treatment. Furthermore, successful class action suits that resulted in systemic reforms in child welfare practices did not differentiate the rights of foster children based on the manner in which they entered foster care, despite the fact that a substantial percentage of plaintiff class members were voluntarily placed.[170] The AACWA[171] provides states with foster care maintenance payments if the state follows its mandates, and the services and protections it prescribes do not discriminate against foster children who entered care voluntarily.[172]

V. CONCLUSION

As a result of the decisions in *Suter v. Artist M.*[173] and *DeShaney v. Winnebago County Department of Social Services*,[174] children not in foster care but under the supervision of a child welfare agency can neither obtain judicial review of state actions in implementing the AACWA nor assert claims of deprivation of constitutional rights when subject to shocking conditions of care. Large sums of federal monies received by the states under the AACWA are allocated to exercising reasonable efforts to keep children at home and to make it possible for those in care to return home.[175] In accepting these funds, states agree to abide by the provisions of the statute. Considering the gross inadequacy of

---

170. See L.J. v. Massinga, 838 F.2d 118 (4th Cir. 1988); LaShawn A. v. Dixon, 762 F. Supp. 959 (D.D.C. 1991); Joseph A. v. New Mexico Dep't of Human Servs., 575 F. Supp. 346 (D.N.M. 1983).

171. Pub. L. No. 96-272, 94 Stat. 500 (1980) (codified as amended at 42 U.S.C. §§ 620-628, 670-679a (1988)).

172. Mark A. Hardin & Ann Shalleck, Children Living Apart From Their Parents, in Legal Rights of Children 353, 358 (Robert M. Horowitz & Howard A. Davidson eds., 1984) ("[The AACWA mandates that] the states . . . provide to all children placed under the supervision of the state protections designed to achieve permanence. These protections include case plans, case review, and services to children and families.").

173. 112 S. Ct. 1360 (1992). See supra part II.C.

174. 489 U.S. 189 (1989). See supra notes 101-105 and accompanying text.

175. Brief for Respondents, supra note 75, at 41-42 (stating that of the $65 million that Illinois receives a year from the federal government "to fulfill its obligations under the Act," millions are spent to provide preventive services from children in their homes).

federal monitoring,[176] the absence of a private right of action under § 1983 or the AACWA allows state child welfare agencies to continue to operate to the detriment of supervised children by accepting federal funds that never actually fuel state compliance with the Act. In addition, the lack of a constitutional remedy deprives these children of any constitutional protection no matter how alarming their predicament.

With regard to foster children, *Suter v. Artist M.* similarly declined to recognize a foster child's right to bring a private action to enforce the provisions of the AACWA. But whether a foster child is constitutionally entitled to adequate care remains an open question. Cases addressing a foster child's constitutional rights often result in structural injunctions that change the way state agencies provide for children in their custody.[177] The continued vitality of such claims depends on the Supreme Court's willingness to define the proper scope of foster children's liberty interests in safety and treatment, including clothing, shelter, and medical care needs.[178]

Because children do not comprise a political constituency, because they are dependent and vulnerable, because the tremendous power child welfare agencies have over the lives of their charges is exercised outside of public scrutiny,[179] and because the failures of child welfare agencies are to some extent a function of their low priority in the battle for legislative funding, the necessity of a Supreme Court decision validating a foster

---

176. House Report, supra note 1, at 3 ("Federal oversight and funding are weak to nonexistent.").

177. Commentators argue that structural injunctions are the superior method of instituting child welfare system reform. Mushlin, supra note 5, at 245-49; Lowry, supra note 4, at 266-67.

178. A report on the condition of the New York City child protection system operated by the Human Resources Administration included findings about the inadequate protections provided children in foster care and those in known abusive situations. Seven children died in 1990 of beatings from family members who the agency had identified previously as abusive. Forty-four children, "whose families had a troubled history known to the agency," died in 1990. Three children who had been placed in foster care by the agency were killed by their foster mothers. The report described "poor evaluations of troubled homes," "inadequate screening of foster parents," and "problems with the training, competency and supervision of child welfare caseworkers." Celia W. Dugger, 7 Deaths in 1990 Point Up Failing of Child Protection System, N.Y. Times, Jan. 23, 1992, at B1.

179. Mushlin, supra note 5, at 214. See also Freedman, supra note 8, at B5.

child's constitutional claim and endowing such a claim with substantive rights is compelling.[180]

The availability of injunctions in private action suits based on constitutional claims would require local governments to implement adequate plans or face court sanctions.[181] Judicial intervention is necessary to ensure that Fourteenth Amendment rights are not violated by administrative failures. A decision by the Supreme Court affirming the constitutional rights of foster children would improve the quality of state care by rendering state child welfare agencies accountable to their charges.[182]

---

180. See Mushlin, supra note 5, at 212-14; Lowry, supra note 4, at 274-75.
181. See Sheryl A. Donnella, Safe Foster Care: A Constitutional Mandate, 19 Fam. L.Q. 79, 97-98 (1985).
182. See Jack M. Beermann, Administrative Failure and Local Democracy: The Politics of *DeShaney*, 1990 Duke L.J. 1078, 1079 (1990).

TERMINATION OF PARENTAL RIGHTS TO FREE CHILD
FOR ADOPTION

In 1955 there were almost 15,000 children under the care of all the voluntary child-care agencies in New York City.[1] Some of them had been left with these agencies permanently, their parents simply being unwilling or unable to care for them.[2] Others had been placed temporarily, for any number of reasons—sickness or death in the family, desertion by one parent, or the necessity of finding some means of support for an illegitimate child.[3] However, it is regrettable how many of these "temporary" placements become permanent. After placing a child in an agency, the parents continue to visit him for a while, then gradually lose interest, and eventually abandon him completely. For many years of his life the child is cared for by an agency or in a succession of foster homes, never knowing its natural parents.[4] Many of these children are what is termed "nonadoptable," *i.e.*, children who will eventually return to their natural parents, or have mental or physical handicaps, or are emotionally disturbed.[5] However, a substantial number, otherwise available for adoption, are deprived of the chance to find a new home solely because their natural parents, although long since foregoing all parental responsibilities, are unwilling to consent to an adoption.[6]

In 1955 the Welfare and Health Council of New York City made a study of 4,021 children in fourteen foster-care agencies—28 per cent of the 14,585 children in the care of all the voluntary child-care agencies of New York City. It was estimated that adoption would be a sound plan for 773 of the children, almost 20 per cent.[7] Of these 773 children, 632—80 per cent—were considered *legally* unavailable for adoption, the primary reason being the difficulty of obtaining parental consent.[8] The figure of 632 children who would be considered good adoption risks if legally available is especially significant when it is remembered that in 1951 there were a total of only 2,133 adoptions in New York City.[9]

---

[1] Welfare and Health Council of New York City, Children Deprived of Adoption 4 (1955) (hereinafter cited as Children Deprived of Adoption).

[2] Id. at 11.

[3] Comment, 59 Yale L.J. 715, 717-18 (1950).

[4] In a study of fourteen foster-care agencies, the Welfare and Health Council of New York City found cases where children had been under foster care for as long as ten to fifteen years without any contact at all with relatives. Children Deprived of Adoption, supra note 1, at 1.

[5] Id. at 2; Study on Adoption of Children, U.N. Doc. No. ST/SOA/17, at 60-61 (1953); Comment, 59 Yale L.J. 715, 717-18 (1950).

[6] Children Deprived of Adoption, supra note 1, at 11.

[7] Id. at 6. The report states that there is no reason to believe that the conclusions reached in the study should not be equally valid for the remainder of the foster-care agencies. Id. at 15.

[8] Id. at 10, 11.

[9] Gellhorn, Children and Families in the Courts of New York City, a Report by a Special Committee of the Association of the Bar of the City of New York 243 (1954). Later figures are unavailable.

Disturbed by the plight of these children, some social workers and members of the legal profession have come to the conclusion that in such cases the parents should be deprived of their parental rights, thus freeing the children for adoption. They recommend that a judicial procedure be established to accomplish this, a procedure which would take place prior to, and separate from, the adoption proceedings.[10] The 1956 Report of the Temporary Commission on the Courts strongly recommends that such legislation be adopted in New York,[11] and the Commission can be expected to propose it shortly. Yet, before any changes can be made in the present adoption law, it is first necessary to understand something of the background and theory of the adoption process itself and the way it has been regarded in New York, as evidenced by statutes and judicial decisions.

I

HISTORY AND OBJECTIVES

The practice of adoption is an ancient one, existing among the earliest civilizations. The Assyrians, the Greeks, the Egyptians, and the Romans all made use of adoption in some form.[12] However, adoption was never part of the common law,[13] and in the United States it was not until the middle of the nineteenth century that adoption statutes were enacted.[14] In England the first adoption statute was not passed until 1926.[15]

In spite of this fairly recent development, however, adoption is of vital importance because of its far-reaching effects. It establishes new legal relationships between the parties involved, drastically altering their personal and property rights. It serves as an efficient social instrument,

---

[10] 1956 Report of the Temporary Commission on the Courts to the Governor and the Legislature of the State of New York 66-67, N.Y. Legis. Doc. No. 18 (1956) (hereinafter cited 1956 Report of the Temporary Commission on the Courts); Notes, 102 U. Pa. L. Rev. 759, 763, 774 (1954), 8 Wyo. L.J. 210, 214-15 (1954). See also Melli, The Children's Code, 1956 Wis. L. Rev. 431, 437-38.

[11] 1956 Report of the Temporary Commission on the Courts, supra note 10, at 66-69.

[12] For an excellent account of the historical roots of the adoption process, see Brosnan, The Law of Adoption, 22 Colum. L. Rev. 332 (1922). The object of ancient adoption laws was not necessarily to protect children unwanted by their parents. The Roman law used adoption to bolster the position of the family by adding strength to it. Gellhorn, supra note 9, at 253; Note, 38 Va. L. Rev. 544, 545-46 (1952). See also Ruggles and Redmond, Adoption and Abandonment of Children 11 (1946).

[13] See Matter of Taggart, 190 Cal. 493, 498, 213 Pac. 504, 506 (1923); Matter of Thorne, 155 N.Y. 140, 143, 49 N.E. 661, 662 (1898); 4 Vernier, American Family Laws 279 (1936). It has been suggested that adoption was unknown to English and Scotch law because of the peculiarities of the English feudal system and English reverence for heirs of the blood of the ancestor. Merrill and Merrill, Toward Uniformity in Adoption Law 299 n.6 (1955); Brosnan, The Law of Adoption, 22 Colum. L. Rev. 332, 335 (1922).

[14] Massachusetts was the first common-law jurisdiction to enact an adoption statute in 1851. Mass. Laws 1851, p. 324. See Ross v. Ross, 129 Mass. 243 (1880). At present, every American jurisdiction has such a statute. See 4 Vernier, American Family Laws 279 (1936).

[15] Adoption of Children Act, 16 & 17 Geo. 5, c. 29.

not only in promoting the welfare of orphaned and neglected children, but also in enriching the lives of their adoptive parents.[16]   In view of these considerations and the ever-increasing volume of adoptions,[17] the United States Children's Bureau has specifically set forth the factors which should be the basis of any adoption statute: protection of the child from unnecessary separation from his natural parents, from adoption by unfit persons, and from interference by his natural parents after he has been established in his new home, protection of the natural parents from hurried decisions to give up a child; protection of the adopting parents from taking responsibility for children of unknown heredity, or physical or mental capacity, and from later disturbance of their relationship to the child by the natural parents.[18]   Balancing these frequently conflicting policies is the objective of modern adoption legislation.

II

PRESENT NEW YORK STATUTE

In General.—The first New York adoption statute was enacted in 1873.[19]   The foundation of the present law was laid in 1896,[20] and in 1938 the statute assumed the form which, with some minor amendments, is the law today.[21]

The procedure begins with the receipt of the child by the proposed adoptive parents, either from an authorized adoption agency or from a private individual, such as a parent, clergyman, or friend.   The latter method is known as "voluntary" adoption[22] and, contrary to popular opinion, accounts for the great majority of adoptions.[23]   After receiving the child into their home, the adoptive parents may present to the court a petition for

---

[16] It has been pointed out that adoptions are also a factor in promoting the welfare of the state by "improving the future quality of the race by furnishing to children better material advantages, better education, better moral background. . . . [F]amilies created because adopting parents were resolute in their desire to build up a family life have something to offer by way of stability and social health." Hanft, Thwarting Adoptions, 19 N.C.L. Rev. 127, 132 (1941).

[17] "Some 75,000 adoption petitions are filed annually in American courts, an estimated increase of more than 500% over the level of twenty years ago." Gellhorn, supra note 9, at 241.   In the period 1940-1949, adoptions in New York State doubled. Id. at 241-42. It has been suggested that some of the factors responsible for the increase were the number of families broken up by death, divorce, and desertion during World War II; the increase in the number of illegitimate children born since 1944; and the growing feeling against institutional care for children. Note, 102 U. Pa. L. Rev. 759, 761 n.20 (1954).

[18] United States Children's Bureau, Essentials of Adoption Law and Procedure 2 (Pub. No. 331, 1949).

[19] N.Y. Laws 1873, c. 830.

[20] N.Y. Laws 1896, c. 272, §§ 60-68.   See Matter of Thorne, 155 N.Y. 140, 143, 49 N.E. 661, 662 (1898) (dictum).

[21] N.Y. Dom. Rel. Law §§ 109 through 118-a.

[22] Id. § 109(5).

[23] Of the 2,133 adoptions in New York City during 1951, only 31% were arranged through adoption agencies. Gellhorn, supra note 9, at 243. In California, from 1949 to 1951, only 16% of the adoption petitions involved agencies. Study on Adoption of Children, U.N. Doc. No. ST/SOA/17, at 27 (1953).

adoption, setting forth detailed information about themselves and the child.[24] Ordinarily, the judge hearing the petition will then direct the persons whose consents are required—the natural parents or anyone having lawful custody of the child[25]—to appear personally before him in order to execute and acknowledge the necessary documents.[26] He may also direct that notice be sent to the natural parents even though circumstances exist which make their consents unnecessary.[27] He must then order an investigation of the new home,[28] unless the adoption was arranged through an authorized agency in which case he may accept a report of the agency in lieu of the investigation.[29] If he is satisfied that the adoption will promote the moral and temporal interests of the child, he will then make an order approving it.[30]

Consent.—As might be imagined, the knottiest legal problems in the adoption proceedings center around the issue of consent. The statute requires the consent of the child, if he is over fourteen years of age, of the parents of a child born in wedlock or the mother of a child born out of wedlock, and of any person or agency having lawful custody of the child.[31] However, consent is not required of a parent who has abandoned the child; has surrendered it to an authorized agency for the purpose of adoption; has been deprived of civil rights; has been divorced because of his adultery; is insane or has been judicially declared incompetent; is a mental defective; or has been adjudged an habitual drunkard or been judicially deprived of the custody of the child on account of cruelty or neglect.[32]

The question of whether a parent has acted in such a way as to render his consent unnecessary does not arise in New York until the adoption proceeding itself. After the child has resided with his new parents, after new emotional attachments have been established, the petition for adoption is filed and the issue of consent is litigated. As a result, the judge in the adoption proceeding is faced with two distinct questions: (1) whether the natural parent has forfeited his right to withhold consent to the adoption, and (2) whether the petitioners should be allowed to adopt the child. These questions present separate problems and involve different policy factors. The mere fact that the child's welfare would be promoted by the adoption is not enough to cut off the natural parents' rights; nor does the unfitness

---

[24] N.Y. Dom. Rel. Law § 112(2).

[25] Id. § 111.

[26] Id. § 112(1).

[27] Id. § 112(6).

[28] Id. § 112(8).

[29] Id. § 113.

[30] Id. § 114. The child must reside with the adopting parents for at least six months before an order of adoption can be made. Id. § 112(7).

[31] Id. § 111. It is usually stated as a general rule that a legitimate child cannot be adopted without the consent of his parents, and that an illegitimate child cannot be adopted without the consent of his mother. Ruggles and Redmond, Adoption and Abandonment of Children 26 (1946); Comment, 59 Yale L.J. 715, 727 (1950).

[32] N.Y. Dom. Rel. Law § 111. For a recent compilation of United States statutes dealing with consent and grounds for dispensing with consent, see Comment 24 Rocky Mt. L. Rev. 359 (1952).

of the natural parents establish the fitness of the adoptive parents.[33]   Yet both questions are decided in the same proceeding. Not only does this result in confusing the legal issues, but it allows the natural parents to learn the identity of the adoptive parents, leaving the door open for interference in the child's new home and perhaps for blackmail by the natural parents.[34] Consequently, child-care agencies will not place a child in a home for the purpose of adoption unless the natural parents have surrendered the child for adoption.[35] They will not take the risk of creating new ties when the child might be taken from its new home in a few months. Thus, in effect, the child is "nonadoptable" as long as the natural parent refuses to sign an *express surrender for the purpose of adoption*. This nullifies the statutory provision dispensing with parental consent in cases where the parent has been guilty of misconduct.

It is for this reason that litigation involving the issue of consent arises only in connection with voluntary or independent placements where the natural parent or a private individual acting on her behalf has delivered the child into the home of the petitioner. In such cases, months or years may go by before the adoption proceedings are brought, and, in the meantime, the natural parent often experiences a change of heart and refuses to consent to the adoption. The court is then faced squarely with the question of whether the parent's consent is necessary.

It is obvious that in any legislation providing for a procedure to cut off parental rights before the adoption petition is filed, the grounds for such termination will be much the same as the present grounds for dispensing with consent. The policy argument is the same: the parent has acted in such a way that he has forfeited all rights in the child or is incapable of caring for the child. The factors which will prompt a court to conclude that such a state of affairs exists will be approximately the same whether the question is decided at the time of adoption or in a prior proceeding. For this reason it will be useful to examine the circumstances under which the court will dispense with parental consent under the present statute.

Dispensing with Consent: Judicial Interpretation.—Although most of the statutory provisions for dispensing with consent have given rise to liti-

---

[33] Comment, 59 Yale L.J. 715, 727 (1950).

[34] Most authorities in the field of adoption believe that litigation involving the termination of parental rights should be kept separate from the adoption proceedings in any case, whether the placement is arranged by an agency or independently. United States Children's Bureau, Essentials of Adoption Law and Procedure 7 (Pub. No. 331, 1949); Note, 102 U. Pa. L. Rev. 759, 773-74.

Uniform Adoption Act § 5(1) provides that consent to an adoption shall not be required of one whose parental rights have been judicially terminated. This termination is to take place in separate proceedings before the adoption proceedings are brought. However, the uniform act does not specify any procedure for such termination since it was felt that this would entail insuperable procedural and policy differences among the states. The act is reprinted as an appendix to an excellent article by Merrill and Merrill, Toward Uniformity in Adoption Law, 40 Iowa L. Rev. 299, 329 (1955). See also Note, 3 N.Y.U. Intra. L. Rev. 57, 63 (1956).

[35] Children Deprived of Adoption, supra note 1, at 10; Study on Adoption of Children, U.N. Doc. No. ST/SOA/17, at 61-62 (1953).

gation, the question of abandonment has caused the real problem. The other provisions have not been invoked as often, although a few of them will be discussed first, principally to indicate the tendency of judges in general to construe this section of the statute very narrowly in favor of the natural parents.

1. Miscellaneous Grounds.—The only provision which is accepted on its face is that providing for dispensing with consent where the child has been surrendered to an authorized adoption agency for the purpose of adoption. It is clear that in such a case, in the absence of fraud or mistake, all rights of the natural parents are terminated and the surrender may not be revoked unless the court is convinced that the child's welfare will be bettered by allowing revocation.[36]

The provision dispensing with consent where a parent has been judicially deprived of custody because of his cruelty or neglect has been narrowly construed to apply only to an adjudication under section 486 of the Penal Law.[37] The remaining grounds, other than divorce for adultery or abandonment, rendering consent unnecessary include loss of civil rights or an adjudication of incompetency, mental deficiency, or habitual drunkenness. These provisions are of little importance since they are rarely used.[38]

2. Divorce for Adultery.—The necessity of obtaining the consent of a parent who has been divorced because of his adultery is rather uncertain, but illustrates in an especially clear way the lengths to which courts will go in order to protect the "natural rights" of parents in their children. The typical situation involves *W* (wife) who has divorced *H-1* (her first husband) on the ground of adultery, the decree awarding custody of the children to *W*, and in some cases giving *H-1* visiting privileges. *W* remarries and *H-2* petitions to adopt the children. *H-1* is given notice of the proposed adoption and objects. In 1921 the Surrogate of New York County held that in such a case *H-1* had a right to oppose the proceedings and denied the petition.[39] He explained that *H-1*'s rights in his children had not been abrogated, but had only been curtailed by the divorce decree which could be modified at any time.[40] This decision was followed for many years, and before the consent of a divorced parent could be dispensed with it was neces-

---

[36] People ex rel. Anonymous v. Rebecca Talbot Perkins Adoption Soc'y, Inc., 271 App. Div. 672, 68 N.Y.S.2d 238 (2d Dep't 1947); People ex rel. Miller v. Butts, 99 N.Y.S.2d 913 (Sup. Ct. 1950); People ex rel. Harris v. Commissioner of Welfare, 188 Misc. 919, 70 N.Y.S.2d 389 (Sup. Ct. 1947).

[37] Matter of Adoption of Antonopulos, 171 App. Div. 659, 157 N.Y. Supp. 587 (2d Dep't 1916); Matter of Adoption of Cohen, 155 Misc. 202, 206, 279 N.Y. Supp. 427 (Surr. Ct. 1935) (dictum); Matter of Connolly, 154 Misc. 672, 278 N.Y. Supp. 32 (Surr. Ct. 1935).

[38] It is possible, however, that they might be used more frequently if they were made grounds for termination of parental rights. The Welfare and Health Council of New York City reported that mental illness prevented securing a consent in 12% of the cases studied in its survey. Children Deprived of Adoption, supra note 1, at 11.

[39] Matter of Adoption of Metzger, 114 Misc. 313, 186 N.Y. Supp. 269 (Surr. Ct. 1921) (custody to *W*, visiting privileges to *H-1* by divorce decree).

[40] Id. at 314, 186 N.Y. Supp. at 270.

sary to prove an abandonment—the divorce had no effect on consent.[41] Some courts simply ignored the statutory provision and determined only whether an abandonment had taken place,[42] or decided the case on other grounds.[43] Others were quite frank in stating that the statute could not be construed literally.[44] One judge wrote:

> It is manifest from a perusal of the cases that there has evolved over the years a construction of the statute which takes into account some phases which a literal reading thereof does not reveal.
>
> . . . .
>
> It is clearly recognized that one who has abandoned his child is not on the same footing morally or legally as one who has been divorced for adultery.[45]

However, in 1952 this line of decisions seemed to be overthrown by an appellate division decision in the Matter of the Adoption of *Greenfield*,[46] overruling a surrogate court's denial of an adoption petition on the ground that there was no proof of abandonment by the divorced parent. In a memorandum opinion the appellate division held that abandonment is not even an issue in a case of this kind; the most the divorced parent is entitled to is notice of the proposed adoption and a chance to show the court that the child's best interests will not be served by the adoption.[47] The only factual distinction, but a vital one, between this case and the previous ones was that the petitioner seeking adoption here was not the new stepparent (*H-2*), but was a neighbor with whom the mother had left the child after obtaining the divorce and being granted custody. In the ordinary case denial of the adoption petition is less drastic in that the child continues to live with its mother and stepfather. In the *Greenfield* case, however, the denial of the petition might have caused the child to lose a good home. In spite of this distinction, shortly after the *Greenfield* case, the Queens County surrogate

---

[41] Matter of Adoption of "Rivers," 201 Misc. 447, 106 N.Y.S.2d 92 (County Ct. 1951). Note that in this case the fact pattern was reversed inasmuch as *H*, the father of the children, had obtained the divorce and was granted sole custody, with no reservation of visiting privileges for *W-1*. *H* had voluntarily allowed *W-1* to visit. *H* remarried and *W-2* desired to adopt the children. See also Caruso v. Caruso, 175 Misc. 290, 23 N.Y.S.2d 239 (Sup. Ct. 1940) (custody to *W*, visiting privileges to *H-1* by decree); Matter of the Adoption of Munzel, 160 Misc. 508, 290 N.Y. Supp. 178 (County Ct. 1936) (custody to *W*, visiting privileges to *H-1* by decree; abandonment proved); Matter of Norris, 157 Misc. 333, 283 N.Y. Supp. 513 (Surr. Ct. 1935) (custody to *W* by decree, *W* voluntarily allowed *H-1* visiting privileges).

[42] Caruso v. Caruso, 175 Misc. 290, 23 N.Y.S.2d 239 (Sup. Ct. 1940).

[43] Matter of Norris, 157 Misc. 333, 283 N.Y. Supp. 513 (Surr. Ct. 1935).

[44] Matter of Adoption of "Rivers," 201 Misc. 447, 106 N.Y.S.2d 92 (County Ct. 1951). See also Matter of the Adoption of Munzel, 160 Misc. 508, 290 N.Y. Supp. 178 (County Ct. 1936) (recognized adultery provision but ignored it, deciding case on abandonment). See note 41 supra for a description of *H-1*'s visiting rights in these cases.

[45] Matter of Adoption of "Rivers," 201 Misc. 447, 449, 106 N.Y.S.2d 92, 94-95 (County Ct. 1951).

[46] 281 App. Div. 887, 119 N.Y.S.2d 442 (2d Dep't 1953) (mem.), reversing 109 N.Y.S.2d 462 (Surr. Ct. 1952) (sole custody to *W* by decree).

[47] Id. at 887, 119 N.Y.S.2d at 443.

granted an order of adoption in a proceeding initiated by the *stepfather*, dutifully following the decision of the appellate division that the divorced father's consent was unnecessary whether or not an abandonment had been shown.[48] Yet, three months later, on exactly the same facts, the surrogate of Bronx County denied an adoption by *H-2* on the ground that abandonment by the divorced parent was an issue and had not been proved.[49] He held that where the divorced parent had *visiting privileges*, the petitioner must show abandonment.[50] It is significant to note, however, that the divorce decree in this case had given *W* sole custody, *H-1* getting visiting privileges only as a result of a private agreement between him and *W*. Considering that adultery is the only ground for divorce in New York, and that parties frequently use it merely as a pretext for separating, it will be a rare case where the divorced parent is not given some right to visit his children, if not by the decree, then by an agreement with the other spouse. In effect, then, in the ordinary case the consent of the divorced parent will not be dispensed with unless he has abandoned the child.

   3. *Abandonment.*—The term "abandonment" has been held to mean neglect and refusal to perform the natural and legal obligations of care and support.[51] If a parent withholds his presence, love, care, and the opportunity to display filial affection, and neglects to lend support and maintenance, such a parent abandons the child.[52] The traditional test of abandonment is whether there has occurred any conduct on the part of a parent which "evinces a settled purpose to forego all parental duties and relinquish all parental claims to the child."[53] However, it is not easy to determine exactly what acts must be present before the court will find that an abandonment has taken place. The "natural rights" of the parents are jealously guarded,[54] and the burden of proof is on the party seeking to prove the abandonment.[55]

---

   [48] In re Adoption of Blachinsky, 127 N.Y.S.2d 553 (Surr. Ct. 1953) (sole custody to *W*, *H-1* required to support by decree).

   [49] In re Adoption of Fischer, 127 N.Y.S.2d 423 (Surr. Ct. 1954) (sole custody to *W*, *H-1* required to support by decree).

   [50] Id. at 425-27.

   [51] In re Anonymous, 80 N.Y.S.2d 839, 845 (Surr. Ct. 1947); In re Davison's Adoption, 44 N.Y.S.2d 763, 765 (Surr. Ct. 1943); Matter of Dein, 135 Misc. 244, 246, 237 N.Y. Supp. 658, 661 (Surr. Ct. 1929); Matter of the Adoption of Hayford, 109 Misc. 479, 481, 179 N.Y. Supp. 182, 183 (Surr. Ct. 1919).

   [52] In re Anonymous, 80 N.Y.S.2d 839, 845 (Surr. Ct. 1947); Matter of the Adoption of Hayford, 109 Misc. 479, 481, 179 N.Y. Supp. 182, 183-84 (Surr. Ct. 1919).

   [53] Winans v. Luppie, 47 N.J. Eq. 302, 305, 20 Atl. 969, 970 (Ct. Err. & App. 1890). See also Matter of Zucker, 277 App. Div. 1077, 1078, 100 N.Y.S.2d 568, 569 (3d Dep't 1950) (per curiam); Adoption of Sanderson, 143 N.Y.S.2d 520, 523 (County Ct. 1955); Matter of Anonymous, 142 N.Y.S.2d 11, 13 (Surr. Ct. 1953).

   [54] Application of Livingston, 151 App. Div. 1, 7, 135 N.Y. Supp. 328, 332 (2d Dep't 1912); Matter of Anonymous, 178 Misc. 142, 146, 33 N.Y.S.2d 793, 797 (Surr. Ct. 1942); Caruso v. Caruso, 175 Misc. 290, 292, 23 N.Y.S.2d 239, 241 (Sup. Ct. 1940).

   [55] In re Anonymous, 85 N.Y.S.2d 358, 362 (Surr. Ct. 1948); Matter of Paden, 181 Misc. 1025, 1027, 43 N.Y.S.2d 305, 308 (Surr. Ct. 1943); Matter of Anonymous, 178 Misc. 142, 145, 33 N.Y.S.2d 793, 796 (Surr. Ct. 1942); Matter of the Adoption of Marks, 159 Misc. 348, 350, 287 N.Y. Supp. 800, 802 (Surr. Ct. 1936).

In 1924 the New York Court of Appeals, speaking through Judge Cardozo, laid down the policy that in order to dispense with a parent's consent to an adoption on the ground of abandonment the evidence must be such "that even though the parents be given the benefit of every controverted fact, a finding of abandonment follows as an inference of law."[56] The acts must be "so unequivocal as to bear one interpretation and one only," namely, an intention to abandon the child.[57] The welfare of the child is irrelevant in deciding whether an abandonment has taken place.[58]

In general, there are three types of cases in which the issue of abandonment is raised: (1) where the natural parents have been divorced and the new spouse of one seeks to adopt the children of the first marriage; (2) where a parent has handed the child over to the new parents and has signed an instrument of surrender or executed a statutory consent; and (3) where the parent has left the child with the new parents, but no documents have been signed.

The first type of case has already been discussed in part in considering whether a parent divorced for his adultery may object to an adoption. The courts will seldom hold that a divorced parent has abandoned his child as long as he has visited it occasionally[59] or made some attempt to visit it.[60] In the few cases where abandonment has been found, the circumstances have been extreme—there has been a complete absence of contact with the child for a period of years[61] or, as in one case, evidence of blackmail.[62]

The case where there has been a written surrender or consent is much more common. The children involved are usually illegitimates, left with the new parents shortly after birth. To protect their interest in the child, they require the mother to sign an instrument surrendering it to them for adoption. It is the legal effect of this instrument which is often in issue. As regards a nonstatutory surrender agreement, if the mother revokes her consent within six months (the period which the law requires that the child be in the new home before an adoption order can be made),[63] the surrender would appear to be worthless.[64] However, this revocation must involve taking positive action to regain custody of the child, either by de-

---

[56] Application of Bistany, 239 N.Y. 19, 21, 145 N.E. 70, 72 (1924).

[57] Id. at 24, 145 N.E. at 71.

[58] Id. at 24, 145 N.E. at 72.

[59] In re Adoption of Fischer, 127 N.Y.S.2d 423 (Surr. Ct. 1954); Matter of Adoption of "Rivers," 201 Misc. 447, 106 N.Y.S.2d 92 (County Ct. 1951); Matter of Anonymous, 192 Misc. 359, 77 N.Y.S.2d 121 (Surr. Ct. 1948); Caruso v. Caruso, 175 Misc. 290, 23 N.Y.S.2d 239 (Sup. Ct. 1940).

[60] Matter of the Adoption of Willing, 298 N.Y. 566, 81 N.E.2d 103 (1948) (mem.).

[61] Matter of Lieblich, 207 Misc. 793, 141 N.Y.S.2d 473 (Surr. Ct. 1955) (eight years); In re Adoption of Resnick, 127 N.Y.S.2d 918 (Surr. Ct. 1953) (three years).

[62] Matter of Anonymous, 142 N.Y.S.2d 11 (Surr. Ct. 1953).

[63] N.Y. Dom. Rel. Law § 112(7).

[64] People ex rel. Flannagan v. Riggio, 193 Misc. 930, 85 N.Y.S.2d 534 (Sup. Ct. 1948); Matter of Anonymous, 178 Misc. 142, 33 N.Y.S.2d 793 (Surr. Ct. 1942); Matter of the Adoption of Cohen, 155 Misc. 202, 279 N.Y. Supp. 427 (Surr. Ct. 1935).

manding its return from the new parents[65] or, if necessary, by bringing habeas corpus proceedings.[66] If the natural parent takes no steps to regain the child until after the six-month period, the court is more likely to find an abandonment.[67] Yet, even in a case where nine months had passed, the court was not willing to base a finding of abandonment on the passage of time alone, but coupled it with evidence of blackmail.[68]

As regards a consent executed in accordance with the statute,[69] the law is unsettled at the present time.[70] Some cases hold that revocation is possible anytime before the final adoption order is signed as a matter of strict legal right.[71] Others allow it within the six-month probationary period.[72] The present tendency is to restrict the power of revocation, forbidding arbitrary withdrawal and making it depend on all the circumstances of the case, including the moral, physical, and financial condition of the natural parent, the circumstances under which the consent was given, the length of time elapsing, and the attitude of the foster parents toward the child.[73]

Where there is no written surrender involved, any attempt to reconcile the cases is hopeless. In those cases, an adoption usually was not contemplated at the time the child was left with the foster parents, but after a few years they became attached to the child and decided to adopt it. No two courts agree on the "unequivocal acts" which will spell out an abandonment. Traditionally, the natural parent has to do very little to indicate that he does not have a settled intent to abandon the child. Visiting him at intervals[74] and even reserving the right to custody on the death of the new parents[75] have been enough to prevent a finding of abandonment. Mere unwillingness to take responsibility for the child does not seem to constitute

---

[65] Matter of the Adoption of Anonymous, 178 Misc. 142, 33 N.Y.S.2d 793 (Surr. Ct. 1942).

[66] Matter of the Adoption of Cohen, 155 Misc. 202, 279 N.Y. Supp. 427 (Surr. Ct. 1935).

[67] Matter of the Adoption of Marino, 168 Misc. 158, 5 N.Y.S.2d 328 (Surr. Ct. 1938); Matter of Dein, 135 Misc. 244, 237 N.Y. Supp. 658 (Surr. Ct. 1929).

[68] Matter of the Adoption of Marino, 168 Misc. 158, 160, 5 N.Y.S.2d 328, 330 (Surr. Ct. 1938).

[69] N.Y. Dom. Rel. Law §§ 111(1)-(4).

[70] The question of whether a parent may withdraw his consent, once given, is the subject of an interesting Note in 30 St. John's L. Rev. 75 (1955).

[71] People ex rel. Anonymous v. Anonymous, 195 Misc. 1054, 91 N.Y.S.2d 591 (Sup. Ct. 1949); In re Anonymous, 85 N.Y.S.2d 358 (Surr. Ct. 1948).

[72] In re Burke's Adoption, 60 N.Y.S.2d 421 (Surr. Ct. 1946).

[73] Matter of the Adoption of Anonymous, 198 Misc. 185, 189, 101 N.Y.S.2d 93, 97 (County Ct. 1950). This latter view was reinforced by a recent decision of the appellate division holding that a statutory consent cannot be revoked at will even if attempted within six months. Matter of the Adoption of Anonymous, 286 App. Div. 161, 143 N.Y.S.2d 90 (2d Dep't 1955).

[74] Application of Bistany, 239 N.Y. 19, 145 N.E. 70 (1924).

[75] Matter of the Adoption of Marks, 159 Misc. 348, 287 N.Y. Supp. 800 (Surr. Ct. 1936).

an abandonment,[76] unless the circumstances are particularly sordid, involving immorality and drunkenness[77] or exploitation of the child.[78]

An exception to this policy can be found in a recent decision of Surrogate Moss of Brooklyn which held that a mother had abandoned her child even though she had visited it twice a year for eight years and had brought habeas corpus proceedings in which, although she had been denied custody, she had been given the right to visit it once a month.[79]   This is a startling result inasmuch as no other court has found an abandonment where such a degree of contact still existed between parent and child.

It is important to remember that every case of abandonment that has been discussed so far has involved an independent placement.   As has been pointed out, the question has not arisen in agency placements since the agencies will not release a child for adoption unless the parent has surrendered it expressly for this purpose.   A significant step towards remedying this situation was taken a few months ago by two child-caring agencies which petitioned the Surrogate's Court of Brooklyn for a decree of guardianship over two children in their care and for a declaration that their parents had abandoned them and that in any future adoption the consent of the parents could be dispensed with.   The children, brother and sister, had been in the care of the agencies for eleven years.   The parents had visited them regularly for the first six months, but gradually the visits fell off to less than once a year.   The girl had not been visited at all for the last two years, and the boy for the last seven.   In a decision, the importance of which cannot be overestimated, Surrogate Moss granted the petitions of the agencies.[80]   While recognizing the natural rights of the parents as sacred, and while extending them the benefit of every controverted fact, he found that by their conduct they had abandoned the children. He pointed out that the procedure established in this case should serve as a guide to child-care agencies in hundreds of cases where children have been deposited with them by parents who take little or no interest in them but who never the less refuse to consent to their adoption.[81]

III

PROPOSED LEGISLATION

Although the decision of Surrogate Moss is a step in the right direction, it is certainly not the final answer to the problem.   The legislature should take action to indorse the procedure and to encourage its use.

Several states have recently set up statutory procedures to terminate

---

[76] See Adoption of Sanderson, 143 N.Y.S.2d 520 (County Ct. 1955) (no abandonment although mother went west with new husband and only occasionally sent small sums of money to foster parents).

[77] Matter of "Tommy," 1 Misc. 2d 378, 148 N.Y.S.2d 39 (N.Y. Dom. Rel. Ct. 1956); Matter of the Adoption of Davis, 142 Misc. 681, 255 N.Y. Supp. 416 (Surr. Ct. 1932).

[78] Ibid.

[79] Matter of Anonymous, 142 N.Y.S.2d 313 (Surr. Ct. 1955).

[80] Commitment of Knapp, 156 N.Y.S.2d 668 (Surr. Ct. 1956).

[81] Id. at 672.

parental rights in a child.[82]   Pennsylvania, for instance, provides that where an approved agency has had the care of a child for thirty days, and it appears that it has been abandoned for at least six months, the agency may petition the court for a finding of abandonment.   The court must then fix a time for a hearing, and the natural parents must be given at least five days notice by registered mail sent to their last known address.   At the hearing, if the court finds that there was an abandonment, it will issue a decree giving the agency custody of the child and the power to consent to any future adoption without notifying the natural parents.[83]

The Pennsylvania statute has been criticized on two grounds.   It has been suggested that the provision for notifying the natural parents is not only questionable, but possibly unconstitutional.[84]   Besides the lack of any requirement of personal service, it does not even specify that publication or proof of mailing is necessary.[85]   Secondly, a judicial determination of abandonment prior to adoption proceedings can occur only where the child is in the care of an agency.   There is no reason why foster parents who receive a child through an independent placement should not themselves be able to petition for a finding of abandonment and settle the issue before they become strongly attached to the child.[86]

---

[82] Del. Code Ann. tit. 13, §§ 1101-11 (Supp. 1956); Mich. Stat. Ann. §§ 27.3178(598.1) through 27.3178(598.22), particularly § 27.3178(598.20) (Callaghan Supp. 1955) [in connection with the Michigan statute, see Virtue, Study of the Basic Structure for Children's Services in Michigan 310 (1953)]; N.J. Stat. Ann. §§ 9:2-18 through 9:2-20 (West Supp. 1955); Pa. Stat. Ann. tit. 1, §§ 1.1-.2 (Purdon Supp. 1956); Wis. Stat. §§ 48.40-.47 (1955).

[83] Pa. Stat. Ann. tit. 1, § 1.2 (Purdon Supp. 1956).   In 1953 Pennsylvania completely revised its adoption laws.   For a comprehensive discussion of the changes, see Note, 102 U. Pa. L. Rev. 759 (1954).   See also Note, 59 Dick. L. Rev. 57 (1954); Comment, 15 U. Pitt. L. Rev. 150 (1953).

[84] Under the due process clause of the fourteenth amendment to the Constitution, notice to the natural parents and opportunity to be heard are indispensable in an abandonment proceeding.   Sullivan v. People ex rel. Heeney, 224 Ill. 468, 79 N.E. 695 (1906); Petit v. Engelking, 260 S.W.2d 613, 616 (Tex. Civ. App. 1953) (dictum); Schiltz v. Roenitz, 86 Wis. 31, 56 N.W. 194 (1893).   The New York courts are in accord: "To hold that the State may permit its courts to determine without notice to the parent that he has forfeited his natural rights to the custody of his child is nothing less than to assert that the powers of the State over the child are in their nature legally superior to the natural rights of the parent." Application of Livingston, 151 App. Div. 1, 7, 135 N.Y. Supp. 328, 332 (2d Dep't 1912).   See also Matter of the Adoption of Oddo, 186 Misc. 359, 360, 59 N.Y.S.2d 612, 614 (Surr. Ct. 1946); Matter of the Adoption of Davis, 142 Misc. 681, 689, 255 N.Y. Supp. 416, 425 (Surr. Ct. 1932).

[85] Note, 59 Dick. L. Rev. 57, 59-60 (1954).   The writer of the note outlines the possibility that under the Pennsylvania act a judge could take a child from its parents without the latter ever receiving notice or without any sincere effort being made to notify them of the action.

[86] Note, 102 U. Pa. L. Rev. 759, 774 (1954).   The 1953 act has also been criticized as incorporating a too stringent definition of "abandonment," in that it requires "conduct on the part of a parent which evidences a *settled purpose* of relinquishing parental claim to the child and of refusing or failing to perform parental duties." Pa. Stat. Ann. tit. 1, § 1 (Purdon Supp. 1955). (Emphasis added.)

Wisconsin has also set up termination proceedings, but its statute is of wider application than the Pennsylvania one.[87]   The right to petition for the termination of parental rights is not limited to authorized agencies, but anyone may bring the action.[88]   The grounds for such termination are not confined to abandonment but also include lack of care or protection, absence of support, habitual use of drugs or liquor, and mental deficiency.[89]   A hearing is of course required, and notice must be served personally on the parents at least ten days before the date of the hearing unless the court is satisfied that personal service cannot be effected, in which case notice may be sent by registered mail at least twenty days prior to the hearing together with publication in a newspaper once a week for three weeks.[90] Then, after the hearing has been held, if the court finds that any of the conditions outlined in the statute exists, it may terminate the parent's rights.[91]

It is suggested that the broader Wisconsin statute might serve as a guide to New York in drafting similar legislation.   Either an agency or an individual having actual custody of the child should be able to petition to terminate the natural parents' rights.   The grounds for such termination should not be limited to abandonment, but, with one exception, should be the same as those which at present allow the court to dispense with the parents' consent to an adoption.   The provision which should not be carried over is that rendering unnecessary the consent of a parent who has been divorced because of his adultery.   It has already been pointed out that the court has practically nullified that provision as it now stands.[92]   Considering how common divorce is in New York today, and looking behind the bare decree, it would seem unjust to deprive a parent of all rights in his child merely because he was divorced by his spouse.[93]   The legislature should not give new strength to this harsh provision by incorporating it in a termination proceeding.

The present method for giving notice to the natural parents, which at least in theory leaves the matter in the discretion of the court,[94] should not be followed.   Personal service should be required, or, where this is impossible, service by registered mail accompanied by publication.[95]

In accord with these suggestions, a statute setting up a procedure to terminate parental rights might read as follows:

---

87 The Wisconsin legislature, after 1½ years of study by its child welfare committee, adopted a completely new children's code in 1955. Wis. Stat. c. 48 (1955). See Melli, The Children's Code, 1956 Wis. L. Rev. 431.

88 Wis. Stat. § 48.40 (1955).

89 Ibid.

90 Id. § 48.42.

91 Id. § 48.43.

92 See text at notes 38-48 supra.

93 Asch, A Critical Appraisal of Adoption in New York State, 20 Brooklyn L. Rev. 27, 48 (1954).

94 Actually, notice must be sent to the natural parents and this is done in practice. See note 82 supra.

95 Where service is accomplished by registered mail, the petitioner should be required to produce a return receipt. See Note, 59 Dick. L. Rev. 57, 60 (1954).

§ *1. Grounds for termination of parental rights.*—The court may, upon petition, terminate all rights of parents to a minor if it finds that one or more of the following conditions exist:

(a) that the parents have abandoned the minor; or

(b) that the parents have surrendered the minor to an authorized agency for the purpose of adoption under the provisions of the social welfare law; or

(c) that the parents have been deprived of their civil rights; or

(d) that the parents are insane or have been judicially declared incompetent or are mental defectives as defined by the mental hygiene law; or

(e) that the parents have been adjudged to be habitual drunkards; or

(f) that the parents have been judicially deprived of the custody of the child on account of cruelty or neglect.

§ *2. Procedure in terminating parental rights.*—The termination of parental rights under § 1 shall be made only after a hearing before the court. The court shall have notice of the time, place, and purpose of the hearing served on the parents personally at least ten days prior to the date of the hearing; or if the court is satisfied that personal service, either within or outside the state, cannot be effected, then such notice may be given by registered mail sent at least twenty days before the date of the hearing to the last known address of the parent, if an address is known, and by publication thereof in a newspaper within a county once a week for three weeks prior to the date of hearing. Where notice is given by registered mail, the court shall require proof of mailing.

This statute would free many formerly nonadoptable children for new lives in good homes. At the same time, it would protect the rights of the natural parents.

It is important to consider one possible result of such legislation. In setting up a separate termination proceeding, the question of abandonment in many cases will not be the subject of a dispute between the natural parents and the foster parents, but between the natural parents and an agency which has custody of the child. In the past the courts have often justified their very strict requirements for a finding of abandonment on the ground that although there was no abandonment and consequently no adoption order could be made without the natural parents' consent, custody of the child nevertheless might be given to the foster parents.[96] In an adoption proceeding where the consent of the natural parents is sought to be dispensed with, the question is whether the facts warrant the court in completely severing all ties between the parents and the child, and the welfare of the child is not controlling. In a custody proceeding, on the other hand,

---

96 Application of Bistany, 239 N.Y. 19, 145 N.E. 70 (1924); Matter of Paden, 181 Misc. 1025, 43 N.Y.S.2d 305 (Surr. Ct. 1943); Matter of Adoption of Marks, 159 Misc. 348, 287 N.Y. Supp. 800 (Surr. Ct. 1936); Matter of Norris, 157 Misc. 333, 283 N.Y. Supp. 513 (Surr. Ct. 1935); Matter of the Adoption of Cohen, 155 Misc. 202, 279 N.Y. Supp. 427 (Surr. Ct. 1935).

the child's welfare is paramount.[97]   Therefore, in the past, the court could allow the child to remain with the foster parents while at the same time not completely terminating the natural parents' rights.   Under the proposed new statute, however, reluctance in finding an abandonment will have much graver consequences.   The child will be denied the possibility of being placed in a new home and becoming part of a family.   For many years he will be cared for in an institution or will be transferred from foster home to foster home.   This might be a sobering thought to judges who espouse an extremely strict definition of abandonment.[98]

JEAN P. RITZ

---

[97] Ibid.

[98] One judge has defined abandonment in this way: "Abandonment connotes *leaving on a doorstep*, putting out of sight and mind, putting away without regard to consequences." People ex rel. Flannagan v. Riggio, 193 Misc. 930, 932, 85 N.Y.S.2d 534, 536 (Sup. Ct. 1948).   (Emphasis added.)

STATUTORY NOTE

INFANTS—Termination of Parental Rights.—Kan. Stat. Ann. § 38-824 (1964) provides for disposition of children found to be dependent and neglected as defined by Kan. Stat. Ann. § 38-802(g) (1964). In the absence of an order terminating parental rights, the juvenile court may make such children wards of the court and transfer legal custody of the children to the parents or to persons, associations, or agencies specified by the statute. The court may permanently terminate parental rights, if the parents are found and adjudged to be unfit to have custody of such dependent and neglected children. Upon making such an order, the court must commit the children to the guardianship of specified persons, associations, or agencies. Such guardians are authorized to consent to the adoption of the child, in lieu of parental consent.[1]

The principal statute, enacted in 1957 as part of the Juvenile Code,[2] differs considerably from the statute which it repealed.[3] The earlier statute provided that a child found to be dependent and neglected could be committed to the care of certain persons or organizations who, by authority of a companion statute,[4] were empowered to assent to adoption of the child. Thus, in effect, a finding of dependency and neglect was all that was required permanently to terminate parental rights.[5] By the enactment of 38-824, the legislature clearly recognized that permanent termination of the parent-child relationship is justified only in certain cases of dependency and neglect. The determinative factor is parental unfitness. In a recent Attorney General's opinion,[6] the question was asked: "Must the court make an order finding the parent, or parents, to be an 'unfit person,' before it can permanently sever parental rights?"[7] The Attorney General answered in the affirmative. He recognized that the term "unfit person" is harsh, but pointed out that it is a term of art, with a particular connotation and meaning which substitute phrases do not convey. It was pointed out that "by using this term in the code, the legislature has restricted the court's power to permanently sever parental rights to one situation, i.e., where the parent or parents have been found to be 'unfit persons.'"[8] Anything short of such a finding would leave the court without authority permanently to sever parental rights. Thus, when the parents are *not* found to be unfit persons, the court must act within the provisions of clause (b) of 38-824. If the court finds that the parents *are* unfit and orders permanent deprivation of their parental rights, as authorized by clause (c), the court must provide for the child in accordance with clauses (c) and (d).

The legislature did not specify what conditions must be found to adjudge a parent to be an unfit person. It is certain, however, that if the distinction made in 38-824 is to have meaning, two standards must be used—one to determine dependency and neglect and another to determine parental unfitness. The Attorney General's opinion[9] on the instant statute did not offer a definition of the term "unfit person."

The Kansas Supreme Court has on only one occasion directly or indirectly applied the principal statute. In *Lennon v. State*,[10] a mother's rights to a dependent and neglected child were permanently severed. While the court referred to the Juvenile Code as a whole, no express mention was made of 38-824. The court seemed to decide the case under the re-

---

[1] Kan. Stat. Ann. § 59-2102(5) (1964).
[2] Kan. Stat. Ann. §§ 38-801 to -838 (1964).
[3] Kan. Sess. Laws 1905, ch. 190, § 7.
[4] Kan. Sess. Laws 1905, ch. 190, § 8.
[5] Adoption of a child severs "forever and conclusively the legal rights and interests of the natural parents. . . ." Jackson v. Russell, 342 Ill. App. 637, ..., 97 N.E.2d 584, 585 (1951).
[6] 62-98 Ops. Att'y Gen. 358 (1962).
[7] *Id.* at 358.
[8] *Id.* at 360-61.
[9] *Ibid.*
[10] 193 Kan. 685, 396 P.2d 290 (1964).

pealed statutes, in complete disregard of the 1957 enactment. Parental rights were permanently severed, but no mention was made of parental unfitness. The child was committed to the State Department of Social Welfare, but no mention was made as to whether this department had authority to consent to the adoption of the child.

Recognizing the absence of both legislative and judicial construction of the term "unfit person," this note will suggest a positive interpretation of the term. First, however, certain definitions of unfitness applied in other proceedings must be distinguished. In divorce actions[11] or proceedings upon a writ of habeas corpus, where parents are disputing custody of their children, courts universally apply the "best interests of the child" test.[12] The welfare of the child is viewed as paramount to the rights, desires, and wishes of the parents[13] and is said to be best served by giving custody to a fit parent.[14] Parental fitness or conversely, unfitness, is judged by positive values such as financial resources, a proper home, and interest in and affection for the child.[15] In proceedings for the determination of custody of minor children between the parents and a third party, parental rights and the welfare of the children are both important. Parents are preferred over third parties if they are fit persons to care for their children.[16] To remove custody from the parent, the third party must show parental unfitness with clear and convincing evidence.[17] Parental unfitness in this context has been defined by the Kansas Supreme Court in *In re Vallimont*.[18] After recognizing the absence of any statutory definition of unfitness, the court stated: "We think it entirely plain that misconduct on the part of parents which would empower a juvenile court to take jurisdiction of a child as 'dependent and neglected'[19] is likewise such breach of parental duty as to make the parents unfit to be entrusted with the custody and rearing of their child in a custody award matter."[20]

Parental unfitness within these definitions is not such unfitness as to adjudge a parent to be an unfit person within the context of 38-824. The *Vallimont* definition, if used as the standard, would resurrect the statutes repealed by 38-824. Parental rights could again be terminated upon proof of dependency and neglect alone. This would clearly defeat the legislative purpose behind the enactment of 38-824.

Further, the consequences on the parent-child relationship when parental unfitness is proven are much less severe in custody award suits than in proceedings under the principal statute. Legal custody[21] and guardianship[22] of minor children are the only questions resolved in the former. Permanent termination of parental rights is not a consequence. "Both an award of legal custody and an order of guardianship of the person are serious limitations upon parental rights, but both are temporary and partial limitations as contrasted with termination which is permanent and complete severance of the relationship of

---

[11] Kan. Stat. Ann. § 60-1610 (1964) authorizes termination of parental rights for unfitness in divorce proceedings. The statute does not define unfitness and there are no cases which have construed unfitness in the context of the statute.
[12] Simpson, *The Unfit Parent: Conditions Under Which A Child May Be Adopted Without The Consent Of His Parent,* 39 U. Det. L.J. 347, 356 (1962).
[13] Hurt v. Hurt, 315 P.2d 957, 959 (Okla. 1957).
[14] Tucker v. Finnigan, 139 Kan. 496, 499, 32 P.2d 211, 212 (1934).
[15] Johnstone, *Child Custody,* 1 Kan. L. Rev. 37, 44 (1952).
[16] *Id.* at 39.
[17] Pinney v. Sulzen, 91 Kan. 407, 413, 137 Pac. 987, 989 (1914).
[18] 182 Kan. 334, 321 P.2d 190 (1958).
[19] Kan. Stat. Ann. § 38-802 (1964).
[20] 182 Kan. at 339, 321 P.2d at 195.
[21] Legal custody denotes "those rights and responsibilities associated with the day to day care of the child. It includes the right to the care, custody and control of the child. It includes the duty to provide food, clothing, shelter, education, ordinary medical care and to train and discipline." U.S. Dep't of Health, Educ., and Welfare, Standards for Specialized Courts Dealing With Children 15 (1954).
[22] Guardianship of the person includes the powers and duties as defined under legal custody. A guardian has the additional power to "make major decisions affecting the long-time planning for the child, including such things as the right and duty to consent to marriage, to enlistment in the armed forces, major surgery, and to represent the child in some legal actions before the court." *Id.* at 18.

parent and child."[23] This is equally true in actions brought by a state to have a child declared dependent and neglected. A finding of dependency and neglect gives the juvenile court jurisdiction to assume guardianship and to award legal custody of the child to designated persons.[24] Certain parental rights and responsibilities remain however, such as the right to consent to the adoption of the child and the responsibility to help support the child.[25] It is these parental rights which the legislature has protected by requiring the additional showing of unfitness.

Other jurisdictions have recognized the difference between deprivation of custody and guardianship in contrast to complete termination of all parental rights. It has been said that "the concept of unfitness and neglect must be viewed with more flexibility when custody is involved, as distinguished from permanent termination of parental rights . . ."[26] and that "[T]ransitory failures and derelictions of the parents might justify temporary deprivation of custody but seldom the permanent deprivation of parental rights . . . ."[27] Wisconsin has an enlightened children's code which clearly distinguishes between conditions sufficient to find a child to be dependent and neglected, and parental unfitness such as to justify permanent termination of parental rights. One section[28] defines dependent or neglected in terms very similar to Kan. Stat. Ann. § 38-802 (1964). A second section[29] provides for disposition of children found to be dependent or neglected. This statute allows legal custody transfers only. A third section[30] provides that if the juvenile court has made an order transferring legal custody of a dependent or neglected child, that juvenile court shall have jurisdiction to hear a petition for termination of parental rights. The termination of parental rights statute[31] specifies the following grounds:

. . . .

    (2) (a) that the parents have abandoned the minor; or

          (b) that the parents have substantially and continuously or repeatedly refused to give the minor necessary parental care and protection; or

          (c) that, although the parents are financially able, they have substantially and continuously neglected to provide the minor with necessary subsistence, education or other care necessary for his health, morals, or well-being or have neglected to pay for such subsistence, education or other care when legal custody is lodged with others; or

          (d) that the parents are unfit by reason of debauchery, habitual use of intoxicating liquor or narcotic drugs, or repeated lewd and lascivious behavior or conviction and confinement for a felony . . . , which conduct or status is found by the court to be likely to be detrimental to the health, morals or the best interests of the minor.

. . . .

These grounds, while basically similar to those required to find a child to be dependent and neglected under 38-802, differ greatly in degree. The parental misconduct must be

---

[23] U.S. Dep't of Health, Educ., and Welfare, Legislative Guides for Termination of Parental Rights and Responsibilities and Adoption of Children 9 (1961).

[24] "It is the legal custody of the child which is normally transferred to an agency in cases where a child is found to be neglected. . . ." U.S. Dep't of Health, Educ., and Welfare, supra note 21, at 15.

[25] These rights have been called "residual parental rights and responsibilities." U.S. Dep't of Health, Educ., and Welfare, supra note 21, at 18.

[26] Application of Mittenthal, 37 Misc. 2d 502, ..., 235 N.Y.S.2d 729, 739 (Family Ct. 1962).

[27] Roy v. Holmes, 111 So. 2d 468, 471 (Fla. Dist. Ct. App. 1959).

[28] Wis. Stat. Ann. § 48.13 (Supp. 1965).

[29] Wis. Stat. Ann. § 48.35 (Supp. 1965).

[30] Wis. Stat. Ann. § 48.41 (1963).

[31] Wis. Stat. Ann. § 48.40 (Supp. 1965). For construction and application of this statute, see In re Johnson, 9 Wis. 2d 65, 100 N.W.2d 383 (1960).

substantial, continuous, or repeated before parental rights will be severed. The Missouri statute[32] is very similar but in addition requires a showing of wilfulness.

Certainly, had *Lennon v. State*[33] been decided under the Wisconsin statute, the mother's rights would not have been permanently severed. The evidence showed that the mother was careless of her appearance and personal hygiene. She had a violent temper and was to some degree emotionally unstable. There was evidence of criminal activity by the mother twelve years prior to the action. The most damaging evidence against the mother was that she had been married three times, that her third husband had deserted, and that the child in question was illegitimate. However, there was no evidence that the mother had abandoned the child. Rather, the child was taken from her fifteen days after birth. There was evidence that the mother loved, adequately fed, and adequately housed two older children. There was no evidence of substantial and continuous neglect or of repeated lewd and lascivious behavior. It is submitted that these facts would not justify permanent termination of parental rights under the Wisconsin or Missouri statutes and should not justify permanent deprivation under Kan. Stat. Ann. § 38-824 (1964).

The principal statute represents a balancing of interests by the legislature. On the one hand, the state as parens patriae[34] is concerned with the welfare of minors. This interest is served by granting the juvenile court broad discretion as to the determination of dependency and neglect and as to the measures to be taken upon such a finding. On the other hand, parental rights require protection.[35] The statute affords such protection by the requirement that parents must be found to be unfit persons before permanent termination is authorized.

Such a balance can be achieved only if proof of substantial and continuous misconduct is required to find a parent to be an unfit person. Parental misconduct which results in conditions sufficient to find dependency and neglect, continued over a period of time sufficient to negate any reasonable possibility of parental reform should be the standard applied for determining a parent to be an unfit person. Duration of time, parental motive, and absence of reform and rehabilitation should be the primary factors in applying this standard.

The principal statute should by judicial construction or by legislative amendment be corrected to specify sufficient grounds to determine parental unfitness, as distinct from conditions upon which dependency and neglect orders may be made. Temporary and permanent deprivation of parental rights are clearly different, and should be recognized as such.

JAMES M. WHITTIER

---

[32] Mo. Rev. Stat. § 211.441 (1959). For construction of this statute, see *In re* Burgess, 359 S.W.2d 484 (Mo. Ct. App. 1962).
[33] 193 Kan. 685, 396 P.2d 290 (1964).
[34] *In re* McCoy, 184 Kan. 1, 8, 334 P.2d 820, 826 (1959).
[35] The right to bring up children is among those guaranteed by the fourteenth amendment. Meyer v. Nebraska, 262 U.S. 390, 399 (1923).

THE REQUIREMENT OF APPOINTMENT OF COUNSEL FOR INDIGENT PARENTS IN NEGLECT OR TERMINATION PROCEEDINGS: A DEVELOPING AREA

Robert S. Catz* and John T. Kuelbs**

A rapidly developing area of case law that has received recent attention in both the state and federal courts is the recognition of the right to counsel, at state expense, of indigent parents faced with a proceeding to terminate parental rights.[1] Developments in this area of the law reflect the proposition that the Due Process and Equal Protection Clauses of the fourteenth amendment require that an indigent parent in a child neglect or parental rights termination proceeding be afforded counsel at no cost, and also that the parent in such proceeding be advised of this right.

A logical discussion of the development and current status of the indigent parent's right to counsel in neglect or termination proceedings requires an analysis of the constitutional arguments raised. Such analysis will demonstrate that the rights and interests of the parents which are jeopardized

* A.B., 1967, University of Southern California; J.D., 1970, Golden Gate University; LL.M., 1973, University of Missouri. Member of the bars of Nebraska and the District of Columbia, and the National Legal Aid and Defender Association. Staff Attorney, Migrant Legal Action Program, Inc., Washington, D.C.

** B.S., 1965, St. John's University; J.D., 1973, Creighton University; LL.M. (candidate), University of Virginia. Member of the Nebraska bar, and the United States Court of Military Appeals. Captain, Judge Advocate General's Corps, United States Army. [The opinions and conclusions expressed herein are those of the authors and do not necessarily represent the views of the Judge Advocate General's Corps or the United States Army.]

[1] State v. Jamison, 251 Ore. 114, 444 P.2d 15 (1968); Chambers v. District Court, 261 Iowa 31, 152 N.W.2d 818 (1967); *In re* Karren, 280 Minn. 277, 159 N.W.2d 402 (1968); In the Matter of B, 334 N.Y.S.2d 113, 285 N.E.2d 288 (1972); Cleaver v. Wilcox, 40 USLW 2658 (N.D. Cal. 1972); White v. Green, 70 Misc. 2d 28 (N.Y. Fam. Ct. 1971); *In re* K, 105 Cal. Rptr. 209 (1972); Danforth v. State Department of Health and Welfare, 303 A.2d 794 (Me. 1973); State v. Caha, 190 Neb. 347, 208 N.W.2d 259 (1973).

in a neglect or termination proceeding are such that due process and equal protection of the law demand that an indigent parent be given court appointed counsel. The necessity for granting such a right becomes particularly apparent when one considers the seriousness and permanency of the consequences of such proceedings, the resources of the state in comparison with those of the parents, and the complexity of issues and questions involved in such proceedings.

I. THE APPLICATION OF THE DUE PROCESS CLAUSE

Since the right to be a parent is a fundamental aspect of personal liberty and the legal consequences of neglect proceedings are both grave and lasting, the due process clause logically requires the appointment of counsel to indigents. The term "liberty" as used in the fifth and fourteenth amendment to the United States Constitution has been broadly applied by the United States Supreme Court and not limited solely to physical confinement. The right of a parent to the custody, care and upbringing of his child is among the fundamental rights guaranteed to citizens under the United States Constitution. The parental relationship and the responsibility of raising children as citizens of this society are basic elements of the social, economic and legal fabric of our state and nation. The term "liberty" as used in the fifth and fourteenth amendments to the United States Constitution has been interpreted as:

> . . . not merely freedom from bodily restraint but also the right of the individual to contact, to engage in any of the common occupations of life, to acquire useful knowledge, *to marry, establish a home and bring up children*, to worship God according to the dictates of his own conscience, and generally to enjoy those privileges long recognized at common law as essential to the orderly pursuit of happiness by free men.[2] [emphasis added].

On a number of occasions the United States Supreme Court has commented on the status of the family by expressing that parental rights are protected under the penumbras of the Bill of Rights and the fourteenth amendment. Re-

---

[2] Meyer v. Nebraska, 262 U.S. 390, 399 (1923).

cently, in *Ginsberg v. State of New York*,[3] the Court stated:

> . . . [C]onstitutional interpretation has consistently recognized that the parents' claim to authority in their own household to direct the rearing of their children is basic in the structure of our society. . . .

Indeed, in *May v. Anderson*,[4] the Court declared that:

> . . . Rights far more precious to appellant than property rights will be cut off if she is bound by the Wisconsin award of custody.

More recently the United States Supreme Court has reasserted its recognition of the special interest of the parental relationship.[5]

State courts have likewise affirmed the fundamental nature under natural law of a parent's rights to the custody of the children:

> There is probably no action known to the law more worthy of judicial consideration and careful determination than a proceeding affecting the custody of a little child. Claims of a parent should not be regarded in the removal of a child from the control

---

[3] 390 U.S. 629, 639 (1968).

[4] 345 U.S. 528, 533 (1953).

[5] In *Stanley v. Illinois*, 405 U.S. 645, 650, the Court elaborated on the special status accorded the filial relationship:

The private interest here, that of a man in the children he has sired and raised, undeniably warrants deference and, absent a powerful countervailing interest, protection. It is plain that the interest of a parent in the companionship, care, custody and management of his or her children 'come[s] to this Court with a momentum for respect lacking when appeal is made to liberties which derive merely from shifting economic arrangements.' Kovacs v. Cooper, 336 U.S. 77, 95 (1929). The court has frequently emphasized the importance of the family. The rights to conceive and to raise one's children have been deemed 'essential,' Meyer v. Nebraska, 262 U.S. 390, 399 (1923), 'basic civil rights of man,' Skinner v. Oklahoma, 316 U.S. 535, 541 (1942), and '[r]ights far more precious than . . . property rights,' May v. Anderson, 345 U.S. 528, 533 (1953). 'It is cardinal with us that the custody, care and nurture of the child reside first in the parents, whose primary function and freedom includes preparation for obligations the state can neither supply nor hinder.' Prince v. Massachusetts, 321 U.S. 158, 166 (1944). The integrity of the family unit has found protection in the Due Process Clause of the Fourteenth Amendment. *Meyer v. Nebraska, supra*, at 399, the Equal Protection Clause of the Fourteenth Amendment, *Skinner v. Oklahoma, supra*, at 541, and the Ninth Amendment, *Griswold v. Connecticut*, 381 U.S. 479, 496, (1965). [parallel citations omitted].

of its parent if the parent is clearly unfit or has by misconduct forfeited his right to the custody of the child and if such drastic action is for the welfare of the child. However, the devotion, care, and guidance of a normal parent and child are invaluable to his child and the relationship of parent and child should not be severed or disturbed unless the facts justify it. The interest of all parties concerned require, when the issue is contested in court, that the facts be shown by competent evidence.[6]

While no one can dispute that neglect or termination proceedings are necessary expressions of state interest in the protection of children, these proceedings can be of a decidedly coercive nature, capable of producing the most profound consequences to parents summoned to appear therein. It is obligatory that the fundamental and basic interest, that of being a parent, be protected from the acts of the state by appointment of counsel in such proceedings. In most neglect and termination proceedings, a parent stands accused by a governmental party possessing substantial financial and investigative resources. Such proceedings are not contests between private litigants seeking to advance private interests or to achieve personal gain; nor are they contests over custody between two parents. One commentator has adequately depicted the nature of the process;

. . . [N]eglect laws, as with delinquency and criminal statutes, are not an attempt to resolve disputes between private litigants but are an expression of a definite state interest, and the state uses a panoply of resources to vindicate its interests.[7]

Parents appear *pro se* in most neglect and termination proceedings and are confronted by social caseworkers, attorneys representing them and their agencies, and medical and other expert resources which such agencies have at their disposal.[8] At least in areas of vital concern to an individual,

---

[6] *In re* Godden, 158 Neb. 246, 250, 63 N.W.2d 151, 155, (1954).

[7] Note, *Representation in Child-Neglect Cases: Are Parents Neglected*, 4 COLUM. J. OF LAW AND SOC. PROBS. 230, 250 (1968).

[8] Close to 60% of the petitions in neglect and abuse cases filed in the judicial year 1969-1970 were brought by "institutional" petitioners, most being officers or employees of governmental entities [Report of Administrative Board of Judicial Conference State of New York for Judicial year July 1, 1969 through June 30, 1970, 336, 359-61 (1970)]. A study of cases in Kings County Family Court, New York, discloses that during 1966, over 80% of the petitions in neglect were filed by social

particularly where parental custody is in issue, there is a substantial and growing body of opinion with the view that where the state is involved in the litigative process, the indigent defendant should have an unqualified right to counsel:

> Among the clearest cases of injustice in the civil process are those in which the state brings suit against an indigent and unrepresented defendant and whether in its role as tax-collector, condemnor of property, landlord, or *parens patriae*. The defendant, unable because of his poverty to present his case properly, is overborne by lawyers and other litigative resources paid for out of the public treasury.[9]

Statistical data compiled in a recent study[10] reveals that where parents went unrepresented against institutional petitioners, 79.5% of the proceedings resulted in neglect adjudications and 16.6% of the petitions were either withdrawn or dismissed; whereas, where the parents were represented, 62.5% of the proceedings resulted in neglect findings, and 37.5% of the petitioners were withdrawn or dismissed. Moreover, in cases where neglect was necessarily found, dispositions of "placement" for the children occurred far less frequently where the parents were represented by counsel; 40.6% without counsel, 18.2% with counsel. Referring to this statistical study, the commentator stated:

> Since there is no evidence indicating that the average respondent who can retain counsel is better or less neglectful than one who cannot, the conclusion seems inescapable that a significant number of cases against unrepresented parents result in findings of

---

welfare agencies, and 66% were by governmental officials or employees. These petitioners were all represented by legal counsel while 76% of the respondent-parents were not represented at any stage of the proceedings. 4 COLUM. J. OF LAW AND SOC. PROBS. *supra* note 7, at 236-37.

[9] Note, *The Indigents Rights to Counsel in Civil Cases*, 76 YALE L.J. 545, 556 (1967). *See also* Note, *Child Neglect: Due Process For the Parent*, 70 COLUM. L. REV. 465, 477-78 (1970); Brisbois, *Trumpets in the Corridors of Bureaucracy: A Coming Right to Appointed Counsel in Administrative Adjudicate Proceedings*, 18 U.C.L.A. L. REV. 758, 777 (1970); Note, *The Right to Counsel in Civil Litigation*, 66 COLUM. L. REV. 1322 (1966); Willging, *Financial Barriers and the Access of Indigents to the Courts*, 57 GEORGETOWN L.J. 253, 286 (1968); Carson, *In the Matter of Ella B—A Test For the Right to Assigned Counsel in Family Court Cases*, 4 COLUM. HUMAN RIGHTS L. REV. 451 (1972); Comment, *Indigent Access to Civil Courts: The Tiger Is at The Gates*, 26 VAND. L. REV. 25 (1973).

[10] *See* note 7 *supra*, at 241, 243.

neglect solely because of the absence of counsel. In other words, assuming a basic faith in the adversary system as a method of bringing the truth to light, a significant number of neglect findings (followed in many cases by a taking of the child from his parents) against unrepresented indigents are probably erroneous. It would be hard to think of a system of law which works more to the oppression of the poor than the denial of appointed counsel to indigents in neglect proceedings.[11]

Another difficulty for the indigent parents confronted with an accusation of neglect is that the proceedings are exceedingly complex and accusations made cannot be adequately met and understood by a parent without counsel. The burden on the parent appearing *pro se* to competently litigate in a neglect or termination proceeding is extraordinarily heavy. Fitness of a home is a relative concept. It cannot be adequately determined except by an appraisal of all available evidence bearing upon the child, parents and their environmental circumstances. The issues involve not only what has happened on certain occasions, but how circumstances have affected and may in the future affect the child's development.[12] These considerations are expressed in the rule of "neglect" that:

> In neglect proceedings, the Court's duty is to determine whether, despite any past deficiency, children are at the time of the hearing suffering or likely to suffer from neglect. . . .[13]

Medical and psychiatric evaluation and evidence are of the utmost importance to determine the truth of the petition, whether the aid of the court is required, and to render a proper disposition if neglect has been established.[14] Therefore, the parents' need for legal counsel is basic to obtain independent medical opinion, test the accuracy of medical evidence and present argument thereon. Due both to the social and psychological aspects of such proceedings and to the broad definitional concepts of this area of the law and the

---

[11] *See* note 9 *supra*, at 476.

[12] Kay and Phillips, *Poverty and the Law of Child Custody*, 54 CALIF. L. REV. 717, 737 (1966).

[13] Matter of Vulon Children, 56 Misc. 2d 19 (N.Y. Fam. Ct. 1968).

[14] *See* Sargent, *Problems in Collaboration Between Lawyers and Psychiatrist*, 11 WAYNE L. REV. 697, 700-01 (1965).

purpose of the neglect statutes, the issues are often vague and difficult for the unrepresented parent to prepare to meet. When the allegations involve "environmental" neglect, assessments of minimum standards of conduct are particularly difficult to define.[15] The courts must apply society's standards of proper child care to the facts of a particular case in such a way as to assure that the child is not and will not be harmed while at the same time acknowledging that the parents not only have a primary right to custody but also possess a wide latitude in determining how to care for and rear their child. The problems entailed in this judicial duty of determining reasonableness of parental conduct are often delicate and subtle and always require a full and total understanding of all circumstances. Frequently all the circumstances are not presented since parents without counsel are seldom in a position to present their case.

The focus in a neglect or termination proceeding is not on the child's behavior, but on the parents' conduct and capacities. The parents have the knowledge to answer governmental accusations.[16] The contribution which the parents' legal counsel can make in a neglect proceeding, therefore, is doubly significant. The operative facts relate to the parents' conduct and the consequences befall both parents and child.[17] Without counsel, there is hardly a chance that the parent in a neglect or termination proceeding would be able to cope with procedure, discovery and rules of evidence. Speaking of the need of parents to be represented by legal counsel, the Council of Judges of the National Council on Crime and Delinquency has stated:

> A neglect adjudication, like a delinquency adjudication, must be

---

[15] ". . . [I]n terms of health and psychosocial dimensions, legal neglect is essentially a policy issue which requires judicial determination as to when the state ought to intervene . . . ." Tamilia, *Neglect Proceedings and the Conflict Between Law and Social Work*, 9 Duquesne L. Rev. 579, 586 (1971). *See also* Sullivan, *Child Neglect: The Environmental Aspects*, 29 Ohio St. L.J. 85 (1968).

[16] 66.7% of the Family Court judges responding to a questionnaire indicated that a respondent's failure to obtain counsel hindred the court's development of the facts. 4 Colum. J. of Law and Soc. Probs., *supra* note 7, at 235.

[17] *See* Isaacs, *The Role of the Lawyer in Representing Minors in the New Family Court*, 12 Buffalo L. Rev. 501, 519 (1962).

based on facts adduced at a hearing that comport[s] with the requirements of due process. The adjudication must be based on evidence, not on conjecture, and the classic role of a lawyer in any proceeding is to present and contest testimony and exhibits which are to become evidence . . . . Trying these [jurisdictional] facts in a neglect case requires a lawyer's skills to the same degree as does trying the allegations of a delinquency petition.[IX]

Various procedural safeguards have historically been dependent upon the designation of a proceeding as "criminal" or "civil". However, this traditional distinction should no longer be decisive unless it allows for accurate categorization of proceedings requiring different treatment. Thus, whether the Constitution requires appointment of counsel in a neglect or termination proceeding should turn on the question of whether the assistance of counsel in such proceedings has become so necessary to this area of the civil judicial system that—as in criminal cases—its absence deprives the litigant of his right to a fair hearing. Increasingly, courts are rejecting the traditional distinction and holding that due process of law demands the availability of free counsel for indigent parents in neglect or termination proceedings notwithstanding that such proceedings are denominated as "civil."[19] The Supreme Court's depiction of a fair hearing is well known and has been applied by these courts:

> The right to be heard before being condemned to suffer grievous loss of any kind, even though it may not involve the stigma and hardship of a criminal conviction, is a principle basic to our society . . . .[20]

In determining what procedures satisfy concepts of due process, it is necessary both to delineate

---

[IX] N.C.C.D. Council of Judges, Provision of Counsel in Juvenile Courts—A Policy Statement, 11-12 (1970).

[19] State v. Jamison, 251 Ore. 114, 444 P.2d 15 (1968); Chambers v. District Court, 261 Iowa. 31, 152 N.W.2d 818 (1967); *In re* Karren, 280 Minn. 277, 159 N.W.2d 402 (1968); In the Matter of B, 334 N.Y.S.2d 133, 285 N.E.2d 288 (1972); Cleaver v. Wilcox, 40 USLW 2658 (N.D. Cal. 1972); White v. Green, 70 Misc. 2d 28 (N.Y. Fam. Ct. 1971); *In re* K, 105 Cal. Rptr. 209 (1972). Danforth v. State Department of Health and Welfare, 303 A.2d 794 (Me. 1973); State v. Caha, 190 Neb. 347, 208 N.W.2d 259 (1973).

[20] Joint Anti-Fascist Refugee Committee v. McGrath, 341 U.S. 123, 168 (1951).

the precise nature of the government function as well as of the private interest that has been affected by governmental action . . . [Cafeteria and Restaurant Workers Union v. McElroy, 367 U.S. 886, 895 (1961)] and to ensure that "the opportunity to be heard . . . is tailored to capacities and circumstances of those who are to be heard . . . ."[21]

Based on the foregoing discussion, it is submitted that we are dealing with rights just as paramount as a man's personal liberty not to be confined. Moreover, in exercising its vital function to safeguard the welfare of children and yet sustain the parent-child relationship except in exigent circumstances, the government's interest in thoroughly testing the merits of its own allegations against a parent is fully as great as in many criminal prosecutions. Here also, we have significant disparities between a governmental petitioner with its resources and an unrepresented parent in a judicial proceeding.

In *Powell v. Alabama*,[22] quoted approvingly in *Gideon v. Wainwright*,[23] the Court stated:

> The right to be heard would be, in many cases, of little avail, if it did not comprehend the right to be heard by counsel. Even the intelligent and educated layman has small and sometimes no skill in the science of law . . . . He requires the guiding hand of counsel at every step in the proceedings against him. Without it, though he be not guilty, he faces the danger of conviction because he does not know how to establish his innocence.

Among the decisive factors in *Gideon* were the state initiative, state coercive power, and the resources available to the state.[24] These factors are involved in most neglect and termination proceedings. Since *Gideon*, the right of an indigent to court-appointed counsel has been extended to persons accused of having committed misdemeanors,[25] to children accused of wrongdoing (even though their confinement is considered "treatment" rather than "punishment"),[26] and to

---

[21] Goldberg v. Kelly, 397 U.S. 254, 268-69 (1970).

[22] 287 U.S. 45, 68-69 (1932).

[23] 372 U.S. 335, 344-45 (1964).

[24] *Id.* at 344.

[25] Argersinger v. Hamlin, 407 U.S. 25 (1973).

[26] *In re* Gault, 387 U.S. 1 (1967).

persons allegedly in need of hospitalization for mental illness, a matter traditionally labeled both "civil" and "treatment" oriented rather than accusatorial.[27] In *Boddie v.
Connecticut*,[28] involving an indigent-plaintiff's inability to
pay for court fees and for service of process in a divorce action, the Court ruled that Connecticut statutes effectively
prevented indigents from utilizing the divorce courts and
therefore violated plaintiff's rights to due process of law. The
Court emphasized two factors in the case; that the marriage
relationship is a fundamental one in our society and that the
courts are the sole means of resolving a dispute of this type.
The relationship between parent and child is also fundamental in our society and is similarly protected as a basic human
liberty. Moreover, the concern of the state is in protecting
children from their parents, if necessary; but otherwise it is
in promoting and maintaining the parental relationship and
is certainly no less important than its interest in the bond
between a husband and wife. Obviously, there are occasions
when state intervention in these relationships is appropriate,
but whether such intervention be passive, as in divorce, or
active, as in neglect and termination proceedings, it is the
judiciary to which society looks for the resolution of such
disputes. The analysis in *Boddie*[29] begins with the assumption that when "the judicial proceeding becomes the only
effective means of resolving the dispute at hand . . . denial
of a defendant's full access to that process raises grave problems for its legitimacy." *Boddie* concludes that:

> Just as a generally valid notice procedure may fail to satisfy due
> process because of the circumstances of the defendant, so too a
> cost requirement, valid on its face, may offend due process be-
> cause it operates to foreclose a particular party's opportunity to
> be heard. The state's obligations under the Fourteenth Amend-
> ment are not simply generalized ones; rather, the State owes to
> each individual that process, which in light of the values of a free
> society, can be characterized as due.[30]

---

[27] Heryford v. Parker, 396 F.2d 383 (10th Cir. 1968).

[28] 401 U.S. 371 (1971).

[29] *Id.* at 376.

[30] *Id.* at 380. *Contra*, United States v. Kras, 409 U.S. 434, (1973) rejecting the
application of the *Boddie* doctrine to bankruptcy proceedings.

As discussed, neglect and termination proceedings entail a broad and complex scope of inquiry, often involving subtle issues of policy and frequently difficult psychiatric questions of motivation and capacity to love and care for children. Thus, following a termination, the parents can no longer nurture the child's growth and the child's warmth and companionship. The relationship to the child is legally dead. Following a termination of parental rights, the children may be adopted without the natural parent's consent. Children, once adopted, cannot be located at any time in the future by the natural parent, as adoption and social service agencies and the courts shield their records from the natural parents. Thus, in these cases, the legal death of the child to the parent is tantamount to a natural death of the child. These considerations taken with the parents' deprivation of liberty by the state in a neglect or termination proceeding and considered within the matrix of cases cited, mandate the availability of counsel to indigent parents in all such proceedings as a matter of basic and fundamental fairness. The interest of a parent to the child is so fundamental to personal liberty that it must be accorded the fullest protections of the law, which include the appointment of counsel.

II.   THE APPLICATION OF THE EQUAL PROTECTION CLAUSE

The educated, economically independent family is rarely involved in neglect or termination referrals.

For the many parents too poor to hire an attorney in neglect proceedings, the opportunity to hire an attorney at their own expense is a cruel sham; the protection it confers is a fiction.[31] The poor are subject to a triple jeopardy in such proceedings. First, the administrative processes through which most neglect petitions result are focused upon the poor, mainly recipients of public assistance; second, quite often, poor parents' care for their children may seem adequate in one cultural setting (namely that of the ghetto), yet

---

[31] "Not only do they (the poor) not know what remedies exist for wrongs done them and not only are they ignorant of the procedures for availing themselves of these remedies, but their attitude toward the courts is one of fear." O'Conner v. Matzdorf, 76 Wash. 2d 589, 595, 458 P.2d 154, 160-61 (1969).

may seem appalling from a different cultural viewpoint; and third, it is the poor parent who is unable to hire an attorney to defend his parental rights in the juvenile court.[32]

Ordinarily, a classification which is made to support a valid state purpose and which is reasonably related to such purpose meets the constitutional standard of equal protection of the law.[33] But when a fundamental right is impaired by a classification based on wealth, the classification is subject to strict scrutiny to determine whether it is supported by a compelling state justification.[34] The fact that the juvenile court acts are apparently neutral does not immunize them from challenge by impecunious parents whose ability to defend is thereby curtailed. The Supreme Court in *Boddie* stated:

> Our cases further establish that a statute or rule may be held constitutionally invalid as applied when it operates to deprive an individual of a protected right although its general validity as a measure enacted in the legitimate exercise of a state power is beyond question . . . the right to a meaningful opportunity to be heard within the limits of practicality, must be protected against denial by particular laws that operate to jeopardize it for particular individuals. . . .[35]

The juvenile courts, by not providing court appointed counsel for indigent parents, effectively deprive a large class of respondents of the vital role which counsel play in neglect or termination proceedings. So, while a fundamental liberty of the parent is at stake, the means to an effective opportunity to cross-examine, introduce evidence and present argument are withheld.

In other areas of the law, the right of the indigent to

---

[32] *See* Paulsen, *Juvenile Courts, Family Courts, and the Poor Man*, 54 CALIF. L. REV. 694 (1966).

[33] McGowan v. Maryland, 366 U.S. 420, 425-26 (1961).

[34] *See* Harper v. Virginia Board of Elections, 383 U.S. 663, 668 (1966) (financial burden on right to vote invalidated). "Lines drawn on the basis of wealth or property . . . are traditionally disfavored . . . ." *See also* Note, *Development in the Law, Equal Protection*, 82 HARV. L. REV. 1065, 1180-81 (1969); Note, *Discrimination Against the Poor and the Fourteenth Amendment*, 81 HARV. L. REV. 435, 437-38, 451-52 (1967).

[35] *See* note 28 *supra*, at 379-80.

legal counsel has been more fully recognized and articulated. The recent trend in criminal cases reflects the developing attitudes of the courts that economic circumstances should not be a factor in obtaining justice.

Griffin v. Illinois[36] is the seminal case in a series of cases where the court granted relief to indigents observing that "there can be no equal justice where the kind of trial a man gets depends on the amount of money he has. . . ."[37] In *Douglas v. California*,[38] the court ratified this basic tenet in ruling that indigents are also entitled to free counsel on appeal from a felony conviction. "[D]enial of counsel on appeal to an indigent would seem to be a discrimination at least as invidious as that condemned in [*Griffin v. Illinois*] . . . ."[39]

The scope of the *Griffin* and *Douglas* decisions has been expanded by subsequent cases which have ruled out any requirement that the indigent convict first show "articularized need" to obtain the means to effective appellate review.[40] The United States Supreme Court, again relying on *Griffin v. Illinois*, and its progeny and referring to the "unreasoned distinctions" where poverty precludes perfection of an appeal, extended the relief granted in *Griffin* to an indigent convicted of a petty offense for which a maximum sentence of ninety days incarceration was possible.[41] While the indigent's rights gradually increased, the arbitrary distinc-

---

[36] 351 U.S. 12 (1956).

[37] *Id.* at 19.

[38] 372 U.S. 353 (1963).

[39] *Id.* at 355, quoting Chief Justice Traynor of the California Supreme Court.

[40] *See* Draper v. Washington, 372 U.S. 487 (1963); Britt v. North Carolina, 404 U.S. 226 (1971). *See also, e.g.*, Burns v. Ohio, 360 U.S. 252 (1950) (filing fee to file motion for leave to appeal invalidated); Smith v. Bennett, 365 U.S. 708 (1961) (filing fee for appeal and habeas corpus applications invalidated); Lane v. Brown, 372 U.S. 477 (1963) (right to free transcript and counsel on appeal in *coram nobis* proceeding); Long v. District of Iowa, 385 U.S. 192 (1966) (transcript must be provided in connection with appeal in habeas corpus proceedings); Gardner v. California, 393 U.S. 367 (1969) (convict entitled to free transcript to aid him in preparation of habeas corpus); Tate v. Short, 401 U.S. 395 (1970) (substitution of jail confinement when indigent is unable to pay a fine after conviction is denial of equal protection).

[41] Williams v. Oklahoma, 395 U.S. 438, 459 (1969).

tions regarding criminal sanctions continued to be mechanically applied with respect to the right to counsel.

A significant gap was bridged in the applicability of the Equal Protection Clause to indigents in judicial proceedings in *Mayer v. Chicago*.[42] In that case the appellant sought a free transcript in order effectively to appeal from convictions of violating city ordinances prohibiting disorderly conduct and interference with a police officer. Under the applicable ordinances, the maximum penalty is a five hundred dollar fine for each offense. Relying on *Williams v. Oklahoma City*, the *Mayer* Court viewed the claimed distinction between felony and non-felony as unreasoned, and stated, ". . . the size of the defendant's pocketbook bears no more relationship to his guilt or innocence in a non-felony than in a felony case."[43] The Court was not impressed by the distinction between incarceration and fine, for the court went on to say that the City's reliance on conserving public funds as a superior interest to the accused's interest in avoiding a fine was misconceived:

> Griffin does not represent a balance between the needs of the accused and the interests of society; its principle is a flat prohibition against pricing indigent defendants out of as effective an appeal as would be available to others able to pay their own way. . . . Arbitrary denial of appellate review of proceedings of the State's lower trial courts may save the State some dollars and cents, but only at the substantial risk of generating frustration and hostility towards its courts among the most numerous consumers of justice.[44]

Additionally, the Court pointed out that:

> A fine may bear as heavily on an indigent accused as forced confinement. The collateral consequences of conviction may be even more serious as when . . . the impecunious medical student finds himself barred from the practice of medicine because of a conviction he is unable to appeal for lack of funds. . . .[45]

The Supreme Court has held for the first time that the prin-

---

[42] 404 U.S. 189 (1971).
[43] *Id.* at 415.
[44] *Id.* at 416.
[45] *Id.*

ciple of *Griffin v. Illinois* applies in a case where there is no possibility of incarceration or continued confinement. Mere denomination of *Mayer* as "criminal" or "quasi-criminal" should not, by some talismanic effect, blind us to the essentiality that rich and poor alike possess the tools of effective defense, at least when the liberty of the parent to the custody of his child is at stake.[46]

Far from promoting the purposes expressed in most juvenile court legislation, absence of a right to counsel to indigents works to disable the important state interests in these proceedings. While in the past juvenile courts have often been viewed as overly informal tribunals, the notion that such courts function better without lawyers has been thoroughly discredited.[47] Poverty does not constitute child neglect, and the financial ability of a parent to hire an attorney does not rationally relate to his legal adequacy as parent. An attempted justification for the classification might well be based upon a desire to conserve public resources by avoiding the payment of counsel fees in neglect cases. However, this is not a compelling state interest. In terms of financial impact, it is fair to conclude that neglect or termination proceedings are numerically of far less significance than other proceedings in the juvenile courts of most states. The conservation of public funds should not defeat an indigent parent's right to counsel in such proceedings. The states must consider the parent's interest which is at stake and the often "brutal" need which a parent has for counsel. Compare the Court's language in *Goldberg v. Kelly*,[48] which may be appropriately recalled here:

---

[46] *See* Goodpaster, *The Integration of Equal Protection, Due Process Standards and Indigent's Right of Free Access to the Courts*, 56 IOWA L. REV. 223, 263-64 (1970).

[47] Kent v. United States, 383 U.S. 541 (1966); *In re* Gault, 387 U.S. 1 (1967); Heryford v. Parker, 396 F.2d 393 (10th Cir. 1968).

[48] 397 U.S. 254, 261 (1970). *Compare* Shapiro v. Thompson, 394 U.S. 618, 633 (1969), where durational residence requirements for welfare benefits were invalidated as an impermissible burden on the fundamental right to travel; the Court stated as to cost justification: ". . . but a state may not accomplish such a purpose by invidious distinctions between classes of its citizens . . . ." and *Mayer v. Chicago, supra* note 42.

Against the justified desire to protect public funds must be weighed the individual's overpowering need in this unique situation not to be wrongfully deprived of assistance. . . .

Consequently, the state's interest in protecting the welfare of the children and its intent that the parents' right to counsel in neglect or termination proceedings be expressed by the courts, coupled with the parents' constitutionally protected liberty to the custody of their children mandate that *all* parents enjoy a real opportunity to legal representation unrelated to their ability to hire an attorney. Certainly, the state can no more allow denial of counsel in these types of proceedings than it can withhold a transcript needed to effectively appeal a conviction for disorderly conduct.[49] This is not to say that the state must supply every "accoutrement" of litigation which an affluent party may possess; nor that counsel need be provided to the poor in all types of litigation, either to defend or prosecute.[50] But when the right to the custody of one's child is subjected to a state initiated and prosecuted judicial proceeding, discrimination based on wealth which may be otherwise rational but which substantially impairs the ability of a parent to respond to the allegations and evidence of neglect should be condemned and disallowed. Thus, an indigent parent in a neglect or termination proceeding who is not afforded free counsel is denied the equal protection of the law.

III. Recent Developments

The modern trend has been to recognize the indigent's right to appointment of counsel in neglect and termination proceedings.[51] Since 1968, a number of courts have begun to

---

[49] *See* note 42 *supra*.

[50] *See* Slade v. Valley National Bank, 406 U.S. ___ (1972), *cert. denied*, which raised the issue of "right to counsel" where an indigent debtor being sued by creditors defended the action in a *pro se* proceeding.

[51] Although most states do not yet furnish appointment of counsel in neglect-termination proceedings, the trend is developing. Legislative provision for court-appointed counsel has now been enacted in twelve jurisdictions. *See* Colo. Rev. Stat. Ann. § 22-1-6 (1963); Ga. Code Ann. § 24-2418.1 (1971); Idaho Code § 16-1631 (Supp. 1973); Iowa Code Ann. § 16-1631 (Supp. 1973); Iowa Code Ann. § 232.28 (1969); Kan. Stat. Ann. § 38-820 (1964); Minn. Stat. Ann. § 260-155 (1971); N.D. Cent. Code § 27-20-26 (Supp. 1973); Ohio Rev. Code § 2151.351

recognize the need to provide safeguards to the indigent parent in neglect and termination proceedings. In *State v. Jamison*,[52] the Oregon Supreme Court squarely held that there is a constitutional due process right of an indigent parent to the appointment of a lawyer in a dependency hearing for the parent's child. Upon appeal from an order of an Oregon juvenile court terminating her parental rights and awarding custody to the County Public Welfare Commissioner, the mother of five children born out of wedlock asserted as an assignment of error, the failure of the juvenile court to advise her, an indigent person, that she was entitled to the assistance of court appointed counsel. Although there was no decision in Oregon which required the juvenile court as a matter of constitutional due process to supply counsel to indigent parents,the court concluded that:

> The permanent termination of parental rights is one of the most drastic actions the state can take against its inhabitants. It would be unconscionable for the state forever to terminate the parental rights of the poor without allowing such parents to be assisted by counsel. Counsel in juvenile court must be made available for parents and children alike when the relationship of parent is threatened by the state. If the parents are too poor to employ counsel, the cost thereof must be borne by the public. . . .[53]

The *Jamison* Court stressed the basis for its decision on the type of hearing that was held without the parent being represented:

> The importance of the aid of counsel in a termination case involving the poor is well illustrated by the record in this case. Without counsel, the informality usually associated with ex parte hearings prevailed. The juvenile court was led to proceed on the basis of incompetent evidence and evidence that had remote, if any, connection with the issues made up by the petition. We need not be detained now by the numerous assignments of error that have been urged in this appeal. In a hearing in which both sides had been represented by counsel, most, if not all, of the alleged errors would not have been allowed.[54]

(1971); OKLA. STAT. tit. 10, § 1109 (6) (1951); ORE. REV. STAT. § 419.498(2) (1971); S.D. COMP. LAWS ANN. 26-8-22.2 (1967) and UTAH CODE ANN. § 55-10-96 (1953).

[52] 444 P.2d 15 (1968).

[53] *Id.* at 17.

[54] *Id.*

In *Chambers v. District Court of Dubuque County*,[55] the Supreme Court of Iowa held that the Constitution requires that an indigent parent appealing from a finding of dependency be afforded both legal counsel and a transcript:

> The right of appeal without both of them [counsel and transcript] is a mere sham and fails to meet constitutional requirements . . . .[56]

In *In re Karren*,[57] the Supreme Court of Minnesota held that an indigent parent appealing from a finding of dependency is entitled to a free transcript. The Court cited and quoted *Chambers*, approvingly, thus underscoring the constitutional basis of the right. The court further stated that the *Gault* decision would cover this situation even though not within the precise facts of *Gault* itself. The right to counsel was not itself at issue (the appellant had been represented by the Legal Aid Society at the neglect trial) but the Court's language, and discussion of *Gault* and *Chambers* clearly indicated that the Court would have recognized that right had it been at issue.

The Court of Appeals of New York (the court of last resort for that state) recently held that indigent parents were entitled to appointed counsel in juvenile neglect cases:

> The determination must be reversed. In our view an indigent parent, faced with the loss of a child's society, as well as the possibility of criminal charges . . . is entitled to the assistance of counsel. A parent's interest in the liberty of the child, as well as in his care and control, is too fundamental an interest and right . . . to be relinquished to the state without the opportunity for a hearing, with assigned counsel if the parent lacks the means to retain a lawyer. To deny legal assistance under such circumstances would as the courts of other jurisdictions have already held [citations omitted] constitute a violation of his due process rights, and, in light of the express statutory provision for legal representation for those who can afford it, a denial of equal protection as well.[58]

Another recent decision of the United States District

---

[55] 261 Iowa 31, 34, 152 N.W.2d 818, 821 (1967).
[56] *Id.*
[57] 280 Minn. 277, 159 N.W.2d 402 (1968).
[58] In the Matter of B, 334 N.Y.S.2d 133, 285 N.E.2d 288 (1972).

Court for the Northern District of California held that California juvenile courts must appoint counsel for indigent parents in neglect proceedings. That court noted that:

> [W]hether the proceeding be labelled 'civil' or 'criminal,' it is fundamentally unfair, and a denial of due process of law for the state to seek removal of the child from an indigent parent without according that parent the right to the assistance of court-appointed and compensated counsel . . . . Since the state is the adversary . . . there is a gross inherent imbalance of experience and expertise between the parties if the parents are not represented by counsel. The parent's interest in the liberty of the child, in his care and in his control, has long been recognized as a fundamental interest . . . . Such an interest may not be curtailed by the State without a meaningful opportunity to be heard, which in these circumstances includes the assistance of counsel.[59]

Two of the most recent and interesting cases, for purposes of comparison and discussion, are the *Danforth*[60] and *Caha*[61] cases. Although each case established the right to court appointed counsel for indigent parents, the collateral doctrine of waiver was discussed only in *Danforth*. The Nebraska Supreme Court, in *Caha*, held that an indigent parent, upon *request* is entitled to counsel at the expense of the county.[62] Although the Nebraska Supreme Court mentioned that the judge is required to advise the minor and his parents "of their right" to counsel at county expense in juvenile proceedings, no mention was made of such a requirement by the judge in neglect or parental rights termination proceedings.[63] The Maine Supreme Court, on the other hand, held in the *Danforth* decision that:

> An indigent parent or parents against whom a custody petition is instituted under 22 M.R.S.A. 3792 is entitled to have counsel appointed at the State's expense unless the right to counsel is *knowingly* waived. We say this is so because the Constitution of

---

[59] Cleaver v. Wilcox, 40 USLW 2658 (N.D. Cal. 1972). *See also* White v. Green, 70 Misc. 2d 28 (N.Y. Fam. Ct. 1971); *In re* K, 105 Cal. Rptr. 209 (1972) (where the courts similarly held that counsel for indigent parents is constitutionally required in neglect or termination proceedings).

[60] Danforth v. State Department of Health and Welfare, 303 A.2d 794 (Me. 1973).

[61] State v. Caha, 190 Neb. 347, 208 N.W.2d 259 (1973).

[62] *Id.*

[63] *See* note 63 *supra*, at 260.

the United States and the Constitution of Maine compel such conclusion.[64]

In *Danforth* it was noted that the "[a]ppellants were at no time advised by the District Court of any right to court-appointed counsel and were not aware that any such right might exist."[65] In *Caha*, the court noted that "the appellant stated she was not represented by counsel; she did not 'have any money to afford one'; and she requested the court to appoint one."[66]

Very simply stated, the distinction is that in Nebraska an indigent parent in a neglect or parental termination proceeding must ask the court to appoint counsel before that parent's right to counsel arises. An indigent parent in Maine, however, has the right to counsel and to go unrepresented must knowingly and intelligently waive that right. This means that a Maine Court is under a specific duty to clearly advise the indigent parent of his right to counsel whereas a Nebraska Court is apparently under no such compulsion.

The distinction between these two cases is critical since many poor people are simply unaware of their various rights. The Maine standard, being clearly defined, would naturally seem the most appropriate since it would protect those indigent parents unaware of the existence of any actual or potential right to counsel.

As has been discussed, the indigent parent faces complicated issues at trial which necessitate the assistance of counsel to develop and explore, but this problem is aggravated by the parent being confronted by possible criminal prosecution which compels appointment of counsel to avoid the prospects of self-incrimination.

A parent's exposure to possible self-incrimination and criminal prosecution frequently occurs in a termination hearing because the operative acts used to terminate parental rights may also support a criminal charge against the

---

[64] *See* note 62 *supra*, at 795.
[65] *Id.*
[66] *See* note 63 *supra*, at 260.

parent to the extent the termination proceeding involves facts which, if true, would subject a parent to criminal prosecution. The parent is placed in legal jeopardy at the hearing and needs the vital protection of counsel. Thus, the complexity of the issues at these proceedings coupled with potential criminal prosecution flowing from the facts adduced, necessitates the appointment of counsel to represent the indigent parent.

The impact of the parent's possible self-incrimination is not difficult to assess. What has been, for an unrepresented parent, a complicated hearing to maintain rights to the family, suddenly can become an ominous proceeding wherein the parent can justifiably fear that he might implicate himself criminally, resulting in a subsequent criminal prosecution.[67] This is not unlikely since the state agency that performs the prosecutorial function usually institutes the initial neglect proceedings. In such cases, the indigent parents need the guiding hand of skilled counsel to steer them between the Scylla of a contempt finding for invoking the fifth amendment privilege prematurely, and the Charybdis of waiving the fifth amendment privilege by invoking it too late, if at all, and providing obviously incriminating answers. Not only can counsel help in making timely decisions as to when the privilege should be invoked, but also, and probably more importantly, counsel can gauge the probabilities of a criminal prosecution and, depending on his assessment, prepare the parents for appropriate trial posture (i.e., openness, guardedness, silence or some other demeanor). The attorney can minimize the obvious distortions of a parent's trial demeanor resulting from unreasoned alarm over possible self-incrimination and criminal prosecution.

---

[67] At this point, the question arises whether or not the *Miranda* warnings should be given, since these include the warning of a right to appointed counsel. It is merely suggested that if the probability of incriminating statements at such hearings is high, then perhaps the fifth amendment privilege against self-incrimination will provide a bridge to court-appointed counsel that is independent of equal protection, procedural due process or the sixth amendment right to counsel.

IV. CONCLUSION

The legal trend has been to recognize the indigent parents' constitutional right to the appointment of counsel in neglect and termination proceedings. The essentiality of such a right becomes apparent when one considers the precarious position of the indigent in such proceedings. Parental rights to children involve a natural and fundamental aspect of personal liberty. Moreover, the proceedings involve issues and questions of great complexity pitting the parent against the vast and overwhelming resources of the state. In the final analysis, a parent's right to his or her own child is as paramount and important if not more so, than his desire not to be confined in jail. With regard to the latter, the fourteenth amendment guarantees the appointment of counsel.

To deny this right to indigent parents in neglect or termination proceedings is to completely ignore the mandates of the fourteenth amendment. Justice is ill-served when the hopes of indigent parents are rudely snuffed out at a proceeding where they stand alone and uncounseled.

STATUTORY STANDARDS FOR THE INVOLUNTARY TERMINATION OF PARENTAL RIGHTS

ORMAN W. KETCHAM*

RICHARD F. BABCOCK, JR.**

In 1970, Charles and Darlene Alsager were adjudged unfit by an Iowa juvenile court which terminated all parental rights and ordered the removal of five of the six Alsager children from their parents' care. Five years and fifteen foster homes later, a federal district court ordered the return of the children to their natural parents and declared that the statute under which Iowa had terminated the Alsagers' parental rights was unconstitutionally vague under the due process clause of the fourteenth amendment.[1] The Iowa statute permits termination of parental rights where, *inter alia*, the court finds "conduct . . . likely to be detrimental to the physical or mental health or morals of the child,"[2] or that "the parents have substantially and continuously or repeatedly refused to give the child necessary parental care . . . ."[3] The federal court found that this statute, on its face and as applied, failed to give proper notice of the standards which a parent must meet in order to avoid involuntary termination of parental rights and was therefore susceptible to arbitrary application.[4] The court pronounced a caveat regarding termination statutes generally:

> The state's interest in protecting children is not absolute . . . . It must be balanced against the parents' countervailing interest in being able to raise their children in an environment free from government interference.
>
> . . . .
>
> . . . Termination is a drastic, final step which, when improvidently employed, can be fraught with danger. Accordingly, to preserve the best interests of both parents and children, the Court deems that terminations must only occur where more harm is likely to befall the child

---

* B.A., 1940, Princeton University; J.D., LL.B., 1947, Yale Law School; Judge of the Superior Court of the District of Columbia; formerly Judge of the Juvenile Court of the District of Columbia; Adjunct Professor of Law, University of Virginia Law School.

** B.A., 1969, Dartmouth College; J.D., 1974, University of Michigan Law School; Law Clerk to Judge Ketcham, 1974-75; Member of the Bar of the State of Illinois; presently reporter for *The Record*, Hackensack, New Jersey.

1. Alsager v. District Court, Civil No. 73-79-2 (S.D. Iowa, Dec. 19, 1975).
2. Iowa Code Ann. § 232.41 (2)(d) (1969).
3. Iowa Code Ann. § 232.41 (2)(b) (1969).
4. Alsager v. District Court, Civil No. 73-79-2, at 17 (S.D. Iowa, Dec. 19, 1975).

by staying with his parents than by being permanently separated from them.[5]

The experience of the Alsager family epitomizes tragically the problems inherent in the formulation and administration of statutes authorizing the involuntary termination of parental rights. These statutes deal, first, with the standards for a finding of unfitness or neglect and, second, with the disposition following such a finding.

This Article will discuss guidelines for drafting and applying a statute authorizing involuntary termination of parental rights.[6] In drawing up these guidelines, the authors have had three main purposes in mind. First, we seek to limit the circumstances under which involuntary termination can be ordered to those cases in which this drastic step is genuinely warranted. Second, we hope to aid a court confronted with a termination petition to focus on those questions which are relevant to its incipient decision. Both these purposes are probably self-obvious principles of sound legislative drafting, but in the discordant fields of parental and juvenile rights, they are easily overlooked. Third, to minimize the child's ordeal, we wish to reduce the time for making and administering decisions to terminate parental rights.

I. PARENTAL RIGHTS VS. THE NEEDS OF THE CHILD

Terminating parental rights by court order means severing all legal bonds between the biological parent[7] and child.[8] In the eyes of the law, a parent whose rights have been terminated becomes a stranger to the child, with no right to custody, visitation, or communication.[9] Court-ordered termination can be either voluntary, as when a parent consents

---

5. *Id.* at 18-22.
6. For a discussion of the frequency with which the question of termination of parental rights arises, see Gordon, *Terminal Placements of Children and Permanent Termination of Parental Rights: The New York Permanent Neglect Statute*, 46 ST. JOHN'S L. REV. 215, 218-20 (1971) [hereinafter cited as Gordon].
7. "Parent" as used in this article can refer to either or both parents.
8. *See generally* V. DE FRANCIS, TERMINATION OF PARENTAL RIGHTS—BALANCING THE EQUITIES (1971) [hereinafter cited as DE FRANCIS]; S. KATZ, WHEN PARENTS FAIL 115-21 (1971) [hereinafter cited as KATZ]; W. SHERIDAN, STANDARDS FOR JUVENILE AND FAMILY COURTS (1966) (Children's Bureau Publ. No. 433-1966) [hereinafter cited as SHERIDAN]; U.S. DEP'T. OF HEALTH, EDUCATION AND WELFARE, LEGISLATIVE GUIDES FOR THE TERMINATION OF PARENTAL RIGHTS AND RESPONSIBILITIES AND THE ADOPTION OF CHILDREN (1961) (Children's Bureau Publ. No. 394-1961) [hereinafter cited as LEGIS-LATIVE GUIDES]; Gordon, *supra* note 6; Simpson, *The Unfit Parent: Conditions Under Which a Child May be Adopted Without the Consent of His Parent*, 39 U. DET. L.J. 347 (1962) [hereinafter cited as Simpson].
9. *See* Dobson, *The Juvenile Court and Parental Rights*, 4 FAM. L.Q. 393, 405 (1970) [hereinafter cited as Dobson].
It should be noted that an order terminating parental rights also entails a loss of rights to the child. Primarily, "[t]he child's right to be with his natural parents and siblings is wiped out in the process." DE FRANCIS, *supra* note 8, at 10.

to place a child for adoption,[10] or involuntary, as when the court orders the termination over the objections of a natural parent.[11]

The fields of parental and juvenile rights are replete with conflicts and confusion emanating from the very organizations and governmental bodies[12] designed to facilitate such rights. No one seems able to agree on a suitable legal explanation of a biological parent's rights in his child. In the nineteenth century, these rights were likened to property rights, with the child having the status of a chattel.[13] Such an analysis seems to have been discarded in this century.[14] The right has also been likened to a trust relationship, conferred by natural law on the biological parent but revocable by the state in certain circumstances.[15] More recently, a parent's relationship to a child has been conceived of as a compact, with the parent's rights balanced against certain obligations owed to the child.[16] Still another line of analysis describes the natural parent's rights in his child in terms of the bundle of rights encompassed by parenthood.[17] Included in this bundle are the right to have custody, the right to visit, the right to determine education, the right to choose the child's name, the right to consent to marriage, the right to appoint guardians, and the right to consent to adoption.[18] These rights dwindle as the child approaches maturity; several or all of them may be abruptly terminated by court action.[19]

Despite confusion regarding the exact nature of parental rights, our society overwhelmingly agrees that a natural parent has a special interest in his child.[20] This interest needs to be recognized in legislatures, as it

---

10. *See, e.g.*, Iowa Code Ann. § 232.41(1) (1969); Minn. Stat. Ann. § 260.221(a) (Supp. 1976).

11. *See, e.g.*, Iowa Code Ann. § 232.41(2) (1969); Minn. Stat. Ann. § 260.221 (b) (Supp. 1976).

12. *See generally* Dobson, *supra* note 9; Eekelaar, *What are Parental Rights?*, 89 Law Q. Rev. 210 (1973); Foster & Freed, *A Bill of Rights for Children*, 6 Fam. L.Q. 343 (1972) [hereinafter cited as Foster].

13. *Cf. In re* W, 29 Cal. App. 3d 623, 629, 105 Cal. Rptr. 736, 740 (1972); H. Clark, Domestic Relations § 18.5 (1968) [hereinafter cited as Clark]; Carrigan, *The Law and the American Child*, in The Legal Rights of Children (S. Katz ed. 1974).

14. *Cf., e.g.*, Boone v. Boone, 150 F.2d 153 (D.C. Cir. 1945); Appeal of Goshkarain, 110 Conn. 463, 148 A. 379 (1930); Parker v. Kutterman, 208 Ore. 680, 302 P.2d 717 (1956).

15. 3 J. Story, Equity § 1760 (14th ed. 1918). *See also* Wald, *State Intervention on Behalf of "Neglected" Children: A Search for Realistic Standards*, 27 Stan. L. Rev. 985, 990 (1975) [hereinafter cited as Wald].

16. *See In re* Lutheran Children & Family Serv., 456 Pa. 429, 321 A.2d 618, 621 (1974); *In re* Willis, — W. Va. —, 207 S.E.2d 129, 137 (1973).

17. *See, e.g.*, Nevelos v. Railston, 65 N.M. 250, 254, 335 P.2d 573, 576 (1959).

18. *See* De Francis, *supra* note 8, at 1; Legislative Guides, *supra* note 8, at 6; Dobson, *supra* note 9, at 394-96.

19. Legislative Guides, *supra* note 8, at 10-11.

20. *See* Clark, *supra* note 13, at § 17.5; Wald, *supra* note 15, at 989-1000. It has frequently been said that the separation of biological parent and child is "unnatural."

Courts must not be tempted to interfere with the natural order of family life, except in special cases of extreme urgency. In a case like this a court should not

has been consistently protected by the courts.[21]   The United States
Supreme Court with Justice White writing for the majority in *Stanley v.
Illinois*[22] said: "The Court has frequently emphasized the importance of
the family.   The rights to conceive and to raise one's children have been
deemed 'essential,' . . . 'basic civil rights of man,' and rights far more
precious . . . than property rights' . . . ."[23]

Although frequently called upon to sever one or more of the rights
encompassed in parenthood, courts often express a particular reluctance
to terminate permanently all rights of the biological parent in his child
against the will of the parent, since such action severs absolutely the
"primordial bond"[24] between parent and child.[25]   It is widely recog-

---

arrogate to itself the right to determine by its standards the welfare and benefit of
the child, but should have a conscientious regard for the natural law, from which
we learn that the father, as a rule, knows far better what is good for his child than
a court of justice can know.   Paternal control of the family has been a fundamental
principle in the history of mankind, and its free exercise, restricted only in the interest of humanity and good morals, is essential to the highest development of the
race.   What influence more likely to lead to despondency and self-destruction than
the unnatural separation of a parent from his child, and what greater stimulus to
worthy ambition and noble endeavor on the part of a father than the care and companionship of his motherless girl?   It is needless to elaborate argument.   The father
has not relinquished nor forfeited his rights as a parent, and the faults found with
his habits are not of such unusual and serious character as to disqualify him from
discharging his parental duties, or to make him an unfit associate of his own child.
Gilmore v. Kitson, 165 Ind. 402, 410, 74 N.E. 1083, 1085 (1905).

21. *In re* Luscier, 84 Wash. 2d 135, 524 P.2d 906 (1974).   The Washington
Supreme Court gave the following account of the United States Supreme Court's
protection of parental interests:

The family entity is the core element upon which modern civilization is founded.
Traditionally, the integrity of the family unit has been zealously guarded by the
courts.   *See, e.g., Ginsberg v. New York*, 390 U.S. 629, 639 . . . (1968); *May v.
Anderson*, 345 U.S. 528, 533 . . . (1953).   The safeguarding of familial bonds is
an innate concomitant of the protected status accorded the family as a societal institution.   The fundamental nature of parental rights as a "liberty" protected by the
due process clause of the Fourteenth Amendment was given expression in *Meyer
v. Nebraska*, 262 U.S. 390, 399 . . . (1923), wherein the court stated:
"While this Court has not attempted to define with exactness the liberty thus
guaranteed, the term has received much consideration and some of the included
things have been definitely stated.   Without doubt, it denotes not merely freedom
from bodily restraint but also the right of the individual to contract, to engage in
any of the common occupations of life, to acquire useful knowledge, to marry, establish a home and bring up children, to worship God according to the dictates of
his own conscience, and generally to enjoy those privileges long recognized at common law as essential to the orderly pursuit of happiness by free men."   The essential right to procreate and raise children was acknowledged in *Skinner v. Oklahoma*,
316 U.S. 535, 541 . . . (1942), to be among "the basic civil rights of man.   It is
cardinal with us that the custody, care and nurture of the child reside first in the
parents . . ."   Prince v. Massachusetts, 321 U.S. 158, 166 . . . (1944).   And, in
Stanley v. Illinois, 405 U.S. 645 . . . (1972), the court recognized the fundamental
right of a father to custody of his children.
84 Wash. 2d at 136-37, 524 P.2d at 907-08.

22. 405 U.S. 645 (1972).

23. *Id.* at 651.

24. *In re* Garnet, Civil No. 515 (Ct. Spec. App. Md., Sept. 1974).

25. *See, e.g.*, Bell v. Leonard, 251 F.2d 890, 895 (D.C. Cir. 1958); People *ex rel.*
K.S., 33 Colo. App. 72, 76-77, 515 P.2d 130, 133 (1973).

nized that "both by law and by nature parents have the primary right as against the world to their children."[26]   Thus, involuntary termination of all parental rights is ordered only when absolutely necessary to the child's welfare.[27]

Any statute which authorizes a judge to terminate involuntarily all parental rights will have to ensure that the parent's interest is not unnecessarily infringed by arbitrary state action[28] and that the parent is provided with the full panoply of legal rights necessary before termination is ordered.[29]   At a minimum, this requires that the basis for the state's intrusion on family autonomy is clearly delineated.[30]   In addition, the parent who is brought to court in a termination proceeding must receive notice[31] and a fair hearing,[32] including representation by counsel,[33] an opportunity to cross-examine witnesses, to present evidence, and, if necessary, to appeal.[34]

Of course, the special interest of the natural parent in a child is not unbounded.   The philosophical alternative to absolute parental rights in a child was traditionally thought to be the benevolent state, or *parens patriae* concept, which reached its apotheosis in the juvenile court movement from about 1900 to 1955.[35]   Under this historically dubious English doctrine, adherents reasoned that the state should intrude into private family life when necessary to assure that the welfare of the child was being served.[36]   In the past two decades, concepts of *parens patriae*

---

26. *E.g.*, S.K.L. v. Smith, 480 S.W.2d 119, 123 (Mo. App. 1972).
27. See *In re* Adoption of Child, 124 N.J. Super. 272, 274, 306 A.2d 467, 468 (App. Div. 1973) ("We believe that the umbilical of natural parenthood is so sacred that only in the most exceptional cases will anything other than self-destruction by the natural parent sever it.").
28. *See* Wald, *supra* note 15, at 991-1000. *See generally* Note, *State Intrusion into Family Affairs: Justifications and Limitations*, 26 STAN. L. REV. 1383 (1974) [hereinafter cited as *State Intrusion*].
29. *In re* Luscier, 84 Wash. 2d 135, 137, 524 P.2d 906, 908 (1974).   Although nominally civil, it has been suggested that actions by the state to sever parental bonds bear many of the earmarks of criminal proceedings and must be closely scrutinized in order to assure procedural due process. *See* Note, *Child Neglect: Due Process for the Parent*, 70 COLUM. L. REV. 465, 475-85 (1970).   See text accompanying notes 30-34 *infra*.
30. *See* State v. McMaster, 259 Ore. 291, 296-301, 486 P.2d 567, 569-71.
31. *In re* Willis, — W. Va. —, 207 S.E.2d 129, 138 (1973).
32. *Id.*
33. *See, e.g.*, Shappy v. Knight, 251 Ark. 943, 945, 475 S.W.2d 704, 706 (1972); State v. Caha, 190 Neb. 347, 349-51, 208 N.W.2d 259, 260-61 (1973); *In re* Ella B., 30 N.Y.2d 352, 356, 285 N.E.2d 288, 290, 334 N.Y.S.2d 133, 136 (1972); State v. Jamison, 251 Ore. 114, 117, 444 P.2d 15, 17 (1968); *In re* Luscier, 84 Wash. 2d 135, 138, 524 P.2d 906, 908 (1974). *See also* Comment, *The Indigent Parent's Right to Appointed Counsel in Actions to Terminate Parental Rights*, 43 U. CIN. L. REV. 635 (1974).
34. *See In re* Gault, 387 U.S. 1, 57-58 (1967).
35. *See id.* at 14-19. *See also* Kleinfeld, *The Balance of Power Among Infants, Their Parents and the State, Part III*, 5 FAM. L.Q. 64, 66-71 (1971).
36. *See In re* Gault, 387 U.S. 1, 14-19 (1967).
The question of whether the state's power to terminate parental rights is of solely

have been challenged and found wanting.[37]   Instead, there has been a
growth of the idea that the child is a person whose full individual rights
the state and its legal system should recognize.[38]   In the quasi-criminal
setting of juvenile delinquency hearings, this has resulted in laws that

---

statutory origin, or whether that power existed under the common law, is open to dispute.
It is clear that the *parens patriae* doctrine became a part of the English common law
several centuries ago.   At the time of the famous custody case of *Wellesley v. Wellesley*,
4 Eng. Rep. 1078, 1080 (11 Bligh N.S. 124) (H.L. 1828), in which the legality of the
exercise of *parens patriae* was affirmed, Lord Redesdale stated that English chancery
courts had been assuming an authority for the care of children for at least 150 years.
However, while it is conceded by all that the state could take custody and control of
children under *parens patriae*, it is unclear whether that doctrine gives the state sufficient
authority to terminate all residual parental rights.   In fact, the issue seems never to have
come up directly.   Terminating all parental rights is very much a product of the need to
free a child for adoption.   Since adoption was unknown to the English common law and
unpracticed in England until the twentieth century, *see* Brosnan, *The Law of Adoption*,
22 COLUM. L. REV. 332, 335 (1922), it might be assumed that no English court was
called upon to sever all residual bonds between parent and child prior to a statutory
authorization.   At any rate, the authors have not located any early English cases on
point.
    In the United States, the authors have located only a few cases, all involving
adoptions, in which the common law power to terminate parental rights was considered.
These cases are not in accord.   In *Appeal of Woodward*, 81 Conn. 152, 166, 70 A. 453,
459 (1908), the court stated in dicta that the rights of a father in his child "cannot be
destroyed as between himself and his child, except by force of statute."   Similarly, it was
said in *In re Cozza*, 163 Cal. 514, 523-524, 126 P. 161, 165 (1912):

> As the act of adoption is to sever absolutely the legal relation between the parents
> and child; to destroy their reciprocal relations and create entirely new ones between
> the adopting parent and the child, the law, recognizing the natural and sacred rights
> of natural parents to their children, will permit this to be done only with the con-
> sent of the parents, unless under exceptional conditions, which it itself prescribes,
> such consent is declared unnecessary.

Cf. Sayre, *Awarding Custody of Children*, 9 U. CHI. L. REV. 672, 673 (1942) ("The
plain truth is that the unqualified granting of rights in the parent-child relationship is not
possible under the common law, and is equally restricted in courts of equity, where most
of the rights of parent and child are usually determined.").   See also *In re* C.A.P., No.
9365 (D.C. Cir., Apr. 1976).
    On the other hand, in *Nugent v. Powell*, 4 Wyo. 173, 33 P. 23, 28 (1893), the
Supreme Court of Wyoming endorsed the natural rights theory that there is "no parental
authority independent of the supreme power of the state, but the former is derived
entirely from the latter."   This view is in accord with at least one authority. L.
HOCHHEIMER, CUSTODY OF INFANTS § 2 (1899).   Moreover, in a few states, carelessly
drawn adoption statutes have authorized the adoption of a child without any statutory
basis for dispensing with the consent of the natural parent.   In a few cases, courts, apparently drawing on some unspecified common law power to terminate parental rights,
have proceeded to grant adoption over the objections of the natural parent.   *See* 14 U.
CHI. L. REV. 303, 305-06 (1947).
    37. *See In re* Gault, 387 U.S. 1, 14-19 (1967).   *See also* P. MURPHY, OUR KINDLY
PARENT—THE STATE *passim* (1974); PRESIDENT'S COMM'N ON LAW ENFORCEMENT AND
THE AMINISTRATION OF JUSTICE, THE CHALLENGE OF CRIME IN A FREE SOCIETY 80
(1967); W. STAPLETON & L. TEITELBAUM, IN DEFENSE OF YOUTH 23-27 (1972);
Thomas, *Child Abuse and Neglect* (pt. 1): *Historical Overview, Legal Matrix, and
Social Perspectives*, 50 N.C.L. REV. 293 (1972).
    38. *See* S. DAVIS, RIGHTS OF JUVENILES (1974) [hereinafter cited as DAVIS] (sum-
marizes the rights now extended to juveniles in a juvenile court setting).   *See also* Foster
& Freed, *A Bill of Rights for Children*, 6 FAM. L.Q. 343 (1972) [hereinafter cited as
Foster & Freed]; Levin, *Guardian Ad Litem in a Family Court*, 34 MD. L. REV. 341,
351-55 (1974).

assure each child most of the same legal protections afforded to adult criminal defendants.[39]   Of equal importance, however, has been the development of neglect[40] and termination laws intended to protect the basic human needs of children.[41]

In a termination proceeding, the paramount concern of the court should be the child's need to receive the consistent love and care of an adult in an environment conducive to successful personality development.[42]   This is essential for all children.[43]   It should be emphasized, however, that the love and care to which a child is entitled need not come from the biological parent.   Our society expresses a preference for the natural parent, but children are fully capable of thriving under the loving care of a nonbiological parent.[44]   This, of course, is the basis of adoption.   In their seminal book, *Beyond the Best Interests of the Child*, Joseph Goldstein, Anna Freud, and Albert Solnit use the term "psychological parent" to describe an adult with whom the child develops a consistent, loving relationship.   They point out that this relationship is based upon "day-to-day interaction, companionship and shared experiences.   This role can be fulfilled either by a biological parent or by an adoptive parent or by any other caring adult—but never by an

---

39. *See* DAVIS, *supra* note 38, at 123-43.

40. "Neglect" in this article includes what is commonly referred to as "abuse" and "abandonment."

41. *See, e.g.*, the Purpose Clause of the Connecticut statute designed to protect children from abuse which states:

>   to protect children whose health and welfare may be adversely affected through injury and neglect; to strengthen the family and to make the home safe for children by enhancing the parental capacity for good child care; to provide a temporary or permanent nurturing and safe environment for children when necessary; and for these purposes to require the reporting of suspected abuse, investigation of such reports by a social agency and provision of services, where needed, to such child and family.

CONN. GEN. STAT. ANN. § 17-38a(a) (1975). *See also* CAL. CIV. CODE § 232.5 (West Supp. 1975), which states that the provisions of the statute authorizing the involuntary termination of parental rights "shall be liberally construed to serve and protect the interests and welfare of the child;" Katz, *supra* note 8, at 56-58.

However, the framers of neglect statutes and the courts which have interpreted the statutes have historically overlooked the needs of the children in many regards.   For an interesting history of the development of neglect intervention, see Areen, *Intervention Between Parent and Child: A Reappraisal of the State's Role in Child Neglect and Abuse Cases*, 63 GEO. L.J. 887, 894-917 (1975) [hereinafter cited as Areen].   Even today, most neglect and termination statutes focus more on parental failure than on the needs of the child. *See* Wald, *supra* note 15, at 1000-04; text accompanying notes 91-93 *infra*.

42. *In re* Eugene W., 29 Cal. App. 3d 623, 629, 105 Cal. Rptr. 736, 740 (1972). *See also* Foster & Freed, *supra* note 38, at 349.

43. *See* Goldstein, *Psychoanalysis and Jurisprudence*, 77 YALE L.J. 1053, 1076 (1968).

44. J. GOLDSTEIN, A. FREUD, & A. SOLNIT, BEYOND THE BEST INTERESTS OF THE CHILD 16-21 (1973) [hereinafter cited as GOLDSTEIN]; Foster & Freed, *supra* note 38, at 349-50. *See also* Note, *Alternatives to "Parental Right" in Child Custody Disputes Involving Third Parties*, 73 YALE L.J. 151, 158-59 (1963) [hereinafter cited as *Alternatives*].

absent, inactive adult, whatever his biological or legal relationship to the child may be."[45] It is clear that a child separated from his psychological parent for a significant period of time suffers intense trauma and possibly permanent emotional damage.[46]

The termination proceeding, therefore, is an essential legal mechanism for assuring to a child his right to a "psychological parent," in cases where his natural parent has failed to establish a loving and caring relationship. While this need of the child to remain with the psychological parent lacks the venerable legal credentials of the natural parent's hereditary right to the child, it is an interest that is being increasingly considered and recognized by the courts.[47] Except in very rare circum-

---

45. GOLDSTEIN, *supra* note 44, at 19.

46. *See id.* at 31-34; Foster & Freed, *supra* note 38, at 350; Wald, *supra* note 15, at 994. *See also* D.M. v. State, 515 P.2d 1234, 1237 (Alas. 1973), in which a psychiatrist offered the following psychological evaluation of the effects of removing a child from his foster home:

> Removing [D.M.] from the [R's] home and replacing him with his mother . . . would constitute an extreme and unconscionable psychological assault upon him, removing him from the only family he has ever known and from people with whom he has profound and healthy emotional attachments and placing him into a home where he is a total stranger, where a quite different style of life is practiced and where fairly extensive and continuing family stresses . . . are prominent.

47. *See, e.g., In re* Jennifer "S", 69 Misc. 2d 942, 946, 330 N.Y.S.2d 872, 876-77 (Sur. Ct. 1972):

> Too often a preoccupation with parental rights tends to blur the essential right of an infant to end the limbo of foster care (or shelter boarding care) and secure a permanent parental home either with his natural or adoptive parents. Parental "rights" must not be emphasized to the point of denying the child a parental "home." The courts have tended to evade or avoid the superior right of an infant to the protection of a permanent home as the most essential element of its emotional well being, by repeated assertions that the best interests of an infant always rest with the blood-related parent, unless the parent is unfit, or has surrendered the child irrevocably for adoption, or has "abandoned" the child intentionally. This may be so, if the concept of abandonment be construed by the courts liberally enough so that the constitutional rights of the infants, rarely asserted, are not derogated or infringed. That the courts have sometimes harkened sufficiently to infants' constitutional rights, is illustrated not only by the parental unfitness doctrine, but also by the strong probative weight given to older infants' expressed desire for a home other than the parental home, if such other home is suitable and reasonable.

See also Lloyd v. Schutes, 24 Md. App. 515, 332 A.2d 338 (Ct. Spec. App. 1975); *In re* Lutheran Children & Family Serv., 456 Pa. 429, 321 A.2d 618 (1974).

The notion that a child has a right to remain with adults with whom he has formed strong emotional bonds is not new. Over a century ago, Judge Hoar of the Massachusetts Supreme Judicial Court stated:

> . . . If by misfortune, the child has made new relations in life, so deep and strong as to change its whole nature and character, the father has no right to reclaim it. I am satisfied that this is a sound proposition. The child is not the father's property. It is a human being and has rights of its own. The father has a right to the custody of the child, because from general experience, the natural and trained affections of the child attach to the father and those of the father to the child. If the father has left the child at an age too early for it to remember him, and it is placed in circumstances so that it must perish unless cared for, and other persons have expended money and become attached to the child, and the child has formed such associations as cannot be severed without injury to it, then the father has no legal right to sunder those ties.

In re Jerremiah O'Neal, 3 AM. L. REV. 578, 580 (1868-69).

stances, a child should never be removed from the adult psychological parent.

The need of a child to receive love and care from an adult is both crucial and urgent. This need must be fulfilled at an early age to insure normal emotional growth.[48]   A child who is without parental care and affection suffers profound and immediate damage.   Hence, Goldstein, Freud, and Solnit think that courts must act with "all deliberate speed" to place the child with an adult who is or can soon become a "psychological parent."

> The courts, social agencies, and all the adults concerned with child placement must greatly reduce the time they take for decision. While the taking of time is often correctly equated with care, reasoned judgment, and the assurance of fairness, it often also reflects too large and burdensome caseloads or inefficiently deployed resources. Whatever the cause of the time-taking, the costs as well as the benefits of the delay to the child must be weighed. Our guideline would allow for no more delay than that required for reasoned judgment.   By reasoned judgment we do not mean certainty of judgment.   We mean no more than the most reasonable judgment that can be made within the time available—measured to accord with the child's sense of time.   Therefore, to avoid irreparable psychological injury, placement, whenever in dispute, must be treated as the emergency that it is for the child.[49]

As a result of the potentially countervailing interests of parent and child, there are two major conflicts which can arise in the involuntary termination proceeding, one substantive and the other procedural. The substantive conflict pits the parent's hereditary interest in a child against the child's need to receive love and care from a suitable psychological parent.[50]   This is the underlying conflict in all involuntary termination cases.   In its starkest form, it arises when a neglected child is placed with a substitute or foster parent with whom the child develops a psychological parent-child relationship.   The substitute parent then requests the court to terminate the parental rights of the natural parent so that the substitute parent can adopt the child.   The natural parent, in the meantime, may have modified life patterns and may be prepared to

---

48. GOLDSTEIN, *supra* note 44, at 31-45.

49. *Id.* at 42-43.

50. It is frequently said that there are three concerned parties in domestic relations cases: the parent, the child, and the state. *See* Areen, *supra* note 41, at 890-94; Pound, *Individual Interests in Domestic Relations*, 14 MICH. L. REV. 177, 182 (1916). The primary interests of the state are usually held to be the preservation of the autonomous family unit and the protection of dependent persons to insure the development of well-bred citizens. *Id.* at 182.   In the termination proceeding, these interests are represented respectively by the parent and the child.   However, there may be certain relatively insignificant interests of the state which differ from the interests of either the parent or the child. *See* State *ex rel.* Juv. Dept. v. Wade, 19 Ore. App.—, 527 P.2d 753 (1974), *dismissed for want of federal question*, 96 S.Ct. 16 (1975), in which the court noted that in a termination proceeding the state had an interest in increasing the pool of adoptable children while potentially reducing welfare costs. *See also* Areen, *supra* note 41, at 893-94.

show a capability of providing a suitable home for the child and thus be able in time to become a psychological parent.[51]

The recommended procedure in cases of this type requires the court to consider two questions, one loosely styled "jurisdictional" and the other "dispositional."[52] The jurisdictional question is whether the biological parent, by behavior, has forfeited all rights in the child.[53] The dispositional question is whether terminating parental rights would be in the best interests of the child.[54] The first question focuses on the action, or inaction, of the natural parent. The second focuses on the placement which will be most beneficial to the child. If it is first decided that the parent has forfeited his rights in the child, then the court moves on to the second question. On the other hand, if it is decided that the biological parent's behavior does not violate minimum standards of parental conduct so as to render the parent unfit, then the analysis ends and termination is denied.[55] In these latter instances, the court never reaches the question of whether the child's future well-being would be better served by placement with the substitute or psychological parent.

This traditional approach, which focuses first and foremost on the actions of the parent, is justified in the broad sense because of the primary right our society grants natural parents in their children.[56] Clearly, no court should be permitted to intrude on a parent-child relationship to decide what placement would be in the best interests of the child, except in special, carefully delimited circumstances.[57]

But the traditional parent-centered approach often affords to the natural parent a seemingly irrebuttable entitlement to maintain legal ties

---

51. *See, e.g.,* D.M. v. State, 515 P.2d 1234 (Alas. 1973); Lloyd v. Schutes, 24 Md. App. 515, 332 A.2d 338 (Ct. Spec. App. 1975).

52. Although this two-stage process is not explicitly mandated by any statute, it has been adopted as a method of proceeding by courts. *See In re* Adoption of Children by D, 61 N.J. 89, 293 A.2d 171 (1972); *In re* Willis, — W. Va. —, 207 S.E.2d 129 (1973). *See also* DE FRANCIS, *supra* note 8, at 15-16; Simpson, *supra* note 8, at 355.

53. DE FRANCIS, *supra* note 8, at 15-16.

54. *Id.*

55. *E.g., In re* Willis, — W. Va. —, 207 S.E.2d 129, 142 (1973), in which the West Virginia Supreme Court stated: "No court is warranted in applying the 'polar star principle' [of the best interests of the child] until the natural parents' rights have been lawfully severed and terminated."

56. One commentator has noted that since parenthood could be classed as a "fundamental interest," an argument could be made that the government should not restrict that interest absent a compelling state interest. The author goes on to suggest, however, that strict scrutiny review of state action is inappropriate in domestic relations cases in which competing personal interests are at stake. *State Intrusion, supra* note 26, at 1384-94.

57. It has been pointed out that if every family were scrutinized under the best interests of the child concept, the result could be a "redistribution of the entire minor population among the worthier members of the community . . . ." Simpson, *supra* note 8, at 355.

to the child. In cases where the child, after having been separated from the natural parent, has developed a positive relationship with a psychological parent, the right of the child to remain with the psychological parent should also be considered by the court. It is exactly in such cases, where the child has established a loving, consistent relationship with another adult, that a court can best predict which placement will be in the future best interests of the child.[58] It would be tragic if the disposition that would clearly give the child the best chance to lead a happy, productive life could not be considered simply because the natural parent's action, while neglectful, was not deemed sufficiently heinous to justify terminating parental rights. This has not been an uncommon result, however.[59]

The Oregon case of *State v. McMaster*[60] demonstrates the point. The child, having been born out of wedlock in June 1965, was taken from her mother at the age of two months under a complaint alleging that she was not receiving proper care. Several months later she was made a ward of the court and placed with foster parents. At the time the Oregon Supreme Court handed down its decision in the case, the child had lived virtually all of her six years with the foster parents, who wished to adopt her. When the child was four, a trial court had ordered termination of the rights of the natural parents (who had subsequently married) under an Oregon statute which provides for such termination if parents are found to be "unfit by reason of conduct or condition seriously detrimental to the child . . . ."[61] That order was affirmed by the appeals court,[62] and the natural parents appealed to the Oregon Supreme Court. That court acknowledged that the natural parents have suffered from "mutual instability . . . , probably paramount, and numerous separations and lack of concern . . . for anyone else that might be living in the home . . . ."[63] The natural father rarely held a job and frequently absconded with the welfare check, leaving the natural mother destitute. The family frequently moved. The foster parents, on the other hand, were the "complete antithesis—stable, consist-

---

58. The record of courts and social agencies in finding suitable placements for neglected children is poor. *See* Wald, *supra* note 15, at 993-96 and sources cited therein. When such placements do occur children often find it exceedingly difficult to form a lasting relationship with an adult in the foster home and frequent changes of foster home placement are likely to occur. *Id.* It would be sadly ironic if the court were unable to make permanent those psychological parent-child relationships which do take seed and grow.

59. *See, e.g., In re* Clear, 58 Misc. 2d 699, 296 N.Y.S.2d 184 (Fam. Ct. 1969); State v. McMaster, 259 Ore. 291, 486 P.2d 567 (1971); Mahoney v. Linder, 14 Ore. App. 656, 514 P.2d 901 (1973); *In re* Willis, — W. Va. —, 207 S.E.2d 129 (1973).

60. 259 Ore. 291, 486 P.2d 567 (1971).

61. Ore. Rev. Stat. § 419.523(2) (1973).

62. 4 Ore. App. 112, 476 P.2d 814 (1970).

63. 259 Ore. 291, 302, 486 P.2d 567, 572 (1971).

ent, and mutually supportive."[64] The court further acknowledged that taking the child from her foster parents at this time in her life would have a "serious detrimental effect" upon her. Nonetheless, the court reversed the appeals court.

We are of the opinion that the state of the McMaster family is duplicated in hundreds of thousands of American families—transiency and incapicity, poverty and instability. The witness was undoubtedly correct when he stated that living in the McMasters' household would not "allow this child to maximize her potential." However, we do not believe the legislature contemplated that parental rights could be terminated because the natural parents are unable to furnish surroundings which would enable the child to grow up as we would desire all children to do. When the legislature used the phrase, "seriously detrimental to the child," we believe that they had in mind a more serious and uncommon detriment than that caused by the conduct of parents such as the McMasters. The best interests of the child are paramount; however, the courts cannot sever the McMasters' parental rights when many thousands of children are being raised under basically the same circumstances as this child. The legislature had in mind conduct substantially departing from the norm and unfortunately for our children the McMasters' conduct is not such a departure.[65]

Society has set limits on the right of a natural parent to preserve his special interest in a child.[66] Time was that only extremely aberrant conduct by the natural parent was thought to exceed that limit.[67] But today this attitude is being reassessed. If the child's relationship to the natural parent has been severely damaged and the child is prepared to enter into, or has already entered into, a psychological parent-child relationship with another adult, then the rights of the natural parent should approach their limits.[68] In analyzing the interplay of rights it might be helpful to view the interests of the parent and the needs of the child not as fixed and immutable, but as points along connected continui. When the parent is engaged in a healthy psychological parent-child relationship with the child, his legally protected interest in the child is very strong and the need of the child to be free of ties to the natural parent is slight. When the biological parent-child relationship has deteriorated, however, the rights of the parent in the child are reduced at the same time that the need of the child to be freed from pa-

---

64. *Id.*

65. *Id.* at 303-04, 486 P.2d at 572-73.

66. *See* note 36; text accompanying notes 35-41 *supra.*

67. *See generally* text surrounding notes 47-54 *supra. See also* Simpson, *supra* note 8, at 354-55.

68. *See* authorities cited in note 46 *supra. See also Alternatives, supra* note 44; Comment, *Custody of Children: Best Interests of Child v. Rights of Parents,* 33 CAL. L. REV. 306 (1945) [hereinafter cited as *Custody of Children*]. This view is by no means widely accepted by courts, however. *See, e.g., In re* Willis, — W. Va. —, 207 S.E.2d 129, 142 (1973).

rental ties increases. The natural parent's rights reach their nadir when there is no longer any participation on the part of the parent in a psychological parent-child relationship. And where the child has already entered into a psychological parent-child relationship with another adult, the need to have the biological parent-child ties severed is greatest.

The procedural conflict involved in a termination proceeding concerns time. Any statute that authorizes that termination of parental rights must provide the natural parent with every reasonable legal right in the presentation of his case.[69] The exercise of these rights, especially the right to appeal, can take considerable time unless expedited by statute or court rule. On the other hand, because of the immediate damage that a child will suffer when it lacks the love and care of an adult even for a short period,[70] the termination statute should minimize the time that a child's home life is disrupted or the child is without parental care. The statute must, therefore, ensure that justice be done, but swiftly. Even the wisest and most humane disposition may be in vain if the child is forced into limbo for too long.

Thus, the termination statute will need to balance the natural parent's special interest in his child against the child's need to receive consistent love and care from a supervising adult. Additionally, such legislation will need to provide the parent with the full range of legal rights which is his due, but minimize the time during which the status of the child is uncertain.

II. The Need to Couple Termination with Adoption

For both the parent and the child, the essence of the law's function in termination proceedings is to provide the greatest permanence of parent-child relationships and thereby insure that the child is receiving necessary love and care.[71] Termination of parental rights should not be used as a judicial sanction or expression of community censure for parental inadequacy.[72] Nor is termination usually necessary to protect the immediate welfare of the child since, in most instances, that function is served by neglect statutes.[73] A decision to terminate parental rights should not simply extinguish an unsuccessful parent-child relationship without making provision for the creation of a more promising relation-

69. *See* text accompanying notes 28-34 *supra.*
70. *See* text accompanying notes 42-49 *supra.*
71. *See* text accompanying notes 42-47 *supra.*
72. *See* Legislative Guides, *supra* note 8, at 19; Simpson, *supra* note 8 at 370.
73. Under all neglect statutes, courts are given a variety of possible dispositions. *See, e.g.,* Conn. Gen. Stat. Ann. § 17-38a(a) (1975), *quoted in part at* note 41 *supra.* Thus, to protect the welfare of the child, a court could take custody of the child and appoint a guardian ad litem for the child, without having to resort to termination of parental rights. *See* Sheridan, *supra* note 8, at 101. *See also* De Francis, *supra* note 8, at 15.

ship.[74]   Yet current termination statutes usually do not require the court to plan for or even look into the child's future adoption.

It is the authors' position that the ultimate purpose of a termination process is the assurance of the child's adoption.   A child is better served by continuing ties to the natural parent than by severing all rights of the natural parent with only the vague hope that the child will one day be adopted.   The record of social service agencies in finding suitable adoptive placements for troubled children is too uncertain to presume that the child will eventually be adopted.[75]   No termination proceeding should make a child an orphan moving from one institution or foster home to another, without even nominal ties to a natural parent.[76]

Since termination proceedings should be limited to situations where there are real prospects for the child's adoption,[77] the veil of secrecy, which has traditionally surrounded adoption proceedings,[78] should be lifted sufficiently for the presiding judge to be apprised of the child's adoptive prospects.[79]   There should be no administrative impediment to a judge's efforts to obtain the salient facts of the proposed plan for the child's adoption.   If no specific future placement has been planned, the court should require the production of a detailed program to effect the adoption of the child.

In addition, the judge should enter an interlocutory or provisory order

---

74. *See* SHERIDAN, *supra* note 8, at 101-02.

75. *See* R. GEISER, THE ILLUSION OF CARING 81-86 (1973); A. KADUSHIN, ADOPTING OLDER CHILDREN 3-7 (1970); H. MOAS & R. ENGLER, CHILDREN IN NEED OF PARENTS 366-69 (1959).   The incidence of adoption of "hard-to-place" children may have increased recently, however.   *See* Haring, *Adoption Trends: 1971-1974*, 54 CHILD WELFARE 524, 525 (1975).

76. It is well documented that such an indeterminate status seriously and perhaps irremediably affects the child's well-being.   *See* Wald, *supra* note 15, at 993-96 and sources cited therein.

77. *See* SHERIDAN, *supra* note 8, at 101-02.   *See generally* DE FRANCIS. *supra* note 8, at 3-4; LEGISLATIVE GUIDES, *supra* note 8, at 25-28.   Sheridan argues strenuously, however, that the termination order should not be conditioned on the adoptability of the child, since there are situations in which the child cannot be adopted and yet no possible benefit can accrue to the child from continuing the natural parent-child relationship. SHERIDAN, *supra* note 8, at 101.   The authors question whether even in these rare situations termination should go forward in the face of the nonadoptability of the child. Since in cases where it is warranted, the court can assume custody and control of the child, and appoint a guardian for it, terminating parental rights to the nonadoptable child would not seem to benefit any party and could eliminate the slight chance that the natural parent might become sufficiently rehabilitated to resume exercising parental rights.

Nonetheless, because of the novelty of the question, the present authors are open to evidence that in certain cases the rights of the natural parent should be terminated despite the fact that the child cannot be adopted; and, in our suggested standards for termination, we do not wish to preclude the possibility that termination might be appropriate, although rarely, under such circumstances.   *See* note 115 and accompanying text *infra*.

78. *See* CLARK, *supra* note 13, at § 18.3.

79. SHERIDAN, *supra* note 8, at 100-01.

terminating the rights of the natural parent conditional upon the successful adoption of the child.[80]   The court would then retain jurisdiction of the case for a specified period of time.   If at the end of that period the child had not been adopted, the court could rescind the termination order and restore parental rights to the natural parent.   Ideally, the child whose ties to the natural parent had been severed on an interlocutory or conditional basis would be swiftly placed in an adoptive home. If the adoptive home has been tested and found satisfactory, the court will be asked to approve the final order of adoption, thus closing the last link in the proceeding and justifying the court in making the termination order final and irreversible. Should the agency responsible for placing the child be dilatory, the court, through its continuing jurisdiction, would have the supervisory power to spur it on.   Furthermore, the placement agency would be working under a deadline, the date the interlocutory order expires, and, therefore, would have a continuing incentive to find an adoptive home as quickly as possible.

The authors recommend that an interlocutory termination order, authorized by statute, be used as a standard procedure in most, if not all, proceedings for the involuntary termination of parental rights.   It should serve as a procedural mechanism for insuring both that the child is provided with new and better parents through adoption and that the adoption is effected swiftly enough to comport with the child's heightened sense of the passage of time.

III.   THE ESSENTIAL ELEMENTS OF AN INVOLUNTARY TERMINATION ADJUDICATION

Under existing statutes in different jurisdictions, termination of parental rights is authorized in any of three proceedings.[81]   In some states, the rights of the natural parent can be terminated following an adjudication that the child is neglected.[82]   In a second group of states, statutes authorize severance of parental rights, after a special hearing,[83] under a remarkable variety of circumstances: neglectful or abusive behavior by

---

80. For several objections to this procedure, see LEGISLATIVE GUIDES, *supra* note 8, at 27. It is argued therein that an interlocutory termination order will leave the parents in a state of uncertainty for a period of time, will put the social service agency in an awkward position, and could raise practical difficulties in enforcing support liability in the event the natural parent has left the jurisdiction when the termination order is rescinded. It is submitted that these administrative difficulties, which, at worst, are temporary in nature, are outweighed by the advantage of allowing the court to retain jurisdiction and to require the placement agency to act swiftly.

81. *See* Areen, *supra* note 41, at 928.

82. *See id.* at 928-29. *See, e.g.,* KAN. STAT. ANN. § 38-824(c) (1973); NEB. REV. STAT. § 43-209 (1974).

83. *See* Areen, *supra* note 41, at 929; *cf., e.g.,* KY. REV. STAT. ANN. § 199.600 (Supp. 1975); N.C. GEN. STAT. § 7A-288 (1969).

the parent,[84] depravity,[85] open and notorious adultery or fornication,[86] mental illness,[87] intoxication or habitual use of drugs by the parent,[88] failure to provide financial support,[89] and divorce.[90]   Finally, some jurisdictions provide that the rights of the natural parent can be extinguished in an adoption proceeding by permitting the court to waive the necessity of consent to the adoption by the natural parent.[91]   These statutes authorize such waiver when the child has been abandoned,[92] the consent is being withheld contrary to the best interests of the child,[93] or the parent has been declared "unfit."[94]

With one exception, these statutes all emphasize the conduct of the natural parent in setting standards for the termination decision.[95]   This can be disadvantageous to the parent, when the court is influenced by his "immoral" conduct.   Moreover, such legislation can also be disadvantageous to the child, when the court fails to consider adequately the child's circumstances because of judicial concern with the misconduct of the parent.   Professor Michael Wald has recently argued that neglect statutes should "abandon concepts of parental fault and . . . focus on the child if we wish to limit the intervention to cases where it will likely do more good than harm."[96]   This admonition is equally relevant to termination proceedings where a court must make a decision about the permanent future status of a child.   Instances of past misconduct by the parent or examples of specific harms which have befallen the child should be considered only to the extent that they assist the court in estimating the child's future well-being under alternative placements.

---

84. *See, e.g.,* CAL. CIV. CODE § 232(a)(2) (West Supp. 1975); HAWAII REV. STAT. § 571-61(b)(3) (Supp. 1974); N.C. GEN. STAT. § 7A-299(4) (1969).

85. *See, e.g.,* ILL. ANN. STAT. ch. 4, §§ 9.1-1D(h), 9.1-8 (Smith-Hurd 1975).

86. *See, e.g.,* ILL. ANN. STAT. ch. 4, §§ 9.1-1D(i), 9.1-8 (Smith-Hurd 1975).

87. *See, e.g.,* ILL. ANN. STAT. ch. 4, § 9.1-8(e), (f) (Smith-Hurd 1975).

88. *See, e.g.,* IOWA CODE ANN. § 232.41(d) (1969); MO. ANN. STAT. § 211.441(1)(2)(d) (Vernon 1962).

89. *See, e.g.,* IND. ANN. STAT. § 31-3-1-6(g)(1) (Burns Supp. 1975); *cf.* MINN. STAT. ANN. § 260.221(b)(2) (Supp. 1975).

90. *See, e.g.,* N.J. STAT. ANN. § 9:2-19 (1960).

91. *See* Areen, *supra* note 41, at 928. *See, e.g.,* MASS. ANN. LAWS, ch. 210, § 3 (Supp. 1974); VT. STAT. ANN. tit. 15, § 435 (Supp. 1972).

92. *See, e.g.,* IND. ANN. STAT. § 31-3-1-6(g)(1) (Burns Supp. 1975); VT. STAT. ANN. tit. 15, § 435 (Supp. 1972).

93. *See, e.g.,* D.C. CODE ANN. § 16-304(e) (1973); MASS. ANN. LAWS ch. 210, § 3(a)(ii) (Supp. 1974).

94. *See, e.g.,* ILL. ANN. STAT. ch. 4, § 9.1-8 (Smith-Hurd 1975).

95. One section of the Connecticut termination statute provides that the court may terminate parental rights when:

. . . [t]here is no ongoing parent-child relationship, which means the relationship that ordinarily develops as a result of a parent having met on a day to day basis the physical, emotional, moral and educational needs of the child and to allow further time for the establishment or reestablishment of such parent-child relationship would be detrimental to the best interest of the child . . . .

CONN. GEN. STAT. ANN. § 17-43a(a)(4) (1975).

96. Wald, *supra* note 15, at 1001.

This information should not be used by the court or community to express disapprobation of the parent's conduct. The emphasis in a termination proceeding should be on questions concerning the existence or nonexistence of an ongoing psychological parent-child relationship and the termination statute should properly focus the court on those questions.[97]

The authors suggest that there are two factual bases for the involuntary termination of parental rights. These bases focus on the status of the child's relationship to his natural parent (Basis I) and the condition of the child's relationship to another adult (Basis II). In a Basis I situation, which would require a special hearing following an adjudication of neglect, the factual conditions can be summarized as follows: the conditions which led to the neglect adjudication are likely to continue, or have continued, despite social service intervention and consequently the natural parent will be unable to participate, or is not participating, in a psychological parent-child relationship. In a Basis II situation, which would require a special hearing in connection with a pending adoption petition, these are the factual conditions: the natural parent is not participating in a psychological parent-child relationship and the adult who seeks to adopt has developed such a relationship with the child. The authors submit that every case in which termination of parental rights is warranted falls within one of these two categories.

A. Basis I—Special Hearing Following an Adjudication of Neglect

In many cases where there has been an irremediable breakdown of the natural parent-child relationship, there is an urgent need to free the child from natural parental ties in order for the child to find a new psychological parent, usually through adoption. In such cases it is important that there be a separate, prior adjudication that the child is neglected. There are several reasons why this neglect adjudication should be reached first and separately.[98] A properly drawn neglect law[99] should isolate those conditions which indicate a possible breakdown in the nat-

---

97. See Alternatives, supra note 44, at 157; cf. Custody of Children, supra note 68, at 310-11.

98. All fifty states, as well as the District of Columbia, Guam, Puerto Rico, and the Virgin Islands, have enacted neglect statutes. For a comprehensive survey of every state neglect and termination statute as amended through August 31, 1974, see Katz, Howe, & McGrath, Child Neglect Laws in America, 9 FAM. L.Q. 1 (1975).

99. Many neglect statutes have been criticized recently. See, e.g., Areen, supra note 41; Wald, supra note 15. We agree with many of the proposed reforms, particularly the suggestions, in which both Professors Areen and Wald seem to concur, that standards for neglect intervention should focus on the needs of the child and that the primary thrust of neglect intervention should be to strengthen family bonds. Redrawing current neglect statutes to comport with these reforms would improve a termination statute that relied in part on a prior neglect adjudication.

ural parent-child relationship. For example, the District of Columbia neglect statute[100] defines a "neglected" child as one:

(A) who has been abandoned or abused by his parent, guardian, or other custodian;

(B) who is without proper parental care or control, subsistence, education as required by law, or other care or control necessary for his physical, mental, or emotional health, and the deprivation is not due to the lack of financial means of his parent, guardian, or other custodian;

(C) whose parent, guardian, or other custodian is unable to discharge his responsibilities to and for the child because of incarceration, hospitalization, or other physical or mental incapacity; or

(D) who has been placed for care or adoption in violation of law.[101]

The conditions specified in the statute are the same conditions which, if severe or continuous, could destroy the emotional bonds between parent and child. The prior determination that these conditions exist, thus establishing the court's right to intervene,[102] should help the court to concentrate on those questions which are most germane to a termination proceeding, such as the likelihood that the child will continue to be neglected if left with the parent, whether the natural parent-child relationship has broken down beyond rehabilitation, and the child's prospects for adoption by another family.

Another advantage of a prior neglect adjudication is that the court considering the termination petition will have had jurisdiction of the child and presumably will have tried to overcome the neglect through the intervention of social services. Thus, the court will not order termination of parental rights where there is a possibility of remedying the unsatisfactory environment.

Finally, requiring that the neglect adjudication be separate and prior to the termination proceeding should serve as a barrier to unwarranted judicial intrusion into the autonomy of the family.[103] The power to sever the bonds between parent and child is an awesome infringement on this autonomy and it should be carefully circumscribed and rooted in factual conditions, rather than in judicial speculations about what is best for the child. The finding of neglect should establish whether conditions exist that justify the further intrusion by the court in family life.[104]

---

100. D.C. CODE ANN. § 16-2301(9) (1973). This statute is based largely on the statute recommended by the Children's Bureau of the Department of Health, Education, and Welfare. *See* W. SHERIDAN, LEGISLATIVE GUIDE FOR DRAFTING FAMILY AND JUVENILE COURT ACTS 5 (1969) (Children's Bureau Pub. No. 472-1969).

101. D.C. CODE ANN. § 16-2301(9) (1973).

102. *See* text accompanying note 99 *supra.*

103. *See State Intrusion, supra* note 28, and sources cited therein.

104. Wald, *supra* note 15, at 988. The conditions which warrant a finding of neglect are not the same as those that warrant terminating parental rights.

After the neglect hearing the court should hold a factfinding hearing to determine whether, despite social services intervention, the conditions which led to the adjudication of neglect are likely to continue, or have continued, and whether the natural parent will thus be unable to participate, or is not participating, in a psychological parent-child relationship with the child. The question is stated in alternative tenses because in some instances the determination will be made prospectively. In cases where the child has been abandoned or severely abused, for example, it may be clear immediately upon the completion of the neglect adjudication that, despite the availability of social service assistance, the harmful condition will continue if the child remains with the natural parent, with a consequent destruction of the emotional ties between parent and child. In such cases, the termination proceeding should commence immediately. In other cases, these facts can only be established after a social service agency has attempted unsuccessfully over a period of time to remedy the conditions which led to the neglect adjudication.

Continued, irremediable neglect justifies termination of parental rights under many existing termination statutes.[105] This is appropriate, as far as it goes, because in most cases in which the child is suffering from such neglect the natural parent-child relationship has already been permanently damaged. Requiring a showing that the conditions of neglect will continue despite efforts of a social service agency to assist will afford the troubled but concerned parent an opportunity to reestablish a viable household and preserve the relationship with the child.[106] However, most statutes do not add the further proviso suggested above: that, as a result of the continued neglect, the natural parent is not participating in a psychological parent-child relationship with the child. This proviso is necessary because there may well be instances, such as the case of the parent who is incarcerated but remains in regular, concerned contact with the child,[107] where the child continues to be legally neglected but the bonds between the parent and the child are still strong. Hence the statute which authorizes the termination of parental rights under Basis I should require the court to find not only that the neglect is likely to continue despite social service intervention, but also that

---

105. See notes 92-94 and accompanying text *supra*.

106. The state should be required to provide some social service assistance to attempt to repair the parent-child relationship when such intervention would be potentially useful. However, requiring the state to adhere to a statutory standard of effort can create more problems than it solves. *See In re* Clear, 58 Misc. 2d 699, 296 N.Y.S.2d 184, 186 (Fam. Ct. 1969) (interpreting the New York termination statute which conditions the termination decree upon the showing that "the authorized agency has made diligent efforts to encourage and strengthen the parental relationship and specifying the efforts made"). *See also* Gordon, *supra* note 6, at 235-37.

107. *See In re* Adoption of Riggs, 10 Misc. 2d 617, 175 N.Y.S.2d 388 (Sur. Ct. 1958). *See also* Staat v. Hennepin County Welfare Bd., 287 Minn. 501, 178 N.W.2d 709 (1970).

the natural parent is not participating in a psychological parent-child relationship with the child.

B. *Basis II—Special Hearing in Conjunction with a Pending Adoption*

The majority of states authorize the termination of parental rights when the child is sought for adoption and the natural parent refuses to consent.[108]   In most jurisdictions having such a statute, the point at which the natural parent forfeits the right to veto an adoption of the child is said to be reached when the child has been constructively abandoned, when the consent of the parent is being withheld contrary to the best interest of the child, or when the parent has been declared "unfit."[109]   These standards are either too narrowly defined or too loosely interpreted to provide the necessary guidance in determining whether termination is warranted under the facts of a specific case. Abandonment or constructive abandonment of a child has developed a very complex meaning in the law and is difficult to prove.[110]   A few isolated expressions of interest in the child by the parent, for example, can rebut abandonment, even when the child has not seen the parent for months or years.[111]   But concerned observers may fear that "consent withheld contrary to the best interests of the child" may be so broad a standard as to justify virtually any discretionary decision made by a judge.[112]   Similarly, "unfitness" as a ground for terminating parental

---

108. *See generally* text accompanying note 93 *supra.*

109. *See* text surrounding notes 91-93 *supra.*

110. CLARK, *supra* note 13, at § 18.5. The frequently cited definition of child abandonment is:
. . . any wilful and intentional conduct on the part of the parent which evinces a settled purpose to forego all parental duties and relinquish all parental claims to the child, and to renounce and forsake the child entirely.
Logan v. Coup, 238 Md. 253, 258, 208 A.2d 694, 697 (1965). The question of abandonment is said to be largely one of intent. Bevis v. Bevis, 254 S.C. 345, 175 S.E.2d 398 (1970). *See generally* Annot., 35 A.L.R.2d 662 (1954). *See also* Note, *Child Abandonment: The Botched Beginning of the Adoption Process*, 60 YALE L.J. 1241 (1951).

111. *See In re* Adoption of Porras, 13 App. Div. 2d 239, 215 N.Y.S.2d 778 (1961). *See generally* Annot., 35 A.L.R.2d 662.

112. . . . [T]he courts which use the more prevalent best interest test operate in a comparatively free-wheeling manner. In determining best interest courts evaluate any of a large number of factors including moral fitness of the competing parties; the comparative physical environments offered by the parties; the emotional ties of the child to the parties and of the parties to the child; the age, sex, and health of the child; the desirability of maintaining continuity of the existing relationships between the child and the third party; and the articulated preference of the child. The multiplicity and complexity of these factors, the tendency of the courts to emphasize different factors in each case, and the failure to adopt procedures designed to aid this factual inquiry and thus to fulfill the expressed concern for the child, has led to some feeling that the test may be unworkable or a mere cloak for the operation of judicial intuition.
Comment, *Alternatives to "Parental Right" in Child Custody Disputes Involving Third Parties*, 73 YALE L.J. 151, 153-54 (1963). *See also State Intrusions, supra* note 28, at 1391.

rights is a vague and moralistic concept which provides a court with little guidance in reaching a decision.[113]   In fact, conduct, such as promiscuity, which is sometimes cited as demonstrating that the parent is "unfit," may have little or no bearing on the child-parent relationship or on the child's ability to prosper with its natural parent.[114]

When termination of parental rights is ordered in conjunction with a pending adoption, the order should be based on facts established concerning the child's relationships with both the natural parent and the prospective adoptive parent.   Hence, the authors suggest that Basis II for the termination of parental rights exists when the natural parent is not participating in a psychological parent-child relationship and when the child has established a psychological parent-child relationship with the person seeking to adopt.

It should be noted that the breakdown of the biological parent-child relationship can arise in a different context under Basis II than under Basis I.   Whereas Basis I was directed specifically at the situation in which the child needed to be freed from natural parental ties in order to develop a psychological parent-child relationship, Basis II focuses on the case of the child who has *already* entered into a psychological parent-child relationship with another adult.   The purpose of terminating the rights of the natural parent under Basis II is to give permanence to the already existing emotional bonds between adoptive parent and child by permitting the adoption to go forward.   Under Basis I, the primary indication of the natural parent's inability to furnish love and care to the child is the continuation of conditions in the home which caused the child to be adjudicated neglected.   Under Basis II, on the other hand, it is not necessary to show that the natural parent cannot provide an adequate home for the child.   Hence, Basis II would be applicable to a variety of cases not petitionable under Basis I.   For example, it would apply where the child was adjudicated neglected and the parent subsequently eliminated the conditions which led to the neglect adjudication, but in the meantime the child had become emotionally attached to another adult and the natural parent had not reestablished a relationship with the child.[115]   It would apply where a parent voluntarily left the child with other adults for an extended period of time without maintaining regular psychological contact with the child, al-

---

113. *Cf.* Johnstone, *Child Custody*, 1 U. KAN. L. REV. 37, 44 (1952).   Professor Johnstone contends that in custody disputes courts often rely on parental unfitness to justify exercising broad discretion in placing children.

114. *See In re* Dake, 87 Ohio L. Abs. 483, 485, 180 N.E.2d 646, 648 (Juv. Ct. 1961), in which the court terminated parental rights because the mother was "so devoid of morals and intelligence as to bring forth a series of illegitimate children who must be supported by public funds . . . ," despite the fact that the children were in good physical condition and adequately cared for by the mother.

115. *See, e.g.,* D.M. v. State, 515 P.2d 1234 (Alas. 1973); *In re* Lem, 164 A.2d 345 (D.C. Mun. Ct. App. 1960).

though not abandoning the child under the technical legal definition of that term.[116] And it would apply where custody of the child was awarded to one parent following a divorce and that parent subsequently remarried a person with whom the child developed strong emotional ties, while the noncustodial natural parent maintained little or no contact with the child. In this circumstance, if the step-parent petitions the court to adopt the child, the case would be brought under Basis II.[117]

There are three facts which need to be established in order to warrant terminating parental rights under Basis II: that a petition for adoption is pending,[118] that the natural parent is not participating in a psychological parent-child relationship with the child, and that the prospective adoptive parent is participating in a parent-child relationship with the child. The burden of proving these three circumstances should be adequate protection against unwarranted state intrusions on family autonomy under Basis II. In the first place, Basis II is initiated by an adoption petition, an act not easily controlled by the state. In addition, the required breakdown of the bonds between natural parent and child will almost always arise as the result of the natural parent's failure to provide consistent attention, concern, and affection for the child: a course of conduct which is controlled by the parent. Finally, the requirement that the child be participating in a psychological parent-child relationship with the prospective adoptive parent, a relationship that is fostered and nurtured by steady regular contact and care, should limit the instances in which Basis II can be established to those few in which the child has found it necessary to turn from the natural parent to the adoptive parent to fulfill basic needs.

The development of a psychological parent-child relationship between the child and the prospective adoptive parent is, of course, crucial to Basis II. The existence of this relationship may justify terminating the rights of the natural parent without a showing that the child has been neglected by the natural parent. The child's emotional investment in the psychological parent-child relationship and the threat of irremediable harm that would be suffered by the child if that relationship were extinguished increases the child's need to be free from ties to the natural parent and at the same time reduces the natural parent's claims to the child.[119] Factual circumstances, the relative strength of the competing

---

116. *See, e.g., In re* Adoption of Christian, 184 So. 2d 657 (Fla. App. 1966); *In re* Bair's Adoption, 393 Pa. 296, 141 A.2d 873 (1958).

117. *See, e.g.,* Adoption of Minor, 258 N.E.2d 567 (Mass. App. 1970); *In re* Adoption of Jagodzinski, 444 Pa. 117, 281 A.2d 868 (1971).

118. In some cases, it may be preferable to prevent the adoptive parents from coming in contact with the natural parents. This can be accomplished by holding a bifurcated hearing in which the testimony is taken from the natural parent and the adoptive parent at separate times or places. *See In re* J.S.R., Nos. J-0084-69, 8501-72-A (D.C. Super. Ct., Jun. 18, 1974), *reported in* 102 DAILY WASHINGTON L. REP. 1393 (1974).

119. See text surrounding notes 66-71 *supra*.

relationships, and the child's individual needs will fashion the result in these most difficult of judicial decisions.

Under both Basis I and Basis II, in order to terminate parental rights involuntarily, the court would be required to make determinations as to the condition of the relationship between an adult and a child. To do this, the court will need to take evidence from the adults involved and from the child whenever he is able to articulate needs and feelings. Social workers should be called upon to investigate and to make preliminary reports on the respective relationships and testimony can be taken from knowledgeable relatives and friends of the families. In addition, insight into the quality of the relationships involved may be provided by certain easily established facts, such as the frequency of contact between the natural parents and the child as well as the length of residence of the child with the psychological parent. On the whole, the determinations regarding the quality of relationships required by a judge under either basis will be difficult, but not more difficult than the myriad other decisions that a family court judge is called upon to make regularly. These determinations should not be beyond the ability of a conscientious judge supported by subpoena and investigative authority.

The authors believe that the conditions necessary for terminating parental rights enumerated under Basis II will serve to focus the court on those factors which justify termination and perhaps restrict the total number of cases in which termination is authorized in conjunction with adoptions. Nonetheless, we recognize that because Basis II does not require a prior adjudication of neglect—let alone a prior finding of significant parental fault—it may be perceived as a broadening of the circumstances in which termination is authorized. The problem lies in determining the point at which the state is justified in intruding on the autonomy of the private family. We are satisfied that the conditions set out in Basis II appropriately define that point, while giving consideration to the respective rights of parent and child. Because of the complexity of the issue, however, we briefly note the following alternative resolutions of the problems which we considered and ultimately rejected.

First, Basis II might be eliminated entirely as a ground for termination. Termination would thus only be permitted where there was a finding of continued neglect, as in Basis I. The difficulty with this alternative is that there are a few cases in which termination is certainly justified to permit adoption, but the child is not suffering from continuing neglect. *See* text accompanying notes 115-117 *supra.* The situation may be aggravated in such cases because, without the prior adjudication of neglect providing a statutory basis for the court's jurisdiction, the court may be forced to award immediate custody to the natural parent to the grave disadvantage of the child. *See In re* Adoption of Farabelli, — Pa. —, 333 A.2d 846 (1975).

A second alternative would be to add a further condition, grounded on parental fault, to Basis II. We considered, as a criterion, a finding that the natural parent had failed for a defined period of time to maintain regular, ongoing contact with the child. (Because of the complexities of proving legal abandonment, however, that concept is specifically rejected as a condition). The difficulty with this formulation is that courts may dwell more on the actions and inactions of the parent than on the quality of the parent-child relationships involved, however difficult that may be to ascertain. Nevertheless, a legislature considering enactment of a termination statute might wish to consider these alternatives.

C. The Best Interests of the Child

A finding that the elements of either Basis I or Basis II are established would authorize, but would not require, the court to enter an order terminating the rights of the natural parent. Once it has been established that the facts of a given case justify a termination order, the court would then decide which of the available alternative dispositions is in the best interests of the child.[120] This choice will require inevitably fallible predictions, but, if the step-by-step factual determinations required by Basis I or Basis II have been made, much of the speculation would be removed from the ultimate determination. The court will already have before it the essential facts regarding the child's relationship with his natural parent and, in some cases, with his psychological parent. At this point the court will not be balancing the parent's rights against the interests of the child. The question, quite simply, will be which of the alternative placements will give the child the best opportunity to lead a happy, productive life. The authors suggest that, in most cases in which that question is finally reached, the answer will be relatively clear.

D. The Element of Time

The authors have already adverted to the fact that petitions for termination of parental rights come to the court with an urgency not present in most other cases.[121] This urgency stems from the child's heightened sense of the passage of time.[122] What may seem an acceptable delay to an adult can be a profoundly damaging period of loneliness and lovelessness to a child.[123] Since the status of the child is the gravamen of the termination proceeding, that proceeding should be conducted according to the demands of a child's sense of time, not an adult's.

Several of the guidelines for termination of parental rights advanced herein have had as one of their main purposes the prodding of those

---

120. Goldstein, Freud, and Solnit have suggested that the traditional standard might be more appropriately termed the "least detrimental alternative," a change in appellation that they maintain should

. . . enable legislatures, courts and child care agencies to acknowledge and respond to the inherent detriments in any procedure for child placement as well as in each child placement decision itself. It should serve to remind decisionmakers that their task is to salvage as much as possible out of an unsatisfactory situation. It should reduce the likelihood of their becoming enmeshed in the hope and magic associated with "best," which often mistakenly leads them into believing that they have greater power for doing "good" than "bad."

GOLDSTEIN, *supra* note 44, at 63.

121. *See* text accompanying notes 48, 49 *supra*.
122. GOLDSTEIN, *supra* note 44, at 40-45.
123. *See id.* at 40-41.

responsible to make swift decisions regarding the future of the child. In particular, the use of the interlocutory termination order should spur the responsible social service agency into dealing with the child's indeterminate status with all deliberate speed. In addition to internalized incentives, the termination statutes should explicitly authorize the court to hear the termination proceeding on an expedited basis. Only such time as is necessary to provide for adequate representation should be permitted between the filing of the petition and the hearing of the case. Once a decision has been reached by the trial court, the appeals process should also be expedited. Statutory language to insure suitable time limits is recommended.

Goldstein, Freud, and Solnit have persuasively argued that durational standards are artificial where children are concerned since the "process through which a new child-parent status emerges is too complex and subject to too many individual variations for the law to provide a rigid statutory timetable."[124] It is true that the court should not be concerned with questions of the passage of arbitrary periods of time, but with whether the child's relationship with his natural parent is irreparably damaged, or whether the child has entered into a new psychological parent-child relationship. However, until behavioral scientists can provide more objective criteria for the determination of such factors, more traditional time concepts acceptable to the judicial system may be necessary. For the sake of both the parent and the child, there should be some outer limit to the period of time during which a decision to terminate can be effected. While durational "limits" of this sort too frequently become timetables for acting rather than the cut-off points they were intended to be, such limits are necessary either to encourage the responsible social service or placement agency to act promptly in those cases in which termination may be warranted, or to remove the threat of termination from the natural parent whose child has been adjudicated neglected.

It is recommended that the interlocutory termination order be limited to six months for a child under six years of age and to one year for a child who is six years of age or older.[125] If at the end of that period of time an adoption has not been effected, the termination order should be rescinded. In the case of a termination petition brought under Basis I, it is recommended that it must be brought within one year after the neglect adjudication. This period of time should give a social service

---

124. *Id.* at 48.

125. These time limits are not based on any scientific data, but rather reflect the authors' balancing of several relevant factors, including the child's need for a swift, permanent placement; the amount of time a conscientious placement agency will require to find a suitable placement for a child; the length of the time that the child needs to reside with the prospective adoptive parents before the placement can safely be considered satisfactory; and unavoidable court delays.

agency ample time to attempt to remedy the conditions which led to the adjudication of neglect and to attempt to repair the biological parent-child relationship. If the prospects for recovery are not good within a year, then some action should be taken to give the child a fresh start with a new parent.

IV. CONCLUSION

The authors have attempted to set out several of the basic conflicts underlying the decision to terminate involuntarily all rights of a biological parent in his child and to suggest guidelines for a statute authorizing such a decision. The elements of the two grounds for involuntary termination that we propose can be summarized as follows:[126]

Basis I

1. The child has been adjudicated neglected within one year prior to the filing of the petition for termination of parental rights.

2. Despite social service intervention, the conditions which led to the neglect adjudication have continued (or are likely to continue) and consequently the natural parent is not participating (or will be unable to participate) in a psychological parent-child relationship with the child.

3. Termination of parental rights is in the best interests of the child.

4. The termination order is entered on an interlocutory basis pending adoption.[127]

5. If an adoption of the child is not effected within six months in the case of a child under six years of age or within one year in the case of a child over six years, the termination order is dissolved.

Basis II

1. A petition for adoption of the child is pending.

2. The biological parent is not participating in a psychological parent-child relationship with the child.

3. The child has entered into a psychological parent-child relationship with the prospective adoptive adult.

4. Termination of parental rights is in the best interests of the child.

5. The termination order is entered on an interlocutory basis pending adoption.

---

126. These elements are guidelines only. They need to undergo further refinement and definition based on experience to avoid problems of vagueness in a statute.

127. The authors do not want to dismiss the possibility that there could be rare cases in which termination would be warranted despite the nonadoptability of the child. *See* note 77 *supra.*

6. If the adoption of the child by the psychological parent is not effected within six months in the case of a child under six years of age or within one year in the case of a child over six years, the termination order is dissolved.

As a final caveat, it should be emphasized that the authors believe that neither governments nor judges are possessed of omniscient wisdom and that both are capable of and sometimes guilty of causing more problems by intruding on a private family than they resolve. Our theme throughout this discussion has been the principle that the involuntary termination of parental rights is an awesome exercise of judicial power, reserved for rare circumstances in which it is genuinely warranted. If our proposed statutory guidelines diverge from this principle, we hope this article prompts further discussion. The rights and needs here concerned are precious and ephemeral. They deserve far more attention from our society than they have to date received.[128]

---

128. *See* Dembitz, . . . *And Thwarting a Life of Crime*, N.Y. Times, Aug. 9, 1975, at 15, col. 2.

Effect of the Adoption Act of 1970 on Termination of Parental Rights

Richard L. Placey*

I. Introduction

There has been concern in Pennsylvania among governmental agencies and private institutions, as well as the bench and the bar, that too many children are required to maintain 'a parent-child relationship with parents who have little regard for the child's welfare, or who are unable to provide a minimum standard of proper parental care.[1] The Pennsylvania General Assembly addressed this problem in 1970 when it extensively revised the Adoption Act[2] by expanding the grounds for involuntary termination of parental rights.[3] In addition to broadening the grounds of abandonment,[4] a new ground, section 311(2), became part of the adoption law.[5]

The official comment to the new section indicates that its purpose is to focus judicial inquiry upon the welfare of the child.[6] Some courts have held, however, that in the absence of sufficient evidence of parental fault, the question of the welfare or best interest of the child is not a consideration.[7] The lower courts are understandably confused as to the state of the law under section 311(2):

---

* LL. B. 1955, Dickinson School of Law; Former Chairman, Family Law Section, Pa. Bar Association; Partner, Placey & Wright, Harrisburg.
1. Article by the Honorable Hugh C. Boyle, Chairman of the Subcommittee on Adoption of the Joint State Government Commission Decedents' Estates Laws Advisory Committee which appeared in Fiduciary Review, September, 1970.
2. PA. STAT. ANN. tit. 1, § 101-603 (Purdon Supp. 1976-77).
3. Section 311 replaced section 1.2.
4. PA. STAT. ANN. tit. 1, § 311(1) (Purdon Supp. 1976-77).
5. The new section allows the termination of parental rights when
the repeated and continued incapacity, abuse, neglect or refusal of the parent has caused the child to be without essential parental care, control or subsistence necessary for his physical or mental well-being and conditions and causes of the incapacity, abuse, neglect, or refusal cannot or will not be remedied by the parent.
Id., § 311(2).
6. JOINT STATE GOVERNMENT COMMISSION, OFFICIAL COMMENT, ADOPTION ACT § 311 (1970).
7. Adoption of McAhren, 460 Pa. 63, 331 A.2d 419 (1975); Richardson Adoption, 23 Pa. Fiduc. 489 (C.P. Erie 1973); Peternel Adoption, 24 Pa. Fiduc. 204 (C.P. Alleg. 1974). *See also* Adoption of M.P., 24 Pa. Fiduc. 210 (C.P. Lanc. 1974).

709

[W]e are not certain whether the welfare of the child is a factor we should consider in a proceeding to terminate parental rights involuntarily . . . . With the law at the present time being rather inconclusive, we feel that it would be inappropriate for us to reach a decision based solely upon the best interests or welfare of the child, although in our minds we are well satisfied that this should be not only a consideration but the most important consideration.[8]

This article will explore various interpretations adopted by the courts in construing the grounds for termination of parental rights and will suggest a broadening of the application of the new ground set forth in section 311(2).[9]

II. Historical Background

Under the 1925 Adoption Act, the primary ground for termination of parental rights was abandonment, defined in the Act as "conduct on the part of a parent which evidences a settled purpose of relinquishing parental claim to the child and of refusing or failing to perform parental duties."[10] The cases construing the section made clear that an intent to escape parental responsibility was an essential element of abandonment.[11] If the parent's conduct, however undesirable it was and whatever adverse effect it had upon the welfare or best interest of the child, fell short of that standard, termination could not be decreed. The welfare or best interest of the child was not a consideration until the abandonment had been found.[12]

In 1951 a task force of the Joint State Government Commission undertook a review of the procedures for placement of children. In 1953 the National Conference of Commissioners on Uniform State Laws recommended a Uniform Adoption Law. Although Pennsylvania's 1925 Adoption Act was amended in 1953 to meet some objections,[13] the subject lay dormant until the 1960's. Then, in 1962, the Joint State Government Commission Task Force and Advisory Committee on Decedents' Estates Laws was asked to formulate amendments to the 1925 Act. At the same time, officials of public and private welfare agencies, the Family Law Section of the Pennsylvania Bar Association, and the Pennsylvania Department of Public Welfare began to revise the adoption laws.

---

8. *In re* Rinehart, 70 Pa. D. & C.2d 739, 746 (C.P. Adams 1975).

9. Section 311(3) allows the parental rights of the presumptive but not natural father of the child to be terminated upon establishment of the fact that he is not the natural father. This ground is not treated in this article.

10. Adoption Act of Apr. 4, 1925, P.L. 127, § 1, *as amended*, PA. STAT. ANN. tit. 1, § 1(a) (Purdon 1963).

11. Rettew Adoption Case, 428 Pa. 430, 239 A.2d 397 (1968); Snellgrose Adoption case, 425 Pa. 258, 228 A.2d 764 (1967).

12. Jacano Adoption Case, 426 Pa. 98, 231 A.2d 295 (1967); Gunther Adoption Case, 416 Pa. 237, 206 A.2d 61 (1965).

13. Act of Aug. 26, 1953, P.L. 1411.

In 1967 and 1969 bills were introduced to revise the Adoption Code but were not adopted. Late in 1969 the Honorable Hugh C. Boyle, Chairman of the Subcommittee on Adoption of the Joint State Government Commission Decedents' Estates Laws Advisory Committee, at the direction of the Task Force and Advisory Committee, called a series of meetings to conclude a satisfactory adjustment of outstanding objections to the legislative proposals previously presented. The proposed legislation embodying the subcommittee's recommendations was introduced in the General Assembly on May 14, 1970, and became law on July 24, 1970, as the Adoption Act of 1970.[14]

III. Grounds for Involuntary Termination of Parental Rights Under the Adoption Act of 1970

A. *Parental Intent to Abandon*

Section 311(1) of the Act initially appears to restate the abandonment provisions of the 1925 Act.[15] Closer scrutiny, however, reveals that through use of the disjunctive (*or*) two distinct grounds for termination are set forth:

(A) A settled purpose of relinquishing the parental claim to a child, or
(B) A refusal or failure to perform parental duties.[16]

Intention to abandon is no longer the essential element in cases in which termination is based on refusal or failure to perform parental duties.[17] Under the present law, abandonment is established if either (A) or (B) above is proven. Under (B) there will be cases in which a parent may lose parental rights despite a desire to maintain them, or in which there is no settled purpose of relinquishment of parental claim.[18]

B. *Abrogation of Parental Duties*

The courts have continued, and properly so, to apply a rule to a section 311(1) termination that had been applied in abandonment cases under the 1925 Act. This rule provides that the best interest of the child is not a consideration in cases arising out of that section until abandonment has been found.[19] Section 311(1) now applies to all cases in which there is an abandonment coupled with an intention to abandon, or in which there is willful failure or refusal to perform parental duties without regard to intent. This section requires that the parent be at fault for a six-month period.

---

14. Act of July 24, 1970, P.L. 620, No. 208, *codified in* PA. STAT. ANN., tit. 1, §§ 101-603 (Purdon Supp. 1976-77).
15. PA. STAT. ANN. tit. 1, § 311(1) (Purdon Supp. 1976-77).
16. Castell Adoption, 55 Pa. D. & C.2d 307 (C.P. Fay. 1972). Owen Adoption, 51 Pa. D. & C.2d 761 (C.P. Mercer 1971).
17. Adoption of JRF, 27 Som. 298 (Pa. C.P. 1972).
18. Adoption of Croisette, — Pa. —, 364 A.2d 263 (1976).
19. Adoption of McAhren, 460 Pa. 63, 331 A.2d 419 (1975).

Section 311(2), which had no counterpart under the 1925 Act, was suggested by section 19(c) of the revised Uniform Adoption Act.[20] The official comment of the Joint State Government Commission states that the import of this section "differs from 'abandonment' in that it centers judicial inquiry upon the welfare of the child rather than the fault of the parent."[21] Section 311(2) provides:

> The repeated and continued incapacity, abuse, neglect, or refusal of the parent has caused the child to be without essential parental care, control, or subsistence necessary for his physical or mental well-being and the conditions and causes of the incapacity, abuse, neglect, or refusal cannot or will not be remedied by the parent . . . .[22]

For the most part, the treatment accorded section 311(2) by the courts has been confusing. For example, the existence of this section as a separate and distinct ground for termination of parental rights has largely been ignored. The confusion was initiated by the Joint State Government Commission's official comment to the section, which indicates that its purpose is to focus inquiry on the welfare of the child rather than on the fault of the parent. The section itself, however, does not do this. The Pennsylvania Supreme Court as well as the lower courts, have augmented the confusion by not clearly distinguishing between the second ground for termination in section 311(1) and the ground set forth in section 311(2).[23] The following discussion will illustrate the construction given to section 311(2) since its enactment.

Most cases hold that a statutory prerequisite to considering the welfare of the child is a finding that there is and will continue to be nonperformance of affirmative parental duties or parental fault of some sort.[24] *Jones Appeal*,[25] an early case construing section 311(2), set the tone for what was to follow:

> While the new Adoption Act must be viewed as an expansion of the courts' powers to terminate parental rights under the proper circumstances, the statutory standard of evidence necessary to support termination is nonetheless demanding. The legislative enactments [embodied in section 311(2)] demonstrate that the courts should not disturb the parent-child relationship in the absence of compelling evidence of '*repeated and continued incapacity, abuse, neglect or refusal*' to provide essential parental care.[26]

---

20. Uniform Adoption Act, 9 U.L.A. § 19(c) (Master Edition 1973).
21. JOINT STATE GOVERNMENT COMMISSION, OFFICIAL COMMENT, ADOPTION ACT (1970).
22. PA. STAT. ANN. tit. 1, § 311(2) (Purdon Supp. 1976-77).
23. *See* Adoption of McAhren, 460 Pa. 63, 331 A.2d 419 (1975); Appeal of Diane B., 456 Pa. 429, 321 A.2d 618 (1974); discussion of cases accompanying note 24 *infra*.
24. Adoption of McAhren, 460 Pa. 63, 331 A.2d 419 (1975); Shaeffer Appeal, 452 Pa. 165, 305 A.2d 36 (1973); Peternel Adoption, 24 Pa. Fiduc. 204 (C.P. Alleg. 1973); Richardson Adoption, 23 Pa. Fiduc. 489 (C.P. Erie 1973).
25. 449 Pa. 543, 297 A.2d 117 (1972).
26. *Id*. at 547, 297 A.2d at 119 (emphasis in original).

No attempt was made to distinguish between failure or refusal to perform parental duties—constituting grounds under section 311(1)—and repeated and continued incapacity, abuse, neglect, or refusal by the parent to provide essential parental care—purported grounds for termination under section 311(2). The activities or situation of the parent are central to both.

In other decisions the court has held similarly. The court remanded the *Shaeffer Appeal*[27] case for the lower court to consider terminating parental rights under section 311(2). The lower court was instructed to receive evidence of a *"continued and irremediable parental incapacity as would justify a decree of involuntary termination under Section 311(2) . . . . ."*[28] Such an inquiry into parental incapacity would be required to establish grounds for termination because of refusal or *failure* to perform parental duties.[29] The court apparently considered this inquiry of primary importance for the establishment of grounds under section 311(2).

A possible explanation of the court's holding lies in its statement that the parent's fitness as a parent has no relationship to the issue of abandonment under section 311(1).[30] Hence, the court draws a distinction between "parental fitness," stating that this is relevant under section 311(2), and "failure to perform parental duties," which is properly considered under section 311(1). The line of demarcation between the two is less than clear, however, since "parental unfitness" can only result from a failure to perform parental duties, regardless of the underlying reason for the failure.[31] Therefore, while the court in *Shaeffer* was unwilling to find abandonment of the child on a showing of unfitness of the parent, it would have been justified in doing so under section 311(1) depending on the duration and degree of the incapacity.

The most recent, and the clearest, supreme court construction of section 311(1) came in *Adoption of McAhren*.[32] In unequivocal terms, the court stated that "in the absence of sufficient evidence to satisfy the statutory requirements for involuntary termination, the question of the best interest of the child never arises."[33] The court searched for conclusive evidence of refusal or failure to perform parental duties as a prerequisite for termination under section 311(1). As a result, then, the court required a finding of parental fault as the nexus of section 311(1) grounds for termination. It declined to specifically consider the child's welfare despite the causal relationship between parental fault and child welfare.

---

27. 452 Pa. 165, 305 A.2d 36 (1973).
28. *Id.* at 171, 305 A.2d at 40 (emphasis in original).
29. *See also* PA. STAT. ANN. tit. 1, § 311(1) (Purdon Supp. 1976-77).
30. Shaeffer Appeal, 452 Pa. 165, 168, 305 A.2d 36, 38-39 (1973).
31. "Parental unfitness" may be interpreted in a neutral sense. A parent incapable of performing parental duties is just as parentally unfit as one who refuses to perform the duties.
32. 460 Pa. 63, 331 A.2d 419 (1975).
33. *Id.* at 70, 331 A.2d at 422.

C. The Best Interests Criterion

The "best interests of the child" criterion has been applied, in accordance with the official comment, in some cases construing section 311(2). In *Appeal of Diane B*,[34] the court delved into that inquiry in considering the section 311(2) grounds for termination. It held that parental rights may be terminated under the section despite a desire on the part of the parent to keep the child.[35] The parent has a positive duty to provide care, control and subsistence for his or her child, as well as a duty to love, protect and support the child.[36] Thus, when it is shown that a child is not receiving the parental care essential to normal development and a minimal level of well-being, parental rights may be severed.[37] Judicial inquiry focused upon fulfillment of the child's needs as well as upon the fault of the parent.[38] Even in the *Diane B* case, however, the evidence tended to emphasize the fault of the parent in denying the child essential parental care. This is attributable to the inevitably close relationship between parental fault and the child's well-being.

In summary, while most Pennsylvania cases construe section 311(2) to require a showing of parental fault, there is some authority for the proposition that consideration of the well-being of the child is relevant.[39] Under the present state of the law, however, termination of parental rights cannot be achieved solely because it is in the best interests of the child.

IV. Effect of Section 311(2) in Termination Proceedings

It is necessary to view section 311(2) as a distinct ground for termination of parental rights.[40] Failure to recognize it as such, but to treat it instead as abandonment grounds treated under section 311(1), reduces its impact and ignores the legislative purpose.

In *In re Geiger*[41] the court pointed out that under section 311(2) three things must be shown before the natural parent's rights in the child will be terminated:

> (1) repeated and continued incapacity, abuse, neglect or refusal must be shown;
> (2) such incapacity, abuse, neglect or refusal must be shown to have caused the child to be without essential parental care, control or subsistence; and

---

34. 456 Pa. 429, 321 A.2d 618 (1974).
35. *Id*. at 434-35, 321 A.2d at 621.
36. *Id*. at 433, 321 A.2d at 620.
37. PA. STAT. ANN. tit. 1, § 311(2) (Purdon Supp. 1976-77). *Accord*, Loar Adoption, 56 Pa. D. & C.2d 618 (C.P. Mercer 1972); Janusek Adoption, 23 Pa. Fiduc. 59 (C.P. Alleg. 1972).
38. Appeal of Diane B., 456 Pa. 429, 433-34, 321 A.2d 618, 620 (1974).
39. Janusek Adoption, 23 Pa. Fiduc. 59 (C.P. Alleg. 1972); Adoption of JRF, 27 Som. 298 (Pa. C.P. 1972).
40. *In re* Geiger, 459 Pa. 636, 331 A.2d 172 (1975).
41. *Id*.

714

(3) it must be shown that the causes of the incapacity, abuse, neglect or refusal cannot or will not be remedied.[42]

Although this section is an expansion of the court's power to terminate parental rights,[43] all three elements must be established by compelling evidence.[44] There can be no termination without the presence of all three.

The second element enumerated in *Geiger*, deprival of essential parental care, control, or subsistence, has presented the most problems.[45] The confusion arises out of the imprecise official comment to the section, which reads too much into it. Earlier lower court decisions that construed the official comment reasoned that the best interest and welfare of the child is an important consideration.[46] While the best interest and welfare of the child are the central considerations in a custody case, they were not material to the termination of parental rights under the 1925 Act.[47] Nor does section 311(2), read in its entirety, make it the central issue, notwithstanding the official comment.[48] Until the role played by the child's welfare in determinations under this section is clearly articulated, confusion in the lower courts will continue.[49] Reference in the section to "essential parental care" permits adoption in cases where it would not be possible under section 311(1).

The parent's obligation to the child is a positive duty that requires affirmative performance.[50] A parent must provide care, control, and subsistence and has the duty to love, protect, and support the child.[51] In *Adoption of JFR* the court focused on parental duties:

> Parenthood is not . . . mere biological status, or passive state of mind which claims and declines to relinquish ownership of the child. It is an active occupation, calling for constant affirmative demonstration of parental love, protection and concern.
>
> . . . [A parent] must exert himself to take and maintain a place of importance in the child's life, and must exercise reasonable firmness in declining to yield to obstacles. Otherwise, he cannot perform the job of parent, and the parent-child relationship will deteriorate as the absent parent more and more gives his thoughts, attentions, concern and priorities to his own life and associates.[52]

---

42. *Id.* at 639, 331 A.2d at 174.
43. *Id.* at 639, 331 A.2d at 173, *citing* Appeal of Jones, 449 Pa. 543, 547, 297 A.2d 117, 119 (1972).
44. *Id.*
45. *In re* Rinehart, 70 Pa. D. & C.2d 739 (C.P. Adams 1975).
46. Adoption of JRF, 27 Som. 298 (Pa. C.P. 1972).
47. Jacano Adoption case, 426 Pa. 98, 231 A.2d 295 (1967); Gunther Adoption case, 416 Pa. 237, 206 A.2d 61 (1965).
48. JOINT STATE GOVERNMENT COMMISSION, OFFICIAL COMMENT, ADOPTION ACT § 311 (1970).
49. *In re* Rinehart, 70 Pa. D. & C.2d 739 (C.P. Adams 1975).
50. *See, e.g.*, Smith Adoption Case, 412 Pa. 501, 194 A.2d 919 (1963).
51. Appeal of Diane B., 456 Pa. 429, 321 A.2d 618 (1974); Wischmann Adoption case, 428 Pa. 327, 237 A.2d 205 (1968).
52. Adoption of JRF, 27 Som. 298, 304-05 (Pa. C.P. 1972).

Viewed in this light, section 311(2) opens a wide range of possibilities. There are many cases in which the parent does the minimum necessary to avoid termination under 311(1), such as provide support, undertake occasional visitations, and show minimal concern.[53] Minimal conduct that does not give the child essential parental care would not preclude a termination under this section.[54] The section would apply when the parent is permanently incapacitated, either mentally or physically,[55] and, in the author's view, when a parent is a long-term prisoner who does the minimum necessary to avoid termination under 311(1).[56]

The section applies to cases in which a child is in the custody of one parent and a step-parent, and the other natural parent never sees, communicates with, or in any way interacts with the child other than to pay ordered support. While payment of support was held to preclude termination under prior law,[57] it would not preclude termination under section 311(2), since the parent's neglect "to take and maintain a place of importance in the child's life"[58] would deprive the child of that parent's essential care.[59] The fact that someone else is providing for the needs of the child does not excuse the performance of the parent.[60]

A review of cases that have considered section 311(2) reveals that some of the problems encountered arise from the character of the proof offered rather than from a refusal of the court to apply section 311(2). In *Appeal of Jones*[61] the evidence offered in support of termination included the natural mother's guilty plea to a charge of being an accessory to the rape of one of her daughters. The other evidence was two written documents, both admitted into evidence by the lower court over the objection of the natural mother's counsel. The one was a summary of the child welfare agency's history of the natural mother and her children and contained a recounting of "facts" accumulated by the agency. The "facts" alleged in the summary were not proved by collateral evidence and the report was held to be hearsay by the supreme court. The other

---

53. *See, e.g.*, Vaders Adoption case, 444 Pa. 428, 282 A.2d 359 (1971) (decided under the 1925 Act).
54. Appeal of Diane B., 456 Pa. 429, 321 A.2d 618 (1974).
55. Adoption of M.P., 24 Pa. Fiduc. 210 (C.P. Lanc. 1974); Loar Adoption, 56 Pa. D. & C.2d 618 (C.P. Mercer 1972); Adoption of Szopinski, 56 Erie 78 (Pa. C.P. 1972).
56. *In re* Adoption of McCray, 460 Pa. 210, 331 A.2d 652 (1975). Here the court suggests that the father could have avoided termination under section 311(1) if he had taken advantage of his visitation rights or made a sincere effort to inquire about his child.
57. Vaders Adoption case, 444 Pa. 428, 282 A.2d 359 (1971) (decided under the 1925 Act).
58. Adoption of JRF, 27 Som. 298, 304 (Pa. C.P. 1972).
59. The essential parental care referred to is the care required of the parent himself and not someone else. A parent should not be deemed to have provided that care if he simply provides the financial support and neglects the greater portion of those other duties that the court in *JRF* outlines. *See* Adoption of JRF, 27 Som. 298 (Pa. C.P. 1972).
60. Smith Adoption Case, 412 Pa. 501, 194 A.2d 919 (1963) *In re* Lightner, 60 Pa. D. & C.2d 64 (C.P. Lyc. 1972).
61. 449 Pa. 543, 297 A.2d 117 (1972).

document was a written statement of a physician made the day before the hearing:

> At the time I examined Mrs. Jones I felt that she was definitely psychotic and incapable of appropriate reasoning. Also, I indicated that I felt this problem was not situational, but rather of long duration, or having prior occurrence. I further felt that the prognosis was poor unless immediate treatment was utilized.

> Without a current psychological examination and evaluation I would be unable to comment on her present condition; however I feel certain that she is a very unstable individual who is incapable of assuming the responsibilities of homemaker and wife. Her ability to be an adequate mother would appear to be against reason and good judgment.[62]

The court ruled this evidence inadmissible as hearsay, but did point out what its affect would have been, had it been properly adduced at trial.

> [The physician's] statement is illuminating. It represents precisely the quality of evidence substantively necessary to support a finding of continued and irremedial parental incapacity—the quality of evidence capable of sustaining an order of involuntary termination of parental rights under the 1970 Adoption Act.[63]

Similarly, in *Shaeffer Appeal*[64] the court reversed a termination under section 311(1) because it felt that under the circumstances there was insufficient evidence of a settled purpose of relinquishing parental claim. It then remanded the case to the lower court to allow the adopting parents to pursue the issue whether the natural parent had evidenced such a continued and irremedial parental incapacity as would justify a decree under section 311(2).[65]

An example of the successful use of section 311(2) is the *Appeal of Diane B.*[66] Even though the petition for adoption in that case was cast in the language of section 311(1), the court approved termination of parental rights under section 311(2). Although the facts in that case would not support a termination under section 311(1) because there was evidence of support and visitation sufficient to defeat the six month requirement of that section, the court had no difficulty in finding that this minimal conduct on the part of the parents would not defeat a termination under section 311(2). This suggests that proper preparation and reliance on section 311(2) will enable the courts to broaden its application when there is continued and irremedial parental incapacity, abuse, neglect or refusal.

---

62. *Id.* at 550-51, 297 A.2d at 121.
63. *Id.* at 551, 297 A.2d at 121.
64. 452 Pa. 165, 305 A.2d 36 (1973).
65. *Id.* at 171, 305 A.2d at 40.
66. 456 Pa. 429, 321 A.2d 618 (1974).

V. Conclusion

The foregoing discussion reflects the impact of the Adoption Act of 1970 on broadening the grounds for involuntary termination. Although the welfare and best interest of the child have not become determinative considerations, children who lack essential parental care, but who have not been totally abandoned, are more adoptable than ever before.

Parental fault remains, as it should, a significant element. An adoption, unlike a custody matter, is a final decision on the parent-child relationship. Unless we totally ignore parental rights and focus on what the state may deem best for the child, some concept of fault or inability of the parent must be maintained as part of the termination process.

718

Antecedents and Consequences of Parental Rights Termination for Abused and Neglected Children

ROBERT BORGMAN

A study of relationships between parental rights termination and placement demonstrates that adoption practice does not guarantee permanency for neglected and abused children, who may successfully resist or disrupt adoptive plans unacceptable to them.

Six-year-old Karen and her older brother have lived together in three foster homes since the court declared them neglected and ordered them removed from their mother's care three years ago. Their mother has failed to establish a home and has visited the children only twice. Officially, the father's whereabouts are unknown. After unsuccessful work with the mother, the protective service agency, which has legal custody of the children, petitioned the court for termination of the parents' rights so that these children might have the opportunity for permanent security in an adoptive home.

This sequence of planning and services has been recommended repeatedly in recent years and is now an accepted part of federal and state policy in child welfare services [7:571–80; 6:401–7; 11:22–25]. But will ter-

---

Robert Borgman, Ph.D., is Psychologist at The Children's Home, Winston-Salem, NC.

0009-4021/81/060391-14 $01.25 © Child Welfare League of America

mination of parental rights, followed by adoptive planning, guarantee Karen and her brother the security of "no more here and there" [3]?

Of those children placed in adoptive homes, an estimated 15%, the majority placed after age six [1:505–12; 8:32–38], will experience termination or disruption of the adoption and return to the placement agency [13:23–27]. What procedures would lead to more stable adoptive placement for older neglected or abused children? What alternatives are available for those children whose adoptions have failed or who have not been placed for adoption after a prolonged period of legal availability?

The purposes of this exploratory study are twofold: To identify consequences of parental rights termination (PRT) for neglected or abused children in relation to antecedent characteristics of children and parents and circumstances in the foster care process, and to indicate alternative plans for those children whose parental rights termination has not been followed by permanent adoptive placement. The author hopes that this knowledge will result in more constructive permanency planning for children and families who enter the foster care system.

Factors Influencing Adoption

Critics repeatedly allege that the foster care system is inattentive and indecisive about permanent planning for foster children, so that the child is neither returned to the family nor placed in an adoptive home [14:2–5]. This allegation raises questions about what specific relationships among foster families, children, biological families, and the agency retard the movement toward adoption or restoration of the child to the family.

Despite the inadequacies of the foster care system, the majority of children are returning to their parental families, usually within a year [5:467–83]. The question is why the minority remains in foster care. The quality of service surely affects whether a child returns home; so do the characteristics of the child and the family, as well as their external resources.

If child welfare workers follow the recommended sequence of service goals—first, attempts at rehabilitating the child's own family; then placement with relatives; and finally adoptive planning—foster children who become available for adoption are a residual group from the foster care population. Their families may have few internal and external resources for providing child care. Children who are not returning to their families are likely to have acquired the scantiest inner resources in early life for adapting successfully to an adoptive family. In addition, multiple changes in foster homes during prolonged foster care may compound whatever problems in behavior or personality the child brought into foster care.

Research Design

Records were reviewed for all 29 children placed in a group care setting from 1970 to 1979 whose parents' parental rights had been terminated either before or during this placement. The biological parents had lost all residual rights, and the children were available for adoption. The children's home served a 43-county area in the Piedmont region of the South, an industrial, urbanized area of small- and medium-sized cities.

These children had been placed in the custody of county protective service agencies following adjudication of neglect, abuse, or dependency. (The term "dependency" refers to a legal adjudication. In practice it encompasses children neither of whose parents could be located by the agency investigating a neglect or abuse complaint; or those children so adjudicated to avoid stigmatizing labels of neglect and abuse, or to avoid legal complications in proving neglect or abuse.) The children in this study represented a residual foster care population, having been placed in group foster care because of failure to adapt successfully in foster family care.

This group consisted of 13 boys and 16 girls. The parents of 25 were divorced, separated, widowed, or never married to each other at the time the child entered foster care. Their ages, characteristics of their foster care experience, and other attributes of their parents are presented in the section on results below.

These children formed three subgroups:

1) Ten had never entered an adoptive placement, although they were legally available for adoption. They had spent a median of 5 years, 9 months in foster care after termination of parental rights.

2) Nine had experienced an adoptive placement that was disrupted. Only two of these were subsequently placed in another adoptive family. These two are also included in the third group.

3) Twelve (including the two who had experienced a disruptive adoption) were discharged from the children's home into an adoptive family. These adoptions have been completed and at present appear stable.

Age and Foster Care Duration

Table 1 (see pages 400–401) compares the three subgroups according to variables of age and length of time in various periods of foster care, and also according to certain characteristics of parents and children and type of parental rights termination.

The results show no significant relationship between status of adoptive placement and the age of the child at entry into foster care, at termination of parental rights, or at adoptive placement. There is also no significant difference among subgroups in the length of time in foster care before PRT and between PRT and adoption, and in the total amount of time spent in foster care. There is no difference in the number of foster care placements experienced by the majority of children in each subgroup.

Typically, these children entered foster care shortly before kindergarten age, experienced PRT midway through elementary school, and entered an adoptive home on the brink of adolescence. The majority waited somewhat longer than a year for an adoptive home after they became legally free for adoption.

Characteristics of Parents

None of the mothers of these 29 children had ever been regularly employed at the same job for more than a year. The vocational history of nearly half of the fathers was unknown. Of those fathers whose employment was recorded, only one worked regularly at a skilled occupation. Three others worked regularly at unskilled laboring jobs. The others had no consistent employment record.

The median education for all mothers was ninth-grade, substantially below the twelfth-grade median of the adult population in the area. No mother in the total group had more than a tenth-grade education. Median education of fathers was also ninth-grade but was unknown for nearly half the fathers. Only one father was a high school graduate, and one had an eleventh-grade education.

There is considerable evidence that the educational attainment and employment records of parents are directly related to the quality of child care they provide [12:115]. Thus, the parents of these children available for adoption may represent a residual group of the least adequate parents, who neglect or abuse their children.

Nevertheless, there is a significant difference between the educational levels of mothers of children who had stable adoptive placements and mothers whose children's adoptions were disrupted (p < .05 by Fisher's Exact Test). The mothers of children in stable adoptions had the least adequate educations. Perhaps the mother's and the child's perceptions of maternal inadequacy helped both to accept adoption. In contrast, children whose mothers had more adequate educations may have been more likely to question the need for adoptive placement and retain stronger ties to the parent.

Characteristics of Children

Half of the 29 children showed intelligence levels significantly below average at PRT. However, there was no significant relationship between intellectual adequacy and adoptive status. Three youngsters obtained IQ scores below 70; one was involved in a stable adoption and the other two had disrupted adoptive placements.

Gross behavioral deviations were reported for 13 of the 29 children during foster care before PRT. Each of the 13 showed at least one of the following behaviors: public displays of heterosexual or homosexual sex acts, significant vandalism or repeated stealing, fire setting, assaultiveness upon adults, or running away.

Reported presence of at least one of these conduct disorders was significantly related to whether the child entered an adoptive placement; eight of the ten children with no adoptive placement showed such behavior in foster care, whereas only five of the 19 who entered adoptive homes did (p < .05 by Fisher's Exact Test).

Foster Care Experience

Initial placement for all these children was foster family care, which proved highly unstable. Twenty-four of the 29 children had lived in at least three foster homes before PRT. Reasons for moving children from foster home to foster home included unacceptability of the child's behavior to the foster family; poor communication and mutual distrust between foster parent and agency worker, with concomitant closing of the foster home; and crises within the foster family, such as death, serious illness, or marital conflict and separation of the foster parents.

Casework service rendered could best be described as a succession of expedient crisis interventions designed to ensure children a roof over their heads by sundown. With only a few exceptions, casework service did not appear to move in any goal-oriented direction either to rehabilitate the child's family, to terminate parental rights, or to seek remedies for the child's behavior or emotional problems.

This lack of planning did not seem to result so much from the foster care worker's inattention or indecisiveness as from the overwhelming need to stabilize the foster care placement or to locate another one. Workers also quite reasonably seemed hesitant to introduce the possibility of parental rights termination in the midst of upsets in the foster care placements. In view of the child's unstable foster care experience, the agency worker often lacked leverage (or feared she did) in relationships with the child's own family.

Policies of the foster care agencies prohibited the child's family from visiting at the foster home; the parents usually were not told where the child was living. The rationale for this policy was to protect the foster home from unplanned or disorderly intrusions by the family. Visits between child and family were arranged through the agency worker and took place either in the agency office or at some neutral location, usually during normal business hours, when the worker was available to furnish transportation.

Parents were usually reluctant or antagonistic about going through the agency for visits with their children in foster care. Their feelings were understandable, in view of the adversary nature of the neglect or abuse adjudication and the agency's participation in giving evidence to the court. Thus, in practice, children in foster care were officially inaccessible to their parents.

Some parents dealt with this by simply not visiting. But older children did know where their parents were, and often would call and visit them surreptitiously, sometimes with the collusion of the foster parents. (There was clear evidence of surreptitious visits between seven children and their parents.) Thus, children who were thought to have been officially abandoned were actually having much contact with their families outside the agency's influence. This pattern of surreptitious visits had important consequences for the child after parental rights termination.

Parental Rights Termination

Initiation of the process to terminate parental rights typically occurred about three years after the child entered foster care. The type of parental rights termination was strongly associated with stability of the adoptive placement. Both parents of seven of the 12 children in stable adoptive placements had signed voluntary consents for adoption. In contrast, parents of 18 of 19 children whose adoptions had been disrupted or who had remained without adoptive placement had had their rights terminated involuntarily by court order ($p < .01$ by Fisher's Exact Test). Parents and children may regard voluntary consent to adoption as a valuable gift to the child; they usually consider involuntary PRT a hostile act of disapproval by the agency and the court, and they may retaliate by undermining adoptive planning.

The mothers of all 18 children were located and attended their PRT hearings; the fathers of only five children attended. The parents of seven children appealed the initial court decisions, which were all upheld after a delay of about two years.

After the initial court order terminating parental rights, the protective service agencies invariably forbade any contact between parents and their children and often attempted to limit the children's involvement with other relatives and unrelated families as well. It was usually six months to four years before the child arrived in an adoptive home; during this time the child lacked officially sanctioned emotional support outside of the foster caretaker. In addition, the child was usually transferred to a specialized adoption worker or referred to a private adoption agency, losing even the support of the familiar foster care worker who had gone through the PRT process with him. Transferring the case caused additional delay, since the adoption worker also needed to become acquainted and form a relationship with the child. Occasionally, she was diverted into further efforts to stabilize the foster home placement, a task outside her specialty.

The time between PRT and arrival in an adoptive home was a stressful period for the child and foster parents, frequently marked by eruption of behavior problems. Those children who had been seeing their parents surreptitiously continued to do so after they became legally free for adoption.

Adoption

As adoptive planning proceeded, children showed understandable anxiety and suspicion about the unknown and a reluctance to move again. Some voiced concern about losing activities and relationships in the community that were important to them. Some were unwilling to relinquish contact with siblings and other relatives to whom they were attached when they were told, honestly, that continuation of such relationships could not be guaranteed in an adoptive home. Many felt that acceptance of adoption would be an expression of disloyalty toward the biological family, and older children often influenced their younger siblings in this belief.

The stable adoptive placements were more likely to reflect a resolution of these concerns. Previously mentioned was the finding that more children in stable adoptions than in the other subgroups had become legally adoptable by voluntary consent of their parents, which may have reduced their guilt about accepting adoption. In addition, stable adoptions were more likely to be in families with whom the child was already familiar. Seven of the 12 children in stable adoptions had been placed with families already known to the child: relatives, former foster parents, and, in one case, a family in which the adoptive mother had served as "big sister" to the child for three years. Only two of the nine children in disrupted adoptions had known the adoptive family before the placement.

All 12 of the children in stable adoptions had retained the same social worker through foster care, PRT, and adoption. Six of these had been placed by a private adoption agency whose social worker worked jointly with the foster care worker on the adoptive placement. In contrast, only two of the nine children whose adoptions had been disrupted had retained the same worker throughout the process.

Disrupted Adoption

Adoptive placements were disrupted for one or more of the following reasons: child's behavioral problems were neither remediable nor tolerable to the adoptive family; child could not accept adoption and/or the adoptive parents; the adoptive parents had crises such as debilitating illness or marital separation.

One year was the median time the child spent in adoptive placement before it was terminated. During this time the adoption workers provided support to the adoptive family and obtained mental health services for the child. Service to the child invariably focused upon changing the child's behavior, encouraging him or her to accept adoption, or modifying adoptive parents' feelings or reactions to the child's conduct.

The two children who entered adoption with gross behavioral deviations continued to display that behavior; an additional three youngsters began to show one or more of the gross behavioral problems specified above after they arrived in the adoptive home. In contrast, the gross behavioral problems of three youngsters in stable adoptions disappeared after the placement.

Table 2 (see page 401) shows the final placement for those children whose adoptions were disrupted and for those who never entered an adoptive placement. Three children whose initial adoptive placement was terminated were placed in a second adoptive home that proved stable for two. The second adoption attempt was also disrupted for one child, who was then returned to her initial adoptive family!

The Unadopted

Eight of the ten children never adopted continued to show serious behavior problems throughout their foster care experience. For three of them this resulted in their eventually being sent to a residual institution such as a mental or correctional facility. Failure to find adoptive placements for children with serious behavior problems is often ascribed to the deficient commitment, efforts, or skill of social workers in seeking such placements. However, the behavior problems of these children resulted in such instability of foster care placements that the worker was diverted from efforts either to seek treatment or to prepare for adoption, and was forced simply to prevent the child from being homeless.

In addition, these ten children persistently showed physical as well as psychological resistance to adoptive planning by running away and by physically refusing to meet prospective adoptive parents. Four eventually initiated a return to their mothers' homes with de facto planning from the protective service agency. All had surreptitiously visited their mothers during foster care.

Two other children never resolved their separation from their former foster parent, who was deemed too elderly to provide suitable care for them. They ended up in a residual institution. Two others entered a free foster care arrangement with community families who had befriended them over a period of time. One remained in group foster care until emancipation age.

Legal and social statuses are highly ambiguous for children with PRT who remain unadopted. They are officially parentless. While they may be nominally in the legal custody of the protective service agency, the majority in this study were beyond the effective care and control of that agency, but without sanctioned relationships to their parents. Laws

TABLE 1

Characteristics of Children by Adoptive Status

Variable	No. of children	Median IQ of child	Median education of mother, in grades	Median number homes before PRT
No adoptive placement	10	81	9th	4
Disrupted adoption	9*	84	10th	4
Stable adoption	12	84	8th	4
Total for sample	29	85	9th	4

*Includes two children who subsequently entered a stable adoption.

Age and Time in Years-Months

Variable	Median age entering foster care	Median age at PRT	Median age at adoption	Median time of foster care before PRT completed	Median time between PRT and adoption	Median time in foster care before adoption
No adoptive placement	4-11	9-11	–	3-4	–	–
Disrupted adoption	3-2	8-2	9-5	3-2	1-3	4-7
Stable adoption	4-1	9-0	11-3	2-11	1-3	5-6
Total for sample	4-11	9-11	11-8	3-4	1-3	4-7

Variable	% involuntary PRT	% with behavioral problems during foster care	% with behavioral problems in adoption
No adoptive placement	100	80	–
Disrupted adoption	89	22	56
Stable adoption	42	33	0
Total for sample	72	43	21

TABLE 2
Final Placement of Unadopted Children

Variable	Returned to biological mother	Free foster home	Licensed foster home	Emancipation	Subsequent adoption	Residual Institutional care
No Adoptive placement	4	2	–	1	–	3
Disrupted adoption	–	1	2	–	3	3
Total	4	3	2	1	3	6

governing PRT need clarification regarding children who have not been adopted. One scholar has proposed that no parental rights termination become final until the child is legally adopted [9:530–64].

Conclusions

First, much of the difficulty in permanency planning for children in this study appeared traceable to the instability and inappropriateness of the initial placement in foster family care. An alternative might have been an initial, time-limited placement in a small, professionally staffed group care facility accessible to visits by the child's parents. In this context, reactions to the child's behavior problems might be more constructive and corrective, and problems arising in parental visits might be used constructively in attempts to rehabilitate the child's family. The stability of such an initial placement would thereby free protective service workers to pursue plans to reestablish the family or to select other long-term arrangements for the child.

Second, the majority of children in this study strongly resisted adoption, either explicitly, or implicitly through the emergence or exacerbation of behavioral problems when adoption was proposed or took place. Behavioral problems in this context have sometimes been viewed as defenses against pain and grief about "losing" the biological parents [2:196–99; 10:175–81]. For some children, permanent guardianship might have been more appropriate than adoption [4:1165–94]. Under permanent guardianship, as under adoption, the biological parents are legally prevented from ever asserting claims to resuming custody of the child. The placement is also freed from supervision or control by the court or agency. However, unlike adoption, parents and children retain residual rights specified in the court order granting the guardianship. These may include parents' and relatives' rights to visit the child, the child's right to retain the family's name, and the right to inherit property from the family. Permanent guardianship allows children to expand relationships and broaden psychological identity without having to lose a heritage of relationships and rights.

Third, involuntary termination of parental rights by court order seemed to create more serious problems for the children than it solved. The adversary nature of the proceedings and their length left the child in a limbo of anxiety and heightened loyalty conflicts in relation to the parents, grief about losing them, and hostility toward the agency seeking the termination. The effort invested by the agency in such proceedings might have been more effectively spent in developing relationships with the parents to obtain voluntary consent to the child's adoption.

Last, the final resting place for nearly all these children, adopted or not, was with familiar families: relatives, former foster families, or persons with whom the child had developed relationships long before parental rights were terminated. The unpleasant alternative was life in a residual institution. In view of this, the author believes that efforts to place older children in adoptive homes far from their communities of origin are at best of questionable value.

This study demonstrates that termination of parental rights, whether or not followed by adoptive placement, is no guarantor of permanency and security for the child. In theory, all children may be potentially "adoptable," but in practice the probability is unacceptably low for finding adoptive parents who are willing and able to cope constructively with children who show grossly unacceptable behavior. This study also demonstrates the persistence and resourcefulness of children in successfully determining their own ultimate placement when adoptive planning is unacceptable to them. ♦

References

1. Bass, Celia. "Matchmaker-Matchmaker: Older Child Adoption Failures." Child Welfare LIV (July 1975).

2. Boyne, John. "A Mental Health Note in Adoption of School Age Children." Child Welfare LVII (March 1978).

3. Carney, Ann. No More Here and There. Chapel Hill, NC: University of North Carolina Press, 1976.

4. Derdeyn, Peter; Rogoff, William; and Williams, Robert. "Alternatives to Absolute Termination of Parental Rights After Long Term Foster Care." Vanderbilt Law Review XXXI (October 1978).

5. Fanshel, David. "Children Discharged from Foster Care in New York City." Child Welfare LVII (September/October 1978)..

6. Jones, Martha L. "Aggressive Adoption: A Program's Effect on a Child Welfare Agency." Child Welfare LVI (June 1977).

7. _____. "Stopping Foster Care Drift: A Review of Legislation and Special Programs." Child Welfare LVII (November 1978).

8. Kadushin, Alfred, and Seidl, Frederick. "Adoption Failure: A Social Work Postmortem." Social Work XVI (July 1971).

9. Ketchener, Oscar, and Babcock, Richard. "Statutory Standards for the Involuntary Termination of Parental Rights." Rutgers Law Review XXIX (April 1976).

10. Littner, Ner. "The Importance of the Natural Parents to the Child in Placement." Child Welfare LIV (March 1975).

11. Pike, Victor. "Permanent Planning for Foster Children: the Oregon Project." Children Today V (November/December 1976).

12. Polansky, Norman; Borgman, Robert; and DeSaix, Christine. Roots of Futility. San Francisco: Jossey-Bass, 1972.

13. Rooney, Rita. "When Child Adoption Doesn't Work." Parade Magazine (March 4, 1979).

14. Wiltse, Kermit T. "Decision Making Needs in Foster Care." Children Today V (November/December 1976).

(*Address requests for a reprint to Robert Borgman, P.O. Box 993, Winston-Salem, NC 27102.*)

JOURNAL OF FAMILY LAW
University of Louisville School of Law

Volume Twenty	1981-82	Number Two

REPRESENTING ABUSED AND NEGLECTED CHILDREN: WHEN PROTECTING CHILDREN MEANS SEEKING THE DISMISSAL OF COURT PROCEEDINGS

by Douglas J. Besharov*

I. Introduction

In the past six years, over forty states have changed their laws or court procedures to provide for the independent representation of children who are the subjects of child protective proceedings.[1]

---

* J.D., 1968, New York University; LL.M., 1971, New York University. The author was the first director of the National Center on Child Abuse and Neglect. He is presently Guest Scholar at The Brookings Institution. The opinions expressed herein are solely those of the author.

[1] *Oversight Hearings on Title I—Child Abuse Prevention and Treatment and Adoption Reform Act of 1978, Before the Subcommittee on Select Education*

Formal descriptions of the role of the child's representative in a child protective proceeding are unanimous in stating that the representative, whether an attorney or a lay guardian ad litem,[2] must make an independent appraisal of the facts and then "exert his efforts to secure an ultimate resolution of the case which, in his judgment, will best serve the interests of his client."[3]

Although such statements suggest that the child's representative may decide that continuing the court proceeding itself is not in the child's interest, there is an almost universal tendency to assume that he will support the need for court action. This is a natural assumption since the impetus to appoint independent representatives for children has come from cases in which the court's failure to protect obviously endangered children led to their further injury and even death.[4] Furthermore, there is a reasonable assumption that if a child protective agency has filed a petition the child's interests must require court action. All regular participants in court proceedings know that child protective agencies initiate court action "only as a last resort"—when other efforts to protect the children through

---

of the House Committee on Education and Labor, 96th Cong., 2d Sess. 198 (1980) (statement of Cesar A. Perales). *But compare* Johnson, *Statutory Provisions Regarding the Guardian Ad Litem Mandate: Some Findings from a Regionwide Survey of Judges in the Southeast*, 3 Juv. & Fam. Ct. J. 15 (1979), reporting on some deficiencies in implementation.

   [2] A word on terminology: Statutes and court rules differ among the states on whether an attorney or a lay guardian ad litem should be appointed. Because this Article treats their roles as essentially equivalent when it comes to seeking the dismissal of the proceedings (*see* the text accompanying note 36, *infra*), it uses the neutral term: the "child's representative."

   [3] Isaacs, *The Role of the Lawyer in Representing Minors in the New Family Court*, 12 Buffalo L. Rev. 501, 504 (1963); *see also* Fraser, *Independent Legal Representative For The Abused And Neglected Child: The Guardian Ad Litem*, 13 Cal. W.L. Rev. 16, 29 (1976-77), stating that the guardian ad litem is "to do everything in his power to insure a judgment that is in the child's best interests." *But see* Family Court Branch, New York Legal Aid Society, Manual For New Attorneys 218-19 (undated), discussed in the text accompanying note 45, *infra*.

   [4] *See, e.g.*, Comment, *A Child's Right To Independent Counsel In Custody Proceedings: Providing Effective "Best Interests": Determination Through The Use of a Legal Advocate*, 6 Seton Hall L. Rev. 303, 303-04 (1975).

voluntarily accepted services have failed.[5] (Nationally, less than twenty percent of all cases reported to the authorities reach the court.)[6] Even defense counsel acknowledge that most cases that do not belong in court are diverted by this extensive screening.

However, this diversionary process does not keep every inappropriate case out of court. The process may have malfunctioned or may have been bypassed, new facts may have been discovered, or the parents' improved ability to care for the child may have gone unnoticed during the pendency of the proceeding. Hence, in certain limited—but by no means uncommon—situations, court action may not be in the child's interest. In fact, because of the unavoidable emotional trauma of formal court proceedings and the often severe deficiencies of existing treatment programs, formal court action may be potentially harmful. In such circumstances, representing the child, and protecting his interests, may mean seeking the dismissal of the proceedings.

To adequately protect the children he represents, the child's representative must be able to recognize such situations and deal with them effectively. Unfortunately, this aspect of the role of the child's representative has received scant attention because the more common problem he faces is to ensure that prompt and effective court action is taken to protect an endangered child. As a result, the child's representative is frequently unprepared to mount the effort needed to get an inappropriate case dismissed. He may feel unqualified to disagree with the "experts" in the child protective agency, especially if he lacks wide experience in child protective proceedings. After all, if he is wrong, he could jeopardize the child's safety and future development. Institutional and collegial pressures to go along with the

---

[5] For a further discussion of this process, *see* text accompanying note 23, *infra.*

[6] U.S. DEP'T OF HEALTH AND HUMAN SERVICES, NATIONAL CENTER ON CHILD ABUSE AND NEGLECT, NATIONAL ANALYSIS OF OFFICIAL CHILD NEGLECT AND ABUSE REPORTING 38 (1980).

system make such decisions even more difficult to reach and sustain.

By identifying the five major types of cases in which the child's interests may require the dismissal of the proceeding, this Article seeks to assist and support the child's representative in making this fateful decision.

II.   CASES WHERE THE CHILD'S INTERESTS MAY REQUIRE DISMISSAL

A.   Case #1: When There Is No Persuasive Evidence That The Child Is Abused or Neglected

One purpose of the extensive pre-court screening of child protective cases is to ensure that only legally sufficient cases are brought to court. But, because the decision to file a petition is usually made by a protective worker or someone else not trained in the legal requirements of evidentiary proof, in many cases: (1) the allegations fall outside the jurisdictional statute, or (2) there is insufficient admissible evidence to prove the allegations. Even when legal counsel reviews cases before they are filed, institutional and community pressures in serious cases (as well as carelessness and plain mistakes) can lead to the filing of an unprovable case.

What should the child's representative do if, after his own assessment of the case, he concludes it is legally insufficient? Some authorities suggest that he do nothing. One New York court, for example, stated that:

> At the outset of the case, a Law Guardian [the title of the lawyer who serves as the child's representative], who in addition to his role as counsel, advocate and guardian serves also in a quasi-judicial capacity in that he has some responsibility, at least during the dispositional phase of the proceeding, to aid the court in arriving at the proper disposition, should, like the judge, be neutral. At some point in the hearing he has a right to formulate an opinion and then to attempt to persuade the Court to adopt that disposition which, in his judgment, will best promote his ward's interest. But certainly the Law Guardian's conclusions in these matters should not be reached in advance of a hearing and

without knowledge of the facts.[7]

The troubling aspect of this decision is that by holding the child's representative cannot form an opinion concerning the interests of the child in advance of an adjudicatory hearing, it seems to equate obtaining "knowledge of the facts" with the actual court hearing. However, unlike the judge, whose knowledge of the facts is limited to the evidence which is introduced during court proceedings, the child's representative can and should learn a great deal about the case prior to the trial—by informally reviewing the evidence with the petitioner, by interviewing the child, and by performing his own further investigation. It is naive to expect him to withhold judgment about the merits of the case, and it is unfair to the child to deny him the benefit of his representative's informed advocacy.

Therefore, the child's representative has an affirmative obligation to determine the legal sufficiency of the case, albeit a tentative one, and to take such action as is required. If the child's representative can correct the legal insufficiency, he should seek to do so. Many times, crucial evidence has been overlooked by the child protective agency (after all, their primary purpose is to provide social services, not to be legal investigators). Hospital records, school teachers, neighbors and relatives can often provide persuasive evidence in support of the petition.

If the legal insufficiency cannot be corrected, what should the child's representative do? Ordinarily, he can expect the parents' attorney to seek a dismissal. But if the parents are not represented, or if for some reason their attorney does not seek a dismissal, the child's representative must decide whether he should do so. A trial that results in a dismissal is not in the child's interests (nor in anyone else's) since it needlessly causes emotional stress and uncertainty. A trial can rupture already fragile family structures, especially if relatives are forced to testify against each

---

[7] *In re* Apel, 96 Misc. 2d 839, ___, 409 N.Y.S.2d 928, 930 (Fam. Ct. 1978).

other. Forcing a child to testify against his parents can be even more devastating. On the other hand, failure to pursue a case, even if it is technically insufficient, may leave an endangered child unprotected.

Hence, in deciding whether to seek the dismissal of a legally insufficient case, the child's representative must carefully assess the nature of its insufficiency. If the failure of proof is caused by the inadmissibility of otherwise persuasive evidence, and if the child's representative believes that the child is in danger, as the *child's* representative, he is under no obligation to seek the dismissal of the case, although a prosecutor might be.[8] In such cases, the child's representative should allow the case to continue, while pressing efforts to find supporting evidence. (Nevertheless, it may be advisable to attempt to convince the parents to accept a referral for voluntary treatment services,[9] especially since the case is probably in court only because they refused a prior offer of services.)

Cases on the borderline of legal sufficiency should also go to trial. At the trial, the child's representative "should seek to introduce all relevant evidence, pro and con, which has been overlooked by, or is unavailable to, other counsel or the court, and challenge by appropriate objection and cross examination the reliability of all evidence, pro and con, which is offered by other counsel or the court—to the

---

[8] The response of the child's representative to a motion by the parents to dismiss such cases must be determined on a case by case basis, but certainly it must be governed by his obligation to fully and candidly present the facts, as he understands them, to the court. *Compare* AMERICAN BAR ASSOCIATION, CODE OF PROFESSIONAL RESPONSIBILITY EC 7-13 (1970): "The responsibility of a public prosecutor differs from that of the usual advocate; his duty is to seek justice, not merely to convict." *See also* Brady v. Maryland, 373 U.S. 83 (1963): "Society wins not only when the guilty are convicted but when criminal trials are fair; our system of administration of justice suffers when any accused is treated unfairly . . .. The [prosecution] wins its points whenever justice is done its citizens in the courts." *Id.* at 87.

[9] The reasons this is possible are discussed in connection with the case when the child can be adequately protected by parents' voluntary acceptance of services, beginning at text accompanying note 23, *infra.*

end that the court will have all (and only) reliable evidence upon which to make its decision . . .."[10] Once again though, the best resolution of such situations may well be a referral for voluntarily accepted services.

However, if the child's representative finds no evidence—whether legally admissible or not—to support the petition, then he has no reason for believing that the child is in danger. If there is no reason to believe that the child is in danger, then there is no justification for putting the child and the family through the emotional trauma of a court trial—and the child's representative should seek dismissal of the case.

B. Case #2: When The Child, Although Previously Abused or Neglected, Is In No Danger of Further Maltreatment

The reason society intervenes in situations of child abuse and neglect is obviously to protect children. That is why it is called "child protective intervention." But from what are children being protected? The aim can certainly not be to protect them from harm that has already occurred (although government intervention is sometimes needed so that the effects of past maltreatment can be remedied, and the severity of past maltreatment sometimes requires the criminal prosecution of the parents).[11] Rather, civil child protective proceedings seek to protect children from *further or future harm.* For example, Georgia law describes the purpose of its child protective procedures to be "the protection of children whose health and welfare are adversely affected *and further threatened* by the conduct of those responsible for their care and protection."[12]

---

[10] MANUAL FOR NEW ATTORNEYS, *supra* note 3, at 218.

[11] Even criminal prosecutions have as their justification "prevention"—prevention before the maltreatment occurs through the deterrent effect penal sanctions are said to have on the population generally, and prevention of a reoccurence of the maltreatment through the incarceration of the offending parent or the provisions of rehabilitative services.

[12] GA. CODE ANN. § 74-111(e) (Supp. 1978) (emphasis added).

Civil statutory definitions of "child abuse" and "child neglect," however, do not focus solely on the question of whether the child is sufficiently "endangered" to justify state intervention. Although they all are careful to include children whose health or well-being is endangered or threatened with harm, statutes tend to concentrate on descriptions of past parental conduct which has already harmed the child. Indeed, simply calling the child an "abused child" or a "neglected child" suggests that the abuse or neglect has already happened.

Since the purpose of child protective intervention is to protect endangered children, such definitions are frequently criticized as examples of fuzzy thinking. The Institute of Judicial Administration - American Bar Association Juvenile Justice Standards Project, for example, proposed that this entire area of court jurisdiction be relabeled "child endangerment."[13] But the focus on past maltreatment has a valid purpose. To decide that a child is endangered, that is, in danger of future maltreatment, one must make a *prediction of future parental* conduct. Such predictions are no more than probabilistic assessments based on our admittedly shaky ability to understand the forces that shape future human behavior, and they make most child protective professionals and courts uncomfortable. Hence, to minimize the ethical and practical pitfalls of such blatant predictions of human behavior, definitions focus on the past maltreatment. This adds one concrete element to an otherwise amorphous decisionmaking process because past parental conduct is a valid indicator of future parental conduct.

This focus on the past maltreatment tends to obscure the reason for child protective intervention—the need to protect the child from future harm. Consequently, agencies and courts sometimes intervene when there is no danger of

---

[13] JUVENILE JUSTICE STANDARDS PROJECT, INSTITUTE OF JUDICIAL ADMINISTRATION/AMERICAN BAR ASSOCIATION, STANDARDS RELATING TO ABUSE AND NEGLECT 48 (Tent. draft 1977). *See also* N.Y. PENAL LAW § 260.10 (1980), entitled "Endangering the welfare of a child."

future of further maltreatment. The IJA/ABA Juvenile Justice Standards Project described two such situations:

> First, there may be some cases where the child was injured by a parent, but the evidence indicates there is little danger of future harm. For example, a child may be physically injured by a parent in a moment of anger, but all evidence indicates that this was a one-time event and supervision is unnecessary to protect the child.
>
> Second, coercive intervention may be inappropriate in cases where the parents' and child's situation has changed from the time the court petition was initially filed. For example, a very young child may not have been adequately protected because his/her parent worked and left the child without a caretaker. However, since the filing of the petition, the child has been placed in a day care center and now is adequately protected.[14]

Some observers have responded to such situations by saying that it does not hurt to take jurisdiction over them. They reason that, if the danger to the child is small, it is unlikely that the child will be removed from the home, and court supervision is a painless way of ensuring that the child will be safe in the future. But it is not painless. In addition to the unavoidable stress of court proceedings, the stigma of a formal adjudication can have a devastating effect on the family and, therefore, on the child.[15] Moreover, the process of court supervision, though not as traumatic as removal, can place an added strain on an already tenuous family situation.

> The presence of a caseworker supervising parental behavior can interfere with the psychological system of the family. For example, caseworkers may pressure parents into substituting the caseworker's views regarding childrearing for their own. Yet, the caseworker may not allow for cultural differences in childrearing, or take into account the way in which a child has adapted to "bad" parental behavior. As a result of external pressure, a parent may become uncertain in dealing with the child and move from one pole to another in behavior management techniques—from permissiveness to authoritarianism—or begin to

---

[14] IJA/ABA ABUSE AND NEGLECT STANDARDS, *supra* note 13, at 63-64.

[15] *See generally* E. M. SCHUR, LABELLING DEVIANT BEHAVIOR: ITS IMPLICATIONS (1971).

"scapegoat" the child, who is seen as the source of trouble.[16]

Lastly, there is still the possibility that the child will be removed—as child protective and court officials overreact to the severity of the past maltreatment.

Because these are the unavoidable costs of court intervention, the IJA/ABA Juvenile Justice Standards require that: "In order to assume jurisdiction, a court should . . . have to find that intervention is necessary to protect the child from being endangered in the future."[17] Similarly, since 1962 the New York Family Court Act has authorized the court to dismiss a petition even if "facts sufficient to sustain the petition" are established, if "the court concludes that its aid is not required on the record before it."[18] *In re G.*[19] dramatically illustrates the degree of discretion this section vests in the family court—no matter how serious the maltreatment. The case came to the attention of child protective authorities after the respondent mother placed her newborn child in a waste receptacle on Wall Street and left the infant there. The infant was taken to a hospital where it was found to be in good health. Two weeks later, after the child protective agency had made a home visit, and with the court's permission, the infant was returned to the mother's custody. Two months later, the respondent, *joined by the attorney for the child,* moved to dismiss the petition on the ground that "it failed to state that the court's aid or assistance was in any way required under Section 1051(c) . . .."[20] Even though this issue is usually addressed at the conclusion of the factfinding hearing, the court held a hearing to consider the respondent's motion.

---

[16] Wald, *State Intervention on Behalf of "Neglected" Children: A Search For Realistic Standards,* 27 Stan. L. Rev. 985, 999 (1975) (footnotes omitted).

[17] Standard 2.2, IJA/ABA Abuse and Neglect Standards, *supra* note 13, at 63.

[18] N.Y. Fam. Ct. Act § 1051(c) (McKinney 1975). It should be noted that this authority is limited to cases of child neglect; it does not apply to cases of child abuse.

[19] *In re G.,* 91 Misc. 2d 911, 398 N.Y.S.2d 975 (Fam. Ct. 1977).

[20] *Id.* at 912-13, 398 N.Y.S.2d at 976.

The court heard extensive evidence from a variety of law enforcement, child protective, and social services agencies as well as the respondent's babysitter. (The child protective agency had made eight home visits during the two-month period; the Visiting Nurse Service had made five visits.) All agreed that there was "no present neglect but, on the contrary, a normal, healthy and affectionate parent-child relationship."[21] Holding that there was "no evidence in this record to persuade [the] court that respondent or her children are presently or will in the future be in need of [the] court's aid or assistance," the court dismissed the petition.[22]

Admittedly, situations in which a previously abused or neglected child is not in danger of further maltreatment are rare—and rightfully difficult to prove. But when they arise, the child's representative must be prepared to protect the child's interest in being free from unnecessary state intervention. Even in the absence of a statute which gives the court the explicit authority to disregard instances of past maltreatment, the child's representative should not hesitate to seek the dismissal of the proceeding, *if* it can be established that the child is not in danger of further maltreatment. Most courts are willing to consider this common sense approach, for they too are aware of the serious harm that even well meaning state intervention can cause.

C. Case #3: When The Child Can Be Adequately Protected By The Parents' Voluntary Acceptance Of

---

[21] *Id.* at 914, 398 N.Y.S.2d at 977.

[22] *Id.* While there is no reason to question the soundness of the court's determination, given the extreme level of emotional disturbance (and disregard for her child's safety) reflected in the mother's original behavior in abandoning her newborn on a city street, it is unfortunate that the court's opinion does not explain why the court did not expect the mother to engage in similarly dangerous behavior in the future. The disturbance may well have been a transitory one, but the evidence supporting such a conclusion is neither described nor alluded to in the opinion. *Compare In re* Forman, 75 Misc. 2d 348, 349, 347 N.Y.S.2d 319, 320 (Fam. Ct. 1973), in which the court described how the respondent had "fully rehabilitated herself."

Services[23]

Many abusive or neglectful parents can be helped to adequately care for their children without resort to court action. In fact, treatment services are most effective when they are voluntarily accepted. When parents understand their need for help and willingly accept it, they are more motivated to make the personal commitment required for treatment to work.

Recognizing this, child protective agencies seek the voluntary participation of parents in treatment by offering a range of services designed to help them meet their child-rearing responsibilities. Many of these services, such as day-care, are a concrete effort to relieve the pressures and frustrations of parenthood. Individual and family counseling services are also used to relieve personal or psychological problems and marital tension. Referrals are also made to family service agencies, mental health clinics, hospitals, and other social and child welfare agencies. Recently, a large number of Parents Anonymous groups have been established, and often a referral is made to one of them. If the parent is an alcoholic or drug addict, he may be referred for detoxification and rehabilitation. Although foster care for children is also considered a "service" that is "offered" to parents for their voluntary acceptance, it is deemed necessary in only about fifteen percent of all cases.[24]

Therefore, even in cases of serious maltreatment where there is ample evidence to establish court jurisdiction, unless the parents are deemed to need a structured treatment atmosphere that only the court's authority can provide (which is rarely the case), most child protective agencies in-

---

[23] This section describes the process through which a case is dismissed as the result of the parents' agreement to accept voluntary, non-court treatment services. It does not discuss plea negotiations in which the charges are reduced (or the allegations softened) in return for a parental guilty plea or admission of responsibility.

[24] NATIONAL ANALYSIS OF OFFICIAL CHILD NEGLECT AND ABUSE REPORTING, *supra* note 6, at 36.

itiate court action only when parents refuse treatment ser-vices.[25] Hence, in almost all cases, court action is com-menced only because: (1) the parents have refused to accept treatment services (including foster care), and, (2) the child protective agency decides that, to protect the child, it needs the court's authority either to remove a child from the home or to impose treatment services. (Court action to ob-tain services that are otherwise not available to the child protective agency seem utterly inappropriate. While this is necessary in some states, the preferable procedure, if not the constitutionally mandated procedure, is to offer these services without the harmful impact of a court adjudication.)

Given this commitment to prior offers of treatment ser-vices, many practitioners assume that by the time a case reaches court it is no longer possible to divert a case for voluntarily accepted services. But this is far from true. Di-version is always possible, even after an adjudication. First, despite the system's general commitment to pretrial diver-sion, in a particular case no real effort may have been made to offer the services that would have prevented court action. For example, the case may have been especially serious or notorious, or the person who made the report may have in-sisted that a petition be filed, and no one in the child pro-tective agency may have been willing to accept responsibil-ity for an informal referral. However, by the time the case reaches court, cooler heads may be willing to treat the situ-ation normally.

Second, as the prospect of a trial approaches, the par-ents may be much more amenable to accepting a service they previously rejected. It is not just a question of their agreeing to the placement of their children in foster care, although that frequently happens. A surprising number of

---

[25] Sometimes, initial parental cooperation is not enough to keep a family out of court; the parents' care of the child may not improve or may even worsen dur-ing the period of contact with the child protective agency, but they may refuse to "voluntarily" place their child in foster care, thereby necessitating court action.

parents are brought to court because they rejected relatively innocuous services such as day care and homemakers. While parents have a right to reject even these beneficent governmental intrusions, most will change their minds when the nature of the service and the consequences of their refusal are explained to them. (Explaining these realities is an important function of the parents' counsel.) If it appears that a voluntary referral is possible, the child's representative therefore may explore it with the parents' attorney as well as the petitioner. If the parents are not represented, approaching the parents may be practically and ethically more difficult, but, if a voluntary referral is in the child's interest, the effort should be made.

Third, the child protective agency can sometimes be convinced to accept an informal resolution of the case different from the one it originally offered the parents. The "service" most often rejected by parents is, of course, foster care. But even in such cases, where the child protective agency has presumably concluded that removal of the child is essential to his protection, the agency may be willing to modify its position if it is persuaded that the initial decision was wrong or that the family situation has changed since the initial decision was made. If the legal sufficiency of the case is in doubt, the agency has an additional incentive to seek an informal resolution that at least provides some treatment services to the family.

Such opportunities to divert a case, when coupled with the emotional trauma that unavoidably accompanies formal court action, place an affirmative obligation on the child's representative to assess the viability of an informal resolution of the proceeding. In doing so, he must keep in mind that such referrals for voluntary services remove the family from the child protection system's formal monitoring, poor as it might be. If the parents do not do well in treatment—or drop out of treatment altogether—it is unlikely that corrective action will be taken, unless the family happens to be reported again. Hence, in deciding where the child's interests lie, the child's representative must assume that, unless some kind of child protective agency followup can be arranged,[26] the child and his family will be on their own. Despite this troubling reality, he may decide that the child's interests can be adequately protected by the parents' voluntary acceptance of treatment services.

D. *Case #4: When The Harmful Effects Of Intervention Outweigh The Danger The Child Faces From His Parents*

Child protective proceedings are initiated, as their name implies, to "protect" the victims of child abuse and neglect. The early identification of cases resulting from the recent dramatic increases in reporting has prevented many thousands of children from suffering serious injury and death. As Ruth and Henry Kempe note: "Not only are more cases being reported—they are of a milder nature, suggesting that families are being helped sooner. In Denver, the number of hospitalized abused children who die from their injuries has dropped from 20 a year (between 1960 and 1975) to less than one a year."[27] This improvement is not limited to Denver, which has long been the center of much innovation in the field. In New York State, for example, under a comprehensive reporting law that also mandated the creation of specialized child protective units, there has been a fifty percent reduction in fatalities, from about 200 a year to under 100.[28]

Unfortunately, while courts and child protective agencies are increasingly able to protect children from immediate or life threatening harm, they usually can do so only by removing the child from the home. Existing programs often are unable to provide the treatment services needed to break patterns of intergenerational abuse and neglect by helping parents provide the physical, emotional, and cogni-

---

[26] *Compare* N.Y.FAM. CT. ACT § 1039 (McKinney 1975), which provides for a judicially monitored "adjournment in contemplation of dismissal."

[27] R. S. KEMPE & C. H. KEMPE, CHILD ABUSE 8 (1978).

[28] N.Y.S. DEPT. OF SOCIAL SERVICES, CHILD PROTECTIVE SERVICES IN NEW YORK STATE, 1979 ANNUAL REPORT, Table 8 (1980).

tive care that children need. More disquieting than the inability of existing programs to improve family situations is the undisputed evidence that they often harm the children they are meant to protect. Too many families suffer the trauma of home investigation, are forced to agree to treatment, and then are forgotten. Although only about fifteen percent of the children in the system are placed in foster care, for these children, it may be years before they are returned home. (More than half of the children placed in foster homes remain in this "temporary" status for over two years; more than twenty percent are in foster care for more than six years.) During this time, many of them are placed in a sequence of ill suited foster homes, denying them the consistent support and nurturing they so desperately need. The resulting emotional scars that many of these children carry into adult life make them a continuing burden on the full range of community welfare, mental health, and social service systems. With good cause, Goldstein, Freud, and Solnit, in their book, *Before the Best Interests of the Child*, concluded: "By its intervention the state may make a bad situation worse; indeed, it may even turn a tolerable or even a good situation into a bad one."[29]

Therefore, in deciding whether court action is in the child's interest, his representative must weigh the danger the child faces from his parents against the possible harmful effects of intervention. The notion that child protective intervention should be authorized only when it will "do more good than harm"[30] is not a new one; neither is the notion that the child's representative must balance the relative benefits and harms involved. For example, North Carolina law specifies that one of the "duties" of a guardian ad litem is "to serve the child and the court by protecting and promoting the best interests of and the least detrimental

---

[29] J. GOLDSTEIN, A. FREUD & A. SOLNIT, BEFORE THE BEST INTERESTS OF THE CHILD 13 (1980).

[30] IJA/ABA ABUSE AND NEGLECT STANDARDS, *supra* note 13, at 40.

alternative for the child . . .."[31]

Discussions of the need to avoid a harmful intervention usually operate on the implicit assumption that some "lesser" intervention will be in the child's interest, assuming that the child is indeed in danger. However, there are times when *any* conceivable intervention will cause more harm than the child otherwise faces. For example, an older adolescent who has weathered the storms of parental abuse and neglect may be ready or about ready to leave home. For him, even casework supervision may complicate a tense family situation that is best left alone. Similarly, when the cause of the abuse or neglect is the parent's inability to cope with the child's developmental disabilities, the child may be better served by enrollment in a special education program.

There are times when the child's interest in being free of court intervention is clear. But, in most cases, the balance of harms and benefits is far more ambiguous. First, predicting the quality of the parents' future care for the child, and the harm that it may cause, is a subjective and uncertain process.[32] Second, it is often equally difficult to predict the effects of the intervention; many parents and children are helped by court-imposed treatment services. Further complicating matters is the fact that there may be two, three, four, or more children in the same family, each of whose interests may conflict. Although an adjudication may not be in the interests of an older child ready to enter adult society, the safety of younger children in the same family may well depend on an adjudication and a proper order of disposition.

Because of these ambiguities—and the hesitancy everyone feels about saying a child is better off if society does nothing—many cases in which intervention may do more

---

[31] N.C. GEN. STAT. § 7A-283 (Supp. 1977) (repealed). Similar provisions are now contained in N.C. GEN. STAT. § 7A-586 (Cum. Supp. 1979).

[32] *See* text accompanying note 13, *supra*.

harm than good are resolved through the parents' referral
to voluntary services. Unlike the situations discussed in the
previous section, such referrals give the illusion of doing
"something" to protect the child when they are really only
a practical escape from a no-win situation. Many patently
improbable referrals are made because the charade of a referral allows the system to ignore its inability to help the
child. But such referrals tend to obscure the true consideration at stake, namely, that given the deficiencies of existing
treatment programs, the child is likely to be harmed by societal intervention. When a meaningful referral is not possible, this obfuscation makes it doubly difficult for the child's
representative to convince the "system" that the child's interests require an outright dismissal of the case.

E. Case #5: When A Child Of Sufficient Maturity Requests That The Petition Be Dismissed

Up to now, in discussing the circumstances that may
require the dismissal of court proceedings, this Article has
ignored the wishes of the child. If the child is an infant or
of tender years, his representative necessarily must make a
decision in the absence of any guidance from the child,[33]
although children as young as four or five can often shed
significant light on the quality of the home situation and
the consequent need for court intervention.

At some point, the child reaches sufficient maturity so
that his wishes—whether or not in agreement with those of
his legal representative—must be taken into account, even
if he wants the proceeding dismissed. For example, if a sixteen year old who has been beaten by his father concludes
that he would rather not have his family put through the
strain of a full-blown trial, if he thinks he would be better
off if the incident is simply forgotten, perhaps he is right.[34]

---

[33] For a discussion of whether the child's representative should make such
decisions on his own, *see* text accompanying note 44, *infra*.

[34] Actually, older children often wish to be placed out of their homes, so that
they can escape what they consider to be an impossible family situation. However,

In any event, he has a right to have his point of view forcefully expressed to the court. As Vincent DeFrancis, long a strong advocate for more effective intervention in child abuse and neglect cases, points out:

> Children have very real and legitimate feelings and are entitled to have those feelings respected. At minimum, this requires procedures which ensure that the child has meaningful input into the process which determines his future. Since it is the judicial process which ultimately makes such a determination, the child needs someone to serve effectively as an advocate for his wishes and feelings in the judicial forum.[35]

The need to respect the wishes of a sufficiently mature child is usually discussed in relation to his representation by an attorney. For example, the IJA/ABA Juvenile Justice Standards provide that: "Where counsel is appointed to represent a juvenile subject to child protective proceedings, and the juvenile is capable of considered judgment on his or her own behalf, determination of the client's interest in the proceeding should ultimately remain the client's responsibility, after full consultation with counsel."[36] However, even if the child's representative is a lay guardian ad litem, it seems difficult to deny that at some age the child has a right to have his views considered. Would that not be the role of a wise parent or guardian? In child custody litigation, consideration of a sufficiently mature child's wishes is sometimes expressly guaranteed. California has a typical statute; it provides: "If a child is of sufficient age and capacity to reason so as to form an intelligent preference as to custody, the court shall consider and give due weight to his wishes in making an award of custody or modification thereof."[37]

---

such cases are beyond the scope of this Article.

[35] V. DeFrancis & C. Lucht, Child Abuse Legislation in the 1970's, 186 (rev. ed. 1974).

[36] Institute of Judicial Administration/American Bar Association, Juvenile Justice Standards, Standards Relating to Counsel For Private Parties, 79 (1980) (Standard 3.1(b)(ii)[b]); *compare* ABA Code of Professional Responsibility EC 7-7 (1974).

[37] Cal. Civ. Code § 4600 (West Supp. 1974); *see also* Ga. Code Ann. § 30-127

This does not mean that the court should be bound by the desires of even a mature child. It still must make its decision on the basis of the law and the child's interests as it determines them. Rather, the child's wishes should bind *his representative* and should shape the position he takes before the court. If a child of sufficient maturity wishes the proceedings to be dismissed, the child's representative, whether a lawyer or lay guardian ad litem, is under a moral and practical obligation to pursue that end. "Although [he] may strongly feel that the client's choice . . . is unwise, and perhaps be right in that opinion, [his] view may not be substituted for that of a client who is capable of considered judgment . . .."[38]

The child's ability or inability to reach a "considered judgment" is often quite clear. Unfortunately, many children before the court are on the borderline of maturity. There are no easily applied rules of thumb such as those contained in child custody statutes which sometimes specify the age at which a child is deemed to be of sufficient maturity.[39] In the absence of such rules, the child's representative often feels ambivalent about the degree to which he should be bound by the child's wishes. Consequently, he temporizes, at one moment supporting the child's express desire and at the next moment arguing against it. The result is a troubled attorney or guardian, a dissatisfied court, and a confused and hostile child-client.

The only way to lessen the difficulties inherent in borderline cases is for the child's representative to adopt a policy that respects the child's fundamental right to be heard by the court before a decision is made concerning his future. The framework enunciated by the United States Supreme Court in *Bellotti v. Baird* serves as an apt model. In *Bellotti*, the Court held that a minor has a right to decide

---

(1969).

[38] IJA/ABA Standards Relating to Counsel for Private Parties, *supra* note 36, at 81. *Accord* ABA Code of Professional Responsibility EC 7-7 (1974).

[39] *See, e.g.*, Ga. Code Ann. § 30-127 (1969) (specifying age 14).

whether to have an abortion if she can show: "(1) that she is mature enough and well enough informed to make her abortion decision, . . . independently of her parents' wishes; or (2) that even if she is not able to make this decision independently, the desired abortion would be in her best interests."[40] Therefore, even if the child's representative is not sure that the child is sufficiently mature to make a decision about the course of the proceeding, he should nevertheless "help him express his wishes to the court . . .."[41] While doing so, he should also seek the fullest presentation of the facts concerning the allegations of the petition and the family's present situation. Then, as in the case of a minor's decision about an abortion, it would be up to the court to decide whether the outcome desired by the child is in his interests.

III. CONCLUSION

Many child protective cases reach court that do not belong there. Usually, this happens because the system's diversionary procedures did not operate as they should have. The legal sufficiency of the case may not have been carefully assessed; the relative safety of the child's present situation may not have been recognized; the parents' willingness to voluntarily accept treatment may not have been adequately pursued; the likely benefits of intervention may not have been weighed against its possible harmfulness; or the child's own wishes, if he is of sufficient maturity, may not have been taken into account. For any of these reasons, formal court action may be contrary to the child's interests, and actually harmful to the child.

The person representing the child, whether an attorney or lay guardian ad litem, has an affirmative obligation to determine whether court action is in the child's interest and, if it is not, to seek its dismissal. As the American Bar

---

[40] Bellotti v. Baird, 443 U.S. 622, 643-44 (1979).
[41] N.J. STAT. ANN. § 9:6-8.23(a) (West 1976); *accord* N.Y. FAM. CT. ACT § 241 (McKinney 1975).

Association Code of Professional Responsibility states: "If the disability of a client [and the absence of a legal guardian] compel the lawyer to make decisions for his client, the lawyer should consider all circumstances then prevailing and act with care to safeguard and advance the interest of his client . . .."[42]

In a surprising number of cases, the child's representative will be able to convince the petitioner of the need to dismiss the case. However, there are times when he will have to adopt a straightforwardly adversarial posture vis-a-vis the petitioner. He may be forced to make a formal motion to dismiss, accompanied by appropriate supporting briefs and documents and perhaps amplified by an evidentiary hearing. (Such motions should be made as soon as their need becomes apparent.)[43]

Some authorities have disagreed with the kind of active representation of children this Article advocates. Unless the child is mature enough to decide what position his representative should take, they assert that the representative should remain "neutral concerning the proceeding."[44] They argue that for the child's representative to decide what is in the child's interests, "and then tailor his representation in the light of that decision, is a self-serving exercise in which the lawyer has in reality judged the ultimate issues in the case and then set out to implement his own judgment."[45]

No one can disagree that determining where a child's interest lies is a subjective and dangerous task (although, of course, judges do so every day). And no one can deny that opposing the pressure to go along with the system requires professional and personal courage. Nevertheless, adopting a "neutral" posture about the need to dismiss a case leaves unprotected the child for whom court intervention may be

---

[42] ABA CODE OF PROFESSIONAL RESPONSIBILITY, EC 7-12 (1974).
[43] *See, e.g., In re* G., 91 Misc. 2d 911, 398 N.Y.S.2d 975 (Fam. Ct. 1977).
[44] IJA/ABA STANDARDS RELATING TO PRIVATE PARTIES, *supra* note 36, at 80 (Standard 3.1(b)(ii)[c][3]).
[45] MANUAL FOR NEW ATTORNEYS, *supra* note 3, at 218-19.

harmful. (While the parents can be expected to resist court intervention, unless they are represented, it is unlikely that they can effectively raise the issues discussed here. Even if they are represented, their interests too often diverge from those of their children for them to be adequate spokesmen for their children's interests). Especially in serious or notorious cases, everyone in the system, from the child protective worker to the judge, is hesitant to consider a dismissal, even if it appears to be in the child's interests. For, while there is always the danger of negative media publicity if the child is subsequently injured or killed, no one of any consequence will later complain if the child is permanently scarred as a result of unnecessary intervention. That is why, at the time this crucial decision is made: "The child is entitled to a spokesman and an advocate who totally, unequivocally, and actively pursue his rights and interests."[46]

---

[46] U.S. Dep't of Health and Human Services, National Center on Child Abuse and Neglect, Representation for the Abused and Neglected Child, 1 (1980).

NOTES

THE RIGHT TO COUNSEL FOR INDIGENT PARENTS IN TERMINATION PROCEEDINGS: A CRITICAL ANALYSIS OF LASSITER V. DEPARTMENT OF SOCIAL SERVICES

I. INTRODUCTION

In 1981, the U.S. Supreme Court ruled 5-4 in *Lassiter v. Department of Social Services*,[1] the fourteenth amendment to the United States Constitution does not require states to provide indigent[2] parents with state-paid counsel in all proceedings to permanently terminate parental rights.[3] Instead, the Court held the trial court should determine on a case-by-case basis what process is due an indigent parent in a termination proceeding so long as the proceeding is fundamentally fair.

While all states have a mechanism for permanent termination of parental rights,[4] thirty-four states and the District of Columbia provide, by statute, counsel to indigent

---

[1] 452 U.S. 18 (1981).

[2] For the purposes of this Note, it is assumed that the parent is indigent and lacks the means for securing counsel to defend him or her in a termination proceeding. For a discussion of the determination of indigency on a federal and state-to-state basis, see 51 A.L.R.3d 1108.

[3] Hereinafter referred to as "termination proceedings."

[4] *See, e.g.*, N.C. GEN. STAT. §§ 7A-289.24, 7A-289.25(6), 7A-289.27, 7A-289.28, 7A-289.29, 7A-289.30, 7A-289.34 and 7A-587 (Supp. 1979).

parents in such proceedings.[5] In these jurisdictions, thirty-two states[6] guarantee an absolute right to counsel, while two states[7] give the trial court discretion to determine whether provision of counsel is necessary.[8] In the remaining states with no statutory right to counsel for indigent parents in termination proceedings, two states[9] have current case authority holding an absolute right to counsel exists. One state[10] has current case authority holding no right to counsel exists for indigent parents in termination proceedings.

This Note will critically examine the majority and minority opinions in *Lassiter,* the previous case law on right to counsel in termination proceedings, the empirical findings on the effect of counsel in termination proceedings,

---

[5] *See* ALA. CODE § 23-15-63(b) (1975), Alaska Rules of Court Procedure and Administration, Children's Rules, Rule 15 (1977), ARIZ. REV. STAT. ANN. § 8-225 (Cum. Supp. 1979), CAL. CIV. CODE § 237.5 (West Cum. Supp. 1980), COLO. REV. STAT. § 19-1-106(1)(b)(ii) (1973), CONN. GEN. STAT. ANN. § 17-66b(b) (West Supp. 1976), D.C. CODE ANN. § 16-2304(b) (Supp. V 1978), IDAHO CODE § 16-2009 (1979), ILL. REV. STAT. ch. 37, § 701-20(1) (Cum. Supp. 1979), IND. CODE § 34-1-1-3 (1973), IOWA CODE § 232.28 (1969), KAN. STAT. ANN. § 38.820 (Supp. 1974), KY. REV. STAT. § 199.600(7) (1977), LA. REV. STAT. ANN. § 13:1602(c) (West Supp. 1974), ME. REV. STAT. ANN. tit. 22, § 3792 (Supp. 1979), MD. CTS. & JUD. PROC. CODE ANN. art. 119, § 29 (Cum. Supp. 1980), MASS. GEN. LAWS ANN. ch. 119, § 29 (West 1975), MICH. STAT. ANN. JCR § 6.1 (Supp. 1980), MINN. STAT. § 260.155(2) (1971), MISS. CODE ANN. § 43-21-17 (1972), MO. ANN. STAT. § 211.562 (Vernon Supp. 1980), MONT. CODE ANN. § 61-320 (Supp. 1977), NEB. REV. STAT. § 43-205.06 (1943), NEV. REV. STAT. § 62.195 (1979), N.H. REV. STAT. ANN. § 170 - C:10 (1977), N.J. STAT. ANN. (West Cum. Supp. 1979), N.D. CENT. CODE § 27-20-26 (1974), OHIO REV. CODE ANN. § 2151.352 (Page 1976), OKLA. STAT. tit. 10, § 1109(a) (Cum. Supp. 1979), R.I. GEN. LAWS § 14-1-31 (1970), UTAH CODE ANN. § 55.10-96 (1974), WASH. REV. CODE ANN. § 13.34.090 (Supp. 1974), WIS. STAT. ANN. § 48.23 (West Cum. Supp. 1981).

[6] All states in note 5 except Minnesota and South Dakota.

[7] Minnesota and South Dakota.

[8] Factors that are considered are the difficulty of the proceedings and the need for counsel. A more detailed discussion follows in section III of this Note.

[9] Washington and West Virginia. *See In re* Welfare of Myricks, 533 P.2d 841 (Wash. 1975) and Lemaster v. Oakley, 203 S.E.2d 140 (W. Va. 1974).

[10] Maryland. *See In re* Cager, 251 Md. 473, 248 A.2d 384 (1968). The court gave no reason why there was no right to counsel, but held that so long as the parents received notice and were given opportunity to be heard, due process was satisfied.

and the Court's precedents on the parameters of procedural due process. It is the purpose of this Note to determine whether the right to counsel should presumptively attach to termination proceedings and whether a case-by-case determination of the right to counsel in termination proceedings can protect the fundamental rights of parents and families. The analysis in this Note is limited to termination proceedings where the state seeks permanent termination of parental rights. While there are temporary termination and custody proceedings, this Note does not analyze them.

Section II of this Note discusses the parent's constitutional right to marry and raise a family and the state's legitimate interest in protecting children from neglect and abuse. Next, it examines the procedural protections of counsel and due process when the parent's and state's interests converge in a termination proceeding. Section III analyzes the rule the right to counsel attaches only in proceedings resulting in actual imprisonment of the defendant. It examines prior Court precedents on the right to counsel and empirical authority on the effect of counsel in termination proceedings. Section IV analyzes the *Lassiter* case-by-case determination of the right to counsel rule and suggests a procedural due process framework for case-by-case analysis. Section V is the conclusion.

II. THE RIGHTS AND RESPONSIBILITIES OF THE PARTIES IN TERMINATION PROCEEDINGS

A. *The Parent's Right to Custody*

It is unquestioned that the privacy and integrity of the family is one of the most cherished and fundamental freedoms preserved in our Constitution. While not explicitly mentioned in the Constitution, courts have upheld continuously the fundamental rights of the family. In *Meyer v. Nebraska*[11] the Court suggested the fourteenth amendment preserved the individual's right to marry, establish a home

---

[11] 262 U.S. 390 (1923).

and bring up children. In *Stanley v. Illinois*[12] the Court proclaimed:

> The private interest here, that of a man in the children he has sired and raised, undeniably warrants deference and, absent a powerful countervailing interest, protection. It is plain that the interests of a parent in the companionship, care, custody and management of his or her children "come[s] to this Court with a momentum for respect lacking when appeal is made to liberties which derive merely from shifting economic arrangements."[13]

A parent's fundamental right to the custody of his or her children is not absolute. The state has a legitimate interest in protecting children from neglect and abuse.[14] The

---

[12] 405 U.S. 645 (1972).

[13] *Id.* at 651. The fundamental right to raise a family has been deemed "far more precious than property rights," May v. Anderson, 345 U.S. 528, 533 (1933); "essential to the orderly pursuit of happiness by free men," *Meyer* at 399; and has been labeled a fundamental interest worthy of protection of the fourteenth amendment of the U.S. Constitution in Smith v. Organization of Foster Families, 431 U.S. 816, 845 (1977); Moore v. East Cleveland, 431 U.S. 494, 499 (1977); Prince v. Massachusetts, 321 U.S. 158, 166 (1944); Pierce v. Society of Sisters, 284 U.S. 510, 534-35 (1925); and Wisconsin v. Yoder, 506 U.S. 205, 232-34 (1972) (recognizing the natural parent's constitutional interest in controlling the details of his or her child's upbringing). This fundamental rights analysis may be appealing to one advocating that the rights of parents trigger strict scrutiny envisioned by the equal protection clause of the fourteenth amendment to the U.S. Constitution. For a discussion of the equal protection implications of the indigent parent's right to counsel in termination proceedings, see Catz & Kuelbs, *The Requirement of Appointment of Counsel for Indigent Parents in Neglect or Termination Proceedings: A Developing Area*, 13 J. FAM. LAW 223, 233-38 (1973). For a discussion of the right to counsel in paternity actions see Note, *The Right to Appointed Counsel in Paternity Actions*, 19 J. FAM. L. 497 (1980).

[14] *See* Santosky v. Kramer, 50 U.S.L.W. 4333 (1982). The Court wrote:
In addition to the child's interest in a normal homelife, the State has an urgent interest in the welfare of the child. . . . Few could doubt that the most valuable resource of a self-governing society is its population of children who will one day become adults and themselves assume the responsibility of self-governance. A democratic society rests, for its continuance, upon the healthy, well-rounded growth of young people into full maturity as citizens, with all that implies. . . . Thus, the whole community has an interest that children be both safeguarded from abuses and given opportunities for growth into free and independent well-developed citizens.
Id. at 4345 (Rehnquist, J. dissenting, parallel citations omitted).

nature of this parens patriae role of the state is to assure children are given adequate opportunities to grow into well adjusted and mature adult citizens.[15] Accordingly, all states conduct judicial proceedings to terminate parental rights when the child's safety is jeopardized by his or her parents.[16]

In a termination proceeding, the state's interest in protecting the child from alleged neglect and abuse converges with the parent's right to custody of the child. If the state prevails, the parent-child relationship is severed permanently. The courts have recognized generally the severity of an adverse ruling to a parent in a termination proceeding. In *Davis v. Page*[17] the Fifth Circuit Court of Appeals declared:

> Loss of a child is one of the severest possible sanctions that can be taken against a parent; it is a deprivation which can be equated with the imposition of a fine or imprisonment through criminal proceedings. Indeed it is not unlikely that many parents would rather choose to serve a prison sentence than lose the companionship and custody of their children. In addition, the determination that a parent has abused or neglected a child may lead to criminal proceedings against the parent and certainly carries with it a stigma which may be as traumatizing to the parent as imprisonment.[18]

B. *Procedural Requirements in Termination Proceedings*

Parental rights are fundamental but not absolute.

---

[15] *See supra* note 14. *See also* Prince v. Massachusetts, 321 U.S. 158 (1944) and Ginsberg v. New York, 390 U.S. 629 (1968).

[16] The state must show parental unfitness in some way. In Quilloin v. Walcott, 434 U.S. 246 (1978) the Court wrote:

we have little doubt that the Due Process Clause would be offended if a State were to attempt to force the breakup of a natural family, over the objections of the parents and their children, without some showing of unfitness and for the sole reason that to do so was thought to be in the children's best interest.

Id. at 255. *See also* Smith v. Organization of Foster Families, 431 U.S. 816, 862-63 (1977) (Stewart, J., concurring).

[17] 618 F.2d 374 (1980) [Davis I], *aff'd in part, rev'd in part*, 640 F.2d 599 (5th Cir. 1981) [Davis II].

[18] 618 F.2d at 379.

However, the permanent termination of fundamental parental rights is sufficiently severe to invoke the need for constitutional protections. Courts have recognized consistently the need for procedural protections when persons face the risk of deprivation of important interests. In *Goldberg v. Kelly*,[19] the Court declared "the extent to which [a person] may be condemned to suffer grievous loss"[20] determined the procedural protection to be granted to that person.

Two separate but related strands of constitutional law are relevant in determining the level of procedural protection due unrepresented indigent parents in termination proceedings: the right to counsel and procedural due process.[21]

1.   The Right to Counsel

The goal of our judicial system is equal justice under the law. Our legal system is adversarial; thus, the quest for justice depends on the reasoned clash of opposing advocates before an impartial judge and/or jury. Most lawyers are privately employed; thus, access to the legal system requires economic resources indigent persons may lack.

Justice Black believed indigency should not prevent a person from having his or her day in court. He wrote "there can be no equal justice where the kind of trial a man has depends on the money he has."[22] While indigent litigants never have been guaranteed provision of counsel in all judicial proceedings, the Court has found a right to counsel in certain judicial proceedings.

---

[19] 397 U.S. 254 (1970).

[20] *Id.* at 263.

[21] The Court has recently ruled all states must use at least "a clear and convincing" standard in determining the state's burden of proof in a termination proceedings. This ruling was based on procedural due process analysis. *See* Santosky v. Kramer, 50 U.S.L.W. 4333 (1982).

[22] Griffin v. Illinois, 351 U.S. 12, 19 (1956).

The sixth amendment[23] to the U.S. Constitution guarantees the provision of counsel to all defendants in criminal prosecutions in federal courts.[24] This right was applied to states for the first time in *Powell v. Alabama.*[25] There, the Court held a defendant accused of a capital offense must be guaranteed counsel. The right to counsel was extended to all federal and state felony criminal proceedings in *Gideon v. Wainwright*[26] and to any felony or misdemeanor criminal proceeding potentially resulting in incarceration of the defendant in *Argersinger v. Hamlin.*[27] In *Scott v. Illinois,*[28] the Court refused to extend the right to counsel in proceedings where the defendant was not sentenced to jail, although the offense was punishable by jail sentence. The *Scott* Court ruled the right to counsel attaches automatically only when the defendant faces actual imprisonment. The Court has repeated many times the significance of the right to counsel in *Powell, Gideon, Argersinger* and their progeny when they claim "the right to be heard would be, in many cases, of little avail, if it did not comprehend the right to be heard by counsel."[29]

In judicial proceedings that do not meet the "actual imprisonment" standard of *Scott,* the Court has decided the right to counsel question on a case-by-case analysis of the substance and nature of the particular proceedings. In so doing, the Court avoids merely characterizing those proceedings as criminal or civil,[30] and instead focuses on the

---

[23] U.S. CONST. amend. VI provides in part "in all criminal prosecutions, the accused shall enjoy the right . . . to have Assistance of Counsel for his defense."

[24] Johnson v. Zerbst, 304 U.S. 458 (1938). The right to counsel can be waived if the waiver is "knowingly and intelligently made." For a discussion of waiver of right to counsel in termination proceedings, *see* 80 A.L.R.3d 1141 at 1163.

[25] 287 U.S. 45 (1932).

[26] 372 U.S. 335 (1963).

[27] 407 U.S. 25 (1972).

[28] 440 U.S. 367 (1979).

[29] 287 U.S. 45, 68-69 (1932).

[30] *See, e.g.,* McKeiver v. Penn, 403 U.S. 528, 541 (1970) ("Little, indeed, is to be gained by any attempt simplistically to call the juvenile court proceeding 'civil' or 'criminal.' The Court has carefully avoided this wooden approach."). *See also* Mastin v. Fellerhoff, 526 F. Supp. 969, 973 (S.D. Ohio 1981) ("[t]o characterize a

risk of deprivation of personal liberty from those proceedings.

For example, *In re Gault*[31] extended the right to counsel to juveniles in delinquency proceedings. While delinquency proceedings were considered to be "civil" in nature, the Court decided the serious consequences of a finding of delinquency warranted provision of counsel.[32]

In *Gagnon v. Scarpelli*,[33] the Court refused extension of an absolute right to counsel to parole and probation revocation proceedings because revocation hearings were not criminal trials. The Court ruled provision of counsel "[depended] not from the invariable attributes of those hearings, but rather from the peculiarities of particular cases."[34] Thus, the Court found a case-by-case determination of the right to counsel in revocation hearings satisfied due process because unlike *Scott* defendants, who faced actual imprisonment, *Gagnon* defendants were already imprisoned and thus, did not possess similar liberty interests. Thus, in civil and criminal proceedings, the Court will find an absolute right to counsel only when the defendant faces the consequences of actual imprisonment or deprivation of personal liberty.

In *Vitek v. Jones*,[35] the Court extended an absolute right to counsel for indigent inmates being involuntarily transferred to a mental institution. The *Vitek* Court focused on the massive curtailment of liberty and the stigma involved in commitment to a mental institution in its ruling the right to counsel attached to those proceedings.[36]

---

proceeding as civil rather than criminal is a distinction without a difference if the end result is loss of physical liberty.").

[31] 387 U.S. 1 (1967).

[32] *Id.* at 36.

[33] 411 U.S. 778 (1973).

[34] *Id.* at 789.

[35] 445 U.S. 480 (1980).

[36] *Id.* at 492-94. Justice Powell concurred with the majority. He refrained from ruling the right was representation by legal counsel and instead ruled the right was representation by qualified experts. *Id.* at 498-500.

The Court's right to counsel decisions concerning criminal and civil proceedings focus on its interpretation of the due process clause of the fourteenth amendment. Thus, the analysis of the right to counsel is based on whether provision of counsel is a necessary procedural safeguard whon a person's liberty interests may be deprived. In this analysis, two constitutional questions are important: one, "where does the right to counsel presumptively attach?"; and two, "what factors are relevant in weighing the interests of the state and the defendant?"

In *Lassiter,* the Court ruled an absolute right to counsel presumptively attaches only in proceedings where the defendant will be incarcerated if he or she loses the litigation.[37] The Court relied on *Scott* in drawing the line at "actual imprisonment." Furthermore, the Court used the *Gagnon* analysis that a defendant not facing incarceration possessed a limited liberty interest to be weighed by the trial court on a case-by-case basis.[38]

2. *Procedural Due Process*

Also in *Lassiter,* the Court ruled the interests of the state and the indigent parent should be weighed by the due process test articulated in *Matthews v. Eldridge.*[39] In *El-*

---

[37] 452 U.S. at 25. *See also* Alsco-Harvard Fraud Litigation, 523 F. Supp. 790, 799 (1981).

In *Lassiter* there was no risk that criminal charges could be brought against Ms. Lassiter as a result of the termination proceeding. Thus, the petitioner could not argue Ms. Lassiter faced potential incarceration from the termination proceeding and needed counsel for that reason. *See* Brief for Respondent at 15-17.

[38] 452 U.S. at 32.

[39] 424 U.S. 319, 335 (1976). This test is hereinafter referred to as "the *Eldridge* test." In *Lassiter,* only Justice Stevens refused to use the *Eldridge* test. He wrote in a separate dissenting opinion, "[the *Eldridge* test] is an appropriate method of determining what process is due in property cases." 452 U.S. at 18 (Stevens, J., dissenting).

Two *Lassiter* commentators have criticized the Court's use of the *Eldridge* test. *See* Schecter, *The Pitfalls of Timidity: The Ramifications of Lassiter v. Department of Social Services,* 8 N. Ky. L. Rev. 435 (1981) and Jackson, *Lassiter v. Department of Social Services: The Due Process Right to Counsel Left Hanging Uneasily in the Matthews v. Eldridge Balance,* 8 N. Ky. L. Rev. 513 (1981).

dridge, the petitioner challenged HEW's administrative procedures for termination of his Social Security benefits. The Court ruled the petitioner's property interests deserved some procedural protection to guarantee fairness and prevent error. The Court wrote:

> identification of the specific dictates of due process generally requires consideration of three distinct factors: First, the private interest that will be affected by the official action; second, the risk of an erroneous deprivation of such interest through the procedures used, and the probable value, if any, of additional or substitute procedural safeguards; and finally, the government's interest, including the functions involved and the fiscal and administrative burdens that the additional or substitute procedural requirements would entail.[40]

The Court has adopted the *Eldridge* test as its "formula" for weighing the various interests of private and state actors in cases calling for procedural due process. The fundamental question in *Lassiter,* as seen by the Court, was whether unrepresented indigent parents were denied procedural due process per se when they were not provided with state-paid counsel in termination proceedings. For eight of the Justices, the result in *Lassiter* was based on their interpretation of the *Eldridge* test.[41]

An analysis of *Lassiter's* majority, concurring and minority opinions, as well as the previous right to counsel and procedural due process precedents interpreted in *Lassiter,* reveals two important problems with the decision. One, the Court's ruling that the right to counsel presumptively attaches only in proceedings where the defendant faces actual incarceration is based on unsound constitutional interpretation and reasoning. Two, there is serious doubt whether the case-by-case approach announced in *Lassiter* can protect the liberty interests of indigent parents in termination proceedings. These problems are discussed in sections III and IV.

---

[40] 424 U.S. at 335.
[41] *See supra* note 40.

III. The "Actual Incarceration" Standards and the Right to Counsel in Termination Proceedings

A. The Court's Right to Counsel Precedents

In *Lassiter*, the Court misapplied prior right to counsel precedents. In using the "actual imprisonment" standard to determine the right to counsel, the Court relied on *Scott*.

In *Scott*, the Court ruled an unrepresented defendant fined $50 and not sent to jail was not denied necessary procedural protection of his liberty interests. The *Scott* majority's analysis, however, was limited to the particular misdemeanor proceedings at bar. In that context, the Court wrote "actual imprisonment is a penalty different in kind from fines or the mere threat of incarceration . . . and warrants adoption of actual imprisonment as the line defining the constitutional right to appointment of counsel."[42]

Misdemeanor proceedings are not analogous to termination proceedings. In termination proceedings, indigent parents do not face a mere fine or small jail sentence, but rather the permanent termination of the fundamental right to custody of their children. Termination of parental rights is one of the most severe sanctions our society can impose. For some parents, the risk of termination is worse than the threat of incarceration.[43] In fact, it is difficult to consider many consequences of greater magnitude than the loss of one's children.[44] Even the *Lassiter* majority characterized termination of parental rights as "a unique kind of deprivation . . . and a commanding [parental interest]."[45]

The Court's precedents do not support "actual imprisonment" as the trigger for a right to counsel. In *Gagnon*, the Court failed to find a right to counsel in parole revocation proceedings, even though the petitioners were faced with the prospect of cancelled parole or probation and con-

---

[42] 440 U.S. at 373.
[43] *See supra* note 18 and text accompanying.
[44] Crist v. Division of Youth, 320 A.2d 203, 211 (N.J. 1974).
[45] 452 U.S. at 27.

tinued incarceration. Instead, the Court focused on the liberty interest of the petitioners and the substance and nature of revocation proceedings. The Court found counsel was not procedurally required in every revocation proceeding and since the petitioners in revocation proceedings were already incarcerated, their liberty interests were less substantial than a criminal defendant facing incarceration.[46]

Revocation proceedings are not analogous to termination proceedings. In termination proceedings, the parent faces a loss recognized as greater than revocation of parole. No court has characterized the parent's interest in a termination proceeding as the "limited liberty interest" of the *Gagnon* petitioners. In fact, the Court has recently recognized that as the state moves towards termination of parental rights, the parent's need for procedural protection becomes greater.[47] Nor can the parent's interests be deemed lessened because the family unit is already broken down since that is the issue to be decided in the termination proceeding.[48]

In *Vitek,* the Court found a right to counsel when the petitioner did not face incarceration, but instead commitment to a mental institution. The Court recognized the loss of personal liberty involved in commitment and the stigma the petitioner would receive upon commitment to a mental institution. In commitment proceedings, the Court felt presence of counsel was necessary in light of the expert medical testimony and hearsay evidence common to such proceedings.

Like commitment proceedings, the indigent parent faces a serious loss of liberty even though no incarceration is threatened. To be sure, an adverse determination in a termination proceeding creates an onerous stigma for the parent. One Court noted "[the state] attempt[s] to demon-

---

[46] 411 U.S. at 485-89.
[47] 50 U.S.L.W. at 4335. *See also* Cleaver v. Wilcox, 499 F.2d 940 (9th Cir. 1974).
[48] 50 U.S.L.W. at 4335.

strate that the parents' conduct has failed to measure up to a socially and legally acceptable norm."[49] Another court wrote "the defendant is charged with conduct—failure to care properly for her children—which may be criminal and in any event is viewed as reprehensible and morally wrong by a majority of society."[50] It would seem the analysis in *Vitek* would command a similar result in *Lassiter*. Furthermore, termination proceedings commonly feature expert testimony and hearsay evidence[51]—complex issues requiring an attorney's expertise.

In *Lassiter*, the majority attempted to distinguish *Vitek* on grounds the defendant's personal freedom triggers the right to counsel.[52] In dissent, Justice Brennan replied "physical confinement is [not] the only loss of liberty grievous enough to trigger the right to counsel."[53] Instead, Brennan read *Vitek* as permitting other deprivations of liberty, such as loss of parental rights, to justify the right to counsel.

More importantly, the erroneous analogy of *Scott* to termination proceedings and the misanalysis of the petitioners' liberty interests in *Gagnon* and *Vitek* resulted in the failure of the *Lassiter* majority to use the substance and nature of termination proceedings as the test of the right to counsel.[54] Accordingly, Justice Brennan found the "actual imprisonment" presumption "insensitive" and "inflexible."[55]

By focusing on the substance and nature of termination proceedings, rather than the threat of incarceration, the analysis of the right to counsel is in harmony with prior

---

[49] 320 U.S. at 208.

[50] Danforth v. State Dep't of Health, 303 A.2d 794, 801 (Me. 1973).

[51] 452 U.S. at 30.

[52] *Id.* at 25.

[53] *Id.* at 40 (Brennan, J., dissenting) (weighing due process by the extent to which the litigant risks deprivation of important interests).

[54] *Id.* at 41-42. *Cf.* Goldberg v. Kelly, 397 U.S. 254; *See also supra* notes 19-20 and text accompanying.

[55] 452 U.S. at 42 (Brennan, J., dissenting).

precedent.[56]

B. *The Substance and Nature of Termination Proceedings*

Termination proceedings are governed by state statute.[57] Typically the action is brought by the state, the other parent, a foster parent or a private social agency. Grounds for termination range from physical abuse and neglect to inability to perform as a parent. If a parent is unsuccessful in a termination proceeding, the result is permanent loss of all rights and duties as parent of the children. Also, the children are permanently separated from their parents. They may be adopted or placed in a foster home.[58]

1. *The Imbalance of Resources in Termination Proceedings*

Some termination proceedings operate as informal ex parte proceedings, while other termination proceedings resemble a formal trial. Regardless, in any termination proceedings, the parent must proceed against an array of state resources and agencies. In *In re Welfare of Myricks*,[59] the Supreme Court of Washington wrote:

> in [termination] proceedings, the indigent parent has to face the superior power of state resources. The full panoply of the traditional weapons of the state are trained on the defendant-parent, who often lacks formal education, and with difficulty must present his or her version of disputed facts, match wits with social workers, counselors, psychologists and physicians and often an adverse attorney; cross-examine witnesses (often expert) under rules of evidence and procedure of which he or she usually knows nothing; deal with documentary evidence he or she may

---

[56] *Id.* at 44.

[57] *See, e.g., supra* note 4.

[58] 50 U.S.L.W. at 4338 n.15. For a discussion of the harm to children removed from their original family and placed in foster or adoptive homes, see Wald, *State Intervention on Behalf of 'Neglected' Children: A Search for Realistic Standards*, 27 STAN. L. REV. 985 (1975), particularly notes 45-59 and text accompanying. *Id.* at 993-96.

[59] 533 P.2d 841 (Wash. 1974).

not understand and all to be done in the strange and awesome
setting of the juvenile court.[60]

The imbalance in resources is inherent to termination
proceedings. In *Santosky v. Kramer*,[61] the Court wrote "the
state's ability to assemble its case almost inevitably dwarfs
the parents' ability to mount a defense."[62] Accordingly, any
discussion of the nature and substance of termination proceedings must acknowledge this intrinsic inequity between
the litigants.

2. The Accusatorial Nature of Termination Proceedings

Termination proceedings are also characterized by the
accusatorial nature usually associated with criminal proceedings. The parent is accused of criminal-like conduct,
and the state presents its case the same way it does in a
criminal proceeding. Furthermore, the accusatorial nature
of termination proceedings may overwhelm the indigent
parent, who by fear, lack of education or intimidation by
authority figures may be unable to present an articulate defense against the state. Unfortunately, this is the rule, not
the exception, as one court noted "the persons most likely
to be subjected to a termination proceeding are frequently
on the lesser end of the scale of intelligence and resourcefulness."[63] In termination proceedings, parents are accused
frequently of not meeting accepted social norms[64] or engaging in reprehensible conduct.[65] Also, parents may actually
be charged with criminal conduct.[66]

---

[60] *Id.* at 842.
[61] 50 U.S.L.W. 4333 (1982).
[62] *Id.* at 4337.
[63] 320 A.2d at 210.
[64] *Id.* at 208.
[65] 303 A.2d at 801.
[66] *See supra* note 38. Other courts have found the risk of criminal prosecution to be an integral part of the private interests portion of the due process equation. In *Crist*, the Superior Court of New Jersey said at 208 "we cannot dismiss
the possibility that a parent appearing in a neglect hearing without assistance of
counsel might make self-incriminating statements that could result in a criminal

3.   The Risk of Error in Termination Procedures

In addition to the accusatorial nature of termination proceedings, lack of counsel for the indigent parent intensifies the existing risk of erroneous factfinding. In *Santosky,* the Court wrote:

> [p]ermanent neglect proceedings employ imprecise subjective standards that leave determinations unusually open to the subjective values of the judge . . . . In appraising the nature and quality of a complex series of encounters among the agency, the parents, and the child, the court possesses unusual discretion to underweigh probative facts that might favor the parent. Because parents subject to termination proceedings are often poor, uneducated, or members of minority groups, such proceedings are often vulnerable to judgments based on cultural or class bias.[67]

Other courts also conclude lack of counsel in termination proceedings increases intolerably the inherent risk of erroneous factfinding. In *Cleaver v. Wilcox,*[68] the Ninth Circuit Court of Appeals noted:

> Despite the informality of the juvenile dependency hearings, the parent, untutored in the law, may well have difficulty presenting his or her version of disputed facts, cross-examining witnesses or working with documentary evidence. [Thus], the greater the probability of removal, based on the facts of the case and the social worker's recommendations, the more pressing will be the need for appointed counsel. . . . The more complex the case, the more counsel can contribute to the hearings.[69]

While the *Cleaver* court adopted a case-by-case rule, it went on to hold that, in any permanent termination proceeding, an absolute right to counsel exists.

---

prosecution." In *In re* B., 285 N.E.2d 288, 290 (1972), the New York Court of Appeals wrote "In our view, an indigent parent faced with . . . the possibility of criminal charges is entitled to assistance of counsel (parallel citations omitted)."

[67]   50 U.S.L.W. at 4337.

[68]   499 F.2d 940 (9th Cir. 1974).

[69]   *Id.* at 945. The *Cleaver* court held that provision of counsel for indigent parents in termination proceedings be made by the trial court judge on a case-by-case basis. The court ruled "the determination should be made with an understanding that due process requires the state to appoint counsel whenever an indigent parent, unable to present his or her case properly, faces a substantial possibility of the loss of custody or prolonged separation from a child." *Id.*

In *State v. Jamison*,[70] the Supreme Court of Oregon held:

> without counsel, the informality usually associated with *ex parte* hearings prevailed. The juvenile court was led to proceed on the basis of incompetent evidence and evidence that had remote, if any, connection with the issues made up by the petition. . . . In a hearing in which both sides had been represented by counsel, most, if not all, of the alleged errors would have been avoided.[71]

One court depicted the crucial issues and evidence in a termination proceeding as "beyond the understanding of the ordinary person."[72] Another court noted the indigent parent had found the proceeding "incomprehensible."[73] In *Davis*, the court wrote "the uncounseled parent, ignorant of governing substantive law, was little more than a spectator in the proceeding and sat silently through most of the hearing . . . fearful of antagonizing the social workers."[74]

---

[70] 444 P.2d 15 (Or. 1968).

[71] *Id.* at 17. In *Lassiter,* the majority opinion downplayed the rule of hearsay evidence in the decision to terminate Ms. Lassiter's parental rights by indicating that "while a lawyer might have done more with the argument that William should live with Ms. Lassiter's mother . . . but the evidence . . . though controverted, [was] sufficiently substantial that the absence of counsel did not render the proceedings fundamentally unfair." *Id.* at 33. Brennan's dissenting opinion was in sharp contrast to the majority view. He wrote

> the legal issues posed by the state's petition are neither simple nor easily defined. The standard is imprecise and open to the subjective values of the judge. A parent seeking to prevail against the state must be prepared to adduce evidence about his or her personal abilities and lack of fault, as well as proof of progress and foresight as a parent that the state would deem adequate and improved over the situation underlying a previous adverse judgment of child neglect. The parent cannot possibly succeed without being able to identify material issues, develop defenses, gather and present sufficient supporting nonhearsay evidence and conduct cross-examination of adverse witnesses.

Id. at 45-46.

[72] 303 A.2d at 799.

[73] 444 P.2d at 17.

[74] 618 F.2d at 376. Two excellent articles that have been cited in many of the termination decisions discuss the problems of the indigent parent in the courtroom. *See* Schetky, Angell, Morrison & Sack, *Parents Who Fail: A Study of 51 Cases of Termination of Parental Rights,* 18 J. AM. ACAD. CHILD PSYCH. 366 (1979) and Paulsen, *Juvenile Courts, Family Courts and the Poor Man,* 54 CAL.

The *Davis* court explained further:

> the dependency proceeding is complex in terms of the procedural, evidentiary and substantive law applicable to the hearing . . . . Those representing the state have experience in legal proceedings and the ability to examine witnesses, present evidence, and argue skillfully that the child should be adjudicated dependent. Unrepresented parents, in contrast, will normally not cross-examine witnesses, submit evidence, call witnesses or present a defense. They do not understand the rules of procedure or substantive law. They do not object to improper questions or move to strike improper testimony. As the trial court here found to be true of Hilary Davis, they may not even understand the legal significance and effect of the proceedings.[75]

C. The Effect of Counsel in Termination Proceedings

While there has been little empirical investigation of the relationship between counsel and the outcome of termination proceedings, the results of the reported studies favor provision of counsel. In 1966, the *Columbia Journal of Law and Social Problems* conducted a study of docketed neglect proceedings in the Kings County, New York, Family Court. The purpose of the study was to determine what effect, if any, counsel had in the outcome of termination proceedings.[76] The study found that 72.2 percent of the judges who presided over termination proceedings felt that when a parent was unrepresented it was more difficult to conduct a fair hearing and 66.7 percent of the judges felt it was more difficult for unrepresented parents to develop the facts. The study also found parents represented by counsel had a higher rate of dismissed petitions (25% to 7.9%) and a lower rate of neglect adjudications (62.5% to 79.5%) than unrepresented parents.[77] Other courts[78] have cited the Kings County study as empirical authority for the proposi-

---

L. REV. 694 (1966).

[75] *Id.* at 380-81.

[76] The complete study along with methodology and results is published in *Representation in Child Neglect Cases: Are Parents Represented?*, 4 COLUM. J. OF LAW & SOC. PROBS. 230 (1968), hereinafter referred to as the Kings County Study.

[77] *Id.* at 241.

[78] *See e.g., Crist, Danforth* and *Lassiter.*

tion indigent parents have a right to counsel in termination proceedings.

In *Lassiter*, the Respondent's Brief on the Merits referred to an unpublished North Carolina study of the effects of counsel on termination proceedings.[79] That study found that represented parents prevailed in 5.5 percent of the termination proceedings while unrepresented parents prevailed in only 0.15 percent of the termination proceedings.

In *Lassiter*, the Court admitted the previously discussed factors "may combine to overwhelm an uncounseled parent,"[80] but was convinced "presence of counsel for Ms. Lassiter could not have made a determinative difference."[81] The Court suggested the lack of criminal allegations, expert testimony or troublesome points of law proved Ms. Lassiter did not need counsel.[82] The Court dismissed the Kings County study and the North Carolina study findings that presence of counsel made a determinative difference as "unilluminating."[83]

The majority view in *Lassiter* that provision of counsel does not make a determinative difference in termination proceedings is analytically unsound. In fact, there are no empirical findings supporting the *Lassiter* majority. Justice Brennan, dissenting in *Lassiter*, wrote:

> while these statistics hardly are dispositive, I do not share the Court's view that they are 'unilluminating.' Since no evidence indicates that the defendant who can retain or is offered counsel

---

[79] The complete study along with methodology and results is produced in Respondent's Brief on the Merits at 38-39 and 25a-31a, hereinafter referred to as the North Carolina Study.

[80] 452 U.S. at 30.

[81] *Id.* at 33.

[82] *Id.*

[83] *Id.* at 30 n.5. *See also* Note, *Child Neglect: Due Process for the Parent,* 70 COLUM. LAW REV. 465, 476 (1970) (suggesting the conclusion [that a sizable number of cases against unrepresented parents end in termination solely because of absence of counsel] seems "inescapable" and "it would be hard to think of a system of law which works more to the oppression of the poor than the denial of appointed counsel to indigents in neglect proceedings.")

is less capable than one who appears unrepresented, it seems
reasonable to infer that a sizable number of cases against unrepresented parents end in termination solely because of absence of
counsel.[84]

Furthermore, the *Lassiter* majority failed to prove that
indigent parents are not overwhelmed by the state in termination proceedings. To be sure, almost every court prior to
Lassiter found provision of counsel a necessary prerequisite
to a fair and accurate termination proceeding.

The *Lassiter* Court's analogy to *Gagnon*, where the
prisoners' limited liberty interest did not warrant an absolute right to counsel in revocation hearings, is misplaced.
Given the majority's explication of the fundamental nature
of parental rights and the societal value of parental freedom, the indigent parent in a termination proceeding has
more than a limited liberty interest. In fact, the proper
analogy is to *Gault* and *Vitek,* where an absolute right to
counsel was found based on the nature and substance of the
individual proceedings and the serious consequences of an
adverse determination in that proceeding.

Termination proceedings, by their very nature, are proceedings where the unrepresented indigent parent is overwhelmed and outnumbered by the state. The legal issues
are complex and confusing to the layman. Presence of counsel has been proven to have a determinative effect on the
outcome of termination proceedings. Furthermore, the overwhelming majority of legal opinion has concluded there is
no more severe sanction than the permanent termination of
the family unit. Thus, it is imperative that fundamentally
fair procedures be used in termination proceedings. This
problem is addressed in section IV.

IV.   PROCEDURAL DUE PROCESS AND THE CASE-BY-CASE
DETERMINATION OF THE RIGHT TO COUNSEL IN TERMINATION

---

[84]   452 U.S. at 46 (Brennan, J., dissenting).

PROCEEDINGS

Once the *Lassiter* Court placed the presumption of the right to counsel at "actual imprisonment," it addressed the question of whether due process mandated provision of counsel to indigent parents in termination proceedings. The majority found no absolute requirement and ruled the right to counsel for indigent parents in termination proceedings should be determined on a case-by-case basis by the trial court, subject to appellate review.[85] However, the weight of the parent's interests coupled with the inherent risk of error in termination proceedings where the parents are unrepresented do not support a case-by-case determination of the right to counsel.

A. The Requirement of Procedural Due Process

The fifth amendment[86] and the fourteenth amendment[87] to the U.S. Constitution provide that no federal or state government "actor" may deny any citizen "due process" under the law. The Court admits the term "due process" is incapable of precise definition.[88] It can be discerned from the Court's decisions that "due process is an uncertain enterprise which must discover what 'fundamental fairness' consists of in a particular situation."[89] As such, the requirements of procedural due process are that "procedures [be] tailored, in light of the decision to be made, to the capacities and circumstances of those who are to be heard, to in-

---

[85] 452 U.S. at 32.

[86] U.S. CONST. amend. V provides in part "no person shall be . . . deprived of life, liberty or property, without due process of law."

[87] U.S. CONST. amend. XIV provides in part "no state [shall] deprive any person of life, liberty or property, without due process of law."

[88] Justice Frankfurter wrote in Joint Anti-Fascist Refugee Committee v. McGrath, 341 U.S. 123, 162-63 (1951)

> due process . . . is not a technical conception with a fixed content unrelated to time, place and circumstances . . . . Due process is not a mechanical instrument. It is not a yardstick. It is a process. It is a delicate process of adjustment inescapably involving the exercise of judgment by those whom the Constitution entrusted with the unfolding of the process.

[89] 452 U.S. at 24-25.

sure that they are given a meaningful opportunity to present their case."[90]

A parent's fundamental right to custody of his or her children is not absolute.[91] While states may conduct proceedings to terminate a parent's right to custody, the state must use procedures that protect the parent's fundamental rights. Generally, the Court requires that in proceedings in which a person can be deprived of fundamental rights, courts must use "fundamentally fair" procedures.[92] This requirement of protection of a person's fundamental rights is called procedural due process. The Court uses the *Matthews v. Eldridge* test[93] for weighing the interests of private and state actors in cases calling for procedural due process.

The *Lassiter* Court ruled a case-by-case determination of the right to counsel in termination proceedings satisfied due process. The question now is whether, using the *Eldridge* test, a case-by-case determination of the right to counsel in termination proceedings can sufficiently protect the parent's fundamental right to the custody of his or her children. Furthermore, the question becomes in light of *Lassiter,* how can the states best protect the fundamental rights of indigent parents and their families?

B. The Matthews v. Eldridge Analysis of Termination Proceedings

The three *Eldridge* factors as applied to termination proceedings are: one, the private interests of the parents at stake in termination proceedings; two, the parens patriae and administrative interests of the state at stake in termination proceedings; and three, the risk that procedures used in termination proceedings could result in erroneous deprivation of fundamental rights. While each factor is examined in isolation, the Court also analyzes the interrelationship of

---

[90] 424 U.S. at 349.
[91] *See supra* notes 14-16 and text accompanying.
[92] *See supra* note 91.
[93] *See supra* note 40 and text accompanying.

these factors in its due process analysis. Accordingly, the Court seeks flexibility rather than mechanical precision in determining the parameters of procedural due process.[94]

1. Parental Rights

The *Lassiter* Court recognized the great interest of the parents in termination proceedings. The rights to marry, to raise children and to privacy of the family were deemed fundamental and worthy of procedural protection.[95] Furthermore, the risk of criminal charges of abuse and neglect stemming from an adverse ruling in a termination proceeding was deemed a valid parental interest, although the issue was not relevant in *Lassiter*.[96]

2. State Rights

The state's interests at stake in termination proceedings are the administrative costs of provision of counsel and the desire to expedite termination proceedings. The *Lassiter* Court was unpersuaded the state had a weighty administrative interest which outweighed the parents' interests when they noted "the state's pecuniary interest is hardly enough to overcome private interests as important as those here, particularly in light of respondent's concession that the potential costs of appointed counsel in termination proceedings is *de minimus* compared to the costs in all criminal actions."[97]

Additionally, the state has a parens patriae interest in protecting children from neglect and abuse.[98] However, the

---

[94] *See supra* note 90.

[95] *See supra* note 13 and text accompanying.

[96] *See supra* notes 38 and 67.

[97] 452 U.S. at 28. Similarly, other courts have not accorded the state's administrative interest any real due process value. In Cleaver v. Wilcox, 499 F.2d 940, 945 (9th Cir. 1974), the Ninth Circuit Court of Appeals held "the state's interest in saving public money does not outweigh society's interest in preserving viable family units and the parent's interest in not being unfairly deprived of control and custody of a child."

[98] *See supra* note 14 and text accompanying.

question of neglect and abuse is one of the central questions
to be answered in the termination proceeding. Thus, the
state's parens patriae interest does not overcome the parent's interests prior to the decision in a termination proceeding, especially when provision of counsel for parents results in more accurate findings of fact in termination
proceedings.[99]

3.   The Risk of Error

The third *Eldridge* factor, the risk procedures used will
lead to erroneous deprivation of parental rights, was the basis for the *Lassiter* majority's case-by-case rule and the
Lassiter dissenters' call for an absolute right to counsel in
termination proceedings. The majority felt there was no
risk of criminal charges being brought against Ms. Lassiter,
there was no expert testimony and there were no troublesome points of law such that provision of counsel would alter the outcome of the trial.[100] Accordingly, the court felt
while the parents' interests were great and the state's interests were small, there was little risk of an erroneous decision when the decision of whether or not to appoint counsel
was made by the trial judge, subject to appellate review.

The *Lassiter* majority's analysis of this third *Eldridge*
factor is illogical and unsupported by any empirical evidence or the Court's previous decisions. Also, the majority's
analysis contradicts the findings of almost every court

---

[99] *See* Santosky v. Kramer, 50 U.S.L.W. 4333 (1982).

[100] There were four sharp dissenting opinions in *Lassiter*. In Justice Brennan's dissent it is said
> the risk of error is severalfold. The parent who has actually achieved the
> improvement or quality of parenting the state would require may be un-
> able to establish this fact. The parent who has failed in these regards
> may be unable to demonstrate cause, absence of willfulness, or lack of
> agency diligence such as justification. And errors of fact in the state's
> case may go unchallenged or uncorrected. Given the weight of the inter-
> ests at stake, this risk of error assumes extraordinary proportions. By
> intimidation, inarticulateness or confusion, a parent can forever lose all
> contact and involvement with his or her offspring.

452 U.S. at 46-47.

which had previously analyzed the risk of error in termination proceedings. The overwhelming legal and empirical concensus is the risk of error is significant in termination proceedings where indigent parents are not assisted by counsel. Furthermore, the majority does not show how the need for counsel could be determined in advance or how an erroneous decision could be identified and corrected by appellate review. Indeed, there are no guidelines for the trial court in making a prospective determination of the right to counsel. It is not clear how there is little risk of error when the trial court makes a case-by-case determination of the right to counsel in termination proceedings.

While the majority characterized Ms. Lassiter's temination proceeding as simple and raising no troublesome legal questions,[101] four Justices disagreed sharply. The dissenters noted the legal issues raised in any termination proceedings were complex, imprecise and subjective. Furthermore, the *Lassiter* minority argued that in any termination proceeding, a parent must identify material issues, develop defenses, gather and present non-hearsay evidence and cross-examine adverse witnesses.[102] Additionally, the imbalance of resources against the indigent parent[103] and the tendency for indigent parents to be uneducated and inarticulate, intimidated by authority figures and confused in termination proceedings[104] led the *Lassiter* dissenters to conclude "errors of fact or law in the state's case may go unchallenged and uncorrected. Given the weight of the interests at stake, this risk of error assumes extraordinary proportion."[105]

The majority's analysis of the risk of an erroneous deprivation of an uncounseled indigent parent's termination proceeding was based solely on the factual circumstances of

---

[101] *Id.* at 32.
[102] *Id.* at 45-46 (Brennan, J., dissenting).
[103] *See supra* notes 60-63 and text accompanying.
[104] *See supra* notes 64-67 and text accompanying.
[105] 452 U.S. at 46-47 (Brennan, J., dissenting). *See also Danforth, Crist, Davis, Cleaver* and *Jamison.*

Ms. Lassiter's termination proceeding. They conceded hearsay evidence was admitted, the parent's defenses were incomplete and a lawyer might have been more articulate.[106] However, the *Lassiter* majority concluded Ms. Lassiter would have lost custody of her child even if she had been represented by counsel.[107] The majority opinion did not discuss how the Court was sure counsel would not have made a difference in the *Lassiter* case. Moreover, the *Lassiter* majority did not argue why the question "would the outcome of Ms. Lassiter's hearing have been different if she had been provided counsel?" was relevant in determining whether there was a right to counsel in termination proceedings. To the contrary, the Court's procedural due process precedents suggest the question, "was the proceeding fundamentally fair?" was the only relevant question.

Again, the dissenters disputed the majority's conclusions. Justice Brennan felt "the problem of inadequate representation was painfully obvious in the case."[108] To support his conclusion, he laid out the history of the case, the inadequacy of the state's evidence, the admission of inadmissible hearsay evidence and Ms. Lassiter's inability to present her case, cross-examine witnesses and make a closing argument.[109] As such, he found the majority's conclusion Ms. Lassiter's termination proceeding was fundamentally fair to be "virtually incredible" and counter to the Court's previous precedents.[110]

C. The Failure of Case-by-Case Determination of the Right to Counsel to Guarantee Procedural Due Process in Termination Proceedings

The majority's reasoning that the *Lassiter* termination proceeding demonstrates a case-by-case determination of

---

[106] 452 U.S. at 32-33.
[107] *Id.* at 33.
[108] *Id.* at 52 (Brennan, J., dissenting).
[109] *Id.* at 52-56.
[110] *Id.* at 57.

the right to counsel satisfies procedural due process is illogical. First, the confinement of the analysis to only the *Lassiter* termination proceeding begs the entire question whether there should be a per se right to counsel rule in all termination proceedings. By engaging in case-by-case analysis prior to its determination of a case-by-case right to counsel rule, the majority bypassed the Court's traditional analysis of the proceedings at hand in determining the parameters of procedural due process.[111] In short, the majority inferred a general rule of law from the unique facts of one termination proceeding. Accordingly, the reasoning that counsel for Ms. Lassiter would not have altered the outcome of her termination proceeding does not justify the conclusion her termination proceeding satisfied the Court's requirement of procedural due process. The majority's focus on the result alone while ignoring the means by which the result was reached contradicts the goal of procedural due process to devise "procedural norms to ensure that justice be done in every case and to protect litigants against unpredictable and unchecked government action."[112]

Second, the majority misapplies the *Eldridge* test. In using the *Eldridge* test to analyze only Ms. Lassiter's termination proceeding and to declare a case-by-case right to counsel rule, the majority ignores the *Eldridge* command "procedural due process rules are shaped by the risk of error inherent in the truthfinding process as applied to the

---

[111] *Id.* at 49. Justice Brennan wrote:

This conclusion is not only illogical, but it also marks a sharp departure from the due process analysis consistently applied heretofore. The flexibility of due process, the Court has held, requires case-by-case consideration of different decisionmaking *contexts,* not of different *litigants* within a given context. In analyzing the nature of the private and governmental interests at stake, along with the risk of error, the Court in the past has not limited itself to the particular case at hand. Instead, after addressing the three factors as generic elements in the context raised by the particular case, the Court then has formulated a rule that has general application to similarly situated cases.

Id.

[112] *Id.* at 50.

generality of cases, not the rare exceptions."[113] The *Lassiter* majority never demonstrates Ms. Lassiter's termination proceeding fits the generality of cases. In fact, the overwhelming conclusion of the courts and experts indicate the general termination proceeding is fundamentally unfair when the parent is unrepresented.[114] Furthermore, there is serious dispute with the majority's factual determinations of Ms. Lassiter's termination proceeding.[115] In fact, the majority admits the distinct possibility in any given termination proceeding that provision of counsel would be compelled.[116] Thus, the majority's case-by-case approach is undermined by the very test used to justify the rule.

Third, a case-by-case approach will not guarantee protection of fundamental rights. Justice Brennan wrote

> determining the difference legal representation would have made becomes possible only through imagination, investigation and legal research focused on the particular case. Even if the reviewing court can embark on such an enterprise in each case, it might be hard pressed to discern the significance of failures to challenge the state's evidence or to develop a satisfactory defense. Such failures, however, often cut to the essence of the fairness of the trial, and a court's inability to compensate for them effectively eviscerates the presumption of innocence. Because a parent acting *pro se* is even more likely to be unaware of controlling legal standards and practices, and unskilled in garnering relevant facts, it is difficult, if not impossible, to conclude that the typical case has been adequately presented.[117]

Furthermore, the majority does not discuss how a trial court or reviewing court can determine the right to counsel question in any given termination proceeding. Given the concern of procedural due process with the manner in which fundamental rights may be deprived and the Court's failure to find an absolute right to counsel in termination proceedings, it seems essential that lower courts possess

---

[113] 424 U.S. at 344.
[114] *See generally supra* Section III B and C of this Note.
[115] *See supra* notes 110 and 111.
[116] 452 U.S. at 31.
[117] *Id.* at 51 (Brennan, J., dissenting).

standards and guidelines in making the case-by-case determination of the right to counsel. Since there are no such guidelines, there is no guarantee the *Lassiter* rule will protect the fundamental rights of unrepresented indigent parents in termination proceedings.

D. Recommendations

While the *Lassiter* Court held the United States Constitution did not require providing indigent parents with counsel in every termination proceeding, the Court did indicate the state statutes and state court decisions providing higher standards of due process were "both enlightened and wise."[118]

In light of *Lassiter,* it is now the responsibility of the states to protect the fundamental rights of indigent parents. Thirty-four states and the District of Columbia require by statute provision of counsel in all termination proceedings. The remaining sixteen states should enact similar legislation. To date, three states have adopted the Uniform Juvenile Court Act (UJCA) which provides counsel for indigent parents in termination proceedings.[119] The sixteen states which do not statutorily provide counsel in all termination proceedings can adopt the UJCA or use its provisions as a model for their own statute.

Furthermore, litigants in state courts should pursue interpretation of state constitutional provisions to guarantee the right to counsel in all termination proceedings. *Lassiter* was limited to federal constitutional interpretation. State constitutions may provide greater constitutional safeguards.

Finally, trial courts saddled with the burden of making case-by-case determinations of the right to counsel in termination proceedings should weigh the three *Eldridge* factors in light of court precedent and expert authority and

---

[118] 452 U.S. at 34.

[119] UNIF. JUVENILE COURT ACT § 26(a), 94 U.L.A. 35 (1979). The states which have adopted this Act are Georgia, North Dakota and Pennsylvania.

lean strongly towards providing counsel in all cases, instead of a narrow focus on the particular facts of the case at bar. In so doing, the flexibility of procedural due process determinations will be preserved.

V. Conclusion

Unfortunately, indigent parents may find themselves forced into court to defend their familial relationships more often than their middle class and wealthy counterparts.[120] There is a serious risk of erroneous termination of one of our most cherished and important rights—the right to raise a family—when indigent parents must alone combat the panoply of state resources in a termination proceeding. In fact, it is hard to think of a system of law which works more to the oppression of the poor than the denial of appointed counsel to indigent parents in termination proceedings.[121]

Indigency, inarticulateness and lack of legal acumen are inexcusable reasons to break up a family. On the contrary, poverty and ignorance should invoke greater protection from the legislatures and the courts. Justice Harlan wrote once "there is an obligation in the courts to lift the handicaps flowing from differences in economic circumstances when litigants appear before us."[122] If we believe there can be no equal justice where the kind of trial one receives depends on the money one has,[123] then surely, there can be no equal justice where the right to one's family depends on the money one has.

---

[120] *See* Paulsen, *Juvenile Courts, Family Courts and the Poor Man*, 54 CAL. L. REV. 694, 699 (1966) (writing "jurisdictional provisions of a juvenile court are likely to reach a disproportionate number of the children of the poor . . . . Poor children fall into the 'neglect' category more frequently than offspring of the well-to-do . . . . A child of parents who are very poor stands in danger of a court-ordered separation from his parents to the extent which children of the middle and upper classes do not.").

[121] Note, *Child Neglect: Due Process For the Parent*, 70 COLUM. L. REV. 465, 476 (1970).

[122] Griffin v. Illinois, 351 U.S. 12, 34 (1956) (Harlan, J., dissenting).

[123] *See supra* note 23.

It is now the duty of the state legislatures and courts, in their "enlightened wisdom," to lift the handicap of poverty when indigent parents appear in court to defend their right to their families and to receive their right to equal justice.

GARY T. PADGETT

RECENT DEVELOPMENT

SANTOSKY v. KRAMER: DUE PROCESS AND THE INTEREST OF THE CHILD IN PERMANENT NEGLECT PROCEEDINGS

The fourteenth amendment provides that no state shall "deprive any person of life, liberty, or property, without due process of law."[1] The right to establish a home and raise a family is a liberty afforded such protection.[2] The Supreme Court has explained that the Constitution protects the integrity of the family because of the important role that institution has played in our history.[3] Nevertheless, the right to family integrity is not inviolable. A parent's right to raise his child carries with it the corresponding duty to care properly for that child.[4] In general, parents must see to it that their children are pro-

---

[1] U.S. Const. amend. XIV, § 1.

[2] Meyer v. Nebraska, 262 U.S. 390 (1923). Subsequent to *Meyer,* which struck down a statute prohibiting the education of children in a foreign language on the ground that it unreasonably interfered with parents' right to direct the upbringing of their children, a line of Supreme Court cases has addressed the rights incident to the establishment and maintenance of the family. *See, e.g., Moore v. City of East Cleveland,* 431 U.S. 494 (1977) (articulating fundamental right to live in an extended, as opposed to nuclear, family); Loving v. Virginia, 388 U.S. 1 (1967) (invalidating state miscegenation statute as interfering with fundamental right to marry); Griswold v. Connecticut, 381 U.S. 479 (1965) (holding that right to use contraceptives is an incident of marriage which falls within constitutionally protected zone of privacy); Pierce v. Society of Sisters, 268 U.S. 510 (1925) (invalidating statute requiring children to attend public schools on the ground that it deprived parents of their right to select school).

The right "to establish a home and bring up children" is protected even where the relationship between the parents has not been legitimated by a marriage ceremony. In Stanley v. Illinois, 405 U.S. 645 (1972), the Court invalidated a statute that, upon the death of the mother, deprived unwed fathers of custody of their children without a hearing and proof of neglect. *Id.* at 658.

[3] Moore v. City of East Cleveland, 431 U.S. 494, 503-04 (1977). Specifically, the Court stated that its "decisions establish that the Constitution protects the sanctity of the family precisely because the institution of the family is deeply rooted in this Nation's history and traditions. It is through the family that we inculcate and pass down many of our most cherished values, moral and cultural." *Id.* (footnotes omitted).

For a discussion of the role of the family in Western society, see Hafen, *Children's Liberation and the New Egalitarianism: Some Reservations About Abandoning Youth to Their "Rights,"* 1976 B.Y.U. L. Rev. 605, 613-19.

[4] In Pierce v. Society of Sisters, 268 U.S. 510 (1925), the Supreme Court declared that "[t]he child is not the mere creature of the State; those who nurture him and direct his destiny have

vided with such essentials as food, clothing, shelter, education, freedom from physical abuse, and perhaps even emotional support.[5] Because of society's transcendent interest in the welfare of its children,[6] the state has an interest in enforcing these parental obligations.[7] The state has the power, under the Constitution, to interfere with the parent-child relationship where the physical or mental health of the child is in jeopardy.[8] Under certain circumstances, as where a child is abused or neglected, the state may exercise its police power and intervene to protect the health, safety, and best interests of that child.[9]

Apart from the parental right of family integrity, and the interest of the state in the welfare of its children, children themselves have certain constitutionally protected rights. In *Bellotti v. Baird*,[10] for example, the Supreme Court invalidated a statute that required parental consent before a minor could obtain an abortion. The Court held that the minor must be given the opportunity to demonstrate that she is mature enough to decide independently of her parents that an

---

the right, coupled with the high duty, to recognize and prepare him for additional obligations." *Id.* at 535.

[5] *See* Note, *In the Child's Best Interests: Rights of the Natural Parents in Child Placement Proceedings*, 51 N.Y.U. L. REV. 446, 450-51 (1976). *See generally* Comment, *The Rights of Children: A Trust Model*, 46 FORDHAM L. REV. 669 (1978) (analogizing the parent-child relationship to a trust imposed upon the parents by the state in its role as *parens patriae*). For a discussion of the doctrine of *parens patriae*, see Rendleman, *Parens Patriae: From Chancery to the Juvenile Court*, 23 S.C. L. REV. 205 (1971).

[6] *See* Ginsberg v. New York, 390 U.S. 629, 640 (1968); Prince v. Massachusetts, 321 U.S. 158, 165 (1944). In the past, some courts went so far as to assert that it was

> settled doctrine in American courts that all power and authority over infants are [sic] a mere delegated function, intrusted by the sovereign state to the individual parent or guardian, revocable by the state through its tribunals, and to be at all times exercised in subordination to the paramount and overruling direction of the state.

Fladung v. Sanford, 51 Ariz. 211, 217, 75 P.2d 685, 687 (1938) (citation omitted). Other courts have been less absolute, maintaining only that "[t]he right of parental control is a natural, but not an unalienable one" that "remains subject to the ordinary legislative power." *Ex parte* Crouse, 4 Whart. 9, 11 (Pa. 1839).

[7] Prince v. Massachusetts, 321 U.S. 158, 166 (1944). Because of the peculiar vulnerability of children, the power of the state to regulate their activities may exceed its power to legislate for the protection of adults. *See, e.g.*, Ginsberg v. New York, 390 U.S. 629 (1968) (upholding a statute prohibiting the sale of pornography to minors).

[8] Parham v. J. R., 442 U.S. 584, 603 (1979). Despite its recognition of the state's inherent power to protect its children, the *Parham* Court upheld a Georgia statute that allowed parents voluntarily to commit their children to state mental hospitals without a pre-commitment hearing. The Court was persuaded that periodic review by the physicians and staff satisfied the requirements of due process. *Id.* at 649.

[9] *See, e.g.*, Boone v. Wyman, 295 F. Supp. 1143 (S.D.N.Y. 1969). For a comparison of state statutes which provide for intervention on behalf of an abused or neglected child, see Katz, Howe & McGrath, *Child Neglect Laws in America*, 9 FAM. L.Q. 1 (1975).

[10] 443 U.S. 622 (1979).

abortion would best serve her interests.[11] Similarly, in the criminal context, the Constitution requires that a child be accorded the same procedural protection an adult would receive.[12]

Family law has traditionally been the province of the states, which formulate their own standards for intervention in the family relationship.[13] Such intervention, however, often directly conflicts with the constitutional right of family integrity.[14] Due process therefore requires that the procedures chosen by the state be designed to minimize unfair or mistaken deprivations.[15]

In *Santosky v. Kramer*,[16] the Supreme Court was faced with the question whether due process mandates an elevated standard of proof in a proceeding to terminate parental rights on the ground of permanent neglect.[17] The Court held that the standard of proof by a fair preponderance of the evidence is unconstitutional in such a proceeding,[18] thereby striking down section 622 of the New York Family

---

[11] *Id.* at 647. *See also* Ginsberg v. New York, 390 U.S. 629, 638 (1968) (acknowledging that minors have constitutionally protected rights).

[12] *See, e.g., In re* Winship, 397 U.S. 358 (1970) (holding that when juvenile delinquency proceedings are based on charges of alleged criminal activity, a finding of delinquency must be supported by proof beyond a reasonable doubt); *In re* Gault, 387 U.S. 1 (1967) (holding that child has a right to fair procedure in a delinquency hearing, including notice of the charges and a right to counsel).

[13] Matters of family law are generally viewed as "local" concerns. There is, therefore, "a long history of state predominance and federal deferral" in this area. Sylvander v. New England Home for Little Wanderers, 584 F.2d 1103, 1112 (1st Cir. 1978). Only where "clear and substantial" federal interests are at stake will state family law be overridden. United States v. Yazell, 382 U.S. 341, 352 (1966). For a discussion of the evolution of constitutional limits on family law, see Note, *The Constitution and the Family*, 93 HARV. L. REV. 1156 (1980) (the Constitution protects not the family *per se*, but the family as a collection of individuals, each possessing intrinsic, often conflicting, rights).

[14] *In re* Leon RR, 48 N.Y.2d 117, 124, 397 N.E.2d 374, 378, 421 N.Y.S.2d 863, 868 (1979) (citing Pierce v. Society of Sisters, 268 U.S. 510, 535 (1925)). In *Leon*, the court admonished that notwithstanding the child's best interests, "parents who are fit to raise their child are constitutionally entitled to do so." *Id.* (citing Stanley v. Illinois, 405 U.S. 645, 657-58 (1972)).

[15] Fuentes v. Shevin, 407 U.S. 67, 97 (1972). It is therefore necessary that the procedures relied upon provide a true test of the validity of the state action. *Id.*

[16] 102 S. Ct. 1388 (1982).

[17] *Id.* at 1392-93. Under New York law, a "permanently neglected child" is

a child who is in the care of an authorized agency and whose parent or custodian has failed for a period of more than one year following the date such child came into the care of an authorized agency substantially and continuously or repeatedly to maintain contact with or plan for the future of the child, although physically and financially able to do so, notwithstanding the agency's diligent efforts to encourage and strengthen the parental relationship when such efforts will not be detrimental to the best interests of the child.

N.Y. Soc. SERV. LAW § 384-b(7)(a) (McKinney Supp. 1981-1982).

[18] Santosky v. Kramer, 102 S. Ct. at 1397. This was a 5-4 decision with the Chief Justice and Justices Rehnquist, White and O'Connor dissenting.

Court Act.[19] This Recent Development will present the background of *Santosky*, discuss the application of the New York Family Court Act, and analyze the Court's decision. Finally, it will will argue that, had the Court recognized the interests of the child in a termination proceeding, and had it examined the standard of proof in the context of New York's statutory scheme for termination, it would have found that proof by a fair preponderance of the evidence was fundamentally fair in such a proceeding.

I. Background of *Santosky*

A. *History of the Santosky Family*

John and Annie Santosky are the parents of five children, three of whom have been adjudicated to be neglected within the meaning of article 10 of the New York Family Court Act.[20] The eldest, Tina, now age ten, was in foster care from November 1973; John III and Jed, ages eight and seven, from September 1974.[21]

In September 1973, Tina was brought to the hospital with a broken leg for which the attending physician recommended hospitalization.[22] Refusing medical treatment for their child, the Santoskys preferred to apply a homemade splint.[23] Two weeks later, after responding to a neighbor's complaint, the police returned Tina to the hospital where

---

[19] N.Y. Fam. Ct. Act § 622 (McKinney Supp. Pamphlet 1981-1982) (amended 1982). At the time the Santosky children were adjudicated to be neglected, § 622 provided, in part, that during the fact-finding hearing in a proceeding to terminate parental custody on the ground of permanent neglect, the standard of proof should be "a fair preponderance of the evidence." *Id.* In light of *Santosky*, the legislature amended the statute, raising the standard of proof to "clear and convincing." 1982 N.Y. Laws ch. 123, sec. 2, § 622.

[20] *In re Apel*, No. B-3-4-5-78, slip op. at 2 (Fam. Ct., Ulster County, March 12, 1979). Article 10 of the Family Court Act provides for temporary removal from the home of abused or neglected children either with or, in cases of emergency, without the consent of the parents. N.Y. Fam. Ct. Act §§ 1021, 1024 (McKinney Supp. Pamphlet 1981-1982). A "neglected child" is one
  whose physical, mental or emotional condition has been impaired or is in imminent danger of becoming impaired as a result of the failure of his parent or other person legally responsible for his care to exercise a minimum degree of care
  (A) in supplying the child with adequate food, clothing, shelter or education . . . or medical, dental . . . or surgical care . . . or
  (B) in providing the child with proper supervision or guardianship, by unreasonably inflicting or allowing to be inflicted harm, or a substantial risk thereof, including the infliction of excessive corporal punishment . . . .
Id. § 1012.
[21] *In re Apel*, No. B-3-4-5-78, slip op. at 2 (Fam. Ct., Ulster County, March 12, 1979).
[22] Brief for Respondent at 1-2, *Santosky v. Kramer*, 102 S. Ct. 1388 (1982).
[23] *Id.* at 2.

it was discovered that she had severe bruises on her upper arms, fore-head, flank, and spine, as well as cuts on her thigh.[24] As a result, Tina was temporarily removed from the custody of her parents to the care of the Ulster County Department of Social Services (the Agency).[25]

Not quite a year later, John Santosky III was hospitalized for severe malnutrition.[26] Not only was John underfed, he had also been pinpricked repeatedly as "discipline" for refusing to sit up in his high chair.[27] The following month, the Agency temporarily removed the boy from the custody of his natural parents.[28] That same day, Annie Santosky gave birth to a third child, Jed, who was immediately transferred to a foster home on the ground that removal was necessary to insure his well-being.[29]

Over the next four years, the Agency, in addition to providing financial assistance, encouraged the parents to participate in a number of programs designed to prepare them to assume responsibility for raising their children.[30] These services included psychological, vocational, nutritional, and planned parenthood counseling.[31] When prolonged efforts to rehabilitate the Santoskys were unsuccessful, the Commissioner of Social Services filed a permanent neglect petition with the Ulster County Family Court and sought termination of the

---

[24] *Id.*
[25] Santosky v. Kramer, 102 S. Ct. at 1393.
[26] Brief for Respondent at 2, Santosky v. Kramer, 102 S. Ct. 1388 (1982).
[27] *Id.*
[28] *In re* Apel, No. B-3-4-5-78, slip op. at 2 (Fam. Ct., Ulster County, March 12, 1979).
[29] Santosky v. Kramer, 102 S. Ct. at 1393.
[30] In its attempt to reunite the family, the Agency arranged for and urged the Santoskys to accept eleven different social services. These included:
  (a) Visits with the children on an average of twice a month, the children being brought to [the Santoskys'] home.
  (b) Attendance by [the mother] at the Child Enrichment Program offered by the Family Service Center to mothers with pre-school children, which program included the use of a parent aid. Transportation was provided.
  (c) Psychological evaluations of both [parents], and a complete neurological evaluation of [the father].
  (d) Follow-up psychiatric and psychological services to both [parents].
  (e) Counseling sessions for [both parents] with [a] certified social worker.
  (f) Birth control counseling at Planned Parenthood.
  (g) Vocational training [for] John Santosky.
  (h) Educational assistance to [the father].
  (i) Nutrition Aid Services to [the mother] since November 1977.
  (j) Homemaker Service to help the [parents] immediately prior to and after the birth of their fourth child in June 1978.
  (k) Public Assistance, Food Stamps and Medicaid.
In re Apel, No. B-3-4-5-78, slip op. at 20-21 (Fam. Ct., Ulster County, March 12, 1979).
[31] For a complete list of the services provided, *see supra* note 30.

Santoskys' parental rights in the children.[32]

B. Application of the Family Court Act to the Santoskys

New York's Family Court Act requires the inclusion of several spe
cific allegations in a petition to terminate parental custody.[33] First, it
must detail the steps taken by the Agency to foster the parent-child
relationship.[34] Second, it must allege that the parents have failed for
more than a year to maintain contact with the child or plan for his

---

[32] *In re* Apel, No. B-3-4-5-78, slip op. at 1 (Fam. Ct., Ulster County, March 12, 1979). Once
before, on September 8, 1976, the Commissioner had filed permanent neglect petitions with
respect to these children. *In re* Santosky, 89 Misc. 2d 730, 393 N.Y.S.2d 486 (1977). The court
was satisfied that although the Agency had "made diligent efforts to encourage and strengthen
the parental relationship," *id.* at 733, 393 N.Y.S.2d at 489, the Santoskys had been only "superficially cooperative." *Id.* at 738, 393 N.Y.S.2d at 492. The Family Court Act, however, requires
that the agency prove that the parents have failed to plan for the future of their children
"although physically and financially able to do so." N.Y. FAM. CT. ACT § 614(1)(d) (McKinney
Supp. Pamphlet 1981-1982). Because the Santoskys were recipients of full public assistance, the
court concluded that they were not "financially able" to plan for the future of their children. *In
re* Santosky, 89 Misc. 2d at 741, 393 N.Y.S.2d at 494. The Santoskys' "very eligibility for full
public assistance," the court held, "presupposes that they are 'financially unable.'" *Id.* The
Santoskys' failure to plan for the future of their children was thus excused by reason of their
poverty. Accordingly, the court dismissed the petition and instructed the Agency "to redouble
its efforts to raise the parents to an acceptable minimal level of competency." *Id.* The appellate
division affirmed on the ground that the Santoskys' good faith effort to comply with the
Agency's plan "constituted planning by conduct." *In re* John W, 63 A.D.2d 750, 751, 404
N.Y.S.2d 717, 719 (1978). The appellate court, however, rejected the family court's conclusion
that eligibility for full public assistance rendered the parents "financially unable." The court
held that unless it is shown that a parent is receiving inadequate public assistance, the fact that
he receives such assistance does not, in itself, excuse him from planning for the future of his
child. *Id.*, 404 N.Y.S.2d at 718.

[33] The Family Court Act provides that:

A proceeding for the commitment of the guardianship and custody of a child on the
ground of permanent neglect is originated by a petition alleging:

. (a) the child is a person under eighteen years of age;

(b) the child is in the care of an authorized agency;

(c) the authorized agency has made diligent efforts to encourage and strengthen the
parental relationship and specifying the efforts made or that such efforts would be detrimental to the best interests of the child and specifying the reasons therefore;

(d) the parent or custodian, notwithstanding the agency's efforts, has failed for a period of more than one year following the date such child came into the care of an authorized agency substantially and continuously or repeatedly to maintain contact with or
plan for the future of the child, although physically and financially able to do so; and

(e) the best interests of the child require that the guardianship and custody of the
child be committed to an authorized agency or to a foster parent . . . .

N.Y. FAM. CT. ACT § 614(1) (McKinney Supp. Pamphlet 1981-1982).

[34] As required by § 614 of the New York Family Court Act, the Agency provided numerous
services to the Santosky family over a period of several years prior to the permanent neglect
proceeding. *See supra* note 30.

future.[35] Finally, the petition must aver that the best interests of the child dictate permanent termination.[36] The statute is narrowly construed; New York recognizes that in seeking to terminate a natural parent's rights, the state assumes a burden of constitutional dimensions.[37]

In concluding that the Santosky children were permanently neglected, the Ulster County Family Court first reviewed the Agency's efforts on behalf of the family. The court found that the Santoskys had failed "in any meaningful way" to take advantage of the social

---

[35] The phrase "maintain contact with or plan for" is stated in the disjunctive, N.Y. FAM. CT. ACT § 614(1)(d) (McKinney Supp. Pamphlet 1981-1982); thus "a finding of a failure to plan, in and of itself, suffices to support a determination of permanent neglect." In re Orlando F., 40 N.Y.2d 103, 110, 351 N.E.2d 711, 715, 386 N.Y.S.2d 64, 67 (1976).

The New York Social Services Law provides that
"to plan for the future of the child" shall mean to take such steps as may be necessary to provide an adequate, stable home and parental care for the child. . . . In determining whether a parent has planned for the future of the child, the court may consider the failure of the parent to utilize medical, psychiatric, psychological and other social and rehabilitative services and material resources made available to such parent.

N.Y. Soc. SERV. LAW § 384-b(7)(c) (McKinney Supp. Pamphlet 1981-1982). The court may not impose its own subjective values. The standards by which it evaluates the parents' plan for the future of the child must be tailored to the financial and social circumstances of those parents; it must not be "evaluated with reference to unrealistically high standards." In re Leon RR, 48 N.Y.2d 117, 125, 397 N.E.2d 374, 379, 421 N.Y.S.2d 863, 868 (1979). See also In re Orlando F., 40 N.Y.2d 103, 111, 351 N.E.2d 711, 716, 386 N.Y.S.2d 64, 68 (1976). It is not necessary that the plan be consummated; the law requires only that the parents " 'formulate' a plan and 'act to accomplish' it." In re Santosky, 89 Misc. 2d 730, 740, 393 N.Y.S.2d 487, 493 (1977) (quoting In re Orlando F., 40 N.Y.2d 103, 110, 351 N.E.2d 711, 715, 386 N.Y.S.2d 64, 67 (1976)).

[36] N.Y. FAM. CT. ACT § 614(1)(e) (McKinney Supp. Pamphlet 1981-1982). It is important to note that a statutory ground for termination must be present before the child's best interests may be considered. Statutory grounds for termination include abandonment, abuse, neglect, and the mental illness or retardation of the parents. N.Y. Soc. SERV. LAW § 384-b(4) (McKinney Supp. 1981-1982). To the extent that Bennet v. Jeffreys, 40 N.Y.2d 543, 356 N.E.2d 277, 387 N.Y.S.2d 821 (1976) has been construed as creating a "no-fault" ground for termination in the best interests of the child, that case has been overruled. In re Sanjivini K., 47 N.Y.2d 374, 382, 391 N.E.2d 1316, 1320-21, 418 N.Y.S.2d 339, 344 (1979). Thus, while there was once confusion over the "no-fault" issue, it is now clear that New York law requires that termination proceed along statutory grounds. For a discussion of the "no-fault" termination theory which was spawned by Bennett, see Judge Elwyn's opinion in In re Apel, No. B-3-4-5-78, slip op. at 16-17 (Fam. Ct., Ulster County, March 12, 1979).

A permanent neglect proceeding in New York consists of two phases: a factfinding hearing and a dispositional hearing. N.Y. FAM. CT. ACT §§ 622, 623 (McKinney Supp. Pamphlet 1981-1982). It is only during the latter phase, after the child has been found to be permanently neglected, that the court takes into account the child's best interests. Thus, even a finding of permanent neglect does not necessarily entail termination of parental rights. See, e.g., In re Roy Anthony A., 59 A.D.2d 662, 398 N.Y.S.2d 277 (1977).

[37] Corey L. v. Martin L., 45 N.Y.2d 383, 386-87, 380 N.E.2d 266, 267, 408 N.Y.S.2d 439, 440 (1978) ("Despite recent changes in statutory law, there remains a heavy burden of constitutional magnitude on one who would terminate the rights of a natural parent . . . ."). See supra notes 1-3 and accompanying text.

and rehabilitative services urged upon them.[38] In fact, the Director of the Family Services Center, who had been most sympathetic to the parents' predicament, was forced to conclude that the Santoskys' passivity and reluctance to cooperate with the Agency precluded the possibility of a reunion "in any foreseeable future."[39] Finding that the Agency had met its statutory burden of making diligent efforts to foster the family relationship by providing myriad services,[40] the court turned to the question whether the Santoskys had failed to plan for the future of the children.[41]

The court determined that the Santoskys had never formulated their own plan for the children and that they had failed for three years to cooperate with the Agency's plan.[42] Judge Elwyn therefore concluded that the record established, by a preponderance of the evidence, that the Santoskys had failed to plan for their children's future as required by the statute.[43] Upon a separate dispositional hearing, the court decided that the best interests of the children required the permanent termination of the parents' right to custody.[44]

The Santoskys challenged the constitutionality of the Family Court Act, contending that the standard of proof prescribed was so low as to deprive them of due process of law.[45] Following their unsuc-

---

[38] *In re* Apel, No. B-3-4-5-78, slip op. at 27 (Fam. Ct., Ulster County, March 12, 1979).

[39] *Id.* at 27-28.

[40] *Id.* at 20-21. The court held that the Agency's burden of showing that it had made "diligent efforts" to reunite the family had been "*amply* met by a preponderance of the evidence." *Id.* at 22 (emphasis added). *See supra* note 30.

[41] *In re* Apel, No. B-3-4-5-78, slip op. at 23 (Fam. Ct., Ulster County, March 12, 1979). *See* N.Y. Fam. Ct. Act § 614(1)(d) (McKinney Supp. Pamphlet 1981-1982). For a discussion of the meaning of the requirement that the parents plan for the future of the child, see *supra* note 35.

[42] *In re* Apel, No. B-3-4-5-78, slip op. at 27, 29 (Fam. Ct., Ulster County, March 12, 1979). ("Even giving them credit for their miniscule efforts to comply with the Agency's plan . . . is no longer enough to save them from the loss of their children, for the statute states that 'good faith effort shall not of itself, be determinative.' ").

[43] *Id.* at 30. *See supra* note 35.

[44] *In re* Apel, slip op. at 2 (Fam. Ct., Ulster County, April 10, 1979). The court noted that John and Tina could be expected "to have psychological difficulties in adjusting to any home situation," and therefore conditioned its order on the Commissioner's agreement to provide "supportive help" in order that each child might achieve a healthy, permanent family relationship. *Id.* at 2-3.

[45] This was the sole question on appeal. *In re* John AA., 75 A.D.2d 910, 427 N.Y.S.2d 319 (1980). Although the due process challenge was raised at the permanent neglect proceeding, *In re* Apel, No. B-3-4-5-78, slip op. at 17-18 (Fam. Ct., Ulster County, March 12, 1979), the court did not reach the constitutional question on the theory that courts of the first instance should refrain from declaring an act of the legislature unconstitutional except in rare instances involving life and liberty where the invalidity of the act is apparent on its face. *Id.* (citing N.Y. Statutes § 150 (McKinney 1971)). The case was therefore disposed of according to the standard of proof prescribed in the Family Court Act: a fair preponderance of the evidence. *In re* Apel, No. B-3-4-5-78 slip op. at 19 (Fam. Ct., Ulster County, March 12, 1979).

cessful appeals in the New York courts,[46] the Supreme Court granted the parents'. petition for writ of certiorari and gave them leave to proceed *in forma pauperis*.[47]

II. The Supreme Court's Decision in *Santosky*

After describing the statutory procedure for termination of parental rights in New York and reviewing the facts of *Santosky*,[48] Justice Blackmun, writing for the majority, noted that due process requires the state to provide parents with fundamental fairness in any action to sever familial bonds.[49] In *Mathews v. Eldridge*,[50] the Supreme Court announced a protocol for procedural due process analysis

---

[46] *In re* John AA., 75 A.D.2d 910, 427 N.Y.S.2d 319, *appeal dismissed sub nom. In re* Apel, 51 N.Y.2d 768, 411 N.E.2d 801, 432 N.Y.S.2d 1031 (1980).

[47] Santosky v. Kramer, 450 U.S. 993 (1981). The question of standard of proof in termination proceedings came before the Supreme Court in a recent case which was dismissed for want of a properly presented federal question. Doe v. Delaware, 450 U.S. 382, *reh'g denied*, 451 U.S. 964 (1981). Justice Stevens dissented from dismissal, finding the federal question concerning standard of proof to be "squarely at issue," and prophesied that it was "certain to reappear." 450 U.S. at 396. Perhaps the Court's true motivation in dismissing *Doe v. Delaware* was a belief that it would be a poor test case: the five children involved were the product of an incestuous relationship. *In re* Five Minor Children, 407 A.2d 198 (Del. 1979). The fact that the Santoskys were given leave to proceed *in forma pauperis* is evidence of the seriousness with which the Court viewed the question.

[48] Santosky v. Kramer, 102 S. Ct. at 1392-93.

[49] *Id.* at 1394. Specifically, Justice Blackmun observed that "[i]f anything, persons faced with forced dissolution of their parental rights have a more critical need for procedural protections than do those resisting state intervention into ongoing family affairs. When the State moves to destroy weakened familial bonds, it must provide the parents with fundamentally fair procedures." *Id.*

[50] 424 U.S. 319 (1976). In *Eldridge*, the Court was faced with the question whether due process requires an evidentiary hearing before a recipient of Social Security disability benefits may be deprived of such benefits. *Id.* at 323. Despite its recognition that "the interest of an individual in continued receipt of these benefits is a statutorily created 'property' interest protected by the Fifth Amendment," *id.* at 332, the Court in *Eldridge* held that termination of benefits without a prior hearing does not violate due process. *Id.* at 349.

The Court distinguished *Eldridge* from Goldberg v. Kelly, 397 U.S. 254 (1970), which held that an eligibility hearing is required before a state may terminate an individual's welfare benefits. *Id.* at 264. A significant factor in *Goldberg* was the desperate situation an individual might face during the period after termination and before an eligibility hearing could be held. The plight of the Eldridge family was no less desperate. After termination of the disability benefits, the mortgage on their home was foreclosed and their furniture was repossessed, requiring the entire family to sleep in one bed. 424 U.S. at 350 (Brennan, J., dissenting). *Eldridge* evidences the Supreme Court's reluctance to expand the "entitlement" theory advanced in *Goldberg* and similar cases. *See* L. Tribe, American Constitutional Law § 10-10, at 522-32 (1978); Marshaw, *The Supreme Court's Calculus for Administrative Adjudication in* Mathews v. Eldridge: *Three Factors in Search of a Theory of Value*, 44 U. Chi. L. Rev. 28 (1976).

which it has followed in a number of subsequent cases.[51] Accordingly, the *Santosky* Court undertook the *Eldridge* analysis, which calls for a balancing of three factors: the private interest involved, the risk of erroneous deprivation through the procedures chosen, and the governmental interest at stake.[52] An understanding of the *Santosky* decision therefore requires a detailed consideration of each of these factors.

A. The Private Interests Involved in a Termination Proceeding

The *Santosky* Court envisioned a termination hearing as a simple adversarial proceeding between the parents and the state.[53] The Court therefore identified the private interest involved as the *parents'* "fundamental liberty interest" in the custody and care of their children,[54] a compelling interest that demands heightened procedural safeguards.[55] An interest of this magnitude, the Court concluded, militated against the use of the preponderance standard in a permanent

---

[51] *See, e.g.,* Lassiter v. Department of Social Servs., 452 U.S. 18 (1981) (right to counsel in termination proceedings); Memphis Light, Gas & Water Div. v. Craft, 436 U.S. 1 (1978) (procedural safeguards for customers of government operated utility prior to termination of service); Smith v. Organization of Foster Families, 431 U.S. 816 (1977) (procedures governing removal of child from foster home).

In *Lassiter,* another 5-4 decision, the Court weighed the *Eldridge* factors and concluded that due process does not require appointment of counsel for indigent parents in all termination proceedings. Such a decision, the Court held, may be left to the discretion of the trial court "subject . . . to appellate review." 452 U.S. at 32. At the time her child was removed from her custody, the petitioner in *Lassiter* had neither counsel nor "the benefit of the 'clear, cogent and convincing' evidentiary standard." *Id.* at 29 n.4. Nevertheless, due process was not offended. If litigation without counsel under a preponderance standard was fundamentally fair, then a hearing under the same standard with counsel appointed for both parent and child as required in New York, *see* N.Y. FAM. CT. ACT §§ 249, 262(a)(v) (McKinney Supp. 1981-1982), should not present a due process problem. *See infra* text accompanying notes 81-82.

[52] Mathews v. Eldridge, 424 U.S. 319, 335 (1976). Specifically, the Court stated that its prior decisions indicate that identification of the specific dictates of due process generally requires consideration of three factors: First, the private interest that will be affected by the official action; second, the risk of an erroneous deprivation of such interest through the procedures used, and the probable value, if any, of additional or substitute procedural safeguards; and finally, the Government's interest, including the function involved and the fiscal and administrative burdens that the additional or substitute procedural requirement would entail.

Id. at 334-35. Professor Tribe feels that the Court's reliance upon the "utilitarian balancing test" of *Eldridge* represents an abdication of its judicial responsibility to safeguard individual rights. L. TRIBE, *supra* note 50, §10-13, at 542-43.

[53] Santosky v. Kramer, 102 S. Ct. at 1398. The Court stated that "the factfinding hearing pits the State directly against the parents." *Id.* at 1397.

[54] *Id.* at 1394. *See supra* note 2.

[55] Santosky v. Kramer, 102 S. Ct. at 1397.

neglect proceeding.[56]

In sharp contrast to the majority opinion, the dissent recognized that the child has an interest in a stable and loving homelife.[57] When this interest, which the state shares,[58] is balanced against the parents' interest in the custody of their child, it may be constitutionally permissible for the state to require that the parties bear the risk of error equally.[59] Justice Rehnquist, writing for the dissent, maintained that a proper due process inquiry requires an examination of *all* the procedural protections afforded the parents.[60] The dissent therefore concluded that, in light of the state's "fundamentally fair" scheme for handling neglect, New York's reliance on the standard of proof by a preponderance of the evidence did not violate due process.[61]

---

[56] *Id.* According to the Court, "the first *Eldridge* factor—the private interest affected—weighs heavily against the use of the preponderance standard at a State-initiated permanent neglect proceeding." *Id.*

[57] *Id.* at 1412 (Rehnquist, White, O'Connor, J.J., & Burger, C.J., dissenting). Justice Rehnquist took issue with the Court's conclusion that the child has no interest at stake in a termination proceeding. *Id.* at 1412 n.13. Consistent with this view, the dissent maintained that it is permissible for the standard of proof to balance "the interests at stake in a particular case." *Id.* at 1411. Thus, "[o]n one side is the interest of the parents in a continuation of the family unit and the raising of their own children. . . . On the other side of the termination proceeding are the often countervailing interests of the child." *Id.* at 1412. The dissent also stressed the need to safeguard the child's "physical, emotional and spiritual well-being." *Id.*

[58] *Id.* at 1413. The dissent maintained that " 'the State has an urgent interest in the welfare of the child.' " *Id.* (quoting Lassiter v. Department of Social Servs., 452 U.S. 18, 27 (1981)). *See supra* notes 6-9 and accompanying text.

[59] Santosky v. Kramer, 102 S. Ct. at 1413. According to the dissent, "a State constitutionally may conclude that the risk of error should be borne in roughly equal fashion by use of the preponderance of the evidence standard of proof." *Id.*

[60] *Id.* at 1405. The Justice reasoned that

[d]ue process of law is a flexible constitutional principle. The requirements which it imposes upon governmental actions vary with the situations to which it applies. . . .

Given this flexibility, it is obvious that a proper due process inquiry cannot be made by focusing upon one narrow provision of the challenged statutory scheme. Such a focus threatens to overlook factors which may introduce constitutionally adequate protections into a particular government action.

Id. According to Justice Rehnquist, the Court's refusal to examine the standard of proof in context

denies the flexibility that we have long recognized in the principle of due process; understates the error-reducing power of procedural protections such as the right to counsel, evidentiary hearings, rules of evidence, and appellate review; and establishes the standard of proof as the *sine qua non* of procedural due process.

Id. at 1406 n.4.

[61] *Id.* at 1414. The majority refused to consider New York's statutory scheme for termination of parental rights as a "package." *Id.* at 1396 n.9. The dissent, on the other hand, stressed that due process is a flexible doctrine. Accordingly, "[c]ourts must examine *all* procedural protections offered by the State and must assess the *cumulative* effect of such safeguards." *Id.* at 1405. In the context of the New York procedure for termination, proof by a fair preponderance of the evidence does not result in a deprivation of "fundamental fairness." *Id.* at 1405-06 &

The Court noted that the child shares his parents' interest in avoiding the erroneous termination of the family relationship.[62] The parental interest involved in a termination proceeding, however, is not merely the disinterested prevention of "erroneous termination." If it were, the same parents would presumably have no interest in retaining custody of their children where termination would not be erroneous. Rather, the parents' sole interest lies in retaining the custody of their child.[63] As the dissent pointed out, the child shares that interest only where preserving the family unit will not constitute a harm to him.[64] Thus, while "the State cannot presume that a child and his parents are adversaries,"[65] neither can the state presume that they are not.

In choosing to ignore the child, and in characterizing the termination proceeding as a simple contest between parents and state, the Court overlooked the fact that protecting the child's welfare is the very reason for state intervention in cases of neglect. Society does not require parental competence for the sake of the parents. If the child does not have a significant interest at stake in such proceedings, it is difficult to justify any degree of state intervention in the family.

B.   The Risk of Erroneous Termination

Turning to the second *Eldridge* factor, the Court examined the question whether the standard of proof by a fair preponderance of the evidence fairly allocated the risk of error between the parents and the state.[66] In finding that it did not, the Court cited several factors which it felt magnified the risk of error in a permanent neglect proceeding. Among these were the discretion allowed the family court, the disparity between the resources of the litigants, and the

---

nn.3-4.

[62] *Id.* at 1398. The Court cautioned that, at the factfinding, the state cannot presume that parents and child are adversaries. *Id.* Rather, they "share a vital interest in preventing erroneous termination of their natural relationship." *Id.*

[63] *See supra* text accompanying note 54.

[64] *Santosky v. Kramer*, 102 S. Ct. at 1412 n.13. As Justice Rehnquist observed:
To be sure, "the child and his parents share a vital interest in preventing *erroneous* termination of their natural relationship." But the child's interest in a continuation of the family unit exists only to the extent that such a continuation would not be harmful to him. An error *in the factfinding hearing* that results in a failure to terminate a parent-child relationship which rightfully should be terminated may well detrimentally affect the child.
Id. (citation omitted).

[65] *Id.* at 1398. *See supra* note 62.

[66] *Santosky v. Kramer*, 102 S. Ct. at 1398.

"striking asymmetry in their litigation options."[67] These factors will be considered separately.

1. Discretion of the Court

Decrying the unusual discretion[68] possessed by the family court in a permanent neglect proceeding, Justice Blackmun pointed to two specific instances in which the court is given such latitude. First, New York allows the court to excuse the Agency from attempting to reunite the family where such efforts would be harmful to the child.[69] Second, in considering whether the parents have planned for the future of their child, the court may disregard any plan that is unrealistic in light of the physical and financial resources of the parents.[70] The dissent was satisifed that the discretion vested in the family court was not overly broad.[71]

While the Court correctly pointed out that the trier of fact has discretion in a termination proceeding, it must be remembered that such discretion does not exist in a vacuum. New York's avowed purpose is to preserve the family whenever possible.[72] The provision allowing the court to excuse the Agency from making efforts to reunite the family where those efforts would be detrimental to the child's welfare is a mechanism for providing protection to the child in the extreme case where, for example, the parent physically abuses him during the initial visits after removal.[73] Since the Agency is required to specify its reasons for declining to attempt to reunite the family,[74] the possibility that the Agency will base its decision on inappropriate

---

[67] *Id.* at 1399.

[68] *Id.* Specifically, the Court remarked that the trial court "possesses unusual discretion to underweigh probative facts that might favor the parent." *Id.*

[69] *Id.* at 1399 n.12; N.Y. FAM. CT. ACT § 614(1)(c) (McKinney Supp. Pamphlet 1981-1982). *See supra* note 33.

[70] Santosky v. Kramer, 102 S. Ct. at 1399 n.12. *See* N.Y. SOC. SERV. LAW § 384-b(7)(c) (McKinney Supp. 1981-1982). *See also supra* note 35.

[71] Santosky v. Kramer, 102 S. Ct. at 1410 n.11. Justice Rehnquist stated that "the 'unusual' discretion of the family court judge to consider the 'affectio[n] and concer[n]' displayed by parents during visits with their children . . . is nothing more than discretion to consider reality." *Id.* The dissent saw no basis for the Court's characterization of the state "as a wealthy and powerful bully bent on taking children away from defenseless parents." *Id.*

[72] N.Y. SOC. SERV. LAW § 384-b(1)(a)(ii) (McKinney Supp. 1981-1982). For a discussion of the efforts made by the Agency to reunite the Santosky family in particular, see *supra* note 30 and accompanying text.

[73] Practice Commentary to N.Y. Soc. SERV. LAW § 384-b (McKinney Supp. 1981-1982) (by J. Carrieri). *See, e.g., In re* Terry D., 53 A.D.2d 957, 385 N.Y.S.2d 844 (1976).

[74] N.Y. FAM. CT. ACT § 614(1)(c) (McKinney Supp. Pamphlet 1981-1982).

grounds is avoided.

Under New York's statutory scheme, the family court judge is not free to impose his own values; rather, he must evaluate the plan with respect to the financial and social resources of the parents.[75] Given that the standard which the court must apply is so clearly defined, the mere fact that the court may reject an unrealistic plan does not vest it with "unusual" discretion. As the dissent noted, this is merely the discretion to consider reality.[76]

2. Disparity in Litigation Resources

Contributing to the Court's decision that due process requires an elevated standard of proof in termination proceedings was the majority's concern that the ability of the state to prepare its case "almost inevitably dwarfs the parents' ability to mount a defense."[77] The Court was concerned that the state's "expert" attorney, who has full access to the public records concerning the family, might spend unlimited sums to prosecute a particular termination proceeding.[78]

The dissent found nothing in the record to support the majority's fear that the state was bent on persecuting innocent parents.[79] In particular, Justice Rehnquist emphasized the fact that New York's statutory scheme for termination requires that indigent parents be provided with counsel throughout the proceedings.[80]

It is difficult to reconcile the *Santosky* Court's concern over the disparity between the litigation resources of the parents and the state with the Court's earlier decision in *Lassiter v. Department of Social*

---

[75] *See supra* note 35.

[76] *See supra* note 71.

[77] Santosky v. Kramer, 102 S. Ct. at 1399.

[78] *Id.* The Court went on to observe that "the primary witnesses at the hearing will be the agency's own professional caseworkers whom the State has empowered . . . to testify against the parents." *Id.* This indicates that the Court believed that, from the outset, the Agency had no intention of providing services to reunite the family. Rather, the Agency employed these caseworkers merely to build a case against the parents. The Court also suggested that, because the child was in the custody of a state agency, the state would use its "power to shape the historical events that form the basis for termination." *Id.* The Court did not, however, adduce any support for this proposition.

[79] Santosky v. Kramer, 102 S. Ct. at 1410 n.11. *See supra* note 71.

[80] Santosky v. Kramer, 102 S. Ct. at 1410 n.11. Justice Rehnquist stressed the fact that "if parents lack the 'ability to mount a defense,' the State provides them with the full services of an attorney." *Id.* (citation omitted). Furthermore, the parents' access to public records concerning the family equals that of the state. *Id.* The dissent was thus persuaded that the New York statutory scheme as a whole was fundamentally fair to the parents. *Id.* at 1410.

Services.[81] In *Lassiter,* the Court held that the decision whether to appoint counsel for an indigent parent in a termination proceeding should be left to the states.[82] Where the disparity in the adversaries' resources is not so severe that due process requires the appointment of counsel in a proceeding to terminate parental rights—a step that would go far toward putting the litigants on an equal footing—it is unclear why this factor should weigh heavily in considering the standard of proof in such proceedings.

3.   Asymmetry in Litigation Options

The *Santosky* Court noted that once the parents are found to have met the minimum statutory level of fitness, they have no "double jeopardy" guarantee that they will be safe from subsequent state efforts to terminate their parental rights.[83] This concern with "double jeopardy" is inappropriate. While the fifth amendment protects the individual against multiple trials for the same offense,[84] separate acts or abuses are separate offenses; a "repeat offender" is not immune from multiple prosecutions. Providing a "double jeopardy" defense in neglect proceedings would lead to absurd results. Once a parent had been found "not guilty" of neglecting his child, the state would be powerless to intervene regardless of the parent's future treatment of that child.

While the majority found that the foregoing factors, coupled with a preponderance standard, heightened the risk of erroneous termination,[85] the dissent stressed that the function of a standard of proof is

---

[81] 452 U.S. 18 (1981).

[82] *Id.* at 31-32. *See supra* note 51.

[83] Santosky v. Kramer, 102 S. Ct. at 1399-1400. Justice Blackmun compared termination proceedings to criminal proceedings in his dissenting opinion in *Lassiter.* Lassiter v. Department of Social Servs., 452 U.S. at 42-43. There, the Justice carried the analogy further, remarking that a termination proceeding "has an obvious accusatory and punitive focus." *Id.* at 43. But the purpose of termination is not to "punish" parents. Rather, it is to make the best of the unfortunate situation that arises where "positive, nurturing parent-child relationships no longer exist" by "freeing the child for adoption." N.Y. Soc. SERV. LAW § 384-b(1)(b) (McKinney Supp. 1981-1982).

[84] U.S. CONST. amend. V.

[85] Santosky v. Kramer, 102 S. Ct. at 1400. The Court reasoned that, even if the appellate division was correct in suggesting that the preponderance standard properly balanced the interests of both parents and child, the parents' interest in avoiding erroneous termination outweighed any interest the child might have in avoiding an erroneous failure to terminate. *Id.* at 1400-01. The Court remarked that

  [f]or the child, the likely consequence of an erroneous failure to terminate is preservation of an uneasy status quo. For the natural parents, however, the consequence of an errone-

not merely to minimize the risk of error.[86] Rather, since errors in factfinding affect all parties concerned, it is crucial that the risk be minimized as to those interests which are most important.[87] Taking issue with the majority's conclusion that the child has no interest in the termination proceeding, Justice Rehnquist pointed out that a failure to terminate the parents' custody might well have detrimental effects upon the child.[88] The dissent therefore concluded that, in balancing the interests of the child and the state against those of the parents, it is constitutionally permissible for the parties to share the risk of error equally where the overall statutory scheme affords the parents adequate procedural protection.[89]

---

ous termination is the unnecessary destruction of their natural family. A standard that allocates the risk of error nearly equally between those two outcomes does not reflect properly their relative severity.

Id. (footnote omitted). At the very least, this position is debatable. Authority exists for the proposition that there is a direct correlation between the severity of emotional problems encountered in adopted children and the age of the child at the time of placement. *See* 3 H. KAPLAN, A. FREEDMAN & B. SADOCK, COMPREHENSIVE TEXTBOOK OF PSYCHIATRY 2756 (3d ed. 1980). *See also* Santosky v. Kramer, 102 S. Ct. at 1412-13 (Rehnquist, White, O'Connor, J.J. & Burger, C.J., dissenting). The duration of this "uneasy status quo" is actually precious time during which the child is vulnerable to becoming psychologically and socially impaired. If such consequences are taken into account in calculating the risk of error, it is not at all clear that an elevated standard of proof is appropriate in termination proceedings.

[86] Santosky v. Kramer, 102 S. Ct. at 1411. Justice Rehnquist explained that "[i]n determining the propriety of a particular standard of proof in a given case, . . . it is not enough simply to say that we are trying to minimize the risk of error. Because errors in factfinding affect more than one interest, we try to minimize error *as to those interests which we consider to be most important.*" *Id.* (emphasis added). The disagreement between the majority and the dissent on this point stems from the fact that, unlike the majority, the dissent recognized that the child has an interest at stake in a termination proceeding. *Compare id.* at 1397 *with id.* at 1412 n.13 (Rehnquist, White, O'Connor, J.J., & Burger, C.J., dissenting).

[87] *Id.* at 1411. *See supra* note 86.

[88] Santosky v. Kramer, 102 S. Ct. at 1412 n.13. The dissent was convinced that
   children who are abused in their youth generally face extraordinary problems developing into responsible, productive citizens. The same can be said of children who, though not physically or emotionally abused, are passed from one foster home to another with no constancy of love, trust or discipline. If the Family Court makes an incorrect factual determination resulting in a failure to terminate a parent-child relationship which rightfully should be ended, the child involved must return either to an abusive home or to the often unstable world of foster care.

Id. at 1412-13 (footnotes omitted). *See supra* note 85.

[89] Santosky v. Kramer, 102 S. Ct. at 1413. Specifically, the dissent maintained that
   [w]hen, in the context of a permanent neglect termination proceeding, the interests of the child and the State in a stable, nurturing homelife are balanced against the interests of the parents in the rearing of their child, it cannot be said that either set of interests is so clearly paramount as to require that the risk of error be allocated to one side or the other. Accordingly, a State constitutionally may conclude that the risk of error should be borne in roughly equal fashion by use of the prepondernce standard of proof.

Id.

C. The Governmental Interest

In analyzing the final *Eldridge* factor, the Court noted that there are two state interests at stake in a termination proceeding: a fiscal interest in minimizing the cost of the proceedings, and a *parens patriae* interest in the welfare of the child.[90] The Court found that both these interests are promoted by a standard of proof more stringent than a preponderance of the evidence.[91]

As the Court noted in *Lassiter,* the state has a relatively insignificant pecuniary interest in a termination proceeding.[92] It is therefore of little consequence that elevating the standard of proof might place an added financial burden on the state. It is the state's second interest, that of safeguarding the welfare of its children, which deserves greater consideration in this context. In a termination proceeding, the state appears in order to protect the welfare of the child. Where this interest, which child and state share, is balanced against the parents' interest in custody, there is no apparent reason for the state to bear a greater risk of error. As the dissent noted, where the overall scheme is fundamentally fair to the parents, the state may constitutionally require the parties to share the risk of error equally.[93]

---

[90] *Id.* at 1401.

[91] *Id.* The Court remarked that, at the factfinding, the state's *parens patriae* goal of providing a permanent home for the child is best served "by procedures that promote an accurate determination of whether the natural parents can and will provide a normal home." *Id.* There was no showing in *Santosky,* however, that the family court's determination was inaccurate. As the dissent noted,

> the State's extraordinary four-year effort to reunite petitioners' family was not just unsuccessful, it was altogether rebuffed by parents unwilling to improve their circumstances sufficiently to permit a return of their children. At every step of this protracted process petitioners were accorded those procedures and protections which traditionally have been required by due process of law. Moreover, from the beginning to the end of this sad story all judicial determinations were made by one family court judge. After four and one-half years of involvement with petitioners, more than seven complete hearings, and additional periodic supervision of the State's rehabilitative efforts, the judge no doubt was intimately familiar with this case and the prospects for petitioners' rehabilitation.

Id. at 1410.

[92] Lassiter v. Department of Social Servs., 452 U.S. 18, 28 (1981). In view of the efforts made by the state to reunite the Santosky family, *see supra* note 30, it is apparent that cutting costs was not a motivating force in these proceedings. In fact, once before when the Agency filed permanent neglect petitions in this case, the family court ordered the Agency to "redouble its efforts" on behalf of the Santoskys. *See supra* note 32.

[93] Santosky v. Kramer, 102 S. Ct. at 1413. *See supra* note 89.

III. Conclusion

A termination proceeding is actually a three-party action involving the interests of parents, child, and state. New York law presumes that it is in the child's best interest to remain with his natural parents and therefore makes every effort to foster the family relationship.[94] It is clear, however, that "parental rights are limited by the legitimate rights and interests of their children."[95] Where the child has been in the custody of an agency for a year or more,[96] his own rights to stability and to "proper custody" take on increasing significance. Due process requires that the child's interest be expressly considered in any proceeding which affects his all too precarious position. The child's right to fair process cannot simply be ignored in favor of his parents' rights.

Under New York's statutory scheme, a proceeding to terminate parental rights cannot occur until the child has been in the care of an authorized agency for more than one year.[97] In addition, the agency must make diligent efforts to reunite the family,[98] counsel is provided for both parents and child,[99] and, even if the child is found to be permanently neglected, there must be a separate dispositional hearing to terminate parental rights.[100] Since the termination proceeding is but one part of a comprehensive statutory scheme for handling the problem of child neglect, the applicable standard of proof should not have been examined in isolation. When it is viewed in the context of the New York statutory scheme for termination, it seems clear that the standard of proof by a preponderance of the evidence does not offend fundamental notions of fairness. Moreover, when the interest of the parents in raising their child is balanced against the child's interest in proper custody and the state's interest in the welfare of its children, it cannot be said with certainty that the parents' interests are so clearly superior as to require that a greater risk of error be imposed upon child and state.

---

[94] New York's Social Services Law provides that "the state's first obligation is to help the family with services to prevent its break-up or to reunite it if the child has already left home." N.Y. Soc. Serv. Law § 384-b(1)(a)(iii) (McKinney Supp. 1981-1982).

[95] Parham v. J. R., 442 U.S. 584, 630 (1979). *See id.* at 603-04 (Due process rights of parent and child are not identical in cases of child abuse or neglect.).

[96] The Santosky children, for example, were in foster care for nine years. *See supra* text accompanying note 21.

[97] *See supra* notes 17 & 33.

[98] N.Y. Fam. Ct. Act § 614(1) (McKinney Supp. Pamphlet 1981-1982). *See supra* note 30.

[99] N.Y. Fam. Ct. Act §§ 249, 262 (McKinney Supp. Pamphlet 1981-1982). *See supra* note 51.

[100] *See supra* note 36.

Although a finding of permanent neglect may result in the permanent severance of the parent-child relationship, the purpose of such a proceeding is not to punish the parents; it is to free the child from what has become a hopeless situation in order that he might find stability in an adoptive home. Tina Frances Apel, now ten years old, was in foster care for nine years.[101] During this time, while the Santoskys made indifferent efforts to become responsible parents, Tina and her brothers were left in a kind of limbo. Surely these children, and others like them, deserve the same degree of consideration afforded their parents under current law. It is time they were given a chance to find security and what remains to them of a "normal childhood."

CATHERINE B. GABRIELS

---

[101] On remand from the United States Supreme Court, the judgment permanently terminating the Santoskys' parental rights was affirmed by the appellate division. *In re* John "AA," 89 A.D.2d 738, 453 N.Y.S.2d 942 (1982) (mem.).

The Legal Representation of Children in Protection Proceedings: Some Empirical Findings and a Reflection on Public Policy*

ROBERT F. KELLY AND SARAH H. RAMSEY**

In the last two decades federal and state governments have become increasingly concerned with child abuse and neglect. One result of this concern has been the passage of legislation in many states providing legal representation for children in protection proceedings. While this legislation presumes that attorneys will provide a benefit for children, there are few empirical evaluations of this assumption. This study reports on an evaluation of legal representation for children in the state of North Carolina. The evaluation is based on a random sample of child protection cases and attorneys who served in these cases. Using information concerning the court's custodial disposition, a scale of judicial coercion was developed and used as a basis for evaluating the performance of attorneys. A multivariate model of judicial coercion was estimated. Based on this model it was found that attorneys in general produced no significant benefit for the children represented. However, particular types of attorneys who were effective are identified. Recommendations for improving the provision of services to abused/neglected children are presented.

Introduction

In the last two decades there has been a great increase in concern over child abuse and neglect. One outgrowth of this concern was a federal requirement that the states provide representation for children in abuse/neglect judicial proceedings. This requirement was indirectly imposed through a funding mechanism in the 1974 Child Abuse Prevention and Treatment Act. A majority of states responded to this requirement by providing attorneys for children in these proceedings.

*Paper presented at the 10th International Congress of the International Association of Child and Adolescent Psychiatry and Allied Professions, Dublin, July 27, 1982. Research for this article was supported by a grant from the Z. Smith Reynolds Foundation and NIMH Grant No. 5T32 NIH I 5188-02.
**Assistant Professor of Sociology and Director, Program in Applied Sociology and Urban Policy Studies, Wayne State University, Detroit, MI 48202.
Associate Professor of Law, College of Law, Syracuse University, NY 13210.

Key Words: abuse, children, custody, evaluation, law, neglect, policy.

(Family Relations, 1985, 34, 277-283.)

The policy of requiring that attorneys be appointed to represent children in protection proceedings is based on the assumption that attorneys will provide a significant benefit to allegedly abused and neglected children. It is this assumption which justifies spending scarce public funds on lawyers for children rather than, for example, additional social, medical or psychiatric services for these children and their families. However, to date there have been few efforts to empirically evaluate this assumption due at least in part to the formidable difficulties in developing a standard for judging the impact of representation and in gaining access to confidential court records on abuse and neglect cases.

This article suggests one type of standard which would appear to be appropriate for judging attorney performance in court systems that are highly interventionistic in nature. Using data from the first sixteen months of operation of a statute providing for the use of attorneys for children in the state of North Carolina, this standard is applied to evaluate the performance of attorneys. Discussions are presented of the development of the standard of benefit and the methodology used to gather data for the analysis. Next a description of the use of the standard as part of a multivariate evaluation of the impact of attorneys for children is provided. The paper concludes with a reflection on public policy strategies for improving services for abused/neglected children based on the results of the evaluation.

Developing a Standard of Effective Representation

Decisions concerning custody (removal from or return of children to parents or guardians) are central to judicial strategies for handling abused and neglected children. However, since such decisions have an enormous impact on the lives of parents and children, they should be carefully made. Two factors militate against removing a child from his home except in extraordinary circumstances; first, the harm caused by removal and second, the principle of family integrity.

When a child is allegedly abused or neglected the first impulse is to rescue the child from the poor home environment by removing the child and not returning custody until progress has been demonstrated in the home. However, removing the custody of a child from his caretakers can be very harmful to both child and parents, and therefore should not be the automatic response of the court in a child protection case. While removal may protect the child from certain types of harm, it may also be more emotionally damaging to the child than nonremoval and result in harmful reductions in the parent's and child's self esteem (Littner, 1956; Mnookin, 1973). Additionally, the safe homes to which children are often removed, usually foster care, generally have many negative aspects in themselves (Gil, 1974; Mnookin, 1973, 1975; Wald, 1975, 1976).

Thus, since removal is harmful, removal should be a remedy of last resort used only if less intrusive forms of intervention cannot prevent harm. This stance against removal is also supported by the Constitutional protections extended to the family against unreasonable state interference. The integrity of the family unit and maintenance of the parent-child relationship are among the fundamental rights of Americans. Since removal of a child from the custody of a parent infringes on these rights, the court should have a strong reason for ordering such an action.

An example of legislation which contains this policy stance against removal is the Federal Adoption Assistance and Child Welfare Act of 1980 (P.L. 96-272) which conditions a state's receipt of Federal funds upon the development of service programs designed to keep families together. This and related legislation allows a reduction in a state's federal foster care funds if the state has not implemented "a preplacement preventive ser-

vices program designed to help children remain with their families."[1]

Hence the policy against removal is supported by research suggesting that removal may be harmful and by the principle of protecting the family from unreasonable state interference. Additionally, the concept that removal should be a remedy of last resort has been widely accepted. The next question that must be considered is how to turn this macropolicy into an evaluation tool for a particular piece of legislation—in this instance legislation which provided for the appointment of attorneys.

For this evaluation, a measure of the degree of state intervention was developed. This measure is *judicial coercion* and it is defined as the propensity of a court to intervene in the lives of families in which abuse or neglect is alleged by removing the child from the home and once removed, keeping the child out of the home for a substantial period of time. While the term coercion may possess a certain value-laden connotation, it is used here only to refer the court's use of the most forceful strategy available to it. The use of coercion is, of course, a relative matter. Minimally it must be judged relative to the weight of factors which would justify its use and relative to the amount of force normally used under similar circumstances.

In the North Carolina sample used in the present analysis, custody was removed from parents in 87% of all abuse/neglect petitions which were brought before the court (Sample N = 210). The North Carolina sample was representative of the entire state caseload of child protection cases handled by the courts. Of the 183 cases in which custody was removed, it was returned to parents in 67 cases (37%) during the time period studied.[2] Using the distribution of custodial decisions, an ordinal scale of *judicial coercion* was formulated in which *low coercion* was represented by cases in which custody was not removed (27 cases, 13%), *high coercion* was represented by cases in which custody was removed and not returned during the period studied (116 cases, 55%), and *medium levels of coercion* were represented by those cases in which custody was removed but subsequently returned (67 cases, 32%).

---

[1] 42 U.S.C. 627 (b)(3)(Supp. 1975).

---

[2] Data were collected from March through June, 1979 for cases in which a petition was filed between September 1977 and December 1978. For those cases in which custody was returned during this time period, the average number of days that cases were under court supervision was 90. Thus, nearly all of the cases in the sample had court data available for far in excess of 90 days.

The next important question is the feasibility of using the scale, *judicial coercion*, as a measure of attorney impact on abuse/neglect cases in North Carolina. In this respect it is instructive to note that the statutory scheme by which abuse/neglect cases were handled in North Carolina made it relatively easy to remove a child, even prior to a full hearing on the merits of the allegation. Additionally, return of custody was not encouraged.[3] In fact removal occurred in a large majority (87%) of North Carolina cases whereas nationally only one-third to one half of court proceedings assessing child maltreatment result in removal (Aber, 1980). Thus, the North Carolina system may be characterized as highly interventionist in its use of removal as compared to the national average.

But there may well be conditions under which this significantly higher than average use of *judicial coercion* would be justified. Two such conditions would be that the North Carolina cases were significantly worse than other cases nationally and/or that the North Carolina court system had strong therapeutic grounds for its decision to remove custody and not return it. There is no research available to support a suggestion that North Carolina's cases were any worse than those in other states in terms of the problems which brought the cases to the court's attention. Indeed since a much higher percentage (33%) of substantiated abuse/neglect cases are brought to court in North Carolina than are nationally (14%), the North Carolina court caseload should have comprised a broader range of cases. Additionally, a statistical trend exists in the North Carolina data indicating that unnecessary and apparently unjustified removals occurred on a systematic basis. In the analysis reported here and elsewhere (Kelly & Ramsey, 1983) no statistically significant relationship was found to exist between a measure called *removal risk* which gauges the severity of the alleged problems, and the exercise of *judicial coercion* (Table 1).[4] What this means is that high and low risk cases were equally likely to be removed and not returned to parents. These findings are similar to those reported by Runyan et al. (1981) based on a different sample of North Carolina protection cases.

However, relationships shown in Table 1 do indicate that *judicial coercion* was exercised to a significantly greater extent when families

had a long social service history and when several categories of problems were alleged in the petition. The image that emerges from these findings is that *judical coercion* was largely exercised as a function of how troublesome families were to local departments of social services, rather than as a function of potential serious and immediate harm to children.

With these considerations as a rationale it is proposed that the measure *judicial coercion* may be used, at least in the case of a judicial system such as North Carolina's, as a standard by which to evaluate attorney impact. It is suggested that attorneys, *ceteris paribus*, produce a benefit for population of child clients to the extent that they are able to reduce *judicial coercion*. Thus, in a system such as North Carolina's in which a great deal of judicial intervention is used without strong diagnostic/therapeutic bases for this use, there should be a statistical tendency toward less coercion in cases in which children have attorneys. These attorneys would not reject custody removal *a priori* but rather, acting in the child's interests, they would independently scrutinize interventionistic tendencies both of social services and the courts. This approach is consistent with the intent of much of the legislation which provides for attorneys in protection proceedings and it is consistent with current public policy. It is also consistent with the underlying principles of more innovative programs which have sought to provide legal services for children in protection proceedings. O'Shea, in a description of Child Advocacy Unit (CAU) of the Family Court of Philadelphia, has noted that:

> It is a basic philosophy of the Unit that a child belongs with its own parents, in his own home and with his own siblings (1980, 278).

Note that the standard is probabilistic in that it is posed in terms of population tendencies rather than individual cases. As such, the standard does not reject the fact that removal and non-return is undoubtedly justified in certain individual cases. Indeed, the occurrence of such cases in average numbers would not invalidate the use of *judicial coercion* as a measure of attorney impact.

Thus the proposed standard of attorney effectiveness has the merit of being a tool for measuring program impact which is consistent with current public policy. While this standard may be at variance to some degree with clinical ideologies which emphasize the need for removal and professional therapy and supervision, it is a standard with which clinicians should be familiar, for in the last instance their practices operate within a macro-institutional and legal policy environment. Additionally, the statistical model presented here will be of value to family practitioners because it

---

[3]For a full discussion of this process see Kelly & Ramsey (1983).

---

[4]Analysis of discrete types of problems indicated that problems of physical violence, sexual abuse, substance abuse and abandonment were no more or less likely to result in removal or return of custody than problems strictly related to poverty or "status offenses" by parents (Kelly & Ramsey, 1983).

Table 1
Regression Model of the Determinants of Judicial Coercion[a]

Independent Variables	Standard Coefficients	Level of Statistical Significance
Attorney for Child (ATT) Appointed (Yes = 74%)	−.009	.89
Average Hours Worked by ATT (M = 10.5 hours)[b]	−.111	.09
Children Matched with ATT by Race (Yes = 38%)[b]	−.126	.09
ATT Believes That Attorneys Should Be Automatically Appointed in ALL Abuse/Neglect Cases[c] (Definitely or Probably No = 31%)	−.108	.09
Parents or Guardian Has Counsel (Yes = 24%)	−.142	.03
Petition Indicates That Family Has Long Social Service History (Yes = 24%)	.142	.06
Removal Risk: Number of Reasons That Might Justify Removal Cited in Petition (M = 1.9)	.057	.37
Number of Types of Problems Mentioned In The Petition (M = 1.9)	.133	.048
Custody Removed by Immediate Custody Order (Yes = 58%)	.281	.00
Father Named As Source of Petition Problems (Yes = 12%)	−.142	.03
Days In The Court System[c] (M = 4.58 weighted days)	.138	.04

Note: n = 210; variance explained (R^2 = .23); correlation matrix available upon request.

[a]A high score on the judicial coercion dependent variable indicates that custody was removed but not returned (high coercion). A low score indicates that custody was not removed (low coercion) and a medium score indicates that custody was removed but subsequently returned (medium coercion).

[b]For cases in which an attorney was not appointed, attorney level missing values are set to the mean in order to minimize the loss of cases for the analysis.

[c]This variable is calculated as the number of days from petition date to the last date noted on the court record. It is weighted by the number of potential days a case could have spent in the court system as of the petition date for the period of time under study. The unweighted number of days under court supervision is 91.1.

analyzes the determinants of custodial dispositions by the courts and thereby provides useful information on how courts respond to cases of child abuse and neglect.

Methodology

In order to evaluate the impact of the presence of attorneys on the disposition of abuse and neglect cases in North Carolina a statewide stratified random sample of abuse/ neglect cases was collected. Sampling was conducted in two stages. First a sample of twenty of North Carolina's one hundred counties was drawn and evaluated for its representativeness. With the assistance of the State Administrative Office of the Courts access was granted by district court judges to juvenile court records in each of the twenty counties— a response rate of 100%. In the second stage of sampling, information was gathered from randomly selected juvenile court case records for 210 cases involving 375 children. To be in-

cluded in the population from which the sample was drawn an abuse/neglect petition had to have been filed between September 26, 1977 and December 31, 1978, the first sixteen months of operation of the representation statute. Data were collected on the outcomes of these cases through June of 1979. To supplement case-level data two additional sets of information were collected. It was decided that analysis would be improved if the purview of the inquiry could be expanded beyond the question; "Do lawyers make a difference?", to the broader question; "Are there specific types of attorneys who make a difference?" Thus an extensive survey of the attorneys who actually handled the cases was conducted.[5] In addition

'The attorney survey was conducted by Samuel Streit, Esq. of the Bush Institute for Child Development at the University of North Carolina at Chapel Hill. We gratefully acknowledge this contribution to the study.

442

to case and attorney information, structural/ contextual socioeconomic, demographic, and social service and judicial-administrative data were collected for each of the 20 counties. Case level, attorney level and county data are integrated in the analysis.

For the purposes of evaluating the impact of representation, the North Carolina data possess a distinct advantage. Since legal reforms are normally implemented on a universal and mandatory basis, evaluation of the impact of change is often difficult to carry out because, in an experimental sense, there is no variance (experimental group, control group) in the independent variable—namely the legal reform. However, in North Carolina attorneys were not always appointed and, because it was possible to statistically control for the factors which influenced appointment decisions the North Carolina data may be analyzed in a quasi-experimental fashion.

Determinants of Judicial Coercion: Analysis and Findings

Table 1 presents the results of an ordinary least-squares regression analysis of *judicial coercion*.[6] At various stages in the analysis several types of variables were scrutinized with respect to their ability to explain the variance in *judicial coercion,* the dependent variable in the model. Categories of variables analyzed include: characteristics of the court's treatment of the case, characteristics of the problems that brought the case to court, characteristics of the children named in the petition (e.g., race, age, sex), characteristics of the parents and family of the child,[7] characteristics of the attorney who served as the child's representative, and characteristics of the county in which the abuse/neglect petition was filed. The final model presented in Table 1 allows an assessment of the impact of attorneys by using the standard of benefit. None of the variables which were found to influence the appointment of an attorney was found to have a significant impact on judicial coercion nor was their inclusion in the model found to meaningfully alter its results.

---

[6]The dependent variable, *judicial coercion*, may be viewed as an ordinal measure. There are difficulties involved in the use of the ordinary least squares model for the analysis of ordinal variables. This is especially problematic in the present case because the ordinal measure is constructed from qualitative/ categorical scores based on custodial dispositions. As such the probit mode of analysis would normally be the method of choice (Goodman, 1978). However, because the sample size is relatively small, and because the probit model requires relatively large ratios of cases to independent variables, and finally because the complexity of judicial processes literally require a large number of independent variables, ordinary least squares regression was used to estimate the model.

---

[7]Unfortunately it was impossible to obtain a reliable measure of mother's age.

It is notable that slightly less than a quarter of the variance ($R^2 = .23$) in *judicial coercion* is explained by the model. While this figure is low in absolute terms, when the model is compared to other attempts to predict child abuse/neglect treatment outcomes, its explanatory power is quite strong. For example, Runyan et al. (1981) used approximately 40 variables in a very sophisticated attempt to model the determinants foster care as an outcome in child protection cases in North Carolina and were able to explain only seventeen percent of the variance.

The most important finding in Table 1 is that the appointment of an attorney, in itself, had no significant impact on *judicial coercion*. However, it was found that certain types of attorneys, most notably those who spent more than the normal number of hours on their cases, were able to significantly reduce the court's interventionist tendency. It was also found that for cases in which attorneys and children had been matched by race (i.e. black attorneys with black children and white attorneys with white children), there was an increased likelihood that custodial interventionism would be reduced. Finally it was found that those attorneys who were most skeptical about the need for universal appointment of attorneys in abuse/neglect cases were also more able to reduce *judical coercion*.

Taken as a whole the findings present few surprises. There is a substantial empirical literature indicating that legal representation alone seldom provides benefits either for children or other similar categories of clients (Clarke & Koch, 1980; Scheff, 1966). The explanation for this absence of impact is multifaceted. First, attorneys are seldom paid for their work in protection cases at a rate which is competitive with their private practices. As a consequence lawyers tend to view their child protection work as charitable in nature. Such an arrangement is unlikely to generate an adequate supply of either high quality representation or time commitments to cases. Second, the role of the child's representative is typically undefined and therefore the expectation that the attorney will act in the vigorous and independent fashion that the standard implies and the proponents of the enacting legislation envisioned is likely to be frustrated. The ambiguous role of the attorney is heightened by the fact that traditionally it was the role of the court, not attorneys, to represent the child and to act in the child's best interest (Ryerson, 1978).

It is encouraging, however, that when attorneys were highly committed to their cases (as measured by average hours worked on cases), they could produce benefits as measured by the standard of *judicial coercion*. The finding that racial matching between attorney and child was associated with beneficial out-

443

comes may be explained by the fact that attorney-child as well as attorney-parent communication and cooperation are likely to be enhanced where fewer social and cultural barriers exist. Since so much of the lawyer's trade and craft is premised on the ability to correctly read the intent of the client, it is understandable that racial matching would manifest some influence on lawyer-child relationships. This interpretation is supported by much of the research literature on the bias which is introduced into the social survey interview situation by racial mismatching (Dohrenwend et al., 1968). Attorneys who were skeptical about the need for guardians in every abuse/neglect case were also more likely to serve their clients well. These attorneys may have felt that they could not have an effective role in some cases, perhaps those in which there were almost no choices about disposition. They also may have understood the interventionist nature of the court system and the frustrations involved in any attempt to restrain the interventionist tendency. It should be noted that these skeptical attorneys were those who were likely to work more hours on their child protection cases than other attorneys. This interpretation is reinforced even further by other analyses which showed that those attorneys who were most independent of the court's interventionist milieu were best able to serve their clients (Kelly & Ramsey, 1983).

Variables other than those measuring the impact of representation on the child contribute significantly to the explanation of the use of *judicial coercion*. Parents who had representation themselves were able to significantly reduce the court's tendency to intervene. This finding is important because it shows that the courts in North Carolina were susceptible to the pressures that might be brought to bear by parties to the proceeding who had counsel.[8]

When the child's father was identified as the major source of the problem *judicial coercion* was less likely to be used. This relationship may be explained by the fact that the courts probably viewed mothers rather than fathers as the primary caretakers of the children, and thus to remove the child from the troublesome father's care might unjustly punish the mother and deprive the child of its mother's care. It may also be the case that the courts were sexist and simply rejected the idea that fathers could seriously harm their children. It is likely that some combination of these explanations accounts for the court's tendency to be more lenient when fathers were the source of the problem.

Finally, two variables which characterize the courts' treatment of the cases, namely whether an immediate custody order had been issued[9] and the number of days that the case was under the courts' supervision, are included in the model. Neither of these variables is of special theoretical or policy relevance in the evaluation of the impact of representation but their inclusion provides additional statistical controls of possible selection biases and thus increases confidence that the model is properly estimated.

Conclusion: Strategies for Change, Public Policy and Standards

Using the measure *judicial coercion* as a standard for evaluation showed that taken as a whole attorneys representing children had no beneficial effect, at least not in a state such as North Carolina which was characterized by high levels of judicial custodial interventionism.[10] Although disappointing, this result was not surprising. Attorneys appointed in North Carolina to represent children typically had no specialized training in juvenile law or child welfare. They spent little time on the cases and received compensation which they thought was inadequate. Additionally survey data indicate that there was confusion both in the minds of the attorneys and the judges as to the role and purpose of the child's representative. This approach is quite distinct from well thought out team approaches to representation used on a limited basis in other jurisdictions (O'Shea, 1980).

What is interesting, however, is that some attorneys did produce a beneficial effect, and the characteristics of these attorneys suggest changes that might be made in the representation system. First, the representation system needs to provide both independence and incentives for an adequate time commitment. Attorneys who spent more time on cases and attorneys who displayed independence accomplished more.

Second, attorneys need a clearer definition of their role and they need to understand what their goal is in a particular case. Attorneys for parents presumably took the standard role of advocate and had a clear goal, reunion of the

---

[8]When various attorney/client representation interactions such as parent represented/child not represent, were examined the single variable relationships discussed above were unaltered and no interaction had a significant impact on judicial coercion.

[9]This is a decision allowing speedy removal prior to a hearing on the merits of the case. The measure of judicial coercion is based on custodial decisions made subsequent to the hearing on the merits.

[10]In a separate analysis the question of whether the presence of an attorney representing the child altered the likelihood that the court would order therapeutic services for the child and the child's family was examined. Using this standard, a standard based on the notion that attorneys who serve their clients well are able to get services such as therapy for their clients, it was also found that attorneys represented no significant benefit to their child clients (analysis available upon request).

444

family. As a consequence, they were able to provide effective representation for their clients. Arguing by analogy from the case of legal representation for parents, it is reasonable to suggest that attorneys who represent children need to have their role as independent advocate clarified and reinforced. But for the child's representative to develop clear goals for individual cases reinforcement of the advocacy role will not alone suffice. Representatives require specialized and extensive training in child welfare and information about the difficulties inherent in representing children in protection proceedings (Ramsey, 1983). Indeed, it has been suggested that lawyers should act as members of teams including lay representatives and other professionals whose goal would be to represent the child's interests to the court. Analysis of field experiments which have attempted to assess the impact of such strategies should soon be available (Duquette & Ramsey, 1984).

Some consideration also needs to be given to how attorney performance could be monitored. As previously suggested, the measure *judicial coercion* used in this analysis is only applicable to highly interventionist systems. It would not work in a system that already treated removal as a remedy of last resort and expedited return. Thus more sophisticated and refined measures need to be developed for assessing attorney effectiveness. As the analysis of the North Carolina system has shown, representation for children without some kind of monitoring runs a serious risk of failing to provide effective representation. In developing such measures serious consideration must be given to the impact of representation—whether by solo practitioner or multidisciplinary teams—on the child and his or her family. Too often representation projects and programs are uncritically assumed to be successful simply because a representative is provided or because the relevant professionals communicate more with each other. This may be good for the professionals and it should be good for the children, but these are suppositions which require empirical testing.[11]

As this analysis showed the provision of attorneys for children in protection proceedings may well be a waste of preciously scarce resources if these attorneys are merely thrown together with children without regard for the complexity of such cases and the resources required to adequately represent the child. This information is important for family practitioners who may be influential in the development or monitoring of representation programs. Also, they should be aware that the mere presence of a representative, even though inadequate, may provide a false sense of protection for the child which will make others in the proceeding less vigilant.

This demonstration of the need for evaluation of the performance of attorneys has implications for other professionals as well. Although family clinicians operate in a world defined by the immediacy of each child's needs, their activities are also governed to a large degree by institutional public policy. From a policy perspective, the provision of family practitioners *per se* would not provide a benefit to children or families unless the practitioners implement the policy which was the motivating factor in their procurement. Also, measures need to be developed so that the effectiveness of family practitioners can be gauged, for it is demonstrable implementation and measured impact which are ultimately goals of both public policy and clinical practice.

REFERENCES

Aber, J. (1980). The involuntary child placement decision: Solaman's dilemma revisited. In G. Gerbner, C. Ross, & E. Zeigler (Eds.), *Child abuse, an agenda for action* (pp. 156–182). New York: Oxford University Press.

Clarke, S. & Koch, G. (1980). Juvenile court: Therapy or crime control, and do lawyers make a difference. *Law and Society Review, 14,* 265–308.

Dohrenwend, B. S., Colonbotas, J., & Dohrenwend, B. O. (1968). Social distance and interviewer effects. *Public Opinion Quarterly, 32,* 410–422.

Duquette, D., & Ramsey, S. (1984). Representation of children in child abuse and neglect cases: an empirical look at what constitutes effective representation. Ann Arbor, MI: The Child Advocacy Clinic, The University of Michigan Law School.

Gil, D. (1974). Institutions for children. In A. Schorr (Ed.), *Children and decent people* (pp. 53–81). New York: Basic Books.

Goodman, L. (1978). *Analyzing qualitative/categorical data.* Cambridge, MA: Abt Books.

Kelly, R., & Ramsey, S. (1983). Do attorneys for children in protection proceedings make a difference?—a study of the impact of representation under conditions of high judicial intervention. *Journal of Family Law, 21,* 405–455.

Littner, N. (1956). *Some traumatic effects of separation and placement.* New York: Child Welfare League of America.

Mnookin, R. (1973). Foster care—in whose best interest? *Harvard Education Review, 43,* 599–638.

Mnookin, R. (1975). Child-custody adjudication: judicial functions in the face of indeterminacy. *Law and Contemporary Problems, 39,* 226–293.

O'Shea, A. T. (1980). The child advocate attorney—the mental health professional: a current "courtship." *Journal of Marital and Family Therapy, 6,* 277–283.

Ramsey, S. (1983). Representation of the child in protection proceedings: the determination of decision making capacity. *Family Law Quarterly, 17,* 287–326.

Runyan, D. K., Gould, C. L., Frost, D. C., & Lada, F. A. (1981). Determinants of foster care placements for the maltreated child. *American Journal of Public Health, 71,* 706–711.

Ryerson, E. (1978). *The best laid plans: America's juvenile court experiment.* New York: Hill and Wang.

Scheff, T. J. (1966). *Being mentally ill: A sociological theory.* Chicago: Aldine & Atherton.

Wald, M. (1975). State intervention on behalf of neglected children: a search for realistic standards. *Stanford Law Review, 27,* 985–1040.

Wald, M. (1976). State intervention on behalf of neglected children: standards for removal of children from their homes, monitoring the status of children in foster care, and termination of parental right. *Stanford Law Review, 28,* 723–706.

---

[11]"For example, O'Shea stated that "any representation is better than none" and that: "Continual exposure to the CAU approach has sensitized both legal and mental health personnel to one another's disciplines. Such growth can only produce better service to children" (1980, p. 282).

by Karen Dorros and Patricia Dorsey

Whose Rights Are We Protecting, Anyway?

John first came to our early intervention program when he was six months old. A cherubic youngster with blonde hair and hazel eyes, he had first come to the attention of Child Protective Services because of his mother's neglect. Apparently, he had had a minor cold and fever that developed into serious pneumonia requiring a lengthy hospitalization. During this period it became apparent that there was overall neglect of this infant while in his mother's care.

After a few months in foster care, Johnny was returned to his natural mother. They, along with his three brothers, lived in one room of a welfare motel well known for its poor conditions and ongoing violence. Moreover, the mother was mentally retarded and had poor parenting skills. Because Johnny was already showing signs of developmental lags, he was referred to our program. Our job was not only to take care of Johnny's developmental needs, but to counsel his mother as well. In reality, this was quite impossible not only because of her limited understanding, but more importantly because of the dreadful environment that the family was exposed to daily.

Over the next two years, Johnny continued in the program. He would often sleep in school or come to school needing a bath. He was frequently inadequately dressed or brought snacks that were barely edible. On occasion, a cockroach might be found in his lunch bag. Behaviorally, he was difficult to handle, subject to strong and physical temper tantrums. His tantrums could be so violent that many of our staff had difficulty controlling him, even though he was still a toddler. In spite of all this, he was developing well and loved to come to school. Apparently, it was the one secure, safe place in his life.

Unfortunately, Johnny's attendance became more erratic, his physical appearance more dirty, and his behavior more uncontrolled. Finally, unexplained bruise marks were found on Johnny's body; there were clear hand prints. We contacted Child Protective Services, and Johnny was once again removed from the home.

Johnny now began to evidence even more emotional and behavioral difficulties. He was placed with one foster family who could not handle his disruptive, aggressive behavior. Within days, he was placed with another foster family willing to undergo the strain of trying to meet his now extensive needs. After a while and a lot of work, Johnny began to flourish.

Visits with his mother and siblings (who had also been placed in foster care) were established. A court order against the mother's boyfriend was mandated because he

Child abuse is a horror that our society condemns but our legal system perpetuates.

was implicated in the charges of physical and sexual abuse. The mother was found to be negligent. With the help of social services, new quarters were found for the family. The mother promised to terminate the relationship with her boyfriend.

After about a year, the court decided that the mother was ready to care for Johnny and he was sent home. One day, less than a year later, Johnny came to school with more bruises—and also cigarette burns. Child Protective Services was again contacted, and he was again removed from home. Although the physical scars healed quickly, the emotional damage was now extensive. Johnny became extremely hard to handle; he had violent outbursts and poor impulse control. Even for the most seasoned professional, Johnny was—and still is—a tough challenge. He is five years old.

Johnny continues to visit with his mother. After each visit, he is upset and more disruptive. It is quite clear to his preschool teachers that his mother's parenting skills will never be better than they are now. But in all likelihood Johnny will be returned home, only to be bruised and battered again. He will probably never be able to function outside of a self-contained educational setting for emotionally disturbed children. The saddest part of this story is that Johnny's experiences are not unique ... nor the worst. How can we in the helping professions let this happen?

Child abuse is a horror that our society condemns but our legal system perpetuates. Although there is much talk about protecting children, our legal system is far more concerned about protecting parents' rights. Indeed, they should be considered as sacred, but at what cost?

What about our children and their right to protection under the law from abuse and neglect? Should that not take precedence over the biological rights of the parents? We believe that too often it does not. How many times should a child be sent back into a home after abuse has been proven? How does the court ensure that a repeat offender will not abuse the child again? There do not appear to be any specific legal guidelines protecting children from the inevitable damage of being repeatedly sent back into homes where they have already been abused. In fact, our system is set up to return these children to their homes. The problem is that the legal system has not sufficiently provided for their safety once they are returned to their natural parents.

How does the system work? In New York State, we, as early childhood educators, are required by law to report any suspected incidents of child abuse. As in

Johnny's case, we reported the unexplained bruise marks by calling a toll-free 800 number. The county Child Protective Services agency is then notified, and CPS investigates the allegations within 24 hours. If the allegations appear justified, CPS takes action. This may mean removing the child (or children) from the parent and placing him or her in foster care. At this point the court becomes involved. The social service agency and the county attorney are responsible for providing full documentation justifying charges of abuse and removal of the children. Parents are provided counsel and the children are provided a legal guardian. The case is then placed under the auspices of the Department of Social Services.

Typically, the court will order that the social service agency provide the parent with every opportunity to remediate the situation. A complicated, lengthy process to reunify the family then begins. This may involve providing the parent with therapy and/or counseling, financial support, transportation and help in locating suitable housing. For the child, it may involve placement in foster care and the provision of any other services—health care, special education, counseling, etc.—required.

At the same time, the children must cope with a new living arrangement as well as the circumstances that led to their entering foster care. This is extremely stressful for the child, and therapeutic intervention is often necessary. This is when our early intervention program becomes involved.

Usually, a child is referred to us at age two or three because he or she is manifesting signs of developmental delays, emotional/behavioral difficulties, sleep/feeding disturbances, or aggressive/bizarre responses. The child may recently have been placed in foster care as a result of abuse or neglect and is beginning to manifest extreme adjustment reactions. Often, the foster family needs help in understanding and working with the child.

Even by age two, an abused child has learned many maladaptive, dysfunctional behaviors. There may be severe temper tantrums, food hoarding, sleep terrors or many other behaviors that require a tremendous amount of work to modify. It may take weeks to get the child to realize that he will not be beaten if he screams or has a temper tantrum, or to begin to trust that there is something stable and consistent in his life, perhaps for the very first time.

Often, after we have accomplished those beginning steps, the visits with the parent begin. Sometimes we are lucky, and the parent has been able to use the time and resources provided by social services in a constructive way. Unfortunately, most of the time we are not lucky. Too often the system superficially remediates part of the parent's problem by providing new housing, a job or financial support, but no behavioral changes occur.

Social services cannot provide everything—particularly the essential elements that dictate the success of any plan for rehabilitation: the parent's willingness and motivation to change. Without that desire, the provision of services only prolongs a downward spiralling pattern. The victim is the child. Eventually the child is returned home, and the pattern of behavior that led to the child being abused in the first place is repeated. Unfortunately for the little ones, each time they are returned, the scars become deeper and deeper, and harder to heal. The result of this focus on the parents may mean years of foster care for the children, repeated episodes of abuse when they are returned, and, finally, permanent emotional damage.

Termination of parental rights is difficult, if not seemingly impossible, to attain. Our system is not designed with specific guidelines that force abusive parents to show strong evidence of remediation or show that they are capable of caring for a child. It is not uncommon for a parent to contact the child in foster care once in six months, but on the basis of that visit alone, the natural parent's rights would not be terminated. Visiting your child for an hour once in six months seems to be a very poor standard of commitment, particularly for a parent who already has abused a child.

Under these conditions, it is very difficult to understand how the legal system is acting in the best interests of the child. We are all aware of situations where children spend years in foster care, meeting with their biological parents once a week. The parents make no plans to care for the children; they do not improve their parenting skills, and many are not capable of caring for a child on a daily basis. Some covertly continue to abuse drugs and alcohol. During their visits, they may tell the children negative things about the foster parents, or fill the children's heads with false promises about taking them home. After these visits, the foster parents must pick up the pieces.

The social workers are also frustrated. Most agencies are terribly understaffed, and many workers are not trained to handle these problems. Moreover, the court places the burden of proof on the social service agency, when in reality the burden of proof should be on the parents. Social workers are obligated to continue working with dysfunctional parents, even when it is clear that the parents are not moving in a productive way to resume caring for their children. The social workers try—often for years—to build cases. While symptoms of physical abuse or medical negligence are concrete and visible to a judge, emotional abuse and neglect are extremely difficult to prove legally. So workers often have to wait until the child suffers concrete physical damage even though in many cases, like Johnny's, the emotional damage is far more scarring and permanent.

We are even aware of cases where the parent has lost control and harmed the child in front of the social worker during a supervised visit. The result: termination of visits—not rights, but visits. This may be a small step in the right direction, but it's a long way from protecting that child from permanent emotional damage.

It appears that too often the child's needs are only fully considered *after the fact*. Too often, we ask the question of why something was not done earlier. We get angry at the social workers and teachers who should have done something before a child is mutilated or dead, as in the Steinberg-Nussbaum case. But the vast majority of social workers are equally frustrated and angry. They amass volumes of documentation, only to face courts that unwaveringly determine in the parent's favor.

Are there any solutions? It is our belief that the child's right to a protected life and future needs to be weighed more heavily by the courts. Parents who have abused or neglected their children should be given specific guidelines to follow. They should demonstrate improved parenting skills by attending ongoing parenting classes as well as counseling sessions. They should be bound to provide concrete evidence of their positive motivation toward being a parent and the steps that they are taking in that direction. And all of this should be accomplished *before* they get their children back.

We also believe that the children's foster caretakers and therapists should be more involved in the decision-making process. The legal guardian should meet with those involved with the children on a periodic basis to understand what is in the child's best interest. There also should be increased psychological and psychiatric documentation not only about the parents but about the children as well. Finally, cases that have been around for three or four years or longer should be brought to a forced resolution by the courts.

In our preschool program, we see children in the earliest and most formative years of their lives. It is a tragedy that we see children who by age five are damaged not only by their parents but by the system that is supposed to protect them. It is only by forcing the system itself to take a harder line against child abuse and in favor of children's rights that we can begin to find some solutions. ■

Karen Dorros, Ph.D., and Patricia Dorsey are Co-directors of A Starting Place, Inc., Pearl River, New York.

Tighten Standards for Termination of Parental Rights

by Robert Horowitz, J.D.
Associate Director
National Legal Resource Center for
Child Advocacy and Protection,
American Bar Association.

K aren Dorros and Patricia Dorsey's criticism of the legal system, at heart, is that it makes it difficult to terminate parental rights.

This view is a common one, and their example is compelling. While I do not disagree with the general statement, I part company with some of the implications and suggestions of this piece.

The authors state that the "legal system"—read judges—favors parental rights over those of children, as evidenced by its requiring social service agencies to attempt to remediate family problems, and its

tendency to give parents second, third and even more chances. This, they suggest, allows neglectful parents to both maintain custody until the child is seriously injured, or defeat abandonment claims by infrequent, even once every six months visits with their child in foster care. This assertion, however, confuses basic legal and child welfare principles with individual case handling.

To illustrate, the courts do expect

attempts at family rehabilitation. Yet this is not an individual judicial quirk, but a requirement of law. Under Public Law 96-272, the requirements of "reasonable efforts," "preventive services," "case plans" and the like have been widely adopted and accepted. This does not mean, however, that termination is foreclosed. Indeed, an equal thrust of the Act is to review cases periodically and move towards termination quickly when rehabilitation is not possible. Thus the real question becomes one of proof: When is rehabilitation no longer feasible? Here is where individual judges are, perhaps, reluctant to terminate and slow to recognize the seriousness of the emotional harms being done to neglected and abused children.

Or, perhaps, others in the child welfare system are not properly presenting information to the court upon which a termination can legally be based. The example given by the authors involved, at its earliest stages, an infant living in a welfare motel. While this is certainly not an ideal environment, I am assuming that they are not suggesting that welfare—that is, poverty status—is grounds for coercive state intervention. (In a recent report of the American Public Welfare Association, American Bar Association and American Enterprise Institute, *Child Abuse and Neglect Reporting and Investigation: Policy Guidelines for Decision Making*, a diverse group of 38 child welfare professionals concurred that child protection agencies "have not been established as society's response to poverty," although they are often improperly forced to assume this role.)

In the authors' example, the ground for state intervention seems to have been the mother's mental retardation, which caused poor parenting skills. What the authors don't share is the evidence presented at trial. Remember, the bench, while very powerful in some respects, is weak in others. Its biggest weakness is its total dependence on others to present the facts of the case. Paraphrasing an old saying, the judicial opinion (out-

put) is only as good as the quality of the evidence (input). Did the agency present to the court information on the mother's mental capacity and its relationship to parenting—the prognosis—and whether this condition could be alleviated—the diagnosis? Without both aspects, termination is unlikely.

I am not, however, trying to redirect any fault from the bench. Even after being presented with compelling evidence by the state, many judges are too slow to terminate. The harms to the child are those stated by the authors. Their solutions and my responses are that:

● parents of abused and neglected children be given specific guidelines to follow. I agree, and this is the case plan requirement of P.L. 96-272. However, we first must address whether the caseworkers are writing "good plans" which identify the conditions or problems that contributed to the child's placement, select reasonable and achievable goals that address these conditions, and document who will do what and when.

● foster caretakers and therapists be more involved in the decision-making process. While the judge will not relinquish her responsibility to

decide, these persons are critical to the "input."

● cases that have been around several years should be finally resolved by the courts. No dispute. Certainly this is the intention, if not the reality, of P.L. 96-272.

● the burden of proof be shifted to the parents to prove they are fit, rather than the state prove they are unfit.

This last recommendation is the most controversial. It would require altering a constitutionally recognized principle, established by the U.S. Supreme Court in *Santosky v. Kramer* (1982), that the state prove grounds for termination of parental rights by clear and convincing evidence. It is therefore unlikely to pass, but does underscore some of the criticisms of *Santosky*. At issue in *Santosky* was who should be protected from the risk of an erroneous decision being made at termination. Siding with the parents, the Court chose to make it more difficult for the state to prove termination, presumably, therefore, making it more difficult to terminate in inappropriate cases. The criticism, and one that partially validates the authors' basic criticism—that is, that we overprotect parents at the expense of the child—is that the Supreme Court framed termination as a contest between the parents and state, and was thus willing to err in the parents' favor. The child, unfortunately, was not considered, nor the consequences to the child when termination does not occur. One might ask whether the recent decision in *DeShaney v. Winnebago County Department of Social Services*, in which the Supreme Court opined that the child protection system owed no constitutional duty to protect abused children from further abuse at their parents' hands, is another example of the Court's failing to protect children.

Perhaps, therefore, rather than trying to reallocate the burden of proof, the authors should focus on tightening the standards for termination, so that even within this constitutional scheme the state's evidentiary tasks would be less difficult.

10

For example, statutes could clearly state that abandonment exists even when the parent who is able to fails to have *meaningful* visits or communication with their child—in short, shows an intent to abandon.

Finally, I think that much of the problem can be addressed through education. As a recent report by the Governor's (of Maine) Working Group on Child Abuse and Neglect Legal Proceedings observed:

"Presentations on child abuse and neglect are sporadically offered to [the state's] legal community—judges and attorneys—[but] they have no regular opportunity to receive and discuss information about this problem. Without adequate information flowing through the system that responds to child abuse, children will continue to be hurt by the failings of the system." (*Protecting Our Children: Not Without Changes in the Legal System*).

The Attorney General's (of Minnesota) Task Force on Child Abuse Within the Family, in its final report, went one step further, recommending that the state supreme court mandate that all trial court judges receive such training. What this training should consist of, how often it should be given, and whether it will affect individual case outcomes are questions for another time.

Prospective Abuse and Neglect — The Termination of Parental Rights

Introduction

Immediately after his December 1985 birth, a newborn baby boy, W.L.P., was taken from his parents, through a Florida Department of Health and Rehabilitative Services (hereinafter HRS) proceeding. In *Padgett v. Department of Health and Rehabilitative Services*,[1] the court determined that if left with his natural parents, who had been guilty of abuse and neglect with other children, W.L.P. would also be abused and/or neglected.[2] However, since the parents, Thomas Padgett and Mary Hartline Padgett, never had custody of W.L.P., there was no evidence that they ever abused or neglected W.L.P.[3] Nonetheless, in August 1988, the final order of permanent commitment[4] was entered, and the case is currently pending appeal.[5]

On June 1, 1989, pursuant to *Padgett*, the question of whether the concept of "prospective abuse, neglect or abandonment" is a viable one was certified to the Florida Supreme Court as a question of great public importance.[6] The purpose of this article is to evaluate the validity of the concept of "prospective abuse or neglect" and its applicability to the termination of parental rights.[7] Aside from affecting parents and

---

1. Padgett v. Department of Health and Human Serv., 543 So. 2d 1317 (Fla. 5th Dist. Ct. App. 1989).

2. *Id.*

3. *Id.*

4. THE FLORIDA BAR CONTINUING LEGAL EDUCATION, FLORIDA JUVENILE LAW AND PRACTICE, §15-5 (2d ed. 1988) [hereinafter FLA. BAR], defines permanent commitment as "the permanent termination of parental rights."

5. *Padgett*, 543 So. 2d at 1318.

6. *Id.*

7. This article will only discuss the topics of abuse and neglect because in *In re J.L.P.*, 416 So. 2d 1250 (Fla. 4th Dist. Ct. App. 1982), the court stated:

    abandonment may not be considered prospectively in view of the language of section 39.01(1), Florida Statutes (Supp. 1980), which provides: 'Abandoned' means a situation in which a parent who, while being able, makes no provision for the child's support and makes no effort to communicate with the child for a period of 6 months or longer . . . .

children, the Florida Supreme Court's response to this certified question will undoubtedly affect many professionals such as lawyers, physicians, nurses, teachers, social workers, child care workers, and police.[8]

Before discussing "prospective abuse and neglect," this article examines the current United States and Florida laws pertaining to parental termination. This examination will include a brief history of parental rights and termination, as well as the legal and social dilemmas associated with such termination. The next section explores the extent of the child abuse and reabuse problem. Following is a discussion of Florida's parental termination procedures and "prospective abuse" cases and a brief examination of how other states have responded to and analyzed this concept. The next section examines, through the use of psychological articles and studies, the concept of "prospective abuse" to determine if the concept is viable and objective enough to support the termination of an individual's "right" to rear a child. Additionally, this article compares the actual characteristics of individuals whose parental rights have been terminated as a result of actual and prospective child abuse to those characteristics that the psychologists label as predictors of child abuse.

Background - the Right To "Bring Up" Children

In *Meyer v. Nebraska*,[9] the United States Supreme Court held that the fourteenth amendment of the United States Constitution guarantees an individual the liberty to "marry, establish a home and bring up children."[10] Later, in *Moore v. City of East Cleveland, Ohio*,[11] the Court held that "the institution of the family is deeply rooted in this

---

Id. at 1252, n.3.

However, in 1987 the definition of "abandoned" was changed, and the six month requirement was removed. The revised definition states that "[a]bandoned means a situation in which the parent . . . while being able, makes no provision for the child's support and makes no effort to communicate with the child, which situation is sufficient to evince a willful rejection of parental obligations . . . ." FLA. STAT. § 39.01(1) (1987). Therefore, it is possible that the Florida Supreme Court will find that the revised definition of "abandoned" supports a finding of prospective abandonment.

8. For example, social workers and police officers will have to be extremely knowledgeable of the characteristics to predict child abuse since they are often the first to investigate the situations.

9.   262 U.S. 390 (1923).

10.   *Id.* at 399.

11.   431 U.S. 494 (1977).

Nation's history and tradition."[12] Moreover, in *Santosky v. Kramer*,[13] a newborn was immediately taken from his parents on the ground that immediate removal was necessary to avoid imminent danger to his life since three of the Santosky's five children had been adjudicated neglected within the meaning of article 10 of the New York Family Court Act.[14] The *Santosky* Court stated that "[t]he [fourteenth amendment] fundamental liberty interest of natural parents in the care, custody, and management of their child does not evaporate simply because they have not been model parents or have lost temporary custody of their child to the state."[15] Consequently, "[b]efore a state may sever completely and irrevocably the rights of parents in their natural child, due process requires that the State support its allegations by at least clear and convincing evidence."[16]

Parents, then, do not have exclusive control over the lives of their children.[17] When a state intervenes into the "right of family integrity," it is asserting its *parens patriae* authority and its police power.[18] "The parens patriae power . . . is the state's limited paternalistic power to protect or promote the welfare of certain individuals, like young children . . . who lack the capacity to act in their own best interests."[19] Based on their *parens patriae* authority, states may enact statutes to govern guardianship, civil commitment of the mentally ill, juvenile courts, and child abuse and neglect.[20]

The police power is the state's other source of authority allowing it to intervene into the "right of family integrity." That is the state's authority "both to prevent its citizens from harming one another and to promote all aspects of the public welfare."[21] The state's police power

---

12. *Id.* at 503.
13. 455 U.S. 745 (1982).
14. *Id.* at 751.
15. *Id.* at 753.
16. *Id.* at 747-48.
17. Wald, *State Intervention on Behalf of "Neglected Children": A Search for Realistic Standards*, in Pursuing Justice for the Child 246, 248 (M. Rosenheim ed. 1976).
18. Fla. Bar, *supra* note 4, at 15-8; Myers, *Abuse and Neglect of the Unborn: Can the State Intervene?*, 23 Duq. L. Rev. 1, 21-24 (1984); *See also*, Wald, *supra* note 17, at 246.
19. Myers, *supra* note 18, at 22 (citing *Development in the Law -The Constitution and the Family*, 93 Harv. L. Rev. 1156, 1199 (1980)).
20. Myers, *supra* note 18, at 23.
21. *Id.* at 24 (citing *Developments in the Law - The Constitution and the Family*, 93 Harv. L. Rev. 1156, 1198-99 (1980)).

allows it to foster the "public health, safety, morals, or general welfare."[22]

As discussed, when confronted with the threat of parental rights termination, a parent's fourteenth amendment right to rear children is in jeopardy. Consequently, the state may only utilize its powers when it can show a compelling state interest and when no less burdensome alternative is available.[23]

In addition to the legal concerns involved in removing a child from his home, there are also social dilemmas. For example, "the natural rights of parents and children to family integrity operate against the interest of the state in child protection and, sometimes, against the best interests of the child."[24] There are times when a child will definitely be "better off" when parental rights are terminated. However, for that particular child, adoption may not be feasible or available.[25]

In *Santosky*, the United States Supreme Court noted that it is a "hazardous assumption" that termination of the natural parents' rights will invariably benefit the child.[26] "Even when a child's natural home is imperfect, permanent removal from that home will not necessarily improve his welfare."[27] Although there are no answers to these dilemmas, they are constant concerns of social workers, lawyers, and judges—some of the individuals whose services determine the fate of the parents and the child.

The Problem of Child Abuse and Neglect

Child abuse and neglect are both national and local problems. "One of the most disturbing aspects of child abuse is its tendency to reoccur."[28] Reabuse rates of abusers who are in treatment range from

---

22. Village of Euclid v. Ambler Realty Co., 272 U.S. 365, 395 (1926).

23. FLA. BAR, *supra* note 4, at 15-8 (citing Roe v. Wade, 410 U.S. 113, *reh'g denied*, 410 U.S. 959 (1973)).

24. FLA. BAR, *supra* note 4, at §15-14.

25. *Id.* at §15-15.

26. *Santosky*, 455 U.S. at 765, n.15.

27. *Id.* (quoting Wald, *State Intervention on Behalf of "Neglected" Children: A Search for Realistic Standards*, 27 STAN. L. REV. 985, 993 (1975)) "In fact, under current practice, coercive intervention frequently results in placing a child in a more detrimental situation than he would be in without intervention." *Id.*

28. Ferleger, Glenwick, Gaines Green, *Identifying Correlates of Reabuse In Maltreating Parents*, 12 CHILD ABUSE & NEGLECT 41 (1988).

16% to 66.8%.[29] Additionally, post treatment reabuse rates have varied from 18.5% to 33% to 50% to 66.6%, depending on the study[30]

Two approaches to measure abuse repetition are recurrence and recidivism.[31] Recurrence is the "occurrence of one or more abuse incidents after an initial incident."[32] Recurrence can be measured by the frequency count of legal charges of abuse or by the frequency count of verified abuse incidents noted in the case records.[33] Recidivism is a second approach to measure abuse repetition.[34] Recidivism is a "further occurrence of abuse after termination of service to a family following the first citation for abuse."[35] Recidivism, either frequency count of legal charges of abuse or frequency count of verified abuse incidents may be used as a measure.[36]

A 1979 study reported findings on a follow up study of 328 families who were provided services for child abuse in two counties of eastern Pennsylvania during the ten year period of 1967-1976.[37] The study revealed that among the 328 families, 260 had at least one valid charge of child abuse.[38] However, case records of 286 families revealed verified incidents of abuse.[39]

Regarding recurrence, of the 260 families with at least one valid charge, there was a total of 349 citations,[40] and 903 incidents of abuse

---

29. *Id.* "The discrepancy often found between official and unofficial rates of reported reabuse suggests that the true incidence of reabuse is seriously underreported in official tallies." *Id.* (citing Herrenkohl, Herrenkohl, Egolf & Seech, *The Repetition of Child Abuse: How Frequently Does It Occur?* 3 CHILD ABUSE AND NEGLECT 67 (1979) [hereinafter "Herrenkohl"]).

30. Ferleger, *supra* note 28, at 41. *See also* Zuravin, *Fertility Patterns: Their Relationship to Child Physical Abuse and Child Neglect*, 50 J. MARRIAGE AND FAMILY 983 (1988) (citing Daro, Achieving Success In The Treatment Of Child Abuse And Neglect, Paper presented to the 11th Annual Meeting of the American Public Health Association, (Dallas 1983) (unpublished paper)).

31. Herrenkohl, *supra* note 29.

32. *Id.* at 68.

33. *Id.*

34. *Id.*

35. *Id.*

36. Herrenkohl, *supra* note 29, at 68.

37. *Id.* at 67.

38. *Id.* at 68.

39. *Id.* In case records of the twenty-six families for which there was not a validated charge, there was evidence that abuse had occurred. However, for various reasons, including self-referral of the family, there was not a validated charge. *Id.*

40. *Id.*

in the 286 families with verified incidents were reported.[41] As for recidivism, there were 192 cases which closed among the 260 validly cited
families, of the closed cases seventy-three were re-opened.[42] Twenty-
one of the families with re-opened cases were found to have further
incidents of abuse.[43] Among the 286 families with a verified incident,
of which 206 cases had closed, eighty-four were re-opened.[44] Thirty-
eight of the families with re-opened cases were found to have further
incidents of abuse.[45] This number represents 13.2% of all 286 families
or 18.5% of those families who cases had been closed.[46] The degree to
which official reports of abuse potentially underestimate the degree of
recurrent abuse is significant.[47] For instance, for families with identified abuse, the 25.4% low recurrence percentage for official reports as
compared to the much higher percentage for verified incidents 66.8%,
means that the magnitude of the problem is underestimated if recurrence is assessed by means of charges.[48] The researchers suggest that
"a practical consequence of this underestimation may be that the potential for recurrent abuse may not be given the attention it deserves."[49] Despite the methodological shortcomings of the research on
reabuse rates,[50] such rates appear to be high both during and after
treatment.[51]

Of significant importance to the issue of prospective abuse, especially where newborns are involved, is the fact that a significant association exists between recurrence and a child's age. Recurrent abuse occurs more frequently in newborn through five year old children than in
groups of six through eleven year olds or children over eleven years

---

41. Herrenkohl, *supra* note 29, at 69.
42. *Id.*
43. *Id.*
44. *Id.*
45. *Id.*
46. Herrenkohl, *supra* note 29, at 69. This study also explores the following: Indications of Recurrence by Parties to the Abuse, Targets of Abuse, Indications of Recurrence by Types of Abuse, and Whether Recurrent Abuse Occurs in Families with
Younger or Older Children.
47. *Id.* at 71.
48. *Id.*
49. *Id.* at 69.
50. Such shortcomings include, "variability in extent of outreach to detect
reabuse, reliance on subjective assessment of incidence of reabuse, [and] absence of
post-termination follow-up." Ferleger, *supra* note 28, at 41.
51. *Id.*

old.[52]

The terms "abuse" and "neglect" often elicit different meanings from different people. What one parent labels discipline, another will label abuse or neglect. For example, parents are allowed to hit their children; however, it becomes "abuse" when the hitting becomes inappropriate.[53] There is a wide range of variation in the types of situations potentially considered "inappropriate."[54]

Nearly all states have their own set of definitions for abuse and neglect.[55] However, nearly all states' definitions conform to those provided in the Child Abuse and Neglect Prevention and Treatment Act.[56]

Pursuant to a Congressional mandate in the Child Abuse Amendments of 1984,[57] the Study of National Incidence and Prevalence of Child Abuse and Neglect (NIS-2), was commissioned to assess the current national incidence of abuse and neglect and to determine how the severity, frequency and character of maltreatment changed from its earlier 1980 study.[58] The key results of the NIS-2 study estimate that "in 1986, more than one million children nationwide . . . met the stringent requirement of having already experienced demonstrable harm as a result of abuse or neglect."[59] These results represented a sixty-four percent increase in countable cases of abuse and neglect over the estimate of 625,100 provided by the 1980 incidence study.[60] However, the researchers feel that these figures represent an improvement in the pro-

---

52. Herrenkohl, *supra* note 29, at 71.

53. Wald & Cohen, *Preventing Child Abuse - What Will It Take?* 20 FAM. L. Q. 281, 282 (1986). "[T]here is great variation in the types of situations considered inappropriate by people involved in the child protection system." *Id.*

54. *Id.*

55. U.S. DEPARTMENT OF HEALTH AND HUMAN SERVICES, STUDY FINDINGS - STUDY OF NATIONAL INCIDENCE AND PREVALENCE OF CHILD ABUSE AND NEGLECT (1988). [hereinafter STUDY FINDINGS]. The research described in this report was sponsored by the National Center on Child Abuse and Neglect, Children's Bureau, Administration for Children, Youth and Families, Office of Human Development Services, U.S. Department of Health and Human Services, under Contract 105-85-1702.

56. *Id.* at xii. The Child Abuse and Neglect Prevention and Treatment Act is a federal statute which provides basic State Grants. 42 U.S.C. § 5101 (1982).

57. Pub. L. No. 98-457 (1984).

58. STUDY FINDINGS, *supra* note 55. This study was commissioned by the National Center on Child Abuse and Neglect, Administration for Children, Youth and Families in the Office of Human Development Services, Department of Health and Human Services.

59. STUDY FINDINGS, *supra* note 55, at 7-1. Approximately 1,025,900 had already experienced demonstrable harm.

60. *Id.*

fessionals who deal with mistreated children rather than an increase in actual child abuse. The researchers state that

> it seems reasonable to suggest that the findings reported here do *not* necessarily imply an increase in the actual incidence of child abuse and neglect in the nation, but are consistent with the suggestion that, in the interim since 1980, professionals have become better attuned to the cues of maltreatment . . . .[61]

This particular study is unique since, in addition to reporting on actual abuse, it also used revised definitions which included children who had been endangered, but not yet demonstrably harmed, by abuse or neglect.[62] The endangerment standard included cases where a child's health or safety was endangered through abusive or neglectful treatment.[63] Hence, according to the endangered standard, "all cases were considered to meet the revised harm criterion if maltreatment was officially substantiated by CPS [Child Protective Services] or if non-CPS professionals judged the child's health or well-being to have been seriously endangered by the maltreatment they reported."[64]

> For example, a two-year old child who was left home alone for several hours may have emerged from the incident unscathed, but the police officer or other community professional who submitted a data form on the case may have judged this treatment as having seriously endangered the child.[65]

When applying the revised standards, more than one and a half million children were abused or neglected in 1986 throughout the United States.[66] These figures translate into an annual incidence rate of 16.3 children per 1,000 children in the nation who experienced demonstrable harm from abuse and neglect and 25.2 children per 1,000 who are endangered or already harmed as a result of abuse or neglect.[67]

---

61. *Id.* at 7-4 (emphasis in the original).
62. *Id.* Another interesting aspect of the NIS-2 study is its section concerning the relation of abuse and neglect to child, family and county characteristics. That section of the NIS-2 study is be further discussed in this article's section "Predicting Prospective Abuse and Neglect", *infra* at notes 188-234 and accompanying text.
63. STUDY FINDINGS, *supra* note 55, at 2-7.
64. *Id.*
65. *Id.* at 2-7 n.14.
66. *Id.* 7-1. Approximately 1,584,700 children were abused or neglected. *Id.*
67. *Id.*

However, the researchers warn readers that the estimates provided by this study should be regarded as minimum estimates of the numbers of abused and neglected children.[68] In fact, in 1985 more than 1.9 million children were reported to authorities as suspected victims of child abuse and neglect.[69] Another report has estimated that in 1983, approximately 1.5 million children were reported as abused or neglected, representing a 142% increase in the number of reports since 1976.[70]

As mentioned, child abuse and neglect is a local problem as well as a national problem. For instance, since Fiscal Year 1975-76,[71] the number of reports of children abused and neglected in Florida has increased by 168%.[72] However, Florida's total child population increased by twelve percent during this time period.[73] Investigations completed

---

68. STUDY FINDINGS, *supra* note 55, at 7-1-7-2.

These findings should not be interpreted as an estimate of the full extent of child abuse and neglect in the U.S. . . . the study design only tapped into cases known to CPS [Child Protective Services] and recognized by professionals in specific categories of investigatory and non-investigatory community agencies. It made no attempt to assess the incidence of cases known to professionals in other agencies and institutions (e.g., private schools, private physicians, medical clinics not affiliated with hospitals or health departments, clinical social workers or mental health professionals in private practice, etc.). Nor did it attempt to identify cases known to neighbors, relatives, or parents and children themselves.

Id. at 7-1.

69. CHILD ABUSE AND NEGLECT REPORTING AND INVESTIGATION - POLICY GUIDELINES FOR DECISION MAKING (D. Besharov, Rapporteur 1988) [hereinafter POLICY GUIDELINES] The report states that "the following statistics concerning reported cases are derived from various reports of the American Humane Association." *Id.* at 1.

70. DEPARTMENT OF HEALTH AND HUMAN SERVICES OFFICE OF HUMAN DEVELOPMENT SERVICES ADMINISTRATION FOR CHILDREN, YOUTH AND FAMILIES NATIONAL CENTER ON CHILD ABUSE AND NEGLECT, A REPORT TO CONGRESS: JOINING TOGETHER TO FIGHT CHILD ABUSE, (January 1986). [hereinafter JOINING TOGETHER] These statistics are based on the American Humane Association's findings.

71. July 1, 1975 - June 30, 1976.

72. DEPARTMENT OF HEALTH AND REHABILITATIVE SERVICES, CHILD WELFARE SERVICES IN FLORIDA (August 1985) [hereinafter CHILD WELFARE]. This document is the State Plan for Child Welfare Services in Florida for the two year period which began in July 1985. *Id.* at Preface (not paginated). Pursuant to federal regulations HRS must develop a plan describing all child welfare services, regardless of funding source, identifying program deficiencies and indicating major activities planned for strengthening and expanding the range of existing child welfare services. *Id.* The report also states that "the numbers . . . are not unduplicated due to children who may have been reported two or more times during the year." *Id.* at 2.

73. *Id.* at 2.

by HRS during fiscal year 1984-85 revealed credible evidence which would cause a reasonable person to believe that eighteen out of 1,000 children under eighteen years old were abused or neglected.[74]

During January-June 1984, eighty-six percent of all indicated[75] allegations involved parents.[76] Additionally, mothers were most often indicated (48.6%) while males, including fathers (16.3%) and stepfathers (4.6%), accounted for another 20.9%.[77] The American Humane Association found that "43 percent of the reported families were headed by a single female caretaker, compared to only 19 percent of all U.S. families"[78] and that "43 percent were receiving public assistance, compared to about 12 percent of all U.S. families."[79] Forty-one percent of all involved children are five years old or younger, and girls were involved in five percent more of the indicated reports of abuse and neglect than boys.[80]

The Florida HRS report states that "black children, at 28.4%, are overrepresented in relation to their percentage (21.8%) of the total child population of the state." However, this "overrepresentation of minority children has been a common characteristic of national child abuse and neglect reporting data since 1976 [when the American Humane Association first began analyzing national data]."[81] According to the American Humane Association, "possible reasons for this bias are investigative prioritization, biased reporting sources, as well as conditions associated with poverty and unemployment."[82]

There are many types of dispositions available in cases where maltreatment of a child by his or her parents has occurred. The range includes the least intrusive, where no further action is taken beyond the investigation, to involuntary, court ordered supervision of the child and family, to the most intrusive which includes removal and placement of

---

74. *Id.* at 9.

75. "Indicated" means that credible evidence was gathered which would cause a reasonable person to believe a child was abused or neglected. *Id.*

76. *Id.* at 18.

77. CHILD WELFARE, *supra* note 72, at 18.

78. *Id.* However, within the reported statistics of child abuse and neglect, 40% of the cases occur in families headed by single females. JOINING TOGETHER, *supra* note 70, at 5.

79. CHILD WELFARE, *supra* note 72, at 18 (citing the American Humane Association, *1983 Highlights*).

80. *Id.* at 19-20.

81. *Id.* at 19.

82. *Id.* (citing American Humane Association, *1983 Highlights*).

the child in foster care.[83]

Foster care is intended to provide temporary placement of children who are removed from their family due to abuse, neglect or exploitation by the parent or guardian. Its goal is "towards achieving a situation in which a child can return home to his natural parents."[84] "If reunification is not possible, then permanency can be effected either through termination of parental rights for those children who could best be served by adoption, through formalization of long term foster care agreements or by preparing the child for adulthood through an independent living program."[85]

According to HRS's 1984-85 report, four percent of the abused or neglected child population, approximately 2,100 children, were involved in foster care.[86] However, eleven percent of the children in foster care were permanently committed and available for adoption.[87] In other words, the parents of these children have had their parental rights terminated.

As noted, child abuse and neglect is a recurring national and local concern. Accordingly, to protect children from injury, many courts have determined that sometimes removing a child from the "potentially dangerous" environment of its parents will help solve this problem.

Parental Rights Termination - Florida

In Florida, the phrases "termination of parental rights" and "permanent commitment" are basically synonymous.[88] Once parental rights are terminated, HRS or a licensed child-placing agency obtains legal custody of the child and the parents are "legal strangers to that child."[89] The Florida legislature's goal of placing the child in a permanent home can be accomplished since the child is now available for adoption.

The Florida Legislature enacted chapters 39[90] and 409[91] of the

---

83. CHILD WELFARE, *supra* note 72, at 20.
84. *Id.* at 27.
85. *Id.*
86. *Id.* at 20.
87. CHILD WELFARE, *supra* note 72, at 32-33. "Adoption is the permanent plan offering the most stability to the foster child who cannot return to his parents." *Id.*
88. FLA. BAR, *supra* note 4, at § 15-5.
89. *Id.*
90. FLA. STAT. § 39.001 (1987) stating that:
   (2) The purposes of this chapter are: . . . (c) To preserve and strengthen

Florida Statutes to govern permanent commitments and to serve the legislative goals of either reuniting the dependent[92] child with his parent(s) or placing the child in a permanent home as quickly as possible.[93] Florida agrees that "the right to the integrity of the family is

---

the child's family ties whenever possible, removing him from the custody of his parents only when his welfare or the safety and protection of the public cannot be adequately safeguarded without such removal; and, when the child is removed from his own family, to secure for him custody, care, and discipline as nearly as possible equivalent to that which should have been given by his parents; and to assure, in all cases in which a child must be permanently removed from tne custody of his parents, that the child be placed in an approved family home and be made a member of the family by adoption.

See also FLA. STAT. § 39.002 (1987) entitled "Legislative Intent":

It is a goal of the Legislature that the children of this state be provided with the following protections: (1) A permanent and stable home . . . (5) Protection from abuse, neglect and exploitation . . . (8) An independent, trained advocate, when intervention is necessary and a skilled guardian or caretaker in a safe environment when alternative placement is necessary.

91. FLA. STAT. § 409.166 (1987):

(1) Legislative intent - It is the intent of the Legislature to protect and promote every child's right to the security and stability of a permanent family home. The Legislature intends to make available to prospective adoptive parents financial aid which will enable them to adopt a child in foster care who, because of his special needs, has proven difficult to place in an adoptive home . . . .

92. A dependent child means a child who, is found by the court:

(a) To have been abandoned, abused, or neglected by his parents or other custodians. (b) To have been surrendered to the department [HRS] or a licensed child-placing agency for the purpose of adoption. (c) To have been voluntarily placed with a licensed child-caring agency, a licensed child-placing agency, or the department [HRS], whereupon . . . a performance agreement his expired and the parent or parents have failed to substantially comply with the requirements of the agreement . . . .

FLA. STAT. § 39.01(10) (1987). Additionally, the termination of parental rights cannot solely be based on the fact that the child was previously adjudicated dependent. *See* White v. Department of Health and Rehabilitative Servs., 483 So. 2d 861 (Fla. 5th Dist. Ct. App. 1986). *See also infra* note 103, for a description of a performance agreement.

93. *See In re* Baby Boy A., 544 So. 2d 1136 (Fla. 4th Dist. Ct. App. 1989). However, the legislature's goal of reunification was recently questioned as a result of the July 28, 1989, death of two-year old Bradly McGee. The child died of a brain hemorrhage after repeatedly being pushed headfirst into a toilet bowl for soiling his diapers. Gerald Slavens, inspector general for the Florida Department of Health and Rehabilitative Services stated that "it appears that the safety of the child was not the primary concern." He said that workers put the emphasis on keeping the family to-

among the most fundamental rights."[94] However, an individual's parental rights are subject to the overriding principle that it is the best interest of the child which must prevail.[95]

Currently, in Florida, parental rights termination may be based on prospective abuse or neglect when the "evidence establishes that the parent will be unable to provide necessary child care and support in the future, and it is otherwise in the best interest of the child to take such action."[96]

However, the state must comply with specific statutory provisions before terminating parental rights. Initially, a petition for termination of parental rights is filed.[97] This petition can be filed by "an authorized agent of the [D]epartment [of Health and Rehabilitative Service], or by any other person who has knowledge of the facts alleged or is informed of them and believes that they are true . . . ."[98]

Thereafter, several hearings follow the original petition. First, an advisory hearing is set and held fourteen days after the original petition is filed.[99] Here, the date for the adjudicatory hearing is set.[100]

In an adjudicatory hearing on a petition for termination of parental rights, "clear and convincing evidence shall be required to establish the need for such termination."[101] If the court finds clear and convinc-

---

gether instead. Sun-Sentinel, August 15, 1989, at 10A.

As a result of the McGee incident, four social workers were indicted in Polk County, Florida, on charges of failing to report child abuse. The Palm Beach Post, September 1, 1989, at 1A.

94.   Carlson v. State, 378 So. 2d 868 (Fla. 2d Dist. Ct. App. 1979).

95.   *In re* W.D.N., 443 So. 2d 493 (Fla. 2d. Dist. Ct. App. 1984); *In re* J.L.P., 416 So. 2d 1250, 1252 (Fla. 4th Dist. Ct. App. 1982).

96.   *In re* T.D., 537 So. 2d 173 (Fla. 1st Dist. Ct. App. 1989); Spankie v. Department of Health and Rehabilitation Servs., 505 So. 2d 1357 (Fla. 5th Dist. Ct. App.), *rev. denied*, 513 So. 2d 1063 (1987); *In re* J.L.P., 416 So. 2d 1250 (Fla. 4th Dist. Ct. App. 1982).

97.   FLA. STAT. § 39.461 (1987).

98.   *Id.*

99.   FLA. STAT. § 39.466 (1987). The purpose of this hearing is to inform the parties of their legal counsel and *ad litem* rights. *Id. See also* FLA. STAT. § 39.465 (1987).

100.   FLA. STAT.§ 39.466 (1987). The adjudicatory hearing must be set within forty-five days of the advisory hearing.

101.   FLA. STAT. § 39.467(1) (1987). This article's discussion will focus on "prospective abuse or neglect" as grounds for parental termination at the adjudicatory hearing. However, for a complete discussion, including Discovery, Motions, etc., on the procedures relating to the termination of parental rights proceedings *see* FLA. BAR, *supra* note 4, at § 15-35 to § 15-45.

ing evidence to terminate parental rights, it will "enter an order to that effect and shall thereafter have full authority under this chapter [Chapter 39] to provide for the child who is the subject of the adjudication for termination of parental rights."[102] However, if the requisite standard of proof is not met, the court shall "(a) [e]nter an order placing or continuing the child in foster care under a performance agreement[103] or permanent placement plan;[104] or (b) [e]nter an order returning the child to the natural parent or parents with or without protective supervision and other required services or program participation by the parent."[105] Florida Statute section 39.464 enumerates the procedural elements for parental rights termination.[106]

Florida's present support for termination of parental rights based on prospective abuse or neglect is found in Florida Statute sections 39.01(2)[107] and 39.01(37).[108] In section 39.01(2), abuse is defined as "any willful act that results in any physical, mental, or sexual injury that causes or is likely to cause the child's physical, mental, or emo-

---

102. FLA. STAT. § 39.468(1) (1987).

103. A full discussion of performance agreements is beyond the scope of this work. However, a performance agreement is a court ordered plan which is prepared by a social service agency, signed by the parent(s), social service agency, foster parent, guardian ad litem and possibly the child. Essentially, it is a "written plan of action to prevent the recurrence of the facts found in the order which adjudicated the child dependent." See FLA. STAT. §§ 39.01(40) (1987) and 39.451 (1987) for more information on performance agreements. See also Burk v. Department of Health and Rehabilitative Servs., 476 So. 2d 1275 (Fla. 1985), In re C.B., 453 So. 2d 220 (Fla. 5th Dist. Ct. App. 1984). In Burk, the court held that parents must be offered a performance agreement as a prerequisite to permanent commitment proceedings. However, parental rights cannot be terminated solely because of the parents' failure to comply with a performance agreement; the state must still show "clear and convincing evidence of abuse, neglect or abandonment. In re R.W., 495 So. 2d 133 (Fla. 1986). But see FLA. STAT. 39.467(2)(e) (1987) ("[F]ailure to substantially comply is evidence of abuse, abandonment, or neglect, unless the court finds that the failure to comply with the performance agreement is the result of conditions beyond the control of the parent or parents.")

104. A full discussion of permanent placement plans is beyond the scope of this work. However, such plan takes the place of the performance agreement when the parent(s) will not or cannot participate in the preparation of a performance agreement. See FLA. STAT. §§ 39.01(41) (1987) and 39.452 (1987) for further information of permanent placement plans.

105. FLA. STAT. § 39.468(2)(a)(b) (1987).

106. FLA. STAT. § 39.464 (1987).

107. FLA. STAT. § 39.01(2) (1987).

108. FLA. STAT. § 39.01(37) (1987).

tional health to be significantly impaired."[109] Further, neglect occurs

> when the parent . . . deprives a child of, or allows a child to be
> deprived of necessary food, clothing, shelter, or medical treatment
> or permits a child to live in an environment when such deprivation
> or environment causes the child's physical, mental, or emotional
> health to be significantly impaired or to be in danger of being sig-
> nificantly impaired. The foregoing circumstances shall not be con-
> sidered neglect if caused primarily by financial inability unless ser-
> vices for relief have been offered and rejected . . . .[110]

Additional support for prospective abuse is found in Florida Statute section 49.464(2)(b)2 entitled "Extraordinary procedures."[111] In
pertinent part section 49.464(2)(b)2 states:

> (a) Whenever it appears that the manifest best interests of the
> child demand it, the state may petition for termination of parental
> rights without offering a performance agreement[112] or permanent
> placement plan[113] to the parents . . . .
> b) The state may petition under this subsection only under the fol-
> lowing circumstances:
> 2. Severe or continuous abuse or neglect of the child or OTHER
> CHILDREN by the parent that demonstrates that the parent's con-
> duct threatens the life or well-being of the child . . . .[114]

Florida currently allows parental rights termination to be based on
"prospective abuse or neglect" when it is in the best interest of the
child to take such action."[115] On what basis is this clear-and-convincing
evidentiary determination made since no profile exists to accurately
identify prospective abusive and neglectful parents?[116]

As mentioned,[117] the courts have been using the definitions of

---

109. FLA. STAT. § 39.01(2).
110. FLA. STAT. § 39.01(37).
111. FLA. STAT. § 39.464(2)(b)2.
112. *See supra* note 103, discussing performance agreements.
113. *See supra* note 104, discussing the permanent placement plan.
114. FLA. STAT. § 49.464(2)(b)2 (1987) (emphasis added).
115. Spankie v. Department of Health and Rehabilitation Servs., 505 So. 2d
1357 (Fla. 5th Dist. Ct. App.), *rev. denied*, 513 So. 2d 1063 (1987).
116. *See supra* notes 188-234, and accompanying text for a discussion on predicting child abuse.
117. *See supra* notes 107-14 and accompanying text discussing the definitions of
abuse and neglect pursuant to the Florida Statutes.

abuse and neglect to support the concept of "prospective abuse and neglect." Therefore, one may wonder why there is an issue pending before the Florida Supreme Court regarding the viability of this concept. It appears that the Fifth District Court of Appeal may have been anxiously awaiting a case like *Padgett*, since in *Manuel v. Department of Health and Rehabilitation Services*,[118] Chief Judge Sharp wrote a special concurrence stating that "[w]hether 'prospective neglect' or even 'prospective abandonment' are valid grounds for termination of parental rights pursuant to section 39.01 Florida Statutes,[119] are important legal issues which should be addressed by this court in a proper case [and] had this been such a case, I would have done so."[120] Additionally, Judge Cowart's dissent in *Spankie v. Department of Health & Rehabilitative Services*,[121] stated that the allegation of such abuse "is not 'prospective;' it is '*speculative.*' "[122] Further, Judge Cowart compares terminating parental rights based on "prospective abuse" with "justifying the imprisonment of one who has not committed a crime because 'but for' the fact that he was imprisoned he 'would have' committed a crime."[123]

The Second, Fourth and Third District Courts of Appeal have expressly relied on the future tense elements contained in the definitions of "abuse" and "neglect" in Fla. Stat. sections 39.01(2) and 39.01(26) respectively, to support the concept of prospective abuse.[124] However, in his Florida Supreme Court Brief, Lawrence James Semento, counsel for the Appellant, Thomas Padgett, argues that the Florida courts have erroneously relied on the Florida Statutes to support the concept of prospective abuse. He states that

> [t]he Legislature of the State of Florida, responding to the societal need to protect the rights of both parents and children, has set forth a detailed and specific statute to accomplish termination of

---

118. 537 So. 2d 1022 (Fla. 5th Dist. Ct. App. 1988).

119. FLA. STAT. § 39.01 (1987).

120. *Manuel*, 537 So. 2d at 1022-23.

121. *Spankie*, 505 So. 2d at 1357.

122. *Id.* at 1359 (emphasis in the original).

123. *Id.* at 1360.

124. *See W.D.N.*, 443 So. 2d at 495; Yem v. Department of Health and Rehabilitative Servs., 462 So. 2d 1147 (Fla. 3d Dist. Ct. App. 1984); *J.L.P.*, 416 So. 2d at 1252. Also, the First District Court of Appeal may recognize prospective neglect or abuse as a basis to terminate parental rights if such prospective abuse or neglect is sufficiently well-established. *See T.D.*, 537 So. 2d at 175.

parental rights. Prospective abuse, neglect or abandonment, however, are not provided as grounds in that statute.[125]

Further, he states that "the concept of prospective abuse has been
grafted onto the statutory scheme through Florida case law."[126] Thus,
it appears that in response to *Padgett*,[127] and the special concurrences
and dissents of Justices Sharp and Cowart respectively, the Florida Supreme Court has decided to reevaluate this concept to determine if the
concept is "viable."

On August 3, 1989, prior to the Florida Supreme Court's answer
to the certified question, the Fifth District Court of Appeal in *Palmer
v. Department of Health and Rehabilitative Services*,[128] terminated a
father's parental rights solely on the basis of prospective abuse. The
court stated that

> [u]ntil recently,[129] our court has not directly passed on whether
> 'prospective' abuse of a child, however clearly established, is a suffi-
> cient legal basis to terminate parental rights. In the prior cases
> considered by us, there has been an allegation of actual abuse or
> neglect, and proof of the same, with circumstances indicating that
> the abuse or neglect will continue if the child is returned to the
> parent.[130]

The *Palmer* court recognized that the crucial issue is "whether future
behavior, which will adversely affect the child, can be clearly and certainly predicted."[131] However, the court noted that in *Palmer* it was
dealing with pedophilia,[132] a psychological disorder that has been extensively studied.[133] The court further stated that recent "studies show

---

125.   Appellant, Thomas Padgett's Brief at 6, Padgett v. Department of Health
and Human Servs., 543 So. 2d 1317 (Fla. 5th Dist. Ct. App. 1989).

126.   *Id.*

127.   Padgett v. Department of Health and Human Servs., 543 So. 2d 1317 (Fla.
5th Dist. Ct. App. 1989).

128.   547 So. 2d 981 (Fla. 5th Dist. Ct. App.), *appeal dismissed*, 553 So. 2d
1166 (Fla. 1989).

129.   Here, the Fifth District is footnoting to the *Padgett* case.

130.   The court cites *Spankie* 505 So. 2d at 1357; Frederick v. State, 523 So. 2d
1164 (Fla. 5th Dist. Ct. App.), *rev. denied*, 531 So. 2d 1353 (Fla. 1988); and *Manuel*
537 So. 2d at 1022. These cases will be further discussed in this section of the article.

131.   *Palmer*, 547 So. 2d at 984.

132.   "A pedophile is a person who has a preference for repetitive sexual activity
with prepubertal children." *Id.* at 982.

133.   *Id.* at 984.

and experts agree . . . that there is no easy 'cure' for this disorder,[134] and the rate of recidivism from the medical standpoint is extremely high."[135] Consequently, the court affirmed the trial court's finding of prospective sexual abuse.[136] The *Palmer* court compared giving an untreated pedophile, or one who has no prospects for successful treatment, custody of a child as "tantamount to placing matches in a tinderbox."[137]

As mentioned, other Florida courts have applied the concept of "prospective abuse" to terminate parental rights. In *In re J.L.P.*,[138] the earliest Florida case expressly addressing the issue, the court noted that the definition of "neglect" found in Florida Statutes section 39.01(27)[139] supported its holding that "neglect" can be prospective, and the fact that the Appellant never had custody of the child was irrelevant.[140] Consequently, in accordance with *Santosky*,[141] the *J.L.P.* court held that "in order to sustain a final order of permanent commitment because of neglect or abuse, there must be clear and convincing evidence that the child has been or will be abused or neglected."[142] Here, there was evidence of the mother's alleged prior abuse, poverty, "squalid" housing arrangements, limited mental capacity, emotional makeup, and promiscuity.[143] Additionally, a clinical psychologist's testimony revealed that if the child were left alone with the mother, the

---

134. *Id.* at 984 n.5. The *Palmer* court footnotes the following: *See, e.g.*, State v. Coleman, 490 So. 2d 705, 707 (La. App. 1986)).

135. *Id.* at 984 n.6. "The recidivism rate for homosexual pedophilia is second only to exhibitionism, and ranges from 13-28% of those apprehended—roughly twice the rate of heterosexual pedophilia." *Id.* (citing The Merck Manual, Ch. 139, p. 1499 (15th ed. 1987)).

136. *Palmer*, 547 So. 2d at 984.

137. *Id.*

138. 416 So. 2d 1250 (Fla. 4th Dist. Ct. App. 1982).

139.
> [W]hen a parent or other legal custodian, though financially able, deprives a child of, or allows a child to be deprived of, necessary food, clothing, shelter, or medical treatment or permits a child to live in an environment when such deprivation or environment causes the child's physical, mental, or emotional health to be significantly impaired or to be in danger of being significantly impaired.

Id. at 1252 (quoting Fla. Stat. § 39.01(27) (Supp. 1980)).

140. *J.L.P.*, 416 So. 2d at 1252.

141. *Santosky*, 455 U.S. at 753.

142. *J.L.P.*, 416 So. 2d at 1252.

143. *Id.* at 1251-53.

child would be subject to a considerable risk of abuse.[144]

Thus, while noting its sympathy for the mother, the court affirmed the trial court's ruling stating that "[t]he Legislature clearly did not intend to have a child suffer such an experience before a trial court could act."[145]

Similarly in *Yem v State*,[146] the Third District Court of Appeal utilized the *J.L.P.* court's proposition that "the fact that the mother never had actual custody of her child does not foreclose a finding of neglect."[147] The court found that the mother's act of permitting her child to "live in an environment which caused the child's physical, mental or emotional health to be impaired, or in danger of being significantly impaired," justified permanent commitment of the child.[148]

Next, in *In re W.D.N.*,[149] the Second District Court of Appeal held that

> a parent's abuse of some of her children may constitute grounds for the permanent commitment of her other children who also live with the parent . . . . To continue to expose children to abuse by a parent simply because findings of prior abuse by the parent only concerned others of the parent's children would constitute an unacceptable risk to the children where, as here, the mother's propensities in that regard were shown to be beyond reasonable hope of modification.[150]

As mentioned earlier, in *W.D.N.*, the court relied on "abuse" being defined as "any willful act that results in any physical, mental or sexual injury that causes or is likely to cause the child's physical, mental, or emotional health to be·significantly impaired."[151] In *W.D.N.*, the father had abandoned the family leaving the mother with five children. One child died in a fire. Another child, S.N., who was adjudicated depen-

---

144. *Id.* at 1253.
145. *Id.*
146. 462 So. 2d 1147 (Fla. 3d Dist. Ct. App. 1984).
147. *Id.* at 1149 (citing *J.L.P.*, 416 So. 2d 1250).
148. *Yem*, 462 So. 2d at 1149. The facts of *Yem* reveal that the child was born while the mother was imprisoned for the murder of a stepson. The child's grandfather cared for her; however, he was found dead in his home and the child was found wandering the streets. The child was filthy and had a severe case of diaper rash. Additionally, the grandfather's house was filthy.
149. 443 So. 2d 493 (Fla. 2d Dist. Ct. App. 1984).
150. *Id.* at 495.
151. *Id.* (quoting FLA. STAT. § 39.01(2) (1981)).

dent on a finding of child abuse, was permanently committed to HRS for adoption.[152] Subsequently, W.D.N. was adjudicated dependent based on the mother's past abusive behavior toward S.N. and based on the fact that she was unable to provide W.D.N. with necessary medical treatment. Therafter, the mother had twins, C.N. (male) and C.N. (female). Based on findings that C.N. (male) had been abused (three rib fractures) and the past abuse of S.N., the twins were also adjudicated dependent.[153] The mother was provided with all possible helpful programs available, including HRS counseling for parenting problems. However, she did not benefit from the counseling; she did not admit that she had a problem. Since Florida did not have any more programs which could help her, the district court affirmed the trial court's holding that clear and convincing evidence demonstrated that permanent commitment was in the best interests of the children.[154]

Several other Florida cases have upheld "prospective abuse or neglect." In *Spankie v. Department of Health and Rehabilitative Services*, the Fifth District Court of Appeal based the termination of a mother's parental rights on her "history of physical and emotional abuse with little prospect for improvement."[155] In *Spankie*, the mother was unwilling to adjust her lifestyle and consistently denied that abuse had taken place.[156] The abuse consisted of

> malnourishment, whippings, fractures of the child's leg, black eyes and numerous bruises. The mother raise[d] dogs and travel[ed] frequently to show them. The child often smelled of dog feces, was dressed inappropriately (*e.g.*, sundresses in the winter), was unaware of basic hygienic practices (*e.g.*, daily washing) and was left alone all night on at least one occasion. There was also evidence of unsafe and unsanitary conditions at the mother's home and that she locked the child in her room and nailed boards over the windows.[157]

The mother was diagnosed as a passive-aggressive personality since she was angry, hostile, and impulsive. Thus, the mother's parental rights were terminated since the court felt that "clear and convincing evi-

152. *Id.* at 494.
153. *Id.*
154. *W.D.N.*, 443 So. 2d at 495.
155. 505 So. 2d 1357, 1358 (Fla. 5th Dist. Ct. App. 1987).
156. *Id.* at 1358-59.
157. *Id.* at 1358.

dence" existed to show that the child would be further neglected or abused.[158]

Recently, in *In re Baby Boy A.*,[159] a father appealed the termination of his parental rights.[160] The father had been incarcerated for aggravated child abuse upon Baby Boy A.'s older sibling and was in jail when Baby Boy A. was born.[161] Additionally, the father was on parole for manslaughter in New York and was wanted there for parole violation.[162] The Fourth District Court of Appeal found that clear and convincing evidence existed to support a finding of prospective abuse or neglect of Baby Boy A. Its decision was based on the fact that prior to the father's incarceration, he failed to offer supervision or child care *to the older sibling*, although he provided some financial support.[163] The court noted that the father "has no viable plan for the care of the subject child were he free to assume parental responsibility."[164] Further, the court stated that it "need not wait until the prospective abuse or neglect occurs before severing the parental ties because the best interest of the child overrides parental rights."[165]

The decisions discussed constitute the majority of the Florida cases upholding the termination of parental rights or permanent commitment based on "prospective abuse or neglect." Decisions where termination based on prospective abuse or neglect has not been upheld usually involve the additional factor of a parent who is either mentally ill, retarded or borderline mentally retarded.[166]

---

158. *Id.*

159. 544 So. 2d 1136 (Fla. 4th Dist. Ct. 1989).

160. The mother appeared before the court to acknowledge her voluntary placement of the child. *Id.*

161. *Id.* at 1137.

162. *Id.*

163. *Id.*

164. *Baby Boy A.*, 544 So. 2d at 1137.

165. *Id.* (quoting *J.L.P.*, 416 So. 2d 1250). There was a strong dissent in this case by Judge Walden. The basis of the dissent was two-fold. First, the father was never offered a performance agreement. Second, the father presented a child caring plan to the trial court. However, the trial court found his plan unworkable. Judge Walden stated that "[w]hile appellant's proposed plan for the caring for the child may not be comparable to that available from better situated adoptive parents, the appellant should not be expected to do more than his best to provide support for his child, given his circumstances." *Id.* (Walden, J., dissenting).

166. *But see In re* C.N.G., 531 So. 2d 345 (Fla. 5th Dist. Ct. App. 1988) which affirmed the permanent commitment of a mother classified as "mildly retarded" or of "low average intelligence." *Id.* at 345 n.1 (Cowart, J., dissenting) The HRS psycholo-

In *I.T. v. Department of Health and Rehabilitative Services*,[167] the court held that the parents' psychiatric histories, which allegedly showed that they might exercise poor judgment under stress, did not support finding that infant was at risk of prospective neglect.[168] Additionally, in *In re T.D.*,[169] the court held that a parent's chronic mental illness was a condition beyond her control, and was not shown to be a sufficient basis upon which to predicate the necessary finding of prospective neglect, to warrant termination of parental rights.[170] Further, the parent's failure to stimulate the child intellectually was an inadequate basis to support a finding of neglect.[171] However, despite its holding, the court noted that under facts which establish that the parent will be unable to provide necessary child care and support in the future, and it is otherwise in the best interest of the child, termination of parental rights may be based on prospective abuse or neglect.[172]

Prospective Abuse and Neglect In Other States

Many other states have expressly addressed the concept of prospective abuse and neglect. As in Florida, a state court's analysis of the issue often revolves around the particular wording and interpretation of that state's statute.

For example, in *In re Dittrick Infant*,[173] the Dittricks' parental rights of their first child were terminated due to allegations of physical and sexual abuse. Before these rights were teminated, Carol Dittrick became pregnant with the subject child.[174] "Believing that the birth of this present child was imminent, the plaintiff filed a petition in probate court . . . seeking an order of temporary custody pending further hearings."[175] The Michigan Court of Appeals noted that while the probate

---

gist admitted that he had no fear that the mother would ever intentionally neglect or abuse the child. *Id.* at 346 n.9 (Cowart, J., dissenting). The dissent suggested that the question of whether mental retardation of a parent is a ground for termination of parental rights, should be certified to the Florida Supreme Court as a question of great public importance. *Id.* at 347 (Cowart, J., dissenting).

167. 532 So. 2d 1085 (Fla. 3d Dist. Ct. App. 1988).
168. *Id.* at 1089.
169. 537 So. 2d 173 (Fla. 1st Dist. Ct. App. 1989).
170. *Id.* at 175.
171. *Id.*
172. *Id.*
173. 80 Mich. App. 219, 263 N.W.2d 37 (1977).
174. *Id.* at 220, 263 N.W.2d at 38.
175. *Id.*

court could find neglect based on allegations that the Dittricks' abused their first child, the probate court did not have jurisdiction to enter the order of temporary custody since the legislature did not intend for the word "child" to apply to unborn persons.[176] However, where a child is born, the Michigan Court of Appeals consistently holds that when dealing with the termination of parental rights, evidence that a parent mistreats one child is certainly probative of how that parent may treat other children.[177]

In *In re S.L.P.*,[178] evidence supported that the father had a long history of violent behavior and mental illness,[179] and the mother was diagnosed as a paranoid schizophrenic.[180] The Nebraska Supreme Court noted that since neither parent had ever had custody of the child, ..ere was no evidence of actual harm.[181] Nevertheless, the court stated that "a court need not await certain disaster to come into fruition before taking protective steps in the interest of a minor child."[182] Furthermore, it stated that "[i]n termination of parental rights cases, the primary consideration is the best interest of the juvenile."[183]

Based on rationales similar to those discussed above, many other states such as New York,[184] Missouri,[185] Illinois,[186] and Pennsylvania[187]

---

176. *Id.* at 221, 263 N.W.2d at 39. "The probate court jurisdiction in such matters is defined by M.C.L.A. § 712A.2; M.S.A. §27.3178(598.2). Subsection (b) of that statute provides that the probate court has [j]urisdiction in proceedings concerning any child under 17 years of age found within the county . . . ." *Id.* However, the court noted that the present case convinced them that the legislature may want to consider amending the probate code. *Id.*

177. *See In re* LaFlure, 48 Mich. App. 377, 392, 210 N.W.2d 482, 489 (1973). *See also In re* Parshall, 159 Mich. App. 683, 406 N.W.2d 913 (1987); *In re* Futch, 144 Mich. App. 163, 375 N.W.2d 375 (1984); *In re* Kantola, 139 Mich. App. 23, 361 N.W.2d 20 (1984) (adding that such evidence is not conclusive or automatically determinative).

178. 230 Neb. 635, 432 N.W.2d 826 (1988).

179. *Id.* at 636, 432 N.W.2d at 828.

180. *Id.* at 637, 432 N.W.2d at 829.

181. *Id.* at 639, 432 N.W.2d at 830.

182. *Id.* (citing *In re* S.P., N.P., and L.P., 221 Neb. 165, 375 N.W.2d 616 (1985)).

183. *S.L.P.*, 230 Neb. at 639-40, 432 N.W.2d at 830 (citing *In re* J.S., S.C., and L.S., 224 Neb. 234, 397 N.W.2d 621 (1986)).

184. *See Santosky*, 455 U.S. at 1393; *In re* Cruz, 121 A.D.2d 901, 503 N.Y.S.2d 798 (1986) ("a court cannot and should not await broken bone or shattered psyche before extending its protective cloak around a child . . . ."). *Id.* at 903, 503 N.Y.S.2d 801 (quoting *In re* Maria Anthony, 81 Misc. 2d 342, 345, 366 N.Y.S.2d 333, 336 (1975)).

have upheld the concept of prospective abuse or neglect of children. All the states which have expressly dealt with the issue of terminating parental rights based on prospective abuse or neglect have held that the concept is viable as long as clear and convincing evidence is presented to establish such abuse.

Since many states terminate parental rights based on prospective abuse, the ability to predict child abuse appears crucial to determining whether the concept of "prospective abuse or neglect" is viable enough to interfere with an individual's fourteenth amendment right to rear children.

Predicting Prospective Abuse and Neglect

Through the use of psychological information, this article will examine the predictors of abusive and neglectful parents to determine if an "abusive or neglectful parent profile" can be objectively formed to support the termination of an individual's right to rear children.

The previously discussed NIS-2 study[188] compiled and reported the relation of abuse and neglect to child, family, and county characteristics. The report concluded that race/ethnicity and county metrostatus were not associated with maltreatment.[189] However, all other characteristics such as the child's sex, age, family income, and family size did have some impact to the incidence or type of maltreatment.[190] For instance, females were more frequently abused than males.[191] Ad-

---

185. K.S. v. M.N.W., 713 S.W.2d 858 (Mo. Ct. App. 1986) (parental rights were properly terminated upon proof that parents abused child's siblings, even though the siblings did not incur life threatening or gravely disabling injury or disfigurement nor even serious injury).

186. *See In re* A.D.R., 186 Ill. App. 3d 386, 542 N.E.2d 487 (1989). The court found that the physical abuse by the father against the wife-mother, which continued for at least seven years, created an environment injurious to the child. The Court further found that when faced with evidence of prior abuse by parents, the juvenile court should not be forced to refrain from taking action until each particular child suffers an injury.

187. *In re* Black, 273 Pa. Super. 536, 417 A.2d 1178 (1980) (newborn declared deprived even though never in parent's custody since evidence was sufficient to establish that prior deaths of two of mother's children were result of improper care and precautions by parents).

188. *See* STUDY FINDINGS, *supra* notes 55 to 67 and accompanying text.

189. STUDY FINDINGS, *supra* note 55, at 7-6.

190. *Id.*

191. *Id.* (13.1 per 1,000 females vs. 8.4 per 1,000 males).

ditionally, the incidence of abuse, particularly physical abuse, increased with age.[192] However, when the youngest children were abused, they were more likely to experience fatal injury.[193]

"Family income had wide-ranging effects on both the incidence and severity of child maltreatment."[194] That is, "[in 1986] children from families earning less than $15,000 . . . were more likely than those from higher income families to experience maltreatment and injury."[195] Family size was found to be associated with the incidence of maltreatment.[196] "Children from larger families[197] had higher estimated incidence of both abuse and neglect than did their counterparts from smaller families, and were more likely to be regarded as endangered."[198] Since the numbers reflect that a child's sex and age, along with family income and size, have an impact on the incidence of maltreatment, it might appear feasible to create the abusive or neglectful parent profile. If such profile can be objectively formed, the Florida Supreme Court will have support to declare the concept viable.

In Polk County, Iowa, authorities utilized the techniques of "statistical risk-factor analysis" before obtaining an order allowing them to remove a two-month-old child, M. Hall ["M."], from his parents' home.[199] The authorities did not believe that the child had been abused; however, they feared M. would be harmed in the future.[200] "By matching his parents' characters and backgrounds with the findings of scholarly studies, they decided that [M.] . . . faced a precise 40% chance of being abused within the next five years."[201] However, this statement is slightly misleading since Randall Wilson, M.'s attorney, stated that while removing M from his parent's home, the court "was careful not to base its decision solely on the formulas. There was other information available on which it based its decision."[202]

---

192. *Id.* at 7-7.

193. *Id.*

194. STUDY FINDINGS, *supra* note 55, at 7-7.

195. *Id.*

196. *Id.*

197. "Large families" includes those families with four or more children.

198. STUDY FINDINGS *supra* note 55, at 7-7.

199. Los Angeles Times, Feb. 12, 1989, § 1, at 12, col. 1. This article is entitled *Child Abuse: Dilemma of Prevention* [hereinafter *Child Abuse*]. The case was neither appealed nor published in the reporter system.

200. *Id.*

201. *Id.*

202. *Id.*

It was noted that "[t]he Halls are not a terribly winning couple. Joan Hall served time in prison for voluntary manslaughter after she was charged with delivering a blow that killed her daughter in 1982."[203] "Doctors and caseworkers say that both Halls have antisocial personality disorders regarded as untreatable and unlikely to change."[204]

When asked if newborns from all parents who are innately, chronically at high risk would be seized from their parents, Larry Eisenhauer, the Polk County juvenile court judge who ordered M. removed from the Hall's home, stated, "[w]e work under the assumption everything can be remedied. But I know it's coming."[205]

Of particular importance to the present article is the Iowa authorities' determination that M. faced a forty percent chance of being abused within the next five years.[206] This figure was determined by a Consensus Opinion of the Pediatric-Juvenile Court Consultation Committee.[207] The report noted that the same social, marital, family, and environmental factors existed as they did when Mrs. Hall abused and killed her daughter.[208] "This fact by itself places M. . . . at a twenty percent risk of abuse without any consideration of others factor."[209] Additionally, "it has been reported that in a family in which there has

---

203. *Child Abuse, supra* note 199, at 21. M.'s father was not the father of Joan Hall's daughter, Chrissy. The newspaper article reports that in 1979 Joan, eighteen and unmarried, gave birth to her daughter Christina. *Id.* Abuse reports accumulated and Chrissy was placed in a foster home when she was seven months old. *Id.* After two years of foster care, Chrissy was returned to her mother's home. *Id.* At that time, Joan was married (not to M's father) and had another daughter. *Id.* Joan said "she also boozed and did drugs in those days." *Id.* The article states,

> She was speeding on uppers the night Chrissy died. Chrissy had thrown up and wet her pants, Joan explained. So she had gotten angry, lost control and pushed Chrissy against a wall. Chrissy had fallen. She was just lying on the floor, her body moving funny. Joan had called her name but she hadn't answered. Joan pleaded guilty to voluntary manslaughter. A juvenile court judge terminated her right to keep Jessica, [her second daughter].

Id.

204. *Id.* The newspaper article continues to discuss the Hall's past in detail.
205. *Id.*
206. *Id.* at 12.
207. Consensus Opinion of the Pediatric-Juvenile Court Consultation Committee, at 2 (Unpublished Opinion which was Exhibit Number 11 at the August 4, 1988 "Hall" hearing. [hereinafter Consensus Opinion]).
208. *Id.*
209. *Id.* at 1.

been a serious or fatal child abuse case there is a forty percent risk that a second child will be seriously injured."[210] To support these percentages, the Committee relied on an article entitled Identifying Correlates of Reabuse in Maltreating Parents.[211]

The study reported in the above-mentioned article compared twenty-two parent, child and treatment variables which potentially correlated to reabuse by forty-five parents, forty mothers and five fathers, who were in treatment for abuse.[212] Results revealed that a single variable alone was not strongly associated with reabuse; however, interactions involving several variables, such as income source, marital status, and the abuser's personal abuse history significantly differentiated between reabusers and nonreabusers.[213] Other factors including the child's age, the severity of initial abuse, the parent's age, and the length of the abuser's treatment were also associated with reabuse.[214] "For example, while income source did not have a mitigating effect for subjects with a history of having themselves been abused, having some earned income decreased the probability of reabuse for those without a personal abuse history."[215] Additionally, "[i]f treatment lasted less than six months, currently unmarried abusers tended to be less likely to reabuse than currently married ones."[216] It was noted that the marriage may have created stress in the abusers' environment rather than acting as support.[217] An earlier study revealed that family size, family spacing, unplanned conception, parent's age at first birth, and number of children from different fathers are all factors to consider when predicting child abuse and neglect.[218]

Additionally, when the recidivism rate was calculated, it was reported that forty percent of the parents, eighteen of forty five, had been

---

210. *Id.* at 2.

211. *Id.* (relying on Ferleger, Glenwick, Gaines, Green, *Identifying Correlates of Reabuse In Maltreating Parents,* 12 CHILD ABUSE AND NEGLECT 41 (1988)).

212. Ferleger, *supra* note 28, at 41.

213. *See id.* at 43-46 for a technical explanation of the method of data collection, procedures and the statistical analysis.

214. *Id.* at 46-47.

215. *Id.*

216. *Id.* at 47.

217. *Id.*

218. Zuravin, *Fertility Patterns: Their Relationship to Child Physical Abuse and Child Neglect,* 50 J. MARRIAGE AND FAM. 983, 984 (1988). Additionally, this article explores the factor relationships in differentiating abuse from neglect. Such analysis is beyond the scope of this article.

cited for reabuse while they were in treatment.[219] During the follow-up period the rate of reabuse was thirteen percent, sixteen of forty five.[220]

The feasibility and accuracy of identifying parents that are at risk for abusing children is certainly a factor to consider when determining whether the concept of prospective abuse is viable or too speculative. A 1984 study concluded that "prenatal prediction was feasible although the rate of false positive high risk assignment would limit practical application of the interview used."[221] The "[f]easibility of identifying risk for child abuse prospectively was determined by interviewing 1400 expectant mothers and [through objective rating,] predicting that 273 were high risk."[222]

Thereafter, the interviewers, unaware that their subjective comments were going to be used in the study, recorded additional information which they felt would place a mother at risk.[223] Some of the interviewer comments related to statements that the mothers had made. These statements suggested that the mothers had aggressive impulses towards children. Additionally, "[some mothers] implied they had been investigated by protective services for abuse . . . ."[224] In the interviewer's opinion, some of the mothers "seemed to intentionally fail to protect their children . . . from a dangerous situation that occurred while they were being interviewed.[225] Of the thirteen mothers receiving these interviewer comments, six had been reported for abuse.[226] Moreover, of the 273 "at risk" mothers, sixty-seven percent reported nonaccidental child injuries; of the 1127 families who were not labeled "at

219. Ferlenger, *supra* note 28, at 44.
220. *Id.* at 44-45. *See supra* notes 47-50 and accompanying text which discusses the potential for underestimating these rates.
221. Altemeier, O'Conner, Sandler, Sherrod, Vietze, *Prediction of Child Abuse: A Prospective Study of Feasibility*, 8 CHILD ABUSE & NEGLECT 393 (1984) [hereinafter Altemeir].
222. *Id.* The mothers received a thirty five minute interview concerning factors that studies had associated with child maltreatment. *Id.* at 394. Following are the topics covered: mother's childhood nurture, her self-image, support available from others, parenting philosophy, attitude about current pregnancy, and general health related problems including alcohol and drug abuse. *Id.* A modified Life Stress Inventory was used to determine the incidence of twenty one maternal and eleven paternal stresses during the preceding year. *Id.* Several questions explored the mother's knowledge and expectations of child development. *Id.*
223. *Id.*
224. *Id.* at 396.
225. *Id.* These statements reflect the opinion of the interviewers.
226. Altemeier, *supra* note 221, at 396.

risk," one percent had such injuries.[227] Additionally, of the 273 "at risk" mothers, fifty were placed there solely on the research assistant's comments.[228] Of the fifty, four were reported for abuse,[229] illustrating that subjective impressions are important predictors of child abuse.[230] However, the report indicated that prediction was only effective for twenty-four months following the study.[231] Although several reports agree on factors to predict child abuse or reabuse, most note that "the overall approach is unproven and should be limited to investigation"[232] or that "[f]urther research on the correlates of reabuse hopefully will lead to additional clinically relevant recommendations for those attempting to prevent the recurrence of abuse."[233] Moreover, it is virtually undisputed that "despite years of research, there is no psychological profile that accurately identifies parents who, in the future, will abuse or neglect their children."[234]

Actual Characteristics v. Psychologists Predictors

The characteristics of individuals in five of the Florida cases previously discussed[235]—where parental rights have been terminated because of prospective abuse or neglect—will be compared to the psychologists' reported characteristics of potentially abusive and neglectful parents. The purpose of this comparison is to determine if the medical reports predicting abusive and neglectful parents are accurate despite

---

227. *Id.*

228. *Id.* at 395-6.

229. *Id.* at 396.

230. *Id.* at 395.

231. Altemeier, *supra* note 221, at 395, 399.

232. *Id.* at 400.

233. Ferleger, *supra* note 28, at 48. *See also* I. SLOAN, CHILD ABUSE: GOVERNING LAW & LEGISLATION 9-13 (Series of Legal Almanacs #79. 1983) These pages list parent character indicators to be used when considering the possibility of child abuse or neglect. However it is noted that the list is not exhaustive and "[n]either does the presence of a single or even several indicators *prove* that maltreatment exists." *Id.* at 9 (emphasis in the original).

234. POLICY GUIDELINES, *supra* note 69, at 6. *See also*, Wald, *State Intervention on Behalf of "Neglected Children": A Search for Realistic Standards*, in PURSUING JUSTICE FOR THE CHILD 246, 248 (M. Rosenheim ed. 1976) stating that "the few longitudinal studies that have been done all conclude that prediction of future behavior from observation of child rearing practices is extremely difficult."

235. *Spankie*, 505 So. 2d at 1357; *Baby Boy A*, 544 So. 2d at 1136; *Yem*, 462 So. 2d at 1147; *W.D.N.*, 443 So. 2d at 493; and, *Palmer*, 547 So. 2d at 981.

the noted shortcomings of the studies. This brief analysis is unscientific and is based solely on the limited factual information provided by the cases as reported.

As previously discussed, psychological studies reveal that family income, marital status, family size, and spacing are often indicators of prospective abuse.[236] Unfortunately, the reported cases do not provide enough information to adequately analyze these factors. It should be noted though, that in *W.D.N.*, there would have been a family size of six if one child had not been killed in a fire and if two had not been adjudicated dependent.[237] Other cases cited reflect one or two children in the family.

Additionally, children or their siblings who have already been abused or neglected are in clear danger of further maltreatment.[238] It was reported that "in a family in which there has been a serious or fatal child abuse case there is a [forty] percent risk that a second child will be seriously injured."[239] Moreover, if the parent's same social, marital, family, and environmental factors exist as they did when the child was previously abused or if a sibling was abused, the child is immediately at a twenty percent risk of abuse exclusive of the consideration of other factors.[240] It is then reasonable to assume that unless there is a change in circumstances, a parent who has already engaged in harmful conduct toward any child will do so again.[241] On the other hand, common sense dictates that without actual harm, the chances of an erroneous prediction would greatly increase.

Of the five Florida cases examined, all revealed instances where either a sibling or the child himself was previously abused. In *Yem* and *Baby Boy A.*, since a parent's prior abuse of a sibling resulted in death and serious injury, respectively, there is automatically a forty percent chance that the subject children would be abused.[242] In *Spankie*, where the child was fourteen years old at the time of the hearing, there was evidence of a long history of abuse beginning when the subject child was six months old.[243] This evidence clearly demonstrates that the par-

---

236. *See supra*, notes 182 to 198 and accompanying text.

237. *W.D.N.*, 443 So. 2d at 494.

238. Consensus Opinion, *supra* note 207, at 2; POLICY GUIDELINES, *supra* note 69, at 6.

239. Consensus Opinion, *supra* note 207, at 2.

240. *Id.* at 1.

241. *Id.*

242. *Id.* at 2.

243. *Spankie*, 505 So. 2d at 1358.

ent is a continuing threat to the child.[244]

Another similarity in three of the five Florida cases was that psychological testimony illustrated that the abusive or neglectful parent has not benefitted or will not benefit from counseling or therapy.[245] The reasons cited for the poor prognosis are usually that the parent does not accept responsibility for his or her past conduct and shows no remorse for such conduct or that the parent exhibits limited intellectual capacity.[246]

Although it has been noted that an accurate profile cannot be determined, it appears that the parents in these actual cases had many of the same characteristics as those indicated in the psychological journals.

How Far Will the Courts Go?

If courts are given the power to terminate an individual's parental rights based on prospective abuse, how far will the courts carry this power? For instance, what will they do about an individual who is labeled a prospective abuser, and then becomes pregnant?

Some states have addressed this problem. As punishment for leaving two infant sons alone in an apartment for three days, an Arizona woman was sentenced to use birth control for the rest of her childbearing years.[247] The American Civil Liberties Union protested that the order violated her reproductive freedom, and the Roman Catholic Church objected that it violated her religious beliefs.[248] This case was not appealed because the judge had to rescind his order since, while on birth control, the woman became pregnant.[249] Hence, if birth control is not the answer, is sterilization?

Ironically, an Indiana Superior Court Judge suggested that he would reduce a possible twenty year prison term for a woman who poisoned her four-year old son if she were sterilized.[250] Judge Jones

---

244. *See* POLICY GUIDELINES, *supra* note 69, at 6.
245. *See Spankie*, 505 So. 2d at 1357; *W.D.N.*, 443 So. 2d at 493; and, *Palmer*, 547 So. 2d at 981.
246. *Id.*
247. Jacoby, Springen, Lazarovici, *Is Sterilization The Answer? A Controversial Punishment For Abusive Mothers*, NEWSWEEK, Aug. 8, 1988 at 59.
248. *Id.* at 59. Forster is Catholic.
249. Telephone interview with employee of Arizona Civil Liberties Union, July 1989.
250. Jacoby, *supra* note 247, at 59.

stated "[s]he has no need for any more children."[251] Nonetheless, the mother became pregnant again.[252] She voluntarily chose to have sterilization surgery after relinquishing custody of the newborn.[253] During sentencing Judge Jones considered the fact that the mother was sterilized and that she relinquished custody of the newborn as mitigating factors when he sentenced her to ten years in prison rather than the maximum sentence of twenty years.[254]

The United States Supreme Court has addressed the issue of involuntary sterilization. In the 1927 case of *Buck v. Bell*[255] the Court upheld a Virginia statute that permitted involuntary sterilization of the "feeble-minded."[256] However, in 1942, the Supreme Court struck down a sterilization program for prisoners who had been convicted of three felonies.[257] The Court ruled that the statute in question violated the fourteenth amendment's Equal Protection Clause.[258] The Court stated that "[m]arriage and procreation are fundamental to the very existence and survival of the race."[259]

However, *Buck* was never explicitly overruled. Consequently, despite the *Skinner* decision, courts are presently permitting sterilization of the mentally retarded.[260] Since there may be precedent to support involuntary sterilization, it is not inconceivable that the courts will utilize such sterilization in response to the problem of child abuse.

Conclusion

The concept of "prospective abuse and neglect" appears to create an inherent conflict between an individual's constitutional right to rear children and the states' *parens patriae* and police powers. Even though no psychological profile exists to accurately identify a prospective abu-

---

251.	*Id.*
252.	*Id.*
253.	Telephone interview with Superior Court Judge Roy F. Jones, Indiana Superior Court. (August 17, 1989).
254.	*Id.*
255.	274 U.S. 200 (1927).
256.	*Id.*
257.	Skinner v. Oklahoma, 316 U.S. 535 (1942).
258.	*Id.* at 541.
259.	*Id.*
260.	For an article discussing sterilization *see* Stefan, *Whose Egg Is It Anyway?: Reproductive Rights of Incarcerated, Institutionalized and Incompetent Women* 13 NOVA L. REV. 405, 413 (Spring 1989).

sive or neglectful parent, many states expressly permit parental rights termination to be based on "prospective abuse or neglect" when it is in the best interest of the child.

The Florida Supreme Court will most likely follow the direction of other jurisdictions who recite the rationale that "a court need not await certain disaster to come into fruition before taking protective steps in the interest of a minor child."[261] Alternatively, and less likely, the Florida Supreme Court may comply with the request of Lawrence J. Semento, Counsel for Appellant Thomas Padgett, and defer to the legislature to "provide . . . guidelines and standards by which 'prospective,' as opposed to 'actual,' abuse or neglect would provide a legal basis for termination of parental rights."[262]

Since the problem of child abuse and neglect is extremely widespread, this author is persuaded by the rationales expressed by the previously cited jurisdictions."[263] While scientific evidence does not clearly support the concept this is a situation where the emotional appeal is so great that the risk of error is outweighed by the state's interest to protect helpless children. Further, precise guidelines and standards can not be or should not be established since each case is unique. The players and their backgrounds are so very different that precise guidelines would be detrimental to those parents who can benefit from therapy and rehabilitation. However, the inability to determine precise guidelines should not preclude a finding that the concept is viable. It has been accurately stated that "[o]nce the government gets into the business of protecting, there is no alternative but to get involved in the prediction game."[264]

Courts are constantly engaged in the psychological prediction game. The "best interest of the child standard," which Florida courts utilize daily to determine child custody disputes in dissolution proceedings,[265] is based on prediction. For instance, the court considers and evaluates factors including: which parent is more likely to allow the

---

261. *See, e.g., In re* Parshall, 159 Mich. App. 683, 406 N.W.2d 913 (1987); *In re* Futch, 144 Mich. App. 163, 375 N.W.2d 375 (1985); *In re* Kantola, 139 Mich. App. 23, 361 N.W.2d 20 (1984); and, *In re* La Flure, 48 Mich. App. 377, 210 N.W.2d 482 (1973).

262. Appellant, Thomas Padgett's Brief at 10, Padgett v. Department of Health and Rehabilitative Servs., 543 So. 2d 1317 (Fla. 5th Dist. Ct. App. 1989).

263. *See supra* notes 173-187.

264. *Child Abuse, supra* note 199, at 12. Statement by Randall Wilson of the Iowa Civil Liberties Union.

265. *See* FLA. STAT. § 61.13(3) (1987).

child frequent and continuing contact with the nonresidential parent; which parent has the capacity and disposition to provide the child with food, clothing, etc.[266] The court also considers the permanence of the existing or *proposed* custodial home.[267] Further, the mental and physical health of the parents is evaluated.[268]

Judge Cowart's unpersuasive dissent states that prospective abuse is comparable with "imprisonment of one who has not committed a crime because 'but for' the fact he was imprisoned he 'would have' committed a crime."[269] Judge Cowart's analogy is unfair since the potential victim of child abuse is usually living with the abuser; hence, the victim is extremely accessible. On the other hand, a crime victim rarely lives with the criminal; thus, the criminal must seek out his or her victim. Accordingly, since child abuse is a unique crime in that the victim is brought to the offender's home, stringent precautions must be utilized. Thorough case by case analysis combined with expert psychological testimony should provide the courts with adequate information to allow it to decide which parents are habitual offenders beyond recovery. As stated, courts continually engage in the prediction game. Since most state court opinions which terminate parental rights lack thorough analysis and rationale, one can only assume that these opinions are supported by the emotional appeal of the issue combined with the realization that both prediction and speculation encompass most areas of law.

Lori Susan Weiss

---

266. *Id.*
267. *Id.*
268. *Id.* (emphasis added).
269. *Spankie*, 505 So. 2d at 1360 (Cowart, J., dissenting).

ACKNOWLEDGMENTS

Taylor, Delores A., and Philip Starr. "Foster Parenting: An Integrative Review of the Literature." *Child Welfare* 46 (1967): 371–85. Reprinted with the permission of Transaction Publishers. Courtesy of Yale University Law Library.

Katz, Sanford N. "Legal Aspects of Foster Care." *Family Law Quarterly* 5 (1971): 283–302. First published in the *Family Law Quarterly,* copyright 1971 American Bar Association. Courtesy of Yale University Law Library.

Geiser, Robert L. "The Shuffled Child and Foster Care." *Trial* 10 (1974): 27, 29, 35. Reprinted with the permission of the Association of Trial Lawyers of America. Courtesy of *Trial*.

Callanan, Brendan, and Mitchell Wendell. "The Interstate Compact on the Placement of Children." *Juvenile Justice* 26 (1975): 41–46. Reprinted with the permission of the Washington Crimes News Service. Courtesy of Yale University Law Library.

Derdeyn, Andre P., Andrew P. Rogoff, and Scott W. Williams. "Alternatives to Absolute Termination of Parental Rights After Long-Term Foster Care." *Vanderbilt Law Review* 31 (1978): 1165–92. Reprinted with the permission of Vanderbilt University, copyright holder. Courtesy of Yale University Law Library.

Shapiro, Mendel. "Constitutional Protection of Long-Term Foster Families." *Columbia Law Review* 79 (1979): 1191–1208. Reprinted with the permission of the *Columbia Law Review*. Courtesy of Yale University Law Library.

Leashore, Bogart R. "Demystifying Legal Guardianship: An Unexplored Option for Dependent Children." *Journal of Family Law* 23 (1984–85): 391–400. Reprinted with the permission of the *Journal of Family Law*. Courtesy of University of Minnesota Law Library.

Hunner, Robert J. "Defining Active and Reasonable Efforts to Preserve Families." *Children Today* 15 (1986): 27–30.

Reprinted with the permission of the U.S. Department of Health and Human Services. Courtesy of *Children Today*.

Ratterman, Debra. "Judicial Determination of Reasonable Efforts." *Children Today* 15 (1986): 26, 30–32. Reprinted with the permission of the U.S. Department of Health and Human Services. Courtesy of *Children Today*.

Mushlin, Michael B. "Unsafe Havens: The Case for Constitutional Protection of Foster Children from Abuse and Neglect." *Harvard Civil Rights-Civil Liberties Law Review* 23 (1988): 199–280. Permission granted c. 1988, *Harvard Civil Rights-Civil Liberties Law Review*, and by the President and Fellows of Harvard College. Courtesy of *Harvard Civil Rights-Civil Liberties Law Review*.

Shotton, Alice C. "Making Reasonable Efforts in Child Abuse and Neglect Cases: Ten Years Later." *California Western Law Review* 26 (1989–90): 223–56. Reprinted with the permission of the California Western School of Law. Courtesy of Yale University Law Library.

Fein, Edith, and Anthony N. Maluccio. "Permanency Planning: Another Remedy in Jeopardy?" *Social Service Review* 66 (1992): 335–48. Reprinted with the permission of the University of Chicago Press. Copyright (1992). Courtesy of Byrgen Finkelman.

Fried, Arlene E. "The Foster Child's Avenues of Redress: Questions Left Unanswered." *Columbia Journal of Law and Social Problems* 26 (1993): 465–90. Reprinted with the permission of the Columbia University School of Law. Courtesy of *Columbia Journal of Law and Social Problems*.

Ritz, Jean P. "Termination of Parental Rights to Free Child for Adoption." *New York University Law Review* 32 (1957): 579–93. Reprinted with the permission of the *New York University Law Review*. Courtesy of Yale University Law Library.

Whittier, James M. "Infants—Termination of Parental Rights" *University of Kansas Law Review* 14 (1965): 117–20. Reprinted with the permission of the *University of Kansas Law Review*. Courtesy of Yale University Law Library.

Catz, Robert S., and John T. Kuelbs. "The Requirement of Appointment of Counsel for Indigent Parents in Neglect or Termination Proceedings: A Developing Area." *Journal of Family Law* 13 (1973–74): 223–44. Reprinted with the permission of the *Journal of Family Law*. Courtesy of Yale University Law Library.

Ketcham, Orman W., and Richard F. Babcock, Jr. "Statutory Standards for the Involuntary Termination of Parental Rights." *Rutgers Law Review* 29 (1976): 530–36. Reprinted with the permission of *Rutgers Law Review*. Courtesy of Yale University Law Library.

Placey, Richard L. "Effect of the Adoption Act of 1970 on Termination of Parental Rights." *Dickinson Law Review* 81 (1977): 709–18. Reprinted with the permission of the Dickinson School of Law. Courtesy of the *Dickinson Law Review*.

Borgman, Robert. "Antecedents and Consequences of Parental Rights Termination for Abused and Neglected Children." *Child Welfare* 60 (1981): 391–404. Reprinted with the permission of Transaction Publishers. Courtesy of Byrgen Finkelman.

Besharov, Douglas J. "Representing Abused and Neglected Children: When Protecting Children Means Seeking the Dismissal of Court Proceedings." *Journal of Family Law* 20 (1981–82): 217–39. Reprinted with the permission of the *Journal of Family Law*. Courtesy of Yale University Law Library.

Padgett, Gary T. "The Right to Counsel for Indigent Parents in Termination Proceedings: A Critical Analysis of Lassiter v. Department of Social Services." *Journal of Family Law* 21 (1982–83): 83–113. Reprinted with the permission of the *Journal of Family Law*. Courtesy of Yale University Law Library.

Gabriels, Catherine B. "*Santosky v. Kramer*: Due Process and the Interest of the Child In Permanent Neglect Proceedings." *Albany Law Review* 47 (1983): 680–98. Reprinted with the permission of the Albany Law School. Courtesy of the *Albany Law Review*.

Kelly, Robert F., and Sarah H. Ramsey. "The Legal Representation of Children in Protection Proceedings: Some Empirical Findings and a Reflection on Public Policy." *Family Relations* 34 (1985): 277–83. Reprinted by permission. Copyright (1985) by the National Council on Family Relations, 3989 Central Ave. NE, Suite 550, Minneapolis, MN 55421. Courtesy of Byrgen Finkelman.

Dorros, Karen, and Patricia Dorsey. "Whose Rights Are We Protecting, Anyway?" *Children Today* 18 (1989): 6–8. Reprinted with the permission of the U.S. Department of Health and Human Services. Courtesy of *Children Today*.

Horowitz, Robert. "Tighten Standards for Termination of Parental Rights." *Children Today* 18 (1989): 9–11. Reprinted with the permission of the U.S. Department of Health and Human Services. Courtesy of *Children Today*.

Weiss, Lori Susan. "Prospective Abuse and Neglect—The Termination of Parental Rights." *Nova Law Review* 14 (1990): 1171–1204. Reprinted with the permission of the *Nova Law Review*. Courtesy of Yale University Law Library.

SERIES INDEX BY AUTHOR

Please Note: Numbers at the end of each entry refer to the volume in which the article appears.